RICHARD HILLARY

RICHARD HILLARY

THE DEFINITIVE BIOGRAPHY OF A BATTLE OF
BRITAIN FIGHTER PILOT AND AUTHOR
OF *THE LAST ENEMY*

DAVID ROSS

GRUB STREET · LONDON

Published by
Grub Street
The Basement
10 Chivalry Road
London SW11 1HT

British Library Cataloguing in Publication Data
Ross, David
Richard Hillary: the definitive biography of a Second World War fighter pilot
and author of The Last Enemy
1. Hillary, Richard, 1919-1943 2. Great Britain. Royal Air Force.
Squadron, 603 - History 3. Fighter pilots - Great Britain - Biography
4. World War, 1939-1945 – Aerial operations, British
I.Title
940.5'44941'092

ISBN 1-902304-45-4

Typeset by Pearl Graphics, Hemel Hempstead

Printed and bound in Great Britain by
Biddles Ltd, Guildford and King's Lynn

CONTENTS

FOREWORD

by

Lord James Douglas-Hamilton
Lord Selkirk of Douglas PC, QC, MA, LLB, MSP
Honorary Air Commodore to No.603 (City of Edinburgh) Squadron RAuxAF

David Ross contributes a great service in providing an extremely well researched, comprehensive, authoritative and highly readable account of one of Britain's most noteworthy authors.

This biography tells the intensely human story of a young man, who was a powerful athlete, a talented intellectual and a very courageous person.

In the early 1930s the Oxford Union passed a motion to the effect that Oxford students would not fight for King and Country. A few years later Richard Hillary would be one of the former Oxbridge students who would take his place in the foremost position in the front line.

In the Second World War he belonged to 603 (City of Edinburgh) Squadron, and at the beginning of the Battle of Britain, he was posted with his Squadron to Hornchurch in East London. There he found himself in the very eye of the storm.

Each day concentrated attacks were made by massed formations of Luftwaffe bombers, protected by large numbers of fighters. 603 (City of Edinburgh) Squadron sustained heavy casualties, but by the end of that terrific battle 603 emerged as the top scoring squadron in the Royal Air Force and the Royal Auxiliary Air Force.

In that struggle Richard played his part to the full, shooting down a considerable number of enemy aircraft, before being terribly injured, with appalling burns to his face and hands.

Richard Hillary's book *The Last Enemy* published in 1942, is as much a classic as Lawrence of Arabia's *Seven Pillars of Wisdom*. It stands on its own as an outstanding and wonderful piece of writing to describe a traumatic conflict.

After writing *The Last Enemy*, the end of his life had all the ingredients of a Greek tragedy. He was determined to be of further service but the blunt reality is that he should not have been given permission to fly. The risks were unacceptably high, because his hands had been so severely injured. It is of course easy to be wise with the gift of hindsight, and it should be noted that what seems clear today was not perceived as obvious at the time.

The famous plastic surgeon Sir Archibald McIndoe who operated on so many young pilots who had suffered severe burns had written to express his concern and later recorded:

> The station medical officer was away on leave, and my unofficial letter marked 'private' lay on his desk unopened for two weeks. On the night he returned and before he could take action, Richard Hillary met his Enemy face to face. The wheel had come full circle and no-one could stop its remorseless swing.
>
> I often think of him in that last moment – his crippled hands fighting for control of his spinning plane – the cold sweat pouring from his body, the screaming crescendo of the engines, his patchwork face frozen in that mocking twisted smile, his eyes at last gleaming with the supreme knowledge he had so painfully sought and had so short a time to comprehend.

What he left behind was a book which described the first major battle in which the bid of

Hitler and the Nazi High Command met with defeat, at a time when the Third Reich was trying to establish a 1,000 year Empire, based on racial domination, oppression of subject peoples and genocide. All of Richard's friends from Oxford University who became Battle of Britain pilots with him were killed either then or later, and *The Last Enemy* is a fitting memorial to them and their comrades. As was said in times past "For run tomorrow, they gain their today".

After the Battle of Britain Prime Minister Churchill had broadcast the 'Never in the field of human conflict has so much been owed by so many to so few'. Richard was one of those few who put their lives on the line, for the survival of their country. His writing portrays the courage, fortitude and heroism of those involved, and also the pain, the suffering and the anguish which went with it.

It is right that there should be a full and highly accurate account setting in historical perspective the life of a young man of immense promise, who died young. It tells his whole story, including his friendships with women who were both bright and beautiful.

It is the story of the committed patriot, the romantic hero, and the wounded warrior. But it is more than that. It is the life of the distinguished writer who immortalised the Battle of Britain pilots in one of the finest and best works of literature in the 20th Century.

PREFACE

Richard Hillary was a writer who was a fighter pilot, not a fighter pilot who could write. This point was important to him and one which, in his opinion, set him apart from the others with whom he served and who had also written of their experiences. He was aware of his talent, but had it not been for his best-selling book *The Last Enemy* he would merely be one of those who fought in the Battle of Britain and were subsequently killed before the end of World War II. His book was significant in that it provided the public with a glimpse of what life was like for the young pilots fighting in defence of their country in the skies above southern England, sometimes before their eyes. Without the book, the legend would not exist. This is a story that bears so many similarities to others who flew with the RAF during World War II; Richard Hillary, however, was not like other men. During his short, tumultuous life he made possibly the most outstanding literary contribution of the war in any service.

I first read *The Last Enemy* while I was away at boarding school at the age of eleven. My father was an officer in the RAF and serving abroad at the time. I had been brought up on various RAF stations and over the years my appreciation grew for the lifestyle associated with being in such an environment. My love and fascination of flying has never diminished.

When I had finished the *The Last Enemy* I was left wanting to know more about the author. During my research, with the possibility of a book in mind, I realised that much had already been written about Richard Hillary although many inaccuracies have been mistakenly perpetuated. My aim therefore has been to compile as complete a collection of information, anecdotes and photographs as is possible and write the definitive biography on his life, although I am also aware that errors will be inevitable.

In concluding, I believe it is the job of subsequent generations of aviation historians and enthusiasts, with the help of their benefactors, to continue to research and tell the story of 'The Few'. Not that they will ever be forgotten, thanks to the number of authors, researchers, and historians who enthuse over this particular subject, and most importantly we still have those who actually served, should they be willing to assist with research and provide anecdotes after more than 50 years. I am grateful, and am in awe of their courage and achievements.

DAVID M. S. ROSS
April 2000

ACKNOWLEDGEMENTS

'For the Air Force draws you into its secrets and fills your life, even if you live on its edge as I have done, wearing no wings.'

Combat Report by Hector Bolitho

More than fifty years after the Battle of Britain was fought, fighter pilots seem to embody the timeless ideal of the warrior knight. Quintessentially English, they have bequeathed a series of unforgettable images: the carefree young man driving his open-top sports car down country lanes; the dedicated and enthusiastic pilot dashing across the airfield in response to the order to 'scramble'; and the terrified young man whose life flashes before him as he spirals downwards in the burning wreck of his aircraft.

Details of Richard Hillary's life have been hashed and re-hashed time and again, regardless of inaccuracies. The main source of these works is *The Last Enemy* itself, which was also factually inaccurate partly because Richard was in America when he wrote it and did not have research sources available to him at that time. He therefore felt more comfortable referring to his book not as an autobiography, but as a novel.

I have attempted to bring to light some of the inaccuracies. If I myself have made errors, I accept that responsibility and look forward to hearing from anyone who can correct and/or shed further light on the life of Richard Hillary.

* * *

Most of us with an interest in military aviation history will have a particular individual or individuals whose service during the two World Wars has been a source of fascination. I have been fortunate in that, as a boy, I was in the enviable position of being able to meet many such characters. In recent years I have remained in touch with some of the 'Few'.

One of those whom I admire is Wing Commander Geoffrey Page DSO, DFC, RAF (Ret'd). His memories of Richard Hillary, while he was undergoing plastic surgery for his burns in Queen Victoria Cottage Hospital, East Grinstead, were invaluable.

Flight Lieutenant Wilfred Handel 'Andy' Miller DFC and Bar, RAF (Ret'd), had been flying at Charterhall on the night Richard Hillary was killed; and I managed to track Andy down to his home in Northern Ireland. Andy is a kind and very modest man. His memories of the night of 7/8 January 1943 are still very vivid and he was able to provide me with a great deal of detail. Much of what he said could be confirmed by his log-book and notations in conjunction with the available facts and the testimony of others who had been there. Where incorrect details had previously been published, he was able to put the record straight, although all will never be known.

Pilot Officer Philip Cardell, RAFVR, served with Richard in 603 Squadron. He was killed during the Battle of Britain. While I was visiting his grave in Great Paxton, Huntingdonshire, I met Mrs Joan Merton-Jones (nee Palmer), who had been his girlfriend at the time of his death. I thank her for her precious memories of Philip.

I am also grateful to the following for their invaluable assistance: Michael Burn, whose excellent book *Mary and Richard* was an invaluable aid in piecing together aspects of the last year of Richard's life; the staff in the Department of Documents at The Imperial War Museum; staff in the Department of Research, RAF Museum Hendon; Group Captain Tony Stevens RAF (Ret'd) and Mr Steve Clark at the Air Historical Branch (RAF); Christine Marsh at the BBC Sound Archive; Mr Michael Charlesworth OBE and members of the Old Salopian Club for their memories of Richard at Shrewsbury; Mr Alex Tollemache for the memories of his father Tony Tollemache GC; Mrs Margaret Renton for

the memories of her late husband Jim; the Reverend Geoffrey R. M. Fison BA, (Ret'd), for details of his father Wilfrid. The memories of George Frizzel who was first at the scene of the crash; Major General Sir John Swinton KCVO, OBE, and his mother, Mrs Mariora Erskine for their memories of Richard at Charterhall; Mrs Shelley Woodroffe at the RNLI for information about the *J.B. Proudfoot* and her crew; Mr Ken Sandwell; Mr Dick Bright at the Luftwaffe Archive, Imperial War Museum, Duxford; the Richard Hillary Trustees and the Trust Archivist, Captain Anthony Sainsbury VRD, MA, RNR, Mr Dennis Burden, Mrs Clare Hopkins, Mrs Jan Martin, and Dr Mathew Steggle for their invaluable assistance during my many hours of research at the Richard Hillary Trust Archive at Trinity College, Oxford and for providing a copy of Richard's portrait by Eric Kennington, the original of which is held in the National Portrait Gallery; Adrian Samuel at *The Spectator*; Flight Lieutenant Wilfred Handel 'Andy' Miller, DFC and Bar, RAF (Ret'd), for his memories of Richard at RAF Charterhall and the crash; the Deutsche Dienststelle Berlin for details of Hauptmann Eric Bode; Ghislain Malette at the National Archives of Canada; Mr Mark Reece for his expertise on aviation crashes; Mrs Judy Grahame at the VC and GC Association; Wing Commander John Young AFC, RAF (Ret'd), Battle of Britain Fighter Association Historian, Wing Commander Pat Hancock DFC, RAF (Ret'd), Malcolm Smith and the Battle of Britain Fighter Association who welcomed me into their fold during the annual reunions at RAF/USAF Lakenheath; Mr Jonathan Lovat Dickson, son of Rache Lovat Dickson; Mr and Mrs John Meaker and Mr Ian Dykes, past and present owners of Crunklaw Farm and 'Hillary's Field'; Mr Jack Thompson for information about RAF Charterhall; the late Jack Wilkinson for his memories of his time at RAF Charterhall; Mr Ernest Hardy for his expertise at the Public Record Office; Squadron Leader J. Robinson BA RAF, Flight Lieutenant Rosefield and Squadron Leader R.M. Moody RAF at the Oxford University Air Squadron HQ at Manor Road, Oxford; Air Chief Marshal Sir Christopher Foxley-Norris GCB, DSO, OBE, RAF (Ret'd), for his memories of Richard at Trinity College, Oxford and the University Air Squadron; Squadron Leader Lewis Brandon DSO, DFC and Bar for his memories of Richard at Charterhall, and those memories of his good friend and pilot, the late Wing Commander James 'Ben' Benson DSO, DFC and Bar; Mrs Jean Blades (née Waterston) for her memories of her brother Flying Officer Robin 'Bubble' Waterston; my friend Dr George Beckmann, member of Trinity, who carried out research into the life of Richard Hillary and ultimately provided much support; Richard Smith and the Purfleet Military Heritage; Mrs Frank Mileham, a former patient of Sir Archibald McIndoe; John Alcorn for his 'Top Gun' research into the highest scoring RAF squadrons during the Battle of Britain; Miss Jean Cunningham, cousin of 603 pilot Laurie Cunningham; Wendy and Richard Roberts for the exclusive information on Wendy's uncles Ken and Don Macdonald; the 'Children of Tarfside' – Betty Johnstone (née Davie), Mrs Sheila Welsh, the Rogers brothers, Dave Loudon, Charlie Robertson, Dave and Bill Strachan, Graham McCrow, Bill Murray and the irrepressible Angus Davidson and his wife Ruth; Jim Renwick, John Rendall, Harry Ross, Jimmy Skinner, Bob Wilson, Reg Cockell, Alec MacKenzie, Charles 'Chic' Cessford, Bill Smith, John Inkster, John Mackenzie, Bert Pringle and all the members of the 603 Squadron Association in Edinburgh; Wing Commanders Bob Kemp and Alasdair Beaton, former and present commanding officers of No.2 (City of Edinburgh) Maritime Headquarters Unit, now No.603 (City of Edinburgh) Squadron (RAuxAF); George Mullay Jnr; 'Pat' Patterson and Barney Travers; Mr Desmond W. Carbury and the Carbury family for the exclusive information on Brian; Squadron Leader Peter Brown AFC, RAF (Ret'd) for providing information on the Pinckney family; Ted Sergison; Jean Liddicoat; Mrs Fiona Campbell owner of the Sligachan Hotel on the Isle of Skye; the pilots of the 493rd Squadron (F15c 'Eagle') of the 48th Fighter Wing USAF/RAF Lakenheath who brought the Tarfside story full circle; Montrose Aerodrome Aviation Society; Mrs Sheila Wickham; Mrs Pan Nelson-Edwards for permission to quote from her husband's memoirs; and Mr Robin Hope, who was then Richard's closest surviving relative living in England, for his memories of Richard and his assistance, advice and support.
    I would also like to thank the following for their memories of Richard with 603

Squadron: The late Group Captain George Denholm DFC, and his wife Betty; Paul Denholm, Molly Ritchie, Marguerite (Mardi) Morton, Air Commodore Ronald 'Ras' Berry OBE, DSO, DFC and Bar, RAF (Ret'd), Flight Lieutenant Bill 'Tannoy' Read AFC, RAF (Ret'd), the late Squadron Leader Jack Stokoe DFC, the late Group Captain George Gilroy DSO, DFC and Bar, DFC (US), Squadron Leader B.G. 'Stapme' Stapleton DFC, DFC (Dutch), RAF (Ret'd). The information passed on to me by Gerald Stapleton and the hospitality shown to me by him and his wife Audrey is much appreciated and we have become good friends.

The military aviation historians: John Foreman the authority on losses and claims; Squadron Leader Chris Goss; Donald Caldwell; Henry Buckton; John Coleman; Chris Shores; Squadron Leader Bruce Blanche, official historian 603 Squadron RAuxAF; Norman Franks for his time, motivation and expertise in guiding me towards my goal and to Amy Myers and Mr John Davies and the staff at Grub Street Publishing.

It has been a delight meeting them and my apologies to anyone whose name I have inadvertently omitted.

Finally, I would like to thank my family. This book has taken too many years to complete and those around me have provided love, support, expertise and encouragement during good times and bad. If they were ever fed up with this project, they never showed it. To my father Squadron Leader Cliff Ross RAF (Ret'd) for the wealth of information he has gleaned over his many years with the Royal Air Force and a convenient source within my own family; my mother Maureen; Kerry and George Cathro, Alison Bellew and Lynne Robinson.

I wish to acknowledge quotations from: *The Last Enemy* by Richard Hillary, (copyright © The Estate of Richard Hillary, all rights reserved), reproduced by permission of A.M. Heath & Co. Ltd. on behalf of Jonathan Lovat Dickson as the Literary Executor of the Estate; *A Life and The House of Words* by Rache Lovat Dickson, and *The Art of Adventure* by Eric Linklater (Jonathan Lovat Dickson and Macmillan); *Years of Command* by Lord Douglas of Kirtleside (Harper Collins); *Faces from the Fire* by Leonard Mosley (Weidenfeld and Nicolson Ltd); *Merle – The Romantic Life of Merle Oberon* by Charles Higham and Roy Moseley (New English Library); Admiral Jubelin's preface to the French edition of *The Last Enemy* (Editions France Empire); Express Newspapers, for articles concerning Richard Hillary by Robert Pitman and Leonard Mosley; *Duel of Eagles* by Group Captain Peter Townsend (Presidio Press); *Night Flyer* by Lewis Brandon (William Kimber); *Best Foot Forward* by Colin Hodgkinson (Odhams); *Nine Lives* by Al Deere (Wingham Press); *Battle of Britain Day* by Dr Alfred Price (Sidgwick and Jackson); *The Story of 609 Squadron* by Frank Zeigler (Crecy); *Combat Report* by Hector Bolitho (Batsford Ltd); *Beauty for Ashes* by Lady Winifred Fortescue (Blackwood); *Your Uncles* by Roger and Anne Gresham Cooke (private); *A Cauldron of Spells* by Frank McEachran (Greenbank Press); *Spit and Sawdust* by George Nelson-Edwards (Forces Publishing Services); *I Burned My Fingers* by Bill Simpson (Putnams); *The Charterhall Story* by Jack Thompson (Air Research); *Behind the Headlines – An autobiography* by Michael Charlesworth OBE (Greenbank Press); *Mary and Richard* by Michael Burn (Andre Deutsch).

The letters of Richard Hillary, Michael and Edwyna Hillary, Denise Maxwell-Woosnam, Rache Lovat Dickson, and other friends and colleagues of Richard Hillary, along with other papers held in the Richard Hillary Trust Archive, Trinity College, Oxford; the private letters of Mary Booker to Richard Hillary held in the Richard Hillary Trust Archive (permission granted by Michael Burn); papers from the Oxford University Air Squadron; RAF Official Accident Report (RAF Museum, Hendon); 'The Artist and Fascism' (*The Spectator*); No.603 (City of Edinburgh) Fighter Squadron AuxAF, ORB (Air 27) and Combat Reports (Air 50) (Public Record Office, Kew).

As I drove through the derelict domestic site of the old airfield the headlights picked out the deserted buildings. The window panes were broken, doors were hanging off or just simply open, and rendering was missing in patches from the walls of the single-skinned buildings. The long grass hid the pathways. The giant ghostly shape of the hangars emerged alarmingly before me from the swirling mist under the moonlit sky. As I reached the perimeter track I stopped the car, the green glow of the clock showed 23.15. I turned off the lights and engine before climbing out into the sharp chill of the night air. My footing was unsure, the concrete surface of the runways and airfield roads had broken up due to lack of attention over the years since the war. The crunch of gravel sounded loud under each step.

I walked a few yards and stopped. The mist came and went in patches. One moment there was nothing but the luminescent glow from the moon on the swirls in front of me; as it cleared it left just blackness. Then, as the mist drifted it revealed the tall powerful outline of a man just visible under the silver light of the moon as it slipped from behind a cloud, his facial features were not discernible under the peak of a service cap. The bulkiness of his attire indicated he was wearing a flying jacket, with the collar raised. In his right hand he clutched a leather flying helmet and oxygen mask with the RT lead and oxygen hose trailing.

'So you want to know all about me, do you?' said the apparition. The voice was deep, the words clearly and deliberately spoken with concise enunciation, but there was an air of weariness in the tone. 'You pretty much know the whole story, but I would like to put you straight on a few points . . .'

THE FINAL CONFRONTATION

'The last enemy that shall be destroyed is death.'

Corinthians XV, 26
RAF Charterhall,
Berwickshire.
8th January 1943, 01.25 am.

The shepherd sat warming himself in the living room of his farm cottage. He was coming to the end of a very long day. It was the lambing season and he had been busy in the fields with his flock and, until a short while before, had been still attending to a ewe that was about to give birth.

As he sat in the company of his eldest son, on leave from training with the army, he heard several aircraft taking off from the nearby airfield. It was a sound they and all the local people had become used to over the last twelve months. Earlier that night there had been a flurry of night-flying activity and this latest commotion only briefly interrupted the flow of conversation.

The sound of engines became clearer as the aircraft emerged, climbing from behind the hill that separated them from the airfield. Outside they would have seen nothing as the aircraft navigation lights were turned off during night-flying exercise.

In the distance and appropriately on one of the highest points in the area, was a flashing beacon. It was a manned mobile unit that was sent out each evening to its position to the east of the station and it indicated to the pilots the whereabouts of the aerodrome. It was standard practice for aircraft to maintain an orbiting pattern over this beacon. To those in the area, it appeared as a single flashing light suspended in mid-air. Tonight it would be unlikely that they would be able to use it due to the dual-layered cloud cover.

The aircraft had climbed into the cloud but the sound of its engines would always indicate its approximate position.

It was obvious after a few minutes that one of the aircraft was heading back to the airfield and was losing height while another had already taken this familiar course of action in orbiting the beacon. At its nearest point to them, the circling aircraft was practically overhead. The distance from the beacon they knew to be about a mile.

As the aircraft engines droned on, the volume and pitch seemed to be increasing; it was losing height.

In the cockpit the pilot was finding the controls increasingly sluggish and the aircraft difficult to control. The condition of his hands rendered him unable to fight against adversity any longer as the forward speed slowed dangerously to the point of stalling.

As it flew over the farm cottage the shepherd noticed that the engines sounded different from usual, much higher in pitch; there was something wrong. The aircraft impacted with the ground at a fairly shallow angle almost as if the pilot had managed to recover from the dive, but too late to avoid disaster. There was a loud, sickening crash as the aircraft made initial impact by a bend in a burn and flipped on to its back. Wreckage broke free and careered across the field, parallel with the burn, distributing the lightest parts first with the heaviest pieces finally coming to rest against a drainage ditch at the base of a grassy knoll. It had spread debris over a distance of 100 yards. The time was 01.37 am. The flight had lasted just seven minutes.

The fuel from the ruptured fuel tanks ignited immediately and the whole site was enveloped in flames. The flash of the initial ignition not only lit up the surrounding farmland, but the underside of the low cloud as it blew over the site. It was this flash that was witnessed back at the airfield by the other pilots and personnel and the duty staff in the air traffic control tower.

The shepherd and his son emerged from their cottage just in time to see the flash of the fuel tanks erupting following the aircraft's impact with the ground. Back in the house his remaining children, asleep upstairs, awoke with a start.

Instinctively, the two men rushed towards the burning aircraft hoping to help any survivors. It had come down less than 500 yards from the cottage. On arrival at the scene they found that nothing could be done; the flames from the burning aviation fuel were intense and forced them back. The body of a crew member was visible and by its position the shepherd was given the impression that the man had attempted to bale out at the last minute. The body was mutilated and beyond help even if they had been able to get near.

As the two looked on, helpless to assist, the shepherd noticed something on the ground reflecting the light from the flames. As he stooped down to pick it up he realised it was a gold watch. It had been wrenched off the wrist of its owner on impact, and the strap was broken. The back-plate had been engraved and from it he was able to identify the wearer: 'Richard Hillary'.

* * *

Richard Hillary's combat experience in the south of England during the Battle of Britain amounted to just seven days before he was shot down and badly burned. In that time he managed to account for five enemy aircraft destroyed with two 'probables' and one 'damaged'. He himself had been shot down on one previous occasion during this period. In his writings he projects a very introspective nature and seemed to be more sensitive than his fellow fighter pilots. His subsequent recovery was as a result of his existentialism rather than his determination to return to the fight against Nazism.

He was killed 28 months after the Battle of Britain whilst attempting to return to operational flying. He had spent long periods in hospital undergoing many painful operations in order to rebuild his face and attempt to restore the function of his hands. Latterly, between visits to the hospital, he had undergone staff officer training in readiness for a position in administration. It was during his recovery that he wrote his famous best-seller *The Last Enemy*, published in 1942, which tells the story of the early part of his life, his time at Oxford University, his subsequent commission in the RAFVR and his flying training which culminates in his becoming a Spitfire pilot.

The Last Enemy, beautifully written as it is, does not reveal the full story of Richard Hillary, partly because of the times in which it was written, and partly because he may not have wished it to. What follows is an attempt in some way to remedy this.

CHAPTER ONE

THE EARLY YEARS

1919 – 1931

Richard Hope Hillary was born in Sydney, Australia, on 20 April 1919. His middle name was his mother Edwyna Hillary's maiden surname. She later referred to his birth as the arrival of 'our little Easter egg'.

Richard's father, Michael James Hillary, was born in Australia on 20 February 1886 of Anglo-Irish descent. Before the outbreak of war he had been in government service and had joined the army soon after hostilities began, having first to overcome his being refused acceptance into service due to his defective eyesight.

He had a distinguished career. Throughout World War One he served with the Australian Expeditionary Forces in India, Gallipoli and Mesopotamia (now known as Iraq). He attained the rank of colonel and was awarded the Distinguished Service Order, and Order of the British Empire, and was twice mentioned in dispatches in Mesopotamia. He returned home to Sydney at the end of World War I, to find the birth of his son was imminent. Richard was the couple's only child.

Forty-six years later in 1965, at the age of 79, Michael Hillary stated that having only one child was the single greatest regret of his life.

* * *

Richard's mother, Edwyna Mary Evalina Hope, was born in Freemantle or York, north-western Australia in 1881 of Scottish and Spanish descent. Her grandmother was Spanish but the chief blood in the family was Celtic – mainly Scottish. Her father was from Faversham, Kent, although he had actually been born in Australia. She had met Michael Hillary in Melbourne and they were married with Catholic rites on 16 August 1916, although, by the age of twenty Richard was Church of England. They lived in Sydney and during this period Michael Hillary was to spend most of the time serving abroad with the army. After his return, and the birth of Richard, they moved to a small flat in South Yarra, an upmarket inner suburb of Melbourne, and then to a large house in Toorak, still situated in inner suburban Melbourne, where Richard spent the majority of the first three years of his life.

The relationship between Richard and his mother became very close during this period of their lives. Michael Hillary was a friendly and hospitable man up to a point but he had disciplined views on how things should be done. Richard respected his father but was never that close to him and during his early life he was away on business much of the time. It was his mild-mannered mother who provided the warmth of emotional contact; she was devoted to Richard. As Melbourne was an unfamiliar place to Edwyna, she and Richard spent practically all the time in each other's company. Although she was strict on discipline Richard was a spoilt child and various aspects of his personality reflected this. Mrs Beryl Malin, Edwyna's sister, had seen Richard before he was twenty-four hours old and had refused to dote over him:

> There was nothing special to distinguish him from his fellow creatures of similar age. As he grew he became intelligent, mischievous, a rather truculent little boy, usually cheerful and cheeky . . .

Even as a young boy Richard was very self opinionated. He was to develop the ability to wear down those who were intolerant of him and this was a characteristic that was to set him apart from the others. His Aunt Beryl remembers him at this time:

> It was noticeable that he had a good head, fine vivid blue eyes, a ridiculous nose, a large mouth, and a tendency to pout his lower lip. When grieved, he had a habit of screwing his eyes tightly shut, opening his mouth wide, and letting the tears pour down into his mouth without let or hindrance . . .
>
> . . . he had a quick hot temper; was capable of getting literally hopping mad, looking the very embodiment of a small fury. The outbreak quickly spent itself, although sometimes he remained rather petulant until he realised his sulky face was comic, and then he had to laugh in spite of himself.
>
> He learnt to master his temper while still in his teens. I saw so on occasion when he had every justification for being extremely angry. Though scarlet in the face and seething with suppressed wrath, his conduct was admirable.

His temper could be attributed to his father's Irish, and perhaps his mother's Spanish ancestry. His attractive looks were from both his father and mother, two good-looking individuals.

Years later his aunt would add:

> He was fundamentally an honest, straightforward person, but argumentative to the nth degree. He was naturally impatient and intolerant. He had a tremendous zest for life, did everything with great enthusiasm and was, while at Oxford, a handsome, high-spirited, laughing, egoist, with a great deal of charm.

On discharge from the army Michael Hillary went into the government service once again. During this period he was transferred on a three year posting to special duties in Australia House in London. And so at the age of three Richard was brought to England. He was never to return to Australia.

* * *

On arrival in England the Hillary family was accommodated in a flat in Central London and Michael Hillary took up his new position at Australia House. During his first vacation Michael Hillary went looking for a property that he and his family could use as a holiday retreat. He found such a place in Reynolds Road, Beaconsfield, Buckinghamshire, called Shirley Cottage.

These must have been very exciting times for the young Richard. The journey by ship had lasted for several weeks. The transition from Toorak, and the warm open spaces of the Pacific coast beaches of Australia, where the family spent some holiday time, to the relative solemnity of the town of Beaconsfield with its less pleasant climate would have been quite subduing for the tempestuous and demanding young Richard, although he eventually made many friends in the Beaconsfield area. Such was his state of mind that during the first half of 1925 his parents saw fit to send him to stay with his uncle and aunt in Egmanton, Nottinghamshire.

Edwyna's brother, the Reverend Arthur Henry Monger Hope, lived with his wife Kate and two sons, Edmund and Robin, in the vicarage at Egmanton near Tuxford, where he was the vicar at Our Lady of Egmanton parish church in the diocese of Southwell from 1915 until 1926.

The Reverend Hope's two sons, Edmund and Robin, were mostly away at boarding school during Richard's occasional visits to the vicarage. His mother would take him by train as far as Grantham where his uncle would meet Richard and together they would travel across to Tuxford Station. They covered the final half-mile of beautiful countryside from the station to the vicarage by horse-drawn cart. Edwyna would return to Kings Cross having been parted from Richard for the first of many occasions. These partings never became less painful over the years to come.

From his uncle's recollections of Richard's first visit, comes the image of a small boy, with red cheeks, a pair of frosty blue eyes and an exceedingly stiff upper lip, who sat with him in the dog cart, impervious to their ventures at cheerfulness, but momentarily warmed to the semblance of a smile by the news that the mare was named Tavey. The brown hind quarters of Tavey, the comfortable clip-clop of her hooves, the flickering of her sensitive ears, must have been reassuring to the young exile, for Arthur Hope recalls that Richard gazed at her for most of the journey, suddenly cheered up, and subsequently became greatly attached to the horse. He soon adjusted to the lifestyle and surroundings at the vicarage. Richard also thoroughly enjoyed the traditional cooking of his aunt, despite her having been warned by his mother that he was 'tissicky' about food at home:

> He was a little homesick the first night, for he was not quite six, but he soon recovered. He was a little boy who liked to take command of the situation. If one drove with him, he would press to do the driving. One day I took him over to see the water-mill that was in our parish, and coming home he clamoured to take the reins. And when I had given way to him, we were soon on the grass verge! 'You really must let me take the reins, Dick,' I said, but I had to take them . . . No one at that time could have called him a 'dear little boy'.

Richard's Aunt Kate described him as self-assertive, rather disobedient and defiant. His attitude to other children was overbearing and aggressive. The children he liked best were those who stood up for themselves. Any that cried, whined or told tales he loathed. He never sought an adult when beaten in a fight. He was truthful and never tried to cover up a misdemeanour or an act of disobedience.

As a small boy or schoolboy he found it difficult to express sorrow when he was in the wrong. He was not a naughty child in that he got into mischief or scrapes, the trouble came when he couldn't get his own way. In this case his temper got the best of him, which expressed the need for the child of strong character to learn the meaning of discipline.

During his stay at Egmanton he liked reading and being read to. His aunt and uncle said that he sat, '. . . as good as gold, drinking the stories in'. He listened enthralled by the tales of *Alice in Wonderland*, *The Pied Piper of Hamlyn* and *The Knights of the Round Table*. He loved books on animals, and in particular the story of *Robin Hood*. Egmanton was only a few miles away from Sherwood Forest and so was practically in Robin Hood country. Edmund, away at boarding-school, had a book about Robin Hood given to him by one of his godfathers. At night his Aunt Kate would read to Richard from this. He was fascinated by the stories but his aunt was keen to correct the doubtful morality in the stories of Robin Hood and extol the virtues of saints and angels. It is far more likely that he went to sleep enviable of the rude and bluff existence of Robin Hood and his men.

Richard expressed a love for the wildlife and countryside surrounding the vicarage and when the time came for him to return to London he said to his Aunt Kate:'I want to live here, I want to die here, and be buried here. I don't like London and the streets.'

She later said, 'He loved the freedom of the country, the picnics we went on, the pony and the dogs; walks in the woods stirred his imagination, and he got a lot of fun out of them and the games that could be played.' His opinion of the city would change considerably as he grew up.

When this holiday was over, Kate took him to Kings Cross and delivered him into the hands of his mother.

Richard enjoyed a number of holidays with the Hopes over the years of his youth and they enjoyed his company, particularly in the absence of their own sons away at boarding school. The love that Richard's aunt and uncle provided in some way compensated for the love that he missed so much when his own parents left the country.

In 1926 the Reverend Arthur Hope and his family moved away for him to take up the position of rector of Perivale, where he remained until he retired in 1949. Richard did stay with the Hopes again, but they had by that time moved to Perivale.

* * *

During the latter part of his tour in London, Michael Hillary was offered an important and permanent position with the Sudanese government which would ultimately lead to his appointment as auditor-general. He accepted the position and, as he was required to do so, moved to Khartoum with Edwyna and Richard during the winter of 1926.

In September 1927, Michael and Edwyna put Richard, now aged seven, into a preparatory school just outside the village of Haynes Church End, between Bedford and Ampthill, close to the A6. The school was situated in one of the most attractive parts of the Bedfordshire countryside.

Hawnes School had been established in the beautiful mansion that is now known as Haynes Park since the closure of the school some years ago. The grounds included extensive areas of beautiful parkland. A large lake highlights the magnificent view of the house from the village of Haynes Church End. Hawnes School specialised in the preparation of boys for public school and for possible entrance into the Army or Royal Air Force.

Having made their choice Michael and Edwyna drove north, delivered him into the hands of the headmaster and experienced what must have been a very painful parting. Richard remained here until 1931 when his mother and father took him away, one year earlier than had been intended. Richard's parents returned to England for a lengthy summer holiday once every two years. During these holidays, they would spend time at their home in Beaconsfield and travelling to coastal resorts.

Richard did reasonably well at his studies but mathematics was a weakness, the subject terrified him. Despite the efforts of a private tutor hired by his parents, Richard never really grasped the subject. His letters to Khartoum expressed great unhappiness and extreme misery, which must have caused great pain for his mother, being so far apart from her only child. She tried in vain to find another school for him during the summer holiday of 1930, but she failed to do so, and he returned to Hawnes.

Even though he continued to spend his holidays with Arthur and Kate Hope, it must have been terribly hard for a young boy of his age to get used to the fact that his parents were living so far away in another country. This, coupled with the fact that he had left his birthplace, childhood memories, and what few young friends he had, behind in Australia. He also had a doting mother and although she had demanded a high level of discipline from her son during the early years of his life, she could not hide the immense love she felt for him. It was this also that he missed.

CHAPTER TWO

SHREWSBURY SCHOOL

1931 – 37

In 1931 when Richard was twelve Michael and Edwyna took him by car to Shrewsbury School in Shropshire for a preliminary interview with the headmaster. They had been looking for a public school of repute that would provide Richard with all that the preparatory school had apparently been unable to provide. Shrewsbury was, and still is, an excellent public school set in beautiful grounds overlooking the river Severn.

During the journey Richard had expressed his dislike at the idea of being sent there, 'I am going to hate it, I am going to hate it all', he announced.

He may well have been acting like a spoilt child but one can understand his concerns. However, his interview with the soon to retire headmaster, Canon H.A.P. Sawyer, a large rotund uncharismatic man, was nevertheless a success. Richard liked him and answered whatever questions he put to him without hesitation or difficulty.

* * *

Shrewsbury School, where he was to remain until 1937, covers a large area. The main building, which contains the form rooms, is situated on high ground to the south of the Severn valley overlooking the river and boathouses below. Looking across to the north side is the town of Shrewsbury, an attractive, historic town with a pleasant atmosphere. The main school buildings, all in red brick, are situated in a large expanse of beautifully maintained gardens and playing fields, consisting of a church, sports hall, swimming pool, assembly hall and the individual houses in which the boys live.

Richard was put into Churchill House where the housemaster was the Reverend J.O. Whitfield, a short-tempered man during classes but with a genuine concern for the boys in his house shown in the form of acts of unobtrusive kindness and generosity.

Despite Richard's dislike of the traditional educational system, he found that at Shrewsbury he was able to do his own thing and was therefore not unhappy there. He was an individual and an individualist and as such he protected himself by exhibiting a superficial manner that made others think he was supremely confident. He was however, self-reliant. He used his ego to hide and protect his inner feelings. His teachers thought him needlessly provocative, his fellow pupils thought him arrogant and hot-tempered, yet he did not become a solitary figure and underneath there was a sensitivity that few suspected. He expressed cynicism at the objects of a normal boy's interest and enthusiasm.

One of the other new boys was George Nelson-Edwards, whose father and uncle had both been day boys at Shrewsbury. He was one year older than Richard and had just left Mill Read prep school situated on the outskirts of Shrewsbury, close to the family home. Around the time he started at Shrewsbury, his family moved to Worcester, and so he became a boarder. The first person he met as he entered Churchill's, was Richard Hillary:

> Dick Hillary was rather small for his age, an abundant crop of fair hair falling down over a high forehead, squat nose, close eyebrows and full lips with a pronounced pout, especially when disconcerted.
>
> For the first three or four years Dick and I were good friends. Although we usually shared the same study we were never in the same form together, because

5

he took modern languages whilst I remained on the classical side, until my last year when I took history.

Once or twice a year, usually the Christmas or Easter holidays, Dick would come to stay at my parent's house on the river Severn at Hawford Lock, near Worcester. We enjoyed things schoolboys usually enjoy, walking, riding, bicycling, boating on the river and going to the pictures. As we grew older our tastes became, dare I say it, more sophisticated, yet compared with the youth today we were still in the kindergarten stage.

One Easter weekend they went to stay with some wealthy friends of George's family living near Rugeley. It was during this trip that the two did some shooting with a small bore rifle. George took a photograph of Richard deliberately aiming the rifle at the camera:

> They had a beautiful country mansion called Bellamore, and three attractive daughters, Peggy, Sheila and Betty. I had a heavy crush on Sheila, aged about seventeen, but the moment she set eyes on Dick she had no more time for me, yet the strange fact is that Dick displayed only mild interest in her. Nor, for that matter, did he show much interest in Peggy or Betty who used to tease him unmercifully. This infuriated me because I would see Sheila was just wasting her time instead of focusing her attention on me.

It was around this time at the age of 16 that Richard lost his virginity. The response from those who knew him at Shrewsbury was one of incredulous envy. Towards the end of their time at Shrewsbury the two friends started to become a little less tolerant of each other. George Nelson-Edwards became tired of Richard's eagerness to appear independent and argue against popular opinion, usually just for the sake of being different:

> Another study mate of ours in Churchill's was John Keitley, whose father and grandfather were regular officers in the Manchester Regiment. Although army co-ordinated, John was an 'aircraft buff' as he would have been called today.
>
> He had a standing order with W.H. Smith down in the town for the two aeronautical periodicals *Aeroplane* and *Flight*, which he read avidly from cover to cover. We used to sit in our study every Sunday afternoon discussing flying and aviation in general. Photographs of German warplanes like the Me109 were appearing, and already prototypes of the Hurricane and Spitfire were being tested. Most of them looked something like the aircraft in my dream.
>
> Dick always adopted a supercilious attitude towards all this activity, professing to be totally against taking up arms, even vowing that he would be a conscientious objector in the event of war. He scorned patriotism and ridiculed John for his outmoded army traditions and for his unquestioning acceptence of becoming cannon fodder. For my part, I used to read everything I could lay my hands on about the National Socialist ideology, including Hitler's *Mein Kampf* and I came to recognise the evils of the Nazi obsession with world domination.
>
> In 1933 we learnt about the Oxford Union debate when the majority voted for the motion: 'We will never fight for King and Country'. It was the subject of vigorous discussion amongst ourselves and Dick was the only one to side with the Union majority.

Regrettably, Dick Hillary had come increasingly under the influence of a strange master called Frank McEachran, who could have been a 'pre-war hippie'. McEachran's political outlook was Liberal, embracing the teachings of Henry George who preached land reform. His radical leanings were even mildly shared by one or two of the other masters, but in general there was little or no enthusiasm for his doctrinate opinions. During the summer holidays he went as a volunteer to fight for the Republicans in the Spanish Civil War.

It has been said that he played an important part in the formation of Dick's character. Whatever else it did, it tended to alienate Dick from his friends and exposed a rather less attractive side to his nature than the alluring image later attributed to him would suggest.

Eventually we tried out Dick in the Churchill's Four which was shaping exceptionally well. Even in the hour of success Dick had to spoil things by trying to convince me that to excel at sport was old fashioned and a waste of time.

'The value,' he gibed at me, 'to be derived from sitting up late reading Goethe is far more rewarding than snatching beauty sleep to make yourself a top-class oarsman.'

'You can keep your beloved Goethe, Dick,' I countered. 'Don't be a hypocrite. I know full well that you have even surprised yourself by sharing in our rowing success, but you are ashamed to admit it.'

At this Dick lost his temper, grappled with me, and we fell to the floor locked in a bitter struggle. I ordered him to bed and he departed disgruntled and unrepentant. From that moment on we seldom fraternised.

* * *

Michael Hillary had given considerable thought to the future career of his son. With a place at Shrewsbury having been secured he anticipated Richard gaining a place at Oxford. With an adequate academic record and a possible rowing blue he assumed that he would follow him into employment with the Sudanese government, which chose its officials through personal selection. With this knowledge and the backing of his father Richard would have felt that he already had one foot in the door and as long as he gained a reasonable standard of education, and a Shrewsbury and Oxford background would seem to reflect that, he would achieve this goal. This would allow him to adopt a laid-back attitude, which he so openly exhibited, and allow him the flexibility to follow other interests. His future seemed secure and must have given great peace of mind for a while. His urge to be a writer, however, was indeed prevalent at this time, but Richard thought it best not to mention it to his father, perhaps he was still unsure as to his true ability with the pen.

Michael Charlesworth, a contemporary of Richard at Shrewsbury, remembers:

> Dick Hillary was a nice enough person, but temperamental. Whenever you approached him you never really knew what to expect. He had a very sarcastic sense of humour which was often taken the wrong way. I would say he was sardonic. He liked to talk but he was very argumentative.
>
> I personally had no problems maintaining a good friendship with him over the five years that I knew him. After we left Shrewsbury, he went to Trinity College Oxford, while I went to Brasenose, as did my lifelong friend George Nelson-Edwards, and I saw little more of him.

Richard joined the Officers Training Corps (OTC) at Shrewsbury and was a boy sergeant-major in his unit from 1933 until 1937. When he subsequently joined the RAFVR in August 1939, this experience may have been taken into consideration when he was given the rank of sergeant. The OTC later became the Combined Cadet Force (CCF), with Army, Navy and Air Force sections.

The main sport at Shrewsbury included soccer and rowing. Having the river nearby was an excellent facility with the school having its own boathouse, in a beautiful setting, a hundred yards further east along the bank of the river Severn from that of the town. Richard was to row for the Second VIII but was never to gain a place in the First VIII.

Michael Charlesworth recalls:

> He was a very good oarsman. For two years he stroked the Second Eight at Shrewsbury. It seems he either rowed stroke or not at all. Once he had applied himself to the task he gave everything. It was this almost reckless determination that made him successful. Unfortunately he failed to get his colours for the first.

> The coach in charge of the First VIII decided not to include him in the team despite his performances saying, 'He hasn't got racing guts.' I think that it was due to his attitude in general. He gave everyone the impression that he was very 'laid back' and casual about most things and it was probably thought that this would be detrimental to the success of the First VIII. He was also still quite small for his age.

The coach may have simply taken a dislike to this over-confident egoist as Richard was destined never to have the chance to prove himself in the First VIII. However he had gained a reputation as an oarsman which was to precede him when he went up to Oxford.

Richard's academic studies went according to plan. Michael Charlesworth again recalls:

> Dick did quite well. He wasn't that bright but he managed to pass all the relevant exams when they came along. The brighter and more mature boys might spend two years in Upper Sixth, but Richard only spent one year in Lower Sixth. During English classes he was very impressed by the teaching methods of Frank McEachran. McEachran was a comparative newcomer who appeared to teach us – what? I think it must have been divinity but as all came to know as time went on, it was immaterial what Mac taught as it always turned out to be a study and recitation of 'Spells' – his name for wide ranging quotations from literature, which became his hallmark, known to generations of Salopians spread over forty years.
>
> Richard later said that it was through him that he: '. . . got the idea of trying to write good English, and of enjoying books.'

Richard confided in McEachran that he wanted to be a writer and that he wished to model himself on the American novelist John Steinbeck. To some this would be seen as being presumptuous but McEachran provided him with relevant advice and reading material, taking the opportunity to assist one of his pupils genuinely interested in what was being taught him. Later, in July of 1941, during a radio broadcast in America Richard named McEachran as the greatest influence in his life.

McEachran was born in 1900 in the Black Country town of Wolverhampton. His early life was spent moving between a series of homes in the north of England as his father's job as a journeyman joiner meant moving to where work was available.

He was educated at Manchester Grammar School and Magdalen College, Oxford. Following his degree, he went on to a B.Litt on the German philosopher Herder. The late 18th century writer is often regarded as the founder of modern Nationalism; an event which McEachran later came to destest.

The period of hyperinflation in 1923 coincided with McEachran's studying in Leipzig where he spent some time researching Herder. A Dip.Ed, taken after completing his B.Litt, led him to the start of his teaching career. His first teaching post was at Gresham's School, Holt. What initially set McEachran apart from other public schoolmasters during the early years of his teaching career was his literary achievement. Between 1927 and 1934, he contributed around 20 essays to highly prestigious literary periodicals and also had published two books *The Civilised Man* in 1930 and *The Destiny of Europe* in 1932. At that time McEachran may have considered a purely literary career, as the 1920s were a golden age for periodicals which was yet to experience the debilitating effects of the massive expansion of the media industry.

Although some of the descendants of the big Victorian heavyweight reviews were still in the field, at this time there was a new generation of journals, which specialised in literary criticism and were edited by leading figures of the literary critical world. T.S. Eliot's *Criterion*, Cyril Connolly's *Horizon* (McEachran contributed to both, especially the former), and F.R. Leavis' *Scrutiny* being the most obvious. It has been said that it was McEachran's contact with T.S. Eliot in particular, whom he knew quite well, which would have given him an easy route into the world of publishing. It was Eliot's firm of

Faber and Faber that published his two books.

McEachran left Gresham's in 1934 and spent time travelling through Greece and Russia before being appointed to Shrewsbury School in 1935 by the then headmaster H.H.H. Hardy. His diaries from his travels were published as a commemorative volume after his death.

In the Easter holidays of 1937, the time of the Spanish Civil War, McEachran and a Shrewsbury colleague travelled to Republican Spain to try to find a friend whose contact with home had been lost. On reaching Almeria they discovered that the friend had left for England the day before. The trip later added to the McEachran mythology and the tale developed that he actually took part in the war on the Republican side. His dropped shoulder was not in their opinion as a result of poor posture but from having his rifle slung over it! Although this was not the case at all, the image would suit Richard. The affair also matched the reputation for radicalism that McEachran had already acquired.

Of McEachran's own literary achievements, his pupils at Shrewsbury knew nothing. They remember him for his 'spells' and to a lesser extent his screeds (a 'spell' is an incantation and the actual practice of saying the verse out loud is the origin of the term here. The expression is unique to McEachran).

McEachran's spells appealed on many levels. Some always treated them as a joke; others found the style of his teaching unconvincing; others still enjoyed the little pantomime of standing on chairs to recite them, a bit of fantasy which again made them memorable. Some were captivated by the sheer sound of them – which was the main reasoning behind such recitations. McEachran's own definition of a spell, was 'concentrated poetry, of sound or sense'; and perhaps a minority saw deeper than this, to the uniting of sound and sense which is the essence of spells, and of all successful poetry. McEachran emphasised the incantatory nature of spells; they were often not recited individually at all, but chanted in chorus. The extreme example of this must have been the Hitler spell: *'Niemand hat je gesagt, ich wäre feig gewesen'*, where McEachran himself stated in the accompanying note: 'If you want to understand the spirit of Nazism, make a class of adolescents, with teeth clenched, bellow this out.'

No doubt it must have been a memorable experience for the pupils, but one is left to ponder the reaction of other teachers, in particular the colleague teaching next door.

At heart, McEachran was deeply and passionately committed to the ideal of individual human freedom. The great question for him was how an economic system supposedly founded on the principles of Victorian liberalism, which always commanded his loyalty, had gone so disastrously wrong; and he found the answer in the writings of Henry George. George was a nineteenth-century land and tax reformer, whose ideas attracted great interest and provided topic for discussion for a period towards the end of the last century both in this country and in his native America. McEachran's ideas were largely shaped by him, and Richard was also to adopt George as a prophet, while at Shrewsbury and more particularly at Oxford, when others perhaps chose Marx or Keynes.

McEachran had the strongest dislike of and distrust for the state, which he regarded as potentially the most authoritarian and dangerous of all human institutions. From the standpoint of the late 1990s, it should be stated that his ideas were formed against the background of the totalitarian states of the 1930s and 1940s, a time which saw some of the most oppressive, authoritarian institutions ever. He was convinced that freedom was the only valid end of human activity.

Frank McEachran remained at Shrewsbury until his retirement in 1960. It has been said of his humble background that: '. . . Mac never assimilated himself to the public school type – I doubt if anyone would ever have taken him to be a public school old boy, and in many ways he always remained an outsider within the system . . .'. McEachran is probably best remembered as a loveable old eccentric who used to make pupils stand on their chairs and recite poetry. Between retirement and his death in 1975, he continued to hold spell and screed sessions in his flat.

* * *

An interesting point to consider is that Richard, like W.H. Auden and Benjamin Britten, obviously saw something that he admired in McEachran, something that inspired him and gave him the ambition to become a writer. Richard later told an audience of many during a radio broadcast that McEachran was:

> The only master that succeeded in teaching me anything . . . He made me realise
> there might be more important things than toiling on rivers . . .

It should be said that Richard saw himself as being different to everyone else, a bit of a radical, sometimes arguing against, simply because everyone else was for. Could Richard have seen McEachran as a radical, someone to model himself on in some way? I believe he took on the mantle of McEachran whilst he was at Oxford. There are certainly aspects of McEachran's life that impressed Richard to the point that later he would follow the same directions. He travelled abroad and was always eager to mix with the locals, rather than friends or other travellers, and learn as much as possible while he was there.

Richard, like McEachran, became interested in existentialist philosophy. He craved knowledge even at the annoyance of others. In hospital recovering from his burns he would enquire as to the experiences of his fellow patients, even at a time when their suffering was great and on the verge of death itself. They were angered and surprised at his questions at such an inappropriate time. But he had to know what they were feeling. He asked his plastic surgeon, Archibald McIndoe, if the patient who was close to death was aware of its inevitability. What did they feel? This question stuck in the mind of the great plastic surgeon for many years. Such was Richard's inquisitive and eager to learn nature. He has been remembered as a child that questioned everything, sometimes to the annoyance of those around him. This trait was never to leave him.

It may be that Richard included 'spells' of Verlaine and Goethe in *The Last Enemy* as the result of McEachran's influence on him, but we have no reaction from McEachran about the book on record.

McEachran later wrote of his recollections of Richard's outstanding qualities of character, and how they manifest themselves in boyhood: 'Toughness, courage, tenacity. He was hard – bitter and individualistic to a degree.' Of his defects he wrote: 'Slightly cynical and egotistical; critical of others, and a little grudging. He disliked discipline.' McEachran then went on to add:

> Richard's mind was greatly developed by coming into contact with modern
> literature in the form of T.S. Eliot and the contemporary school of poets . . . He
> came to school early and exhausted the possibilities too soon . . . Also, he was
> disappointed in the Sixth Form, which did not really manage him well . . . Oxford
> had a good effect, and definitely turned him the direction of writing.

* * *

Shrewsbury had to some extent disciplined Richard. He was a very independent individual and would never want to be seen to fully conform and was quick to contradict anything that he didn't agree with, or argue against, just for the sake of it. He could be very obstinate and argumentative. His housemaster, Mr Whitfield, recalls:

> He seemed to dislike the conventional views of things, often merely because they
> were conventional. He would often express views merely because he thought
> they were contrary to those of his companions, and would be disappointed if his
> ideas were accepted without argument.
>   He hated above all being treated as young, as though he was not a man of the
> world. He liked shocking people in a mild way.

One occurrence did illustrate this point. A Board of Education inspector visited Shrewsbury school and lunched at the head table in Richard's house. The inspector sat on Mr Whitfield's right, and Richard opposite him. Richard leaned across the table and opened the conversation with the remark: 'You have come to inspect the masters here, not the boys, haven't you?'

He had taken the opportunity to dispute the value of the public school system with the inspector of education such was his enjoyment of argument and under the eye of his housemaster. But everyone just laughed as if it had been a joke.

* * *

In the absence of his parents during the summer of 1932, when Richard was thirteen, his parents reluctantly agreed to allow him to travel abroad on his own during his school holiday. He travelled through France to Germany where he stayed in various pensions. He took advantage of the situation to improve his French and German and very likely got an insight into the attitudes and beliefs of some of the German youth during those pre war years.

It must have been exciting for him to pass on details of his adventures to his fellow pupils back in Churchill House once the new school year began. Was he being pretentious? Very likely, but it was only natural that all the boys would talk of their respective adventures during the summer holiday. Richard probably knew however that his adventures would be unsurpassed.

To be allowed so much independence and for Richard to make so much of the opportunity gives us an insight into just how mature he was at just thirteen years of age and also how much strength of character he had. Try and imagine a 13 year-old of today undertaking such a trip, unaccompanied. He preferred the company of older boys to those of his own age and he was also sexually advanced. Clearly his travels and the time spent away from his parents had contributed greatly to this early maturity.

Richard also enjoyed the occasional reuniting and subsequent holiday with his father and mother. During the summer holiday of 1933, they went on holiday to the Mumbles in South Wales, where he spent much of the day swimming and diving off the cliffs into the sea. However, the long periods away from his parents must have taken their toll having to face the reality of their almost continued absence, and forcing him to be able to survive without the love of a doting mother. Once he was in the position to see her more frequently, during his time at Oxford onwards, they became closer than ever before.

Whatever criticism may have been levelled at him as a person in the years to come, this must have been a contributing factor in the development of a hard, self-preserving aspect to his personality that set him apart from his associates. He has often been described as having a 'chip on his shoulder'. Maybe this would, to some extent, explain the reason for this perception.

There was a warm side to him too, however. Richard had friends, although he would be inclined to choose them and not the reverse. At Shrewsbury, Oxford and when he joined the RAFVR he would surround himself with a small band of loyal friends. At Shrewsbury he came to know David Woodrow, a member of the school rowing team who achieved further success in the successful Trinity College VIII in which Richard was stroke. One of Richard's closest friends at Shrewsbury was Frank A.L. Waldron, a tall, good looking, blond haired, athletic young man who was also an excellent oarsman. The three went up to Oxford and rowed together in the successful Trinity College VIII of 1938-39. Richard and Frank Waldron joined the University Air Squadron. In *The Last Enemy* Richard wrote:

> Frank Waldron had rowed No.6 in the Oxford crew. He stood six-foot-three and had an impressive mass of snow-white hair. Frank was not unintelligent and he was popular. In my first year he had been president of the Junior Common Room. The girls pursued him, but he affected to prefer drink. In point of fact he was unsure of himself and was searching for someone to put on a pedestal. He had a great personality and an undeveloped character. Apart from myself, he was the

laziest though most stylish oarsman in the university, but he did a minimum of work, knowing that it was essential to get a second if he wished to enter the Civil Service, but always finding some plausible argument to convince himself that the various distractions of life were necessities... he was in a way representative of a large number of similarly situated young men. He had many unconscious imitators who, because they had not the same prowess or personality, showed up as the drifting shadows that they were.

The friendship with Frank was to become one of the longest in Richard's short life, and it would seem they were very close. Frank was actually five years older than Richard and while it may seem unusual that a junior should have a senior as a close friend, Richard preferred the company of the older boys. The school photograph taken in 1934 clearly shows the difference in years between the two. Perhaps there was a little hero worship from Richard here towards this tall, good-looking athlete. Regardless, the two were to remain friends during their time at Trinity, where age was not a qualifying factor for friendship.

Richard's sense of humour could sometimes be very cruel, as mentioned by Michael Charlesworth. Certain individuals who did not know him well were left feeling very hurt and resentful, as was to be the case when he was in East Grinstead hospital being treated for his burns just over two years later. Many fellow patients were sometimes to experience cruel, sarcastic comments and thumb-nail sketches but were unaware, at that time, that this was his means of escape, an outlet for his own disconsolate feelings. But as Geoffrey Page, one of Richard's companions at that time, told me:

> There was never any hatred towards him, it was just that he could be so bloody annoying, and at times when you could least tolerate it. Most of us knew that there was also an immensely charming side to his personality and I saw much evidence of that too.

Richard's early predilection for flying first truly emerged when he was 14. It was during the summer holiday of 1933, when his parents were home from Khartoum that Richard had his first flight, followed promptly by a second. Sir Alan Cobham's 'Flying Circus' had advertised its intention to perform a flying display and offer pleasure flights ('the five bob flip') at High Wycombe, close to the Hillary home at Beaconsfield, as part of his National Aviation day tour which took place each year from 1932 until 1935. Michael Hillary took Richard to the venue and paid for his son to have a short flight, which turned out to be a simple circuit of the airfield. Richard was somewhat disappointed at the duration of the flight, but his appetite had been whetted. For the finale of loops, slow and fast rolls the team offered a member of the audience a front seat in one of their aircraft. Michael Hillary succumbed to his son's clamouring and allowed him to take part. Richard was given neither helmet nor goggles and despite the additional discomfort of having a loose attaché case belonging to the pilot in the cockpit which dug painfully into him, he did not go green, was not sick, and enjoyed the experience tremendously.

After six years at Shrewsbury his final exam marks did not reflect outstanding academic ability but were adequate to ensure acceptance into Oxford, although his father's influence and the reputation of the school were also contributing factors. He celebrated his last night at the school by driving an assortment of cars on to the cricket-pitch. Such pranks were not unusual, but Richard was full of remorse when he found out that a match that, unbeknown to him, had been planned for the next day, had to be cancelled due to the damage on the batting strip. He was never to re-visit the school and was to express the opinion that they would not have allowed him to do so anyway because of this prank.

CHAPTER THREE

OXFORD

1937 – 1939

Richard left Shrewsbury during June 1937, and spent some time at the family's holiday home in Beaconsfield, Buckinghamshire before travelling to Khartoum to visit his parents. In October, he entered Trinity College, Oxford, as an undergraduate. His degree course was on Modern Greats of History, with an intended duration of three years. His tutors were Melville Patterson and Reggie Weaver, of whose teaching it was said that, 'Patters can't and Reggie won't'.

Richard would have felt those familiar pangs of homesickness and trepidation at what lay ahead but after only a very short period of time at Trinity he must have become aware that this was going to be a very enjoyable and fulfilling experience. It was an environment that had a great deal to offer this egocentric and it was here that a softening of the harder side of his personality took place, as he became more and more aware of the value of friendship. He became less truculent. In many ways the sardonic side of his personality was a defence mechanism that prevented him from being emotionally hurt or vulnerable to emotional hurt.

In the absence of his parents he had become strong and independent; the people around him were to his liking. He felt comfortable in their company and was happy to reveal the charming side of his personality, wishing to gain their friendship not cast it aside. They were certainly attracted to him and admired his self-assurance. It has been said that he was more mature than most of his fellow undergraduates, certainly he was fortunate in that he had more experience of life than most of them. They saw him as sophisticated, charming, lacking in fear, and athletic, someone who rose to the physical challenge. On one occasion he climbed out of a second floor window overlooking Garden Quad, over 20 feet above the courtyard below, and climbed along the ledge to the next window to the amazement of his onlooking friends. He knew he could impress but, unbeknown to them, he also knew his limitations. They also saw him as extremely good-looking. It has been said that many of the young female undergraduates were attracted to Richard over all the other male students at that time.

Trinity had few, if any, of the rules and disciplines that he had experienced as being so restrictive during his years at Shrewsbury. The oppressive rules and supervision of the masters was lifted. Not that he had been unable to adjust and make the most of his time there, but he now had the opportunity to exploit his enthusiasm to the full in an environment that encouraged just that. Richard was no longer a child, he was an adult in an adult environment.

The harsher side of his temperamental personality to which many of his friends and colleagues refer, should be weighed up against the fact that he was undoubtedly a popular individual at Trinity: tall, with an athletic physique, self assured, confident and with a keen sense of humour. He also displayed much prowess in the sporting activities at Trinity.

He became part of a very loyal group of like-minded friends who had much in common with Richard and who understood him or tolerated him for what he was, the nicer aspects of his personality outweighing the less pleasant aspects. Those on the outside of this group may well have felt very differently about him, vulnerable to his sardonic nature and perhaps years later jealous of his success and reputation.

13

* * *

Trinity is a small college which comprises a president, 30 fellows, approximately 270 undergraduates and 80 graduate students. In Richard's day it was much smaller and, as it is today, thought to be wealthier and more aristocratic than it actually was, giving it an air of privilege and status. Nearly all the undergraduates at Trinity had come from public schools (Richard claimed from the 'better' public schools) and from many different parts of the country. He wrote in *The Last Enemy*:

> It was often said that the President of Trinity would accept no one as a commoner in his college who was not a landowner. This was an exaggeration, but one which the dons were not unwilling to foster.

Richard would later boast that during his time at Trinity:

> We had the president of the Rugby Club, the secretary of the Boat Club, numerous golf, hockey, and running blues and the best cricketer in the university. We also numbered among us the president of the University Dramatic Society, the editor of *Isis* [the university magazine], and a small but select band of scholars.

The college's athletic achievements dwarfed its fairly meagre academic achievements.

By comparison Richard and his friends at Trinity described their attitude as one of 'alert Philistinism', although they were probably no different from others from the same background. They made no attempt to be deliberately offensive or snobbish in any way to the scholars of the college, for that was not the way they felt about them; they had little in common with them, however, and communication would be strained and therefore pointless. According to Richard, 'They were earnest, technically knowing, and conversationally uninteresting.'

Whether they were athletes or scholars any decent sort of individual was welcomed into the house. It was not uncommon for most students to be less interested in academic study and pay more attention to self-definition. The imminent war gave a sense of urgency to that introspection. Richard believed that:

> Trinity was, in fact, a typical incubator of the English ruling classes before the war. Most of those with Blues were intelligent enough to get second-class honours in whatever subject they were 'reading', and could thus ensure themselves entry into some branch of the civil or colonial service.

He was therefore feeling comfortable with his ability to achieve a reasonable standard of education regardless of what he would get up to in the interim and would no doubt be able to get a specific job on graduating. He was determined to enjoy himself. In *The Last Enemy* he wrote:

> We were held together by a common taste in friends, sport, literature, and idle amusement, by a deep-rooted distrust of all organised emotion and standardised patriotism, and by a somewhat self-conscious satisfaction in our ability to succeed without apparent effort. I went up for my first term, determined, without over-exertion, to row myself into the Government of Sudan, that country of blacks ruled by Blues in which my father had spent so many years.

His place within the class structure would ensure that he would get a position of employment with the colonial service with the minimum of effort on his part.

Richard also became one of the staff of *Isis*, whose editor was a member of his college and a friend, thus giving him the necessary introduction. He became the sports editor, his writing talent no doubt being to his advantage in this capacity and allowing him to continue to improve his skills. Perhaps at this stage he saw himself as a journalist.

In the 'Trinity Report' for 1997, under the sub-heading 'Archive Report' it was written:

> We thank Alistair McLay of the Workshop for providing us with an acquisition from another unusual source (beneath a College floorboard). The item in question

is a copy of *Isis* from June 1939, full of mentions of Hitler and debates in the Union. From it, we discover that the Sports Editor was Trinity's own Richard Hillary.

Richard and his friends enjoyed the art of conversation, and the topics were wide ranging: Richard was not homosexual, nor a pacifist, communist, left wing or Tory, in an environment that gained a reputation for producing such individuals. However, although he found politics interesting, he scorned left-wing politics. He believed such individuals who fell under the left-wing politics of the Auden group despised the very people from whom they had received their education, the middle classes, and could not gain entrance to the world of labour they so admired. Richard's criticism of them was more practical than political. He reasoned that their beliefs had rendered them incapable of participating but overlooked the part many had played in the Spanish Civil War when many had fought and died.

Richard would have made his appreciation of Henry George known to those around him, as it was another opportunity to set himself apart from the norm. Despite this, out of all the university societies Richard thought the university debating society to be the most puerile. Although Church of England, he thought little of organised religion and his particular butt was Dr Buckman's Oxford group, whose name had been changed in 1938 to the Oxford Group of Moral Rearmament, calling for Christian regeneration. Richard had once attended one of their revivalist meetings and, in one of his mischievous moods, confessed that his principal weaknesses were 'matrons and Portuguese nuns', which one member actually took earnestly enough to attempt his conversion!

* * *

A number of the university college rowing VIIIs competed annually for the title of Head of the River. It is run on a similar basis to a football league table. Each VIII sets out in pursuit of another and is required to physically 'bump' the boat in front in order to 'win' the race and therefore go above the other VIII in the table. The VIII that finishes at the top is awarded the Head of the River title. The external walls in Garden Quad display the recent success and lists the teams 'bumped'. Unlike its achievements in other sports, up until the time of Richard's arrival, Trinity had yet to make its mark in rowing and for some years had failed in the Head of the River races. Richard, though only as a single member of a team, was to change that, although it didn't always go smoothly; he once engaged in a fist fight with the bow-man of the Trinity boat, Derek Graham.

In June of 1938 Trinity was to prove itself a successful rowing team. For the first time since 1865, with Richard as a freshman rowing stroke, Trinity came to the head of the river. Trinity retained the Headship the following year.

* * *

Following this success, Richard and Frank Waldron decided to write to the German and Hungarian Governments with a view to their providing a rowing team to compete against their own teams in their respective countries. On 3 July 1938 ten of the Oxford oarsmen set off for Bad Ems in Germany, half travelling by car, half by train, arriving with two days for recreation before the race. They duly took full advantage of this time. They had been expected to bring their own boat and only received an inferior boat just before the race began and with no time to practice.

The VIII however did not truly represent the university. It was a team put together from those available for the trip rather than the best oarsman in the university. However, the team was undoubtedly one of some quality. Up against five other German crews, which had shown considerable arrogance towards the seemingly lackadaisical Englishmen prior to the race, the Oxford VIII lagged behind until members of the crowd spat on them. Sammy Stockton, who was stroking the boat, reacted accordingly and took them across the winning line two-fifths of a second ahead of the others. When you consider that the country was on the verge of war it must have meant a great deal to these young men when they won the prestigious Hermann Goering Cup, much to the chagrin of the Germans. Richard remarked in *The Last Enemy*:

> General Goering had to surrender his cup and we took it back with us to England. It was a gold shell case mounted with the German eagle and disgraced our rooms in Oxford for nearly a year until we could stand it no longer and sent it back through the German Embassy. I always regret that we didn't put it to the use which its shape suggested. It was certainly an unpopular win. Had we shown any sort of enthusiasm or given any impression that we had trained they would have tolerated it, but as it was they showed merely a sullen resentment.

In his book Richard intimates that he was one of the rowing VIII that achieved victory in Bad Ems, when he was only a reserve. The team then moved on to Budapest, again travelling by car and train. They were accommodated at the Palatinus Hotel on St Margaret's Island.

Up against four Olympic crews, the makeshift Oxford VIII was defeated due to the combined effects of the heat and over-indulgence at the hands of its hospitable Hungarian hosts. Richard wrote in *The Last Enemy*:

> The Danube, far from being blue, turned out to be a turbulent brown torrent that made the Tideway seem like a mill-pond in comparison. Out in midsteam half-naked giants, leaning over the side of anchored barges, hung on to the rudder to prevent us being carried off downstream before the start. We had to keep our blades above the water until they let go for fear that the stream would tear them from our hands. Then at the last moment Sammy Stockton, the one member of our rather temperamental crew who could be relied upon never to show any temperament, turned pale green. A combination of heat, goulash and Tokay had proved too much for him and he came up to the start a very sick man.

A photograph was taken of the Oxford boat during the race and shows Richard stroking the VIII.

* * *

Following his return from Europe, Richard decided to visit France, and in particular Brittany. It is almost as if he were aware of the possibility that time was running out for him and that unless he sought to live his life to the full now the opportunity might never arise again. Many of us have undertaken such trips sometime during our early life and experienced much adventure, but not with the shadow of war hanging over us. That was the difference.

This trip would be a family motoring holiday with his mother and father. After travelling back to his parents' holiday home in Beaconsfield they set off on their journey via Abbeville, Rouen, Rennes, Quimper, finally ending up at the tiny fishing village of Beg Meil on the west coast of Brittany:

> My main object was, I must admit, food. I saw before me possibly years of cold mutton, boiled potatoes and Brussels sprouts, and the lure of one final diet of Cognac at fourpence a glass, oysters, coq-au-vin, and soufflés drew me like a magnet.

It was quite a journey for someone to satisfy their culinary longings, and by the time they had returned to England they had travelled over 1300 miles.

Richard and his parents were in Rouen, on the last stage of their return journey, the night of Hitler's final speech before Munich. Hitler's speech and the fanatical '*Sieg Heils!*' of the audience were broadcast from external speakers and echoed around the walls of the seemingly dormant cathedral city. The locals looked resigned to the inevitable. The Hillary family returned to England on the day of the Munich conference, September 1938.

Richard made one last trip to France before the war. He travelled to Cannes as spare man for the Oxford rowing VIII, where Oxford and Cambridge had been invited to row in the bay. In *The Last Enemy* he wrote:

> Cafe society was there in force; there were fireworks, banquets at Juan-les-Pins, battle of flowers at Nice, and a general air of all being for the best in the best in all possible worlds. We stayed at the Carlton, bathed at Eden Rock and spent most of the night in the Casino. We gave a dinner for the Mayor which ended with Frank and the guest of honour rolled together in the tablecloth singing quite unintelligible ditties, much to the surprise of the more sober diners. We emerged from some night club at seven o'clock in the morning of our departure with a bare half hour left to catch our plane. Over the doorway a Union Jack and a Tricolour embraced each other in a rather tired entente cordiale. Frank seized the Tricolour and waved it gaily above his head. At that moment the smallest Frenchman I've ever seen rushed after us and clutched hold of Frank's retreating coat-tails.
>
> '*Mais, non, non, non!*' he screeched.
>
> '*Mais, oui, oui, oui,* my little man,' said Frank, and, disengaging himself, he belaboured the fellow over the head with the emblem of his Fatherland and cantered off down the road, to appear twenty minutes later on the airport, a sponge bag in one hand and the Tricolour still firmly clasped in the other.

These young men clearly took full advantage of the quality of life that had been bestowed upon them by the class into which they had been born. They certainly lived life to the full and were labelled by the press as 'The Lost Generation', a phrase from the First World War and originally used to describe the countless young men that failed to return. During the years between the wars the meaning of the phrase rather interestingly shifted in its use to refer to those that were left and returned home, describing the rootlessness of that second generation. Ernest Hemingway used the phrase as an epigraph for his novel *The Sun Also Rises* to characterise that generation's selfish concern for a good time. They gratefully accepted the title as Richard recorded in *The Last Enemy*:

> We were not displeased. Superficially we were selfish and egocentric without any Holy Grail in which we could lose ourselves. The war provided it, and in a delightfully palatable form. It demanded no heroics, but gave us the opportunity to demonstrate in action our dislike of organised emotion and patriotism, the opportunity to prove to ourselves and to the world that our effete veneer was not as deep as our dislike of interference, the opportunity to prove that, undisciplined though we might be, we were a match for Hitler's dogma-fed youth.

For Richard the war gave him the opportunity to temporarily stop worrying about what career to follow, something he was still undecided about and clearly troubled by. He was pressured by society into making a decision he was clearly not ready to make just yet.

In fact his keenness to travel extensively and make the right career choice when he felt he had satisfied certain desires first is prevalent in so many students today. The war solved all problems of a career and promised a chance for self-realisation that would normally take years to achieve.

In the run-up to the 1939 Oxford and Cambridge University Boat Race, Richard and George Nelson-Edwards were both included in the Oxford University Trial Eights which took place on Saturday 26 November 1938 and was rowed from Marsh Lock to Hambledon Lock. The team was coached by Dr P.C. 'Pat' Mallam, a former student of Lancing College who had been sent up to Queen's College, Oxford, where he rowed in the 'Blue' boat from 1921 to 1924. He went on to become an Olympic oarsman. Richard was in the 'B' crew rowing No.2 while Nelson-Edwards rowed No.4 in the 'A' boat which won by one and a quarter lengths. Neither was to gain a place in the 'Blue' Boat, and the war prevented any further chance of their achieving this. They did however both gain a place in the Oxford University second eight, the Isis crew. Although he would have been unable to gain a place in the team of older colonial postgraduate oarsman of the modern day team, Richard was by this time six feet one inch tall and, as a result of the strict training regime, thirteen and a half stone in weight. He was at his strongest, fittest and heaviest, as photographs taken during this period indicate.

Pat Mallam, who had a practice in Oxford, and George Nelson-Edwards, became good friends and on one occasion Pat Mallam asked him if he would like to go to London to see the World Light-Heavyweight Championship fight at Harringay between Larry Gains and an up and coming boxer called Len Harvey. Over dinner they talked about the fight and the Trial Eights. George later recalled the conversation and the thoughts it generated:

> 'Hal [George's nickname to his colleagues at that time] what's your opinion of Dick Hillary?' Pat asked suddenly. 'You were at Shrewsbury with him, you must know him pretty well.'
>
> 'I should say so! We were in the same house together, once upon a time we were good friends.'
>
> 'I've noticed you don't seem very matey, on or off the river. Why's that?'
>
> 'I'm not sure, Pat, maybe its because he once swiped my girl friend.'
>
> 'Tell me more.'
>
> 'Well,' I said, 'He was staying with us on summer holidays, when I introduced him to some very wealthy friends of my parents. I was mad keen on one of their daughters, but as soon as she saw him she didn't want to know me any more.'
>
> 'You can't blame Dick for that, you know,' Pat countered, 'but I can see that he's a very conceited young man.'
>
> Of course I knew there was more to it than just youthful rancour.
>
> Motoring back to Oxford late that night in Pat Mallam's car, along the Western Avenue through Beaconsfield, High Wycombe and Stokenchurch, I pondered on this evident anomaly of having an old friend who suddenly disowns me, yet we still share the same friends in our small world of rowing and training for the Boat Race. My thoughts rambled on and I began to feel resentful at Dick's self-assured egocentric attitude. The tragedy is that his life was cut short before the final reckoning.
>
> In retrospect, I realise that I attributed to him faults which I now know I shared with him – lust, envy, jealousy and covetousness. In other words, in our heedless materialistic young lives there was little to choose between us, and the war which was about to erupt around us was to change everything. . . .
>
> . . . . In those carefree days, London was irresistible if one had money. A favourite haunt for pleasure-seeking undergraduates was the Cavendish Hotel in Jermyn Street, run by a well known lady called Rosa Lewis. She was reputed to be the illegitimate daughter of King Edward VII.
>
> She encouraged young debutantes and moneyed ladies to patronize the Cavendish, and engineered illicit unions between them and approved Oxford and Cambridge undergraduates. Dick Hillary was one of Rosa's favourites and the Cavendish Hotel was where he used to foregather with his friends, among them a young wealthy Armenian called Noel Agazarian. There was no way I could raise the ante to join the Cavendish set.

During this period Richard used to impress his friends by taking them to a fairly sordid little club called the Bag of Nails, which used to be in Beak Street, Soho. Here a small band played as the customers drank over-priced warm champagne at the dimly lit tables or danced with the girls that made themselves available. Richard's youthful friends stood awkwardly, impressed by his familiarity and relaxed attitude in such an environment, more so because they remember him always leaving with the best-looking girl who, they suspected, did it for free with Richard. The others left with nothing more than empty pockets and the breezy call of the owner, Millie, to 'remember the dear old Bag'.

* * *

The University Air Squadrons were formed between the wars. They were intended both to encourage undergraduates to take up the Royal Air Force as a career and to create a reserve of partially trained officer pilots who could quickly be brought to operational standards in the event of war. The UASs were financed by the Government at no cost to the students. On 24 January 1939, Richard began a course which he hoped would lead to his achieving the Air Ministry Proficiency Certificate for flying. During this period he told a colleague that he did not think that the country would go to war with Germany, but that it was just as well to be prepared. He also said, 'Hitler and I share the same birthday, I wonder if we were born under the same star.'

Although in 1933 the Union at Oxford had concluded that it would be against fighting for King and Country, by 1939, with the German threat mounting, the students responded to the call with enthusiasm. Many had fathers who had fought in the trenches of the First World War. Their sons were aware of their sacrifice and the reasons why they had gone to war, and *The Last Enemy* reflects on the mood at this time.

The Oxford University Air Squadron was established in 1925 for 100 members. Student pilots were chosen by a selection committee made up of senior members of the university and selection boards were held several times a term. There was always a good response when vacancies arose with many left on the waiting list for the next course.

The Oxford UAS Headquarters was established in Manor Road where, during set evenings in the week, the students would undertake lectures on air navigation, rigging, airmanship and engines. The commanding officer at Oxford UAS HQ while Richard was there was Wing Commander F.L.B Hebbert, who had been a WWI fighter pilot. The squadron adjutant was Flight Lieutenant H.J. Kirkpatrick who happened to be an old friend of H.H. Hardy, Richard's headmaster at Shrewsbury. George Nelson-Edwards joined the OUAS shortly before Richard and remembers his interview with the CO:

> In March 1938 I was invited down to Manor Road for an interview with the CO. I couldn't help noticing how his hands trembled and his lips twitched as he lit a cigarette. Is that what flying does to you, I asked myself? I need not have bothered. He was no freak. He knew exactly what he was about and, having accepted me, gave a complete run-down on the squadron's function. I wasn't to know then of course, but almost exactly fifteen years later I would be sitting in the same office, in the very same chair, when I returned to Manor Road as the commanding officer.

Each pilot received an average of nine flights per term, totalling five hours 45 minutes (dual and solo). Each flight was of about 35 minutes' duration.

The course culminated in the examinations which were set to test the student's practical flying skill and academic knowledge. The written exams were individual papers on the various topics studied. If they were successful they were awarded the Air Ministry Proficiency Certificate. From here they could apply for a commission in the RAFVR and remain in situ, or apply for a permanent commission which, in either case, would mean being sent to an Elementary and Reserve Flying Training School, E&RFTS. There was also a Volunteer Reserve Centre in Oxford to which members of the RAFVR could report for duty, if required to do so.

Practical flying training was available during approximately 50 days of each term, but many of these days were lost due to bad weather. When the weather was favourable they would spend several afternoons a week flying, and as the possibility of war became ever more likely the student pilots spent all available time improving their flying skills. During the summer of 1939 the squadron was very busy.

At Flight HQ at RAF Abingdon they were given ground instruction and taught to fly by means of practical flying lessons and flight simulation. In those days flight simulation was known as 'synthetic training'; anything that did not involve risking men and machines actually flying sorties. Such a device used was the Link trainer, designed by the American, Albert Link, for training pilots in 'flying blind' at night, or in cloud. It was installed at Abingdon for use by the UAS pilots on 1 January 1939.

The Link Trainer, known as the 'Blue Box' because of its colour, was a working model of an aircraft cockpit in which the trainee pilot could sit, with control column and accurate but basic instrumentation similar to that which would be found in an aircraft. The miniature aircraft (for it had wings and tail with rudder and ailerons that responded to the controls) was mounted on four supporting bellows contained within a turntable mounted upon a square base. A system of pivoted rods connected the bellows, or air operated jacks, to the cockpit which were operated by movements from the pilot's control column. These four bellows worked in pairs, being inflated or deflated as appropriate, in conjunction with a vacuum turbine, by means of what was then an intricate system of valves which were in turn operated by movements of the pilot's control column. The fuselage therefore moved in response to the stick and assumed appropriate attitudes, being tilted forward in a dive, to right or left when banking, and so on. Turning was accomplished by means of a reversible motor connected by an endless belt to the turntable. This motor responded appropriately to movements of the rudder bar. The compressed air movement provided a realistic feel. There was a pantograph system popularly known as the 'crab', tracing the progress of the 'aircraft' across a map on the instructor's table close by, where there was also a second instrument panel harmonised with that of the pilot. The pilot and instructor were linked together by telephone.

The Link trainer saved valuable hours of instruction in the air, as well as lives and aircraft and instruction was given at every stage of a pilot's training. As Richard was to later appreciate, when the weather was bad it was a very cosy way to improve your flying skills!

This coursework was interspersed with actual flying. Dual at first, in one of ten Avro Tutors that were available to the squadron, with an instructor doing the flying, progressing to the student being allowed to take the controls. Finally the student would be allowed the exciting and rewarding prospect of flying solo, if assessed as being capable enough. Ultimately, pilots would be tested on flying solo as part of their Air Ministry Air Proficiency Certificate flying examination. Having gone solo they could then undertake Advanced Training. Unfortunately, appropriate type aircraft were no longer available for such instruction. The three Hawker Harts used for this purpose had been withdrawn from the UAS station flight at Abingdon in 1937 and they were to continue without their use to the beginning of the war. This made it difficult for those who had gained the Air Ministry Air Proficiency Certificate to make further progress. The only way of gaining the advanced qualification was during summer camp. During the Hilary Term of 1939 16 pilots joined the RAFVR and undertook advanced training at the RAFVR Flying School at nearby Kidlington, which had been set up, not by the Air Ministry, but by a civilian, Arthur Marshall. He had established the Marshall Flying School at Cambridge where there was another VR unit, having foreseen the need to train more pilots for impending war. He was one step ahead of the ministry.

All of the training was provided by full time RAF instructors. The aircraft available at Abingdon during this period were: Avro Tutors, Hinds, Harts, if available, and an Audax, the supercharged version of the Hart.

A weekly flying programme was posted in the lodge of each college and also on the noticeboard in the squadron headquarters in Manor Road. George Nelson-Edwards remembers that:

> Transport was provided my means of two magnificent Rolls-Royce motor cars on hire to the squadron from a firm called Humphries, long since extinct. These two Rolls-Royce cars were nicknamed Castor and Pollux, presumably by some bright Greek scholar, after the two sons of Zeus each of whom, the legend says, lived every other day! Each Rolls-Royce was used on alternative days and they were almost identical, so it was very difficult to distinguish which was Pollux and which was Castor. We used to take bets on it with the driver. These limousines created a favourable impression amongst our fellow undergraduates. We felt very grand and superior to be seen riding in luxury, clutching a black leather flying

helmet and wearing the squadron blazer with gold RAF buttons. Daily the 'duty' Rolls would call at each college lodge where members were waiting to be picked up for the short ride to Abingdon, and then to be returned to college after flying.

Among those befriended by Richard was Lord David Douglas-Hamilton. As with Frank Waldron, David was a number of years older than Richard and had undergone training with the UAS prior to Richard joining the squadron and well before the outbreak of war. Lord David Douglas-Hamilton was sent to an initial training wing at Hastings with Richard.

Michael Judd was also in the UAS, and had been for some time before Richard started his training. Richard later recorded in *The Last Enemy*:

> Michael thought and felt as egocentrically as I did about everything, but his reaction to the war was different. It did not fit into his plans, for he had just won a travelling fellowship at All Souls; to him the war was in fact a confounded nuisance.

Richard would later meet Michael again on arrival at Montrose, where he had been posted with 603 Squadron, and where Michael had been posted to be an instructor with No.8 Flying Training School.

Two more of Richard's closest friends had also decided that they would follow the same direction into the services, Peter Howes and Noel Agazarian. Both left an indelible impression on Richard and were significant characters in *The Last Enemy*.

Peter Howes was from Wadebridge in Cornwall and was educated at Oundle School and St John's College, Oxford, where he read natural science. Peter was the same age as Richard and they joined the OUAS and subsequently the RAFVR at the same time, having completed their training together. Richard wrote of him in *The Last Enemy*:

> Peter Howes, lanky and of cadaverous good looks, had been reading for a science degree. With a permanently harassed expression on his face he could be a good talker, and was never so happy as when, lying back smoking his pipe, he could expound his theories on sex (of which he knew very little), on literature (of which he knew more), and on mathematics (of which he knew a great deal.) He was to prove an invaluable asset in our Wings Exam.

He had joined the UAS simply because his friends had done so and now that war loomed he became aware of just how much his reading for a science degree would be affected. He had not wanted his friends to realise just how hard he had been working to this end and decided that he would just have to apply himself to the aeronautical and less to the scientific. This group of individuals gave to the RAF the same ironic, detached interest they had offered to Oxford. He soon adjusted and his personality blossomed.

Richard and Noel Agazarian shared a disrespect for discipline. Richard wrote:

> Noel, with his pleasantly ugly face had been sent down from Oxford in 1939 over a slight matter of breaking up his college and intended reading for the bar. With an Armenian father and French mother he was by nature cosmopolitan, intelligent, and a brilliant linguist, but an English education had discovered that he was an athlete, and his university triumphs had been of brawn rather than brain. Of this he was very well aware and somewhat bewildered by it. These warring elements in his make-up made him a most amusing companion and a very good friend.

Noel le Chevalier Agazarian had been born on 26 December 1916 and was known as 'Aggie' to his friends. Three years older than Richard, five feet nine inches tall, strong and athletic, Noel was the third of four sons born to his Armenian father and French mother, who were living in Knightsbridge at that time. The photograph of the UAS summer camp of 1937 on the wall at OUAS headquarters, shows him as being not particularly good-looking and quite slim. By early 1941 he had put on weight and a photograph taken at that time appears to contradict any previous opinion that he was anything but attractive.

In 1923, when Noel was seven, his mother bought a 1914-18 War Sopwith Pup for £5 at a Croydon auction and installed it at the bottom of the garden. This much-loved 'toy' was to exert a lasting influence on the Agazarian family.

Noel and his brothers were educated at Dulwich College from where he left the Modern VI with a reputation as a fine athlete. In 1935, he was sent up to Wadham College, Oxford where in 1938 he gained an honours degree in jurisprudence and his blue in boxing.

* * *

Noel had joined the UAS and was commissioned in the RAFVR as a pilot officer on 14 February 1939, eventually becoming a pilot officer RAF on 26 September 1939.

He had originally been proposed for Trinity but the president had written back to his headmaster regretting that the college could not accept Mr Agazarian, and pointing out that in 1911, when the last coloured gentleman had been at Trinity, it had proved most unfortunate! Noel was softly spoken with just enough foreign intonation to make him irresistible to girls. After the Battle of Britain he grew a small Errol Flynn moustache to enhance the image.

Another brother, Levon, also flew fighters and Noel's older brother Flight Lieutenant Jack Agazarian RAFVR, was seconded from the RAF and became a member of the Special Operations Executive (SOE). After being trained as a wireless operator Jack with his wife Francine was returned to France to work with the resistance under the command of Major Francis Suttill DSO and his operation code-named 'Prosper'. After a chance encounter with two Germans posing as Dutch agents involved in counter-espionage, he and his wife were brought back to England by Lysander aircraft for a rest.

Suttill's organisation was to suffer during the next period. During 1943 the Germans had infiltrated Prosper and their agents and those connected with them were arrested by the Gestapo. Many were tortured and executed. Suttill himself was captured on 24 June 1943. Just prior to this Jack had been called back from his leave earlier than had been intended. Owing to a shortage of newly trained wireless operators he was asked to return to France despite the fact that he had been pulled out of a very dangerous situation only a few weeks before. After only one week in Paris on this, his second, mission, Jack investigated an address known to be suspect and was captured. He heroically resisted brutal torture under interrogation, was imprisoned for the next year and a half before he was executed by firing squad at Flossenburg, near the German-Czech border, six weeks before the end of the war.

Monique Agazarian, sister to the four men and youngest member of the family, also nicknamed 'Aggie', worked as a VAD on the wards at East Grinstead during the early part of the war and helped nurse the burned and injured pilots under Archibald McIndoe's care.

* * *

At the same time as Richard was learning to fly, two students of Cambridge University were also undergoing further flying training with the RAF Volunteer Reserve (VR), Flying School at Marshall's Flying School near Cambridge. Their names were Peter Pease and Colin Pinckney. They had already completed *ab initio* training with the Cambridge UAS.

They had met while at Eton College some years before and had remained firm friends ever since. They had begun flying lessons with the CUAS a year earlier than Richard and by September 1938 Peter had flown solo and been commissioned in the RAFVR. Colin was to achieve the same by December of that year. Richard, Peter Pease and Colin Pinckney were to form the 'triangle of friendship' referred to in *The Last Enemy*, and with Peter Howes and Noel Agazarian they would become collectively known as 'The Long Haired Boys', the nickname generally given by the regular officers to reserve officers with an 'Oxford attitude to life', a superior and lazy attitude exhibited by some towards all that they did.

They were from a similar middle-class background with parents who were reasonably well off, allowing some of them to have cars, and had a general attitude that their place in society was assured. The only exception was Peter Pease, who was from landed gentry, wealthy landowners and a genuinely upper-class background. They knew that as a result of the ineptness of 1930s politicians throughout Europe, war was imminent and were all united in their determination to throw themselves into combat as soon as they were required to do so, and to do it in as undisciplined a way as possible – as fighter pilots.

Despite their ambition to do so, it should be said that not everyone who set out to become a fighter pilot succeeded in flying fighter aircraft. As well as Fighter Command there were Bomber and Coastal Commands into which pilots could be drafted. This particular group however, was successful in that they did become fighter pilots. Richard wrote in *The Last Enemy*:

> In a fighter plane, I believe, we have found a way to return to war as it ought to be, war which is individual combat between two people, in which one either kills or is killed. It's exciting, it's individual, and it's disinterested. I shan't be sitting behind a long-range gun working out how to kill people sixty miles away. I shan't get maimed: either I shall get killed or I shall get a few pleasant putty medals and enjoy being stared at in a night club.

He discussed his intentions with a friend from another college, David Rutter. In *The Last Enemy* Richard mentions two meetings with him at which the topic of conversation is their own individual input into the war. The first meeting is at Oxford, the second during 1942 at Rutter's home. The intended input of David Rutter, or lack of it, is clear-cut, he is a pacifist, appalled by war, and will not fight. Richard is equally committed to what he believes in.

It is possible that David Rutter did not exist. There seems to be no evidence of a David Rutter having been at Oxford at that time and research has not uncovered any information to indicate otherwise. If such a friend did exist, then it is possible that Richard used a pseudonym to avoid him any embarassment over such a sensitive subject. If he did not exist then why did Richard invent such a character? It is possible that he spent much time deliberating his own actions in going to war, weighing-up the reasons fore and against. After he had been shot down we know he gave a great deal of thought to returning to operational flying, by which time all of his closest friends had been killed in combat. By now he was feeling less sure about his commitment to the war, and what he would do next. The character David Rutter, real or otherwise, gave him the chance to consider his actions thoroughly, without having to discuss such a sensitive subject with his close friends who were united in their belief that they should fight.

* * *

Throughout his life Richard was very fortunate in that he made the acquaintance of many influential people who could open doors for him, which in some cases was his intention. It would seem that many such people were either vulnerable to his charms or genuinely impressed at what he had to offer. Certainly his ability to charm the women in his life was exceptional, and his worldly experience was advanced for his age. His school holidays to Europe had given him the perfect opportunity to improve his practical use of German and French, he had met people from many different walks of life and been free from parental and official supervision to exploit these situations to the full. His interpersonal skills were indeed outstanding, when he put his mind to it. Equally, if he was uninterested he could be painfully dismissive. If you knew him well enough you could understand this reaction, if you were unfamiliar with his personality then you could be left feeling hurt and with a somewhat scathing opinion of him. An interesting point to note is that Richard was clearly aware of the sort of personality he was and that it was not easy for people to get on with him. He was to describe in *The Last Enemy* his thoughts as he floated in his Mae West waiting for death:

> It is often said that a dying man re-lives his whole life in one rapid kaleidoscope.
> I merely thought gloomily of the Squadron returning, of my mother at home, and
> of the few people who would miss me. Outside my family I could count them on
> the fingers of one hand.

Richard began his first term with the UAS on 24 January 1939. He had originally filled in the official application form to join the squadron on 14 March 1938, and by 27 April, he and 13 other colleagues who started with him on this new course had already been accepted. The most likely reason for such a delay was because the courses were always full up in advance.

The squadron strength at this time was 97, of whom 16 were now flying with the RAFVR at Kidlington. Six members were supernumerary as candidates for permanent commission and there were 75 ordinary members.

There was very little flying for the first four weeks of the term because of bad weather. It rained heavily with strong winds and low cloud. Having had to wait nearly ten months to start the course things did not seem to go well for this latest enthusiastic group of *ab initio* flying pupils. Out of the available fifty flying days of this term, only thirty-seven were suitable for flying, and only eight included morning flying. It must be remembered that it was a university rule that there was to be no morning flying during term time. Morning flying was only allowed during the week prior to the start of term time, and for the week after the term had ended. Flying therefore only took place on 29 afternoons.

Out of the 36 *ab initio* pilots who had not gone solo by the end of the previous term, 18 had gone solo early in the new course, 17 would soon go solo and the remaining pilot was to resign. No advanced course flying was available owing to their having no Harts, and it was because of this that 16 senior members were to transfer to the RAFVR, which would enable them to continue with their training at the 'VR' Flying School at Kidlington.

During this first term that Richard was at last actively undergoing flying training, he flew dual in the Avro Tutor. That term the UAS amassed the following hours on this type:

	Hours	Mins	No. of flights
Dual	357	45	682
Solo	230	15	380
Total	**588**	**00**	**1062**

	Hours	Mins	Flights
Average per member	8	28	15
Average per flight	–	34	–

Richard's committment to rowing clashed with his UAS training. He also had a girlfriend, Anne Mackenzie. His practical flying training was also to suffer when he had to miss his first experience of dual flying at Abingdon, which was due to an interview his father had arranged for him, for a job with the Sudan Political Service. A career that he was now no longer interested in.

On 13 June 1939, whilst still undergoing training with the OUAS, Richard was successfully passed fit by the medical board and on 15 June 1939 he enlisted in the RAFVR as an aircraftman second class (AC2), pilot under training (U/T), Service No.754280, for a period of engagement of five years with a registered service expiry date of 14 June 1944. Richard had attended the RAFVR centre in Oxford with Peter Howes who had also passed the medical and been accepted for the RAFVR as AC2 u/t pilot, No.754281. On his application forms Richard describes himself as being six feet half an inch tall with a 37 inch chest, fair hair, grey eyes, a fresh complexion with a scar under his chin.

By this time Michael and Edwyna Hillary had moved to a new holiday home, leaving Shirley Cottage, Reynolds Road, for Long Meadow Bungalow, also in Beaconsfield. Richard was promoted to sergeant on 16 June 1939, the day before the summer camp.

* * *

Each summer the university air squadrons would go away on their summer camp. The training was more intensive, offering the members an opportunity to advance their flying skills considerably in a short space of time. The young pilots were accommodated in the reasonable comfort of tents and were taught by the very experienced RAF officers of the UAS and from the station flight at Abingdon. These camps were enormously beneficial for both the RAF and the student pilots in determining who would be suitable for a career in the RAF. They were also great fun. The young men would have a great time enjoying the competitiveness and comradeship that such courses were designed to generate.

In *The Last Enemy* Richard mentions Frank Waldron, Dick Holdsworth and Michael Judd, contemporaries of his who were older and had already qualified as pilots. They had attended the summer camp of 1938, and Noel Agazarian the summer camp of 1937. Dick Holdsworth was, like Richard and Frank Waldron, a Shrewsbury old boy and had rowed in the Oxford Blue boat in 1931-32 and 1934.

Richard's first and only summer camp was at Lympne, Kent, where he attended a two week course between 17 June and 29 July that year. To miss any part of the training, Richard would have needed a good excuse, otherwise he may not have been allowed to continue with the squadron. The usual acceptable excuses were visiting family abroad, examinations and commitments with the rowing team. It must be remembered that apart from his studies, which he admits were being neglected, Richard spent most of his spare time from March to June training for and competing in the Head of the River races for which his college was favourite to retain the title, as well as assisting in the preparation of the Oxford crew.

Richard's commitment to flying, therefore, would not have become complete until the summer camp and the period before his call-up. In fact his student file with the UAS holds a number of letters of apology sent to his CO and the subsequent replies sent in response. His flying training, up to the period of the summer camp, is so fragmented it is likely that had it not been for the fact that he was so busy training with the rowing team, he would have been forced to resign. As it was, the CO was well aware of his situation, and did a great deal in helping Richard, not only to remain in the squadron, but to further his training whenever the situation arose.

Richard was aware that nearly all of his contemporaries whom he mentions in *The Last Enemy* had already become capable pilots. The exception was Peter Howes who, as a novice, was progressing through each stage of flying training with Richard.

While Richard was lagging behind, he did not seem to be unduly bothered. Had it not been for the rowing, his keen competitive attitude would have had him alongside his friends in the squadron, eager to prove his ability against theirs in attempting to become a pilot. He was to show the same competitiveness against Noel Agazarian later, at Kinloss and Aston Down. He had, after all, been achieving glory status while representing the college on the river, something his contemporaries would have been envious of.

The summer camp was at Lympne but the ground base would be at RAF Hawkinge. It was attended by a total of 97 members and divided into three separate two-week courses for the students. Initially, ground personnel moved by road and rail to Hawkinge on 9 June and erected tents as barracks. The tents were painted with camouflage paint which cut out all light from within, which created a very dull depressing atmosphere to start with, but after a few days went unnoticed. On Saturday 17 June the aircraft from Abingdon were ferried to the camp and consisted of: one Audax, five Hinds and 14 Tutors. Ten of the Tutors were flown independently by members of the squadron who were then ferried back to Abingdon by the Battles of No.40 Squadron, to await their allotted course time. The allotted time for the camp was divided into three separate courses:

Course 1. 18 June – 1 July
Course 2.   2 July – 15 July
Course 3. 16 July – 29 July

On Sunday, 18 June, the first course began. The instructional staff from UAS HQ, Wing Commander Hebbert and Flight Lieutenant Kirkpatrick, attended and from Station Flight at Abingdon, Squadron Leader Cracroft. The officers' mess was catered for under private arrangements.

Each course was divided into two flights for flying training: service type and elementary. Attention was given to navigation, cross-country and instrument flying. Unfortunately, apart from the second and fourth week, the weather was very poor with low cloud, mist and rain. Fortunately the weather was fine during Course No.3 which Richard attended. During these periods of inactivity the trainee pilots were ferried to Rochester for a fascinating guided tour around the factory of the aircraft manufacturers Short Brothers. Nevertheless they still managed to amass a great number of flying hours.

A total of 1690 hours was flown during all three courses, with 465 hours carried out on Hart types, of which approximately 270 hours were solo by 29 members. Before going to camp 21 members had not gone solo, but on leaving 19 members had gained their 'A' Licence and had carried out cross-country flights. One failed to go solo owing to bad weather, and one failed to reach the standard required and was expected to resign. Of the 56 new members, 48 gained their Air Ministry Proficiency Certificate.

The organisation and supervision of flying by Squadron Leader Cracroft, CFI, was exceptional, and ensured that the members received the maximum amount of flying that the weather permitted.

The weekly flying times were as follows:

	Week			**Days flying**	
1st Camp	1	154		2	
	2	338	**Total 492**	4	
2nd Camp	1	313		3	
	2	390	**Total 703**	4	
3rd Camp	1	258		3	(This was the course that
	2	237	**Total 495**	3	Richard attended)
Total no. of hours			**1690**	**19 (out of 33)**	

The practical training quite understandably had its share of minor accidents, particularly during the flying-intensive summer camps, but on 21 July, during this summer camp and the course that Richard was attending, the Oxford UAS suffered its first fatality since the squadron was formed in 1925. Pilot Officer D.C. Lewis RAFVR was killed whilst flying solo in a Hind. He was flying a short map-reading flight between Dover and Dymchurch when his aircraft was struck from above and astern at an angle of 45 degrees, by a Gypsy Moth piloted by the chief flying instructor of Kent Flying Club with a member of the Civil Air Guard as pupil. Both aircraft crashed five miles west of Deal and all were killed.

George Nelson-Edwards remembers the event and could relate his feelings to the day at Shrewsbury when Harris was killed falling from the dormitory window:

> When I saw Percy Byrton climbing down from his aircraft and walking towards
> me as I stood outside the mess tent at Lympne, the first thing I noticed was from
> how far away I could see his face, because it was deadly white, I thought perhaps
> Percy had cricked his neck or something.

'What's up, Percy?' I called to him. He was groping into his pocket for a match, a cigarette trembling between his lips.

'I've just seen something pretty ghastly, I think it was a collision in mid-air but it happened so quickly I couldn't take it all in.'

My God, I thought, suddenly remembering that someone had said David Lewis was a few minutes overdue. David was one of the most experienced pilots in the squadron, there should be no need to start worrying about him yet.

'I saw a large yellow panel,' Percy continued, 'gyrating down like an enormous sheet of cardboard. Then I saw other pieces falling past my port wing tip, though I couldn't see anything recognisable'.

As Percy spoke, several members came out of the mess tent. Suddenly 'Crackers', Squadron Leader Cracroft, the chief flying instructor, appeared, demanding to hear more details. With that he dashed into the tent and grabbed the phone looking pretty ghastly, I thought. Things started to swim before my eyes and I felt an acute twist in the pit of my stomach. Quite a crowd had gathered now, the atmosphere was tense. It seemed like an eternity until 'Crackers' appeared again and looked at us. There was silence. 'It now seems certain,' he said, 'David Lewis has had a mid air collision. Two planes are reported to have crashed about half an hour ago near Canterbury. There is no trace of David having landed anywhere, and he certainly wouldn't have had any gas left by now.'

He gave us a sidelong glance and turned away muttering under his breath.

Although, like myself, David was an Old Salopian, we were acquaintances rather than friends. I came to know him better at Oxford, especially after I joined the OUAS where we often met in the squadron bar at Manor Road.

Within a few minutes it was known that David had collided with a plane flown by an instructor and a pupil of the Civil Air Guard. All three were killed. It suddenly dawned on me that I was probably the last person to see and talk to David. I remember I spoke to him just before he climbed into the cockpit of his Hart, I had picked up his goggles which he had accidentally dropped; they were expensive ones and he was very proud of them. It struck me at the time that I could do with a pair of goggles like that.

So for one evening death was near us all, perhaps a timely reminder that the younger generation were not at liberty to fly planes indiscriminately around the sky without a single thought for anyone or anything. After a spirited game of tennis and hoisting a few beers aboard in Folkestone that evening, we all felt better. The David Lewis incident faded from memory but he was never forgotten; we knew we had learned another lesson albeit at the cost of his life. This and countless other lessons we learned at Lympne that summer.

There were three other minor accidents involving the Avro Tutors that occurred during this camp, without injury. One hit a flashing boundary light at the north corner of Lympne aerodrome. One damaged a wheel during an approach to the subsidiary airfield at Littlestone, near Hawkinge, and turned back towards Lympne where it turned over on landing. It was being flown by the instructor at the time. The final accident occurred when a pilot flying solo, got lost, ran out of fuel and crashed at a disused rifle butts at West Runton. He was uninjured.

Ground instruction classes for the new pupils included lessons on rigging, engines, engine-starting, airmanship, air navigation and maintenance.

During his time at Hawkinge and Lympne Richard's attitude towards the system did not make him any friends among the instructional staff, although the CO had striven to keep him in the squadron despite his poor attendance record. Richard wanted to do things his way. In *The Last Enemy* he mentions the time when he infuriates the CO of Station Flight and chief instructor Squadron Leader 'Crackers' Cracroft, by not paying any attention to his instructions.

The penalty was that he was required to carry out more flights with an instructor before being allowed to fly solo. His progress was slow but he does not seem duly bothered. Such problems must have caused Cracroft to consider removing him from the course, as was the norm. However, perhaps he saw potential and kept him in the squadron.

His summer camp assessment form reflects his attitude at this time:

Oxford University Air Squadron
Annual Summer Camp, Lympne

Name   Mr Hillary

Aircraft Types	HIND	AUDAX	TUTOR
Hours Dual	–	–	11.00
Hours Solo	–	–	3.15

Total number of hours flown to date. 23.15
(Dual 20.00 and Solo 3.15)

Remarks by instructor:

'This member proved very difficult to get off solo. He would not relax on the controls he just held on like a vice. But once off solo, he has improved rapidly'.

L.J. James. Flight Sergeant.

Classification and remarks by the Chief Flying Instructor:

'A very casual pupil who has been slow to learn, he lacks keenness and I do not consider that he has any real interest in flying. His instructor has been most patient with him'.

Exceptional
Above average
Average
Below average   YES

Date 30th July 1939   P.D. Cracroft S/Ldr.,
                                                              Chief Flying Instructor

Richard had achieved his pilot's 'A' Licence with 20.00 hours on dual and 3.15 on solo in his log book. It was a damning report for someone who, by that time, wished to become an officer in the RAFVR. It indicates that he would have not made a good officer had he intended to join the RAF on a permanent commission. However, with the war looming and with his intention to join the RAFVR, to fight against the Germans alongside his friends, his ability to perform in combat, his blind courage, coupled with his reckless abandon when he was up against overwhelming odds, were what brought him success during the brief period he was in combat. It was also this, I believe, that endeared him to so many.

By the time Richard was called up he, unlike some of his contemporaries, had not finished his flying training. With his rowing commitments now at an end he became committed to flying, but by then it was late into the summer of 1939.

Richard successfully passed the Proficiency Certification test on 28 August 1939, and was registered a sergeant/pilot u/t (under/training) No.754280 in the RAFVR.

* * *

Richard had met Anne Mackenzie at a university party during the summer of 1938 when the college rowing VIII had triumphed at the Head of the River. Richard Hillary would have been very much under the spotlight at that time with his new found success, along with the rest of the team.

He became a great deal more committed to the romance than Anne and, quite naturally, wanted a greater commitment from her. Something which he was destined never to get. Some of the letters from that period reflect his longing for something greater from Anne that was forthcoming. It has been written that his early letters are those of a youth in the first frenzy of youthful passion. His letters to Mary Booker written during the last year of his life reflect also the feelings of a man who wants constant reassurance of her love.

Not unnaturally, Richard's letters to Anne seem to be those of an immature schoolboy infatuated by a female for the first time, but who has no inhibitions about expressing his true feelings. His writing shows a level of despair and sentimentality that would have embarrassed his close friends at Trinity. He is very concerned with himself and I think there is little difference between those written in 1938 and those written to Mary in 1942.

Anne was a beautiful young lady and Richard was in love with her, but the relationship died just before the Battle of Britain started. The following two letters provide an insight into Richard's activities and attitude at that time:

April 22nd 1939

Why haven't you got a telephone number – or if you have, am I allowed to know what it is? I feel sure the dance will be dull, and I shall have no compunction about leaving it early. Can you come out later in the evening? There is a friend of mine going along, and he and his partner can make up a foursome. Do say you will come. I would suggest another night, but I cannot get permission off during training for Eights week more than once in a blue moon. We galley-slaves are wedded to our oars and only a temporary disaffection is allowed.

Our Common Ball is on June 20th, so don't cross the Atlantic before then will you?

Do send me your telephone number as I hate writing letters – even to you. (That, I suppose, you label technique – but I can't cure myself all at once.)

Oxford now in the sunshine is quite delightful – largely as I have had no work to do, and spend most afternoons flying. I suppose you are being the social butterfly and flitting from one dance to the next. Don't become too old and bored before I see you again, and don't forget of London night life that 'Plus ca change, plus c'est la meme chose'.

I must stop before I start writing you a treatise on my favourite topic.

Love,
Richard Hillary.

16th July 1939

Last night I decided that I could not possibly stay at home so I went out with a couple of men from Cambridge.

It was the worst thing I could have done as we went to a fair and the awful roundabout ground out 'Deep Purple' all night. So I came home early to hear 'wishing will make it so' being played on the wireless. That was too much and I just gave up and went to bed. I'm afraid its going to be a case of

Music when soft voices die

Vibrate in the memory.

Was it a good ball last night? I spend all my time thinking of you, and trying to imagine what you're thinking and how you're looking. But it is very difficult and I cannot see you clearly at all. You're almost there all the time but it's rather like an awful nightmare. I can almost reach you but not quite, as there is a thick veil in between just blurring you. I wish I had a photograph and then at least I'd have a permanent image of you. All sorts of unpleasant people whom I don't want to think about at all keep popping into my mind with fearful clarity but they won't go away and let you in instead.

I hope you're going to be happy and forget, if that is what you want to do – because there is no good in us both moping around on opposite sides of the Channel.

Sometimes now I wish there would be a war – as I feel then that so many things would clarify themselves and you and I could be together again anyhow for a short time and there would be no false values and muddled thinking. Life would have a purpose while it lasted. I'm afraid that I'm becoming very heavy and rather boring. But a young man in love was ever a pitiable object. I wish I could be with you now – have you in my arms, but the day when I shall be able to do that again seems very remote.

Richard

Whilst at the OUAS summer camp, Richard had written to Anne stating that he actually contemplated borrowing an aircraft, breaking the three mile limit from the aerodrome, and flying to France to see her: 'If I crashed in France I should get kicked out of the Reserve, straight into the militia for six months – which obviously wouldn't do at all.'

The consequences of such an action would indeed have curtailed his flying career there and then. His intention was very likely to impress her and he had never seriously considered such action.

Richard failed his first solo test for his pilot's 'A' licence during this period and in one of his letters to Anne he wrote:

I haven't been doing any solo flying lately as when I had my solo test with the Squadron Leader he started yelling and shouting down the speaking tube, so I disconnected him, thinking he was a thoroughly bad thing for the nerves. I could see him gesticulating wildly in front, and when I landed I gathered that he was trying to get me to do right-hand turns. He failed entirely to take the big view, and a tentative suggestion on my part that it was rather funny did not seem to have the hilarious effect that I had hoped for, and I now fly under strong supervision. Were it possible to crowd two instructors into the plane he would do it. However, la, la and vum! vum! it cannot be helped!

From this, one can appreciate the state of mind of the CFI when he wrote the aforementioned summer camp assessment of Richard's performance.

Flying solo he had a near miss when his aircraft got into a spiral dive:

On Friday I scared myself out of my wits. I was supposed to be practising climbing turns on my own when I got into a spiral dive. I came tearing through the clouds to find the earth looming up at a most alarming rate so I counted my buttons and muttered a prayer to the Only person who means anything to me and who I thought might hear me and sure enough the plane flattened out at 100 feet and glided like a bird.

This is an odd letter to write to a girlfriend when Richard refers to God as: 'the Only person who means anything to me.' What is interesting about this part of his letter is the fact that he expresses belief in God, whilst in *The Last Enemy* he says that when faced with death:

What did gratify me enormously was to find that I indulged in no frantic abasements or prayers to the Almighty. It is an old jibe of God-fearing people that the irreligious always change their tune when about to die: I was pleased to think that I was proving them wrong.

The couple carried on writing to each other until April 1940 whilst Richard was at No.14 Flying Training School (FTS), at Kinloss in Scotland. He would have been busy with classes and with the task of improving his flying skills to a level that would qualify him as a fighter pilot. The Phoney War was at an end, Hitler had invaded Denmark.

He was also in the company of Noel Agazarian and Peter Howes, whose companionship would have made their drifting apart easier to accept. Anne was still in his thoughts and he actually considered proposing to her, but perhaps the distraction was too great with such an adventure ahead of him. After Richard had been shot down and burned Anne tried to visit him in hospital. It is not known if she did so.

Geoffrey Page, who was at East Grinstead at the same time as Richard and knew him well says:

> Richard was charming with the women. He always seemed to have several beautiful girls on the go at the same time! There were a number of occasions when we saw a pretty girl rush from the ward, handkerchief clutched to her mouth, crying her eyes out because Richard had jilted her. He seemed to be able to get any girl he wanted, and he knew it. We were very envious of him.

An interesting comment coming from another pilot who was also very handsome. Richard's talent lay with his ability to turn on incredible charm and win over the affections of women so quickly.

One other point that should be considered is that Richard also used people to his advantage, in particular to get to know a number of very well known members of society. The list of well known people to whom he was introduced is very impressive; Merle Oberon, George Bernard Shaw, Lady Winifred Fortescue and J.B. Priestley to name just a few. They quite possibly saw aspects of Richard that they found attractive and appealing, particularly in the case of Merle Oberon.

* * *

During the summer of 1939 Richard was feeling the strain of the commitment demanded from members of the rowing team, and his attitude at this time perhaps adds some credence to the earlier decision by the rowing coach at Shrewsbury to leave him out of the first VIII. He became unhappy with the limited lifestyle and due to his state of mind was removed from the crew for, 'lack of enthusiasm and co-operation'. He languished in the second VIII for a while. He later wrote in *The Last Enemy*:

> I had a number of intelligent and witty friends; but a permanent oarsman's residence at either Putney or Henley gave me small opportunity to enjoy their company. Further, the more my training helped my mechanical perfection as an oarsman, the more it deadened my mind to an appreciation of anything but red meat and a comfortable bed. I made a determined effort to spend more time on the paper [the *Isis* magazine, as sports editor] and as a result, did no reading for my degree. Had the war not broken I fear I should have made a poor showing in my finals. This did not particularly worry me, as a degree seemed to me the least important of the University's offerings. Had I not been chained to my oar, I should have undoubtedly read more, though not, I think, for my degree.

CHAPTER FOUR

CALL UP/FLYING TRAINING

Initial Training Wing and Flying Training School
3 October 1939 – 14 May 1940

On Monday 4 September, three days after Hitler's invasion of Poland, Richard reported to the RAFVR Centre in Oxford in response to a radio call-up. He and Frank Waldron spent the night before at Trinity in Frank's old rooms, with the walls still adorned with the memorabilia from his years there. Frank was 25 and had now finished his last year at Oxford. As they lay reminiscing about life thus far, they must have experienced both excitement and trepidation at what lay ahead of them. They pondered the fact that wherever their respective talents lay it certainly was not, as yet, with flying. They would have to learn a great deal in order to survive. It was this thought that caused concern.

At this time Richard had been at Trinity for two years and would have still had one year to go for his degree in Modern Greats of History, had war not been declared on the 3rd.

Richard and his friends were put on stand-by and told to report every fortnight until such times as they were required for further training. For this they would be paid. The next day, Richard collected and signed for his flying log book from the Oxford University Air Squadron.

Following a further period of waiting, during which he continued to report to the RAFVR centre in Oxford, Richard was drafted to one of the initial training wings (ITW), established in certain colleges that had been seconded for use, and whose main objective was drilling, route marching and lectures. Richard was sergeant u/t pilot No.754280, due possibly to his experience as a boy sergeant at Shrewsbury, and for two weeks Sergeant Hillary carried out the drilling of his flight. When he was unsure of what to do, he operated the democratic principle of consultation with the flight and vote by the showing of hands to determine the next move. He noted: 'My fellow sergeants were certainly tough: they were farmers, bank clerks, estate agents, representatives of every class and calling, and just about the nicest bunch of men it has ever been my lot to meet.' A glowing tribute indeed.

On 2 October Richard was discharged as a sergeant in the RAFVR in order to take up the appointment to commission the next day. As a result of the score achieved on his Proficiency Certificate gained with the UAS, Richard was commissioned as Pilot Officer Hillary, RAF No.74677. The promotion was gazetted on 10 October. The prospect of flying seemed no nearer but spirits were high.

With the promotion came a move to another wing, where Richard found himself in the company of his friends, Frank Waldron, Noel Agazarian and Michael Judd of the UAS. Richard and his companions rented a large hotel room near to their ITW in Oxford where, much to their displeasure, it was intended for them to spend the next six weeks undergoing more drilling and route marches. They had joined the RAF to fly and Richard later recorded their response to the marching: 'Prominent and eager at the start we were never to be seen by the end.'

This posting came to a sudden and premature end. On 3 October 1939, they were to move again, this time as supernumeraries to 1 ITW at Hastings, on the south coast.

Richard travelled down to Hastings with Frank Waldron in his old Alvis Speed Twenty-Five and along with several other friends he was billeted in a traditional seaside boarding house on the sea front. Within two days he was convinced that the legend of sea-side boarding houses was true: 'There it all was, the heavy smell of Brussels sprouts, the aspidistras, the slut of a maid with a hole in her black stockings and a filthy thumb-nail in the soup, the communal table in the dining room which just didn't face the sea, the two meals a day served punctually at one o'clock and seven thirty.'

No.1 ITW wing was commanded by Acting Air Commodore Critchley, whose headquarters was situated in the requisitioned Marine Court flats on the sea front at St Leonards on-Sea where many of the trainees were also accommodated. The wing had only recently been opened as an aircrew receiving centre. Several hundred young men from Oxford, Cambridge and London Universities, resplendent in their new officers' uniforms bought with the ministry allowances, were accommodated in Marine Court and other suitable hotels and apartment blocks requisitioned by the Air Ministry. They were then split into smaller groups of about 40 with the senior member of each group in charge. Under the command of regular RAF instructors, including Ryder Cup golf team captain, Pilot Officer L.G. Crawley, and Test cricketer Pilot Officer Wally R. Hammond, they were taught parade ground drill and physical training for several hours a day for the duration of the eight week course on nearby Palace Pier and the spacious promenade right opposite the accommodation. If the weather was inclement the underground car-park adjacent to Marine Court was used. (Richard mistakenly referred to the course's duration being only two weeks.)

The instructors had to work hard. At the time they would have seemed merciless. There was no protection from the obvious contempt with which the commissioned breed was held by the NCO physical training and drill instructors assigned to each group.

George Nelson-Edwards was also posted to Hastings at the same time as Richard, and he remembers:

> The majority of the staff officers originated from the Greyhound Racing Association, as did the CO who had been the head, and they were more used to training greyhounds than an unruly body of recalcitrant undergraduates and the like. The RAF had requisitioned a very large underground car park beneath the promenade where we were made to march in threes up and down, morning and afternoon.
>
> At roll call every morning there would always be a few of us missing, mostly in London. We developed an almost foolproof system of answering for the absentees. The authorities were either unable or too uninterested to do much about it; consequently we enjoyed more than a little freedom.
>
> The warrant officer in charge of drill instruction was a Mr Hoy, whose favourite and frequent expression was, 'Nothing in it, like my front room!' For some inexplicable reason this would trigger us off into uncontrollable paroxysms of laughter which gave him enormous pleasure. He turned a blind eye to our comings and goings, he had to, he had little choice in the matter!

Geoffrey Page was at 3 ITW at this time; his memories paint an amusing but accurate picture of the haste which needed to be applied in order to get these young men trained ready for Flying Training Schools (FTS). Regarding the instructors:

> No one escaped the sarcasm in their spat commands to march and counter march over the seaside promenade that was used as a parade ground or urge us to greater gymnastic effort. Almost any insult was permissible, as long as the regulation compliment was paid to the King's commission at the end of each diatribe. 'When I say right turn, I mean right turn – air force right turn – not some fancy university right turn. . . . SIR!' As greenhorns we tolerated the situation. It was, of course, essential to mould a band of individualistic students into acceptably fit and disciplined military units, and the NCOs did astonishingly well to create some order out of the chaos of our first few days in uniform, when we could hardly be said to know our left feet from our elbows.
>
> At the end of the first week the Medical Branch claimed our attention. We joined a slow moving line of young men with tunics off, their right arms bared to

the shoulder, filing past a pair of bored looking medical orderlies playing darts with a couple of hypodermic needles, the older of the two prefacing each jab with a muttered 'just a little prick'. I never felt the injection!

When I recovered consciousness, the two orderlies were supporting me. There was no sympathy in their faces.

'What's going to happen when he sees real blood?'

Wiping the moisture from my forehead with the back of my hand, I did indeed wonder. Was I really cut out to be a pilot, let alone a cool, efficient killer? At that moment I could have thrown in my hand and run home to mother.

Wherever we gathered over the next few days the medical orderlies score was plain to see. Saluting was agony and it seemed to us that NCOs and men were deliberately going out of their way to return their obligatory compliments. The bastards!

The evidence was just as marked when we were off duty. In the bar of the Grand Hotel everyone, with the exception of the rare civilian, clutched his glass with the left hand and winced at the slightest collision of the right arms. But the tenderness did nothing to dampen our spirits.

Our conversations varied little. Though serious at times, it was more often light-hearted. Flying and aeroplanes predominated. Without exception we all knew that the majority of RAF squadrons were sadly lacking in modern equipment. We also knew from Army friends that Britain's land forces were in the same boat – dangerously short of the sort of equipment needed to stand up to an assault by a modern military machine.

But youth has a wonderful facility for switching away from the unpleasant. We would almost inevitably drift into talking about sex, of which we knew and had experienced as little as we had of flying, and yet we held forth with the authority of Socrates! Our parents would have been left speechless had they even caught snatches of the conversations that drifted through the babble in the bar; '. . . all she said was that sexual intercourse was not a socially acceptable form of introduction!'

The barmaids responded to the passes, ribaldry and invitations with marvellous humour.

'Oh you raf boys are all the same. If you're not doing it, you're talking about it!'

Many of the 'raf' boys, like me, had only recently left the protective shelter of home for the first time, and despite the brave phrases and the jargon, we were very unsure of ourselves.

I have since wondered about the underlying motive that led us to don uniform without hesitation to range the skies in defence of the homeland. Was it for King and Country? Or was it more fundamental than this well-worn recruiting cliché would have anyone believe?

Most of them, I knew, had learned to fly because of an insatiable urge that is most peculiar to all airmen – not because they wanted to go to war, but because they wanted to fly. And yet, it did not explain our readiness to man the front lines and sacrifice our high-spirited and joyful lives without asking why. I never once heard anyone voice a motive for fighting the enemy. I tried to analyse my own reasons for taking up arms. But I never did produce a satisfactory answer.

In addition to Frank, Richard was billeted in the boarding-house with three other individuals, Nigel Bicknell, a former Cambridge student whose family were from the north-east, Dick Holdsworth and Bill Aitken, son of the then Minister for Aircraft production, Lord Beaverbrook, and brother of Max Aitken, who himself became a distinguished wartime fighter pilot. In *The Last Enemy* Richard recalled:

Nigel was a year older than I [21 years]. He had been editor of the *Granta*, the University magazine at Cambridge. From Nigel's behaviour . . . it will be seen that the attitude of Cambridge to the war was the same as ours. He had had a tentative job on the *Daily Express*, and by the outbreak of the war he had laid the foundations of a career. For him as for Michael Judd, the war was a confounded nuisance.

Bill Aitken was older. He had the Beaverbrook forehead and directness of approach. He was director of several companies, married, and with considerably more to lose by joining the RAF as a pilot officer than any of us. The immediate pettiness of our regulations and our momentary inactivity brought from him none of the petulant outbursts in which most of us indulged, nor did he display the same absorption with himself and what he was to get out of it.

Dick Holdsworth had much the same attitude. He was to me that nothing short of miraculous combination, a First in Law and a rowing Blue. He too, was several years older than most of us and considerably better orientated: his good-natured compliance with the most child-like rules and determined eagerness to gain everything possible from the course ensured him the respect of our instructors. But the others were mostly of my age and it was with no very good grace that we submitted to a fortnight's pep course.

Dick Holdsworth also became a 'Guinea Pig' as a result of injuries received in the war.

* * *

At the end of the training at Hastings, Richard, Dick Holdsworth, Peter Howes and Noel were posted to No.14 Flying Training School (FTS) situated at RAF Kinloss, close to RAF Lossiemouth on the north-eastern coast of Scotland. They were to take their places on No.4 Course, which started on 20 November. There is a large gap between the end of the training at Hastings and the start of this FTS course, a not uncommon occurrence, and I can find no record of where Richard was during this period. It is safe to assume that he returned home for a period before rejoining Peter Howes and Noel for the journey north.

Kinloss was actually an operational training unit (OTU) for Bomber Command but had recently added the FTS facility. The total time spent at FTS was six months and was split into two parts. The first part, initial training school (ITS), sometimes referred to as the 'junior' course, included drilling, lectures and a progressive syllabus of intensive flying training which amounted to approximately 50 hours' flying time which Richard would add to the 23 hours 15 minutes already in his flying log book. At the beginning of the ITS course, the students were each given 23 textbooks which provided all the information in preparation for the final exams. In Richard's case the ITS would run from November 1939 to February 1940.

During the early part of March 1940 he and Noel went on leave before resuming the second part of the course with advanced training school (ATS), sometimes referred to as the 'senior' course. This period would involve approximately another 50 hours' flying time for the students to add to their log books and also included a mixture of lectures and flying, but the flying would involve specialist tasks including: blind flying cross country, formation flying, height test, night flying and gunnery school when they carried out live firing. This took Richard from February to May 1940.

In addition to passing out with successful completion of the flying practicals, the candidate had to obtain passes in written papers on: airmanship, navigation, armament, law and discipline, air frames and rigging, engines, meteorology and organisation of the RAF. There was also oral examinations on some of these subjects. The aggregate for a pass was 60%.

On 15 February 1940, Richard and his friends became entitled to wear the flying badge, 'wings' brevet. He had passed his flying practical, initially on the Avro Tutor, but in the main flying Harvard F1587. Richard's report however, was far from complimentary:

> Flying ability average. Has ability but is inclined to be casual. He'd improve under supervision. Must overcome lack and sense of discipline.

However, he found flying intoxicating and his speed of reaction was a useful asset when he later became a fighter pilot.

* * *

Richard, Peter and Noel drove up to RAF Kinloss together and after reporting to the station adjutant they were billeted off-camp in the neighbouring village of Kinloss. Although, once again, Richard was in unfamiliar surroundings, he was with good friends and with the likelihood that they would be flying very soon his spirits were high in anticipation of what lay ahead.

At this time there was resentment towards the volunteer reserve officers from the regulars of the RAF. The Oxford attitude, which they were aware that they exhibited, put them even more at a disadvantage: 'We were expected to be superior; we were known as week-end pilots; we were known as the Long Haired Boys; we were to have the nonsense knocked out of us.'

Richard, Noel and Peter were on course No.4, and underwent initial assessment on Avro Tutors before moving on to the Harvards, American two-seater fighter trainers, which they flew for the vast majority of their flying time. Dick Holdsworth was put on bombing training.

The other officers and airmen on Richard's course varied in age from 18 to 32, and came from all walks of life. There was a lawyer, school teacher, merchant seaman, existing RAF Reservists and young men looking for their first job. These men were eager and willing to take their place with Fighter, Bomber or Coastal Command. Generally Richard felt that he was academically lacking in comparison in that they had some sort of work experience that would assist them with their flying and academic studies. He was making good progress with the practical side of the course but the final exam would require a considerable effort on his part. Although he felt that in some departments he was inferior to some of the other pilots he possessed skills that made him every bit as good as the rest. Despite the fact there were also less talented pilots than him, the challenge to do better was always there:

> I was cheered to discover that Charlie Frizell, the most competent pilot on the course, was almost as mathematically imbecile as I. He had, however, an instinct for flying and a certain dash which marked him out as a future fighter pilot. He was nineteen and had joined the Air Force because he wanted a job.

Indeed he did become a fighter pilot. Charlie Frizell, who was actually only 18, was a Canadian who joined up on a short service commission in August 1939. His memories of Richard are vivid and he responds to the comments Richard wrote about him:

> Although during the winter of 1939-40 we would meet almost every night in the Mess at the RAF Station, Kinloss, and in late 1941 for a few days in the RAF Hospital, Torquay, we never became what I would regard as personal friends. Nevertheless, being almost three years younger than he, I rather admired his truculent attitude towards service discipline and enjoyed the patronage of his company.
>
> I use the word patronage because even in those days Dicky had something of star quality about him. He was the centre of that little coterie of Oxford University pilots – which included Noel Agazarian and Peter Howes – that joined our course. . . . Because of his good looks, youthful arrogance and almost unashamed vanity, he was of course warmly disliked by some members of the course. I can provide you with three anecdotes of our time together:
>
> We all observed that Dicky spent some time grooming his hair which he wore rather longer than the regulations permitted, and we knew he dreaded the day when some senior officer would order him to have it cut shorter. One night a few of us, including Agazarian and Howes, got together in the mess before Dicky arrived and agreed to play a trick on him by approaching him independently and brushing imaginary dandruff off his shoulders. When we went into dinner, Dicky had disappeared, and indeed missed the meal. We later learned that he had

returned to his room to wash his hair. When we told him we had played a trick on him about the dandruff, he blushed a little but accepted the joke in good spirit.

On an another occasion we were at a lecture on armaments given by a regular Warrant Officer instructor who was obliged to treat us neophytes as officers. He was a cockney who referred to bomb-hooks as 'bomooks.' When he asked if there were any questions, Dicky asked what these 'bomooks' were. It was unkind and unnecessary of him to do this because, although it afforded us a smile, it embarrassed and angered the old Warrant Officer.

The next anecdote is one that I have never passed on to anyone, until now. I have always had a small talent for drawing portraits. At a Christmas party which was going to be held in the mess at Kinloss, I decided to do a number of profile caricatures of some of the personalities, with appropriate captions, to hang around the walls. With his long auburn hair and blue eyes, he had a distinctively cherubic face in those pre-burn days, so that it was not difficult for me to caricature him by accentuating the length of his hair and his somewhat full and slightly protuberant bottom lip. He was most concerned with what I had done with his lip and implored me to modify it on the grounds that I had gone beyond the limits of recognizable distortion. It was generally agreed by the others that it was a fitting caricature, though of course it did not really flatter, which is what concerned Dicky. I teased him for some time with this by doing little replicas of this caricature on scraps of paper and magazines around the mess for the remainder of the time we were at Kinloss. Whenever he saw them he would tear them up.

After Kinloss our paths did not cross until I met him again, and for the last time, in late 1941 at the RAF hospital in Torquay.

Although we never flew together while at Kinloss, Dicky wrote of me that I was 'nineteen, the most competent pilot on the course . . . and a mathematical imbecile'. I was neither of the latter, nor was I nineteen until October 1940, almost a year later.

Pilots like Chas Frizell had joined the RAF on short service commissions for one or more of three reasons: they were bored with their jobs and wanted to make a new career move, were preparing for war or quite simply loved to fly. Thirty-eight were to successfully complete the course.

* * *

During the early part of the course the weather was very inclement, quite normal for the region, and despite overcast skies, strong winds, drizzle, wind-driven rain and snow, flying went ahead with relative frequency.

A great competitiveness developed between Richard and Noel. One wished to prove himself better than the other. It just so happened that a similar competitiveness also existed between their two flying instructors. Sergeant Robinson and Sergeant White, Richard's instructor. They both good friends and a rivalry existed whereby they would compete to see who could turn their student into a pilot first. Richard describes Sergeant White:

> White was a dour taciturn little Scot with a dry sense of humour. I liked him at once.

Richard undertook several weeks of flying training under the guidance of Sergeant White, who was ever keen to express his feelings when his pupil failed in any way. (It is interesting to note that most of the instructors were more or less of the same age as the pupils but that was never to cause problems.)

> Then one day he called down the inter-comm, 'Man you can fly at last. Now I want you to dust the pants of Agazarian and show our friend, Sergeant Robinson, that he's not the only one with a pupil that's not a half-wit'.

Richard then progressed to solo cross-country flying, cloud and formation flying. Formation flying was the most popular. Richard was now in the advanced part of his flying course and thoroughly enjoying his experiences in and out of working hours.

It was an exciting time; the thrill and challenge of the flying, the possibility that he would have to fly against enemy aircraft, superb flying conditions and scenery which created a stunning back-drop. Richard's writing exudes an overall feeling of well-being. Three years later he would, once again, undertake a flying course in the Scottish border countryside. This time the weather was freezing cold, the aircraft were, in some cases, almost impossible for him to fly and he had no familiar faces from his earlier experiences to turn to. This time he was faced with great adversity which he fought bravely to overcome.

By March 1940 they had completed the junior part of the course and during the senior coursework they were granted a few days' leave. Richard and Noel decided to get away to the Isle of Skye for four days. They drove across country and took the Skye ferry from Kyle of Lochalsh to Kyleakin. After a 25 mile drive on the rough single track road, they booked into the Sligachan Inn at the foot of the Cuillin mountains. In *The Last Enemy* Richard writes beautifully of this experience including an unscheduled mishap in one of Skye's mountain streams:

> Over dinner we told the landlord of our novel descent. His sole comment was 'Humph', but the old man at the window turned and smiled at us. I think he approved.

Certainly the old man approved when he overheard the two recounting their adventures to the landlord John Campbell at dinner. He was the brilliant mountaineer and scientist Norman Collie.

Norman Collie was born in 1859 and made his first climb aged eight when the Collie family was living in Deeside. His deep interest in climbing in Scotland was to centre on Skye, which he visited first in 1886 as a young chemistry teacher and to which he later retired.

*   *   *

On his return to Kinloss Richard continued with the advanced flying course which was again a mixture of flying and lectures but with the emphasis on classroom work and the specialist subjects. His flying would now be entirely on the Harvard. The night flying practical was the most stressful part of the course. Richard also mentions in *The Last Enemy*, that the night he successfully flew the Harvard solo and was passed by Sergeant White, another young pilot met his end.

> We found him on the shore. The machine half in and half out of the sea. The officer in charge of night flying climbed on to the wing and peered into the cockpit. 'In coarse pitch,' he said, 'as I thought.' Then after a slight pause, 'Poor devil.' I remembered again that moment of blind panic and knew what he must have felt. In his breast pocket was ten pounds, drawn out to go on leave the next day. He was twenty years old.

The pilot was Acting Pilot Officer P Ross who had been flying Harvard N7010 when it crashed on the 15 December 1940. In fact Richard was not even at Kinloss when this crash occurred.

Crashes were inevitable, as with any flying training, and there were a number while Richard was at Kinloss as there were at nearby Lossiemouth:

> It was after an armament lecture in one of the huts when we heard, very high, the thin wailing scream of a plane coming down very fast. The corporal sat down and rolled himself a cigarette. He took out the paper and made of it a neat trough with his forefinger, opened the tin of tobacco and sprinkled a little on to the paper, ran his tongue along the paper edge and then rolled it. As he put it in his mouth we heard the crash, maybe a mile away. The corporal lit a match and spoke: 'I remember the last time we had one of those. I was on the salvage party. It wasn't a pretty sight.'

We later learned that the man had been on a war-load height test and had presumably fainted. They did not find much of him, but we filled up the coffin with sand and gave him a grand funeral.

The 14 FTS and station Operational Record Books contain much detail and this accident to which Richard refers was probably the one that occurred on 18 December 1939, in which Acting Pilot Officer I.R. Wilson was killed when Harvard P.5801 crashed at Alves.

Richard and his companions were now enjoying service life. Whenever they went off the base into the local village or town for a beer, they always looked forward to returning to the familiar surroundings and comradeship of the RAF station that they had grown used to. They felt they were part of a great team that was responsible for achieving the same objective. In conversation they spoke the same language, off base they had little in common with those on the outside.

A change was evident amongst the trainees. None more so than with Peter Howes who had reluctantly agreed to go along with his friends rather than try to finish his degree:

> The change in Peter Howes was perhaps the most interesting, for he was not unaware of what was happening. From an almost morbid introspection, an unhappy preoccupation with the psychological labyrinths of his own mind, his personality blossomed, like some plant long untouched by the sun, into an at first unwilling but soon open acceptance of the ideas and habits of the others.

At 15 FTS at nearby Lossiemouth four other student pilots were currently undergoing the same training as Richard. Sergeant Pilots Alfred Sarre and Jack Stokoe and Pilot Officers Bill Read and Philip Cardell had arrived on 29 December, for flying training on 2 January. They were all destined to serve together in 603 Squadron. Like Richard, Jack Stokoe would also receive debilitating burns but completed an outstanding wartime career in the RAF and left not long after as a squadron leader.

Another interesting character who knew Richard while he was at Kinloss was Maurice 'Mark' Mounsdon who would later serve with No.56 Squadron during the Battle of Britain. Both he and fellow squadron member Geoffrey Page were to receive treatment for burns at East Grinstead at the same time as Richard and would once again make his acquaintance. Maurice recalls:

> I first met Richard at Kinloss. There were six that came from the University Air Squadron at the end of October, early November 1939, including Noel Agazarian and Peter Howes. They were a nice bunch of fellows who initially kept to themselves but then gradually spread out, so to speak. I became quite friendly with Richard at this time, as did the others, and we went about together. Two thirds of the course were on bomber training and one third were on fighter training and that included myself, Hillary, Agazarian and Howes. During the flying exercises I flew with Hillary on three occasions. We all did our training together and that included formation flying, cross-country, reconnaissance, aerobatics and it was during three of these flights that Hillary and I shared an aircraft. I flew half an hour as pilot and then we changed over. I got on with him perfectly well.

Maurice Mounsdon's logbook records the following advanced training flights as having been flown with Richard:

29th February.....Cross-country
1st March...........Cross-country
27th March.........Formation practice

Maurice continued with his recollections:

> There were probably half a dozen of us who had cars or managed to buy old cars locally really cheaply. This gave us the freedom to drive into the countryside,

where we would walk. It was very beautiful where we were situated and we used to drive along the River Findhorn, Findhorn Valley and the Culbin Sands. Sometimes we went into Nairn or further afield to Inverness. Occasionally we went over to Elgin and met some of the characters undergoing the same training at RAF Lossiemouth, which was just next door.

We also went shooting. A number of us had .22 rifles and pistols and we used to go to the coast, shoot rabbits and give them to our batmen. Typical antics of young men at that time, of course. We used to go to dances, when we could find them. We had dances at the station and girls appeared from somewhere or another and we all had a good time. They threw a Burns night on the station and events like that.

The isolation was a good thing because it kept us all together. If we had been based in the home counties, every time someone took leave they would just disappear. Being out in the sticks kept us together, which was a good thing and we all enjoyed ourselves. I certainly did. We used to spend half the day in class and the other half flying.

Now and again we had parades when they attempted to smarten us up a little, but we didn't have the usual passing-out parade. At the end of the course we were rushed off; me to Meir.

Occasionally operational bomber squadrons would land to use Kinloss and Lossiemouth as their base for carrying out raids on Norway. This was the trainee pilots' first glimpse of men and aircraft on operational duties, and provided an opportunity to observe and appreciate any reaction from the crews to the stresses and strains of wartime operations. One day a Spitfire squadron flew in and gave Richard, Peter and Noel a chance to look over the machine that they all hoped they'd be flying very soon.

In February 1940, their hard work culminated in the final examination. Richard was grateful for some assistance from his more academically minded friends: 'I, thanks to Peter's knowledge of navigation and Noel's of armament, just scraped through.'

* * *

The intense advanced flying programme continued and by 20 April, the conclusion of flying training at Kinloss, Richard had approximately 130 hours' flying time in his log book.

The course concluded on 11 May, and prior to such an occasion as the end of an FTS course, the newly qualified pilots would normally return once again to drilling on the parade ground in readiness for the passing out parade and the inspection by area officer commanding (AOC). With perhaps, on the day in question, the AOC giving his address in the mess after tea, not a congratulatory speech concerning their achievements but, a fairly dour talk on what was expected of them and what lay ahead. The parade and inspection would then take place, the men marching, resplendent in their uniforms, rifles with bayonets fixed, feeling elated, justifiably proud at their achievements, retiring to the officers' mess and a celebration of their success. Unfortunately, time was short and they were sent away for the next stage of their training without this experience.

They had now completed their training and, with their pilot's 'wings' on their tunic, were fully aware of the glances such an emblem would attract in a public place. Three tall, good-looking RAF officers with wings on the left breast of their tunic would be more than most young ladies could resist! They had learnt a little of how to fly and how to handle themselves as officers and squadron members.

* * *

The strategic importance of Kinloss and Lossiemouth was becoming evident. The increasing number of bomber detachments interrupted the FTS flying and it was decided to send No.15 FTS to Middle Wallop in its entirety. During 9 and 11 April sightings of aircraft flying over the station were made. They were unidentified. But on the 16th an aircraft sighted over Kinloss and Lossiemouth was identified as a Ju88. Blenheim aircraft from 254 Squadron were sent up from Lossiemouth but they failed to locate the machine. Later the same day a warning order was received from the Air Ministry which read:

> 16th April 1940.
>
> It has been decided to transfer the FTS's from Lossiemouth and Kinloss to Middle Wallop and a station to be selected by Bomber Command. Move to be completed by 20th April. Detailed orders will be issued by Headquarters Training Command.

Training Command took over Middle Wallop on 20 April 1940 from 11 Group Fighter Command.

Flying at 15 FTS at Lossiemouth ceased forthwith. The station administrative officer left for Training Command and arrived at Middle Wallop the next day.

> 17th April 1940.
>
> Following message received from HQTC:
>   14 FTS at Kinloss to move to Cranfield (Bedfordshire) and 15 FTS to move to Middle Wallop. No, repeat, no M.T. to be taken. All aircraft to be flown to new stations within 48 hours.

The records indicate an anomaly here. Documents show that whilst 14 FTS was ordered to move from RAF Kinloss to RAF Cranfield by 20 April 1940, Course No.4 did not end until 11 May. While there is evidence to confirm that 15 FTS had completed the move by the required date, it is possible that 14 FTS did not move until later, thus allowing the pilots to complete their course. Alternatively, Richard and his colleagues may have completed the practical part of their course and with only lectures and the final written exam, they remained in situ. The final possibility is that Course No.4 was completed at Cranfield.

* * *

Meanwhile the RAF was experiencing a massive increase in action over France. One hundred Hurricanes of the RAF's Advanced Striking Force and Air Component, allied with the French Armée de L'Air and small air arms of neutral Belgium and Holland, were attempting to repel the invasion of northern France by Germany. They faced the might of the Luftwaffe and its 3500 serviceable aircraft. In a twelve-day period (May 10th-21st 1940), the RAF claimed 500 victories with the loss of 200 Hurricanes. Fifty-six pilots were killed, 36 were wounded and eighteen became POWs. These losses were significant. Unknown to Richard and his friends their future as fighter pilots was now assured.

CHAPTER FIVE

LIZZIES, NOT SPITS!

No.1 School of Army Co-operation, Old Sarum
15 May – 22 June 1940

Great disappointment awaited the trio. Only Charlie Frizell was to be posted to fly fighters. Six weeks' further training at Old Sarum would finally see Richard, Peter and Noel operational on Lysanders, otherwise known as the 'Lizzie', or 'flying coffins' as Peter Howes referred to them.

At this stage there had been few casualties in Fighter Command. The Battle for France was changing that and creating openings for the newly qualified, but inexperienced, pilots to achieve their ambition and fly fighters.

The No.1 School of Army Co-operation was established at Old Sarum in 1920, on the site of the WWI airfield Ford Farm, built in 1917, two miles north of Salisbury. It was appropriately situated right on the edge of Army country.

The objective of the school was to train crews for tactical reconnaissance squadrons equipped with Westland Lysanders, a high winged, single-engine monoplane. They also trained crews for the night and strategic reconnaissance squadrons that operated the twin-engine Blenheim. Many of these units were called to France with the Air Component of the field forces shortly after the outbreak of war.

At Old Sarum the school was reorganised and a reserve pool was formed to which Richard and his contemporaries may well have been added if fate had not played its hand.

Initially the combined school aimed to train 72 pilots, 37 observers and 72 air-gunners on a six week course that included 48 hours of flying. Having established these guidelines these course times could vary greatly depending on the experience and individual capabilities of the students. Some would last the full six weeks and others only four weeks. The aircraft available were 12 Lysanders, 12 Hectors, 12 Ansons and 15 Blenheims. The unit became known as the Army Co-op Group Pool.

Old Sarum became too small and while the single-engine training remained at Old Sarum the twin-engine training was reformed at Boscombe Down and Andover as the No.2 School of Army Co-operation. At No.1 School the pilots flew solo on Hectors at the beginning and progressed to supervised exercises on the Lysander before flying the Lysander solo. Having completed this they then undertook flying exercises using the Lysander.

Richard, Noel and Peter left Scotland on 14 May to drive down to Old Sarum. It must have been quite saddening for them to leave Scotland after the last six months. Richard and Noel spent the night in London en route, possibly at Richard's parents' flat in Knightsbridge Court, and were picked up by Peter Howes the next morning. During the drive they tried to elevate each other's enthusiasm for what lay ahead.

* * *

Old Sarum is situated in the attractive Wiltshire countryside. On the way down they couldn't help but notice the spire and instantly recognisable landmark of Salisbury Cathedral. Their course was known as Army Co-operation War Course No.7. They had five days before it began on 20th May and were registered as 'Supernumeraries Pending Course' during that interim period.

Richard's days of instruction at Old Sarum were long, from nine in the morning until seven in the evening, alternating between lectures and practical work flying initially the Hector and progressing to the Lysander, on which they would become operational at the end of the course. Not exactly the glamorous fighter pilot image that they had envisaged they would be fulfilling.

It must be said however, that many great airmen undertook to fly the Lysander operationally. It was an outstanding aircraft and had very specific uses during WW2, conveying agents to and from occupied France under the cover of darkness, and delivering vital supplies. One such pilot was Hugh Verity who flew with 161 Squadron from Tangmere and Tempsford, and who once, he recalls, met Richard Hillary's fiancée!

He had been on a train journey in England, during WW2, and had begun a conversation with a young lady in his carriage. She was in uniform and told Hugh that she was French, which he had already noted from her accent, and had come to England in order to further her fight against the Nazis. When Hugh detected a note of dissatisfaction in her voice he said that he would attempt to get her into the Special Operations Executive (SOE). The work would involve strenuous training and ultimately clandestine operations back in France. The young lady was pleased at the opportunity and was successful, thanks to Hugh. Unfortunately she found the training too demanding and opted out of the course.

During the train journey she had mentioned that she was Richard Hillary's girlfriend and that they had recently become engaged. Although it has been said that Richard was at one time engaged to Barbara Dewar, who has yet to enter the story, it would be easy to accuse the young lady of spinning a yarn, but he was not a celebrity at this time! Geoffrey Page has already said that Richard had many girlfriends during his stay at the Queen Victoria Hospital at East Grinstead, and perhaps she was one of them.

* * *

After a few days, several familiar faces appeared on the course. Bill Aitken had been sent from RAF College SFTS (Service Flying Training School) Cranwell. Richard had not seen him since the ITW at Hastings. He brought the news that Frank Waldron, Richard's friend since his Shrewsbury days, and Nigel Bicknell, had been unable to live with the discipline of the RAF College. Frank had applied for a transfer to the Scots Guards and had eventually been accepted. Cranwell and its strict regulations had not agreed with him, as had been the case with Richard, Noel and Peter when they first arrived in Scotland. Also, every time that Frank flew in an aircraft he unfortunately became airsick. To cap it all he overslept on the morning of his wings exam!

Nigel Bicknell was later awarded the DFC when, with his Blenheim flying on only one engine, he had successfully pressed home his attack on a French target. During the return trip, and in darkness, the other engine had cut out and he was forced to ditch in the sea. For six hours he held up his observer until, at dawn, they were spotted by a boat and picked up.

At Old Sarum, Richard formed a triangle of friendship that meant a great deal to him. He admired Colin Pinckney and Peter Pease greatly. In *The Last Enemy* he wrote:

> Peter was, I think, the best-looking man I have ever seen. He stood six-foot three and was of a deceptive slightness, for he weighed close on thirteen stones. He had an outward reserve which protected him from any surface friendships, but for those who troubled to get to know him it was apparent that this reserve masked a deep shyness and a profound integrity of character. Softly-spoken, and with an innate habit of understatement, I never knew him to lose his temper. He never spoke of himself, and it was only through Colin that I learned how well he had done at Eton before his two reflective years at Cambridge, where he had watched events in Europe and made up his mind what part he must play when the exponents of everything he most abhorred began to sweep all before them. Colin was the same height but of broader build. He had a bony, pleasantly ugly face and openly admitted that he derived most of his pleasure from a good grouse-shoot and a well-proportioned salmon. He was somewhat more forthcoming than Peter but of fundamentally the same instincts. They had been together since the beginning of the war and were now inseparable.

They had actually been together throughout their schooling at Eton. Richard was hand-some and arrogant enough to describe Peter as 'the best-looking man I have ever seen'.

Peter Pease was born in London on 15 February 1918. The eldest son of Sir Richard and Lady Pease of Richmond, Yorkshire, Peter was educated at Eton from 1931-36 in the House Group of C.J. Rowlatt. At Eton he had been a talented schoolboy; initially he was renowned for his beautiful treble voice and he recorded 'O for the Wings of a Dove'. Later, he edited the school magazine. His academic and social achievements at Eton were outstanding.

In 1936, he was sent up to Trinity College, Cambridge, where he read history. He and his close friend Colin Pinckney, whom he had first met met at Eton, joined the University Air Squadron. By September 1938, he had applied for and been granted a commission in the RAFVR and undertook further flying training at Marshall's Flying School.

Peter had been in his final year at Cambridge when he was called up during early October 1939. He was sent to No.1 ITW at Jesus College, Cambridge, after which he continued flying training at No.22 E&RFTS, Cambridge. His beliefs in his country, his society and his place within it were firm and secure and he was prepared to risk his life for them. Beneath his surface shyness he was well aware of the privileged life into which he had been born. It was accepted that he had the mental ability, the self-discipline and the inclination to follow a career of his choice in the diplomatic service. He is remembered as being modest, shy and utterly conventional. It was Peter's steadfast, deep-rooted beliefs that Richard admired and the fact that he was willing to die for what he believed. He also admired his background, which his own family's English (Richard's grandfather had emigrated from Wensleydale, not far from the Pease family seat at Richmond) and his own 'Aussie' beginnings had failed to provide. Both were ultimately prepared to risk death in aerial combat. Unlike Peter, Richard questioned whether it was worth dying for. Peter's beliefs gradually confirmed Richard's feelings towards the fight.

Richard tried to project a superior image of himself. Many people from outside his group of friends were of the opinion that he was talking down to them, just making sure that they knew their place in his company. This would not work with his own friends, they were also from a similar background; he knew it, and they knew it. They also knew Richard. In Peter Pease Richard saw what he believed to be the 'real article', to him he was the ultimate in the world of young men in the better-off classes.

* * *

David John Colin Pinckney, Colin to his friends, was born at the family home called Hidden Cottage in Hungerford on 6 December 1918. He had an older brother Philip, born on 7 April 1915, and three sisters. His father Hugh Pinckney was unable to serve in the First World War owing to his poor eyesight and was in the War Trade Intelligence Department, for which he was made a Commmander of the Order of the British Empire. He was a very intelligent man with a keen wit and a love of country life, being a fine shot and an ornithologist; both Philip and Colin were to enthusiastically follow these same interests. He was to bear the loss of his two sons in World War II with great fortitude and continued to attend to his business interests until a short while before his death in 1964 at the age of 87. His wife Winifred and three daughters survived him. At the time of his death the family had lived in their Hungerford home for 50 years.

Colin's early life was very similar to that of Richard: boarding school from an early age followed by university, a period of extensive travel and death in action with the RAFVR. He was very tall at six foot three inches, just as Richard described, had brown hair and normal build. In contrast his brother was shorter and more rugged, broad, athletic and very powerful. While Philip was easy going and amiable Colin had a more delicate sensibility, was unmechanical and had artistic inclinations. Colin was the more handsome of the two.

Colin was to follow the same route as his father and older brother Philip when, after schooling in St Neots, he was then also sent to Eton where he was in Mr Tatham's (ex-Adie's) House. Here Colin earned a revealing final report from his German master, A.K. Wickham:

Colin is, of course, an incorrigibly idle boy, and I'm afraid that in his year in this division he has learnt but very little German. He, and I too perhaps, have accepted too readily his position as bad boy of the division, and he has looked and acted this part so well that it has been hard to take him seriously. I have given him many punishments, but he has always known how to put away my wrath and to sin slyly again. The best tribute I can pay him, as he leaves, is that I have liked him too much.

This reputation for idleness mitigated by personal charm is borne out by his housemaster:

Colin, perhaps, has mixed feelings on leaving Eton. Mine are not, for I am very sorry that he is going. I know that he has been in a quiet way a good influence in the House, and I have reason to be grateful to him for brave and public-spirited actions on two occasions. . . . He deserved to get further than he did and he deserved rewards that were denied him. I admire immensely his attitude of independence towards public opinion – he never bothered to ingratiate himself with his fellows. . . . If he is somewhat idle, he is one of the best advertisements for idleness I have ever come across, and if he has acquired only a small part of his charm from Eton, his time here has certainly not been wasted.

His idleness did not prevent him from getting seven credits in his school certificate in 1935, or when three years later he sat for his Tripos in Anthropology at Cambridge from coming within a few marks of first-class honours.

Colin was admitted to Trinity College, Cambridge, in 1936, nearly two years after his brother, and graduated in 1939. The memories of Mr G.B. Perrett, a tutor of Selwyn College and a good friend of Colin's while he was at Cambridge, do not agree with the reports of laziness:

I think the reference to his being lazy needs a lot of toning down. Colin was a man of limitless energy when he was interested in anything, and he had abilities of a very high order. If he wanted to do anything, no matter what the obstacles, he did it well. You could always rely on him.

As the situation in Europe deteriorated and became ever more warlike Colin was prompted into making an early return from a holiday in Jamaica to England. He caught a coach north to New York where he found that war had been declared and all shipping to Europe at a standstill. He later wrote: 'I had hoped to return to work, not to war.'

When after a week's delay he embarked for England, his notification of call-up for service with the RAFVR was waiting for him at Hungerford.

* * *

The course at Old Sarum continued and Richard was finding the work interesting. The subject matter was specific to the kind of operations he would find himself on, flying Lysanders. Map reading, aerial photography, air to ground Morse, artillery shoots and long distance reconnaissance. Richard later described the aircraft:

The Lysander proved to be a ponderous old gentleman's plane, heavy on the controls but easy to handle. It seemed almost impossible to stall it.

However, the course still had its share of near misses.

From 26 May until 4 June 1940 the evacuation of Dunkirk, code-named Operation Dynamo, took place, in which 338,226 British and French troops were taken off in vessels of all shapes and sizes and brought to England. One small Watson Class lifeboat made many trips in the shallow waters offshore from the beaches of Dunkirk, to ferry soldiers from the beach to a waiting destroyer situated in deeper water, which had been unable to get in any closer. Its brave crew would be responsible for the rescue of a number of RAF pilots downed in the Channel during the Battle of Britain, which was to follow. One of those pilots would be Richard.

The battle for France continued for another two weeks after the evacuation of Dunkirk, and during this period members of the British and Allied Forces continued to make their way to the west coast of France where ships waited to take them to England. Amongst these soldiers were the remnants of several RAF squadrons.

The losses to the RAF during the Battle of France were staggering. In the 40 days of the Battle of France the RAF lost 959 aircraft, of which 509 were fighters. In addition they lost another 66 in the campaign in Norway, two-thirds of the aircraft delivered to the RAF since the beginning of the war. The arbitrary 52 squadrons deemed necessary to defend the shores of Britain had not been achieved, and these losses in men and machines had to be replaced before the inevitable next stage of the battle began. Richard wrote in *The Last Enemy*:

> Every night at nine o'clock the Mess was crowded with Army and Air Force Officers, men who commonly never bothered to listen to the news, parked around the radio with silent expressionless faces, listening to the extermination of France and the desperate retreat of the British Expeditionary Force. . . . then came Dunkirk: tired ragged men who had once been an army, returning now with German souvenirs but without their own equipment; and the tendency of the public to regard it almost as a victory.
>
> After days on the beaches without sight of British planes these men were bitter, and not unnaturally. They could not be expected to know that, had we not for once managed to gain air superiority behind them, over Flanders, they would never have left Dunkirk alive.

It should not be forgotten either that the air battle high above the beaches, obscured by low cloud, was decisive in ensuring the evacuation of so many men. Hundreds of sorties were flown. Pilots were lost, some that had to take to the 'silk' over the beaches were actually confronted by soldiers that wanted to know where the RAF were when they were being straffed on the beaches!

Al Deere, renowned pilot of 54 Squadron, who was based at Hornchurch when Richard arrived, was confronted by a belligerent army major when he walked hastily to the front of one of the long queues leading out to sea. What the major was unaware of was that if this pilot could return home then he would once again be available to defend the evacuation. Naturally the soldier was in no mood to rationalise and Al Deere resorted to physical force, managing to get onboard a destroyer. Al was back flying again over the beaches soon afterwards.

* * *

In *The Last Enemy* Richard wrote: 'For us the evacuation was still a newspaper story, until Noel, Howes, and I got the day off, motored to Brighton, and saw for ourselves.' This would have brought the plight of these men home to them. British, Belgian and French choked the streets, although it was more likely to have been Dover than Brighton. The three airmen witnessed the locals offering whatever they could to brighten up the return of these ragged and dispirited souls. Richard and Noel acted as interpreters to the French, Peter Howes found himself a young blonde and disappeared with her and the car for the rest of the day!

Retiring to one of the bars, seething with khaki, Richard and Noel faced a barrage of questions asking why they had not seen the RAF defending the skies above. They knew the RAF had been fighting above the cloud and that many lives had been lost with little appreciation for the sacrifice. So did many of the soldiers but the rowdy few sought to make their own point, regardless.

Peter Howes returned in the car and under a moonless sky the three headed back to Old Sarum. During the journey Peter lost control of the car whilst taking a bend at high speed. The car turned over twice wrecking it in the process, but the three drunken pilots were very fortunate to survive the resulting crash without a scratch. Richard later recorded that Peter Howes had said at the time:

> It looks as though Fate doesn't want us to go out this way. Maybe we have a more exciting death in store for us.

Prophetic words indeed.

CHAPTER SIX

SPITFIRES!

No.5 Operational Training Unit (OTU) Aston Down
23 June – 4 July 1940

After France had fallen, the English Channel was all that separated Britain from the Germans and invasion. All leave was cancelled. At the end of the Battle of France and the Dunkirk evacuation six first-line RAF squadrons had to be withdrawn to rest, and two others had been virtually destroyed. Five more equipped with Blenheims and only nominally operational, were learning to defend the airspace by night. Eleven other squadrons, whilst operational, had been equipped with Spitfires so recently that it would be several weeks before they would be truly ready for battle. Of the 52 front-line operational interceptor squadrons that Air Chief Marshal Sir Hugh Dowding had hoped to have ready by this time, he had in fact only 28 fresh, combat-ready, squadrons and only 23 were equipped with Spitfires and Hurricanes. It was perceived as being only a matter of time before the Germans would invade, and that time would be of enormous value to the RAF.

* * *

On the completion of his six week period of training at Old Sarum, Richard was due to be posted to an operational squadron elsewhere or become operational at Old Sarum; either way he would be flying Lysanders. In *The Last Enemy* Richard wrote:

> Owing to the sudden collapse of France and our own consequent vulnerability it had been decided that a number of us were to go to fighter Squadrons. The Air Ministry had ordered fifteen to be transferred. We each looked at our neighbour as though he were suddenly an enemy. There were twenty of us, and the five who were to continue at Army Co-operation were to be drawn from a hat. It was my worst moment of the war, and I speak for all the others.
>
> Bill Aitken and Peter Pease were both drawn with three others. The rest of us almost groaned with relief.

The names were not drawn from a hat but predetermined by their superiors. Richard must have been just as excited but wanted to appear to react differently from the others. According to Richard, Peter Pease was added to the list of those going to fighter training.

The 16 would be going on a two-week course to No.5 Operational Training Unit, Aston Down, situated one and a half miles south-east of Chalford on the A419 near the Welsh border, in the beautiful Gloucestershire countryside. The remaining 'four' would stay at Old Sarum, on Lysanders.

Aston Down was planned and built as an aircraft storage unit, on the same site as the WWI Minchinhampton aerodrome. It was opened as 7 ASU on 12 October 1938 and became No.20 Maintenance Unit (MU) just five days later. Fighter Command decided that Aston Down would make a good training base and formed No.12 Group Pool on 23 August 1939, using Harvards, Gladiators and Blenheims. The unit gave intermediate training to pilots being posted to Group squadrons. A month later Fighter Command took over the airfield, although the MU remained. On 15 March 1940 the Group Pool became 5 OTU using Spitfires, Hurricanes, Blenheims, Defiants, Masters and Battles. On 25

July 1940 one of the Spitfires shot down a Ju88. Aston Down was commanded at this time by WWI night fighter pilot Group Captain G.W. Murlis-Green DSO, MC.

The operations record book for No.1 School of Army Co-operation states that 20 pilots started the course that Richard and his friends had undertaken on 3 June and the same number passed out from No.1 School of Army Co-operation on 10 June and were posted to No.5 Operational Training Unit at Aston Down. There is no mention of any of the pilots remaining to become operational on Lysanders.

No.5 OTU's instructors would be some of the pilots from No.1 Squadron which had recently returned from northern France where, along with other valiant Hurricane squadrons, they had attempted to stem the German advance after the invasion of France. Having been rested from operational flying duties they were posted as instructors to a number of OTUs including Aston Down. They would have to convert from Hurricanes to Spitfires in preparation for their instructional duties.

The achievements of No.1 Squadron are now legendary. No.5 OTU, RAF Aston Down, was commanded by Squadron Leader Patrick J.H. 'Bull' Halahan who had taken No.1(F) Squadron to France in September 1939 and led it during the German advance. One of the squadron's flight commanders was Flight Lieutenant P.R. 'Johnnie' Walker, who was now officer i/c flying at the OTU. On 30 October Pilot Officer P.W.O. 'Boy' Mould scored the RAF's first victory in France, the first of 26 achieved by No.1 Squadron by the end of the Phoney War period. Squadron Leader 'Bull' Halahan lived up to his name. He was an Irishman of medium height, powerfully built, well-muscled and with a square jaw. He was partly responsible for the re-harmonisation of the Hurricane's eight Browning machine guns from 400 yards to 250 yards, ensuring more hitting power at close range; it was also Halahan who recognised the need for armour behind the seats of his unit's aircraft, and they got it.

The other flight commander was Flight Lieutenant P.P. 'Prosser' Hanks, who was also instructing at Aston Down, having enjoyed a short period of leave. Flying Officer Kilmartin, who was in charge of Richard's flight at Aston Down, was the only pilot to return to action during the Battle of Britain.

The course at Aston Down had been cut from four weeks to two weeks, such was the demand for fighter pilots, but the fact of the matter was that a pilot was passed out as and when it was considered fit to do so. The course could last anything from three days to three weeks with flying time on the Spitfire amounting to anything from 10 to 20 hours. The OTU at this stage was really only able to provide conversion experience to operational type. Some may have been lucky enough to practice firing their guns. This would have been done over the sea, with no air-to-air firing. The first air-to-air firing that a pilot carried out was during his first combat, if he hadn't been hit first by an unseen enemy fighter.

On 10 June 1940, 38 new candidates arrived for the next conversion course, which began the following day. Of this number, six were to serve with 603 Squadron at one time or another, and four were to serve with Richard at Turnhouse and Hornchurch. The four that were to serve with him were: Pilot Officers Philip M. Cardell (748036) who became good friends with Richard during the short time that they were together, W.A.A. 'Bill' Read (741635), and Sergeants Alfred R. Sarre (745543) and Jack Stokoe (748661) who spent the next 13 days learning to fly the Spitfire before being posted to 263 Squadron at Drem, North Berwick, Scotland, on 23 June, the same day that Richard and his friends began their course at Aston Down. Significantly, on 11 June Flying Officer J.I. Kilmartin arrived after a period of leave to take up an instructional position with 5 OTU. During Richard's course Kilmartin was his instructor. 'Killy' Kilmartin had been one of the valiant No.1 Squadron pilots who had fought in France. On 29 June another No.1 Squadron 'veteran' arrived back from leave to take up an instructional position with 5 OTU: Pilot Officer 'Boy' Mould (33414).

The new arrivals at Aston Down were already familiar with No.1 Squadron's exploits and were in awe of the battle-weary veterans who were to instruct them. The list of pilots on Richard's course at No.5 OTU, Aston Down, as shown in the ORB, reads:

> F/O J.C. Newbery, P/O's H.S. Lusk, K.C. Campbell, F.S. Gregory, J.T. Jones,
> E.T. Stevens, P.L. Kenner (73032), N. Le C. Agrazarian (*sic*) (72580), A. Finnie,
> M.E. Staples, J.T. Russell, R.H. Hillary, P. Howes (74332), P.F. Mayhew (74336),
> A.P. Pease, D.J.C. Pinckney, S/Lt G.B. Pudney, Mid. 'A' J.H.C. Sykes F.A.A. and
> V.H. Bellamy RN.

They learnt the latest in fighter tactics. Much had changed, for the fighting in France had taught them valuable lessons; the experienced instructors were able to pass on the benefit of this experience, in order to assist the new intake in surviving for as long as possible. The new intake at No.5 OTU were both fascinated and eager to learn. What they saw and admired in the instructors before them, they hoped to one day emulate themselves. In *The Last Enemy* Richard records:

> We learned many things then new, though perhaps no longer true, so swiftly do fighter tactics change. We learnt for the first time the Germans' habit of using their fighter escorts in stepped-up layers all around their bombers, their admitted excellence in carrying out some pre-arranged manoeuvre, and their confusion and ineffectiveness once this was in any way disturbed.
>
> We learnt the advantage of height and of attacking from out of the sun; of the Germans' willingness to fight with height and odds in their favour and their disinclination to mix it on less favourable terms; of the vulnerability of the Messerschmitt 109 when attacked from the rear and its almost standardised method of evasion when so attacked – a half roll, followed by a vertical dive right down to the ground.
>
> We learned of the necessity to work as a Squadron and to understand thoroughly every command of the Squadron Leader whether given by mouth or gesture. We learned that we should never follow a plane down after hitting it, for it weakened the effectiveness of the Squadron; and further was likely to result in an attack from the rear. This point was driven home by the example of five planes over Dunkirk all of which followed each other down. Only the top machine survived.

How prophetic this advice would become for Richard, who still possessed a certain amount of recklessness that Shrewsbury and Oxford had failed to discipline, which would drive him to either succeed in killing or being killed.

> If we were so outnumbered that we were forced to break formation, we should attempt to keep in pairs, and never for more than two seconds fly on a straight course. In that moment we might forget all we had ever learned about Rate-1 turns and keeping a watchful eye on the turn-and-bank indicator. We should straighten up only when about to attack, closing in to 200 yards, holding the machine steady in the turbulent slipstream of the other plane, and letting go with all eight guns in short snap bursts of from two to four seconds.
>
> We learned the importance of getting to know our ground crews and to appreciate their part in a successful days fighting, to make a careful check-up before taking off, but not to be hypercritical, for the crews would detect any lack of confidence at once.

Richard had the opportunity of flying the latest in British fighter technology – the Supermarine Spitfire Mark I. As there was no possibility of any dual instruction on the Spitfire, Richard was taken up in a Miles Magister and then an instrument flight in a Harvard in preparation for his maiden flight. When the time came for him to climb into the cramped cockpit of the Spitfire, he was very nervous.

He found the cockpit very tight and restricting. On his very first flight he decided to keep his flying goggles raised on his forehead to reduce the claustrophobia and increase his all-round field of view. This decision was to cost him dearly later.

After running over the instruments with Richard, Kilmartin instructed him to carry out four circuits and bumps. Richard's flying was almost robotic and he flew as instructed and without any problems. He had been well taught. Immediately after his first flight Richard flew again, but on this occasion he tried some aerobatic manoeuvres, getting used to the flying characteristics of the aeroplane. Subsequent flights included an oxygen climb, an air-to-air firing exercise, formation attacks and dog-fighting. This was a most exciting time for Richard. He could now fly the Spitfire, this most renowned of all fighter aircraft.

It was during one of the dog-fight scenarios that Richard was given the chance of flying with his instructor, Kilmartin, as his adversary. Any elation experienced at having successfully flown the Spitfire must have drained away when he was introduced to the hard reality of his inability to avoid being shot down and to shoot down another aircraft. Kilmartin's extensive combat experience allowed him to play with Richard. Richard could not get him off his tail and neither could he get his sights on Kilmartin's aircraft. But that was the object of the exercise. There was no point in kidding anyone about what they were going to be up against in the skies over Britain very soon. Kilmartin had the necessary experience and intended that his pupils benefited from it. It had been a very sobering moment for the embryo fighter pilots.

Aerobatics would be useless in aerial combat with enemy fighters because they invariably presented the enemy with slower, more visible, targets; the exception being the controlled spin.

This was a time when Richard's competitiveness with Noel came to a head. Whether Noel ever intended that to be the case cannot be confirmed one way or the other. Perhaps it was just that Richard's youthful, sporting, competitive spirit caused him to strive to be every bit as good as his friends. What should also be considered is that Peter Howes, Noel and Richard had been in each other's company for the last ten months, not including their time together at university, and their friendship had become a little strained. Peter just kept himself to himself and saw less of the others. However, due to the quick tempers of the other two, a confrontation was more likely. Such an argument broke out after Noel had successfully flown under the Old Severn Bridge. This bridge with its close-set arches, linking England to Wales, had been a landmark for the student pilots during their stay at Aston Down and gained a reputation for having been flown under by a number of pilots before and after Richard's time with 5 OTU. Richard was certainly aware of its reputation and was also tempted to try to fly under it. It was in his nature to rise to the challenge, but he had felt no great urge to do so until now.

While he was weighing up the possibility of undertaking such a stunt Noel had taken the initiative. Flying low along the Severn valley he had flown between the spans which made up one of the arches`and under the bridge. Richard became determined to do the same. Peter Pease advised him that as so many pilots were doing the same, such a stunt would be 'stupid'. Despite the wisdom of Peter, Richard knew that he was going to do it too. And he did.

The day after, Richard, Peter Pease and Colin Pinckney went to the adjutant's office where they were informed that there were three vacancies with 603 (City of Edinburgh) Fighter Squadron. Knowing that 603 was equipped with Spitfires they duly put their names down.

On 4 July, their postings were confirmed and Richard and Peter Pease left Aston Down in Peter's car. They didn't have to report to Turnhouse until the 6th, so they decided to spend one night in London before travelling to the Pease family home in Richmond, Yorkshire, where they would stop over for another night before reporting. Colin would join them there, later in the evening, having driven up in his own car.

Before they departed Richard was able to make his peace with Noel:

> I piled my luggage into his (Peter's) car and prepared to climb in after it. Then I
> hesitated and turned back. I found Noel packing. He got up as I came in. We were

both embarrassed. I held out my hand.

'Goodbye and good luck,' I said.

'Goodbye, Dick,' he said. 'We've drifted rather a long way apart lately. I'm sorry.'

'Don't let's either of us drift up to Heaven. That's all.'

While he was speaking Peter Howes had come in to say goodbye, too. 'You two needn't worry,' he said. 'You both have the luck of the devil. If the Long Haired Boys are to be broken up, I have a hunch that I'll be the first to go.' We both told him not to be a fool and agreed to meet, all three of us, in three months time in London.

Peter Howes was subsequently posted to 54 Squadron at Rochford reporting on 8 July, and Noel was posted to 609 (West Riding) Squadron at Northolt, reporting on the same day. Eight weeks later, on 11 September, Peter Howes, at his own request, was also posted to 603 Squadron. Richard and Noel never saw each other again.

CHAPTER SEVEN

'GIN YE DAUR' (IF YOU DARE!)

No.603 (City of Edinburgh) Fighter Squadron, AuxAF
6 July – 27 August 1940

No.603 Squadron was one of 20 Auxiliary Air Force squadrons, 14 of which were to play a part in the battle out of an overall total of 66 RAF squadrons. On 16 October 1939 the first German aircraft to be shot down over British territory since 1918, had fallen to the guns of 603's Spitfires. As Auxiliaries, just a few weeks earlier many of the Squadron had been engaged in civilian employment.

In the following pages I shall introduce and devote time and space to a great number of pilots who became important to Richard, whose experiences he shared and whose company he enjoyed and would much later crave to return to. Their views and 'adventures' are so important to the development of Richard's character that I shall also quote from them at length.

* * *

Richard and Peter Pease spent the night in London before departing for Peter's family home in Richmond, Yorkshire. They were both concerned by the fact that they were heading north, with the war about to reach the south of England. The weather had become wet and overcast in the south as they left. In *The Last Enemy* Richard recollected how depressing the industrial areas of the Midlands appeared. The two actually travelled north on the Great North Road and would not have passed such sights.

Arriving at Richmond in the early evening they were joined, half an hour before dinner, by Colin. There were six who sat down to dinner that evening, Sir Richard and Lady Pease, Richard, Colin, Peter and his 18-year-old brother Richard.

Peter was the eldest of four children, three boys and a girl. Richard had noted that night at the meal table just how devastating Peter's death would be to them. They were a devoted family and his loss, when it came, was indeed a terrible blow.

Early next morning the three of them drove on to Turnhouse, driving through Edinburgh to the airfield situated to the west of the city, on the then main Edinburgh to Glasgow road. The skies were bright and clear, they had left the cloud and rain behind in the south.

On reporting to headquarters at RAF Turnhouse they met the acting commanding officer, Squadron Leader George Denholm, affectionately known as 'Uncle' to all who served under him.

Richard and Peter Pease were informed that the squadron was operating further north. 'A' Flight was at Dyce and 'B' Flight had been operating from Montrose since 21 June 1940. Colin was sent to Dyce as there was a replacement Spitfire that needed taking there while Richard and Peter were sent to Montrose.

Whilst both flights had been detached in order to offer some protection to the offshore shipping as well as the coast of Scotland, No.8 SFTS was the main function of the airfield at Montrose and 'B' Flight had the additional duty of protecting the recently expanded flying school and its Miles Magisters from possible attack by enemy bombers from Denmark and Norway. Although the North Sea would tend to prohibit heavy raids, they were nevertheless quite frequent. The two flights protected the vast stretch of coastline from Aberdeen to the Firth of Tay. Richard describes his arrival at Montrose:

The aerodrome lay just beyond the town and stretched parallel to the sea, one edge of the landing field merging into the dunes. For a few miles around the country was flat, but mountain peaks reared abruptly into the sky, forming a purple backdrop for the aerodrome.

By now the number of Scottish personnel in the squadron had been considerably diluted with the influx of regular RAF pilots, and there were only three Scotsmen in 'B' Flight when Richard arrived. The imposition of regular pilots occurred with all Auxiliary squadrons and in the case of 603 it did not meet the approval of all of the stalwarts. However, it proved vital to the success of the squadron in the months ahead.

'Rusty' Rushmer was the flight commander. Amongst the other pilots were: Laurie Cunningham who had been with the squadron since 1935 and was experienced; 'Ras' Berry who had arrived the day after the Firth of Forth raid took place; Ken Macdonald who had also been in the squadron since 1935, and whose brother Don had recently joined 'A' Flight. Don Macdonald had been an undergraduate at Cambridge and in the UAS at the same time as Peter Pease and Colin Pinckney.

There were also Noel 'Broody' Benson, who had arrived at Turnhouse from 145 Squadron at Croydon, having entered Cranwell as a flight cadet in 1938, where he gained his 'wings' and a commission; Boulter who was a Londoner from Barnes; Waterston who joined 603 in 1937 and was studying for an engineering degree when war broke out; Cardell who came to the squadron from Grangemouth on 3 July with Stokoe, Sarre and Read; Gerald Stapleton, a South African, who had a reputation for being tough, and Carbury, a tall amiable New Zealander, who had a fine reputation as an athlete. Richard and Peter Pease made up the flight.

One of the first people whom Richard and Peter were to meet on arrival at RAF Montrose was Michael Judd. Richard had not seen him since ITW at Hastings eight months before. Michael was now an instructor with No.8 SFTS at Montrose where he taught student pilots on Miles Magisters. Having brought each other up to date with the latest news of their mutual friends' progress, Michael then took them to the flight hut situated at the north-west corner of the airfield, to introduce them to the rest of the pilots. 'B' Flight dispersal consisted of three huts: one was the flight commander's office, the second was for RT equipment and technicians; and the third was divided into two for the pilots and ground crew. Richard was led into the third hut by Michael Judd. His memories were recorded in *The Last Enemy*:

> From the ceiling hung several models of German aircraft, on the back wall by the stove were pasted seductive creatures by Petty, and on a table in the middle of the room a gramophone was playing, propped at a drunken angle on a pile of old books and magazines. In a corner there was another table on which there were a couple of telephones operated by a corporal. Two beds standing against the longer walls, and several old chairs, completed the furniture. As we came in, half a dozen heads turned towards the door and Rushmer, the Flight Commander, came forward to greet us.

With introductions complete it was Brian Carbury who suggested that they adjourn to the mess for a drink. There followed a period of settling-in for the new intake. It would be a couple of weeks before they were to become operational and in that time Richard went on practice flights twice a day, every day he was available, if the weather allowed. When he left 5 OTU he had about 170 hours flying time in his log book with just over 16 on Spitfires. By the time he was shot down he would have had nearly 90 hours on type and approximately 240 hours total flying time. Richard and Peter became familiar with the established pilots in their flight. Most of them were very experienced on Spitfires; some had already seen action. The squadron had certainly been regularly involved in combat since October 1939.

On arrival at 603 Squadron Richard had come face to face with people he both liked and respected. These men were his mentors; skilled, experienced pilots, some of whom had already seen action. His fellow pilots also seemed to like him and were keen to take him under their wing. They passed on the benefit of their experience until such times as he would be made operational, and they would continue to assist him even then. His own flight commander, Flight Lieutenant 'Rusty' Rushmer, was one such person. He was to bring out all that was good in Richard's personality too.

Richard also bonded well with the ground crew and other inexperienced new arrivals like himself and in many respects it is hard to define a difference in his feelings for these young men and those he categorised as 'The Long Haired Boys'.

* * *

The Men of 603 Squadron
At the time of Richard's arrival, 603 Squadron consisted of the following personnel:

George Denholm was born at Tidings Hill on the shores of the River Forth at Bo'ness, West Lothian, on 20th December 1908, and joined 603 Squadron AuxAF in June 1933.

With the embodiment of 603 Squadron into the RAF on 23 August 1939, Denholm was called to full-time service. By this time he was an experienced flight commander and had been considering retiring from the squadron at the relatively advanced age of 31. It was the fact that he was older than most of his fellow pilots that gave him the nickname 'Uncle' George. As their leader during the Battle of Britain, his paternalist instincts were evident in his concern for the welfare of his longstanding friends in the squadron, as well as the young, inexperienced newcomers. His nickname, whilst initially relevant to his age, became appropriate for this reason.

A respected and popular member of the squadron, Denholm took his job very seriously. His early experience with the squadron, including the great number of flying hours he had accumulated, put him in good stead for the battle that lay ahead.

Following the raid on the naval shipping in the Firth of Forth on 16 October 1939, Denholm had been credited with a share of the destruction of one of the enemy Ju88 bombers of I/KG30. On 17 March 1940, he damaged a Do17 two miles east of Aberdeen, a He111 probable on 26 June over the Forth Bridge, and a third of a Ju88 on 3 July, 40 miles east of Peterhead.

Promoted to acting squadron leader, Denholm took over command of the squadron from Squadron Leader 'Count' Stevens on 5 June 1940, although this position was not officially confirmed until 1 September, when his promotion was promulgated.

Ivor Arber was a sergeant-pilot, and on 3 July 1940 he shared in the destruction of a Ju88 with Denholm and Stewart-Clark of Red Section, off the east Scottish coast. All three Spitfires were damaged by return fire. On 12 July he shared a He111 with Pilot Officer Gilroy and Sergeant Caister in an engagement over Aberdeen. The enemy aircraft, from 9/KG26, crashed and burned out killing the crew of four.

Noel Benson, from the beautiful Yorkshire village of Great Ouseburn, attended the exclusive Sedbergh School, North Yorkshire, and on leaving chose a career in the RAF entering RAF College, Cranwell, in April 1938 as a flight cadet. He graduated as a pilot officer on 23 October 1939. His first posting was to No.11 Group Pool at St Athan where he spent only one week before being posted to No.145 Squadron at Croydon, which was equipped with Blenheim 1Fs. His squadron moved to Drem on 14 August 1940 and sent detached units to Dyce and Montrose. On 18 December 1939, Benson was posted to 'B' Flight 603 Squadron, then based at Montrose. Noel Benson was affectionately known as 'Broody' by the rest of the squadron. Stapme Stapleton remembers why: 'Broody Benson used to sit for ages in the dispersal hut and stare ahead into space ignoring all that went on around him.'

Despite this, Benson was restless and eager to acquit himself well against the enemy. In *The Last Enemy* Richard wrote: 'Broody Benson, nineteen years old, a fine pilot and possessed of only one idea, to shoot down Huns, more Huns, and then still more Huns.' Benson was very professional in his approach to the job and was always smart and 'clean cut'.

Ronald Berry was born in Hull on 3 May 1917. He became known as 'Ras-Berry' after somebody wrote 'Ras' before his surname on his flying log book and it stuck for the rest of his RAF career.

He was educated locally and at eleven years of age he went to Hull Technical College and afterwards took the position of clerk in the St Andrews Engineering Company at the Hull Docks. After 18 months he went to work at the City Treasurer's Office as a clerk on salaries and income tax. After seeing an advert in a newspaper during the early part of 1937 he and a friend in the same office joined the RAFVR in April 1937. He later recalled: 'It was not easy to get into the RAFVR and I got myself really fit by running around my local park.'

Berry undertook flying training at the weekends at Brough. He recalled: 'Having gone solo I realised that this was going to be something that I was really going to enjoy, but it was only done in spare time and weekends, so I did not take my holiday that year, and doing it everyday I got myself well underway and from then on I never looked back'.

Berry spent his annual leave, from the time that he joined until war broke out, improving his flying skills. In August 1937 alone he flew thirty-five times and was taught aerobatics! Called up as a sergeant in February 1939, Berry was initially sent to No.66 Squadron at Duxford and flew Spitfires.

After three weeks he returned to Brough and Hawker Hinds but the experience had put him in good stead for his next posting. Following a short spell at gunnery school he was posted to 'B' Flight 603 Squadron at Turnhouse on 17 October 1939, the day after the raid on naval shipping in the Forth. He was put on readiness duty almost straight away and in November 1939 he was sent as part of a detachment to Montrose to protect the airfield. Berry's early experiences off the Scottish east coast prompted him to buy a rear view mirror from Halfords. His ground crew duly attached it to his Spitfire.

Berry was commissioned on 1 December 1939. His first taste of combat was on 7 December. The pilots of 603 Squadron drove off two Heinkels and then later a formation of seven He111s at which he fired at three and damaged two.

When Richard met Ras at Montrose he drew a mental thumbnail sketch that he was to include in *The Last Enemy* two years later:

> Pilot Officer Berry, commonly known as Raspberry, came from Hull. He was short and stocky, with a ruddy complexion and a mouth that was always grinning or coming out with some broad Yorkshire witticism impossible to answer. Above the mouth, surprisingly, sprouted a heavy black moustache, which induced me to call him the organ-grinder. His reply to this was always unprintable but very much to the point. Even on the blackest days he radiated an infectious good-humour. His aggressive spirit chafed at the Squadron's present inactivity and he was always the first to hear any rumour of our moving south.

Berry recalls:

> He was a splendid fellow with a university background like four others in my flight. There were two or three more at Dyce.

On 3 July 1940, he claimed a share of a Ju88 shot down 10 miles north of Montrose.

London-born John Boulter spent three years in the RAFO before relinquishing his commission in April 1936 on being granted a short service commission in the RAF. He was sent to 'B' Flight 603 Squadron at Turnhouse on 6 October 1939, to provide some regular RAF experience. Here he acquired the nickname 'Bolster'.

On 16 October he fired at a He111, possibly of I/KG26, east of Aberdour. In March 1940, Boulter was hospitalised as the result of injuries received when his aircraft was involved in a taxiing accident with an Airspeed Oxford at Montrose. This incident was merely a precursor, however, to the accident that later took his life.

On Richard's arrival at Montrose he painted the following thumbnail sketch of 'Bolster' Boulter amongst others he did of his fellow pilots: 'Then there was Boulter, with jutting ears framing the face of an intelligent ferret, always sleepy and in bed snoring when off duty.'

Stapme Stapleton recalls:

> Boulter was an older chap who I remember having big ears. He used to stand
> drinking, leaning on the bar all evening, talking and quietly watching the antics
> of the more active. By the end of the evening, at kicking-out time, he would
> simply release his grip on the bar and fall flat on his face!

James Caister from Edinburgh was 33 years old. He joined the RAF as an aircrafthand
around January 1925 and later applied for pilot training. As a sergeant pilot he
subsequently saw service in Palestine between the wars. Caister, known as 'Bill' to his
fellow NCOs, joined 'A' Flight of 603 Squadron on 29 October 1939, providing regular
RAF experience. He was related to John Mackenzie, one of the ground crew and with
whom he was billeted at Dyce, who remembers him with affection as, '. . . a really nice
chap and a good friend'.

Caister was a well-built, tough Scot who liked to box and frequently sparred with
ground crew Alec MacKenzie (no relation to John) and Arthur Carroll in their billet.

From Dyce he shared in the destruction of a Do215 on 16 April 100 miles east-north-
east of Aberdeen. On 3 July Caister shared in the destruction of a Ju88, a Do215 on the
6th and a He111 on the 12th.

New Zealander Brian Carbury, born in Wellington on 27 February 1918, was 22. By
6 October 1939, following the outbreak of war, Carbury was attached to 'A' Flight 603
Squadron, at Turnhouse to assist the Scottish Auxiliaries in their conversion to Spitfires,
but his temporary position became permanent on the 24th October 1939, following the
outbreak of war.

In *The Last Enemy* Richard wrote:

> Then there was Brian Carbury, a New Zealander who had started with 41
> Squadron. He was six-foot-four, with crinkly hair and a roving eye. He greeted
> us warmly and suggested an immediate adjournment to the mess for drinks.
> Before the war he had been a shoe salesman in New Zealand. Sick of the job, he
> had come to England and taken a short service commission. He was now a Flying
> Officer. There was little distinctive about him on the ground, but he was to prove
> the Squadron's greatest asset in the air.

John Rendall, a member of the 603 ground crew before it moved south, recalls his time
with Carbury:

> In those days I was an LAC Fitter and worked on his Spitfire at times. My most
> abiding memory of him was his height, and his fine manners to all ground crew.
> His man to man approach was very good as, at times, the gulf between officers
> and other ranks was not good – though it improved as the war progressed.

Another of the ground crew wrote:

> I would have been closer to Brian, but for the accursed stupid gulf, which kept
> the Gentlemen apart from the Peasants, which still existed in 1938, until much
> later. However, being a New Zealander, Brian had no time for such senseless
> class-distinction and he fraternised with the NCOs and other ranks, probably to
> the consternation of his seniors – It most certainly surprised me as a long serving
> regular in the RAF.

During combat on 7 December 1939, Carbury claimed a damaged He111 two miles
north-east of Arbroath, and on 7 March 1940 claimed a share of a He111 destroyed 40
miles east of Aberdeen. On 3 July he shared a Ju88 ten miles north-west of Montrose,
and following the squadron's move south, Brian Carbury achieved considerable success,
becoming one of the top-scoring pilots during the Battle of Britain.

John Mackenzie knew Brian Carbury throughout the Battle of Britain and described
the awe in which they held him and his combat ability:

> The 'Carbury Trick' was the expression we gave to his tactic of getting in very

close to the enemy before firing. He didn't mess around firing from distance. He could also push the Spitfire to its limits if the enemy fighters got on his own tail, thus shaking off all but the most experienced German pilots.

Philip Cardell was one of the first VRs to be called-up when war was declared. Having qualified as a pilot in late 1937, he had considerable experience by this time. The decision to commit himself to full time service was his. As a farmer he was in a reserved occupation.

Cardell was at No.15 FTS, Lossiemouth, while Richard was at neighbouring Kinloss and was commissioned as a pilot officer on 10 June 1940. From Lossiemouth he converted to Spitfires at No.5 OTU Aston Down and on 23 June, Cardell, along with Read, Sarre and Stokoe, was posted to No.263 Squadron at Drem in Scotland. The squadron moved to Grangemouth on 1 July and on the 3rd Cardell was posted to 603 Squadron along with Bill Read, Jack Stokoe and Alfred Sarre and sent to the two detached flights at Dyce and Montrose. Philip went to 'B' Flight at Montrose, while Stokoe, Sarre and Read went to 'A' Flight at Dyce. Within three days Cardell would be joined by Richard who described his first impression of Philip as 'bewildered, excited and a little lost'. He became known as 'Pip' to his fellow pilots.

Laurie Cunningham was born in Burntisland, Fife, in 1917 and educated at Edinburgh Academy. On completion of his education he very reluctantly joined the family grain merchant business. He joined the AuxAF in early 1935 at the age of 18. He appears as a fresh-faced young man on the front row of the 1936 squadron photograph. By March 1940 he was a flight lieutenant and one of the experienced members of the squadron. He was Blue Section leader with 'B' Flight when Richard Hillary arrived. Richard later recollected his memories of Cunningham in his book:

> Larry [sic] Cunningham had also been with the Squadron for some time. He was
> a Scotsman, tall and thin, without Rusty's charm, but with plenty of experience.

He was indeed very tall, well over six feet, as were at least half of the squadron.

Stapme Stapleton remembers that in order to look older than their years, a number of the flight were at that time trying to grow a moustache. He later recalled that Cunningham failed miserably:

> Cunningham took his higher rank more seriously than the others. He tried to
> grow a moustache but couldn't because the hair grew so short, tight and curly, it
> looked awful!

Jean Cunningham, Laurie's first cousin, recalls:

> Flying was his great joy in life. His mother had the unpleasant experience of
> being on a train which was left stranded when it was stopped from crossing the
> Forth Bridge during the raid in October 1939. She watched the dogfight between
> 603 pilots and the Germans, knowing that her son was in one of our planes.

On 7 December he had damaged a He111 whilst with 'B' Flight at Montrose and on 20 July 1940 he shared in the shooting down of a Do17 into the sea 30 miles east of Aberdeen.

Edinburgh-born George Gilroy was a sheep farmer and was thus known as 'Sheep' by his fellow pilots. He joined 603 Squadron AuxAF in 1938 and having been involved on 16 October 1939 he was in action again on 28 October when he claimed a share of a He111 which crash-landed at Long Newton farm, Humbie, East Lothian. This was the first enemy aircraft to be brought down on British soil during WWII. Gilroy was thrilled by the practicalities of flying and had little time for administrative duties.

By the end of July 1940, while flying with 'A' Flight from Dyce, he had been involved in the shooting down of seven enemy bombers.

Some years after the war Group Captain Sir Hugh 'Cocky' Dundas DSO and Bar, DFC, described Gilroy as: '. . . . Dour, serious in his habits, uncompromising of men in his judgement of their actions, but also possessed of a quick and puckish sense of humour.'

Claude Goldsmith was from Dersley, Transvaal and one of three South Africans to serve with the squadron during the Battle of Britain. Goldsmith was educated in England at Cheltenham College and Imperial College, London, where he studied mining at the School of Mines. He was a member of the London University Air Squadron in 1936 and was commissioned in the RAFVR in March 1938. Called to full time service he was intially sent to a unit flying the Westland Lysander (the 'Lizzie'). Keen to fly the Spitfire he applied for a transfer and was sent to No.603 Squadron and joined 'A' Flight at Dyce in early July 1940.

John Haig was known as 'Jack' by his colleagues. A papermaker by trade, Haig joined 603 Squadron AuxAF early in 1932. In June 1938 he went onto the reserve of officers (AuxAFRO) and was recalled for full-time service on 24 August 1939. By now Haig was one of the oldest and most experienced members of the squadron and was with 'A' Flight at Dyce when Richard joined the squadron.

'Ken' Macdonald was born in Murrayfield on 24 February 1912. He was educated at Cargilfield and Loretto schools and then Peterhouse College, Cambridge were he gained a reputation as an oarsman. He developed a love of fast cars and fast driving. Ken was described by his sister as: 'Sleepy and laid-back. He attracted the girls in large numbers...'

On graduating from Cambridge in June 1934, Ken complied with his father's wishes and started working as a solicitor. Bored with this he sought excitement, becoming a 'weekend flyer' with 603 Squadron AuxAF in early 1935.

Whilst on a photographic course in London in 1938 he met Marguerite (known as Mardi), and they went out together for the next three years. She recalls:

> He was sort of part poet, part philosopher, part artist. He totally changed my life.
> I only knew him for about three years but I looked at life totally differently. But
> I've always felt that he couldn't cope with what was coming. He had too much
> imagination and he felt terribly frustrated. It was a tragedy waiting to happen.

Mardi eventually married Jim Morton, also a member of 603 Squadron during the Battle of Britain.

Called to full-time service on 24 August 1939, Ken was involved in several of the early engagements of the war over the Scottish east coast. He took part in the action on 16 October when his section leader Flight Lieutenant 'Patsy' Gifford was given the credit for shooting down the enemy raider. On 19 January 1940, Ken shared a He111 followed by another on 7 March, both attacked east of Aberdeen. On 12 March, he was promoted to flight lieutenant, and on 26 June, Ken was duty night-flying pilot at Turnhouse when he shot down a He111 over the Forth. A few days later he broadcast his memories of this combat on BBC radio.

By the start of the Battle of Britain, Ken was with 'B' Flight at Montrose while his brother Don was with 'A' Flight at Dyce. It was Ken whom Richard came to know while they were at Montrose and, according to their older sister Ewen: 'Ken did not like him at all, and thought he was too full of himself.'

Don MacDonald was 22, Ken's younger brother by five years. On his arrival in early July 1940 his navigation was judged to be 'laim' and he was immediately sent on a course at an aerodrome in South Wales. He was described by his sister as 'outgoing, jolly and a bit of a practical joker'.

Jim Morton was a 24-year-old Londoner from Blackheath, whose search for more excitement led to his joining the RAFVR in July 1938, undertaking 'casual training' at RAF Turnhouse, where his instructors were members of 603 Squadron. In May 1939, he joined No.603 Squadron, AuxAF, and was called to full-time service on 24 August 1939. On 16 October, during the raid by the Germans on the Royal Navy shipping moored offshore, he too had shared in the destruction of a Ju88 over the Firth of Forth. Later that same day he shared another Ju88 and damaged a second. For his part in this action he received a Mention in Despatches.

Stapme Stapleton recalls:

> He was nicknamed 'Black' Morton on account of his very dark complexion. He

had to shave twice a day and still had this permanent five o'clock shadow, he was so dark and he stood out against the pale complexion of the red-heads, and there were plenty of those in Scotland!

This was not the reason behind the nickname, although a few of the pilots also believed it was. Others thought his nickname was a play on the coal mining connotation or even that he had 'put up a black' (the RAF expression for gaining a black mark from those in authority), since he had been in the RAF. The real reason was that, whilst he was at school, there were two Mortons, one with blonde hair and Jim with his black hair. As Jim was the junior he got the nickname. He was involved in some of the early action along the east Scottish coast, and on 15 and 17 July 1940, he shared in the destruction of two He111s.

Charles Peel was 21 and the younger son of Lieutenant Colonel W.E. Peel DSO of Haddington, East Lothian. Educated at Cheltenham College Peel began *ab initio* flying training with 603 Squadron AuxAF in December 1937 whilst working locally as an apprentice chartered accountant. Peel, like a number of the other pilots in the squadron, owned a fast sports car. He also possessed a small accordion which he could play. One of the ground crew was also a competent accordionist and Peel kindly leant his instrument to him in order for him to entertain his colleagues. But the most outstanding memory his colleagues have of Peel was of his binges in the mess or in Edinburgh. He would lie on the floor under a convenient table, his head just sticking out, his mouth in line with the edge of the table top. A whisky bottle was then laid on the table with the neck protruding over the edge. The top was removed and Peel would attempt to consume as much as possible as it rained down.

Stapme Stapleton recalls:

> Charlie Peel owned a puppy bull-dog called Shadrak, and when we had a high-ranking visitor one day Charlie got a bit flustered when presented to him and, instead of saying 'sit Shadrak' to his excited pup, he said 'shit Sadrak'! The pup actually bit one of the visitors!

Although Peel was very attached to Shadrak, this incident resulted in him having to send the animal home to be looked after by his parents.

Bill Read was from Palmer's Green, London, and was posted to 'A' Flight 603 Squadron, at Dyce, on 3 July 1940.

Stapme Stapleton recalls:

> Read was tall and lean. We nicknamed him 'Tannoy' because he kept chattering on the radio!

On 24 July Read shared in damaging a He111. Although the fighters managed to stop the port engine it was able to return to its base on the other. Bill Read recalls:

> Dick was posted to 'B' Flight at Montrose whilst I was with 'A' Flight at Dyce. We came together at Turnhouse before proceeding south and then of course I became better acquainted with that remarkable man. His book *The Last Enemy* was a minor masterpiece.

Ian Ritchie was another squadron member who was a solicitor in civilian life.

Born in Edinburgh in 1910, he gained a degree in law at Edinburgh University and went to work in the city. When his local squash club played RAF Turnhouse, he met George Denholm for the first time, who suggested to him that he might like to join 603 Squadron and learn to fly. This he duly did and he began his *ab initio* flying training in December 1937. Ian Ritchie and George Denholm remained great friends for the rest of their lives.

His 603 colleagues gave him the nickname 'Woolly Bear' or 'Bear' on account of his powerful build, but kind, soft demeanour. Like George Denholm, Ian was in his thirtieth year and the two friends were well aware of the large age difference between themselves and the youngsters coming into the squadron, particularly in the case of Ian with his prematurely greying hair. The two friends provided much needed support, stability and a much respected level of experience and maturity for the newcomers.

On 3 July 1940, Ritchie shared in the destruction of a Ju88, and a He111 on the 16th.

Fred Rushmer was 30 years old and nick-named 'Rusty' by his fellow pilots in the squadron because of his dark red hair. Born at Sisland, Norfolk on 12 April 1910, he was the youngest of eleven children and tragically the first to die. The Rushmer family were landowners in farming whose family home was Manor Farm, Thurlton. As a young man he, like so many of his 603 colleagues, had owned a fast sports car. In Rushmer's case it was an MG. He had been an engineering draughtsman in civilian life and, while he was at his first place of employment in Norwich, had won the opportunity to experience flying in a competition entered by all the lads in his office. That first flight was at Horsham St Faith (now Norwich Airport).

He joined 603 Squadron at the age of 24, having moved to Edinburgh to take up a job at Bruce Peebles Engineers Ltd in the city. The sister of Reg Cockell, one of the 603 ground crew, idolised Rushmer, but never let him know.

Called to full-time service Rushmer was one of the most experienced pilots in the squadron at that time and was appointed leader of Red Section. As a flight lieutenant he was made commander of 'B' Flight when it was sent to Montrose. Stapme Stapleton describes Rushmer as:

> A very nice man with bright red hair. He seemed far too nice to be a fighter pilot. It was hard to associate him being in such a profession, it didn't seem to suit him, like so many pilots in 603 Squadron. He commanded great respect from us and was a good leader.'

In *The Last Enemy* Richard describes his arrival at 'B' Flight dispersal and his first meeting with Rusty:

> As we came in, half a dozen heads were turned towards the door and Rushmer, the Flight Commander, came forward to greet us. Like the others, he wore a Mae West and no tunic. Known by everybody as Rusty on account of his dull-red hair, he had a shy manner and a friendly smile. Peter (Pease), I could see, sensed a kindred spirit at once. Rusty never ordered things to be done; he merely suggested that it might be a good idea if they were done, and they always were. He had a bland manner and an ability tacitly to ignore anything which he did not wish to hear, which protected him alike from outside interference from his superiors and from too frequent suggestions from his junior officers on how to run the Flight. Rusty had been with the Squadron since before the war: he was a Flight Lieutenant, and in action always led the Red Section. As 603 was an Auxiliary Squadron, all the older members were people with civilian occupations who before the war had flown for pleasure.

On 30 July 1940 Rushmer shared in the destruction of a He111 south-east of Montrose. His own aircraft was hit by return fire but he managed to return to base.

Alfred Sarre joined the RAFVR during March 1939 and was called up on 1 September 1939. Following ITW he was sent to No.15 FTS at RAF Lossiemouth and along with Pip Cardell, Jack Stokoe and Bill Read he completed flying training, converted to Spitfires and after a short spell with 263 Squadron was posted to 603 Squadron, arriving at 'A' Flight, Dyce, on 3 July. He remained very good friends with Jack Stokoe.

Basil Gerald Stapleton was born in Durban, South Africa on 12 May 1920. He was educated in England at the King Edward VI School in Totnes and, like Richard, his first experience of flying came sometime during 1932-35 when Alan Cobham's (later Sir Alan Cobham) National Aviation Day 'flying circus' was touring the country.

In January 1939, he applied for a short service commission in the RAF and on acceptance into the RAF was sent to the Civil Flying School at White Waltham and 13 FTS at Drem for flying training. Following brief spells with a number of units, he was sent to 603 Squadron in December 1939. He has retained vivid memories of many of the young men who were also members of 603 at that time:

> My closest friends were 'Bubbles' Waterston and 'Razz' [sic] Berry. Bubbles was
> a wonderful happy-go-lucky person who lived life to the full. He was from, what
> I believed to be, a wealthy family but never gave any indication that he was from
> such a background. He was the most popular member of the squadron. Over the
> years, I kept in touch with 'Razz' Berry and 'Uncle' George Denholm.
>
> Peter Pease was a tall chap, six feet two, with light wavy hair. He was very
> good-looking. We used to call him 'Popper' Pease.

John Mackenzie and Bert Pringle were responsible for Stapleton's Spitfire. John told me:

> I remember giving Stapme a fiver to get me some cigarettes when he was going
> into Montrose. I never saw that fiver again. He once went into town in a bowser
> full of 100 octane fuel!

Bert Pringle added:

> Stapme was a sorry looking sight. Everywhere he went he carried all he owned
> in a small scruffy suitcase. Eventually the fastening broke and I tied the lid closed
> for him with a piece of string.

On 26 April 1940, while 'B' Flight was on detachment at Drem, Stapleton was forced to
bale out of his Spitfire at night following the failure of an undercarriage leg.

Injuring his leg in the landing, he kept the matter quiet for fear of being grounded and
subsequently saw combat in defence of the Scottish east coast.

On 5 June, he crashed on landing at Turnhouse in Spitfire N5236 after the failure of
both flaps and brakes and on 3 July shared in the destruction of a Ju88 A-2 of 8/KG30
ten miles north-west of Montrose. The aircraft had been on a weather reconnaisance
from Aalborg when Green Section (Carbury, Stapleton and Berry) had shot it down into
the sea at 14.40 hours. On the 20th he shared a Do17P of 1(F)/120 with Bubble
Waterston. The Dornier crashed into the sea 30 miles east of Aberdeen at 12.05 hours.
Stapleton was close enough to identify the aircraft as A6+HH. Laurie Cunningham, the
Blue Section leader, did not open fire as he led the other two Spitfires into attack. His
reason was recorded in the squadron ORB: 'Cunningham stated that he did not open fire
because he was too close.'

When Richard arrived at Montrose on 6 July one of the pilots who was there to greet
him was Stapleton:

> Another from overseas was Hugh Stapleton, a South African. He hoped to return
> after the war and run an orange farm. He, too, was over six feet tall, thick-set,
> with a mass of blond hair which he never brushed. He was twenty and married,
> with a rough savoir-faire beyond his years, acquired from an early, unprotected
> acquaintance with life. He was always losing buttons off his uniform and had a
> pair of patched trousers which the rest of the squadron swore he slept in. He was
> completely slap-happy and known as 'Stapme' because of his predilection for
> Popeye in the *Daily Mirror*, his favourite literature.

Many pilots along with other members of the British armed forces read the *Daily Mirror*
to keep up with the exploits of Jane, and in actual fact Stapleton's nickname came from
another strip cartoon character along-side Jane and Blondie in the *Daily Mirror* called
Just Jake. In this cartoon there was a character called Captain A.R.P. Reilly-Foull who
wore huntsman's attire, red coat and riding boots, and always had a broken cigarette in
the holder clenched in his teeth. His character was unpleasant and lecherous, hence the
play on words, 'Really Foul'. He was always chasing attractive women, and one of his
expressions when he saw a women was, 'Stap me, what a filly!' He recalls:

> I used to cut out this cartoon every day and stick it on the wall of the dispersal
> hut and that's where I got my nickname from. Everybody in 603 called me that.

As a result, some of the squadron didn't even know my real name. Hillary didn't, for example. When he wrote *The Last Enemy* he called me 'Hugh' Stapleton which was incorrect, and to this day writers that quote from his book, or use his book as a source for research, still make the mistake of calling me Hugh! It wasn't until I left 603 that I lost the nickname. In a way the process started again.

Stapme became great friends with Bubble Waterston, one of the experienced members of the squadron, and together they were responsible for creating what was to become a legend; they spent their free time entertaining the children at Tarfside in Glen Esk, fifteen miles from Montrose.

Dudley Stewart-Clark was one of a number of local men in the squadron. Stewart-Clark was born at Dundas Castle, West Lothian, and a member of the wealthy Coates family, the manufacturers of fine threads, and enjoyed a comfortable lifestyle. He was educated at Eton and joined the RAFVR around May 1939.

He was called up on 1 September 1939, and was with No.602 (City of Glasgow) Fighter Squadron at Abbotsinch before he was posted to 'A' Flight, 603 Squadron, at Dyce. He enjoyed early success. On 3 July 1940, he shared in the destruction of a Ju88 and on the 6th shared a Do17. On 15 and 16 June he shared He111s.

Jack Stokoe, the son of a coalminer, was born on 1 February 1920 in West Cornforth, County Durham. In pursuit of a career he travelled south and took up a position in the chief inspector's department of Buckinghamshire County Council in Aylesbury and in June 1939 in search of an exciting pastime he joined the RAFVR, flying from Kidlington, Oxford.

Called to full-time service at the outbreak of war he attended No.1 ITW at Magdalene College, Cambridge and No.15 FTS at Lossiemouth. where he met Alfred Sarre, Bill Read and Philip Cardell with whom he completed his training and served in 603 Squadron. He joined 'A' Flight at Dyce on 3 July. His most vivid memories of anyone in the squadron were of Peter Pease whom he described as being: '. . . a really very nice chap who seemed to be from a different class of background to everyone else.'

Robin Waterston was born in Edinburgh on 10 January 1917. During his early days with the squadron he was keen to put on an overall; the sight of an officer with his sleeves rolled up working on the engine of one of the squadron Harts was unusual.

Soon after joining 603 Squadron, this good-looking young man was nicknamed 'Bubble' by his fellow pilots on account of his bubbly, effervescent personality and the *Water*-ston connotation. (Some incorrectly assumed his nickname was 'Bubbles', a corruption of the original pronunciation.) No matter what he was involved with, he forever exhibited a joyful, youthful exuberance. His unquestioning acceptance of everyone and his unconscious charm made him the most popular member of the squadron.

As a flying officer, he was with 'B' Flight at Montrose in July 1940, when Richard arrived. Richard later included a thumb-nail sketch of Robin in *The Last Enemy*:

> 'Bubble' Waterson was twenty-four, but he looked eighteen, with his short cropped hair and open face. He, too, had been with the Squadron for some time before the war. He had great curiosity about anything mechanical, and was always tinkering with the engine of his car or motorbike.

On 20 July 1940, Bubble, now with 'B' Flight at Montrose, shared in the shooting down of a Do17, into the North Sea 30 miles east of Aberdeen.

CHAPTER EIGHT

OPERATIONAL FIGHTER PILOT

Montrose 'B' Flight
6 July – 27 August 1940

On Saturday 6 July 1940 the Spitfires of Gilroy, Stewart-Clark and Caister, forming Red Section, shot down a Messerschmitt 110 of Aufkl.Gr.OB.d.L., 100 miles east-north-east of Aberdeen at approximately 13.15 hours. The crew were missing. The Spitfires had been scrambled at 12.29 and landed back at Dyce at 13.37.

This was the day on which Richard, Peter Pease and Colin Pinckney had joined the squadron, having arrived while Red Section was busy with the 110. On entering RAF Montrose they reported to the station CO, Group Captain H.V. Champion de Crespigny. (His office is still there today and forms the main building of the Montrose Aerodrome Museum Society.)

Stapme remembers the arrival of Richard and Peter Pease, and although Colin Pinckney went to 'A' Flight at Dyce, Stapme recalls him from that time as being 'another tall chap and a very nice fella.' It was while he was with 603 Squadron that Colin gained the nickname 'Pinker'.

> We called Pease 'Popper' for a reason I cannot remember. Hillary was a very nice chap; he was a year older than I was. He was very well dressed, very good-looking with a typical university hairdo – long hair! Not long as we know it today, with a pony-tail, but much longer than our hair, although ours wasn't too short. But Hillary's was over his ears and over his collar, and we weren't allowed to have that! He was very well spoken, was always very well-mannered and a very polite chap. The university had given him the finish that we didn't have and he had that air about him. We were a little more brash, I'd say. He'd been polished by the university. He seemed a lot older in manner and maturity than he really was. I didn't mind the 'thumb-nail' sketch of me that he included in *The Last Enemy*!
>
> When they arrived, a number of us were in the process of growing moustaches. It was a trend that I believe came from the fact that a number of older, although not necessarily more experienced, pilots came to us from Army Co-operation squadrons after the battle for France. We simply decided to grow moustaches in order to make us look older. We were conscious of how much younger we looked than them. Those that tried to grow moustaches were successful, all that is except for Cunningham. His hair was too short and curly, and there simply was not enough of it growing on his top lip, and so he gave up!

Stapme still sports a splendid 'Flying Officer Kyte' handle-bar moustache to this day.

> The other chaps in the squadron were of monied parents, not untypical of an auxiliary squadron. Somebody had to pay for the flying, usually it was Dad! The men that made up the nucleus of the squadron were really nice chaps. The two that impressed me most were Bubbles Waterston and Rusty, my flight commander. Rusty seemed to be just too much of a gentleman to be a fighter pilot, in that he was quiet and quite introverted. He didn't seem to handle his authority over us in the usual way. If we said something to him that he didn't

agree with he tended just to ignore the comment. He was an outstanding pilot and
we had great faith in him as a flight commander. He was a lovely chap. We now
know of course that he was killed but at that time and for many years afterwards
all we knew was that he had just disappeared.

When I met Bubble's sister Jean in 1996 she told me that Rusty was someone that her
brother had looked up to. They were very good friends. 'Robin used to bring Rusty back
to the house quite regularly, sometimes with Laurie Cunningham.'
    At this time Rusty was 30 years of age. Stapme continued:

There was a mixture of 'VR' and short service commission officers in the
squadron. I remember that Carbury and I were short service. Carbury was about
six feet two inches tall and very thin. He was an excellent pilot. I used to fly as
his 'No.2'. When Hillary got shot down, I was his No.2 and Hillary was his No.3.
I don't know where they got that information from that says I was with No.54
Squadron that day.

Junior members of the squadron were required to undertake a period of induction before
being made operational. This involved a great deal of practice flying including flights
to the other sector airfields, formation flying, dogfights, formation attacks, local
orientation, local reconnaissance and co-operation flights with representatives from the
searchlight and anti-aircraft units.
    The new pilots also had to undergo a week of practice interceptions and attacks
before being declared operational. Blenheims, capably flown by No.248 Squadron,
played the role of the enemy bombers. Based at Dyce they had a detachment at Montrose
then Sumburgh. One such pilot who carried out this exercise was another Australian
called Lewis Hamilton who played the part of the bandit in Blenheim L9392.
    One other duty that Richard undertook, came about soon after he arrived. 'B' Flight
was on standby for night-flying operations and, as Richard was on duty, it was his task
to light and extinguish the three lamps used to mark the landing ground thus enabling
the two members of the section on night flying operations to take off and land (one lamp
marked the near end of the landing area, while two lamps were positioned side by side
at the far end, but to one side – this enabled the pilot to see the lights, even when the
nose of the Spitfire obscured his vision after touching down). The two fighters took off
to intercept the enemy at ten minute intervals, so the path had to be lit and extinguished
twice. Richard remained in attendance throughout.

                                   *   *   *

While Richard was busy with flying practice, the rest of the squadron saw action.
    On Friday 12 July Yellow Section (Pilot Officer Gilroy, Sergeants J.R. Caister, I.K.
Arber) shot down a He111 of 9/KG26 over Aberdeen sometime between 12.43 and 13.10
hours. Unfortunately, the German bomber crashed onto the town's recently opened ice
rink and the resulting fire destroyed the new building. The crew of four were killed.
    Monday 15 July dawned cloudy and overcast. At 11.55 two Spitfires of Yellow Section
(Pilot Officers Morton and Stewart-Clark) were scrambled from Dyce and at 12.15
spotted a He111 of 2/KG26 as it emerged from the thick cloud near Peterhead. It was to
prove a most unfortunate move by the pilot with such generous cover available. The
Spitfires carried out a hurried three-quarter attack before the German pilot, Oberleutnant
Ottmar Hollmann, managed to disappear into the cloud once again. The Spitfires landed
at 12.34. Although brief, the attack proved extremely accurate. Later that day, four of the
crew, Hollmann, Obergefreiter Probst, Unteroffizer Walz and Obergefreiter Prefzger,
were picked up from their dinghy in the North Sea. The fifth member of the crew,
Feldwebel Reinhardt, had been killed. The crew members later reported having counted
over 200 bullet holes in the Heinkel as they climbed into their dinghy
    On Wednesday 17 July, with the poor flying weather continuing, 603 again saw
action. A raid on the Imperial Chemical Industries factory at Ardeer, Ayrshire, by He111s

of Major Victor von Lossberg's III/KG26, flying from Stavanger, Norway, were heading home in a straggled formation as Spitfires from 'A' Flight, 603 Squadron, caught up with one of them. Red Section (Flying Officer Ritchie, with Pilot Officers Morton and Stewart-Clark) shot the He111, of 9/KG26, down 25 miles east of Fraserburgh at 16.12 hours. Two crew members, Oberleutnant Lorenz and Unteroffizier Beer, were seen by the Spitfire pilots to climb into a rubber boat. They later became POWs but Unteroffizier Liedtke and Gefreiter Heimbach were killed. It was reported that Red 2, Jim 'Black' Morton's Spitfire, was hit in the starboard mainplane by an armour piercing (AP) bullet.

Flying Officer Charles D. Peel, flying with 'A' Flight from Dyce in Spitfire K9916, did not return from a patrol on this day. While on detached duty from 41 Squadron as an instructor Flying Officer John Young (later Wing Commander, and official historian for the Battle of Britain Fighter Association) had recommended that Peel be given further training. But his advice went unheeded.

The exact circumstances relating to Peel's disappearance are still unknown although as the weather was not good for flying he may have lost his way. The North Sea became his grave.

* * *

Thursday 18 July 1940 was a very busy day for the squadron. Generaloberst Hans-Jurgen Stumpff's Luftflotte 5, based in Scandinavia, had started to increase the regularity of operations directed at the north of Britain. At 10.00 hours three Heinkel 111s of KG26 attacked Montrose unopposed. At 10.08 Green 1 (Ras Berry) was ordered to patrol Montrose at cloud base and managed to intercept one of the bombers at which he fired two short bursts. It is not known if he damaged the enemy aircraft. He landed again at 11.20. At 14.17 hours the three Spitfires of Yellow Section (Flying Officer Ritchie, and Pilot Officers Morton and Read) were sent up to intercept a convoy-spotting Dornier Do215 10 miles east of Aberdeen. They all fired at the enemy aircraft but did no apparent damage. Yellow 2, Jim Morton, was again hit, his aircraft sustaining eight bullet holes. They landed back at Dyce at 15.53.

At 16.25 hours two Spitfires from Red Section, Red 1 (Pilot Officer Gilroy) and Red 3 (Sergeant J.R. Caister) were again sent up to intercept a small formation of aircraft from KG26 over Aberdeen. Sheep Gilroy fired all his ammunition but was then hit by return fire from the enemy aircraft, damaging the glycol cooling system of his Spitfire, R6755, forcing him to land near Old Meldrum at 16.40 hours. Red 3 (Sergeant Caister) did not sight the enemy and returned to base at 17.03. Red 2 had trouble taking off and did not take part in the engagement.

Finally, late into the evening, between the times of 22.25 and 22.45 hours, 603 achieved success. During a raid on a convoy off Aberdeen by Ju88s of Major Fritz Doensch's I Gruppe, KG30, Caister attacked a Ju88 and fired four bursts at a range of one hundred yards closing to fifty yards, damaging the enemy aircraft. Caister reported that having fired at the Ju88 it then dived steeply into low cloud and was not seen again. He was confident that it would crash into the sea, but owing to cloud and darkness was unable to follow it. The enemy aircraft later crashed in Aalborg, Denmark, with a wounded crew member on board. To compound what little fortune the squadron had this day, at Montrose a Miles Master trainer, piloted by a student, taxied into a parked 603 Squadron Spitfire N7881.

On Friday 19 July practice flying took place and fighting patrols continued by day and night. Caister was again in action attacking an enemy aircraft but received damage to his own Spitfire K9995.

On Saturday 20 July 1940 Pilot Officer R.G. Manlove, a ferry pilot, was delivering a new Spitfire to 'B' Flight at Turnhouse when he crashed on landing. The aircraft, R6752, was written off as a result of the accident. At 11.35 hours Blue Section took off from Montrose lead by Flight Lieutenant Cunningham with Bubble Waterston and Stapme Stapleton and shot down a Dornier Do17P off Peterhead. The aircraft crashed into the sea in flames, the crew were reported as missing. Stapme's memories of this incident are still vivid:

> Montrose was a very exciting time for us because we had German aircraft to
> intercept. The 20th of July was the first time I fired my guns in anger. We had a
> lot of German aircraft over on reconnaissance missions and that was when I
> shared a Dornier Do17 with Bubbles. There were three of us; Cunningham was
> leading with Bubbles as his No.2 and me as his No.3. Cunningham approached
> the bomber, but for some reason he didn't fire at it. Later, after we had landed, he
> told us that he had gone up to the aircraft to identify it, which was bloody
> nonsense! So Bubbles went in and opened fire and I followed behind and did the
> same. For some reason Bubbles refrained from carrying out another attack but
> when I closed in I could see the dorsal gun pointing straight up, instead of at me,
> which indicated that the rear gunner had been hit! I then flew in close formation
> alongside the aircraft and was able to make a note of its squadron letters and
> numbers before it landed in the sea. I got on the radio to tell them where it was
> so they could get a fix on me and get the Air Sea Rescue crew out to pick up the
> surviving crew members. When I returned to base they told me that they hadn't
> sent anybody out to rescue the crew because the weather was too rough, but it
> certainly was not. I had to land at Dyce after that patrol because, much to my
> amazement, my oil pressure gauge showed naught, but the temperature wasn't
> going up! So I realised that I couldn't have lost my oil because my temperature
> gauge was OK. I remember once when 'Uncle' George was 'A' Flight
> commander at Dyce, he landed and he had what I remember as being a glycol
> leak, and the engine was still going, it hadn't seized. The manufacturer's engine
> identification brass plates fixed to the side of the engine, saying Rolls-Royce etc,
> had melted and were buckled, but the engine was still running! That gives you
> some idea of the quality of the Rolls-Royce engine.

On 21 July Pilot Officer Noel 'Broody' Benson returned from leave having spent the
time with his parents at the family home at Great Ouseburn in Yorkshire. This was the
last time that they were to see him.

The squadron was in action again on Tuesday 23 July. 'B' Flight commander Rusty
Rushmer with Ras Berry and Broody Benson (Blue Section) took off at 14.47 and shot
down a Dornier Do17P 75 miles east of Aberdeen at 15.00 hours. The enemy aircraft
crashed into the sea and all four crew members were killed. The Spitfires of Blue 1
(Rushmer) and Blue 3 (Benson) received hits from enemy aircraft return fire, but despite
the damage to their aircraft managed to nurse their aircraft back over the 70 miles of the
North Sea, landing safely at Montrose at 16.00 hours. That same day the CO, George
Denholm, landed Spitfire, N3026, at Montrose with the undercarriage retracted. The
aircraft was repairable and the CO was unhurt.

On Wednesday 24 July the Spitfires of Red Section (Pilot Officer Gilroy, Flying
Officer Haig and Pilot Officer Bill Read) took off at 06.49 and at 07.00 damaged a
Heinkel He111H-3 of 3/KG 26 out to sea between Aberdeen and Peterhead. The enemy
aircraft's port engine was disabled and the rear gunner wounded. The aircraft began to
circle and lose height, but disappeared into low cloud. It made it back to base with three
wounded on-board and crashed on landing. 'A' Flight, Red Section, landed at Dyce at
07.51 hours.

On Friday 26 July Pilot Officer George 'Sheep' Gilroy escaped injury when his
Spitfire, N3288, tipped onto its nose after landing in mud on the Dyce aerodrome. Both
airfields at Dyce and Montrose were prone to becoming mud-baths after heavy or
persistent rainfall.

* * *

Richard had been getting in some extra hours on the Spitfire when he heard on his radio
that Blue Section had been scrambled to intercept an enemy bomber. Had he followed
procedure he would have returned to base but, listening to Operations vectoring the 603

fighters onto the bomber's position, he used his maps to attempt an interception himself. The opportunity to return to base having destroyed an enemy aircraft was irresistible. Unfortunately he failed to locate the bomber and was himself nearly shot down by Brian Carbury and the rest of his section. Carbury had not been informed of any friendly aircraft in the area, which was correct as Richard was four miles further north at the time. When he saw Richard's aircraft flitting in and out of the clouds, thinking he was the enemy he put his flight into line astern for attack. He pulled his aircraft out of the attack at the last moment, on realisation that it was a friendly aircraft in his sights. The next day Richard and Peter Pease were made operational by 'B' Flight commander Rusty Rushmer, who had stated: 'I think it will be safer for the others.'

It was this sort of intuitive, unorthodox and somewhat reckless behaviour that was a familiar trait of Richard's. His single-minded determination to do things his own way was something that was not going to be disciplined.

* * *

Richard had joined a section with 'Bubble' Waterston and 'Stapme' Stapleton, both experienced pilots, while Peter Pease was in a section with the highly experienced 'Rusty' Rushmer and 'Ras' Berry. All that Montrose had on duty at any one time was one readiness section of three aircraft. With a full complement of pilots available, the rest of the squadron was either 'available' (ready to take off within half an hour of a call) or 'released' (which meant that they were allowed off the aerodrome). The same system applied at Dyce. This meant that at least two pilots were able to get a couple of days a week away from the base. Richard's initial opportunity to gain combat experience was therefore limited. The main source of recreation was with fellow pilots in the mess. Stapme Stapleton remembers the difficulties of recreation so far from home:

> Unlike the local members of the squadron we did not have homes to go to during our time off. Therefore the mess was our home from home, as far as we were concerned anyway. We drank and socialised there, while the local Scotsmen could entertain at their own homes. We would get the occasional invitation but we were unable to offer the same in return, we had nowhere to invite them to. I got married to Joan, my first wife, in Montrose. I was nineteen and the CO, who was 'Count' Stevens at that time, sent a telegram to my father, and he sent a telegram back saying 'Don't be a blundering idiot'! 'Count' Stevens denied ever having seen the response and told me to go ahead and get married, which I did.

Bubble Waterston's youngest sister Jean would soon start training as an occupational therapist at the nearby hospital of Stracathro, just outside Brechin. The work would be hard and she did not have many opportunities to think of her brother as he prepared for war. In fact she was of the belief that he would come back safely. When they did meet it was usually back home with the rest of the family. As far as she was concerned he was doing what he loved most, flying, and in the company of those that meant most to him.

On one occasion Bubble invited her to the mess where she was immediately surrounded by the young pilots, eager to get to know the pretty young sister of one of their fellow pilots. She recalls: 'Very soon there was a line of glasses on the bar containing gin and lime, but I was going to have none of that, despite being very young, and didn't drink them!'

* * *

When Richard did get away from Montrose he and Peter occasionally drove to Aberdeen to have dinner with Colin and on one occasion attended a local dance. On another occasion he travelled to a hunting lodge at Invermark with Bubble and Stapme. Invermark is situated 20 miles inland, in Glen Esk, to the north-west of Montrose. In response to an open invitation from Lord (Simon) Ramsay, the 16th Earl of Dalhousie, they stayed at Invermark Lodge where their host was there to greet them on arrival. Lord Ramsay was born in 1914, educated at Eton and Christ Church College, Oxford. He served in the Black Watch from 1936-39 and was MP for Angus from 1945-50, during which time he was the Conservative Whip from 1946 before he resigned in 1950. He was the governor-general for the Federation of Rhodesia and Nyasaland from 1957-63. The Dalhousie family seat, an earldom that was created in 1633, was based in Brechin Castle and the family owned a vast amount of land in the area, including that in Glen Esk. Today the family are still at Brechin Castle but much of the land has been sold.

The scenery in this area is of outstanding beauty and hard to beat anywhere in the world, and in stark contrast to the muddy, flat airfield at Montrose which was open to the icy winds that blew off the North Sea, just a few yards from the eastern-most edge of the airfield. Here they could relax in the hunting lodge with the option of stalking the hinds (the male stags that needed to be culled seasonally), shooting grouse (which took place during two or three days in August), and fishing in Loch Lee, which was situated just two hundred yards from the lodge which overlooked the water from a prominent position. A number of the officers in the squadron took full advantage of this facility including Brian Carbury, who told of a visit to Invermark in a letter dated 8 August 1940:

> We have a lodge near here, way up in the hills and we usually go up there for one or two days and have lots of good fishing and shooting grouse, hare, rabbits and now stag. Last week I got me a young stag, 24 rabbits and four trout. It is marvellous getting up there away from it all and not having to worry about dress or anything.

In *The Last Enemy* Richard wrote that on one occasion he shot a stag: 'But I am no sportsman and the dying look in the beast's eyes resolved me to confine my killing to the Germans.' He had apparently not enjoyed the stag shoot and sought alternative recreation during his days off. An opportunity arose that he could not possibly have foreseen. Those that knew him well would have struggled to believe that he could find such pleasure in this particular association.

The Children of Tarfside

Richard's description in *The Last Enemy* of his first meeting with the children of Tarfside is delightful, and is in such dramatic contrast to the action he would become embroiled in during the weeks ahead.

Richard had named his Spitfire 'Sredni Vashtar', after the immortal short story by Saki (a pseudonym for the Scottish humorist Hector Hugh Monro who was killed in WWI), a story that he repeated to the children in the hayloft during one visit.

The tough, cocksure attitude that he adopted while at Shrewsbury, in order to give those around him the impression that he was not vulnerable to hurt, was dropped in the presence of the youngsters. It must be remembered that he was only a few years older than the eldest children there, who were Mrs Rhoda Davie's eldest daughter, also named Rhoda, who was 16, and her brother Billy, 17. The war would force Richard to grow up very quickly.

It is easy to imagine the young officers in their late-teens/early twenties surrounded by the delighted children, who idolised these courageous knights of the sky. Even into their twilight years they, who later became known as the children of Tarfside, still hold them in the same light.

To meet the children at Tarfside became a popular getaway for the pilots, and on occasion during practice flights, the odd pair would fly down the valley looking for the children in order to give them the thrill of seeing the aircraft in such a dramatic and beautiful backdrop. The children would respond whenever they heard the sound of the Merlin engines by rushing out into a clearing, from wherever they were playing, waving frantically up at them, confirming recognition.

* * *

The Tarfside kids comprised the children of a number of the holiday-makers staying in holiday cottages; the children of the local inhabitants, like Angus Davidson, who were in the minority; and the evacuees, who were actually accommodated in a farm house called Migvie, under the care of Mrs Rhoda Davie a few hundred yards from where the pilots stayed at the Invermark Lodge. Mrs Davie had spent a number of years residing abroad in India and was now living in Brechin. She cared for children whose parents were working abroad and unable to return to visit them. This situation must have generated feelings of kinship between Richard and these youngsters. He had experienced similar emotional hardship just a few years before, with his own parents having only recently returned to these shores.

The children numbered roughly 20 in all and included the three children of Mrs Davie; Billy the eldest, who could only spend the weekends at Migvie as he was working as a despatch rider, daughters Rhoda, and Betty the youngest at ten years. Rhoda and Betty are still living in the region. Betty, who now lives near Blairgowrie, chose Richard as her favourite companion. They all played in a number of areas in Glen Esk including: Migvie; the tributaries of the river North Esk, which ran down the tree-covered slopes close to the farm; and finally Loch Lee. Loch Lee is situated at the far end of Glen Esk and the slopes of the surrounding mountains lead straight down to its edge, with no forestry on its banks, only heather and rocks. Here in the loch the children and pilots would swim together.

Angus Davidson was nine when he spent three weeks of the summer of 1940 in the company of several pilots from 603 Squadron.

He recalls particularly one bright sunny day towards the end of July when Stapme Stapleton and Bubble Waterston were driving past in Stapme's MG Magna convertible. The local families and holiday-makers were enjoying a picnic on the grass next to the farm while watching the Loch Lee Games, the annual mini highland games. As the two pilots went past they found the atmosphere irresistible and stopped. As they sat and watched the events, Stapme became interested in the tossing of the caber (forever the competitor), and was invited to compete. Thus for the first time, they became involved with the children and their families who, having met and enjoyed the company of these fine young men, were happy to see many return visits sometimes with other pilots including Richard who had become intrigued. It was not just the publication of *The Last Enemy* that brought about the legend of the Children of Tarfside, for even the local newspapers published articles on this happy but unusual mixture of children and RAF fighter pilots, responsible for protecting the air-space above their country. However the publication of Richard's exploits did of course contribute on a world-wide scale.

The pilots that Angus remembers best of all are Stapme, Bubble and Richard, of whom he recalls Billy Davie saying years later that he thought: 'Richard Hillary initially stood apart from the others, and was even aloof, perhaps arrogant.' Angus added: 'He was not as laid back as Stapme and Bubbles, but still good fun.'

* * *

Stapme was the favourite of a number of the children, including Angus who was quite overwhelmed when I informed him that he was still alive and well. Angus had thought they had all been killed in the war:

> He seemed to have a foreign intonation and a very loud laugh. He was very tall. Stapme was great fun and always enjoyed himself to the full. Bubbles was probably the best looking after Richard and, like Stapme, always let himself go. He was also great fun.

Laurie Cunningham also visited the children but he didn't appeal to them in quite the same way:

> Cunningham was older and higher in rank than Bubbles and Stapme, and he was not at all laid back. He was very serious and we called him 'Frizzle-guts'! He got on very well with Rhoda Davie and I think they were quite keen on each other.

> Boulter was also older than the others, he certainly looked a lot older. His ears
> seemed to stick out a long way!

Finally there was 'Ras' Berry, whom Angus remembers as being:

> . . . always jovial and looking for every opportunity to joke around. He seemed
> to have a reputation for being a great pilot.

The young lad of that time who took a shine to Richard, with the unfortunate nickname
'Rat Face', is Graham McCrow who still lives in the region as do the Rogers brothers,
who stayed at Migvie, Charlie Robertson, who lives in Montrose, the Robertson sisters,
one of whom became Mrs Sheila Welsh when she married a famous tennis player of that
period, Dave Loudon, and Bill Murray who told me: '. . . I still have wonderful
memories of those days so long ago in the glen.' According to Bill, the brothers Dave
and Bill Strachan emigrated to Canada.

Angus doubts Richard's claim that he shot a stag: 'I cannot say for sure but, as I know
what was required to achieve such a success, it is very unlikely.' Stapme was later able
to confirm that Richard did not shoot a stag and that he had used, what he called:
'literary licence, or bullshit!'

According to Stapme, when the pilots expressed the urge to go stalking Lord
Dalhousie only issued them with a full-bore .22 rifle, hardly the calibre weapon to shoot
a full grown stag. As Stapme said of their host: '. . . he wasn't daft enough to give us
anything bigger!'

Perhaps Richard chose to credit himself with Brian Carbury's 'kill' when he wrote
about events at Glen Esk in *The Last Enemy*.

Bubble's sister, Jean Blades, told me that when Bubble and Stapme had gone stalking,
initially before Richard had joined them, their fitness had suffered with nearly ten months
free from the exercise that they had been used to. In trying to reach the higher slopes they
had become exhausted and returned to the lodge. They tried again, and on this occasion
Lord Dalhousie loaned them a tractor in order for them to reach the higher slopes!

For the next three weeks, during the month of August, the pilots were seen in the
company of the children on several occasions. They would play a number of games with
them including; throwing a ball onto Migvie's low-level slate-tile roof, and compete to
get to it first as it rolled down; hide-and-seek and 'kick the can'. Angus recalls:

> On one occasion I was hiding and I dislodged something that made enough noise
> to give away my position. Stapme gave chase as I panicked and left my hiding
> place, but as we crossed the yard Stapme ran into a large, very wet, pile of dung.
> He went in up to his knees and he stank! When he later went into the farm house,
> my mother asked me where that dreadful stench was coming from and turned,
> only to be confronted by the bulk of Stapme towering over her, which gave her a
> start! There used to be a large bough from a fir tree that used to hang over the
> road, on the other side of the road from the farm house, and Stapme used to climb
> onto it, put a leg either side, and pretend to be flying his Spitfire. The bough has
> been cut off now but you can still see the tree and from where it was removed.

One other game that Angus remembers, which was documented in *The Last Enemy*, is
when they all climbed into the tiny hayloft at Migvie, the pilots would, in turn, each tell
a story to the children. As Richard mentions, and Angus can confirm, they certainly did
try to compete with each other for telling the best story. Richard told the story of *Sredni
Vashta* the ferret, and the *Wizard of Oz*. Afterwards he confessed that he had seen the
Judy Garland film while in London before he had travelled up to Montrose! As Stapme
was able to confirm:

> Dick Hillary was an excellent raconteur. One story he told to the children was
> about *Sredni Vashta*. Until recently, I had always remembered the story being
> about a red-eyed rat; an unpleasant character that he characterised as being a

German. When the rat spoke, Dick would speak his lines in German and then
translate for the kids. It had a marvellous effect.

Richard spoke only basic German, he was more fluent at French.

One day Richard, Stapme and Bubble turned up in the MG with a surprise for the
youngsters. A German Heinkel bomber had been shot down over the sea while returning
after a raid on a Scottish city. It has been said that the next day the Luftwaffe rubber
dinghy from the downed aircraft was washed up on the beach next to the aerodrome and
salvaged by the pilots. Bubble, Stapme and Richard had brought it with them for the
youngsters to play with on the loch. The weather had been fine and they joined the
children in swimming in the loch and playing with the dinghy. A rare photograph of
Richard was taken there with him lying in the dingy while wearing a light open-neck
shirt, pin-stripe trousers, plus his '36 style flying boots, and laughing ecstatically as he
appears to be looking down between his legs. However, Billy Davie remembers that
Stapme fired into the water around Richard with the .22 rifle which their host had loaned
them. He also remembered him shooting into the floor of the dinghy which would
explain Richard's action in retreating to the far end of the boat; and the way he is looking
in amazement at the leaking puncture holes in the bottom. It was Billy who advised
Stapme to stop before there was an accident! Angus remembers using the inflatable
afterwards, and so it was either repaired or Stapme was not quite so reckless! He
remembers the fun they had with the dinghy but could not actually recollect shooting at
it, although he was quick to add: 'I had been a crack shot with a .303 rifle and if I had
wanted to puncture the dingy without hitting Dick then I would have, but I don't
remember having done so.'

The dinghy was left in the boathouse next to the loch for future use and towards the
end of their visits they took it back to Montrose aerodrome with them.

Whatever the level of fun that these children enjoyed, the best was still to come.
There had been much air activity over the Glen during recent months, with the Miles
Magisters of No.8 FTS at Montrose carrying out training flights over the area. On one
occasion the kids reported seeing a German bomber, and this was confirmed later as
having been the case. One day, the two Spitfires of Stapme and Bubble went looking for
the children. They first flew up Glen Esk at low level and then proceeded to try to pick
them out at one of their favourite haunts. They flew to the loch and not having found
them there, flew back over to Migvie. The lads and lassies were playing in a brook
nearby and on hearing the engines louder than usual, they rushed from the woods, onto
the road, where they saw the Spitfires almost at the same time that the pilots spotted
them. The gang raised their arms in glee and jumped up and down, not really knowing
how to react with such a marvellous sight overhead. The two Spitfires then proceeded
to give them a display of their flying skills. They first flew back down the valley a short
distance and then, turning, headed back towards the children at low level. In fact the
aircraft were lower than they were. It is this picture of the approaching Spitfires that has
stayed clear in the mind of Angus for all these years: 'I think that was the best view
anyone could have of that beautifully-shaped aircraft, head-on and looking slightly
down on it'.

The two aircraft pulled-up in front of them one after the other in a crescendo of noise.
The smell of burnt aviation fuel hit their nostrils and gave them yet another new
sensation to add to the massive flow of adrenaline. As the aircraft climbed steeply over
the forest-covered slopes they banked to the left, the engine noise momentarily dying,
before swooping back down the side of the valley, back over their heads at low level. A
few more minutes of pure magic before they flew by, waving, and departing for
Montrose.

This display was to be repeated a number of times during the three weeks that they
visited the youngsters. The pilots occasionally dropped fruit and presents. Bubble
dropped an orange which 'exploded' on the road. On another occasion, according to
Billy Davie, the wheels of one of the aircraft clipped one of the tall pine trees next to

Migvie. Stapme Stapleton felt sure that this story was most improbable.

In *The Last Enemy* Richard described 'B' Flight's recall to Turnhouse:

> For a moment I thought Rusty had forgotten, but then I heard his voice down the
> R.T., 'Once more, boys,' and in four sections of three we were banking to
> starboard and headed for the mountains.
>
> They had heard the news, and as we went into line astern and dived one by
> one in salute over the valley, none of the children moved or shouted. With white
> boulders they had spelt out on the road the two words: 'Good luck'.
>
> We rejoined formation and once again headed south. I looked back. The
> children stood close together on the grass, their hands raised in silent farewell.

Romantic as it may sound, the fly-by did not take place. The orders to return to
Turnhouse were with immediate effect and the squadron simply departed from Montrose
and Dyce. It would have also been against the Air Ministry rules to pass on details of
their movements. The white stones which defined the road edges outside Migvie and the
other cottages might well have given Richard the idea for his use of literary licence.

From the viewpoint of the children, the holiday period was close to an end and some
of the holiday-makers had already left, having taken their nippers with them, their minds
loaded with precious memories which would have been hard to better in the years since.
The visits by the pilots, their heroes, just stopped and the days became quiet without their
company, the air activity noticeably lessened and the Glen returned to the tranquil, quiet,
isolated place it had always been, for all but a three-week spell of thrills. Invermark
Lodge was closed down for another season. The children had little idea of the
transformation of environments that their fighter-pilot friends were now undertaking.

Angus was to read very little of what happened to the pilots. The death of Richard
was mentioned in the local paper under the heading: 'The Last of the Long-Haired
Boys'. Angus kept the cutting believing that all who had visited the Glen had been
killed. During my initial visit I was able to confirm to him that not all the 603 pilots had
been killed, and thus a resurgence of local interest began.

*   *   *

When I spoke to Stapme about his memories of the visits to Tarfside he was initially
eager to tell me about his car during that time. His interest in 'carburettors' had not
diminished over the years!:

> My car at that time was a blue six-cylinder, two seat, MG Magna, one of the TD
> series of which they made only twelve. A chap called Goldie Gardener did a
> record 202 mph on a German autobahn in 1935, in a version with a special body.
> I bought mine in 1939 at Roland Smiths, a second-hand motor car dealer in
> London. The MG Magna, which means the bigger one, was borrowed by Archie
> Winskill, another 603 Squadron pilot, when I became a prisoner of war on 23
> December 1944.
>
> When Bubbles and I travelled to Invermark for the first time we had our bags
> in the back, and as we drove up in front of this lodge we were met by a tall thin
> chap who took our bags and showed us to our rooms in what was a fourteen
> bedroom shooting lodge. We said that we would like to meet our host, the Earl of
> Dalhousie, to which the tall man replied, 'You're looking at him!' I can't
> remember the exact number of times we went there but it was a quite extra-
> ordinary experience. Bubbles and I took Richard Hillary there on two different
> occasions. We never met the children one by one, there was always at least eight
> to ten of them. I first of all remember meeting a crowd and then the kids were
> fascinated by us I suppose. We were wearing our uniforms then and the kids sort
> of gravitated towards us. I think the parents were quite pleased to have them off
> their hands! They were full of questions. I remember flying over there which we
> were not supposed to do, but there were a lot of things that we were not supposed

to do, and we still did them. We even chased some stags down from summer grazing to winter grazing for Lord Dalhousie, from high up, gently, by flying on one side of them, not too close. They moved down into the lower valleys. He had no ghillies to drive them down. Hillary did not shoot a stag at any time we were there. The effort that would have been required – you would have had to walk for miles and been assisted by those that were skilled. I don't know where he got the idea from but it was wishful thinking and as far as the book is concerned, literary licence. Once, while he was with me, I shot a rabbit with my .22 pistol. I didn't kill the rabbit unfortunately, I only paralysed it. I got hold of its back legs and hit its head against a rock, and Hillary was violently sick! If the incident did occur, then that pistol was the one which I was later to use at the Loch when I fired close to Dick Hillary when he was in the Luftwaffe dinghy.

We used to fly training exercises along the route of Glen Esk, in pairs, not in three's, as has been wrongly suggested. Had we been on patrol we would invariably have been in three's. During the training flights we underwent certain exercises. We carried camera guns and would, in turn, each act as hunter and hunted. It was great fun and valuable experience. We each tried to get on the other's tail, before swapping over. On one occasion I shook off my pursuer by going into a 20-30 degree dive and at 800-1000 feet I did a sharp roll and broke away. He thought I would not be able to pull out of it, but I did, and managed to shake him off my tail, as the evidence on the camera gun film was to show.

Richard 'lost his heart completely to Betty Davie' who, now Betty Johnstone, recalls her memories of the summer of 1940:

We used to play games at Migvie, where we were staying. The games consisted of kick-the-can, hide and seek and rounders, we used the painted white stones from the roadside as bases. We were playing one day when Bubbles and Stapme drove past particularly slowly. They were clearly keen to join in and it was Billy who wandered over and invited them. At that time Billy and Rhoda were both old enough to work, and were only with us at the weekends. When the afternoon was over the two pilots asked if they could come again and as they drove off I remember them waving and shouting, 'We'll be back!' The next time they brought Dick. He got on really well with our mother.

We enjoyed so many picnics in the area. So much so that the daily delivery of bread by our local baker Joe Guthrie each morning became more important than ever. Our mother used to prepare a very large number of sandwiches in order to feed everyone, and we loaded them into a large wicker tomato basket.

On one occasion we went on a picnic to Glen Mark. We all clambered into several cars and made our way over there. Over the river in the glen was a bridge made of two ropes suspended from mountings on either bank. One cable was for standing on, the other was for holding onto with your hands. Stapme made his way over to the other side, I remember what a tall, broad man he was. But then Bubbles and Dick tried to persuade me to go over. I said no! I was very timid. But Bubbles and Dick said they would go across with me, one either side, and urged me to 'Come on!' So I said that, with their assistance, it would be alright. As we made our way across, they bounced on the lower cable to make me feel even more insecure than I already was. Unfortunately, as we neared the other side, the bridge collapsed and we all fell. Bubbles and I fell on the shingle, narrowly missing the water, but Dick fell straight in. He was soaked! He stripped off his wet clothes and we wrapped him in a blanket. For some reason Dick always wore his flying boots, and these took about three days to dry out.

By evening time our adventures in Glen Esk would be curtailed by the swarms of mosquitoes and we retreated to the hayloft at Migvie where the pilots told us stories. The hayloft door was positioned to enable the sheaves to be unloaded from the back of the wagon, but the youngsters discovered that it was

> just the right height to use as a jumping platform. This time of story-telling in the
> hayloft was the perfect opportunity for me to get as close as I could to Dick. I
> really was very fond of him.

After Betty heard that Richard had been shot down she wrote to him at East Grinstead.
She received a reply written by a nurse as his hands were badly burned, but dictated by
Richard. In the letter Betty remembers the line: '. . . if you were here now I'm sure that
you would have something cheeky to say about me'! Betty did not keep the letter as it
was not in his handwriting.

> Although I was very fond of Dick, Bubbles was the kindest of them all. To the
> younger children they were all heroes.

Another of the 'children' was 16-year-old Sheila Robertson and her younger sister.
Today Sheila lives in Edinburgh and has many fond memories of those brief weeks in
Glen Esk. Like Betty Davie, Sheila also wrote to Richard in hospital after he had been
shot down, and again the reply was written by a nurse, having been dictated by Richard.
Sheila recalled:

> I remember it began by saying, 'All of those that you knew at Glen Esk were
> heroes.' He talked of Bubble and how sad he was that he had been killed. The rest
> was more or less small talk. But the fact that he bothered to answer our letters
> gives you some insight as to his character – perhaps a rather complex one I think.
>
> At that time I was a very unsophisticated 15 or 16-year-old and I confess
> Robin and Stapme were my favourites, with Dick a close third. My younger sister
> agrees that Dick was slightly more aloof, although that is perhaps not the right
> word to use to describe him.

*   *   *

In *The Last Enemy* Richard recorded that, having been made operational, one of his first
duties was to fly a Spitfire down to RAF Abingdon, which he completed with one stop
en-route to refuel. He landed after having taken advantage of the situation and circled
Oxford, admiring the architectural beauty of the city. After telephoning his flight
commander, Rusty Rushmer, to confirm his arrival, Richard called a taxi and headed off
to see Oxford and Trinity once more; this despite Noel's recent letter to him warning him
not to go back as it had been a depressing visit for him only a few weeks previously. It
had been almost a year since Richard had been there. Although initially he must have
felt very proud, returning to his old college resplendent in his RAF uniform with the
'wings' brevet on his tunic, unfortunately the trip was to be a depressing one for him too,
and he was pleased to return to Montrose. It had been between terms and Richard found
the emptiness of the college and the absence of friends very saddening. The place now
seemed to be haunted with the memories of so many good times gone by, and of friends,
some of whom were now dead as a direct result of the war. Time had indeed moved on
and he no longer felt a part of the place anymore, and it was to the future that he looked.

The real reason behind Richard's undertaking this flight is unknown – that's if it did
actually take place as there is no record of such a flight in the squadron records. If he
did, it was most likely sanctioned not for official reasons, but for pleasure. His mention
of a visit to the local depot to collect another Spitfire for the squadron was more likely
a cover for what was actually a day-trip. Use of aircraft in this way was not unusual but
in recording the event in his book he presents the authorisation of such a flight in an
official context, thereby avoiding having his superiors presented in a bad light when his
book was published. Richard would have landed at RAF Abingdon, the home of the
Oxford UAS, which had no Spitfires during this period.

I spoke to a number of pilots in 603 Squadron and they were unanimous that this part
of his story was fabricated and no such trip took place. What was more likely was that
Richard spent part of a leave with his parents during which time he travelled back to
Oxford. The flight down in the Spitfire certainly adds romance to the story and would
be in keeping with his tendency to use such licence.

* * *

On Monday 29 July Red Section at Dyce (Sergeant Caister, Pilot Officer Read and Sergeant Stokoe) was scrambled at 11.47 hours. They sighted two He111s 12 miles west of Aberdeen. Red 1 (Caister) fired at the enemy aircraft which jettisoned its bombs into the sea. The German was then lost in the thick cloud with no apparent damage. Red 2 and 3 did not get close enough to open fire. They landed back at Dyce at 12.33.

Next day was again overcast and wet. KG26 mounted a small number of raids against Scottish cities from their base in Norway. At 11.45 hours Red Section led by Rusty Rushmer with Ras Berry and Peter Pease, was scrambled and shot down a Heinkel He 111H-4 of 8/KG26, 40 miles south-east of Montrose. There were no survivors when the aircraft crashed into the North Sea and one body was spotted floating on the surface. Green 1 (Flight Lieutenant Rushmer) and Green 3 (Peter Pease's aircraft) were hit by return fire from the Heinkel but managed to get back to Montrose. This had been Peter Pease's first taste of combat and he was credited with a 'share' or third of the kill. This must have made Richard even more eager for the opportunity to shoot down enemy aircraft. Having the existing 603 pilots around him achieve success was something that he could live with and learn from; they were his mentors. But having one of his closest friends achieve success before him would have put him a position where there were just not enough opportunities for him to meet the challenge, leaving him frustrated. But this would not last for long. Knowing full well that the fighting in the south was becoming heavier, Richard was also of the attitude that he would enjoy Montrose while he had the chance. He knew that life was good at the moment and that all would change very shortly.

By 1st August the RAF Fighter Command order of battle showed that 603 had eleven aircraft ready for combat with four more unserviceable. Twenty pilots were available. No commanding officer is noted at this stage as George Denholm had still to be confirmed as the new CO.

On Friday 2 August 1940 Sergeant I.K. Arber crashed his Spitfire at Inkhorn, Aberdeenshire. The crash was not as a result of combat and, despite the aircraft being a write-off, Arber was unhurt.

The continuing poor flying conditions reduced the number of operations on both sides of the Channel and, similarly, also caused a great number of flying accidents with the experienced as well as trainee pilots. On Saturday 3 August 65 Squadron at Hornchurch (the squadron 603 would replace in just over three weeks) suffered a most unfortunate loss, when their CO was killed in a night take-off accident.

On Thursday 15 August, the day the Germans called *Adler Tag* (Eagle day), the all out attack on the airfields of Fighter Command by the Luftwaffe, Richard was granted six days' leave. It is not known where he went but it is likely that he travelled south to visit his parents. He had enjoyed plenty of opportunity to explore the local places of interest in Scotland and he had not seen his parents for quite some time. Michael and Edwyna Hillary were now back in England with Michael still working for the Sudan government, as auditor general. As he would be working in London he had taken a flat at 36 Knightsbridge Court, Sloane Street, but the house in Beaconsfield continued to be used as a holiday home.

On Saturday 17 August 603 Squadron received orders to prepare for a move south to Hornchurch in Essex, and Richard returned from leave on the 20th. 'A' and 'B' Flights were recalled from Dyce and Montrose on the 23rd in readiness. Richard wrote in *The Last Enemy* that on the 22nd he and Peter were sent to Turnhouse by train to pick up two new Spitfires. Having spent the night at Turnhouse, they flew back to Montrose the next morning just as the fateful message arrived. It had been too late to stop them.

The famous confrontation between Richard and Peter, told in detail in *The Last Enemy*, took place during the train journey to Turnhouse. Richard uses Peter's Christian and patrician idealism as a foil for his own outsider creed:

> 'You', he informs Peter, 'are going to concern yourself after the war with politics and mankind. I am going to concern myself with Richard Hillary. I may or may

not be a man of my time, I don't know. But I know that you are an anachronism. In an age when to love one's country is vulgar, to love God archaic, and to love mankind sentimental, you do all three. Me the mass of mankind leaves cold. My only concern outside myself is my immediate circle of friends, to whom I behave well, basically, I suppose, because I hope they'll behave well towards me.'

According to the squadron operational record book this journey did not happen. The discussion as presented in his book was actually the compilation of several discussions that had taken place between Richard and Peter since they had become friends.

The squadron was to wait anxiously for another four days before the move south was finally confirmed. On 26 August Richard was persuaded to use a gun again when the Station Commander of Turnhouse, Wing Commander The Duke of Hamilton, offered the squadron a couple of days' grouse shooting on his estate. The original party had consisted of Peter Pease and Colin Pinckney with 'A' Flight pilots Sheep Gilroy and Black Morton. Peter had to drop out as he was on duty and Richard decided to take his place. The weather was awful and Richard, cold, wet, and making little attempt to hide his misery, found some consolation in the hospitality on offer. Nevertheless his constant complaining left its mark on the memory of George Gilroy who later recollected that: '. . . Hillary continually stumbled through the wet undergrowth, fell into boggy areas and kept making such comments as: "This is a confounded bore", which was really not the done thing considering the hospitality extended to us.'

Gilroy and Morton had to return for duty that night but Richard and Colin stayed for a hot bath, dinner and the promise of more shooting the next day, if it wasn't raining. At 02.00 hours Richard and Colin were awakened by one of the ghillies who had received an urgent telegram from Turnhouse;

SQUADRON MOVING SOUTH STOP
CAR WILL FETCH YOU AT EIGHT OCLOCK STOP –
DENHOLM.

By ten the next morning they were back at Turnhouse.

During this period the squadron pilots, some having already had a taste of combat, had been eager to become involved in the battle proper being fought in the south of England. Information had filtered back that the squadrons of British and Allied fighters were fighting a desperate battle against a far greater number of Luftwaffe aircraft, but were holding their own. This news only served to agitate and make them all the more enthusiastic to be a part of this great air battle, and to acquit themselves well in combat. Many of the squadron had already gained some combat experience but those that had not felt they still had something to prove, and were keen to acquit themselves well in combat.

For some that first baptism of fire would be so terribly short.

CHAPTER NINE

RAF HORNCHURCH. SOUTH AT LAST!

27 August – 3 September 1940

'. . . think not of us as individuals or personalities, but as a Battle of Britain team.'
Air Chief Marshal Sir Hugh Dowding GCB, GCVO, CMG

Fighter Command was organised geographically by groups under the central operational control of Command Headquarters at Bentley Priory, Stanmore, Middlesex. By this time there were four groups, Nos. 10,11,12 and 13. No.10 Group HQ was based at Rudloe Manor, Box, Wiltshire and commanded by Air Vice-Marshal Sir Christopher Quintin Brand; No.11 Group HQ was at Uxbridge, Middlesex and commanded by Air Vice-Marshal Keith Park; No.12 Group HQ was at Wattnall, Nottingham and commanded by Air Vice-Marshal Trafford Leigh-Mallory and No.13 Group HQ was situated at Newcastle, Northumberland and commanded by Air Vice-Marshal Richard Saul. The group areas were divided into sectors and each sector had a sector HQ. No.10 Group had two sectors where the sector HQ airfields were at Filton and Middle Wallop; No.11 Group had eight sectors with sector HQ airfields at Tangmere, Kenley, Biggin Hill, North Weald, Debden, Northolt and Hornchurch; No.12 Group had seven sectors with sector HQ airfields at Duxford, Coltishall, Wittering, Digby, Kirton-in-Lindsey and Church Fenton; No.13 Group had four sectors with Sector HQ airfields at Catterick, Acklington, Turnhouse and Prestwick.

Hitler believed that if he hit Britain hard enough using his air force then the British would also capitulate like his previous enemies. And so the battle began for Britain from the end of the French campaign, with many initial skirmishes in the air over the south coast during the weeks leading up to the official date of what later became known as the Battle of Britain. In July the Luftwaffe had mounted several small scale actions aimed at disrupting the shipping passing through the Channel and at the same time forcing the RAF to defend them. The fighting had gradually become more intense, and the Luftwaffe began to send free-hunting patrols to engage the RAF over southern England.

The pace of the air battle had continued to increase into August. During the 34 day period from 10 July until 12 August the Luftwaffe lost 261 aircraft while the RAF lost 127 in these skirmishes. This was a period of small scale actions when both sides felt out each others strengths and weaknesses. This gave a loss ratio of 2:1 in favour of the RAF but neither side had been put to any real test. On 2 August the Luftwaffe's Air Fleets 2, 3 and 5 had been issued with orders to begin all-out attacks, aimed at destroying RAF Fighter Command.

This new phase had begun on 13 August and was, as far as the Germans were concerned, the main thrust of the battle. On this first day the Luftwaffe launched 1,485 sorties hitting the naval bases at Portland and Southampton as well as the airfields of Detling and Eastchurch. On the 14th the Luftwaffe attacked several of the airfields in the south again but with a smaller force. The next day Luftflotte 5 attacked the airfields and radar stations of northern England from its airfields in Norway and Denmark with a far greater force. The attacking forces were intercepted and suffered heavy losses the result of which was, with 79 aircraft lost compared to the 34 of the RAF, Luftflotte 5 was to play little further part in the battle. Over the next six weeks a series of large-scale, hard

77

fought battles took place with few breaks. Each action was to contain features unique to that particular battle.

On 18 August, which dawned bright and sunny with scattered cloud, the Luftwaffe attacked four of the most important airfields in south-east England. The airfields were further inland than the airfields they had attacked thus far on a large scale. At the same time a large force of Stukas attacked the radar stations in the Portsmouth area. On this day more aircraft would be destroyed than on any other day during the Battle of Britain and it became known as 'The Hardest Day'. During the three major attacks of the day the Luftwaffe lost 69 aircraft destroyed, with 94 crew members killed, 25 wounded and 40 taken prisoner, while the RAF lost 31 fighters with 11 pilots killed and 19 wounded. The ratio of losses between both sides was representative of those during the major actions over southern Britain.

For a week after the seven days of ferocious fighting, leading up to the evening of 18 August, the weather prevented further large-scale air operations. The Luftwaffe resumed its attacks on 24 August with further large-scale attacks on the RAF airfields. For the next two weeks the combat was intensive, with Fighter Command fighting for its very existence, particularly No.11 Group. On 24 August Manston was put out of action and had to be temporarily abandoned, while Kenley, Biggin Hill and Debden were all heavily bombed.

On Tuesday 27 August at 11.00 hours the pilots of 603 Squadron took off from Turnhouse and flew down to Hornchurch in Essex, and into the heat of the battle. The squadron ORB for this day reads: 'All flying personnel and 38 other ranks proceed to Hornchurch.'

The squadron had acquitted itself well during the previous few months and Fighter Command and the Air Ministry did not hesitate in sending 603 to the harder-fought front line of southern England. They were to relieve the battle-weary 65 Squadron which had only five aircraft and 12 pilots left. No.65 Squadron was sent to Turnhouse via Church Fenton to rebuild, and shortly before the 603 Squadron Spitfires left, 65 Squadron landed.

Richard, Noel Benson, Colin Pinckney, and Pip Cardell were to wait for four unserviceable Spitfires to be repaired, finally leaving Turnhouse at 16.00 hours. Broody led with Colin navigating in the 'pocket'. Richard and Pip flew either side.

According to Richard, on the way down they stopped once at Church Fenton to refuel, whereas, according to the log books of Jack Stokoe and Jim Morton, the rest of the squadron flew for 55 minutes before landing at Linton on-Ouse. They then flew to Church Fenton – 15 minutes away – before flying for a further 50 minutes to Hornchurch.

The weather that day consisted of low cloud and drizzle. Later, the dull, overcast sky gave way to clear skies and sunshine when they finally arrived at Hornchurch at 19.00 hours. Richard recorded in *The Last Enemy* that of the 24 who flew south, only eight would return.

As the Spitfires took off that morning a Bristol Bombay also departed from Turnhouse. Onboard were the ground crew including five riggers and five fitters under the command of Sergeants Gillies and Mackenzie. They had the minimum of equipment with them and had to borrow a great deal on arrival at Hornchurch. Following this initial provision of ground personnel the rest followed on 11 September, as recorded in the ORB: 'Flying Officer Allen Wallace and remainder of squadron travelled by special train to Hornchurch overnight from Turnhouse.'

Peter Pease did not fly down with the squadron but took his car. Peter's girlfriend, Denise Maxwell-Woosnam, had been serving with the ATS on an ack-ack site at Vange, Essex, when she decided to take a week's leave and travel to Edinburgh and stay with an uncle in order to be near Peter at Turnhouse. As she disembarked at Waverley Station, she was greeted by Peter with his bags packed, ready to head south. The couple drove down together, stopping overnight at Prior's House, the Pease family home. Denise recalls:

> It was a pretty grim journey when one looks back on it, as he must have known
> the state of the casualty lists, and I had seen daily the little Spitfires whirling like
> wounded butterflies to the ground. But neither of us said anything – there was

really nothing to say. When we arrived at Hornchurch he had to go straight and
fight – and I saw him about every other day in between battles for an hour or two.

Having travelled to Edinburgh to be near Peter, she was now back at work, only 17 miles
from Hornchurch.

In *The Last Enemy* Richard was mistaken in stating that 603 flew south on 10 August.
The weather for that day was thundery showers sweeping much of northern Europe and
Britain. As this was Goering's intended *Adler Tag* which had to be cancelled due to the
unsuitable flying conditions, it is unlikely they would have flown south in such abysmal
weather conditions. The other point of reference for confirming the date of departure
from Turnhouse is that Cunningham, Don Macdonald and Benson were killed the day
after they arrived at Hornchurch, ie: the 28th.

*   *   *

The eager and confident pilots of 603 Squadron swung their Spitfires over Upminster
before racing in low over the turf of Hornchurch airfield and breaking gracefully
downwind for the circuit and landing.

On arrival at Hornchurch the pilots had been met out on the tarmac by the station
commander, Group Captain C.A. 'Daddy' Bouchier DFC (also nicknamed 'Boy'
Bouchier), who, at the welcome address, told the pilots that they would be given the
following morning off to settle in, but at mid-day they would be put on readiness.
From now on, things were going to be very different from what they had been
used to. Squadron Leader George Denholm, now finally confirmed as CO, spent the rest
of the day in consultation with the commanding officers from the other squadrons. Group
Captain Bouchier later recalled his memories of that first meeting with the pilots of 603:

> I shall never forget their coming! Could this really be a squadron, I thought, as I
> went out to meet them on the tarmac on their arrival. The CO, on getting out of
> his Spitfire, had his little 'side-hat' perched on the back of his head; he
> meandered towards me with bent shoulders, hands in his pockets, followed by,
> what seemed to me then to be, the motleyest collection of unmilitary young men
> I had seen for a very long time. I was not impressed. Good heavens! (I suddenly
> remembered) it's an Auxiliary squadron. Ah! I thought, that explains it, but what
> have I done to deserve it?
>
> How wrong I was! And yet, somehow, I feel that 603 will forgive me for those
> first impressions. You see, the RAF Station at Hornchurch was always my
> spiritual home, and I was very proud of it. I had grown up there in peacetime with
> No.54, 65 and 74 Fighter Squadrons – those early 'regular' squadrons which
> were the first to bear the brunt against the German Luftwaffe, and who fought so
> valiantly during Dunkirk and afterwards. They were truly magnificent. One by
> one, battered and weary they departed from my station in a blaze of glory to
> quieter parts of the country to recuperate and fill up their ranks again, and thus it
> was that there came to Hornchurch other 'regular' fighter squadrons, eager and
> fresh for the fray, to take their place.
>
> Into this line of succession of 'regular' squadrons there suddenly dropped
> No.603, the Auxiliary squadron from Edinburgh. How could they possibly cope
> with what they would be up against? How could they, an Auxiliary squadron, be
> expected to acquit themselves in the same manner as my long line of 'regular'
> squadrons had acquitted themselves? Shades of Malan and Tuck and Bader, and
> hosts of others! – the very salt of the earth; the cream of our fighter squadrons!
> How could 603 live in such company, I wondered. Those were my thoughts as I
> went out to greet them on their arrival.

How mistaken Bouchier was with his initial assessment of the 'week-end pilots'.

The 603 pilots were shown the Intelligence Room, area maps, codes etc., and were
instructed to report back at 11.00 hours the next morning to complete the briefing. The
pilots found the atmosphere to be in stark contrast from the relaxed surroundings of

Montrose and Dyce. Everyone appeared tired out and the mess bar lacked the light-hearted banter. Ras Berry remembers arriving at Hornchurch:

> I was walking around the hangars that night and remember meeting a chap who was to become the top-scoring pilot from New Zealand. His Spitfire had been hit, and what he had to say about being hit is unprintable, so I won't repeat it. . . . 'Fucking hell's snakes he hit me!' He was later in my wing in North Africa.

The New Zealand pilot was Flying Officer Colin F. Gray of No.54 Squadron. Stapme Stapleton also remembers arriving at Hornchurch:

> One of my most outstanding early memories of Hornchurch occurred not long after we had arrived. I watched a Spitfire land and as the pilot walked across from his aircraft I could see that he was wounded and there was blood trickling down his face from his forehead. He was all right, it was just a scratch, but that was my first introduction to what was to come.

The pilot was Flying Officer Tony Lovell of No.41 Squadron who had attained the rank of wing commander by the end of the war with 16 enemy aircraft destroyed, 6 shared destroyed, 2 probables, 9 damaged, 4 shared damaged and one destroyed on the ground to his credit. He served in the Battle of Britain, the defence of Malta and various operations throughout the Mediterranean. He was tragically killed in an accident at Old Sarum immediately after the cessation of hostilities when his Spitfire crashed as he pulled out of the second of two rolls just after take-off. He had flown throughout the war, undertaking one of the largest number of operational tours of any pilot in the RAF, but is unfortunately not as frequently remembered like so many of his contemporaries.

A number of wives also travelled south to be near their husbands. Nancy Berry and Joan Stapleton moved into a house in Romford, from where their husbands travelled to Hornchurch early each day. Both wives were pregnant at this time.

* * *

The squadron line-up had changed somewhat in the last twelve months, since its embodiment into the RAF. As well as the inevitable postings to and from the squadron, Somerville had been killed at Grangemouth, D.K.A. Mackenzie had been killed when he crashed during a night flight, Peel had failed to return from a patrol which had involved combat over the North Sea, and injuries suffered by Graham Thompson in a flying accident at Turnhouse put paid to any further wartime flying.

Most of the squadron had amassed a great many hours flying the Spitfire. Some including Uncle George Denholm, Sheep Gilroy, Stapme Stapleton, Bubble Waterston, Laurie Cunningham, Black Morton, Dudley Stewart-Clark, Ras Berry, Ian Ritchie, Ivor Arber, Jim Caister, Ken Macdonald, and Peter Pease had already seen some action. Richard, Peter and Colin, having been given every opportunity to settle in and improve their flying skills on the Spitfire, travelled south with a total of roughly 75 hours' flying time on Spitfires with approximately 60 hours of that total having accrued since becoming operational. This was a great deal more than many were to receive before being thrust into combat.

Whilst at a disadvantage from the other pilots, this inexperience did not necessarily set them apart from the rest of the squadron, as by the time 603 returned north to be rested two months later, the squadron had inflicted heavy losses on the Luftwaffe, although in doing so it had suffered a terrible mauling of both experienced and inexperienced pilots alike. Benson, Cardell, Cunningham, Dewey, Goldsmith, Peter Howes (who had joined his friends in 603 having been posted from 54 Squadron), Matthews, Ken and Don Macdonald, Pease, Rafter, Rushmer and Waterston had been killed. Caister was a POW after landing in France after combat. Hillary, McPhail, Morton, Stewart-Clark, Dexter and Stokoe were to play no further part in the Battle of Britain due to wounds received. Dexter, Boulter, Colin and Richard were killed later in the war. Boulter died tragically from injuries received after returning to Drem for a rest, after his Spitfire was hit by another aircraft.

It has been said that of the 3,000 pilots that are listed as having flown in the Battle of Britain, approximately only 1,000 actually fired their guns at the enemy during combat. With hindsight it was realised that the newly-arrived pilots needed about five patrols, involving combat, in order to gain the experience to have any idea what was going on around them, ie: to develop situation awareness of the proximity of enemy aircraft; to take *effective* evasive action and therefore avoid being shot down; to handle the aircraft with reasonable aptitude under stressful circumstances; to remain reasonably calm enough to act effectively; and ultimately to mount an attack of their own and survive that particular patrol. An understanding of this would help us to comprehend why experienced and inexperienced pilots were so often shot out of the sky within this initial five-patrol period.

The squadron performed brilliantly throughout the Battle. Brian Carbury was to achieve the highest number of enemy aircraft destroyed by any member of the squadron and was one of the top five highest scoring Allied pilots in the RAF for the same period. He was also one of very few who received both DFC *and* Bar during the battle and his confirmed claims for five enemy fighters destroyed during one day was remarkable.

In Scotland they had been used to having just one section of three Spitfires at readiness. On arrival at Hornchurch they found three squadrons at readiness! The RAF airfields were being bombed, although on 27th August, the day of their arrival, after early reconnaissance activity over much of the south-east by enemy aircraft, no attacks materialised out of the gloom of a dull, overcast and drizzly morning.

Hornchurch was a hive of activity with various squadrons and supporting crews dashing about in lorries or on foot attempting to keep up with their work loads, aircraft taking off and landing with great frequency. What greeted the eyes of the pilots and ground crews of 603 on arrival must have been quite daunting. They were now in the front line.

Ras Berry remembers the new lifestyle to which he had to adjust:

> Half a dozen pilots would sleep at dispersal in readiness for surprise dawn attacks. This entailed being up at 04.30 hours, with the Spitfires warmed-up by 05.00 hours. The first sortie was usually about breakfast time, the last being at about 20.00 hours. We had egg, bacon and beans for breakfast which was sent over from the mess. Other times we ate whenever we could. Some didn't even live to enjoy breakfast.

This description is almost the same as Richard's description in *The Last Enemy*.

As so many pilots in 603, Ras also developed an affinity with the calm, relaxed voice of the Controller at Hornchurch issuing urgent instruction to the pilots, via the tannoy system, with no hint of concern in his voice. It had a lasting effect on those that were fraught with tension at that time. The voice was that of Ronald Adam, who had been a fighter pilot in World War I. On 7 April 1918 he had been shot down by the 'Red Baron', Manfred von Richthofen, wounded and taken prisoner.

Wednesday 28th August 1940

Officially the Battle of Britain was 48 days old by the time 603 arrived at Hornchurch. British airfields were being bombed relentlessly in an attempt to eliminate the RAF in preparation for an invasion. The demand on the RAF fighter pilots and the entire ground crew was enormous. There had to be aircraft and pilots available to deploy against the relentless waves of attack from the far superior numbers of Luftwaffe aircraft, and this while these same aircraft were bombing our fighter bases. The Germans, for their part, had to have air superiority before their invasion.

Since 24 August large numbers of RAF fighters had been ordered into the air against the huge massed formations of Luftwaffe aircraft as they approached the coastal areas of Kent, Sussex and Hampshire. Initially the first fighters to become airborne were usually successful in intercepting the Germans over the coast but the German tactics of splitting their formations once they were over land confused the Observer Corps. It therefore proved impossible to guide subsequent fighters on to the enemy formations with any accuracy, and as a result more than two-thirds of the fighter force failed to make contact with the enemy. To take effect as from 27 August, but used for the first time on the 28th, Keith Park, commander of 11 Group, covering the vital south-eastern defence airfields and approaches to London, instructed his fighter leaders to pass a coherent sighting report back to their controller before going into attack. They were to use the traditional call of 'Tally-ho' and give the position, course, strength, and height of the enemy aircraft. This system was used to great effect from this day.

It is interesting to note that occasionally the 603 pilots used the war-cry 'Rooki, Rooki!' when diving to attack the enemy, but there is nothing Scottish about it. During his service in Palestine, Bill Caister had picked up the expression – which describes how a young boy is seized by the scruff of the neck with one hand while the other hand takes hold of the seat of his pants in order to throw him from the room – and found it expressive of squadron victories. The idea caught on after he mentioned it to his fellow 603 Squadron pilots.

The attacks on the RAF airfields continued, but the might of the Luftwaffe, with its familiar three-phase pattern, was now no longer directed at No.10 and 11 Groups but almost entirely at the airfields of No.11 Group. Park was reliant, now more than ever, on other group commanders for reinforcements to maximise the effort in order for his group to survive.

Apart from the odd confrontation with reconnaissance Dorniers early on the morning of the 28th, the first raid of the day was reported to be building up over the Pas de Calais just after 08.00 hours. The Hurricane pilots of No.79 Squadron were moving forward to Hawkinge at the time, and having sighted the Heinkels of II and III/KG53, provided the controller with the required information before going into the attack. Hurricanes of 501 and 615, and Defiants of 264 Squadron at Hornchurch were sent up to intercept. A total of 44 aircraft attempted to engage the bombers.

Once again the airfields were the target of the German bombers and as they crossed the Kent coast over Deal they split into two groups: the Dorniers of I/KG3 attacked Eastchurch while the Heinkels from KG53 attacked Rochford (later Southend Airport) just after 09.00. The heavy German fighter cover of Me109s overwhelmed the RAF fighters and No.79 Squadron was lucky not to lose any aircraft as it attempted to halt the Heinkel's attack. No.615 lost one Hurricane with the pilot injured as it attempted to attack the Dorniers with 501 Squadron, and 264 was bounced by Me109s. Of the 12 that took off, eight returned and of those only three were serviceable. Two pilots and two gunners were killed. Refuelled and rearmed, the crews of the remaining three were eager to get back at the Germans during the next raid.

Although the bombers managed to get through to Rochford, damage was light due to the flak around the airfield, but one hundred bombs fell on Eastchurch. However, despite extensive damage to the grass airfield and the destruction of several light bombers it was not put out of action.

At 12.35 hours the Dorniers of II and III /KG3 returned to attack Rochford after their failure earlier that morning. RAF fighters of No.1 and 54 Squadrons were scrambled to intercept the raid and achieved limited success with 54 Squadron shooting down a Me109.

While the ground crews were busy refuelling and rearming the aircraft, the South Kent RDF stations reported that a number of high flying enemy formations were approaching the south and south-east. Several flights were protecting the sector airfields and six groups of fighters were vectored on to the incoming raids. These enemy aircraft turned out to be not bombers but five *Gruppen* of Me110 and Me109 fighters, and as wave after wave of enemy fighters approached the coast and No.11 Group sector, a fighter versus fighter confrontation occurred. This was just what the German commanders had intended and just what Park had been trying to avoid. It was the bombers that had to be stopped, while not allowing his fighters to be kept occupied by the Luftwaffe fighters.

No.85 Squadron gave a good account of itself, under the watchful gaze of Winston Churchill, who was visiting the south-east defences. Nos.56 and 151 were not quite so fortunate, each losing two Hurricanes, and 54 Squadron lost a Spitfire. It was during this afternoon raid by the Luftwaffe that 603 Squadron was involved for the first time since moving south from Turnhouse.

* * *

In *The Last Enemy* Richard describes his first taste of combat, during the morning after their arrival, and how it results in his claim for a Me109. He does not say whether it was a 'probable' or 'destroyed' claim. Unfortunately Richard is mistaken in his recollection of these events. The patrol for which he makes his first claim actually took place at 15.15 hours on 29 August, the next day, and was a claim for a Me109 'probable'. Records show that he did not make any claims for enemy aircraft damaged, destroyed or probably destroyed during his first patrol.

In the first full day of action in the south, Richard did not take part until the last patrol of the day at 18.36. It was to be a long day with the nucleus of experienced pilots flying all three patrols, offering their experience alongside the new pilots in the squadron, as and when they were filtered in for an operational sortie.

During this morning Richard met Peter Howes who was with 54 Squadron at Hornchurch:

> On the morning after our arrival I walked over with Peter Howes and Broody. Howes was at Hornchurch with another squadron and worried because he had as yet shot nothing down. Every evening when we came into the mess he would ask us how many we had got and then go over miserably to his room. His squadron had had a number of losses and was due for relief. If ever a man needed it, it was Peter Howes. Broody, on the other hand, was in a high state of excitement, his sharp eager face grinning from ear to ear.

An interesting comparison between Howes and Benson, the man who had been seeing a lot of combat recently and the new arrival, eager for his first experience. He would not have long to wait.

The first defensive patrol took off from Hornchurch at 12.27 and consisted of twelve of the most experienced members of the squadron; Denholm, Ken Macdonald, Rushmer, Cunningham, Ritchie, Boulter, Waterston, Haig, Carbury, Gilroy, Berry and Morton. They were ordered to patrol the Chatham area and when they were 20 miles west of Canterbury they saw approximately 12 Me109s in vics of three at an altitude of 22,000 feet. The Spitfires of 603 were at the same height. The squadron was ordered into sections, echelon starboard. As they approached the enemy aircraft the pilots split up into sections and the German fighters scattered. Dogfights ensued but only Red 1 (George Denholm) was able to engage an enemy aircraft before the rest escaped into the cloud. (The patrols were referred to by several names, sorties, defensive patrols and fighting patrols. I have not used one specific title when referring to such a flight.)

George Denholm, flying Spitfire L1067, Code XT-D, claimed one Me109 probable on landing and his interpretation of events was as follows:

> When 20 miles west of Canterbury we saw 12 Me109 in vics* of three at 22,000 feet. I was at the same height and got onto the tail of a Me109, followed it through a cloud, and fired at a range of 80 yards with a two second burst, firing 240 rounds. The enemy aircraft went into a vertical dive with a long trail of white vapour, which I thought was glycol fumes. After that I did not see the enemy aircraft again. It was noticed that the Me109s had yellow noses, but no yellow wing-tips.

All 12 aircraft returned to Hornchurch, landing at 13.30 hours. Richard and Noel Benson were there to greet the returning pilots, although Richard was mistaken as to the actual day of this action. There were aircraft taking off and landing as Richard arrived but they were not 603's Spitfires returning from combat:

> They started coming in about half an hour after we landed, smoke stains along the leading edges of the wings showing that all the guns had been fired. They had acquitted themselves well although caught at a disadvantage of height. 'You don't have to look for them,' said Brian (Carbury). 'You have to look for a way out.'

At 15.55, the squadron was again sent up on a defensive patrol. On this sortie the pilots were; Denholm, Ken Macdonald, Cunningham, Boulter, Ritchie, Carbury, Gilroy, Morton, with Berry, Read, Don Macdonald and Peter Pease who were given their first opportunity of combat since moving south.

When they were between Canterbury and Dover they saw eight Me109s with yellow noses in lose vic formation, about 15,000 feet above them, with another 30 Me109s above the loose vic formation. No.603 was in sections line astern. A dogfight ensued when 603 attacked the loose vic formation and the other Me109s joined it. Pilot Officer Jim 'Black' Morton, flying Spitfire R6753 code XT-G, claimed a Me109 destroyed:

> As No.2 of Yellow Section flying sections astern in a southerly direction over Canterbury at 24,000 feet I observed about eight Me109's† 2,000 feet above and on the port beam 800 yards away. The enemy aircraft crossed over us into the vein. I pulled up onto one Me109's tail but stalled. On recovery I observed another to the NE of me. I approached this and attacked an Me109 pursuing a Spitfire. He omitted a long trail of white smoke and dived for cloud. I followed and found him SE over the Channel. At 6,000 feet he flattened out a little and I got within range at 300 yards and fired 2 bursts, one of six and one of four seconds, closing to 150 yards. During the second burst flames came from behind the cockpit. I left him at 4,000 feet, burning fiercely and still diving steeply east, as I was approaching the French coast. I returned at sea-level.

Pilot Officer George 'Sheep' Gilroy flying Spitfire N3288, code XT-H, also claimed a Me109 destroyed, it having crashed behind Hawkinge, during this sortie:

> While in a position north-west of Dover at 20,000 feet I observed one Me109 going to attack a Spitfire. I got into position behind it and fired a burst of about six seconds from a range of 150 yards closing to 40 yards. The Me109 put its nose down and I gave a two second burst while allowing for deflection. The enemy aircraft went on fire and the pilot opened his hood, which flew off, and came down by parachute.

---

*RAF combat reports frequently referred to the formations of enemy Me109's as being in vics of three; sometimes in sections of five; when the enemy fighters actually flew in pairs and fours. The RAF pilots simply took it for granted that the Luftwaffe flew the same formations as they did, in sections of three.

During the Battle of Britain the effectiveness of the organisation of a squadron into two flights, each of two sections of three aircraft, was called into doubt. It was, of course, undesirable to make any sweeping change during the Battle, but the weakness lay in the section of three when it became necessary to break up a formation in a dogfight. The organisation should perhaps have allowed for a break up into pairs, in which one pilot looks after the tail of his companion. A squadron might be divided into three flights of four (which would limit the employment of half-squadrons), or it might consist of two flights of eight, each comprising two sections of four.

†The Bf109 and Bf110 were originally designed by Bayerische Flugzeugwerke, of Augsburg, and test flown on the 28th of May 1935 and 12th of May 1936 respectively. Despite the reformation of the BFW company in 1938 as Messerschmitt AG, the designations of the existing products never changed. Despite evidence from nameplates of captured and shot down aircraft, and from the interrogation of captured German pilots, these aircraft were consistently referred to as the 'Me 109' and the 'Me 110'.

Pilot Officer Ras Berry flying his first sortie since arriving at Hornchurch, with 'B' Flight in Spitfire P9459, code XT-N, claimed a Me109 probable:

> When approximately over Dover the squadron split up on sighting several Me109's. Looking above, three Me109's crossed my bow in line astern. Shortly after, on my beam a Me109 was firing and I immediately whipped up my aircraft and round and found myself on his tail, and at close range pumped lead into it until it opened into a heavy cloud of smoke. On returning again, another Me109 was attacking from quarter astern. I steep turned to the right and got on his tail and he dived. I followed him and attacked, some bits fell from the enemy aircraft. As my ammunition was expended I broke off combat and returned to base.

Berry had opened fire at 100 yards, firing 2,800 rounds in three bursts, each of five seconds' duration. His latter day memories of the occasion recall:

> We were off on patrol at 30,000 feet in the Dover area, and it was our first encounter. Unfortunately for me the chap on either side of me got shot down in flames, and that was typical. We were in these vic-three formations and out they came, down out of the sun and that was when we started to learn our fighter combat, from then on. These two just got shot down as quick as that and I turned round and got into a dogfight, I thought I got one Me109, I definitely got another but credited with only a probable.

This was Ras Berry's first encounter with the enemy but the squadron's second of the day. It had been the Section Leader Laurie Cunningham in XT-U (R6751) and Don Macdonald in XT-E (R6752) whom he had seen lose their lives. Their flaming aircraft plunged into the sea off Dover with the pilots, dead or alive, still in their cockpits. Both had been bounced at 16.45 hours, probably by Me109s of II/JG3. The bodies of Cunningham who was 23 and Don Macdonald 22, were never recovered and are remembered on the Runnymede Memorial. Don Macdonald had failed to survive his first combat sortie from Hornchurch. His older brother Ken had been flying the same sortie. Almost exactly one month later he would join his younger brother.

Flying Officer Brian Carbury, flying with 'B' Flight in Spitfire R6835, code XT-W, claimed a Me109, damaged with bits of the wings seen dropping off and white smoke coming from the front of the engine after a beam attack over Hawkinge at an altitude of 30,000 feet:

> Approximately over Dover I sighted the enemy aircraft (six Me109s). As they attacked leading sections, we kept in vic, but broke as Me109 came down, I followed two through the cloud, with three following. I fired a short two second burst at one Me109 from 300 yards closing to 200 yards, smoke emitted from front of cockpit and carried on at about 45 degrees' dive for France, so I left him. I sighted another Me109, gave a full deflection burst but lost him in the cloud. I also lost the rest of the squadron, so returned to base.

Ten Spitfires landed back at Hornchurch at 17.20 hours. There were two aircraft missing.

Flying Officer Ian Ritchie returned to base in Spitfire R6989, code XT-X, which had been badly damaged in combat with the 109s, again possibly those of II/JG3, off Dover at 16.50 hours. Ritchie had received a gunshot wound to the back and was also hit in the hand during the skirmish. He managed to fly his damaged aircraft back to Hornchurch and on landing was admitted to Oldchurch Hospital, Romford, where he remained for ten weeks. His Spitfire received Category 2 damage and was repaired.

In response to the RAF losses caused by being 'bounced' Air Chief Marshal Dowding later wrote:

> Some of our worst losses occurred through defective leadership on the part of a unit commander, who might lead his pilots into a trap or be caught while climbing by an enemy formation approaching 'out of the sun'. During periods of

intense activity promotions to the command of Fighter squadrons should be made on the recommendation of Group Commanders from amongst Flight Commanders experienced in the methods of the moment. If and when it is necessary to post a Squadron Leader (however gallant and experienced) from outside the Command, he should humbly start as an ordinary member of the formation until he has gained experience. Only exceptionally should officers over 26 years of age be posted to command Fighter Squadrons.

Although officialdom decreed his age an apparent disadvantage, George Denholm was held in the highest regard by the pilots in his charge. His paternal instincts towards the younger pilots were evident but he cared greatly for all the men in his squadron. Their subsequent loss was deeply felt by him. As a fighter pilot, he quickly learnt when leading the squadron to initially climb on a reciprocal heading to that given by the controller. Having gained sufficient altitude, he would order the squadron to turn and fly towards the enemy having achieved a height advantage over the enemy, thus reducing the chance of being bounced.

The last patrol of the day occurred at 18.36 hours. The nucleus of Denholm, Rushmer, Ken Macdonald, Haig, Waterston, Stapleton and Berry were scrambled with Richard, Colin Pinckney, Noel Benson and Sergeant Alfred Sarre about to gain their first experience of intensive air-to-air combat. The 11 Spitfires took off from Hornchurch and when ten miles west of Manston they saw ten Me109s at 20,000 feet. The squadron went over the top of them and dived in echelon starboard, attacking them out of the sun. The Me109s had yellow noses and were in vic formation. Squadron Leader George Denholm, leading 'A' Flight in Spitfire N3288 code XT-H, destroyed a Me109 at 19.36 hours which crashed in a field near Dover:

> I singled out a Me109 and made two stern attacks at it, and after the second attack, it appeared to be in difficulties. I was then able to make two quarter attacks and the pilot, who had been heading for France, turned back towards the coast and glided down to land. I saw him hit high-tension wires and crash into a field west of Dover. I fired 1700 rounds.

This dogfight was witnessed by Sid Eade and his 14-year-old son from Truckshall Cottage, just below Beachborough. They watched as the aeroplanes roared over Newington and out to sea where George Denholm gave the 109 another burst. Executing a perfect 'U' turn, the German put on power to clear the terraced slopes of Hythe, just missed Saltwood Castle, and then flew through high-tension cables with a terrific flash before belly-landing near the railway tunnel. The pilot, with bullet-grazed face and head, leapt from the burning machine and walked calmly towards the Eades' cottage, effortlessly jumping a fence en route. The pilot was Feldwebel Otto Schottle of I/JG54 and his Me109E-1 crashed on Copt Hill Farm at 19.15 hours.

Bubble Waterston claimed a Me109 probable while flying with 'B' Flight in Spitfire N3267 code XT-S:

> I saw ten Me109's 5,000 feet below me and attacked one out of the sun. I fired two short bursts at about 150 yards, both astern attacks and saw the Me109 dive vertically, emitting a stream of white glycol smoke. I was unable to follow it as I was attacked by another Me109.

Ten of the eleven Spitfires returned to Hornchurch by 20.12 hours.

One detail that Richard correctly recalled was that during this combat Pilot Officer Noel 'Broody' Benson was shot down and killed in the resulting crash at Great Hay Farm, Leigh Green, Appledore Road, Tenterden. In the few seconds of combat that he had experienced he was not able to fulfil his earnest intention: 'To shoot down Huns, more Huns, and still more Huns'.

He was flying Spitfire N3105, code XT-P and was thought to have been attacked by Me109s of I/JG26 at 20.30 hours. At that time the owners of the Tenterden Post Office witnessed what they believed to be the pilot of a Spitfire, attempt to steer his burning aircraft away from their hamlet before it hit the ground. In respect of this action they displayed a photograph of Noel Benson in their shop for many years. Benson was reported missing, confirmation of his death did not reach the squadron until the next day.

The irrepressibly exuberant Broody Benson had been killed, his young life lost in the crash resulting from severe damage to his aircraft. His aircraft had been seen to go down in flames and he had chosen to try to land rather than bale out. Perhaps the flames reached the cockpit before he could get down, and thus he crashed. It is of course possible he had been wounded and was unable to function properly. Perhaps he was trying to emulate his feat of a few weeks previously when he had brought his damaged aircraft back over 75 miles of inhospitable North Sea. We will never know all the details. Broody was so nicknamed because of his moments of high excitement followed by quiet moments of introspective thought, as Stapme Stapleton had witnessed at dispersal during their time together at Montrose when he had first made his acquaintance. 'Broody' because it was a suitably sarcastic description of one outstanding aspect of what his character exhibited. He was a fun-loving young man and one of a number to die that later left Richard feeling particularly mournful and destined to record details of his time with them in his book. The loss of Broody Benson, Laurie Cunningham and Don Macdonald was of course felt by all, but they had a job to do, as part of a team, a job they wanted to do and felt committed to doing. Richard's terrible injuries, received a few days hence, would leave him to ponder his commitment to the cause, before once again deciding to carry on his fight against the Germans.

Noel Benson's body was recovered from a spot close to the wreckage of his Spitfire and eventually returned under escort to his home in Yorkshire. A service was attended by his family and locals of the village of Great Ouseburn at the church of St Mary's before his body was buried in what was then a new extension to the old churchyard plot at the far end looking out over the valley.

Years later remains of his aircraft were recovered and are on display in the Battle of Britain Museum at Hawkinge. The losses this day were a terrible blow to the men of the squadron. We know now that George Denholm was to mourn the loss of each man in his squadron very deeply indeed and Richard lost someone who had become a friend. It was just the beginning.

* * *

It had been a devastating baptism in the air battle over southern England, and by the end of this first full day at Hornchurch 603 had lost three outstanding pilots. Fifty-six years later Stapme Stapleton told me one of the reasons for the Luftwaffe fighter pilots' superiority over them:

> I remember two relevant reasons why the German victories were so high, apart from skill. The first was that they never went on rest. They had leave, but they were never rested from their particular squadron, i.e.; sent away as instructors. Consequently they were far more skilled with flying in the same squadron, in the same aircraft, or the same upgraded version of the same aircraft, be it the 109E, F, or G variant of the Messerschmitt. I was eventually taken off my favourite aircraft and flew Hurricanes and Typhoons up to the time I was made a POW. The second reason was that so many of the pilots had gained experience in the Spanish Civil War.

Thursday 29 August 1940
After a recent increase in night flying activity by the enemy bombers of all three *Luftflotten*, several British cities were bombed, with particular attention being paid to the industrial sites of the Midlands and the North. The city of Liverpool experienced the heaviest bombing raid yet during the night of the 28th/29th. The cities of Birmingham, Bournemouth, Bristol, Derby, Coventry, Sheffield and Manchester were also bombed,

but by a smaller raid of one or two *Staffeln* strength. Despite there being five Blenheim squadrons on patrol flying more than 80 sorties, there was only one sighting, and that bomber escaped.

However the morning of the 29th dawned with no activity on the radar screens. This allowed time for a re-shuffle by Dowding of a number of tired and weary squadrons, which included No.264 Defiant Squadron at Hornchurch. It was sent to Kirton-in-Lindsey and replaced by No.222 Squadron flying Spitfires.

The weather was reasonable but the morning remained quiet. The first build-up of enemy activity was not until 15.00 hours, at which time a small number of Dorniers and Heinkels were sighted below and ahead of an enormous array of more than 500 Me109s of JG3, 26, 51, 52 and 54 and 150 Me110s of ZG26 and 76. It was a trap to lure the already airborne RAF fighters and to get as many more airborne and into the affray as possible, thus keeping them occupied and away from the large formations of bombers that were to follow.

As No.85 Squadron was ordered to disengage this formation, and in the absence of any subsequent interceptions, it became clear to the German commanders that the RAF was unwilling to suffer the inevitable high number of losses likely when large numbers of Allied and German fighters met in combat. That evening the Germans reverted to a number of free chases by Me109 fighters over the English coast in an attempt to lure the RAF fighters into action. They only met RAF fighters on two occasions, one of which involved the bouncing of twelve Hurricanes of No.501 Squadron by a *Staffel* of 109s who lost two aircraft to their guns.

No.603 Squadron had lost five Spitfires fairly quickly over Romney Marshes. The composite patrol report for the day read:

> At 15.15 hours nine aircraft of 603 Squadron took off to patrol Rochford at about 24,000 feet. When in position they were ordered to Deal. While over the cloud slightly inland from Deal, they saw eight Me109's coming down on them, also a further six Me109's inline astern. These six did not make any attempt to attack. A dogfight ensued, and it was found that the 109's operated in pairs, and when one attacked it dived, No.2 diving as well.

During this patrol Richard claimed a Me109 probable while flying Spitfire L1021, code XT-M.

As the Spitfires attempted to gain as much altitude as possible, the 109s made good use of the height advantage and dived on the 603 fighters as they went into line astern. Leading Richard's section was Brian Carbury whose skill quickly turned the tables and allowed his section to gain a height advantage over the German fighters. Latching on to the leading 109, Carbury fired a burst. The evasive action taken by the German pilot took him into Richard's path and he seized the opportunity, brought his guns to bear and stabbed the gun button with his thumb. Firing a four second burst with full deflection, the 109 flew right through Richard's gun sights and slowed perceptibly as he witnessed the tracer strike home. Suddenly red flame burst from the 109 and it dived from view. The dogfight continued apace with Richard unable to reflect on his first kill for it was a case of self-preservation, but as the Germans headed for France, Richard was able to contemplate his success. He later wrote:

> My first emotion was one of satisfaction, satisfaction at a job adequately done, at the final logical conclusion of months of specialised training. And then I had a feeling of the essential rightness of it all. He was dead and I was alive; it could so easily have been the other way around. I realised in that moment just how lucky a fighter pilot is. He has none of the personalised emotions of the soldier, handed a rifle and bayonet and told to charge. He does not even have to share the dangerous emotions of the bomber pilot who night after night must experience that childhood longing for smashing things. The fighter pilot's emotions are those of the duellist – cool precise, impersonal. He is privileged to kill well.

It was his first claim. Before he was able to find the time to fill out the appropriate combat report, Form 'F', he had also been shot down twice and, as a result of injuries sustained in the second incident, was fighting for his life.

While flying with 'B' Flight, Flying Officer Boulter claimed a Me109 destroyed while flying Spitfire N3267, code XT-S. He delivered his attack over Deal at an altitude of 23,000 feet, at 16.00 hours:

> Whilst on patrol with 603 Sqn I noticed a formation of Me109 aircraft above and to the front. I informed the leader of 603 Sqn of their presence and turned to intercept them. As I did so I received a bullet in the cockpit, distracting my attention from my target.
>
> When trying to rejoin my squadron, I saw five Me109's and engaged one of them. It broke away, and I was able to carry out a quarter attack, causing a trail of grey-white smoke or vapour to pour out of the undersurfaces.

Boulter mentions in his report that his aircraft received damage to the cockpit, which was inflicted while in combat with Me109s of I/JG26 over Deal at approximately 16.10 hours, and he was slightly wounded. His Spitfire was damaged but repairable.

The aircraft that Boulter shot down was a Me109E-1 of III/JG3 flown by Unteroffizier Pfeifer. The pilot was reported as missing.

During this patrol, while flying with 'B' Flight in Spitfire L1024, code XT-R, Pilot Officer Stapme Stapleton claimed a Me109 destroyed:

> When on patrol with 603 Squadron we sighted enemy fighters just south of Deal. P/O Read and myself broke away from the squadron to engage two Me109s who were circling above us. P/O Read engaged the first and myself the second. After firing short deflection bursts the Me109 which I attacked went straight down out of my sight with smoke issuing from the engine. I then broke away and climbed into the sun.

An important point that is worth considering is that one of the major differences between the Spitfire and the Me109 was the fuel injection that the German fighter possessed. If attacked from behind the German pilot could push the 'stick' forward and, with the throttles wide open, dive straight down, under power. The Merlin engine of the Spitfire had a gravity-fed carburettor and such a manoeuvre would lead to a momentary loss of power due to sudden fuel starvation, leaving the pilot unable to effectively pursue his prey and vulnerable to attack himself. The Spitfire pilot would therefore need to roll away and dive at the same time, ensuring the carb received the necessary downward pressure from gravity to provide a continuous flow of fuel. When the Messerschmitt 109 carried out this manoeuvre there was a visible puff of smoke from the exhaust ports, giving an inexperienced pilot, in pursuit of a German, the impression that he had hit him, when he may not have.

Bill Read reported:

> Whilst patrolling as Red 3 at 23,000 feet and still climbing, enemy aircraft were sighted crossing above us. I overshot Red 1 (Stapleton), and made a steep right hand turn, finding a Me109 turning above and in front of me. I pulled up nose and fired a short burst from the port quarter. The e/a turned on its back and fell into a spin. I was quickly engaged by other Me109's and thus lost sight of it. But another pilot saw it spinning down (P/O Hillary). In the course of the ensuing dogfight I fired at three more 109's (head-on and two beam attacks), but could not observe effect of fire as I spun myself .

Rusty Rushmer force-landed at Bossingham following the same combat, thought to be with aircraft of I/JG26. At 16.10, flying Spitfire P9459 code XT-N, Rusty was slightly wounded and his aircraft, although damaged, was repairable. The records show that a Spitfire of 603 Squadron was claimed as having been shot down by Oberfeldwebel Wilhelm Muller of 2/JG26 over Dover. The claim was unconfirmed. At that time Muller had ten confirmed enemy aircraft destroyed to his credit.

> Intelligence Patrol Report, 603 Squadron
> 18.10-19.30 hours.
> 29.8.40.
>
> Ten aircraft of 603 Squadron left Rochford at 18.10 hours. When at 27,000 feet over Manston, they saw about 24 Me109's in line astern, weaving over their heads. The 109's made no attempt to attack, so 603 climbed and attacked. A dogfight ensued.

During this patrol Colin Pinckney was reported to have baled out slightly burned and it was reported that Richard had forced-landed near Lympne. Both had been shot down by Ben Joppien of I/JG51.

The ten Spitfires were flown by Squadron Leader Denholm, Ken Macdonald, Pinckney, Carbury, Pease, Gilroy, Read, Stapleton, Hillary and Stokoe.

While leading Green Section of 'B' Flight, Brian Carbury destroyed a Me109, over Manston at an altitude of 27,000 feet, flying Spitfire R6735 code XT-W:

> I was leading Green Section when enemy aircraft were sighted. We went into line astern, Green 2 and 3 attacked individual enemy aircraft. I climbed and saw two Me109's climbing below, so I carried out a frontal attack with slight deflection. A long burst and the enemy aircraft smoked and then blew up. I returned to base having lost the rest of the formation.

Colin Pinckney's report was written by the intelligence officer on his behalf:

> F/O Pinckney claims a Me109 destroyed over Manston at an altitude of 27,000' while flying with 'A' Flight. He himself had to bale out as four Me109's of I/JG51 shot at him and damaged his machine. He is still in hospital and his report will follow. The Me109 was confirmed by the Observer Corps.

Colin's Spitfire crashed at St Mary's Road, Dymchurch, at 18.42 hours.

Richard did not have the opportunity to complete his combat report before he was shot down and seriously injured on 3 September. Therefore, the intelligence officer (IO) subsequently logged a provisional report of Richard's combat:

> P/O Hillary claims a Me109 destroyed, over Manston at 18.50 hours at an altitude of 27,000', this was confirmed by the Observer Corps. P/O Hillary forced-landed in the sea and is still in hospital.

Flying Spitfire L1021 code XT-M, Richard had his first confirmed destruction of an enemy fighter. He was slightly burnt and his name was included on CC list No.295 'Slightly injured (FB)'.

At 18.16 hours 85 Squadron, led by Squadron Leader Peter Townsend, was ordered to scramble from its base at Croydon and patrol the airspace over Dungeness. It was its fourth patrol of the day. Townsend acknowledged the controller's warning of 'bandits' reported to be in the area and the Hurricanes continued the patrol, with the pilots vigilant in the fading light. Townsend later reported that at 18,000 feet a lone Spitfire had joined them. In his book *Duel of Eagles* he refers to Richard's version in *The Last Enemy* with some consternation, when he blamed the presence of a lone Spitfire for the death of one of his most experienced and outstanding flight commanders:

> It was a foolish, almost criminal act. Our wave-lengths were different and thus we could not communicate. And, end-on, a Spit could be taken for a Me.109. 'Watch him very closely,' I called to our tailguard, our 'arse-end Charlies.

It was New Zealander Pilot Officer Hodgson who noticed that the position of Richard's Spitfire had been taken by a 109 and called out to his colleagues. The formation took evasive action but the damage had been done. The Hurricane of Canadian Flight

Lieutenant 'Hammy' Hamilton was seen to slowly break away trailing smoke and flames before rolling over and plunging five miles into the ground at Winchelsea. One pilot managed to get in a shot at a fleeing 109, but the results were unconfirmed. Townsend later recalled:

> Was Richard Hillary in that Spitfire? The height and position agree. It was only after he 'managed to pull himself together and go into a spin' that he thought of warning the Hurricanes – impossible anyway on his wave-length even had his radio not been shot away. The timing agrees, too. Whoever it was, we felt bitter about the Spitfire. Had it kept on the flank where we could see it, Hammy might never have died.

In his combat report Townsend wrote: 'If this Spitfire pilot can be identified, I would like these facts brought home to him, because his action contributed to the loss of one of my flight commanders.'

The 85 Squadron ORB states:

> The squadron climbed to 24,000 feet and were then joined by a Spitfire and a Hurricane which both began weaving behind the flank sections. Warned of the presence of E/A some miles to the north, the squadron wheeled to attempt interception. While circling, Red 3 (P/O Hodgson) suddenly shouted a warning that E/A were behind. These turned out to be three Me 109's, the leader of which was not identified until he was within range on account of the previous presence of the Spitfire and the strong resemblance at a certain distance of a Spitfire and an Me109 from front view. On receipt of warning, the squadron circled steeply left. Red 3 saw tracer ammunition passing close above him and he saw a cannon shell explode on Red 1's tail unit blowing most of it off. Red 1 (F/L Hamilton), was also seen to lose his starboard wing tip. P/O Marshall attacked one Me109 as it was doing a right hand climbing turn. E/A then dived followed by P/O Marshall who fired again. Engagement commenced at 22,000 feet and was broken off at 5,000 feet when E/A was last seen diving vertically out of control towards the sea ten miles from Dungeness. This was confirmed by P/O English and although the E/A was not actually seen to hit the sea on account of the thick haze and bad visibility, it was claimed as destroyed in view of the circumstances of the combat. Ten Hurricanes landed at Croydon between 19.16 and 19.55 hours. Enemy casualties – 1 Me109 destroyed, Our casualties – 1 Hurricane (F/L Hamilton killed).

Richard later wrote:

> There had been the usual dog-fights over the south coast, and the squadron had broken up. Having only fired one snap burst, I climbed up in search of friendly Spitfires, but found instead a squadron of Hurricanes flying around the sky at 18,000 feet in sections of stepped-up threes, but with no rear-guard. So I joined on. I learned within a few seconds the truth of the old warning, 'Beware of the Hun in the sun.' I was making pleasant little sweeps from side to side, and peering earnestly into my mirror when, from out of the sun and dead astern, bullets started appearing along my port wing. There was an appalling tendency to sit and watch this happen without taking any action, as though mesmerised by a snake; but I managed to pull myself together and go into a spin, at the same time attempting to call up the Hurricanes and warn them, but I found that my radio had been shot away.

The radio is situated, unprotected, in the fuselage behind the pilot. Richard was lucky in that he was alert enough to avoid being killed, and it would seem that the Hurricanes would have suffered even if he had not been present. Townsend mentioned that had Richard remained out on the flank, they would have not been hesitant in realising that they were under attack, but surely the squadron leader and his flight commanders were experienced in having a 'weaver' present? Having realised he was there, his appreciation that his squadron was under attack would have been the same if Richard had not been there. Richard's quick reactions saved his life. Unfortunately, the others were not so lucky. Was it therefore fair to blame him for the sad loss of Flying Officer Hamilton? Richard was inexperienced and likely to make mistakes. I certainly do not think his actions could be referred to as criminal. The young pilots in the Battle of Britain would make many mistakes; they were to be expected under the circumstances, but I believe Richard was carrying out an accepted practice even if it was while tagging on to another squadron. He was unable to contact the Hurricane pilots to let them know, because his radio was u/s. He can hardly be blamed for what took place. The squadron record also shows that Richard, along with the other pilot flying a Hurricane, was in fact weaving out on a flank!

Having been hit, Richard initially tried to make Hornchurch but he soon realised that his aircraft would not make the distance. At first he had thought that no serious damage had been inflicted on his aircraft but, as he started to regain altitude, black smoke began pouring from the engine and he could smell glycol. A short while later engine oil covered the windscreen and obscured his forward view. Hornchurch was no longer an option.

In the vicinity was Lympne, an airfield that Richard was familiar with from his summer camp with the OUAS. The condition of his aircraft deteriorated still further and despite flying at full boost with an airspeed dangerously near stalling, he realised he wouldn't make Lympne either. He chose a cornfield and carried out a successful forced-landing at 19.00 in the same field that Colin was landing by parachute. Fortunately, nothing caught fire, and he remembered procedure and turned off the petrol.

When an ambulance motored across the field towards him he mistakenly believed it had come for him, until the personnel rushed past and made for Colin Pinckney still drifting down under his parachute. Although he had been burnt on his face and hands his condition was not life threatening.

The descent of the two pilots attracted local attention, as Richard recollected in *The Last Enemy*:

> We were at once surrounded by a bevy of officers and discovered that we had landed practically in the back garden of a Brigade cocktail party. A salvage crew took charge of my machine, a doctor took charge of Colin, and the rest took charge of me, handing me double whiskies for the nerves at a laudable rate.

Richard's aircraft, with its name *Sredni Vashtar* painted on the cowling, was not written off. Spitfire I, L1021, 235, first flew on 16 June, went to No.20 Maintenance Unit on the 26th and then to 603 Squadron on 15 August. After Richard had forced-landed in L1021 it was repaired and used by No.57 OTU until it was struck off charge (SOC), on 6 March 1945.

On 2 September, Michael Hillary received notification from the Air Ministry that Richard had received 'slight injuries' while in combat. These were treated at the station hospital.

Colin provided his own interpretation of the events of that day in a letter home which stated:

> I was shot down during a patrol over Kent . . . After shooting down a German aircraft my own aircraft was hit and caught fire. I was forced to jump out of my aircraft at about 1,000 feet . . . Having landed all the local Home Guard were on the spot ready to arrest me, the lone parachutist, in case I was a German spy . . . Soon after I applied to join the Caterpillar Club for airmen who had to land by parachute . . . I also wrote to the Irvin parachute manufacturers to compliment them on the quality of their goods.

The burns to Colin's face and in particular his hands were serious enough to cause a certain amount of pain and disability for the next few weeks. After treatment in hospital he was discharged and granted sick leave.

After seeing him off in an ambulance, Richard was invited to a Brigade cocktail party which was taking place in nearby Lympne Castle, a mansion house requisitioned as the Brigade HQ, owned today by the Aspinall family. Here he dined and was plied with alcohol by his hosts until he was in such a state that he was offered a room for the night; an offer he was in no state to refuse. He blames his condition on the alcohol but shock must have contributed towards his mental state. A short period before this relaxed, welcoming and convivial gathering, he was fighting for his life, and winning his own individual battle, with the German fighter falling to his guns. In the confines of the cockpit with its associated noise and smells, in the open skies high above the sunlit countryside, he had fought his duel. The crackle of voices in his ear-phones, the rush of adrenaline, the fast breathing, the fear and anxiety, the panic at hearing his own aircraft struck by bullets from an unseen assailant – and after all he was able to bring his damaged aircraft to a safe wheels-up landing in a field. It is very likely that he was dazed and confused, as well as shocked.

* * *

Sergeant Jack Stokoe also claimed a Me109 probable while flying Spitfire L1070 code XT-A:

> We were patrolling Manston at 27,000 feet in sections astern, when above us we observed about 24 Me109s flying in line astern.
>
> We climbed to attack and I chased one down about 5,000 feet without getting close enough to fire. I climbed back and closed on the tail of a Me109 which was following another Spitfire. I fired about five long bursts, closing from 800 to 100 yards, white smoke came from the 109, and it spun gently down. I did not observe what happened then, as I was out of ammunition and had to shake a Me109 from my tail.

Stapme Stapleton also claimed a Me109 probable while flying Spitfire L1040 code XT-R, with 'B' Flight, at 18.50 hours over Manston at an altitude of 29,000 feet:

> When enemy fighters attacked our squadron I was separated from the rest. I climbed into the sun to 30,000', I sighted one Me109 just going into a loop, catching him with a full deflection shot of 5 seconds, he continued upwards and did a bunt, going downwards beyond the vertical.

When I spoke to him in 1997 Stapme told me that any irregularities in the fighter pilot's vision could create anxiety:

> Was that just a spot in your vision or was it an enemy fighter? As you glanced around the sky spots in your vision could invariably move more slowly than the speed of your eye movement giving the impression that it could be an enemy fighter. Coupled with marks on your canopy you had to be extremely alert.
>
> I found the enemy aircraft easy to spot against the blue sky. It was our anti-aircraft fire that quite often indicated to us the whereabouts of the incoming enemy aircraft.

Those pilots that were able to make it back to their home base landed at 19.30 hours at the end of what had been a very climactic day after a surprisingly quiet morning.

Fine weather had spread over England during the day and continued into the night making conditions ideal for a continuation of the night bombing campaign. Two hundred bombers hit Liverpool and Birkenhead for the second night in succession; the cloudless sky allowing easy location of the target.

Friday 30 August 1940

The battle was now entering a critical phase with the number and intensity of operations continuing to increase towards what would turn out to be an unimagined climax over the days ahead. The next forty-eight hours would involve the fiercest fighting in the whole of the battle. The weather could not be relied upon to offer any respite as an extensive anti-cyclone was stationary over practically the whole of north-west Europe, and it would remain fine for some days yet. The day had dawned fine with a thin layer of cloud lying at 7,000 feet over south-east England, which caused some difficulty for the Observer Corps. Dowding and Park must have been in some way aware that such a climax was near. Over the next week and a half the resources of Fighter Command would be stretched to the point of exhaustion, with its mere existence on the brink of annihilation.

Soon after dawn on the morning of the 30th a number of attacks were made by the Luftwaffe, mainly against convoys heading north from the Thames Estuary, in an attempt to discover what fighter forces would react and from where. Hurricanes of No.111 Squadron were already airborne having earlier been scrambled to investigate what turned out to be three Blenheims of No.25 Squadron. Having been vectored towards the raid they attacked a relatively small number in comparison with what was to follow in a *Gruppe* of Dornier Do 17s protected by about 30 Me110s. With the sighting reported by radio they managed to damage one before they were joined by three Spitfires of No.54 Squadron from Hornchurch, led by New Zealander Al Deere. The Spitfires damaged two more of the raiders.

The next raid dwarfed the first, in that it consisted of three waves crossing the Kent coast on three sides at half-hourly intervals from 10.30 onwards. The first wave consisted of about 60 Me109s, three *Gruppen*, which crossed at different points; Park, believing there to be large numbers of bombers to follow, did not react, for his intention was to save his fighters at Hornchurch, Rochford, North Weald, Croydon, Northolt, Biggin Hill and Kenley. At 11.00 hours his judgement was proven to be sound when the Observer Corps reported that raids totalling 40 Heinkels, 30 Dorniers, 60 Me109s and 30 Me110s were heading towards the Kent coast. At 10.50 eleven Hurricanes of another newly arrived squadron, No.253, had been scrambled from Kenley to protect the airfield from what was thought to be an impending raid. It failed to materialise and they were vectored south to join the Hurricanes of No.43 Squadron as they attacked the third wave of bombers which were crossing the Sussex coast at Hove.

The Hurricanes of No.151 Squadron were also already airborne when they had been earlier ordered up from Stapleford Tawney to patrol the mouth of the Thames Estuary. At 11.20 they intercepted a group of approximately 70 Heinkels and Me110s, destroying three of the bombers for the loss of three of their own aircraft and the deaths of two of the pilots. One of these Hurricanes had been lost moments before the attack when the pilot became separated from his squadron as it divided into flights and he was bounced by enemy aircraft, shot down and killed. The Hurricanes of No.85 Squadron also joined in the attack on this same raid as it lumbered over the Kent countryside. The RAF fighters carried out a head-on attack which broke up the enemy bomber formation and resulted in various dogfights ensuing over the Kent and Surrey countryside. By 11.45 hours the situation had become so confused that it had become impossible for the Observer Corps to identify which raids had been intercepted, and 48 of them reported dogfights overhead! All of 11 Group's fighters were airborne with ten squadrons in action and Park had to call upon No.12 Group for reinforcements in the form of two squadrons from Duxford to cover the airfields at Kenley and Biggin Hill.

No.222 Squadron, situated at Hornchurch with 603, were hit hard as ten Me109s bounced 'B' Flight. They, like 603, had only recently arrived at Hornchurch from the north and had not been briefed, as they had worked their way up to operational status, on the updated tactics now being applied by those squadrons that had been in the thick of things. They were still flying in a close formation with a weaver. By the end of the day they had eight Spitfires shot down, with one pilot killed, two wounded and five aircraft lost.

With the RAF stretched almost to its limit the third and largest raid crossed the coast shortly after 16.00 hours. For the next two hours the RAF fighters fought against no fewer than 19 *Gruppen* of enemy aircraft as they crossed the English coast over the Thames estuary and Kent. The exhausted ground crews exhibited total dedication towards the task of getting their fighters airborne once again, in the hands of an equally exhausted pilot who had every faith that the men who had been working on his aircraft had done the best possible job in preparing it for further combat. As the ground crew watched the fighters in their squadrons take off they perhaps had a few moments to reflect on what had been and what lay ahead.

* * *

At this stage the Luftwaffe commander Albert Kesselring changed his tactics quite significantly. Instead of waiting two or three hours before mounting his next assault he followed the first with more bombers supported by Me110s and Me109s at lunchtime. This gave the RAF the absolute minimum time to recover from their previous sorties before massive demands were made on the pilots and ground crews to enable the fighters to take once again to the skies. At 13.30 the enemy aircraft once again started to cross the Kent coast at 20 minute intervals. But for the invaluable help from the Observer Corps, Fighter Command would have been blind. There was no assistance from the radar stations at Beachy Head, Dover, Pevensey, Fairlight, Foreness, Rye or Whitstable as the electricity grid had been hit during the morning raids.

This third great aerial assault of the day consisted of 60 Heinkels with an escort of Me110s aimed at Luton, Oxford, Slough, North Weald, Kenley, Biggin Hill and the Handley Page factory at Radlett. Despite the attentions of the Hurricanes of No.242 (sent south from 12 Group), and 56 Squadron (from North Weald), as it crossed the coast north of the Thames at 16.20 hours the raid split, with one group, KG1, bombing the Vauxhall Works at Luton where 53 civilians were killed. The largest part of the formation flew on towards its target while attempting to fight off attacking fighters from 1, 56, 222, 242 and 501 Squadrons. With only a few miles to go to their objective (Radlett) the RAF fighters, low on fuel and out of ammunition, were forced to return to base. With only the anti-aircraft guns to defend it, the factory, which was busy manufacturing the Halifax bomber, fortunately survived any serious damage and production was not affected.

Biggin Hill was badly hit at low level by Ju88s, destroying a hangar and inflicting serious damage on many of the other buildings, gas, water and electricity mains, and killing 39. Six Hurricanes of No.79 Squadron managed to take off in the middle of the raid, and shot down two of the attacking aircraft without loss.

The fighting this day had been the heaviest so far with Dowding's pilots flying 1,054 sorties. The fighting on 15th August had been spread over four Group areas but was nowhere near the intensity of this hot, sunny Friday in August. Twenty-two squadrons had been in action, some as many as four times, almost all at least twice.

After dark, Liverpool was bombed again by 130 aircraft with smaller diversionary raids on Norwich, Colchester, Southampton, Bristol, Cardiff, Birmingham and Sheffield.

* * *

No.603 Squadron's involvement in repelling the bombers consisted of two sorties and began with the very first raid. At 10.35 hours the six Spitfires of Squadron Leader Denholm (XT-D L1067), Flying Officer Boulter (XT-S N3267), Flying Officer Pease (XT-V 6751), Pilot Officer Morton (XT-E R6752), Pilot Officer Berry (XT-W R6735), and Sergeant Sarre (XT-F R6754) took off from Hornchurch to intercept the first wave. Pilot Officer Morton claimed a Me109 probable and a Me110 damaged:

> As rearguard aircraft of the squadron (six a/c), I was above and behind the formation at 32,000 feet over Deal when many bombers with Me110 formations above were seen at 20,000 feet. Squadron went into line astern, and dived. I encountered one ring of Me110's. One was in convenient position and I fired from port quarter above for about two and a half seconds from 400 to 100 yards, when

I had to break away to avoid collision as I was going very fast. A long plume of white smoke came from e/a's port engine and on tailing from my break away, I saw that it had dropped out from the formation and was losing height to the N/E. I then found another ring of Me110's and selected one, attacking from above on the port quarter, from 400 to 100 yards, finishing astern. Two bursts of 3 to 4 seconds each. E/A broke formation with white smoke coming from both engines. Spiralled down through cloud at 4-5000 feet. On emerging from lower side of cloud layer 6/10, I saw e/a about 5 miles S.S.W. Lympne still spiralling at 3000 feet with 2 Hurricanes pursuing it. I therefore left it to them and returned to base.

No return fire from first 110, he probably did not see me. Some accurate fire, probably cannon, from slow rate of fire, from second 110.

Black Morton delivered his attack at 11.25 hours west of Dover at an altitude of 17,000 feet.

Sergeant Sarre returned to Hornchurch with damage to the tail of his Spitfire received in combat with the Me110s of II/ZG26, over Deal at 11.10 hours, as they supported the bombers making their way to Hatfield to bomb the Handley Page Halifax works at Radlett. His aircraft was repaired.

* * *

Squadron Leader George Denholm was forced to bale out at 11.15 hours over Deal after his aircraft was damaged by enemy fire, possibly by the same Me110s of II/ZG26. His aircraft, which was named 'Blue Peter' crashed on Hope Farm, Snargate. On 22 September 1973 the Brenzett Aeronautical Museum recovered many parts from the crashed Spitfire including the instrument panel, most major controls and components together with many manufacturers' plates. They also recovered part of the fuel tank cowling still showing traces of the 'Blue Peter' name. George Denholm was invited down to see the display.

During the morning Richard had made his way back to Hornchurch from Brigade HQ by train arriving shortly after lunch:

I went up to London by train, a somewhat incongruous figure, carrying a helmet and parachute. The prospect of a long and tedious journey by tube did not appeal to me, so I called up the Air Ministry and demanded a car and a WAAF. I was put on to the good lady in charge of transport, a sergeant, who protested apologetically that she must have the authorisation of a Wing Commander. I told her forcibly that at this moment I was considerably more important than any Wing Commander, painted a vivid picture of the complete disorganisation of Fighter Command in the event of my not being back at Hornchurch within an hour, and clinched the argument by telling her that my parachute was a military secret which must on no account be seen in a train. By the afternoon I was flying again.

On the contrary, from all available documentary evidence, it is clear that Richard did *not* fly again that day. Moreover, in *The Last Enemy* he tells us that Bubble failed to return from the evening sortie of the 30th. This is incorrect. Bubble did make it back only to be killed the next day.

The evening sortie took place when the squadron were scrambled at 15.55 hours. The Spitfires led by Flight Lieutenant Ken Macdonald (XT-F, 4238), with Boulter (XT-R, R6709), Haig (XT-E, R6753), Carbury (XT-W, R6735), Waterston (XT-O, X4163), Berry (XT-G, R6773), Read (XT-B, N3056), Morton (XT-N, 3173), Pease (XT-V, R6751), Gilroy (XT-H, N3288), Stokoe (XT-K, R6898), and Sarre (XT-X, R7021) took off to intercept the last and heaviest raid of the day by the Luftwaffe.

Bubble Waterston destroyed a Me109 which was providing fighter cover for I/LG2 over Canterbury at 16.40 hours, but his own aircraft was hit during the combat, returning to base with a punctured oil tank. The aircraft was repairable:

When at 25,000 feet over Deal, I saw three Me109's in a vic at the same height as myself. I attacked the nearest one to me on the starboard quarter, firing a short burst. The Me109 dived steeply, then caught fire and crashed in flames in the Medway.

Bubble Waterston was flying with 'B' Flight when he delivered his attack at 16.30 hours, north of Canterbury.

Brian Carbury, now DFC, having recently received news of the award, celebrated his achievement with the further destruction of another Me109 at 16.45 over London. The Messerschmitt Bf109E-1 was of 3/JG27 and flown by Feldwebel Ernst Arnold who was captured after forced-landing his damaged aircraft at Westwood Court, near Faversham:

I sighted three Me109's north of me, so I attacked the rear aircraft. The leading two aircraft turned for my tail. I got a good burst in and the propeller of the rear enemy aircraft stopped, started and finally stopped, with white vapour coming out behind.

The enemy aircraft went into a glide for the east coast. I veered off as other enemy aircraft were closing in on me.

Brian Carbury was leading a section in 'B' Flight when he delivered his attack at 16.30 hours, north of Canterbury at an altitude of 25,000 feet. The same German aircraft was previously reported to have been shot down by Tom Gleave of No.253 Squadron at 11.55 hours. Carbury's ability to hit the enemy fighter hard from close-in and to pull away from the initial attack and not be tempted to remain to 'mix it' in what was a vulnerable position, gives us some idea of why he was so successful.

Also on this the last patrol on 30 August Sergeant Sarre claimed a Me109 probable and shortly afterwards was hit himself and forced to bale out at approximately 16.55 hours following an encounter with 12 Me109s over Deal. The tail of his Spitfire was shot off in combat possibly by the same Me109s that were protecting I/LG2. His aircraft was written off in the crash at Addington Park, near West Malling. His combat details read:

When on patrol with 603 Squadron at 25,000 feet, we sighted enemy formation at 20,000 feet, with enemy fighters above them. I became detached from the squadron and was attacked by a formation of four Me109's from the starboard quarter. I turned into them and opened fire. I was unable to see the result of my fire as my machine fell into a violent spin. On landing by parachute I was met by F/O Delg of West Malling, who had witnessed the combat through field glasses, and said he had seen one Me109 fall away and enter a steep dive, but had not watched the enemy plane crash.

Alfred Sarre was flying with 'A' Flight and received an injury to his hand in the combat.

* * *

The squadron had been at Hornchurch for only three days, but the intensity of the battle must have made it seem that they had been there for a much longer period. Already they would have been feeling the physical and mental strain. The physical strain coming from the hours without sleep, and the stresses on the human body strapped into the seat of a fast agile fighter being thrown about the sky. The mental strain coming from being in perpetual anticipation of what fate had in store. Would they be hit during the next patrol, would they be shot, burnt or simply blown out of the sky? This constant strain would have certainly taken its toll; remember the mental condition of Peter Howes when Richard and Broody met him at Hornchurch. He had been there longer than they, yet just a few days later they now had a better idea of what he was experiencing. Some individuals would find the tension unbearable, rushing outside from the dispersal hut to vomit. Many looked drawn and tired, dark around the eye. The loss of their companions was not something they could afford to get emotional about. They had a job to do and such thoughts would detract from their ability to do it properly. They were also too busy most of the time to become emotionally involved. After landing it was the job of the CO George Denholm to make a check on who was missing. Sometimes there would be a telephone call from a pilot to say he was safe but inevitably there was the call from a rescue team with the number of an aircraft, and another name was wiped from the board.

Richard wrote: 'At that time the losing of pilots was somehow extremely impersonal; nobody, I think, felt any great emotion – there simply wasn't time for it.'

They had to find an outlet when they were off duty and this they did in the form of heavy drinking sessions in the mess or a night out in London, having piled into the cars brought south by some of the pilots. In the mess they would drink, usually keeping to their own company, usually because they were off when others were on. The nights out in London could be quite wild, some staying overnight but always ready to fly as and when required to do so, albeit sometimes a little worse for wear! Once in the air again and faced with the inevitable confrontation of a life and death situation, a few deep breaths of oxygen would soon have the head reasonably clear again and the senses alert!

Stapme Stapleton told me of the time when he and several of the squadron pilots managed to sneak past a reluctant doorman and into a fairly exclusive club in the West End. It was after hours and they were looking to continue what had already been a lengthy drinking session ('I could drink beer all night without a problem. I never touched anything else'). In the early hours the management tried to turf them out, as it was closing time, but the pilots refused to leave. The manager then threatened to call the provost. It was George Denholm that informed the manager that the Provost Marshal was a squadron leader and so was he, and anyway the provost was currently on leave! The party continued into the daylight of a new day.

Stapme also remembers the function arranged to celebrate the shooting down of the squadron's one hundredth German aircraft:

> We all voted to have a party to celebrate the squadron's one hundredth victory. And what a night it was! We chose to have the function at the Dorchester, and it was very formal. Daddy Bouchier was invited as the CO of the Station. Peter Olver and his sidekick Claude Goldsmith, we called them the 'heavenly twins', and I went into London in my Ford V8 with the dicky seat being used for the third passenger in the back, as it was only a two seater, this was after I had my MG. After the dinner we slipped out from the speeches, because we were getting a bit fed up, and had a night on the town. We went to the Turkish baths in Jermyn Street, which I remember it having Russian and Turkish printed on vertical neon signs outside (which were not lit during the blackout). It was a Turkish bath that also provided accommodation. We went in and had our 'bath' and then lay on our bunks; it cost six shillings and six pence a night, and we didn't have to book-in, unlike the hotels. It was either Olver or Goldsmith, I can't remember exactly who, but as one of them lay naked on their bunk the other got the alcohol rub and poured it over the other bloke's balls! Of course, he took-off, because it burnt like hell. It doesn't burn when its rubbed on a chap's hands when he gave you a massage, but poured over the softer tissues it does. He took off down some wooden steps leading to the plunge pool, but the tiles were wet, and as he tried to get to the soothing water of the pool, he was going so fast he couldn't slow down, and he finished up on the floor against the lagged pipes that provided the heat for the steam rooms. Despite being lagged in asbestos they were still as hot as hell. I got down there in time to see him trying desperately to get away from the heat of the pipes, but his hands and feet were just slipping on the wet tiles as he tried to get up and away. It was the funniest thing I've ever seen in all my life!

Saturday August 31 1940
On this day Fighter Command lost 39 pilots killed in action. RAF airfields were bombed by the Luftwaffe, and most of the important sector airfields were bombed twice.

During the attack on Hornchurch, three more pilots reported for flying duty with 603 Squadron. These were Pilot Officers Brian R. MacNamara and W.P.H. 'Robin' Rafter who had responded to the call from Fighter Command for more fighter pilots by volunteering to move from Nos.614 and 225 Squadrons respectively, both Army Co-operation units based at Odiham, where they had flown Lysanders. They were sent to No.7 OTU at Hawarden where they converted to Spitfires. Flying Officer Jim MacPhail, an ex-army co-operation and No.41 Squadron pilot, had converted to Spitfires at No.5 OTU, Aston Down.

During one of the many infamous mess games at Rochford, Stapme Stapleton sparred with Jim MacPhail who was always involved with any such games. But on this occasion he had certainly met his match in Stapme. When MacPhail dived at him he just bounced off the strong South African, ricked his neck in the process, and fell to the floor. The next day he was shot down in combat. Fortunately he survived but when he next met Stapme he was absolutely furious, blaming his badly bruised and stiff neck on not being able to turn his head adequately, and therefore see the enemy fighter on his tail! MacPhail's enthusiasm for wrestling and de-bagging was somewhat dampened after that. It would not be long before MacPhail was a patient at the Queen Victoria Cottage Hospital, East Grinstead, with Richard.

No.603 Squadron saw action during all four patrols on the 31st. With the RDF stations operational once again, power having been restored, four waves of enemy aircraft, one approaching Dover, the other three flying up the Thames estuary, were reported to Fighter Command HQ operations room at Bentley Priory. The Observer Corps at Dover reported that the raid approaching their section of the Kent coast consisted entirely of Me109s, therefore, not wishing to have his fighters drawn into unnecessary attrition, Park communicated with his controllers to warn the two Hurricane squadrons that had been scrambled to intercept, and to order them to withdraw. No.501 Squadron managed to turn away before engagement took place, but No.1 Squadron RCAF was bounced by a *Staffel* of Me109s, which had dived out of the sun, shooting down three Hurricanes and forcing the pilots to bale out.

The German fighters were presented with no further opposition by the RAF and spent their available time over the Kent coast shooting down all of the Dover barrage balloons. More than 80 per cent of all the Me109s in northern Europe were now based at airfields in the Pas de Calais area of Northern France, under the command of Kesselring. It was his intention to use them at every opportunity, as escort or on free-chases over the south coast.

Park scrambled 13 squadrons from seven airfields around London to intercept a raid consisting of 200 enemy aircraft that had been reported to be approaching the coast by the radar stations at Dunkirk in Kent and Canewdon in Suffolk. The Hurricanes of No.257 Squadron took off from Martlesham Heath and attacked the bomber protection, consisting of 50 Me110s. In the initial head-on attack the Hurricanes claimed two of the Me110s for the loss of two of their own number, which were shot down with one pilot being killed. The Me110s then promptly assumed their defensive circle formation.

No.56 Squadron were also scrambled as another raid was reported to be approaching their airfield at North Weald. It met the enemy near Colchester and engaged the escort. In the space of a few moments the squadron suffered heavy losses, without managing to inflict any losses on the enemy. They lost four aircraft with one pilot killed, a flight commander, and two others wounded. The German bombers forged ahead to North Weald.

At the same time another raid consisting of Dorniers with a massive Me110 escort headed for the 12 Group Sector Station at Duxford. The two resident fighter squadrons at Duxford were not at a state of readiness and the controller, Wing Commander E.B. Woodhall, urgently requested cover as the bombers approached. Park responded by diverting the Hurricanes of No.111 Squadron to intercept the raid. As it happened the Hurricanes were in a perfect position to intercept the enemy aircraft and carry out an initial head-on attack, first on the bombers, then the escort, destroying one of each on the first pass with the loss of one of their own Hurricanes. The escort then assumed its defensive circle formation leaving the Dorniers, which had been forced out of formation and having scattered, to make a dash for home, jettisoning their bomb load with no damage to their intended target. The Hurricanes of No.111 Squadron saved Duxford from attack, and while the satellite airfield of Fowlmere was bombed during WWII, Duxford was never to be attacked.

The third part of this particular raid had Debden as its objective and it was successful in reaching its target without detection. One *Gruppe* of Dorniers hit the airfield with about one hundred 250kg bombs damaging a number of buildings, including three barrack blocks and the station sick-quarters. Four Hurricanes were badly damaged on the ground but the airfield remained operational. There were 18 casualties. The cannon-armed Spitfires of No.19 Squadron based at Fowlmere were sent up to intercept the Debden raid. On reaching the enemy aircraft, two sections engaged the escorting Me110s and suffered the loss of two Spitfires. A further aircraft, which had been hit during the engagement and suffered hydraulic failure, attempted to land back at Fowlmere, without the use of flaps. It turned over on landing and caught fire, tragically trapping the 19-year-old pilot in the cockpit.

Just after 09.00 hours two groups of aircraft approached the north Kent coast. One group consisted of about twenty Dornier Do17s with an escort while the other consisted of a mixture of Me110s and Me109s, which were initially thought to be there to provide an outer protection screen for the bombers. The Dorniers bombed Eastchurch aerodrome causing little damage while the second group straffed the airfield in a number of low-level attacks and then turned its attention to Detling where it did the same, probably seeking to destroy any parked aircraft. This tactic would suggest that although the second group may well have been there to provide an outer protection screen, it also had been given its own targets once the bombers had reached their objective.

The first patrol of the day by 603 Squadron took off at 08.55 hours. (The log books of Jack Stokoe and Jim Morton state the time as being 08.30 for a flight of one hour, five minutes.) The 12 Spitfires led by Flight Lieutenant Ken Macdonald (XT-E, R6752), with Boulter (XT-S, N3207), Haig (XT-P, X4274), Waterston (XT-K, X4273), Carbury (XT-W, R6835), Hillary (XT-M, X4277), Morton (XT-J, L1057), Read (XT-F, R6754), Gilroy (XT-H, N3288), Stokoe (XT-X, X4250), Berry (XT-Y, R6626) and Stapleton (XT-L, L1020), took off to join forces with the many other fighter units in an attempt to intercept the German fighters, thus leaving the bombers at the mercy of the Hurricanes. That was the general plan but in the melee that followed the initial first attack the fighters attacked the nearest available enemy aircraft. This was Richard's first flight in Spitfire X4277, the aircraft in which he would be shot down in almost exactly three days' time.

During this sortie Carbury and Gilroy each destroyed a Me109 while another Me109 claimed 'destroyed' appears in the squadron diary but was unallotted.

On his way to achieving 'ace in a day' Brian Carbury claimed a Me109E shot down over Canterbury:

> We were climbing over Canterbury at 28,000 feet when enemy aircraft were sighted. I warned VIKEN leader, and then led on diving on the near Me109 which turned over and spun in. The pilot jumped out by parachute.

VIKEN leader was Ken Macdonald. The enemy aircraft numbered 20 Me109s and Carbury launched his attack not long after 09.00 hours.

It is possible that with this claim he shared in the shooting down of the ace Oberleutnant Eckhart Priebe (Iron Cross First Class) of I/JG77 with Flight Lieutenant Denys Gillam of No.616 Squadron. Priebe had continued to lead his *Staffel* into combat despite the fact that earlier, having selected a target, he found his own guns had jammed, possibly owing to too much oil. His ploy worked for a while but the British fighters soon became aware of his plight and the unarmed fighter soon received the attention of a number of Spitfires and Hurricanes. The complicated maze of pipes and rubber hoses that circulated the vital coolant in his aircraft was pierced and very soon the bellowing engine began to protest. During one of the final bursts of gunfire that caught his plane, bullets entered the slender fuselage behind the cockpit, one bullet hitting the cabin and ricocheting back, striking him in the forehead.

At 12,000 feet above the beautiful Kent village of Elham, Priebe baled out and opened his parachute. The cut on his face was bleeding profusely and he had to wipe it away in order to read his watch which said 10.23 hours (09.23 hours British time). An RAF fighter flew around him, discharging bursts of ammunition as if in celebration of the victory.

Sheep Gilroy claimed a Me109 destroyed:

> P/O Gilroy attacked a stray Me109 in mid-Channel south of Dungeness. He saw it crash in flames in the sea. Later in the day P/O Gilroy baled out and is still in hospital. Report follows.

This report was written by the intelligence officer and a full report was never written. Gilroy was with 'A' Flight when he attacked the 109 at an altitude of 25,000 feet.

The 603 pilots landed again at 09.35 hours.

* * *

Kesselring tried to tempt up the British fighters by sending over a number of free-chases, but Park did not rise to the bait. This did, however, serve to keep the controllers alert to the possibility of there being further bombing raids following up. The next raid materialised in the form of two waves of Dorniers and Heinkels escorted by Me109s and Me110s, sent by Kesselring to attack Croydon and Biggin Hill. The Dorniers, flying at 2,000 feet, had almost made it to their target at Croydon unopposed, before the Hurricanes of No.85 Squadron took off to intercept them at 12.55, just as the first bombs started to fall on the east side of the aerodrome! Led by Squadron Leader Peter Townsend, the Hurricanes caught up with the Dorniers over Tunbridge Wells, but as they climbed hard to attack the Me110s the Me109s fell on them from out of the sun. In the ensuing combat it was claimed that the Hurricane pilots had destroyed two Me109s and one Me110 for the loss of two Hurricanes with both pilots being injured. One of these pilots was Townsend, who later had a piece of cannon shell removed from his foot and had a big toe amputated. The Dorniers had succeeded in bombing Croydon and one hangar was destroyed in the raid.

Biggin Hill was hit hard by the two *Staffeln* of Heinkel He111s that bombed the aerodrome from 12,000 feet hitting two of the remaining three hangars, messes, living quarters, and more importantly, the operations room. All the repair work that had been carried out after the last raid was undone. Water and electricity mains and telephone lines, were once again cut. Hurricanes of No.253 Squadron intercepted the Heinkels as they made good their escape and managed to shoot down one of their number. As they returned to base independently, as was so often the case after combat, Squadron Leader Tom Gleave was bounced by an unseen fighter near Biggin Hill and was shot down. His Hurricane caught fire and he was wounded and badly burnt before he escaped the flaming cockpit and took to the 'silk'. He spent a great deal of time recovering from his burns at East Grinstead where he met Richard. He too became one of the founder members of the Guinea Pig Club, eventually succeeding to the title of 'Chief Guinea Pig', and it must be said that he was one of its most cherished members. What little Richard mentions of Tom Gleave is a little scathing, but it must be remembered that he too was in great pain at the time he made Gleave's initial acquaintance.

At 08.38 Pilot Officer Maurice 'Mark' Mounsdon of 56 Squadron, was shot down in Hurricane R4197, in combat with fighters over Colchester. He was very badly burned and spent the next nine months in various hospitals. Richard and Maurice were at Kinloss at the same time and would later become good friends during their time together at the Queen Victoria Hospital, East Grinstead.

At 09.30 hours Richard's friend from his days at Shrewsbury and Oxford, Pilot Officer George Nelson-Edwards, was shot down. His Hurricane N2345 crashed at the Grange,

Water lane, Limpsfield. He was slightly injured in the combat and managed to bale out.

Whilst playing poker at dispersal Richard had been enjoying a run of success when 603 was scrambled for the second time that day. Flight Lieutenant Ken Macdonald led 12 Spitfires away from Hornchurch at 12.40 hours. The other pilots were Boulter (XT-S, N3267), Waterston (XT-K, X4273), Carbury (XT-W, R6835), Gilroy (XT-N, X4271), Morton (XT-B, N3056), Stapleton (XT-R, X4264), Read (XT-F, R6754), Haig (XT-P, X4274), Hillary (XT-M, X4277), Stokoe (XT-X, X4250), and Berry (XT-Y, R6626).

The intelligence patrol report reads:

> 12 aircraft of 603 Sqn left Hornchurch to patrol Biggin Hill at 28,000 feet. P/O Gilroy saw enemy aircraft above him, so the squadron climbed, but lost sight of them. They were then ordered to patrol base, where they saw about 14 Dornier Do17's at about 17,000 feet, protected by Me109's and He113's. The squadron went into line-astern and dived to attack. A dogfight ensued. The He113's had white spinners and grey and white speckled camouflage on top of the wings.

The He113s to which the intelligence officer refers were Me109Es, which were amongst the confirmed losses that day. The He113 appeared in all British recognition manuals of the early war period and RAF pilots frequently reported combats with them during the Battle of Britain, but despite claims that 113s had been shot down, no wreckage was ever found. The existence of the He113 was actually an elaborate bluff by the Germans. Before the war the Luftwaffe had rejected the He100 in favour of developed versions of the Me109 and the Heinkel fighter was offered for export. In the spring of 1940, nine He100s were prepared for a remarkable hoax which was intended to convince the Allied intelligence services that a new high-performance fighter had entered service. The aircraft were photographed in lines bearing fictitious unit markings and victory bars. The propaganda ruse worked and during the Battle of Britain several pilots reported combat with the 'He113'.

There were no casualties within 603 Squadron and Ras Berry claimed two Me109s destroyed; Brian Carbury claimed two He113s (Me109s) destroyed. Richard claimed a Me109 destroyed, Ken Macdonald claimed a He113 (Me109) destroyed and Jim Morton claimed a Dornier Do17 destroyed. Richard had now claimed two destroyed and one probable. Brian Carbury had already eight enemy aircraft destroyed to his credit.

Jim 'Black' Morton's combat report was detailed:

> As leader of rearguard action I was above squadron at 32,000 feet when many bombers with escort were seen approaching Hornchurch at about 15,000 feet. Squadron dived to attack. I got in a short burst from starboard quarter on a Do.17 of formation. No results observed. On recovering from break-away I observed a Do.17 slightly apart from the main formation. I made to attack it and it lost height quickly. At 8000 feet I observed a Hurricane also pursuing this a/c. I allowed him to make his attack and followed from the sun. I fired bursts totalling 10 seconds from quarter and astern. E/A was now flying at 500 feet at about 240 m.p.h. After my first burst cabin roof of e/a blew off. I made a second attack and finished my ammunition. E/A was now going slowly very close to the water. It forced landed on the sea near the French coast. I did not wait to see any survivors. No return fire in first attack, slight and inaccurate in second.

Jim Morton was flying with 'A' Flight during this combat and delivered his attack at 13.15 hours at an altitude of 15,000 feet.

Ras Berry reported:

> Patrolling with squadron at 28,000 feet over Biggin Hill, I saw a protective fighter formation above bomber squadron. They formed a circle and soon split into combat. I stuck on the tail of a Me109 and closed in and fired two bursts of four seconds and the enemy aircraft broke up. I then caught up with another 109

and closed in and fired at close range. Pieces fell off the 109 and it sank out of control and broke up.

Berry was flying as Blue 2 of 'B' Flight. The number of German fighters and bombers was estimated as 50. The attack was delivered at 13.15 hours over Biggin Hill, at an altitude of 28,000 feet.

Brian Carbury's report claiming two He113s destroyed reads:

> Enemy aircraft Me109 sighted and the squadron gave chase. I left and went for another formation which turned out to be friendly fighters. Heard over R/T that e/a were bombing home base, set course and saw e/a proceeding east. I was at 25,000', so we came down to attack bombers, but saw fighters He113 and Me109 above. I attacked the He113, he went straight down missing the rear of the formation and crashed straight into the ground. I carried out a beam attack on another He113 off to starboard. After one long burst he went on his back, pilot jumped out by parachute, and e/a crashed and burst into flames in a vacant bit west of Southend.

Carbury was leading a 'B' Flight section against approximately 50 Dornier Do17s, 'He113s' and Me109s in an attack delivered at 13.40 hours, west of Southend, at an altitude of 28,000 feet. He opened fire at 150 yards and closed to 50 yards, firing bursts of two seconds.

Richard's claim of a Me109 destroyed was 'written-up' by the intelligence officer based on available evidence from fellow squadron members and the confirmation of his kill by the Observer Corps:

> P/O Hillary claims a Me109 destroyed, shot down over the Channel. He is at present in hospital. Report to follow.

Richard was with 'B' Flight and was involved in the attack on approximately 50 Me109s over Dungeness, carried out at an altitude of 18,000 feet. He was later able to confirm that he opened fire with 3-5 second bursts at 200 yards and closed to a mere five yards! Accurate shooting from that range would very likely result in success.

Flight Lieutenant Ken Macdonald claimed a 'He113' destroyed while leading the squadron as leader of the Station flight ('A'), George Denholm still recovering from his exploits following the previous morning's combat. Macdonald's report reads:

> After patrolling for some time with the squadron at 30,000 feet we were told to patrol base. On approaching base from the south I saw considerable a/c and anti-aircraft activity over base at about 20,000 feet. I put squadron into line astern and gave the order to attack. I selected an He113 which was coming straight in my direction but below me. I got a momentary burst in from almost vertically above but was unable to allow enough deflection. I then pulled out and did a steep climbing turn and came down again above him and behind him to the south. He broke away from the rest of the battle and turned south east at about 20,000 feet. I followed and after a bit gradually overhauled him. As I approached very close behind him he suddenly made a very steep turn to the right. I gave him a full deflection burst of about 2-3 seconds and he immediately emitted a long trail of white 'smoke' and went into a steep spiral dive. I watched him to see him crash, but at about 4,000 feet he pulled gradually out and proceeded SE flying low. I flew down from 20,000 feet and again overtook him flying at about 1,000 feet and about 350 mph. As I approached again he went into a gradual left hand turn and gave him another burst of about 2 seconds from immediately behind having to pull up very suddenly to avoid him. He then flew down onto a field and rolled over and over. He came down approximately south or south east of Maidstone.
>
> The aircraft was of very good lines and appeared not unlike a Spitfire in shape, but in colour (seen as I always did with the sun behind me), it was easily different from the Spitfire owing to its different green and grey camouflage and

its cross on the fuselage just behind the cockpit. It had a general appearance of
neatness and compactness.

Macdonald was proving to be a capable fighter pilot and leader. His attack was delivered
at 13.15 hours at an altitude of 20,000 feet.

The enemy aircraft he claimed to have destroyed was confirmed as being a
Messerschmitt Bf109E-1 of 1JG/77 flown by Feldwebel Walter Evers. It crashed on
Court Farm, Hunton, Kent at 13.25 hours. Feldwebel Evers was severely wounded and
succumbed to his injuries the next day. He was buried in Maidstone cemetery. This
aircraft had previously been reported as having been shot down by an 85 Squadron
Hurricane flown by Lewis at 19.25 hours.

The squadron landed at 13.56 hours. While it had been on patrol, Hornchurch was
bombed. In contrast with the attacks of the previous day the raiders of Biggin Hill had
flown in over the coast to the west of Folkestone as part of a two-wave formation. The
second wave split from the first near Maidstone and headed for Hornchurch aerodrome
where, as the heat haze east of London had prevented the Observer Corps from passing
accurate plots, the *Gruppe* of Dorner Do17s of II/KG3 had almost reached the airfield
when the Spitfires of No.54 Squadron, led by Al Deere, were just taking off.

The Cf. Form 540, No.54 Squadron, 31 August 1940 reads:

> 13.15 hours. A large formation of enemy bombers – a most impressive sight in
> vic formation at 15,000 feet – reached the aerodrome and dropped their bombs
> (probably sixty in all) in a line from our original dispersal pens to the petrol dump
> and beyond into Elm Park. Perimeter track, dispersal pens and barrack block
> windows suffered, but no other damage to buildings was caused, and the
> aerodrome, in spite of its ploughed condition, remained serviceable. The
> squadron was ordered off just as the first bombs were beginning to fall and eight
> of our machines safely cleared the ground; the remaining section, however, just
> became airborne as the bombs exploded. All three machines were wholly
> wrecked in the air, and the survival of the pilots is a complete miracle. Sgt Davis
> taking off towards the hangars was thrown back across the River Ingrebourne two
> fields away, scrambling out of his machine unharmed. Flt.Lt Deere had one wing
> and his prop torn off; climbing to a hundred feet, he turned over, coming down,
> slid along the aerodrome for a hundred yards upside down. He was rescued from
> this unenviable position by P/O Edsall, the third member of the section, who had
> suffered a similar fate except that he landed the right way up. Dashing across the
> aerodrome with bombs still dropping, he extricated Deere from his machine. All
> three pilots were ready again for battle by the next morning.

The Hornchurch station operations record book states that:

> Mass raids continued to be made against our aerodromes, again starting early in
> the morning. The first two attacks were delivered at 08.30 and 10.30 respectively
> and were directed at Biggin Hill, Eastchurch and Debden. The third attack was
> delivered at Hornchurch, and although our squadrons engaged, they were unable
> to break the enemy bomber formation, and about thirty Dorniers dropped some
> one hundred bombs across the airfield. Damage, however, was slight, although a
> bomb fell on the new Airmen's Mess which was almost completed. The vital
> damage, however, was to a power cable, which was cut. The emergency power
> equipment was brought into operation until repair was effected. Three men were
> killed and eleven wounded. 54 Squadron attempted to take off during the attack
> and ran through the bombs. Three aircraft were destroyed, one being blown from
> the middle of the landing field to outside the boundary, but all three pilots
> miraculously escaped with only slight injuries.

According to surviving ground crew and pilots, the 603 Spitfires landed at Rochford at
13.56 hours, having been diverted as a result of the bombing of Hornchurch. Members

of ground crew recall waiting at dispersal, tools at the ready, for the return of the squadron Spitfires, which did not occur until after the final patrol of the day.

According to the log books of Jack Stokoe and Jim Morton, the squadron flew *four* patrols on the 31 August and not three, as written in the ORB. This point is further confirmed in the private letters of Ken Macdonald. The 'missing' patrol in the ORB was the second of the day (10.25 – 11.30).

Hornchurch and Biggin Hill were bombed again at 17.30 hours, the fourth attack on the RAF airfields that day. *Erprobungsgruppe 210* accompanied three *Staffeln* of Ju88s and Me110s dropping about 30 bombs on each target. Two parked Spitfires were destroyed at Hornchurch and one 603 airman killed, bringing the total to four for the day. But apart from damage to dispersal pens, perimeter track and airfield surface it remained serviceable.

Nos. 54 and 222 Squadrons were airborne at the time attempting to fight off the raid on Biggin, and 603 Squadron was refuelling and rearming at Rochford. Richard was not on the ground during any of the enemy bombing raids on Hornchurch or a witness to these events. He flew Spitfire X4277 on all four patrols, which he later claimed in the opening 'Proem' of *The Last Enemy*, had been damaged during an enemy bombing raid on Hornchurch, necessitating a replacement canopy. According to Richard, it was this canopy that prevented a more rapid escape from his cockpit when he was shot down on 3 September. The 603 Squadron ORB states that Richard flew X4264 during the last patrol, but this is a typing error as that aircraft was flown by Flight Lieutenant Fred Rushmer. The RAF Hornchurch ORB states:

> The fourth attack of the day was also directed at Hornchurch, and once again, despite strong fighter opposition and AA fire, the bombers penetrated our defences. This time, however, their aim was most inaccurate, and the line of bombs fell from them towards the edge of the aerodrome. Two Spitfires parked near the edge of the aerodrome were written off, and one airman was killed. Otherwise, apart from the damage to dispersal pens, the perimeter track, and the aerodrome surface, the raid was abortive, and the aerodrome remained serviceable. Our squadrons, which had a very heavy day, accounted for no less than nineteen of the enemy and a further seven probably destroyed. 603 Squadron alone were responsible for the destruction of 14 enemy aircraft. Although we lost a total of 9 aircraft, either in combat or on the ground, only 1 pilot was lost.

An aerial photograph taken of Hornchurch in 1941 clearly shows where the bombs struck the airfield during the raids of the previous summer. By comparing the photograph with Joe Crawshaw's (No.222 Squadron ground crew) photographs taken of the dispersed Spitfires in 1940, it is possible to pin point the position of Richard's Spitfire, X4277, on the aerial photograph.

Stapme Stapleton remembers hearing about the attack on the airfield from colleagues:

> I remember Al Deere at Hornchurch, he was a lucky fella. During that raid when he took off with two other aircraft the bombs caught up with him! There were about twelve Dorniers on their run-in to bomb the aerodrome and these three Spitfires were just gathering speed. Of course they weren't going faster than the Dorniers were flying, so the pattern of the Dorniers was faster than the Spitfires and the bombs fell behind initially and then overtook them sending Al Deere's aircraft corkscrewing into the air. Another chap was flung onto a sewage farm nearby while the remaining pilot clambered from his wrecked aircraft, which had done a cartwheel wing-tip over wing-tip, and helped free Deere from hanging upside down in his cockpit, unable to get out and with fuel pouring around the top of his head. In 24 hours the airfield was serviceable again. They hit the airfield and not the hangars. It was a grass aerodrome with no actual runways. If they had hit the hangars some damage would have been inflicted.

Daddy Bouchier was the CO and he got everybody onto the airfield filling in the bomb craters. There was one strip left untouched by bombs at the southern edge of the aerodrome, which we could still land on when we returned at the end of the day. More aircraft came over the next day and bombed that area too! I remember Hornchurch being shaped rather like an Easter egg with the southern end as the fattest part and the remaining strip across that part. The next day we were all sitting in the mess, the weather was poor with low cloud and we were on our day off. We suddenly heard the ack-ack firing, which didn't have a chance of hitting the target, as an enemy Ju88 appeared at the last moment from the cloud over the airfield. The enemy pilot must have been as surprised as anybody to suddenly emerge from the cloud to find he was right over an aerodrome. He was also very close to the barrage balloons. Two aircraft managed to take off after him but there was too much cloud about to have any hope of finding him. But he planted his bombs right on that untouched strip!

No.603 Squadron was situated, looking from south to north, half way along on the right-hand side of the aerodrome and the hangars were on the left-hand side, with the administration block and that sort of thing, with the mess further over on the same side. We were very much a squadron, even in the mess, because you were off, the other squadrons were on and you never saw them. We had a wonderful controller, I don't remember his name, he used to say, '603 Squadron please get into the air as soon as possible, please get going chaps', he spoke in such a mellifluous way, there was no urgency in his voice, no panic, nothing. It was a great influence.

As Ras Berry mentioned earlier, the voice was that of Ronald Adam the actor and WWI fighter pilot, and it had had a calming effect on him. Stapme continued:

Uncle George used to cheat when we were 'scrambled'. He would jump into his aircraft and, having started it, he would taxi out. He didn't do his belt up because he knew he had to wait for us. As everybody got into position, before we were airborne, he'd fasten his straps and say over the radio, '603 Squadron airborne'!

Daddy Bouchier was a good chap. He was a little fella who was always willing to assist in any duties in order to keep everyone working as a team. He helped position the little yellow marker boxes on the airfield after the raid on the 31st in order to indicate to the returning pilots a safe strip to land on. The pilots returning from combat remember seeing this little figure scurrying about, hastily positioning these markers to help guide them in.

In December 1940, the Edinburgh newspaper *Sunday Post* ran a feature on the pilots of 603 during that year with the headline referring to the success achieved on 31 August: Edinburgh Boys Bump Off 13 Jerries In One Day. It included photographs of pilots: Ras Berry, Stapme Stapleton, Brian Macnamara, Ludwik Martel, John Boulter and David Scott-Malden. (The article did not actually appear until 8 December 1940, which explains the inclusion of Martel and Scott-Malden who had yet to join the squadron.) The actual score was 14 with the loss of only one pilot and two Spitfires.

* * *

Ken Macdonald (XT-E, R6752), once again led the squadron on the last patrol of the day which took off at approximately 17.51 hours, with the Spitfires of Berry (XT-Y, R6626), Haig (XT-P, X4274), Boulter (XT-S, N3267), Waterston (XT-K, X4273), Carbury (XT-W, R6835), Gilroy (XT-N, X4271), Morton (XT-B, N3056), Read (XT-F, R6754), Stokoe (XT-X, X4250), Stapleton (XT-L, L1020), Rushmer (XT-R, X4264) and Richard flying Spitfire X4277, code XT-M, making up the numbers for this patrol. Over Woolwich they met formidable opposition in the shape of the Me109s of I/JG3, with Carbury claiming another two enemy aircraft destroyed over Southend, but with the tragic loss of the most popular member of the squadron, Bubble Waterston. Bubble's

Spitfire had only been issued to the squadron the previous day as a replacement.

Although Bubble's loss was not witnessed by any of his colleagues, many eye-witnesses on the ground saw the Spitfire descend from the sky above. The most likely cause was that at 18.30 hours he had been shot down by the Me109s of I/JG3 during combat over London and was either dead or unconscious when his aircraft plunged into Repository Road, Woolwich. If he was still alive on impact, Flying Officer Robin McGregor Waterston died instantly in the resulting crash. He was 23 years old. Back in Scotland his youngest sister heard the tragic news when her two young nieces ran up the path outside the family home shouting: 'Uncle Robin's dead, Uncle Robin's dead.' They were too young to appreciate the heartbreak of the news that had been passed to them.

Bubble's remains were removed from the wreckage, returned to his home and cremated at the Edinburgh (Warriston) cemetery. His name appears on Panel 4 of the memorial.

Contrary to popular belief, his aircraft did not break up in mid-air as the result of damage received – it has been previously stated that a wing was seen fluttering down from the Spitfire. However, a Me109 E-4 (1503) of I/JG3 flown by Leutnant Walter Binder was shot down over the same area, and during the early part of its subsequent plunge to the earth it lost a wing. The flaming aircraft spiralled to the ground, while the wing 'fluttered' down nearby, and Binder was found dead in the wreckage. It was this aircraft that had been reported as having been seen breaking up in mid-air and subsequently the details of the two crashes became confused.

Bubble's final direction before impact had been from the north-east and, in order to miss the barracks, at an angle of about 45 degrees, which would have taken his aircraft over the rooftops on the north side of Wellington Street where it caught the trees on the southside next to the barracks before crashing into the middle of Repository Road.

Bombardier John Cross of the Royal Artillery (RA) was at that time based at the Royal Artillery Depot Woolwich, with countless others, waiting to go overseas:

> On the 31st, because of the aerial activity, we were confined to the ground floor of the barrack block when there was the sound of an explosion close to the west of the block. Shortly after, a sergeant announced that there had been a plane crash by the roadside and that a guard was required. I was told to take five gunners with rifles and to block the road at the south end of the incident, the intention being to protect the public from the dangers of live ammunition and to prevent looting. Similarly, another NCO took the north end.
>
> On arrival at the site we were met with a tragic mess. The impact of the crashing Spitfire had resulted in the pilot being thrown through a corrugated parade shed at the side of the road. The impact was so great that his body was fragmented. [His head was found on top of the shed.]
>
> My guard was kept busy holding back the gawping civilians who were arriving in numbers. Civilian undertakers arrived with a coffin, which was no more than a wooden box with a tarpaulin cover. Assisted by several gunners we began the gruesome task of gathering the human remains. The job was carried out very thoroughly and it took us about an hour. During the operation we commented on how the pilot had just missed the north-westerly corner of the barrack block, on the corner of Repository Road and Wellington Street, and so avoided the loss of many lives. The fact that the shed remained unrepaired for many years served as a reminder of the sacrifice made by the brave young pilot.'

Certain members of the public did attempt to encroach on the crash site and John was later reprimanded for pointing his rifle when a civilian took a dislike to the way the bombardier carried out his duty. They were not entirely successful in protecting the site from ghoulish souvenir hunters. A young lad called John Hodnett was shown a piece of RAF tunic by another youngster who told him he had found it at the crash site. Several others also managed to acquire small fragments of the aircraft as souvenirs. This was John Cross's first encounter with death, and 57 years later, the effect that this experience had had upon him was still clearly evident.

The Spitfire practically disintegrated on impact. The Merlin engine was half buried in the road and the wreckage that remained attached was spontaneously engulfed in flames on impact as the fuel tanks ruptured and sprayed a welter of flaming aviation fuel over the immediate area. Such was the devastation that little was left that immediately identified the aircraft as having been a Spitfire. The instantly recognisable elliptical wings were smashed and subsequently burnt in the ensuing flames which ultimately produced the 'white ash' of incinerated aluminium. This casts doubt on the perfectly shaped wing that was later recovered from the Woolwich Arsenal Dump after the crash site was cleared, and was subsequently displayed as the wing from Bubble's Spitfire. Many witnesses were questioned as to the condition of the aircraft and, without exception, they all stated that the wings were severely smashed and crumpled from the leading edges rearwards, or totally incinerated in the ensuing fire.

At 16.00 hours on the 31st, in the back garden of the Thompson family home at 50 Ogilby Street, Woolwich, wedding photographs were being taken. Ada Thompson was the bride and the groom was Eddie Stephenson of the Royal Artillery (RA). They had met while Ada was working in the RA canteen. They had recently returned from the church having been married at 15.00 hours. Ada was 18 at the time. Also present amongst a large gathering was Stan Thompson, Ada's 12-year-old brother. The wedding group photograph was taken a quarter of a mile from the crash site and two hours prior to Bubble's death. Later, from their position in the garden, Stan and a number of the guests had a very clear view of the Spitfire as it came down, practically overhead, and dived towards Repository Road. The pilot could be seen at the controls.

The Me109 flown by Binder lost a wing while still at altitude. Many witnesses in Plumstead witnessed the oddly gyrating object grow steadily larger as the speed of the descent increased. As it got lower they saw that it was a plane rolling crazily with one wing gone and flames pouring from the fuselage. Civilians watching events from the gardens of Anne Street and Robert Street began to panic as they realised that the stricken aircraft was going to drop on them. Moments later, and with a terrifying crash, it fell upon the small gardens between the two streets, spewing the remaining contents of the fuel tank over the immediate area and temporarily trapping residents in their garden shelter. Pieces of burning debris were spread for a large distance all around.

While it cannot be confirmed as to who exactly was responsible for shooting down Bubble, two Luftwaffe pilots claimed to have destroyed Spitfires during roughly the same time period and it is possible that one or other could have shot down the young Scotsman. Major Adolf Galland, CO of JG26, shot down a Spitfire over Gravesend while Unteroffizier Hugo Dahmer of 6/JG26 made an unconfirmed claim for a Spitfire destroyed, also over Gravesend. Galland's kill was his 26th victory, Dahmer had reached seven.

Mr P. Delieu who was 17 at the time also witnessed the aerial action during the evening of the 31st:

> I saw a Spitfire come down after a dogfight over Woolwich. I witnessed the start of the battle with my friends while we were swimming in the Charlton open air lido when the warning went and we had to come out of the water. Right away we saw the battle begin overhead and saw the two planes come down. We ran from Charlton Park to the cross-roads at Repository Road. The Spitfire came in low, weaving and trailing smoke. The pilot must have been trying to land his aircraft on the open common. When we reached the scene the badly burnt plane was in the middle of the road. I have no doubt about the details of this incident and am very familiar with the area. I also went to Robert Street and Anne Street where the Me109 came down.

As the second youngest of eight children Bubble's death was a devastating blow to his family. To Richard another short lived but intense friendship had come to an end. Bubble had attempted to live life to the full, but was his enthusiasm given an extra edge as he became increasingly aware that the war could quite possibly end his life prematurely? The intensity with which he lived his life during those months that led to the Battle of Britain would indicate just that.

A notice announcing Bubble's death appeared in the *Scotsman* on 5 September 1940:

> Waterston – Killed in action in August 1940. Flying Officer Robin McGregor
> Waterston, youngest son of Mr and Mrs Waterston of Haughead Ford, Lothian.
> Funeral on Saturday 7th September. Service at Crematorium, Warriston at noon.
> (No flowers, no mourning).

During the same combat over Southend at 18.30 hours, Brian Carbury's Spitfire was hit by a 20mm cannon shell fired from a Me109 of I/JG3, which knocked out the compressed air system and caused severe damage when an oxygen cylinder exploded. His aircraft, R6835, in which he had shot down eight Me109s between 29 and 31 August – with five of these successes claimed during three patrols flown on the 31st – was eventually repaired and returned to operational use ten months later. Carbury was slightly wounded in the foot but managed to return to base safely and was on patrol again after missing just one flight. His combat report reads:

> Enemy aircraft sighted over London and we attacked. Three of us attacked nine
> Me109's, the first went down straight and burst into flames; attacked four e/a
> which were in pairs, slipped up a beam attack, hit the glycol tank of one and
> rolled over and went straight down hitting a wood. A Me109 got on my tail,
> received one cannon shell and the air system punctured, so came home.

The 'no-frills' combat report of Brian Carbury, was the assessment of someone who was rapidly becoming one of the very best combat pilots of the battle and on this occasion 'ace in a day'. He initiated his attack at 18.25 hours north of Southend at an altitude of 25,000 feet. For each attack he opened fire from 150 yards closing to 50 yards, again firing one three-second burst on each occasion. Very efficient.

Sheep Gilroy had a lucky escape at 18.20 over the Thames, when his Spitfire was hit and set alight by Me109s of I/JG3. A few moments before, he had managed to destroy one of their number. The initial attack of this combat claimed Bubble's life. Ten minutes later the same Me109s damaged the Spitfire of Brian Carbury. Sheep Gilroy managed to escape from his stricken aircraft which eventually crashed onto 14 Hereford Road, Wanstead. The engine fell onto the garden of number 12, but fortunately, or unfortunately, the only casualty was a dog. When Gilroy eventually landed by parachute, he was confronted by an angry mob which mistook him for a German and set about him. It has been said that the Home Guard were intent on lynching him and but for a bus conductress who recognised his expletives, somewhat harder to understand initially owing to his Scottish accent, this might have happened; they eventually had him removed to King George Hospital at Ilford where he was treated for minor injuries and burns. The road was cordoned off for two weeks while the wreckage was cleared.

Richard states in *The Last Enemy* that Sheep Gilroy was in the bath when they were ordered into the air, and that he donned the nearest clothing which did not include his tunic:

> He was sitting in his bath when a 'flap' was announced. Pulling on a few clothes
> and not bothering to put on his tunic, he dashed out to his plane and took off. A
> few minutes later he was hit by an incendiary bullet and the machine caught fire.
> He baled out quite badly burned, and landed by parachute in one of the poorer
> districts of London. With no identifying tunic, he was at once set upon by two
> hundred silent and coldly angry women, armed with knives and rolling pins. For
> him no doubt it was a harrowing experience, until he finally established his
> nationality by producing all the most lurid words in his vocabulary.

George Gilroy was able to confirm he had not been in the bath when the squadron was scrambled but had removed his tunic at dispersal, thus removing the instantly recognisable RAF wings brevet. The number of angry women was also somewhat exaggerated.

The squadron landed again at 19.00 hours with Berry claiming a Messerschmitt destroyed, which was later confirmed as being a Me109E-4 of I/JG3 flown by Oberleutnant Helmut Rau, which he had damaged in combat over the Thames estuary at 18.45 hours. It forced-landed on the beach at Shoeburyness and the pilot was captured:

> As I had no oxygen, I had to leave the squadron at 22,000 feet and waited below in the sun for straggling enemy aircraft.
>
> After patrolling for 30 minutes, I saw a Me109 proceeding very fast. To overhaul him I had to press the emergency boost – indicated speed – 345. I caught the enemy aircraft off Shoeburyness [sic]. I opened fire at close range and fired all my ammunition until the enemy aircraft streamed with smoke and pancaked on the mud at Shoeburyness.

Ras Berry was with 'B' Flight and attacked this Me109 at 18.45 hours as it was returning to France.

Sergeant Stokoe's combat report and his memories of action that day leave little doubt as to the severity of the damage inflicted on the Me109 that he had destroyed over South London:

> We were ordered to patrol base at 12,000 feet. As I was rather late, the formation took off without me. I took-off alone, climbed into the sun, and rejoined the formation which was circling at about 28,000 feet. I observed two Me109's above, and climbed after them in full fire pitch.
>
> The Me's kept close together in a steep spiral climb towards the sun. I pumped several bursts at the outside one from about 200 yards with little effect. I closed to about 50 yards and fired two more long bursts. Black smoke poured from his engine which appeared to catch fire, and eight or nine huge pieces of his fuselage were shot away. He spun steeply away and crashed inside the balloon barrage. I continued climbing after the other Me109, and fired two long bursts from about 150 yards. White smoke came from his aircraft, and he spiralled gently downwards. I broke away as I was out of ammunition, and failed to see what happened to him.

The Me109s had been at 30,000 feet when Stokoe had attacked the first at 18.25 hours. Stapme Stapleton claimed a Me109 probable:

> When patrolling in line astern with the rest of the squadron I sighted bomber formation below us on the port. With two other aircraft I climbed into the sun for a favourable position, to make an attack on the bombers out of the sun, when five Me109's engaged us.
>
> These Me109's came out of the bomber formations climbing into the sun. Flying Officer Carbury engaged three Me109's and I engaged the other two. These two were flying in tight line astern. After giving the rear one a deflection burst of three seconds he pulled vertically upwards with white streams pouring from his engine.

Stapme also attacked the Me109s at 18.25 hours at an altitude of 25,000 feet north of Southend. This 'probable' was in fact the aircraft which crashed and burned near Whalebone Lane Gunsite, Chadwell Heath at 18.50 hours. The pilot of the Messerschmitt Bf109E-4 (5339) of 3/JG3 was Oberleutnant Johann Loidolt who managed to bale out of the stricken fighter. It is possible that he was also attacked by Sergeant F.W. 'Taffy' Higginson of No.56 Squadron as well as Stapleton and Carbury.

That same afternoon a series of low level raids aimed at the CH (Chain Home: long range early warning radar), radar stations in Kent and Sussex, and the CHL (Chain Home Low: shorter range for plotting low level flying aircraft) installation at Foreness, were carried out in an attempt to render the RAF blind once again. However, the damage was light and the units were operating again by the end of the day. That night the bomber offensive continued with Liverpool being hit for the fourth consecutive night. The continued inability of the night fighters to have any effect on the German bombers may have prompted the decision to withdraw the Defiant from daylight operations and train the two squadrons in night fighting. While the daylight losses of Defiants were unacceptably high, this decision was later proved to be valid as the Defiant became an effective night fighting aircraft.

During the previous two days the Luftwaffe had carried out an enormous assault on the fighter airfields of the RAF that guarded London, having flown 2,800 sorties. The intensity of the attacks on the airfields would never be equalled during the rest of the battle and the number of RAF fighters sent to intercept would never again be as great as during those two hot summer days in late August. The RAF flew 2,020 sorties with 65 fighters downed, 39 on the 31st; these were dark days indeed. The average of 115 pilots killed or wounded a week was double the output of the training schools and the actual situation was worse than it looked. Experienced pilots killed or wounded had to be replaced with inexperience. Peter Townsend of No.85 Squadron recalls:

> Our strength was even sapped from within. On the morning of 1st September, Sergeant Geoff Goodman of 85, with only four guns working, shot down a Me109; the air lines to the other four guns had been blocked with matchsticks, sabotaged by some German sympathizer at the depot.

To the pilots and ground crews alike, this one day must have seemed like an eternity. The squadron had been in combat four times; in addition, according to the ORB, their airfield was bombed on three occasions, once in the morning and twice in the afternoon. During the lunchtime raid three 603 ground-crewmen were killed when a bomb fell right in front of their lorry as it dashed around the perimeter track. A fourth was killed during the last raid of the day. Those killed were: LAC Baldie, LAC Dickson, AC1 Dickinson, and AC1 Worthington – all Edinburgh lads. In addition, Sergeants Gillies and Mackenzie, AC1 Forest, AC1 Adams, and AC1 Ritchie were wounded.

Witnesses remember seeing the driver of the lorry blown out of the cab, his body landing a considerable distance away. Although Richard refers to the death of Sergeant Ross in *The Last Enemy*, no sergeant was killed during the bombing of the 31st August. Sergeant Harry Ross, much liked and respected by the squadron members, was uninjured in the raid and survived the war.

Richard also recounts his fortunate survival during the lunchtime attack on the airfield, although he was not there. He flew all four patrols on 31 August and, along with the rest of the squadron, was diverted to Rochford as a result of the bombing at Hornchurch.

The following day the squadron was stood down and the pilots rested during the morning, before they were once again in combat during the afternoon.

* * *

Sunday 1 September 1940
On this day Pilot Officer Dudley Stewart-Clark returned from leave, but he was not included on a patrol until the next day. News reached the squadron confirming that the body found in the wreckage of the Spitfire at Woolwich Barracks was indeed that of Bubble Waterston.

The lessons of the first few days had been very hard for the squadron, and it was decided to adopt a different tactic when first scrambled to intercept the enemy formation. The squadron took off and flew initially on a reciprocal of the course given by the controller. When they reached an altitude of 15,000 feet they would then turn and fly back towards the enemy on the correct course, thus reducing the chance of meeting the enemy while still trying to attain the dominant height factor. It was common knowledge that if the fighters were caught at a height disadvantage they would head for home rather than stay and fight at an obvious disadvantage. They also agreed to attack in pairs with one protecting the tail of his partner, who was the main attacking aircraft.

At high altitude Richard was having problems spotting the enemy fighters in the glare of the sun:

> Sheep's experience on the moors of Scotland proved invaluable. He always led
> the guard section and always saw the Huns long before anyone else.

But the other pilots also wore their goggles. Although the pilots also had darkened lenses attached to their goggles Richard did not wear his because they gave him the feeling of claustrophobia:

> With spots on the windscreen, spots before the eyes, and a couple of spots that
> might be Messerschmitts, blind spots on my goggles seemed too much of a good
> thing; I always slipped them up on to my forehead before going into action. For
> this and for not wearing gloves I paid a stiff price.

It was so important that during the fast turn around of the fighters by the ground crews when the aircraft were refuelled and re-armed, the oxygen cylinder was replaced and any problems with the radio etc, were checked, the canopy and windscreen were wiped and buffed to remove the slightest blemish that could be mistaken for an enemy fighter at that vital moment. The closing speed of two fighters diving head-on to one another had to experienced to be believed! Therefore, a moment's deliberation could be fatal. It was also important that the cloth used to polish the canopy was not in any way abrasive. The sun shining on a scratched perspex surface would be refracted and the glare intensified and magnified.

At 09.00 hours on 1 September the RAF Fighter Command order of battle stated that No.603 Squadron had 13 aircraft that were combat ready with three more unserviceable. It also recorded that the squadron had 18 pilots on state. It actually had 25 available in total at that time: Ken Macdonald, Haig, Gilroy, Stapleton, Caister, Hillary, Stokoe, Ritchie, Morton, Stewart-Clark, Carbury, Berry, Rushmer, MacNamara, MacPhail, Rafter, Boulter, Caister, Pease, Read, Cardell, Pinckney, Sarre, Goldsmith and Dexter. The position of commanding officer was temporarily vacant due to George Denholm still recovering from his experience on the 30th; Ken Macdonald covered his duties.

On the 1st Air Chief Marshal Sir Hugh Dowding AOC in C Fighter Command carried out the re-deployment of a number of squadrons, reflecting the need to bring fresh squadrons into the heat of the battle while re-appointing certain others that had suffered debilitating losses to aircraft and men, giving them the opportunity to re-group. At the same time it was realised that a nucleus of experience had to be maintained. Many of the pilots of the 'experienced' squadrons were both physically and mentally exhausted, vulnerable therefore in their current state. At the same time, to introduce inexperience was presenting the enemy with potential 'cannon-fodder'.

No.603 Squadron had only been at Hornchurch for five days, but in that time they had lost Benson, Waterston, Cunningham and Don Macdonald. Denholm, Sheep Gilroy, Colin Pinckney, Brian Carbury, Pip Cardell, Arthur Sarre, Rusty Rushmer, Ian Ritchie and Richard Hillary had all been fortunate to have escaped from a variety of situations by baling out of or forced-landing their aircraft, some receiving minor burns and wounds. They were already veterans, having to fly their Spitfires skilfully enough to shoot down enemy aircraft and avoid being shot down themselves. All this would have taken its toll and they would be starting to feel drained. The prospect of facing death each time they took off would have made each living second all the more valuable.

At 10.20 the Kent RDF stations reported enemy raids formating over France, and by 10.55 these aircraft were advancing over Dover over a front five miles wide which split into two groups of about 30 bombers each with the same number of fighters. They were heading for the airfields once again, with Detling, Eastchurch and Biggin Hill the targets along with the London Docks. The groups divided again fifteen minutes later, just as the fighters of No.11 Group attacked, but they were unable to break through the heavy layer of protection offered by the Me109s and 110s. Once again Biggin was hit, with a number of aircraft of No.610 Squadron in the process of moving north to re-group being destroyed or damaged. No.85 Squadron was to see action on two occasions on this day, firstly at 11.05 and then 13.50 hours, but time was running out. The squadron had been badly depleted and the pilots and ground crews were near total exhaustion, and today would again bring heavy losses. It was only a matter of time before the squadron, which had been involved from the beginning, was annihilated. In fact by the end of the next seven-day period the equivalent of six squadrons would have been destroyed.

The next raid began at 13.00 and at 13.40, 170 enemy aircraft were reported to be crossing the Kent coast. While 603 were rested during the morning and therefore not involved in the defence from this attack, No.85 Squadron were. The ORB clearly illustrates the ferocity of the fighting at this stage, especially bearing in mind that 85 Squadron had been in the thick of it for quite some time now:

> Squadron again airborne at 13.50 hours to intercept enemy formation approaching Tunbridge Wells/Kenley area. At about 13.55 hours about 150-200 aircraft (Do17, Me109 and Me110) were sighted near Biggin Hill at 15,000 feet. When sighted the squadron was still about 5,000' lower, and while climbing were attacked continuously by the 109's and 110's. Allard attacked a straggling Do17 whose rear gunner baled out and whose pilot attempted a force landing near the railway line at Lydd. Allard's oil pressure dropped so he switched off and landed at Lympne, but while the aircraft was being serviced the airfield was bombed and his aircraft was hit (one groundcrewman was killed and another seriously wounded). P/O English carried out two quarter attacks on a Do17, stopping its starboard engine; the enemy aircraft landed between Ham Street and Hythe and two crew were seen to emerge. Evans attacked and destroyed a Me109 with a seven second burst, and a Me109 with a five second burst but was unable to identify location of crashes. Howes attacked and shot down a Do17 just south of Tunbridge Wells, two crew members baling out; he also damaged a Me109. Gowers was hit by a cannon shell and baled out with severe burns on hands, and wounds in hands and face; his Hurricane crashed at Oxted. Booth's aircraft was hit by cannon shells; he baled out near Purley, and his aircraft crashed at Sanderstead. His parachute did not open properly and he suffered a broken back, leg and arm. Patrick Woods-Scawen was posted missing and his body was found near Kenley on 6th September – his parachute unopened. Sgt Ellis was also killed in this fight. Six Hurricanes, all that remained of the Squadron – landed at Croydon between 14.30 and 15.00 hours, and Lewis had to land wheels-up.

At 15.45 hours nine Spitfires of No.603 Squadron were sent up for the first time this day on a routine operational patrol. Squadron Leader Denholm was once again leading the squadron in X4260, XT-D, with Ken Macdonald (R6752), Boulter (X4277), Rushmer (R6626), Morton (N3056), Hillary (R6721), Cardell (L1020), Stokoe (X4271), and Read (L1057). The intelligence report reads:

> Nine aircraft of 603 Squadron to go to Manston. When over Canterbury, Sgt Stokoe was at 3,000 feet and attacked a single Me109. P/O Cardell forced-landed owing to oil trouble. The rest of the Squadron saw nothing.

Sergeant Jack Stokoe's report while flying with 'A' Flight, claiming one Me109 destroyed in combat over Thanet, reads:

> At about 16.30 we were patrolling Manston at 12,000 feet when control informed us Canterbury was being bombed. About five miles south of the town when at about 3,000 feet a Me109, silver with black crosses, dived past my nose flattened out about 50 feet up and headed south. I executed a steep turn, pushed in boost overide, and sat on his tail. At about 50 yards, I gave him one small burst with little effect, closed to 30 yards, and gave a slightly longer burst. Black smoke

poured from him as I overshot him. The a/c crashed in a field, turned over two or three times and burst into flames in a clump of trees. 70 bullets were fired from each gun.

This Messerschmitt was probably a Bf109-E4 (4020) of III/JG53 flown by Oberleutnant Bauer who was killed in the crash, which occurred south of Chilham. Pip Cardell forced landed at 16.45 hours due to a problem with oil temperature. His Spitfire was written off. This patrol had been his first since moving south from Montrose and had been a real baptism when you consider the intensity of the action in which they had become embroiled.

The squadron landed again at 17.25 hours. No.603 Squadron was not involved when the last phase of attacks were launched around 17.30 hours. Kesselring sent over seven different formations consisting mainly of fighters. Park was not tempted into sending up his valuable pilots and so the Germans set about straffing the defences.

* * *

Monday 2 September 1940

Liverpool, Sheffield and Birmingham were again bombed during the night. By the evening of 1 September the night fighter squadrons of No.25 and 600 were moved nearer London (Martlesham Heath to North Weald and Manston to Hornchurch respectively) in preparation for what was thought by Dowding and Park at Fighter Command to be the imminent night attacks on the capital.

At 07.00 hours just inland from Calais gathered one *Gruppe* of KG 3's Dorniers and one *Geschwader* of Me109s for the first of Kesselring's four phase attacks that were to occur this day. As they approached Deal 60 RAF fighters were scrambled to intercept. Unfortunately only 20 were able to owing to the controllers maintaining standing patrols over the sector airfields. In the Maidstone area the bombers split up and attacked Biggin Hill, Rochford, Eastchurch and North Weald. Gravesend received a few bombs on the outer edge of the airfield. No.253 Squadron had initially failed to penetrate the fighter screen prior to the split, but nine Spitfires did manage to engage the Dorniers and Me110s over Maidstone at 13,000 feet. No.603 Squadron was scrambled to protect Hornchurch but when it was realised that the airfield was not under immediate threat of attack it was ordered forward and caught the Me109s as they withdrew over Kent.

> Intelligence Patrol Report, 603 Squadron
> 07.28 – 0830 hours. 2.9.40
>
> The squadron was ordered to patrol Hawkinge. When at 22,000 feet, they saw three Me109's flying in line astern, which they attacked. Later the guard section attacked a further two Me109's. One pilot lost the squadron and saw tight vic's of about 50 Do17's and Me110's consisting of small vic's. He attacked the outside Me110. The Me110's had no yellow noses, but whitish grey wing-tips.

The patrol took off from Hornchurch at 07.28 hours and consisted of 12 Spitfires led by Squadron Leader George Denholm in Spitfire X4260, with Haig (R6752), Boulter (R6626), Carbury (X4263), Caister (X4185), Pease (P6721), Morton (N3056), Read (L1057), Stapleton (X4274), Berry (X4264), Hillary (X4277), and Stokoe (X4271). This would be Caister's first experience of combat since the squadron had moved down to Hornchurch, and no comparison could be made with his minimal experience gained north of the border a few weeks previously. This would be a shocking introduction to a much greater level of action, despite his service flying experience.

Richard claimed a Me109 destroyed in the combat and, as with other combat reports, unable to complete the paperwork before he was shot down on 3 September, the 603 Squadron intelligence officer prepared the following report for the records:

> P/O Hillary claims a Me109 destroyed, which he shot down into the sea. In a later engagement he baled out and is still in hospital. Report follows.

Richard was flying with 'B' Flight. His attack was delivered at 08.15 hours at an altitude of 26,000 feet, north of Hawkinge. I believe that it was during this flight that Richard chased a Me109 back to a point over the French coast:

> On another occasion I was stupid enough actually to fly over France: the sky appeared to be perfectly clear but for one returning Messerschmitt, flying very high. I had been trying to catch him for about ten minutes and was determined that he should not get away. Eventually I caught him inland from Calais and was just about to open fire when I saw a squadron of twelve Messerschmitts coming in on my right. I was extremely frightened, but turned in towards them and opened fire at the leader. I could see his tracer going past underneath me, and then I saw his hood fly off, and the next moment they were past. I didn't wait to see any more, but made off for home, pursued for half the distance by eleven very determined Germans. I landed a good hour after everyone else to find Uncle George just finishing his check-up.

After the next day's first patrol Richard was never to fly with 603 again; his combat reports were, therefore, unfortunately never brought up to date.

Sergeant Jack Stokoe claimed a Me110 damaged:

> We were patrolling the Channel at 26,000 feet when enemy planes were sighted and I became separated from my squadron. Not contacting any enemy aircraft, I heard control say, gate to homebase 15,000 feet. I climbed to 17,000 feet and observed a mass of enemy bombers flying south towards me at 15,000 feet. They were flying in irregular vic's, but packed very close. There must have been at least 50 Me110's and Dorniers. I executed a steep turn and dived on a Me110 on the right of the formation, putting in two short bursts at about 100 yards range. I did not observe what happened then as my windscreen was hit and perspex was scattered into the cockpit. I slid away under the formation and glanced at my instruments to see if the engine was alright. It seemed normal, so I climbed and attacked another Me110 on the left of the formation, closing from 200 to 75 yards and firing several long bursts until my ammunition ran out. White smoke appeared from the port engine of the Me110 and it was losing height towards the coast. I spiralled down to 1,000 feet and headed for homebase.

Stokoe was flying with 'A' Flight, delivering his attacks at 08.15 north of Hawkinge. His hood was shattered during combat and the flight's likely opponents were the Me109s of I/JG2. Jack Stokoe received a slight wound to the hand from a shard of perspex; his aircraft, XT-X was repairable. Flying Officer Haig, also with 'A' Flight, claimed a Me109 destroyed:

> When on patrol at about 26,000 feet over Hawkinge, I saw two Me109's. I saw another Spitfire diving at the same e/a as me. The e/a dived vertically and then pulled up steeply. As it pulled out I noticed a white stream coming from the port wing. I had not fired up to this point, but as the e/a was still proceeding on a westerly course, I opened fire and saw it burst into flames. Later I ascertained that it was Pilot Officer Berry who had fired at this Me109 before me.

Haig also delivered his attack at 08.15 hours. Ras Berry of 'B' Flight claimed a Me109 destroyed:

> When on patrol at 26,000 feet over Hawkinge, I sighted two Me109's, which half rolled and dived earthwards. I followed one and as it pulled out of the dive I opened fire at 100 yards and fired an eight second burst to close range (50 yards). Smoke poured heavily from the Me109. I broke away and blacked-out. Later I saw a Me109 in flames. After landing I ascertained F/O Haig had also fired at Me109.

It was a rarity for Ras to experience a black-out, since his stocky physique gave him a far greater tolerance to the effects of G-Force than the taller, thinner pilot.

The claim by Berry and Haig was confirmed as being a Me109E of I/JG51 shot down over Kent at 07.50 hours. The pilot, Leutnant Gunther Ruttkowski, was killed and the aircraft was a complete loss when it crashed at Nethersole Park, Womenswold, east of Barham. This aircraft was also claimed to have been shot down by Pilot Officer George Gribble of No.54 Squadron at 08.00 hours.

Three other Me109s were shot down by the Spitfires of 603 but it has not been possible to confirm exactly who was responsible. A Me109E of 8/JG51 was downed over the Channel with the pilot, Leutnant Braun, rescued unhurt by a Seenotdienst (German sea rescue unit). Another Me109E of I/JG51 was shot down over the Kent coast at 08.00 hours and the pilot, Feldwebel Heinz Bar, was rescued by Seenotflugkommando. He was later Oberstleutnant Heinz Bar, Knight's Cross with Oak Leaves and Swords; 220 victories over the Western Front, North Africa and Russia, and killed in a flying accident in 1957. The final aircraft was another Me109E of I/JG51, shot down over Kent at 08.00 hours. The pilot, Leutnant Helmut Thorl, baled out and was captured unhurt. The 109 crashed in flames at Leeds Castle, near Maidstone. It was also thought to have been shot down by Squadron Leader James Leathart of No.54 Squadron. It is possible that one of the two German fighters shot down over the Channel was Carbury's claim, while Richard or Stewart-Clark could have been responsible for the shooting down of the I/JG51 Me109 that crashed at Leeds Castle. But with the Spitfires of No.54 Squadron involved in the same combat it will never be confirmed as to who shot who down. It may well have been one of those occasions that Stapme Stapleton referred to when more than one fighter was responsible for bringing down the same enemy fighter, but still believed that it was he that finally brought it down and each claimed it as his own.

The 603 Spitfires landed back at Hornchurch at 08.30 hours.

* * *

Around midday a larger formation was plotted heading for Dover and this time the controllers sent their squadrons to intercept the enemy from the outset, with success not shown necessarily by the numbers of enemy aircraft shot down but by the fact that the raiding formation was broken early on. Four sections were also vectored from neighbouring sectors and over seventy Hurricanes and Spitfires rushed to intercept the 250 German bombers and fighters over Kent. This attack by the enemy bombers and the following one were aimed at the airfields once again, drawing up all available RAF fighters into the melee.

> Intelligence Report, 603 Squadron
> 12.08-13.35 hours. 2.9.40
>
> Nine aircraft took off to patrol Chatham at 22,000 feet. When five miles east of Sheppey, they saw large sections of Me109's, about 10 vic's with eight or nine in a vic, above them. The squadron went into line-astern and climbed to attack. A dogfight ensued. Below the Me109's there were about 50 Do17's in vic's of five, with Me109's a little above them weaving. The Do17's were doing about 220 mph.

The nine Spitfires were led by 'Uncle' George Denholm once again, flying Spitfire X4260, with Rushmer (X4263), Boulter (X4185), Haig (R6752), Berry (X4264), Hillary (X4277), Stapleton (X4274), Morton (N3056), and Read (L1057). Flight Lieutenant Rusty Rushmer claimed a Do 17 destroyed:

> When on patrol with the squadron at 25,000 feet, a number of Me109's were sighted. In the general melee at this height I became separated from the rest of the squadron and continued to patrol on the fringe of the clouds. AA fire aimed at a formation of 40-50 bombers with Me109's as escort flying at 15,000 feet towards the Isle of Sheppey attracted my attention.
>
> I manoeuvred for a position ahead of the formation and selecting a target dived down and attacked a Do17 from a quarter ahead. I followed through the

dive in the breakaway astern of the bombers and, on climbing up immediately, I saw a Do17 on fire diving into the Thames Estuary. A further attack carried out in a similar manner on a second bomber had no apparent effect.

Rusty had been leading a section in 'B' Flight. His attack was delivered at 12.45 hours, five miles east of the Isle of Sheppey at 15,000 feet.

Squadron Leader George Denholm claimed to have damaged a Me109:

> When on patrol with 603 Squadron at 22,000 feet we saw about ten vic's of Me109's, eight or nine in a vic. I put the squadron into line-astern and climbed to attack. In the dogfight which ensued, I fired a short burst at a Me109 from about 150 yards. The Me109 dived and thick black smoke came from the engine in intermittent puffs. I left the enemy aircraft 30 or 40 feet above the water about ten miles from the French coast.
>
> We then passed a Fw seaplane which was apparently scouting for pilots in the sea. The Me109 then pulled up stiffly and headed back over the seaplane. In the meantime I had broken off and made an attack on the seaplane but found that I had no more ammunition, so we returned home.

Denholm also made his attack at 12.45 hours, five miles east of the Isle of Sheppey at 15,000 feet. He noted on his combat report that he saw approximately 80 Me109s.

Richard claimed a Me109 destroyed during this patrol and on this occasion managed to complete his combat report after he had landed:

> When five miles off Sheppey, I saw a formation of Me109's. I chased one over to France and fired at it. I saw the enemy aircraft perspex hood break up, but as it was a head-on attack I was unable to see anything more of it. I then saw a squadron of Me109's at the same height as myself, 23,000', it was turning in formation. I attacked the outside Me109 with three short bursts and saw it spin down emitting black and white smoke. After a few seconds it caught fire.

Richard was flying with 'B' Flight and delivered his attack at 13.05 hours.

Pilot Officer Jim 'Black' Morton claimed a Me109 destroyed:

> At 20,000 feet below cloud the Squadron encountered about 12 Me109's about 1,000 feet above. They circled to attack us from astern and we turned also. I met one Me109 head-on and gave a short burst with no effect. After a while the general melee became split up. I found one Me109 unattended climbing above me and gave chase. Opened fire from 300 yards on port quarter slightly below at 23,000 feet. Enemy aircraft saw me then and did a steep left hand turn into a dive. I got in a good long burst and observed much white smoke from below the e/a. The e/a then went into a vertical dive and I did not see it again.
>
> Pilot Officer Berry who was in my vicinity reports having seen the a/c dive vertically into the ground. E/A was grey with very light wing tips.

Morton was with 'A' Flight and delivered his attack at 12.45 hours five miles east of Sheppey at 21,000 feet.

The squadron returned to base and landed at 13.35 hours. Haig landed afterwards with his undercarriage retracted owing to damage received by return fire from Do17s possibly of I/LG2, and the Me109s over the Thames estuary at 13.35 hours. Haig was unhurt and his aircraft XT-E repaired.

The last attack of the day approached the coast near Dover at 17.00 hours and consisted of another 250 bombers. Kesselring still had this formidable force available despite the magnitude of the last raid. As the enemy aircraft approached a massive dogfight developed near Ashford between about 70 Hurricanes and 15 Spitfires in action with about 160 Me109s. It only ended when they broke off soon after the Dover barrage commenced firing. Several situations like this occurred during this raid, high flying

Me109s diving out of the sun to attack the RAF fighters. The escorting fighters were flying much higher above the bombers than had been the case during earlier raids. This initially led to the belief that these groups of fighters were in fact a return to the free-hunt tactic, and for some days some controllers held back fighters mistaken in the belief that it was a lure when they actually were the escort. This ploy, although inadvertent, did produce some positive results.

The raids were successful in bombing the airfields once again at Biggin Hill, Kenley, and Hornchurch; Brooklands, where the Hawker and Vickers factory was situated, was bombed for the first time. Despite 100 bombs being dropped on Detling by a *Gruppe* of Do17s not much damage was done, but the smaller raid on Eastchurch resulted in mass devastation because the bomb dump, containing 350 bombs, was hit and exploded. Every building for 400 yards was demolished as well as the severing of the drainage mains and power cables along with the telephone lines.

Dowding's suspicions were confirmed by the Brooklands raid: the Germans would go for the aircraft factories as the RAF combat losses mounted. Park agreed and a standing patrol was maintained. Unfortunately it had been drawn away over into the Kent airspace on this afternoon, so the raid got through.

The final patrol of the day for 603 Squadron occurred in the late afternoon.

> Intelligence Patrol Report
> 16.04-18.20 hours. 2.9.40.
>
> Eleven aircraft climbed over base at 23,000 feet and saw a large solid triangle of about fifty bombers and at least fifty fighters, loose and in vic, stepped up to 20,000 feet. The squadron dived to attack and a dogfight ensued.

The patrol consisted of the eleven Spitfires of Squadron Leader Denholm (X4260), Rushmer (X4261), Morton (X4259), Carbury (X4263), Berry (R6626), Pease (P6721), Stokoe (N3056), Caister (X4250), Cardell (X4274), Stewart-Clark (L1057) and Hillary (X4277). This would be Dudley Stewart-Clark's first combat patrol since his return from leave and the squadron's move south. Richard was flying the same Spitfire as the majority of his patrols from Hornchurch, referred to in *The Last Enemy* as 'his' particular aircraft. Richard claimed a Me109 probable:

> I lost sight of the squadron and saw four Me109's in line astern above me. I climbed up and attacked the rear Me109, getting to about 50′ of him before opening fire. The Me109 went straight down with thick smoke pouring out and I did not see it again.

His attack was delivered at 17.10 hours in the airspace over Hornchurch at an altitude of 20,000 feet. He was with 'B' Flight at the beginning of the engagement.

Pilot Officer Dudley Stewart-Clark claimed a Me110 probable:

> I saw eight Me110's in loose echelon below me. I dived and made a head-on attack at the back Me109, which went into a spin with black smoke pouring out. I did not see the enemy aircraft again.

Stewart-Clark was with 'A' Flight and delivered his attack at 17.10 hours at an altitude of 17,000 feet.

It was quite common for the pilots to agree on a time of engagement after the event, and all record the same time in their reports. It was hardly likely that whilst diving to attack an enemy aircraft they would refer to the clock on the instrument panel and mentally record the time!

Brian Carbury claimed a Me109 destroyed:

> I broke away down when the enemy aircraft jumped on us out of the sun, then climbed again and waited about for other friendly aircraft to join up with. Sighted three aircraft, so chased after them diving, as I was above them, and found them

to be 3 Me109's in line astern going east. Carried out a rear beam attack on last enemy aircraft with no visible effect. I climbed up again and did a slight head-on deflection shot and his cockpit hood disappeared and the enemy aircraft went straight into the sea about ten miles off the coast, between Margate and Ramsgate.

Carbury was leading a section in 'B' Flight and delivered his attack at 18.00 hours, off Margate, at an altitude of 15,000 feet.

The Spitfire of Sergeant Jack Stokoe was hit during combat with the enemy Me110 fighters, which were possibly of II/ZG76, over Maidstone at 17.25 hours. He baled out but had been wounded in the attack and received burns when his aircraft caught fire. He was admitted to the Leeds Castle Hospital and later went to Queen Mary's Hospital, Sidcup. The remaining Spitfires of 603 Squadron landed back at Hornchurch at 18.20 hours.

I had the pleasure of meeting Jack Stokoe in September 1996, at the Purfleet Military Heritage, when he was reunited with Stapme Stapleton for the first time since the war. Jack told me that contrary to popular belief he did not go to the Queen Victoria Hospital, East Grinstead, at any time during his recovery from the burns received during this patrol and did not become a Guinea Pig.

By process of elimination I believe that this is the patrol that Richard refers to as being one of two that led to combat over or near French air space:

> I remember once going practically to France before shooting down a 109. There were two of them, flying at sea-level and headed for the French coast. Raspberry was flying beside me and caught one half-way across. I got right up close behind the second one and gave it a series of short bursts. It darted about in front, like a startled rabbit, and finally plunged into the sea about three miles off the French coast.

CHAPTER TEN

SHOT DOWN!

3 September 1940
RAF Hornchurch
08.00 am

The morning was becoming brighter after a damp and misty start. Ghostly, almost indiscernible outlines lurked at the limits of visibility in the claustrophobic gloom. The shroud of mist that was hanging over the airfield at dawn was being slowly burnt-off by the sun, revealing the Spitfires and Blenheims from various squadrons dispersed around the airfield.

Enemy aircraft had attacked the airfield a few days before and the recently filled bomb craters were clearly visible by the circles of fresh light earth on the lush green grass of the airfield. Ground crews were busy with the Spitfires, carrying out last minute maintenance jobs and ensuring that nothing would go wrong during the next sortie. Fitters and riggers were busy, each with their own aircraft to maintain, while the armourers, electricians and radio tradesmen dealt with each aircraft in turn, as required.

Tug Wilson and Freddy Marsland had finished working on Richard's Spitfire, X4277, XT-M, one of only eight remaining serviceable aircraft in the squadron.

At 10.30 a.m. the calm, concise voice of the controller came over the tannoy system ordering 603 Squadron to take off. A split second later the pilots emerged from the dispersal hut and dashed towards their respective aircraft. As they did so, the fitters climbed into the cockpits and prepared to start the engine while the rigger made ready the accumulator. The Merlin engine coughed, the propeller started to rotate, falteringly at first, flames belched from the exhausts and clouds of blue grey exhaust fumes drifted clear as the propeller gained momentum and the engine roared into life.

With his mae west already on and his helmet, goggles and oxygen mask clutched in his hand, Richard reached his Spitfire and strapped on his parachute which he had conveniently left at the ready on the left tailplane (some pilots preferred it laid out in the cockpit ready to fasten on once they were seated).

Clambering into the cockpit he was assisted by Tug Wilson as he fastened the Sutton harness. Freddy Marsland disconnected the accumulator and moved it clear of the area. Richard then plugged in the oxygen hose and radio transmitter lead.

Communication was established with the others in the flight and having signalled to the ground crew to remove the chocks with an outward wave of two open hands the pilot eased open the throttles with his left hand whilst steering using the rudder bar at his feet. The Spitfire moved off, and the grass behind the aircraft was systematically flattened by the slipstream whilst the dust from the newly filled-in bomb craters was blown into a swirling sepia cloud.

The flight commander led, with his number two and three either side, the sound of the engines increasing almost in unison, the wing-tips of the aircraft jerking up and down out of synchronisation as the wheels of the narrow undercarriage bumped over the airfield.

Richard busied himself with such tasks as switching on the gun-sight, placing his feet in the fastenings on the rudder bar, designed to keep them in position at all times during combat, and checking on his aircraft's performance generally to give him vital assurance of his machine's reliability in battle, while at the same time remaining aware of his position relative to the rest of his flight.

As they climbed away from the aerodrome the eight aircraft formed into two vics of three and one pair. There had been little time to replace the lost aircraft and pilot from their last patrol on the previous day. Richard couldn't help but notice from his cockpit, with the noise and vibration of the Merlin engine situated only a few feet in front, the peaceful beauty of the countryside below. A patchwork quilt of gold, green and brown. Workers in the fields. Horses and farm machinery hard at work, seemingly oblivious to what was going on in the skies above apart from the occasional wave when the pilot was low enough to acknowledge. The contrast between what they were doing and what these pilots were about to do, to endure, was stark. As they climbed, the scene below took on the appearance of a model gradually decreasing in scale. Such peace to possible confrontation with death.

As they climbed through the morning mist until breaking through the cloud above into a clear, bright blue, sunlit sky, the warmth greeted Richard physically and mentally.

The controller provided George Denholm with the necessary information for him to be able to guide his aircraft to intercept the enemy, and at about 22,000 feet, the same height as themselves, they spotted six Dornier Do17 bombers in vic formation with an escort of 12 Messerschmitt Bf109s in close attendance. A few thousand feet above this formation they saw another escort of 12 109s.

George dispensed with ground assistance with the cry of 'Tally Ho', signalling that he had a visual fix on the enemy, having previously informed the other pilots who had not already spotted the enemy aircraft, exactly where they were.

The aircraft were ordered to attack the fighter cover while another squadron would attack the bombers. This involved climbing to try to gain the upper hand. The Me109s had seen them and dived down to meet their disadvantaged foe. The experienced pilots knew that to remain in a head-on attack position would be best. Those that turned away would present a slower, clearer target to the enemy.

The opposing forces met in the clear blue skies above the Channel and the Kent countryside in a confusion of twisting turning machines, each attempting to gain the upper hand. The pilots breathed hard, the adrenaline flowing, the heart racing, their heads turning anxiously from one direction to another looking for a victim and at the same time trying to avoid becoming the victim of an enemy pilot. It was all happening so fast. The veterans would use their skill to try to keep a cool mind to out-fly, out-think and out-manoeuvre the enemy, but their marksmanship would be the ultimate proof of experience. Their alertness to attack from enemy fighters would also be their saving.

To the inexperienced the whole ordeal would be terrifying, for the thought that they could be facing imminent death could cause total panic. The task of merely flying the aircraft would be thrown into disarray, and to try to fight to survive and not become fodder for the enemy fighters would be a very difficult feat indeed. It depended so much on the state of mind and a great deal of luck for all parties involved. Even experience couldn't always ensure survival.

A Spitfire managed to get on to the tail of a 109 and fire a short burst. As the vibration from the eight machine guns ceased the acrid smell of cordite filled the cramped cockpit. The enemy fighter had been badly hit and, spewing glycol and oil, fell towards the pure white cloud below in a seemingly terminal dive, the attacking Spitfire quite correctly rejecting the chance to finish the enemy off for fear of falling to another fighter.

Richard had seen a 109 fly right across the nose of his aircraft from starboard to port and he rapidly flung his control column to his left simultaneously pushing his left foot hard against the rudder bar and maintaining his left hand on the throttle. This raised the Spitfire's starboard wing and rolled it to the left in pursuit of the enemy fighter.

Richard had gained the upper hand and his aircraft came down from above and behind the 109 in the perfect position. He opened fire with a two second burst from about 50 yards. The enemy aircraft was hit and immediately began to lose oil and glycol with the tell-tale trail streaming from the engine and back over the upper and lower wing surfaces. The enemy fighter had been mortally wounded but Richard hung on for another attack, a confirmed kill.

One of Richard's 603 Squadron colleagues had just managed to shake off a 109 from his tail, and the airspace behind was now clear. As he looked for a possible target, he saw Richard's Spitfire attacking a crippled 109 from practically point blank range, but was alarmed to see another 109 that had come to the German pilot's assistance. He yelled a warning to Richard over his radio but knew he was too late. It was all over in seconds. The 109 gained on the Spitfire and as the British fighter filled the Revi gun-sight the German pilot simultaneously opened fire with both cannon and machine guns. Richard's Spitfire slowed perceptibly as the shells struck home at the rear of the engine cowling just in front of the cockpit. With smoke and glycol pouring from the aircraft it started to lose height and dive towards the cloud below. The onlooking pilot confirmed that his tail was clear of any enemy fighters and glanced back at the now flaming Spitfire. Richard had slid open the canopy but instead of baling out, his arms dropped and he slumped back in his seat. The flames could now be seen licking at Richard's face. As he shouted into his radio for Richard to get out he noticed the aircraft start a slow roll onto its back. Richard's head moved perceptibly downwards in the now inverted Spitfire and appeared in the canopy opening momentarily before his body slid slowly out, like a butterfly slipping from its suspended chrysalis cocoon, and fell free at last from the inferno. After a tense delay the parachute was deployed and Richard's 603 colleague, finding the skies now clear of any activity, continued on his heading back towards his airfield, safe in the belief that he had seen Richard escape from his crippled aircraft.

* * *

The coastguard had been watching for any signs of the battle raging in the skies high above the cloud. A few moments before he had seen a 109 appear through the cloud high above the Channel in a dive which culminated in a giant splash several miles off shore. A few moments later a flaming Spitfire also dove straight into the Channel. As he maintained his watch a pilot descended through the cloud on a parachute. He watched until it had landed in the sea and then after estimating the position and distance off-shore notified the lifeboat at the nearest station.

It was 90 minutes before the crew of the lifeboat finally found Richard. Badly burned, blinded by the swollen flesh surrounding his eyes, which had been unprotected because his goggles had been kept raised to reduce his feeling of claustrophobia, he was delirious and entangled in his own parachute lines but still alive.

They made a temporary shelter on the fore deck in which to protect him from the rays of the sun. They administered rum through his badly swollen and blistered lips and there was some degree of grateful acknowledgement for this. However, it was not long before his de-sensitised state brought about by the time spent in the cold sea had been replaced by warmth which ultimately re-established his senses and heightened the effects of shock, bringing excruciating pain from the terrible burns to his face, legs and hands.

* * *

Not long after Richard had descended into the cooling waters of the English Channel, the Luftwaffe fighters landed back at their bases. The pilot of one unit had achieved two confirmed enemy aircraft destroyed during the patrol, both had been shot down over the Channel, both pilots had taken to their parachutes. He had been lucky in some respects but his luck had been due to change for the better. Having descended on the enemy fighters with a height advantage the Messerschmitts had become embroiled in a myriad of dogfights. The first Spitfire to fall to his guns had made the fundamental error of remaining on the tail of his adversary too long and had paid the price. The aircraft had gone down in flames. The second had not seen him until it was too late. He had seen the pilot bale out. The German pilot was Hauptmann Erich Bode, *Gruppe Kommandeur* of II/JG26, a very experienced pilot who had been in the Luftwaffe for many years. As he taxied his aircraft to the dispersal area where his ground crew were waiting, he swung the tail towards them, positioning the aircraft in readiness for the next patrol, and engulfing them in a cloud of dust blown up by the propeller backwash. As Bode looked over towards them he raised two fingers, indicating two kills, and the expression of delight on their faces confirmed that they had understood his signal.

The 603 ORB shows that 603 Squadron suffered the loss of two aircraft with both pilots, Richard and Dudley Stewart-Clark, badly injured. During this combat, while flying Spitfire X4277 Richard was shot down by Bode (pronounced Boder) at 10.04 off Margate. He had been very fortunate indeed in that, although grievously burnt, his unconscious body had fallen free from the cockpit. He had been unable to escape prior to this occurrence. Richard was listed on CC List 297 'Wounded (FB)'.

Just four minutes later Bode struck again at 10.08 when he also managed to shoot down Stewart-Clark in Spitfire X4185, although the RAF pilot managed to maintain control of the aircraft before finally deciding to abandon when he baled out over Creeksea Church, Burnham. He had received a bullet wound to the lower leg and was admitted to Chelmsford Hospital on landing. Two rapid kills by the leader of the Luftwaffe fighter squadron would seem to indicate that both had fallen to the guns of an ace. Although he was an extremely experienced pilot these were the first and second enemy aircraft he had destroyed in combat. It is interesting to note that Feldwebel Hoffmann of 4/JG26 also claimed to have shot down a Spitfire of 603 Squadron at 10.20 am over Hockley. It was unconfirmed.

* * *

Earlier that morning, as recorded by Richard in the 'Proem' in *The Last Enemy*:

> We came out on to the tarmac at about eight o'clock. During the night our machines had been moved from the dispersal point over to the hangars. All the machine tools, oil, and general equipment had been left on the far side of the aerodrome. I was worried. We had been bombed a short time before, and my plane had been fitted out with a new cockpit hood. This hood, unfortunately, would not slide open along its groove; and with a depleted ground staff and no tools, I began to fear it never would. Unless it did open, I shouldn't be able to bale out in a hurry if I had to . . .

The pilots had actually been out at dispersal a lot earlier than eight and the aircraft had not been moved to the hangars – an action that would have contradicted the reasoning behind their being dispersed in the first place. The ground staff were indeed depleted, as a result of the deaths and injuries which occurred during the bombing raid of 31 August.

As previously mentioned, Richard's Spitfire was never on the ground during the enemy bombing raids on Hornchurch. However, Richard's own words, 'We had been bombed a short time before, and my plane had been fitted with a new cockpit hood', imply only that his aircraft had been damaged as a result of the bombing. Richard's Spitfire was attended by his regular ground crew Tug Wilson and Freddy Marsland (Tug Wilson was a qualified fitter air-frame engineer FAE). If Richard's aircraft had needed a new canopy, it would have been they who fitted it, and they and the other members of the 603 ground crew have no recollection of such a job being carried out. Tug and Freddy survived the war and passed away a few years ago.

The eight 603 Squadron Spitfires had been attacked by Me109s of II/JG26 that had arrived over the Essex coast and Thames estuary to cover the bombers' retreat, in an operation intended to make maximum use of the 109's limited range and endurance.

Intelligence Patrol Report, 603 Sqn.
09.15-10.30 hours, 3.9.40.

> Eight aircraft took off from Hornchurch. At 22,000 feet over Manston they saw about six Do17's in vic at the same height and about 12 Me109's; above this formation was a further formation of 12 Me109's. The Squadron attacked the fighters, which they considered to be inferior to any they had encountered before.

The Me109's had no yellow noses. P/O Stapleton took off with 54 Squadron and when south of Harwich, dived on to a Do17 and shot it down.

Despite this record and his own combat report stating that he took off on patrol with 54 Squadron, 60 years later Stapme Stapleton has absolutely no memory of this. He remembers taking off as No.2 to Brian Carbury who was leading the section and Richard as No.3. He also recalled that his Spitfire was hit in combat and Brian Carbury escorted him to Rochford where he landed. This went unrecorded. Richard's version in *The Last Enemy* states that the three took off together on this patrol, confirming Stapme's version: 'I was flying No.3 in Brian's section, with 'Stapme' Stapleton on the right: the third section consisted of only two machines . . .'

The 603 Operational Record Book shows us that eight aircraft did take off, as Richard recorded, with two threes and a pair. To confuse matters further it also states that Brian Carbury did not fly on this patrol. The 54 Squadron ORB states that 12 Spitfires took off on their first patrol but at 10.15, one hour later.

According to the 603 ORB, the Spitfires of Denholm (X4260), Macdonald (X4259), Caister (L1057), Pease (X4263), Stewart-Clark (X4185), Hillary (X4277), Stapleton (R6626) and Cardell (X4274) took off on this patrol. Richard was flying X4277, XT-M, for the fourth patrol in succession.

George Denholm led the squadron at the head of 'A' Flight. Ken Macdonald was Denholm's deputy when he remained on the ground. According to the records, with Carbury absent from this patrol two vics and a singleton flew out. Pilot Officer Caister claimed a Me109 destroyed:

> When on patrol with 603 Sqn, 12 or more Me109's dived on the squadron from above, a few miles east of Manston. Six Me109's broke away east from below and did not enter engagement. I attacked from astern, one Me109 and after a few seconds bursts it climbed steeply; closing up with a long burst I saw the e/a out of control. I had fired a few seconds burst at close range and broke off, and almost stalled. Turning away from the e/a I had attacked, I fired a few seconds burst at another Me109 almost dead ahead. This machine did not break off but passed me within a few yards distance. There appeared to be six streams of fire coming from the e/a. I did not observe any damage. I saw at least two and perhaps a third explosion on the water, either bombs or aircraft crashing. Turning round I looked for somebody of my squadron. I noticed an aircraft in my mirror, but I was too far away for it to start firing. Spiralling down in a steep dive I lost it, and being short of petrol I refuelled at Manston, taking off immediately and returned to base.

Caister had been with 'A' Flight when he delivered his attack at 09.45 hours over the Channel at 20,000 feet. He opened fire at 250 yards and closed to 50 yards, firing a burst of ten seconds.

Peter Pease claimed a Me109 destroyed during this patrol:

> I saw one Me109 over the sea about 5,000 feet below me. I could see no other aircraft above or below me, so I dived to make a beam attack. When I was still out of range, the enemy aircraft did a half-roll and dived vertically. It never pulled out, and crashed into the sea.

Peter Pease was with 'B' Flight when he shot down the Me109 20 miles north-east of Margate at an altitude of 12,000 feet.

Peter Pease's claim was confirmed as being a Messerschmitt Bf109E-4 of II Stab/JG26. The pilot Leutnant Eckardt Roch, the *Gruppen* adjutant, was missing at the time of the report and was later confirmed as having been killed in action. He had four kills to his credit.

Pilot Officer Stapme Stapleton claimed a Dornier Do17 destroyed:

> When patrolling with 54 Squadron, I sighted a formation of 15 Do17's,

accompanied by 20 Me110's. The enemy aircraft were flying in line astern and weaving about in 'S' turns. As we had some 8,000 feet on this formation, the squadron went into line astern and attacked the Do17's. I fired at a Do17 in my first attack, with no visible effect. I climbed up again into the sun and attacked a Do17 which had one engine stopped. I attacked on the starboard side, stopping the other engine with a deflection burst of four seconds.

Stapme delivered his attack 15 miles south-west of Harwich at 09.45 hours at an altitude of 20,000 feet.

At 18.35 hours that evening, 54 Squadron took off from RAF Hornchurch and flew to RAF Catterick.

By 10 September 1940, only seven of the pilots that had flown to Catterick were still with the squadron. Of the 54 Squadron pilots to depart, Pilot Officers Peter Howes and Ludwik Martel were posted to 603 and made a prompt return to Hornchurch. Of the new arrivals, Flying Officer Claude Goldsmith and Pilot Officer Peter Dexter were also destined to move to 603 Squadron at Hornchurch.

* * *

Richard had been hit at approximately 25,000 feet, whilst pursuing an already damaged enemy fighter, when he should have broken off his attack in order to avoid the inevitable attack on his own aircraft. According to Richard, when he had initially tried to open the canopy in order to bale out, it would not move back sufficiently on its runners to enable him to escape what had now become a terrible blazing inferno in the cramped claustrophobic confines of the cockpit. A blow-torch of searing heat blasted back against his body from the leg well, burning his trouser legs off in seconds and scorching his legs, his flying boots offering the only protection. He unfastened his straps in order to get a better purchase on the canopy handles. Richard was not wearing gloves. He had spurned the idea of wearing his Mk IV goggles, apart from during take-off and landing, because he found them restricting. Now he would pay the price. At this time they were raised up on his B Type leather helmet. The fuel-fed flames blew back onto his bare flesh.

After what had been only a matter of seconds, his hands and face were terribly burnt, the pain had started to relent and he was succumbing to what now seemed as the inevitable. The radio lead and oxygen hose were still connected, and the flames had fed on the oxygen flow into his Type 19 oxygen mask, burning his upper lip. The Type 19 mask was a variant on the Type D which was green fabric outer with a chamois lining. What is relevant is that the mask Richard was wearing did not form a seal on the face and, in addition, the flow of oxygen was continuous. When he inhaled, he drew in the flames which fed on the oxygen flow.

He had managed to pull back the canopy far enough in order to bale out, which was, bearing in mind the size of the canopy, practically fully open anyway. But he lost consciousness and fell back into his seat.

Richard later blamed his inability to escape the inferno on the new canopy that had been fitted. It wouldn't run smoothly on its runners when opening or closing. It is interesting to note that by this time the Spitfire Mk I cockpit hood had been replaced by a new updated version with the now familiar bulges which provided a better all-round view. It also had a properly designed jettisoning mechanism which made a great difference when trying to exit the cockpit in a hurry. The jettisoning toggle had been an option for Richard as he struggled to escape. Additionally, the canopy on the Spitfire MkI was more difficult to open at high speed.

Later, in June 1942, during an interview at the BBC, Richard recalled, for the second time on radio, his memories of being shot down. But this time he made no mention of the canopy jamming, inhibiting his escape.

* * *

He was going to die, and the pain would be gone. Richard's last action as he lost consciousness was to move the stick in an attempt to turn the Spitfire onto its back in order to bale out, he then put his hands over his eyes as the seering flames brought fresh agony. Pilot Officer Geoffrey Page was an RAF fighter pilot to suffer very similar burns to Richard and later got to know him in hospital. When recounting his own experiences he told me:

> I screamed in sheer terror when I was hit, but then as the flames overwhelmed me
> I started to lose consciousness and this feeling of complete calm swept over me.
> It must be some kind of safety valve that our body provides.

Richard's burning aircraft had been falling from the sky throughout his attempts to escape, and finally the Spitfire fell into an interminable screaming dive for several thousand feet more before, at a height of approximately 10,000 feet, it rolled over into an inverted position and Richard's prone, apparently lifeless form fell free. His head had smashed against the inside of the canopy frame before he slithered out. It was a wonder his neck was not broken and an even greater wonder how he had escaped death at all.

His Spitfire continued its final plunge into the sea below. Having reached terminal velocity the engine was destroyed long before it hit the water by the excess of revs. It has been said by those that have experienced similar horrors that there are only a few seconds to escape a burning Spitfire or Hurricane cockpit before you succumb to the intense heat and flames. It is very unlikely therefore that Richard would have remained trapped inside his aircraft as it fell 15,000 feet, before he finally fell free. He would have been burnt far more severely, probably to death and if by some miracle he had survived, it is most likely that he would have succumbed to his burns as the result of the other life-threatening physiological problems, symptomatic of severe burns.

Richard's brief period of combat in the Battle of Britain had come to an end, although the biggest battle was still ahead. He had relentlessly thrown himself into combat with that same reckless abandon and determination to succeed that had led to certain individuals suggesting such an attitude may well lead to his demise. But the country may not have survived the conflict without pilots with such an attitude.

* * *

On the morning of 3 September Edwyna Hillary was in a taxi, on her way to her daily part-time job with the Red Cross, when she had a feeling of great foreboding that something had happened to her son. She assessed the situation and was satisfied that she was not ill, and ultimately thought that it was not possible to rationalise her feelings in any other way than to believe that something was indeed wrong. She was also aware that as it was nearly midday the RAF fighters were indeed already in action in the skies above. Edwyna therefore tapped on the glass partition to gain the driver's attention and asked him to take her back to her flat in Knightsbridge Court. Both Richard and her husband had previously joked with her about these feelings she had, but this time she disregarded the possibility of being laughed at again; the feeling was too intense.

Edwyna Hillary sat all day waiting for some kind of notification that Richard had been killed or injured, be it by telegram or telephone. As evening approached the telephone rang. Preparing herself in the belief that the news would not be good she lifted the receiver and the voice of Squadron Leader J.E.A. Frazer the station adjutant, asked to speak to Michael Hillary. The task of breaking the news to a father about a son that had been killed, wounded or was missing was something that Frazer had not grown used to, and understandably so. Even bearing in mind the frequency with which he now had to make such calls, it was still a very difficult task and the disassociation that a pilot could adopt when a colleague was killed was not possible, as his own occupation did not provide the same intensity. Now as he had to break the news to a mother he found the task more difficult than ever. Initially he tried to present the news as gently as he could by praising, perhaps even glamorising, Richard's outstanding achievements in the battle and how highly he was thought of in the squadron, but he was waffling and Edwyna, not one to mince words, cut in and demanded to know what had happened to her son. She asked firstly where her son was and Frazer told her that he was reported as 'missing'. His aircraft had been seen going down in flames that day over the North Sea. But she was not to fear the worst. Boats were out patrolling at all hours, and many survivors had been brought back every day. He hoped to ring again soon with good news.

* * *

Richard regained consciousness shortly after falling free from the cockpit. Instinctively he reached for his ripcord and tugged, oblivious at this stage to any pain or damage to his hands. The silk and risers unravelled and with a crack the parachute filled with air, checking his descent and causing the harness to dig into his groin. He was still at quite a high altitude, time enough to ponder his predicament. As he drifted down towards the surface of the sea, the detail of the wavelets became visible on the surface telling him that he was getting close. Even in a seriously injured and concussed state the now-recognised 'battlefield shock' allowed some relief from the agonies of his injuries. In time this effect would wear off and the true pain acknowledged.

Just before he dropped into the sea he made a failed attempt to unfasten his parachute harness, hoping that he would be able to swim free of the rigging before it ensnared him and dragged him under. A not unnatural reaction. As his body splashed into the sea water, he could not have realised for a moment the long term advantage of having inadvertently immersed his burnt body in saline rather than having landed in some field in Kent. He would later realise how fortunate he had been. After initially being totally submerged, the buoyancy in his life-jacket ensured his head bobbed clear of the water, and kept it there. When he tried to check the time he became aware of how badly he had been burnt. The watch had gone and the burnt, dead, white shreds of skin hung from his wrists and hands. His hands had now become so painful that he gave up his futile attempts to undo his parachute harness. The smell of his burnt flesh was pungent in his nostrils and it made him nauseous. His lips were swelling up, as was the tissue around his eyes. He tried to assess the situation. Believing no one on shore had seen him come down, he felt there was little chance of rescue, and it was unlikely that he would be fortunate to be found by a passing boat. He was also aware that his Mae West was not likely to keep him afloat for an indefinite period. As his body temperature started to drop, the sea now began to feel a lot colder than when he had first entered, and coupled with the effects of shock and the pain from his injuries, he entered the early stages of hypothermia. He tried to keep his spirits up by humming to himself and calling for help. A thousand thoughts went through his semi-delirious mind as he bobbed alone on the surface of a very large sea. The tissue now became so swollen that he believed he had gone blind. The lids had become like that of a boxer that had received more than an acceptable share of punishment to the eyes, swollen and shiny, with the edges stuck together.

Believing that he was going to die, he attempted to override the function of the Mae West and release the air from it. This failed because he was too entangled in his shroud lines which kept him afloat like Sargasso sea-weed. After trying to release the harness once again he lay back, amused at his predicament but by this time no longer in control of his emotions. In *The Last Enemy* Richard later wrote:

> Goethe once wrote that no one, unless he had led the full life and realised himself completely, had the right to take his own life. Providence seemed determined that I should not incur the great man's wrath. It is often said that a dying man re-lives his whole life in one rapid kaleidoscope. I merely thought gloomily of the Squadron returning, of my mother at home, and of the few people who would miss me. Outside my family I could count them on the fingers of one hand.

He began to feel terribly lonely, and then he heard voices in the distance. A line was thrown to him which he grabbed, but as he was hauled in the burnt skin came away from his hands and he lost grip. Eager hands then grasped the lines from his parachute and pulled him to the side of the boat. With Richard too weak to assist, his parachute harness was released with far more ease than he could have imagined and with a great deal of effort he was pulled over the side.

*   *   *

The coastguard had seen a parachutist descend into the sea and ordered the lifeboat out. The report reads:

> Margate, Kent. At 10.15 a.m. on the 3rd September 1940, the coastguard reported a parachutist in the sea seven miles NE of Reculver. The sea was smooth with a light NW wind. The motor life-boat '*J.B. Proudfoot*,' on temporary duty at the Station, was launched at 10.20 a.m. and at 11.45 a.m. found a badly burned airman on the point of collapse, after over an hour in the sea. He was taken into the lifeboat, and the honorary secretary, who was on-board, bandaged him and gave stimulants. Another boat was asked to wireless for medical help to be in readiness, and after a journey at full speed the airman was landed at 1.00 p.m. and taken to Margate Hospital. Rewards £5:12:6. The Civil Service Lifeboat Fund.

The motor lifeboat was a large 46 feet 9 inch Watson Class vessel which was normally based at Dover, but had been seconded to Margate to assist with such rescues in the absense of the regular Margate lifeboat, the *Lord Southborough*, which was being re-fitted at Routledge following damage received during the Dunkirk evacuation. It was usually launched from the boathouse and was frequently in use. It returned to the inside of the harbour arm where the steps allowed the rescue services easy access with a stretcher, as was the case with Richard. During the long return journey (the top speed of the lifeboat was only 8 knots) the crew remembered Richard's terrible condition and pain-wracked words: 'How much further? How much further?' The ambulance crew and a doctor were waiting when the boat docked.

The Honorary Secretary who had helped tend to Richard's injuries and gave him a drop of rum 'with wonderful results' (not Brandy as has been previously stated), was Mr A.C. Robinson, who also used a blanket to erect the temporary shade to protect Richard from the direct sunlight as he lay on the deck. It was not usual practice for the Honorary Secretary to be onboard during a rescue; it was his job to man the telephone at the lifeboat station. The coxswain was a Mr Edward D. 'Trunky' Parker DSM who as skipper of the *Lord Southborough*, with his current crew, had received his award for bravery during the Dunkirk evacuation. The signalman was Mr Dennis 'Sinbad' Price and the winchman/launcher was Mr Henry 'Mussel' Sandwell. Henry Sandwell had spotted Richard in the sea just as they were about to give up the search and helped nurse him on the return journey, while Dennis Price bandaged his burns. By 1952, twelve years after he had dragged Richard out of the North Sea, Dennis Price had become the coxwain of the Margate lifeboat, the *North Foreland*, and had been awarded the Silver Medal following the rescue of two men from the rigging of a wrecked barque. The rest of the *J.B. Proudfoot* crew that day were: H. 'Goosie' Parker, Bowman; T. Harman, 2nd Cox; Alf Lacey (later BEM), 2nd Mechanic (Alf was the crewman who had thrown Richard a heaving line in the attempt to pull him to the side of the lifeboat); A. Morris Buller, Crew; and A. Ladd, Crew.

*   *   *

The *J.B. Proudfoot* reduced revs and slowed for entry into the small harbour at Margate. As the coxwain steered his craft towards its mooring point they could see the ambulance waiting, its doors open ready to receive the injured airman. The ambulancemen were standing on the steps that led down to the water's edge with stretcher at the ready. Once in the ambulance Richard was rushed the very short distance to the Margate General Hospital, just a few minutes drive from the steps where the boat docked. As the hyperthermia began to subside and the warmth returned to his limbs, thus did the pain return to the damaged nerve ends, seared by the flames. The pain was excruciating and the relief of the hyperdermic and its pain relieving morphine which was administered on arrival at the accident and emergency unit must have been immense. The medical staff busied themselves by cutting the remnants of his charred uniform, trying hard not to make unnecessary contact with the white, swollen and shredded skin. Richard was able to mumble his name and next of kin when asked to do so to enable the staff to contact his squadron and let them know that he was still alive, albeit in a bad way. The squadron could then inform his parents.

* * *

For the next few days Richard's life hung in the balance. Severe shock was the greatest threat at this time, with his body weak and the pain insufferable, his physical and mental strength was slowly being sapped from his body. The remains of his eyelids were smeared with gentian violet and his burnt hands had been scrubbed and coated with tannic acid after initial assessment, the salinity of the sea water having proved a more than suitable first treatment. The tannic acid however dried to a hard brittle coating and was to prove to be less suitable than had originally been thought for this purpose. The burns to his legs were somewhat superficial compared with his face and hands but nonetheless painful.

His injuries were bandaged and his arms and legs suspended from a frame which had been erected around the bed, which gave visitors the impression that his whole body had been suspended over the bed. Its purpose was to reduce the blood pressure in these extremities by keeping them in a position above the heart, thus considerably reducing the pulsating agony that would have been endured, had they been on the bed. This practice also served to maintain an even pressure. His face was bandaged leaving just his eyes and mouth exposed. The days ahead were filled with a mixture of delirium, pain and relief as yet more morphine was administered.

The next morning, his parents rushed to be by his bedside, but there was not much to see and he was in no condition to acknowledge their presence. Richard was kept at Margate General Hospital for four days. It was only a clearing station, and a busy one at that, but his condition had to stabilise before he could be moved. The effects of his experience, the physical and mental trauma, and shock as a result of both could still claim his life during those hours after being picked up.

On 10 September Michael Hillary wrote to the RNLI to thank them for saving the life of his son.

* * *

On the evening of that Tuesday, as soon as he found the time, Peter Pease telephoned his fiancée Denise. He confirmed that he had returned unharmed from his latest patrol and gave her the news from what had been an eventful day. At the end of the brief conversation he told her that Richard was 'missing'. Knowing what Richard meant to him she tried to offer some sympathetic support, but with the daily casualty list growing rapidly there was little that could be said. Such eventualities were expected and had now become commonplace. The intensity of the battle had intensified to the point where Peter and Denise met occasionally but communicated mainly by telephone and letter when meetings were not possible.

Meanwhile the squadron, regrouping once again, was licking their wounds; the experienced pilots were trying to give the new arrivals every chance they could to survive their first few encounters, although at the risk of being shot down themselves. They had only been in the front line for a week themselves during which time 14 of their Spitfires had been destroyed with four pilots killed and six more wounded.

Stapme Stapleton remembers the day Richard was shot down, and with great clarity:

> I flew No.2 to Brian Carbury and Hillary flew No.3. I have no idea why it was recorded that I flew with No.54 Squadron that day, because I didn't. We didn't know he had been shot down. I was concerned by the fact that my aircraft had been badly hit and was handling very badly. I hadn't seen the enemy aircraft that hit me, all I had experienced was the noise of the sudden clatter of strikes on my

aircraft. All you hear is the Takka, Takka Tak! as the bullets hit your aircraft. I asked Carbury:

'What does my tail look like?' I knew that it had to have been hit by the lack of response from the controls.

'It looks like a bloody collander!' came the reply from Carbury. I landed at Rochford to find that both my tyres had also been punctured. Hillary's action that day has been well documented but that experience of mine has not been mentioned.

Stapme Stapleton's forced-landing on 7 September 1940, however, was recorded. He added:

We didn't have much to do with Hillary after he had been shot down. Like the other casualties, we missed him, he was a very nice fellow. He couldn't have been a very easy man to get on with after he was injured. That transformation from being a very good-looking young man with a big ego to a man with such injuries must have been terribly difficult. I don't know how he managed to cope with it. He didn't wear his goggles so the burns occurred from the forehead down to his nose. It is possible that his top lip may have been burnt when he took his oxygen mask off, which would have been as stupid as not wearing goggles, but what is more likely is that the flames that seered his lip were drawn in and fed on the flow of the inflammable oxygen that continued to flow to his mask during his attempts to free himself from the inferno of the cockpit. He makes no mention of removing his mask. Nobody warned us of the dangers of the flammability of our oxygen supply in such situations. I was in situations where my aircraft had been hit and the engine was streaming glycol and smoke. I couldn't see a thing looking straight ahead. I was lucky in that my Spitfire never caught fire. But I can appreciate that it would have been like a blow-torch right in your face.

In some rare cases pilots preferred to fasten this style of oxygen mask in position with the nose uncovered. The Type 19 and D variant, with canvas and chamois mask, made it possible to fasten the mask with the top edge across the upper lip.

* * *

In just one week of combat the pilots of 603 Squadron had flown a total of 164 patrols. Although there were squadrons that flew more, it is interesting to have a look at what they had done in those few days Richard was with them.

Each of the pilots of No.603 Squadron flew on average 15 patrols between 28 August, when they arrived at Hornchurch, and 3 September, when Richard was shot down. I have compiled a list indicating the number of sorties flown by each squadron member. The date shown before each pilot's name is the date on which they flew their first patrol from Hornchurch. An asterix denotes they were killed during the last patrol.

28th Benson 1*
28th Berry 12
28th Boulter 12
2nd Sept Caister 3
28th Carbury 10
1st Sept Cardell 3
28th Cunningham 2*
28th Denholm 11
28th Gilroy 7
28th Haig 8
28th Hillary 11
28th Ken MacDonald 11
28th Don MacDonald 1*

28th Morton 12
28th Pease 9
28th Pinckney 2
28th Read 10
28th Ritchie 2
28th Rushmer 7
28th Sarre 4
28th Stapleton 9
2nd Sept Stewart-Clark 2
28th Stokoe 9
28th Waterston 6*

Total: 164 patrols by 24 pilots.

Berry, Boulter and Morton achieved the highest number in this period, with Denholm, Ken Macdonald and Richard achieving the next greatest number. It is interesting to note that while such statistics are only to give the reader some idea of the intensity of the fighting during this period of 603's and Richard's involvement, it does show us how the pilots were rotated in order to give brief rests from combat patrols. Although some flew very little during this time, their period of intense fighting was yet to come.

Ken MacDonald, Rushmer, Cardell and Pease did not survive the Battle of Britain; Pinckney, Stewart-Clark, Boulter and Richard did not survive the war.

The day after Richard had been shot down Michael and Edwyna Hillary received a telegram at 10.25 hours which stated: 4th September 1940 – Richard Hillary 'reported wounded but not believed serious.'

The same day, Sergeant Alfred Sarre forced-landed his Spitfire X4263 at Elstead near Ashford as a result of engine failure, and Pilot Officer Caister shot down a Messerschmitt Bf109E-1 of 3/JG27 off Dunkirk at 10.40 hours. The pilot was Feldwebel Wilhelm Harting who was wounded and later rescued from the sea. A similar flight near the French coast would bring the war to a premature end for Caister a few days later.

CHAPTER ELEVEN

THE LONG ROAD BACK

September 1940 – November 1940

Richard's injuries consisted of serious deep dermal/second degree flame burns to the areas of his face not covered by his oxygen mask, causing full-thickness skin loss signified by the skin hanging in shreds. More particularly, the flesh around his eyes including the eyelids and upper cheek area, the lower forehead not protected by his flying helmet, the bridge of the nose and his top lip were badly burned (flame burns to the face cause the eye area and lips to puff up and close). His eyebrows and lashes had been burnt off. His eyelids would have to be replaced when the time came (ectropion), as there was a very real risk of infection and blindness if his eyes were left without the protection and care of eyelids.

From a practical point of view his worst injuries were to his hands. They had also received deep dermal flame burns, with thrombosed veins, and were terribly burnt, the right being worst affected. As with the face, there was full thickness skin loss, and it was soon realised that no amount of surgery would bring about the return of their full function. He had also received less serious burns to his legs which, although very painful, would recover completely.

Richard's memories of those few days at Margate General Hospital were initially of great pain, delirium and of floating in and out of consciousness. When he regained the ability to assess his position in an apparently rational way he was confronted with his awful predicament.

It must have been a quite terrible experience to be in such great pain and unable to see, and with the acrid nauseating smell of his own burnt flesh in his nostrils. Intermittently waking from fearsome nightmares Richard found himself back in his Spitfire reliving all the horror. He heard the calming voices of the faceless nurses offering reassurance before drifting once more into another nightmare, a nightmare that would be a mixture of the realities of life going on around him and vivid dreams. It would be almost impossible to tell them apart. The tone of their voices and the presence around him were something that he became sensitive to without his sight. Under the tannic acid coating his skin felt taut. Those pilots that received burns so severe that the nerve endings had been destroyed felt less pain from those specific areas. (The skin consists of three layers. The top layer is the epidermis, the secondary layer is the dermis and the third layer of subdermal fat supports a plexi of nerves and blood vessels. Under these layers of skin is a layer known as the fascia and then muscle. It is to the depth of the third layer that the damage to nerve endings occurs.) Richard's burns, although not as disfiguring as those received by some aircrew in WWII, had not been so severe as to have destroyed the nerve ends and it was for this reason that he suffered so much pain. The morphine served to make the pain more tolerable while it was at its most effective, but it failed to eliminate it totally. The use of morphine as it was then has since been reviewed as being unsafe in modern day medicine, but the choice then was to provide pain relief or let the patient die in agony from a combination of the injuries, shock and the resulting exhaustion as the body finally gave out. Richard's condition was that he was so weak and his body so pain-racked that he cared about nothing.

He was fed copious quantities of fluid for the first two days in the form of bottles of ginger beer, in order to avoid the symptomatic dehydration. After two days he was then given liquid food through a rubber tube in an attempt to rebuild his strength.

During the late afternoon of his second day in hospital Michael and Edwyna Hillary had arrived to see their son after a long and arduous journey. Their last few hours had been fraught with worry as to what condition they would find their son in. Met by the matron on arrival they were passed on to the ward sister who took them to Richard. She briefed them by saying that they should not expect to find him looking normal. Richard later wrote:

> The room was in darkness; I just a dim shape in the corner. Then the blinds were
> shot up, all the lights switched on, and there I was. As my mother remarked later,
> the performance lacked only the rolling of drums and a spotlight. For the sake of
> decorum my face had been covered with white gauze, with a slit in the middle
> through which protruded my lips.

There is some doubt as to whether the nurse would have suddenly illuminated the room in this manner, bearing in mind that he was only blind because of the swelling around the eyes and although they were somewhat shielded such action may have been unwise. Edwyna Hillary later remarked that the room was in fact left in semi-darkness. The apparition that lay before his parents must have been terribly distressing. Nothing was recognisable, his body was bandaged from head to foot, his tannic coated face was loosely covered with white gauze but the black coating and the gentian violet around his eyes was visible. His swollen, blistered and scab-covered lips protruded from the slit that had been left in the gauze for his mouth. His bandaged arms were suspended over his chest. His body must have looked somewhat like an Egyptian mummy as it hung in its straps over the bed.

They spoke little and just sat listening to their son rambling for an hour, their emotions almost at breaking point, the sound of his voice reassuring when just a short time before they had been faced with the possibility that they may never see him alive again. Finally they were ushered from the room when the nursing team arrived to change his dressings. It is quite conceivable that although his parents were eternally grateful that Richard had survived such a terrible ordeal, they left the hospital and let their grief overflow, something that they had desperately wanted to do sometime during the previous hour but felt that they had to remain in control while in his company.

Changing the dressings on Richard's wounds needed three orderlies to hold his arms, while matron removed the old dressings, a particularly painful experience as the dressings stuck to the weeping burns and scabs. She would then clean the accessible areas before applying fresh dressings. He mentions in his book that he can never remember there being a doctor present; one would not be needed for this fairly standard routine. In the absence of sight another aspect that Richard became hypersensitive to was his sense of smell. Ether, alcohol, antiseptic, all the familiar smells of a hospital became imprinted in his memory for the rest of his life.

* * *

Believing him to be an ancestor of Sir William Hillary, the founder of their service, the lifeboat crew visited Richard in hospital at this time. Unfortunately he was in too much pain to be able to respond in any reliably coherent manner although he did remember the visit and wrote:

> A visit from the lifeboat crew that had picked me up, and a terrible longing to
> make sense when talking to them. Their inarticulate sympathy and assurance of
> a quick recovery. Their discovery that an ancestor of mine had founded the
> lifeboats, and my pompous and unsolicited promise of a subscription.

As Richard drifted in and out of his pain/drug-induced stupor he suffered the further trauma of nightmares, dreams and premonitions. If somebody mentioned something of interest in his semi-stupefied state he would fall asleep and awake to believe that it had been a dream, and could therefore perceive it as a premonition. This, I believe, was to be the case with the death of Peter Pease. He dreamt that an ambulance was coming to take him to another hospital, when in actual fact one had been organised to do just that. These dreams accompanied the nightmares in which he was back in the cockpit of his Spitfire, or that he had gone blind only to awaken to find that he was! Those few days were filled with pain, sweat, smell, overriding apathy and of seeing the staff at work in his room but in slow motion.

When he was coherent he was read messages from the squadron: humorous, coarse, and with their good wishes, but never sentimental. They didn't include news of losses of squadron colleagues either.

On the fourth day at Margate General he was taken by ambulance to the Royal Masonic Hospital in Ravenscourt Park. The Masons had kindly loaned the services a part of the building but owing to its vulnerable position very few war casualties stayed there very long. As soon as they were strong enough they were moved out of the city.

Two nervous Auxiliary Transport Service (ATS) ladies were to be his driver and escort in the very welcome company of his own nurse from the Margate hospital, who wrapped him up in an old 'grandmother's shawl' before, still blind, he was carried out to the waiting ambulance. The ATS ladies were new to the job and very pleased that their first task was to ferry an injured RAF pilot to another hospital. On the way he dictated letters to his nurse, drank yet more ginger beer and gossiped with the ATS ladies. He even managed to turn on some of his old charm when, within earshot, he asked his nurse if the ATS ladies were pretty: 'I heard her answer yes, heard them simpering and we were all very matey.'

Then, as Richard's limited energy reserves dwindled and the morphine started to wear off, the pain returned to his arms with each jolt he received in the back of the vehicle. The journey became unpleasant and almost more than he could stand: 'I stopped dictating letters, drank no more ginger beer and didn't care if the ATS ladies were pretty or not.' To make matters worse the driver was lost.

They eventually arrived at the Royal Masonic with Richard having apparently helped out with the navigation. Despite being blind he had assisted by asking them to call out street names. If he recognised them, he was able to confirm that they were heading in the right direction. His knowledge of this area must have been outstanding if this aspect of his story is to be believed.

On arrival there was a welcoming committee in the form of efficient nurses and porters who carried him into the hospital. Here he experienced a very emotional parting from his nurse when the two of them shed a few tears; she then returned to Margate. Richard was emotionally and physically exhausted. He mentioned later that he had been in a lousy hospital and that now he was in good hands, since the Royal Masonic was perhaps the best hospital in England. As he still held this opinion when he wrote his book, he obviously thought it a better hospital than the Queen Victoria Cottage Hospital, East Grinstead, which was to be the venue for nearly all of his reconstructive surgery. In fact, in a number of letters he wrote during 1942 to his girlfriend at that time he was very critical of the lack of hygiene at East Grinstead and blamed the failure of some of the skin-grafts on this.

In the Royal Masonic this heroic fighter pilot was to become ridiculously spoiled at the hands of the nurses who couldn't keep their hands off him. The charge nurse met him on arrival and asked him what his name was:

> 'Dick', I said
>> 'Ah,' she said brightly. 'We must call you Richard the Lionheart.'
>> I made an attempt at a polite laugh but all that came out was a dismal groan
> and I fainted away.

On arrival, the house surgeon carried out an initial inspection of his injuries. Not liking the look of Richard's hands, he took the opportunity to have him wheeled straight into surgery, anaesthetised, and the tannic acid chipped off his left hand. With the risk of shock, removing it from both hands in one fell swoop might have been more than Richard was strong enough to endure. The tannic was cracked by now, leaving the wounds open to the bacteria in the air. The burnt tendons were also starting to shrivel up with the result being that the fingers were starting to curl in towards the palm like claws. Although the tannic acid was supposed to provide a protective airtight seal to allow the healing process to begin, there were many cases of septicaemia with pilots who had undergone the same treatment for burns. It has been written that when the plastic surgeon Archibald McIndoe first saw Richard at the Masonic he gave instructions that the tannic acid was to be removed. The great surgeon was responsible for having only the gentian violet removed from his eyes and saline compresses applied in its place, as a more suitable alternative treatment. The tannic acid had already been removed.

Richard was one of the first to have the procedure reversed as they became aware of the problems. The procedure took about fifteen minutes and during this operation Richard wrote in *The Last Enemy* that he saw Peter Pease die in action:

> He was after another machine, a tall figure leaning slightly forward with a smile at the corner of his mouth. Suddenly from nowhere a Messerschmitt was on his tail about 150 yards away. For two seconds nothing happened. I had a terrible feeling of futility. Then at the top of my voice I shouted, 'Peter, for God's sake look out behind!'
>
> I saw the Messerschmitt open up and a burst of fire hit Peter's machine. His expression did not change, and for a moment his machine hung motionless. Then it turned slowly on its back and dived to the ground. I came-to, screaming his name, with two nurses and the doctor holding me down on the bed.
>
> 'All right now. Take it easy, you're not dead yet. That must have been a very bad dream.'

According to Richard, two days later a letter arrived from Colin Pinckney confirming that Peter had indeed been killed.

Peter Pease was actually killed on 15 September, seven days after Richard arrived at the Royal Masonic. I believe that the most likely reason why Richard incorrectly associates this event as having occurred immediately after arrival at the Masonic, was that he was told the news while under the effects of morphine and in a semi-delirious state, during a period when he was suffering great discomfort. Later, in a more coherent state, he remembers the news as if he had had a premonition, a dream, a not uncommon occurrence under the circumstances. If Peter's death did actually coincide with his operation he had failed to remember there being a period of seven days between his arrival, and having the operation to remove the tannic coating from his left hand.

For his first three weeks at the Masonic he apparently did nothing but curse and blaspheme. Not exactly a model patient! He drifted in and out of pain and morphine was administered every three hours. The nurses were made only too aware when the last dose was starting to wear-off.

The long agonising process of changing his dressings caused great upset and heart-ache among the less resilient staff. It was the inexperienced and unqualified members of the Voluntary Aid Detachment (VAD), who struggled, most of all with their emotions, when confronted with this brave, young, fighter pilot now in such a distressed state. On two different occasions VAD nurses fainted while helping with the changing of his dressings and another poor unfortunate girl rushed from the ward in tears bearing the wrath of both Richard and the ward sister as she went.

Initially, according to Richard, Michael and Edwyna Hillary were the only visitors allowed to see him and they came daily. However, he was allowed other visitors during this time, and they called by to see how he was progressing. The hospital was conveniently situated only a short distance from Michael Hillary's place of work and their flat in Knightsbridge Court. His mother would sit by the bed and read to him. To be at his side while he was suffering was the best place for her; she had seen so little of her son over the last fourteen years, but her feelings were as strong as any other loving mother, together perhaps with feelings of guilt that she had not always been there for him. It was during one of these visits that Richard quotes her in *The Last Enemy* as having said:

> You should be glad this has to happen to you. Too many people told you how attractive you were and you believed them. You were well on the way to becoming something of a cad. Now you'll find out who your real friends are.

As has been the case with several aspects of his book, some doubt was cast over whether Edwyna Hillary would have actually said such a thing. Lady Winifred Fortescue later recalled that Richard had said to her:

> I was rather nice to look at once, and I suppose getting a bit uppish and spoiled. She [Edwyna] told me in hospital that perhaps this accident had saved me from becoming a cad.

* * *

The first stage of recovery for Richard was to allow the burnt skin on his face and hands to die and fall off, and then for the new and surviving skin to soften. This layer of burnt skin, which would eventually go naturally, or be surgically removed under general anaesthetic, is called the eschar, which is the close fitting cover consisting of protein exudate and dead desiccated burnt tissue which exfoliates as the burnt tissue underneath begins to heal.

Keloids would form as a result of the burns, which were areas of contracted scar tissue that formed particularly where the skin was drawn taut over prominent boney areas. (The modern-day description for keloids is hypertrophic scarring.) It took perhaps two weeks for eschar to occur on an uncovered burn and several months for keloids to form. Additional keloids would also form after surgery on a graft and flap edge.

With the aid of hindsight and knowledge of modern day techniques it would certainly have been more beneficial if Richard's burns had been left exposed and not sprayed with tannic acid, particularly as he had landed in the sea. The dry eschar would have lifted early and a good recovery of the epidermal adrexae would have been possible. Despite the open state it would have still been safe to allow spontaneous healing for a couple of weeks. The wound would have become slightly deeper. The remaining eschar could have then been removed under general anaesthetic and grafts applied. Atmospheric conditions in which the eschar could be left to dry naturally for two weeks would need to be warm and dry. The wounds would require regular cleaning with antiseptic soap. The disadvantage with this method is that if the conditions are not right, ie., the eschar is left too long, or it comes into contact with the sheets and moist air is trapped against the wound, there is a risk of the colonisation of bacteria under the eschar, leading to infection. Nevertheless, a sharp excision with skin grafts applied without delay would have been more suitable than the application of tannic acid.

A modern day approach to the deep burns to his hands would have been to carry out an escharotomy. When burnt, the back of the hand (dorsum) swells rapidly with the extension of the metacarpophalangeal joints and flexion of the interphalangeal joints. A releasing incision is made along the radial border of the hand with further incisions required to release the dorsum and fingers. Eschartomies release the tension on the hands and fingers which would otherwise result in what was known then as 'airman's claw'.

The loss of the fingernails indicates substantial damage to the neuromuscular bundles within the fingers, with some inevitable loss of finger-length, as was the case with the deep burns Richard had received.

As the healing process took its natural course the amount of dressing that his injuries required was reduced. More of the burnt areas had healed enough to be left open to the elements. The more serious areas such as his fingers, remained covered. Bone was actually protruding from one knuckle where the skin had been so seriously burnt and deadened right through to the bone. There was no skin left for regrowth to occur. In due course plastic surgery would be required, first by the removal of the old hard, shrivelled, scar tissue (keloids), and then by grafting a new layer of skin onto the damaged area from another part of the body.

During this initial period after his arrival Richard received a visit from Archibald McIndoe who would play a very great part in the rest of his life, and whose medical skills were about to confirm his reputation internationally. That fame would continue to be associated with his reconstructive work on burns and crash victims of WWII to this day. This despite the fact that there were indeed other accomplished plastic surgeons at that time, but it was likely to have been this latest charge that ultimately brought him such fame. Richard was to be one of the first of his patients to help publicise the work of this great man through his best-selling book *The Last Enemy*, and give the public an insight into what was happening behind the scenes. The image of the glamorous fighter pilot dashing to meet the foe high in the skies over southern England had a darker side, of course, and through his book, along with a few other patients who also wrote of their own experiences, Richard was able to tell the public about this. McIndoe's specialist medical skill had initially been in stomach surgery but was now in reconstructive plastic surgery. As consultant plastic surgeon to the RAF, he had been travelling around his appointed region in his small Vauxhall car visiting the hospitals and looking for the kind of injuries where his talents could be put to very specific good use. On arrival at the Masonic he had been told of a young fighter pilot who had received burns to his face and hands that would benefit from his attention. Although his work was not known to Richard at the time, he was aware that he was in respected company by the hush that befell the room as he carried out his examination:

> Shortly after my arrival at the Masonic the Air Force plastic surgeon, A.H. McIndoe, had come up to see me, but as I had been blind at the time I could recollect his visit but vaguely, remembering only that he ordered the gentian violet to be removed from my eyes and saline compresses to be applied instead, with the result that shortly afterwards I was able to see.

The compresses had reduced the swelling of the tissue surrounding the eyes including the eyelids, allowing them to separate, and for him to see. The relief of having his sight back and the consequent visual distractions would now aid his recovery. They now carried out regular irrigation of the eyes to keep them clean and healthy, because the eyelids were almost completely burnt away, and what remained could not perform the function of keeping the eyeball moist and clean:

> The nurses were wonderfully patient and never complained. Then one day I found that I could see. My nurse was bending over me doing my dressings, and she seemed to me very beautiful. She was. I watched her for a long time, grateful that my first glimpse of the world should be of anything so perfect. Finally I said:
> 'Sue, you never told me that your eyes were so blue.'
> For a moment she stared at me. Then, 'Oh, Dick, how wonderful,' she said. 'I told you it wouldn't be long;' and she dashed out to bring in all the nurses on the block.
> I felt absurdly elated and studied their faces eagerly, gradually connecting them with the voices I knew.
> 'This is Anne,' said Sue. 'She is your special VAD and helps me with all your dressings. She was the only one of us you'd allow near you for about a week. You said you liked her voice.' Before me stood an attractive fair-haired girl of about twenty-three. She smiled and her teeth were as enchanting as her voice. I began to feel that hospital had its compensations. The nurses called me Dick and I knew them all by their Christian names.

Richard was spoilt by the nurses, something he would miss when he was transferred to his next hospital. Sue was very experienced and was Richard's special nurse because of her previous experience with burns. Anne had been married to a naval officer who had been killed on HMS *Courageous* and had taken up nursing after his death. Between them they changed Richard's dressings every two hours and as this process took over an hour they had very little time off. It was their devotion to duty that quite possibly helped save Richard's hands from amputation. Richard later admitted: 'I was a little in love with both of them'.

There were telephone calls to the hospital asking whether he was strong enough to be moved yet. With the hospital being vulnerable to the bombing raids on the capital, although the area was far from being one of the worst hit, the authorities were eager to transfer Richard to a Royal Air Force hospital. He was enjoying the good company too much and did not wish to be moved, and it was his kind-hearted house surgeon who told them that he was still too sick to be moved just yet, and allowed Richard to take full advantage of the caring hands around him. One individual expressed feelings of jealousy at the sight of Richard being pampered:

> An RASC officer who had been admitted to the hospital with the painful but unromantic complaint of piles protested at the amount of favouritism shown to me merely because I was in the RAF. A patriotic captain who was in the same ward turned on him and said: 'At least he was shot down defending his country and didn't come in here with a pimple on his bottom. The Government will buy him a new Spitfire, but I'm damned if it will buy you a new arse.'

He refers to having his own room during his time at the Masonic but in fact he was on a private ward, set aside for injured servicemen.

One nurse that he enjoyed talking to during the hours of darkness was 'Bertha', the night shift nurse; that was the name by which he referred to her in his book, a name that he believed reflected her size and appearance. But she had a heart of gold and he thought very highly of her. She showed an initial resilience to pampering him in the way the other day nurses did, but she soon found his manner irresistible and succumbed to possibly his most potent attribute, his charm:

> At night when I couldn't sleep we would hold long and heated arguments on the subject of sex. She expressed horror at my ideas of love and on her preference for a cup of tea. I gave her a present of four pounds of it when I was discharged. One night the Germans were particularly persistent, and I had the unpleasant sensation of hearing a stick of bombs gradually approaching the hospital, the first some way off, the next closer, and the third shaking the building. Bertha threw herself across my bed; but the fourth bomb never fell. She got up quickly, looking embarrassed, and arranged her cap.
>
> 'Nice fool I'd look if you got hit in your own room when you're supposed to be out in the corridor,' she said and stumped out of the room.

Richard and the other patients had been moved from their wards, and the outer walls of the hospital building, and into the corridors as a safety measure.

As he continued to recover the doctor responsible for Richard decided that it would be all right for him to get out of bed and therefore undertake, to a greater degree, some of the chores that had until now needed the undivided attention of the nurses. His hands were still bandaged and the rather more personal tasks such as washing and going to the lavatory were still greatly assisted by them. One of the most amusing stories that Richard was to feature in his book was the time he was led to the lavatory by one of his nurses and left sitting in one of the cubicles.

This amusing image of Richard wandering around in his dressing gown with a long gold cigarette holder clenched in his teeth was something that a number of the patients at East Grinstead would remember as an outstanding memory of him, right up until the present day.

Other than his parents, one of the first people to come to see him was a former student friend of Richard's from Trinity, Michael Cary. He, unlike Richard, had successfully managed to complete his course and gained a first in Greats. Cary was then the secretary to the Chief of Air Staff, but shortly after seeing Richard he joined the Navy. Whether it was as a result of seeing Richard is not known.

One of the most welcoming faces that would show up, whenever he had leave from Hornchurch, was Colin Pinckney. He brought news of their colleagues, and of the deaths of Ken Macdonald, Pip Cardell, Peter Pease, Peter Howes and Rusty Rushmer. As he sat beside Richard looking tired and weary, his weight-loss obvious, Colin told of the magnificent fight that the pilots in the squadron were still putting up against the Luftwaffe.

Richard quite naturally still saw himself as part of the squadron and these were his fellow pilots and good friends that were being killed. For a few weeks Richard had shared a unique experience with them and it could even be considered that perhaps by now he had actually grown closer to them than to his other friends, and for this reason I shall relate the events of the days on which they were lost below.

* * *

Thursday 5 September 1940
Rusty Rushmer failed to return following combat with Do17s and an escort of Me109s, possibly of II/JG26, over Biggin Hill at 10.00 hours on Thursday 5 September while flying Spitfire X4261. Rusty was posted as 'missing', and the squadron records state that his loss occurred between 09.34 and 10.34 hours. According to Stapme Stapleton:

> I didn't see what happened to Rusty, he just disappeared. Tannoy Read was the only pilot who reported seeing him go down.

Years later his Spitfire was discovered at Smarden, Kent.

* * *

Pilot Officer 'Robin' Rafter had arrived on 31 August while Hornchurch was being bombed.

On 5 September he was shot down at 10.00 am in Spitfire X4264 over Marden by Me109s, possibly of II/JG26. Rusty was killed while leading his section during the same combat. Seriously wounded, Rafter was admitted to West Kent Hospital, Maidstone. Having been thrown clear of his stricken aircraft he managed to land safely by parachute. He had been wounded in the right leg during the combat and had received serious head injuries when he had been thrown through the canopy of his Spitfire as it plunged out of control. He was out of action until November.

During the same combat in which Rafter had been shot down, Stapme Stapleton brought down the Messerschmitt Bf109E-4 (1480) piloted by the infamous Oberleutnant Franz von Werra of Stab II/JG3. Von Werra was an unpleasant, disingenuous character who was made famous in Kendal Burt and James Leasor's book *The One That Got Away* published by Michael Joseph in 1956. A film of the book was later made and starred Hardy Kruger as von Werra. His aircraft forced landed at Winchet Hill, Love's Farm, Marden at 10.10 hours and he was captured unhurt.

Von Werra's unit, II/JG3, was attacked from above by 41 Squadron between Ashford and Maidstone whilst on a diversionary fighter sweep over Kent and, contrary to early research, it is possible that von Werra's aircraft was initially engaged and damaged by Pilot Officer George 'Ben' Bennions of No.41 Squadron, and not Flight Lieutenant Webster of the same unit. Nos. 41 and 603 Squadrons were both involved in the engagement over North Kent between 09.50 and 10.10 hours.

The 41 Squadron ORB reported that Bennions saw the Me109: '. . . streaming glycol going down eight miles south of Maidstone.'

This information is crucial when considering the other 109s that were brought down during this combat. If this 109 was being flown by von Werra, it had been seen going down in the correct area for Stapme to have latched on to it after Ben had broken off his attack. Stapme fired several bursts and eventually forced it down. His combat report made no mention of any flying characteristics that would indicate that the aircraft had been damaged, or whether it had been streaming glycol when he attacked it.

The 603 ORB reports this combat as being between 09.34 and 10.34 hours and that Stapme:

> . . . dived to attack bombers but was engaged by 109's. Attacked one and saw glycol but was then attacked himself and dived to evade. Attacked a lone 109 which forced-landed, pilot got out and tried to fire his aircraft by setting light to his jacket but was stopped by the LDV.

Interestingly it also mentions that as he attacked the 109: '. . . the pilot broke away, waggling his wings'. In his combat report Stapme recorded:

> I was diving to attack them (the bombers) when I was engaged by two Me109's [the *Rotte*, the typical Luftwaffe tactical formation consisting of leader and wingman]. When I fired at the first one I noticed glycol coming from his radiator. I did a No.2 attack and as I fired I was hit by bullets from another Me109. I broke off downwards and continued my dive. At 6,000 feet I saw a single-engined machine diving vertically with no tail unit. I looked up and saw a parachutist coming down circled by an Me 109. I attacked him (the Me109) from the low quarter, he dived vertically towards the ground and flattened out at ground level. I then did a series of beam attacks from both sides, and the enemy aircraft turned into my attacks. He finally forced landed. He tried to set his radio on fire by taking off his jacket and setting fire to it and putting it into the cockpit. He was prevented by the LDV.

The parachutist being circled by the 109 was Robin Rafter of 603 Squadron. Rumours of the Germans murdering pilots as they hung defenceless in their parachute harnesses existed at this time but Stapme told me:

> I noticed that its airspeed had dropped dramatically and I pressed home an attack, followed by another before allowing the pilot to carry out a forced landing. I remember seeing my tracer strike the 109 and was concerned that I was firing at low level, with a village in my apparent line of fire.
>
> Contrary to the myth that has developed over the years, I have no doubt that the pilot was making no attempt to open fire on Rafter as he hung seriously injured in his parachute harness. He was merely concentrating on self preservation and happened to be circling in the vicinity of Rafter. The 109 was clearly disabled with the pilot looking to evade further damage and get his aircraft down. Why risk murdering the parachutist knowing that his aircraft was damaged and a forced landing, on enemy territory, was imminent?

It would appear that von Werra had had every opportunity to open fire on Rafter, who had also suggested that the German pilot had been in a position to open fire, but had not done so prior to being 'driven off' by Stapme.

Initially on landing Stapme had thought the pilot was waving his jacket up at his victorious attacker and so he waggled his wings. Later, as reports came in, he realised that the wave was a deception by von Werra in order to cover his intention to set fire to his aircraft. Stapme learnt this fact before writing his combat report. Perhaps the 'wave' was an attempt by von Werra to disguise his motive from the pilot of the swooping Spitfire, out of fear of having his plans brought to a premature end! Stapme is also of the opinion that von Werra had perhaps managed to douse his lifejacket in fuel.

At the time Stapme had no idea whom he had shot down:

> It was sometime between the end of the war and when I moved to South Africa that I was told the name of the pilot I had shot down on 5 September, and of his reputation as 'the one that got away'. I was in South Africa when the film came

out and didn't see it until many years later. But I knew of its significance.

It is most likely that the aircraft that Stapme saw 'diving vertically with no tail unit' was X4264, XT-R of Robin Rafter, who had stated in a letter home that '. . . my tail must have been damaged' and after spinning out of control, his aircraft dived suddenly into a nose-down attitude, flinging him through the canopy.

Ben Bennions' report is relevant in that it adds an element of credibility to the claim that he may have carried out an initial attack on the 109 of von Werra. The aircraft was still under control and eventually, and very fortuitously after the attacks by Stapme, it landed at Marden, close to where Rafter had landed.*

* * *

Friday 6 September 1940

Bill Caister was flying Spitfire X4260 when he was brought down by Hauptmann Hubertus Von Bonin of I/JG54 in a sporadic engagement over the Channel off Manston at 13.00 hours. Probably owing to disorientation during combat this engagement did not come to an end in the fields of Kent or in the Channel, but on the wrong side of the water. Due to damage to the hydraulics system of Spitfire XT-D Bill Caister was unable to lower the undercarriage, but still made a perfect landing in a meadow near Guines in northern France, thus giving the Luftwaffe an intact example of the Spitfire. The recently commissioned 34-year-old pilot officer with over 15 years' service in the RAF had a brief meeting with von Bonin in the mess at Guines, after which he was taken away to spend the rest of the war as a POW. His new bride would have to wait five years to see her husband again. The only possible consolation was the fact that he would not have to face the dangers of aerial warfare again during the current conflict.

Sunday 15 September 1940

Today, 15th September is celebrated as 'Battle of Britain Day', not because it was the day on which RAF fighters shot down the greatest number of German aircraft, for it was not, but because the loss of 56 aircraft was decisive in persuading Hitler to postpone plans for an invasion. Having been confronted by over 250 fighter aircraft flown with determination and courage, the morale of the Luftwaffe aircrews was suffering, and they had seen no indication that the RAF had been on its last legs.

---

*At 09.50 hours on 29 November, 603's CO, Squadron Leader 'Uncle' George Denholm, led nine Spitfires away from Hornchurch with instructions to patrol the airspace over Ramsgate. By this time the updated Spitfire Mark II with its increased boost was in squadron use.

The unit made visual contact with a lone Bf110 'A5+AA' of Stab/StG.1, and shot it down over the sea. Both pilot, Oberleutnant R. Pytlik, and gunner/radio operator, Oberleutnant T. Fryer were killed. According to the squadron ORB, the pilots were 'frustrated as being in search of bigger game', and as a consequence this combat was described as something of a 'turkey shoot' with the pilots taking full advantage of the situation. The 'kill' was credited to all nine pilots with the ORB confirming that each man was given a 'ninth'.

Robin Rafter had got his chance to fulfil his intentions as expressed to his mother: 'to get my own back on the Jerries'. Tragically, he was killed during the return flight to Hornchurch when his Spitfire, P7449, inexplicably dived from an altitude of 2,500 feet into a meadow at Kingswood, north-east of Sutton Valence. It had been only his second operational flight with 603. The cause has not been established but it is possible to rule out oxygen starvation (anoxia/hypoxia) as he was not flying high enough to require oxygen (although some pilots opted for a moderate flow from take-off, which they increased to full as they climbed, the actual height at which oxygen becomes necessary is over 14,000 feet). It is conceivable Robin had been hit by return fire, information in the ORB is scarce, but the most likely cause is that he blacked out, a legacy of the serious head injury he had received on 5 September. He was 19 years old.

Earlier tragedy had struck the Rafter family when on 11 October Robin's brother Charles was killed in a flying accident at RAF Stradishall while serving as a pilot with No.214 Squadron. During take-off he lost control of the Wellington he was piloting which subsequently struck a hangar and the entire crew was killed.

The brothers were buried with their father at St Peter's Churchyard, Harborne, Birmingham, close to the family home.

Intelligence Patrol Report = 603 Squadron
14.14-15.30 hours. 15.9.40.
Second patrol of the day

13 aircraft took off to join 41 Squadron, which they did not meet. When at 21,000 feet ten miles south east of Chatham they saw about 200 Me109's and 110's making smoke trails at 18,000 feet, and under them about 15-20 He111's in vic's of five, also another formation to the south. One pilot saw two formations of Do17's, 20 in each, unescorted, flying towards Biggin Hill, the leader of the second formation was white on the undersurfaces. An He111 was seen to land at Dishforth with three red bars on the upper surfaces of its wings.

Pip Cardell was granted four days' leave. Sergeant George Bailey had been posted from 234 Squadron at Leconfield to 603 and had arrived on 10 September. He claimed a Me109 destroyed which crashed south of Maidstone:

When on patrol with 603 Squadron SE of Maidstone, I saw a large formation of enemy aircraft. The squadron attacked and after I lost the squadron. I then engaged a Me109 south of Sheerness, which was flying south at 8,000 feet at about 180 m.p.h. I gave him a burst of about two seconds from dead astern and he immediately left a large column of smoke and fell through the clouds and I saw him crash south of Sittingbourne.

Bailey was flying with 'A' Flight and delivered his attack at 15.00 hours. The aircraft he had shot down was a Me109E of I/JG53; the pilot Unteroffizier Schersand was killed. Bailey survived the war.

Another new arrival in the squadron was the experienced New Zealander Pilot Officer Keith Lawrence who joined on 9 September from 234 Squadron at Leconfield with whom he claimed the squadron's first victory on 8 July 1940. Lawrence claimed his first successes with 603 six days after his arrival on 15 September. An impressive start it was too. One Me109 destroyed and two more damaged:

As Yellow 2 on patrol with 603 Squadron, I went in to attack with the squadron a formation of approximately 30 Do17's and He111's 3000 feet below. Due to the awkward approach and excessive speed on reaching the bombers, I pulled up to engage the Me109's coming down, one of which I chased and opened fire at 75 yards, and after about six seconds, and having closed to about 30 yards, it went up steeply and then fell away in a spin and was still spinning on entering the cloud. The 109 lost control at about 18,000 feet. I used the remainder of my ammunition on two Me109's which dived into the clouds. Range in both cases approximately 30 yards.

Lawrence's ability to get in close before opening fire was sure to bring some success. He was also flying with 'A' Flight when he delivered his attack at 14.50 hours, south-east of Maidstone at a height of 20,000 feet.

Back with one of the familiar faces in the squadron, in this combat Stapme Stapleton claimed one Do17 destroyed. The aircraft was a Do17Z (3405) of 9/KG2 which crashed into the sea five miles north-east of Herne Bay at 15.15 hours. It had been on a sortie to bomb St Katharine's Docks in London when it had been intercepted by Pilot Officer B. Pattullo of No.46 Squadron and Stapme. During the attack its starboard engine had been severely damaged and the crew ditched the bomb load before crashing into the sea. Stapme reported:

When patrolling with my squadron, I sighted 25 He111's and 50 Me109's. While diving to attack, I found myself going too fast to pull out on the enemy, so I continued my dive.

About ten minutes later, I sighted two Me109's in light vic. I fired two deflection bursts at one and glycol streams came from his radiator. They dived into the cloud.

> Later I saw one Do17 over the Thames Estuary heading for the clouds. I did several beam attacks and he dived to 100 feet. He flew very low indeed and pancaked on the sea five miles NW of Ramsgate. I experienced no return fire.

Stapme recorded the time of his attack as being 14.50 hours, ten miles south of Chatham at an altitude of 20,000 feet.

Ras Berry claimed a Me109 probable, last seen in an uncontrollable dive with black smoke, and a Do17 destroyed, although he admits that the Dornier was also being attacked by others prior to him apparently finishing the German off:

> The squadron was patrolling over Rochford at 22,000 feet. I sighted large numbers of fighters, Me109's, above and several vic's of three of He111's below. The squadron went into line astern and peeled off onto the bombers. As I dived I saw a Me109 attacking a Spitfire. I immediately split round and came on the 109's tail and at point blank range fired a long burst. The 109 with heavy smoke pouring out, went into a vertical dive into heavy cloud. Whilst patrolling around land over Southend, I sighted a Do17 homeward bound. A Hurricane and Spitfire approached me. We all attacked in turn. I gave a long burst on starboard engine with success, as I had to break away with oil all over my windscreen from the enemy aircraft. The enemy aircraft then glided down and pancaked in a field on the Isle of Sheppey. The crew of three climbed out and the aircraft began to burn slightly.

Ras Berry delivered his attack at 15.00 hours ten miles south of Chatham, at a height of 18,000 feet.

It is possible that Brian Carbury shot down the Me109E of Stab I/JG77 flown by Oberleutnant Herbert Kunze. The 109 crashed into a dyke near Stuttfall Castle, Lympne, at 15.30. The pilot was killed and buried in the cemetery at RAF Hawkinge.

Brian MacNamara claimed a Do17 damaged, specifically to the rudder and starboard engine:

> After becoming separated from the squadron, I hung about the estuary for stragglers. I soon saw AA fire from the Isle of Sheppey and saw a Dornier just emerging from cloud. I carried out a stern chase and saw my incendiaries hitting his starboard engine and very soon black smoke came from it and the aircraft, which was steering east, started turning towards the Essex coast. I had to break away, as I had run out of ammunition and was troubled by heavy AA fire. I did not see what happened to the Dornier. Throughout this attack I was troubled by heavy AA fire, which did not cease despite the fact that I had commenced an attack on the enemy, and shells were continually bursting very close to my aircraft.

MacNamara delivered this attack at 14.45 hours over the estuary just east of Southend at a height of 10,000 feet.

* * *

Squadron Leader George Denholm had survived having been shot down on a number of occasions. He had also claimed his share of German aircraft. Earlier in the day at 12.05 he had shot down a Me109E of 3/JG53. The pilot, Oberfeldwebel Alfred Muller, was wounded and taken prisoner. During this combat he claimed two Do17s damaged:

> I attacked an He111 with a two second burst, diving from astern, then I fired a short burst at a Me109 but observed no results. Some time later I saw an unescorted formation of Do17's over the coast and made a diving frontal quarter attack on the port flank of the formation from out of the sun. I fired a short burst and dived through the formation and turned to make an astern attack. I saw the two Do17's at which I had fired lagging behind the formation, emitting black smoke. I was then fired at and flames started to come through my instrument panel which was broken, so I baled out.

George Denholm delivered his attack at 15.00 hours south-east of Maidstone at a height of 18,000 feet. His own aircraft R7019 was destroyed when it crashed on Warren Farm, Fairlight, near Hastings. He landed by parachute near Guestling Lodge.

At 14.55 hours while Uncle George was about to deliver his initial attack on the Me109 Peter Pease was diving to attack enemy Heinkel 111 bombers of KG26 that had just dropped their bombs on targets in the West Ham area of London and were on their way back across the Kent countryside. The bombers had had a relatively easy run so far with the loss of just one aircraft that had been forced to break formation due to engine trouble and had been finished off by the RAF fighters. Their escorting fighters had driven off any other attempt to break through to the bombers. Such was Peter's determination to press his attack home that he neglected the defence of his own aircraft and was shot down by Me109s south-east of Maidstone shortly after 15.00 hours. No RAF pilot saw his demise, although it was witnessed by the Heinkel bomber crews and one in particular. Leutnant Roderich Cescotti later recalled the attack on his own aircraft by one lone Spitfire in *Battle of Britain Day* by Dr Alfred Price:

> A few Tommies succeeded in penetrating our fighter escort, I saw a Spitfire dive steeply through our escort, level out and close rapidly on our formation. It opened fire, from ahead and to the right, and its tracers streaked towards us. At that moment an Me109, which we had not seen before, appeared behind the Spitfire and we saw its rounds striking the Spitfire's tail. But the Tommy continued his attack, coming straight for us, and his rounds slashed into our aircraft. We could not return the fire for fear of hitting the Messerschmitt. I put my left arm across my face to protect it from the Plexiglas splinters flying around the cockpit, holding the controls with my right hand. With only the thin Plexiglas between us, we were eye to eye with the enemy's eight machine guns. At the last moment the Spitfire pulled up and passed very close over the top of us. Then it rolled onto its back, as though out of control, and went down steeply, trailing black smoke. Waggling its wings, the Messerschmitt swept past us and curved in for another attack. The action lasted only a few seconds, but it demonstrated the determination and bravery with which the Tommies were fighting over their own country.
>
> Fortunately nobody was hurt, and although both engines had taken hits they continued to run smoothly. Ice-cold air blasted through the holes in the plexiglass. So the navigator, with more bravery than circumspection, opened his parachute pack and cut off pieces of silk which he used to block the holes. It was his first operational sortie and I suppose he thought he ought to do something heroic.

Despite over 30 hits on his aircraft, Cescotti's Heinkel was not seriously damaged and the pilot was able to maintain formation and get home. The flaming Spitfire with Peter Pease still on board crashed at Kingswood near Chartway Street, south-east of Maidstone in Kent. It is not known if he had been wounded during the first attack by the 109 and had decided to press home his attack regardless, instead of pulling out and attempting to save himself and his fighter. I believe that he was prepared to do just that if necessary, for he was totally committed to the cause. He may have been killed after his attack on Cescotti's Heinkel, when the 109 pressed home its second attack.

Peter was initially reported 'missing', and the squadron ORB subsequently recorded that he had been reported killed on 17 September. Official confirmation of his death came on 13 November. His body was eventually returned to his home in Yorkshire for burial in the family plot in the beautiful little churchyard of St Michael and All Angels at Middleton Tyas, Yorkshire.

That afternoon Peter's fiancée Denise had been with a group of her girls at prayer in a church in Vange. On hearing the sound of Merlin engines in the sky outside she glanced at one of the windows and saw a number of Spitfires pass by. She caught a fleeting glimpse of the code on the fuselage of one of the fighters. It was XT-P, carrying Peter on his last patrol. The memory of this incredible coincidence remains with her today. In 1991, on the anniversary of the Battle of Britain, Denise attended a memorial service to her late fiancée, held in a church near to where Peter's Spitfire had crashed in Kingswood, Kent. She accompanied Peter's younger brother Richard who had been at the dinner table the night Peter, Richard and Colin had stopped off on their way to RAF Turnhouse in July 1940. A plaque was unveiled and a kneeler placed in the church in memory of Peter.

Wednesday 18 September 1940
This day passed with more bad news from Colin during his visit to the hospital that evening.

> Intelligence Patrol Report – 603 Squadron
> 0910 – 1020 hours
> 18.9.40
>
> Ten aircraft left Rochford and joined up with 41 Squadron. When over Maidstone at 25,000 feet, 41 Squadron dived to attack something which 603 did not see. 603 then saw Me109's above them and also two vic's of five Me109's 2000 feet below them. A dogfight ensued when the squadron dived to attack the lower formation. One pilot when attacking a Me109 at 28,000 feet, saw six Me109's on his tail. He dived and only three of them followed him to 10,000 feet and then went back to France.

Squadron Leader Denholm claimed a damaged Me109:

> I saw two vic's of five Me109's pass at 20,000 feet underneath us and ordered the squadron to attack. We dived down. The Me109 which I picked out did one or two circles and then dived for home. I fired 1,600 rounds at it at ranges of about 150 yards and lost it in a layer of cloud, when he was emitting black smoke and not flying very fast.

George Denholm's attack was delivered at 09.45 hours over Maidstone at a height of 23,000 feet.

Shortly after Uncle George had seen the damaged 109 make good his escape, Peter Howes was shot down by Me109s of Stab JG/26 and/or III/JG53. His Spitfire X4323 crashed at Kennington, near Ashford, with the 21-year-old still in the cockpit. His remains were taken to the Woking (St John's) crematorium in Surrey.

Peter Howes and Richard had been good friends, having been at Trinity together; both had joined the OUAS and gone through each stage of their training at the same time. Most of Richard's friends had undergone their flying training prior to his having joined the UAS, and Peter was probably the only one to have completed the entire course with him. They had then gone to Hastings, Kinloss, Old Sarum and then Aston Down together before Peter had been posted to No.54 Squadron, then based at Rochford, on 8 July. Like Richard, Peter could speak German, and during his time with 54 Squadron he was called upon to translate for a captured German bomber pilot. Al Deere wrote in his book *Nine Lives*:

> There was a surprise in store for us that evening when we returned to the mess, in the person of a Luftwaffe bomber pilot, who had crash-landed and was under escort in the writing-room. He had made a forced landing not far from the airfield and, together with a crew of three N.C.O.'s, had been brought to Hornchurch for safe custody. Full of curiosity to get a look at this specimen of Hitler's Aryan elite and, if nothing else, to poke faces at him, we hurried into the writing-room to be met by a rather small, dark and jack-booted officer who gave us a most haughty look as if to say, "You can stare, but my turn will come." Through the medium of P/O Peter Howe [*sic*], a squadron pilot who spoke German, we learned that the officer was in no way alarmed at his predicament and, indeed had assured Howe that Hitler would be in London within two weeks. He didn't expect to remain a prisoner for long and for this reason thought it necessary to carry only toilet

requisites in the event of being shot down! . . . The cockiness of this German pilot certainly had the opposite effect from that which he had hoped to convey. To those of us who were feeling low and near breaking point it was like a shot of adrenaline, and with a rejuvenated spirit we faced the next day.

By the time Richard arrived at Hornchurch with 603, Peter had already been there for some time with 54 Squadron. He was physically and mentally exhausted. With so little experience he was struggling to survive against the odds, and unhappy with his lack of success. On 11 September he had been posted to 603 Squadron after 54 had been posted away for a well earned rest. Perhaps he requested a return to the front line as he had still not shot down an enemy aircraft. In response, Peter was initially posted to No.234 Squadron at Middle Wallop, before being sent to 603 at Hornchurch. One week later he was dead. Despite being initially unhappy at having his plans for the future interrupted by the war, he had committed himself passionately to fighting the Germans.

Richard was beginning to feel more and more alone as each of his friends were killed. It would be 17 months before, as the last of the 'long-haired boys', he would join them.

During the same combat patrol in which Peter Howes was killed, Sergeant George Bailey landed back at base with the fuselage of his Spitfire K9803 badly damaged by a 20mm cannon shell received in combat over Maidstone at 10.00 hours.

Friday 27 September 1940

Intelligence Patrol Report = 603 Squadron
11.46-12.56 hours
27.9.40

At 11.46 hours, ten aircraft took off from Rochford to patrol Hornchurch at 18,000 feet. When at 18,000 feet over Maidstone, four Me109's went across the bows of the squadron. The squadron chased them and they turned east. When in mid-Channel, two of the Bf109's turned and came back towards England.

P/O Dexter DFC and P/O Cardell were together when P/O Cardell was fired at by two Me109's. P/O Cardell baled out from 500 feet, 400 yards out in the sea off Folkestone. His parachute failed to open, but he came up immediately and was seen floating head well above the water. The machine crashed near him. P/O Dexter circled for ten minutes calling up rival (other squadrons) and 603 Squadron, but got no reply. There were several people on the beach and he tried to attract their notice. As they showed complete apathy and no boats put out, he crashed his machine on the beach, and after much waste of time, he got a boat from a fisherman, but by then P/O Cardell was drowned. A naval launch arrived on the scene an hour later.

Annoyance is clearly evident in the IO's reporting of the events surrounding the slow response to a pilot in distress, enhanced no doubt by Dexter's own interpretation of events. His anger is understandable.

Pilot Officer Dexter claimed one Me109 destroyed during this patrol and his combat report reads:

Returning home with the squadron, I saw one Me109 making for France. After chasing it for some time, I engaged from the rear and fired until a white stream came from the starboard wing root. The machine rose to 500 feet and the pilot baled out.

At this time, P/O Cardell was engaging another 109, which he destroyed. I saw the aircraft hit the water. Five more Me109's came down at us out of the sun. After a short engagement, I saw P/O Cardell make for home. I followed him and observed him to be having difficulty with his aircraft. He baled out at 500 feet, a quarter of a mile off Folkestone beach, but his parachute failed to open.

I circled for ten minutes and as no attempt was made by the people on the beach to rescue P/O Cardell, I force-landed on the beach, commandeered a rowing boat and picked up P/O Cardell. He had, however, by that time been drowned.

Peter Dexter made his initial attack which resulted in the destruction of a Me109 at 12.00 hours at a height of 500 feet. The squadron intelligence officer filed an 'F' form combat report confirming the destruction of one Me109 on behalf of Pip Cardell, witnessed by Peter Dexter.

It was thought that Pip may have been wounded when he and Dexter were bounced by the five 109s, as he was busy finishing off his 109. His Spitfire, N3244, was also damaged.

Pip initially attempted to re-gain English soil but he was clearly having trouble flying his crippled Spitfire. As his failing aircraft neared stalling speed with the risk of it simply spinning out of control, he was forced to abandon it at 12.45 hours, a quarter of a mile off Folkestone beach, close by the pier. Dexter, knowing that he could do nothing to help, watched in horror as Pip jumped and plummeted into the sea. His parachute left the pack but seemingly failed to deploy by the time he hit the water. Dexter repeatedly flew over Folkestone harbour and any potential rescue boats that were slow to put out. Furious at the attitude of the onlookers, in a better position than he to take action to help the stricken pilot, he made his decision. He lowered his flaps and crash-landed his Spitfire X4250 on Folkestone beach, crashing through barbed wire defences and stopping just yards short of an area where mines had apparently been placed. He climbed out of his cockpit and, still encumbered in his flying gear, ran to a group of six men who were attempting to launch two boats, but they lacked his sense of urgency. Hastily ditching his flying gear he helped to launch the first and jumped aboard the second.

When they reached Pip he was floating in his Mae West but sadly was already dead. It was a calm, windless day and the surface of the sea was smooth. The reason for his parachute not opening completely during his short descent was because the altitude was insufficient for an adequate deployment. The airflow drags the released 'chute from the bag and fills the silk canopy. With insufficient airflow, the expression a 'streamer' could be used to describe the action of the parachute; 500 feet had been too low for him to stand any chance over land. Over the sea, he obviously survived the fall initially but died soon after from several possible causes; drowning (as the IO notes in his report), wounds received in combat or, as is very likely, injuries received from the fall. Hitting the sea from that height would have been akin to hitting a brick wall. His death certificate stated: 'Multiple injuries received due to war service.'

Continuing with the combat patrols from Friday 27 September 1940, George Denholm claimed a Me109 probable out of a formation of four at 12.15 over Maidstone at a height of 18,000 feet:

> I saw four Me109s fly across the bows of the squadron about 400 yards away, so I ordered 'A' Flight to attack. The 109s started to dive for France, except for one which became separated from the rest and of which I lost sight. I selected the nearest of the others and did a series of attacks on it from underneath at a range of about 400 yards, this being the nearest I could get to him. Eventually about half-way across the Channel, the other two which were above, turned back north again, and the one I was attacking, slowed up considerably, so that I was able to get quite close, but by this time my ammunition was exhausted.
>
> From the position in which I finished up, I could not see much, as he was right in the sun, but from reports from other members of the flight, it appears that the 109 was emitting a thick stream of glycol.
>
> I thought I was above at that point, so I dived into the haze which was over the sea and made for home.

Sergeant Brian MacNamara was continuing his run of success in the squadron with a claim of a Me109 damaged. His experience had been rewarded with responsibility:

> I was Guard section leader when the squadron was proceeding north near

Dungeness. I saw a 109 flying very low going south. I peeled off and chased it, firing continuously. I could see my incendiaries bursting on the machine and black smoke began to come from the engine and the enemy began to slow down and turn as if about to land on the water. However two Me109s suddenly appeared 200 yards ahead of me out of the haze and shooting at me. I was forced to turn and run. The enemy chased me till I had crossed the English coast. I flew about 20 feet off the water, taking violent evasive action and the enemy's bursts missed mostly through insufficient deflection. In fine pitch, with full throttle and the red lever pressed, I appeared to be drawing away from the 109's, as their fire slackened for the last mile or two and when I turned, they were further behind me than at the start of the action.

MacNamara's attack was delivered at 12.00 hours between Dungeness and the French coast. The height of the enemy fighter above the surface of the sea was just 50 feet when he attacked it, opening fire from 300 yards.

At 15.50 hours Colin Pinckney claimed a Me109 probable:

When on patrol with 603 Squadron, I saw 30 Me109's flying beneath us at 25,000 feet and after being ordered into line astern, attacked a single machine at the back of the formation. After my first burst from astern, enemy aircraft took evasive action by turning in towards me, with glycol streaming from its engine. I followed him down through cloud to 2,000 feet, attacking it from the quarter astern. Last seen, the enemy was a few feet above the ground near Herne Bay, with engine ticking over.

Saturday 28 September 1940

After this day's combat patrols Colin brought Richard news of the death of Flight Lieutenant Ken Macdonald, deputy to CO George Denholm.

While flying Spitfire L1076 Ken Macdonald had been bounced by Me109s of II/JG26 over Gillingham at 10.20 a.m. His aircraft was probably shot down by Oberleutnant Walter Schneider, CO of the 6th Staffel, crashing on the site of Brompton Barracks, home of the Royal Engineers. Ken had claimed three enemy aircraft destroyed.

Albert Johnson was a 19-year-old Royal Engineer on sentry duty at the barracks and witnessed the whole episode. Macdonald's Spitfire circled overhead and Johnson felt a chill as he realised that the pilot knew he wasn't going to make it back to his aerodrome and was trying to look for a place to land. All that lay below, however, were houses, schools, factories and the barrack blocks stretched out beneath him with the many occupants only vaguely aware of what was happening in the skies outside. If the pilot allowed his Spitfire to crash in a heavily populated area, innocent lives may be lost.

The Spitfire spiralled down to within a thousand feet of the ground, its starboard wing now ablaze. Johnson reported seeing the Spitfire pass level with the Memorial Arch, narrowly missing the machine-gun nest on-top (an under-estimation of the exact altitude). He then saw Macdonald steer his aircraft, trailing thick smoke, away from the buildings and towards the Royal Engineers' barrack parade ground, which was the only open ground in the immediate vicinity. He then proceeded to climb out of the cockpit of his Spitfire onto the port wing and jump from about 400 feet. His parachute had barely left its pack when his body hit the ground. He had been too low and had died instantly in the fall. Johnson had been able to see the pilot clearly when he jumped. The Spitfire crashed onto the parade ground, uprooting one of a row of trees, and narrowly missing the barrack block by a matter of feet. The aircraft crashed in a sheet of flame followed a short while later by the crackle of exploding ammunition.

This brave act was also witnessed by Corporal F.E. Hesslewood, Royal Engineers, who reported that he had seen Macdonald stand up in the cockpit and place his left leg over the side and onto the port wing of his Spitfire in order to bale out, but then climb back in again in order to steer his aircraft away from the populated area. This was one of a number of reports that stated the same. After the war, one of the soldiers that witnessed this event made contact with a member of the ground crew of 603 and passed on this story in order for it not to be forgotten.

Contrary to the eyewitness statements, it was reported that Ken Macdonald's body actually landed on the parade ground of St Mary's Barracks, a quarter of a mile further on from the crash site.

Unusually, the crash made little impression on the surface of the parade ground. Despite the high speed impact the engine was not buried in any way. The ensuing fire scorched the leaves off the nearby trees. The aircraft was annihilated, with only the Merlin engine, a piece of the fuselage and tail section to identify the remains as having once been a Spitfire. A Queen Mary transporter took the wreckage away the following morning, after a number of photographs had been taken, leaving a scorched area with the uprooted tree as a sad reminder of the sacrifice made by Ken Macdonald.

Today the trees around the parade ground are all new. The trees that were there during the war were all blown down during the hurricane of 1987. New saplings have since been planted and have practically reached the same size as their predecessors. It is interesting that the one replacing that which was uprooted by Macdonald's Spitfire is noticeably undersized compared with the rest.

The body of Ken Macdonald was removed from the Queen Mary's Barracks parade ground and taken home to Edinburgh where he was cremated at Warriston crematorium. He was 28 years old and had now been reunited with his younger brother Don. Many years later Albert Johnson was able to confirm the identity of the young pilot who had left such an overwhelmingly sad but inspiring impression on him that day.

The Edinburgh family had lost both sons in aerial warfare. Their mother, Ewen, was so griefstricken that she died on 18 December 1940, of what was described as a broken-heart, having suffered such a terrible shock. The shock was indeed real and harrowing, although in actual fact she allowed a stomach ulcer to become life threatening as a result of her loss of will to live.

In 1979 a letter appeared in the *Sapper* magazine written by Major R.J. Simmons (Ret'd), who had been on a course at Brompton Barracks in 1939, when all courses were stopped. It is entitled 'Spitfire at Brompton':

> Many of your readers will have marched through the 'Memorial Arch'. How many, I wonder, have stood on the top of it?
>
> Whilst awaiting a posting to a Field unit, I was given the job of mounting a sand-bagged Bren Gun 'Ack-Ack' emplacement on top of the 'Memo Arch'. To my great disappointment (and possibly good fortune) the attack never came.
>
> A year later, I was back at Brompton on another course. The afternoon parade had just mustered, with a 'dog-fight' going on over-head. A Spitfire was shot down right on to the Square, caught fire, and bullets flew in all directions. Never was that parade ground cleared so quickly! The only casualty was a cut eye, suffered by somebody in a fall down the basement steps. The pilot parachuted safely [*sic*] on to the parade ground at St Mary's Barracks, a little way down the road.

Later that same day some of the 'old hands' in 603 were to reap further success.

Intelligence Report, 603 Squadron
13.10-14.55 hours.
28.9.40

Eight aircraft of 603 Squadron took off from Hornchurch and joined 222 Squadron on the Maidstone patrol line at 15,000 feet, 603 Squadron leading. They then saw smoke trails going east and climbed to investigate to 30,000 feet, but the smoke trails by that time had disappeared. Still on the Maidstone patrol line, 222

Squadron had to go down to 17,000 feet owing to the lack of oxygen and 603 saw about 16 Me109's in a straggling formation going west at 23,000 feet.

603 went into line astern and dived, chasing the Me109's westwards. The Me109's did not appear to see the squadron till they were fired upon, but Guard 1 of 603 was attacked by a vic of three Me109's, which peeled off and started to dive on him. Cloud cover ten-tenths at 1,000 feet.

Pilot Officer Sheep Gilroy DFC destroyed a Me109 which was seen to go down in flames:

Attack was delivered from astern after following enemy aircraft through a tight half-roll. Smoke followed by flames, issued from the enemy aircraft and it dived vertically with cowling and hood coming off. The pilot was not seen to jump, but he may have delayed opening parachute until reaching cloud.

Gilroy was flying as Red 3 in 'A' Flight when he delivered this attack at 14.32 hours, south-east of London at a height of 23,000 feet.

Flight Lieutenant 'Jack' Haig, one of the longest standing members of the squadron, claimed one Me109 damaged:

When leading 603 Squadron and followed by 222 Squadron, we sighted about fifteen Bf109's below at about 25,000 feet. We dived down from 31,000 feet and came up astern of them. I fired a good burst at one and it dropped out of the formation with white smoke coming from it. I broke away and did not see it again, as one Me109 came diving down on me, and so I was fully occupied.

Haig led the squadron as 'A' Flight commander and delivered his attack at 14.30 hours, in an area north of Maidstone at 25,000 feet.

Pilot Officer Bill Read damaged a Me109:

I was patrolling as Red 2 with 603 Squadron at 31,000 feet when approximately 16 Bf109's were sighted below and to starboard, heading west.

The squadron was ordered into line astern and came round into a gentle dive, attacking the enemy aircraft from dead astern. The Me109 which I engaged did an abrupt stall turn, nearly colliding with another. It then dived and I followed, giving it further bursts. White smoke streamed from its port exhausts and I left it going straight down. I was forced to leave it, being attacked from behind by another Me109.

Bill Read was with 'A' Flight and had attacked the 109 at 14.35 hours, over Sevenoaks at 26,000 feet. Only six of his eight guns had functioned.

On 29 September 1940, 603 Squadron received Signal A236 from the group commander, Keith Park: 'Group commander sends warm congratulations to 603 Squadron on their successful fighting without casualties to themselves, showing exceptional leadership and straight shooting.'

The message was copied into the squadron ORB from that period, which is today kept at the Public Record Office at Kew. The word 'without' has been heavily underlined by a latter-day 'reader' and following the exclamation mark added at the end of the sentence, the same hand had scrawled: '9 killed, 9 wounded, 1 missing, 1 POW – In 30 days!' It is inconceivable that Keith Park had intentionally made such an error. Perhaps such a mistake had occurred during administration.

* * *

No.603 Squadron's involvement continued up until, and beyond, the 'official' end of the Battle of Britain on 31 October 1940.

On Wednesday 2 October at 10.30 am, Pilot Officer Dexter was shot down in Spitfire P9553 by Me109s of III/JG53 over Croydon. He managed to bale out but had received a serious gunshot wound to his leg which would keep him in hospital for some time. A few seconds prior to his aircraft being hit he managed to shoot down a Me109, confirmed as having been destroyed. Spitfire P9553 crashed and burned out. It had been used as a back-drop for a photograph taken of Pip Cardell, just before he was killed. Up until that time its pilots had also included Peter Pease.

On 3 October 1940 Richard's promotion to flying officer was recorded in the *London Gazette*.

On Saturday 5 October Jim 'Black' Morton, now one of the most successful pilots in the squadron, was shot down by Me109s of II/JG53 over Dover at 11.55 hours. He managed to bale out but had been badly burned prior to escaping from the cockpit. His Spitfire, K9807, crashed near Chilham. He would play no further part in the battle.

On 27 October the South African Flying Officer Goldsmith was shot down in a surprise attack by a superior force of Me109s of either II/JG51 or III/JG27, south of Maidstone at 14.05 hours. He had been posted to the squadron in July 1940 having previously flown Lysanders with the Army Co-op. He had been with 'A' Flight at Dyce. On 3 September he had been transferred to No.54 Squadron, also at Hornchurch, but the squadron was then sent to Catterick for rest and to reform. On 28 September, in response to a request for experienced volunteers to return to the harder hit squadrons in the south, he returned to 603 and his now dwindling group of friends. His Spitfire II, P3479, crashed near Waltham and Goldsmith was grievously wounded. His shattered body was removed from the wreckage and rushed to hospital where he died the next day. He was 23 years old and is buried in Hornchurch cemetery.

Two other pilots recently arrived from 611 Squadron lost their aircraft in this combat. Dewey was killed while Maxwell managed to bale out.

It is possible that the two Me109s that fell to the guns of No.603 Squadron were the last to fall to the Edinburgh unit in the Battle of Britain, although a few of its pilots, and many others besides, would continue to fight and yet more would lose their lives before the end of WWII. It must not be forgotten that this aerial battle continued into 1941, when many, including the German pilots, believed the real Battle of Britain ended.

* * *

It had not yet occurred to Richard that the extent of his injuries meant he would never rejoin 603, or fly a fighter again in combat. The news was sad and with the time that he now had available he would brood over the loss of these dear, young men against his own survival. He would spend many hours trying to justify his part in the war, that of his friends, and whether it was all worthwhile. Did his friends deserve to die, did humanity deserve the sacrifice which had been made for it by his friends and ultimately by him too?

When the battle had started, Richard had known exactly what his attitude had been towards the idea of fighting for this country, although he was aware that his commitment was not as great as Peter's. This troubled him. He had made his own conscious decision about what his contribution would be and the spirit in which it would be undertaken. He had also seen the awful side of war but he had survived thus far, achieving an above-average level of success in combat. Richard had admitted to being content with his lot as a fighter pilot. He was satisfied that he had remained steadfast throughout the short period he had been involved. Bearing in mind the deaths of so many that he had known, some of whom had been with him at Trinity, he would now put his reasoning to the test and I believe that, at the end of what would turn out to be a 26-month assessment, he would do the same again if he was required to do so, even with such a high price to pay. But his attitude towards it would be different. He would come to see it as a national historic emergency with moral implications, as had Peter Pease.

These many hours of contemplation were to provide the foundation for his decision to return to flying, in as committed a way as his dearest friends had been.

The good news, amongst such terrible news that Colin brought for Richard, was that Brian Carbury, Ras Berry and Sheep Gilroy had all been awarded the DFC, with Brian about to get a Bar to his. He had been the most successful pilot in the squadron during those hard-fought weeks, and richly deserved the accolade. The squadron's confirmed score was also nearing the 100 mark with the celebration, recounted by Stapme Stapleton, occurring not far from where Richard was lying in his hospital bed.

During November, Colin brought news of the squadron having come up against the Italian air force in combat on 23 November 1940. Eight Spitfires had been patrolling when they sighted 20 Italian Air Force Fiat CR42 fighters, ten miles south-west of Dover, protecting a bomber force of Italian Fiat BR20s, which was retreating, after an unsuccessful attempt to attack our coastal shipping. Seven of the Italian fighters were claimed 'destroyed', with two 'probables' and two 'damaged'. No 603 pilots or aircraft were lost. It was a great morale booster. Ras Berry's memories, as related to me, make this point. Colin told Richard that 603 had been in the air with 41 Squadron at the time when Uncle George called out:

'Wops ahead.'
'Where are they?' asked 41 Squadron.
'Shan't tell you,' came back the answer. 'We're only outnumbered three to one.'
Colin told me that it was the most unsporting thing he had ever had to do, rather like shooting sitting birds, as he so typically put it.

* * *

Shortly after Peter Pease had died, Richard received an unexpected visit from somebody that would become very dear to him indeed, Peter's fiancée Denise Maxwell-Woosnam. It was to Denise that Richard later dedicated *The Last Enemy*. She decided to go and see Richard in hospital and although she had heard much about him from Peter, she had never actually met him. After a nervous start it was therapeutic for them both, and once she began to talk about Peter, Denise felt an intense understanding and sympathy from Richard.

At a time when Richard was still wrestling with the anguish of losing several friends including his best friend and idol, such feelings would have been most comforting. He may well have been looking for an association with Peter, and hypersensitive to any mannerism that he recognised in Denise as being that of his dead friend. Denise recalled that it was an awkward meeting, Richard was in severe pain and she was not sure she should have visited him:

'I hope you'll excuse me coming to see you like this,' she said; '. . . but I was going to be married to Peter. He often spoke of you and wanted so much to see you. So I hope you won't mind me coming instead.'

In his last letter to Denise, written on 14th September, Peter wrote that he had finally found enough time to locate the whereabouts of Richard and that he must go to see '. . . our Mr Hillary' the next day. He had been killed on the 15th.

Richard had been surprised to see her, to come face to face with someone of whom he had heard so much. He was also surprised that she had taken the time to visit him and this would have appealed to his sensitive side. Initially he found that he was unable to say any of the things that he wanted to say, mainly due to the ward being very busy at the time, and lacking in privacy. He seemed to lack the confidence to say anything of importance during that first visit perhaps because of an initial shyness in her company, but more likely owing to the awe in which he held her as he was not known for being shy. She was beautiful, intelligent and he saw in her so many qualities that Peter had possessed. He had seen in Peter what he believed to be perfection and now quite unexpectedly he was witnessing the same qualities in what he intimated was the female equivalent.

Richard was aware of Denise's shyness almost at once. Nevertheless, it was she who did most of the talking during that first meeting. It was Richard's kindness and understanding shown towards her, despite suffering pain from his injuries, which Denise remembered. When she had left the hospital Richard asked a nurse to take a dictation in which he asked Denise if she would come again but give him more warning.

The following day Denise returned and they talked almost entirely of Peter. She left when Richard's tea was brought in. He was unable to feed himself due to his bandaged hands and, as the nurses provided assistance, Denise thought he might feel uncomfortable with her looking on so she left promising to call again the next day. Richard subsequently asked for his tea to be stopped.

Denise was staying in her father's house in Eaton Place with their housekeeper. Her father was to remarry and had moved into the country. Denise had joined the ATS in 1938 and, until recently, had been part of an anti-aircraft battery unit situated close to Peter, within sight of Hornchurch. When Peter had been killed she was granted compassionate leave for a short time, before being posted to the War Office. There she worked as a senior commander for the ATS on recruitment, to which she cycled each morning. Her sister Penny worked in the Admiralty.

During her visits to the Masonic, Denise talked a little about herself, but for most of the time she talked about Peter, and Richard listened intently when she spoke. Although he himself had failed to succeed in getting Peter to open up in a way that would reveal his true self, he now had an opportunity to learn more from Denise. Richard saw many similarities between these two wonderful people. He later wrote that he was of the opinion that Denise was the 'reincarnation of Peter'. He believed that such was the strength of her own spirit he could initially offer very little in words of comfort. For her spirit was far greater than his, and both Peter and Denise had committed themselves to making sure that their freedom, along with that of the rest of the country, was not taken away. Richard felt that his own commitment was lacking by comparison. When Peter had gone to war he had no doubts about the job that needed to be done and the risks that came with it. Although Richard was willing to fight for his own well-being the nagging doubts came when he analysed his commitment to fighting for others. Peter and Denise believed they were fighting for the freedom of the whole world.

Despite her obvious display of courage, Denise had been devastated by the loss of Peter. The time she spent with Richard was an intermediate period of therapy, of gradually coming to terms with her loss supported by her own spirit and strong religious beliefs.

They talked about practical subjects typical of the young people of that era. So many others did the same irrespective of the theatre of war in which they were serving at the time, home or abroad, onboard ships, in the desert or in POW camps. They talked about their hopes for after the conflict. The hope that the opportunity for change would be taken for the better, to improve things from the way they were before the war. To change from the old order and to avoid religious revival. This was what Richard hoped for. He also used Denise as he used Peter, to measure his own beliefs.

He had brought her out of her grief, even if it was for a brief spell, to realise and appreciate that there was hope and happiness in the future, without Peter.

They would occasionally argue, Richard taking the opposite side just for the sake of it. This was something he had always loved to do, and was particularly good at. This personality trait had so often been misunderstood by certain individuals that had known him. It was clear to Denise at that time that Richard's two main passions were flying and writing and his enthusiasm for life was unbounded.

Richard had learnt of Peter's death in a letter from Colin Pinckney and Denise later brought news of how, it was thought, Peter had been killed. When Denise had asked Richard if he would like to hear what had happened, he interrupted her, struggled to sit up due to his bandaged hands, and said: 'Let me tell you. . . .'. Richard told her of the 'premonition' he had had whilst under the anaesthetic, in which he had seen Peter killed. As far as Denise was concerned Richard was correct in every detail. Everything that she had been told featured in Richard's dream, although there is no mention of her confirming these details in *The Last Enemy*.

Perhaps Richard's earlier premonition was as a consequence of being given the news while delirious with pain, under the effects of the morphine. Available details would have been fairly limited and could have been passed on by a friend and colleague who had obtained details from the station adjutant. George Denholm would have been given the news of Peter's death when the crash team had reached and identified the wreckage of the Spitfire and Peter's body. The station adjutant at Hornchurch then passed the dreadful news on to Peter's relatives, as he had when Richard had been shot down. Despite Richard remembering that he was only allowed visits by relatives until he was stronger, others were allowed to sit with him.

* * *

As the weather hardened into winter, Richard spent many hours in thought, staring out of the windows watching the leaves turn to brown, and eventually fall from the trees and cover the paths and flower beds. The sight of the temporary air-raid shelters, barrage balloon and anti-aircraft units ensured that his inadvertent escape from the war was not complete. The skies more frequently cloudy and grey, the people below wrapped up against the elements, their own clothing lacking the bright colours of those of the season now past.

At night the German bombers continued in their attempt to pound London into submission, although Richard saw little of the bombing at the Masonic. The people were enormously spirited and at night continued to fill the restaurants, clubs and pubs, perhaps as an act of defiance, but certainly to escape the horror of what was happening to their city. While many were trying to enjoy themselves, including the wealthy and soldiers, sailors and airmen on leave, there was a far greater number right in the thick of the seemingly relentless onslaught on London by the Luftwaffe bombers. While the citizens of the Capital took cover in the London Underground, basements and purpose built shelters, outside were the many anti-aircraft crews, police, LDV, Red Cross, and other officials bolstered by civilian volunteers busy carrying out their duties. The next morning these same people dusted themselves off and went about their normal daily duties. It was gloomy and Richard sought the company of his family and friends at this time.

The care the nurses provided was something that he held very dear. Denise was in a similar situation. She took one day at a time knowing eventually that the pain must soften, but her faith and the therapy which her friends and Richard supplied was needed. Her flat was visited regularly by friends of both herself and Penny, but also friends of Peter, including Colin, who stopped by to offer support. When they had gone Denise would welcome the solitude to reflect on what might have been had Peter lived, and what the future may hold for her now.

During one of his visits to her flat, Colin announced to Denise and Richard that he was to be posted to No.243 Squadron on 29 December, and they were due to go to the 'near east'. Richard was immediately engulfed with a feeling of dread, that he would lose the last of his closest friends from this period of his life. He tried to persuade Colin to apply to remain in Britain, for he had somehow gained the impression that the odds of him surviving were less over there. In the case of Colin, he was not mistaken. Not long afterwards he left for Singapore.

During the period in which Richard was confined to his bed at the Masonic he began to keep a diary, and this diary apparently formed the basis for *The Last Enemy*. With both hands swathed in bandages he was forced to hold his pencil in his left hand, as if holding a hammer, this despite being right-handed. The left hand was not as badly burned as the right and less heavily bandaged out of the two. Writing proved very difficult for him. From surviving extracts reprinted in Lovat Dickson's biography of Richard, that which he wrote in his diary certainly seems to have been far franker than what appeared in his book. It certainly lacks the finish that the book received before publication. Unfortunately, no such diary has been seen since.

Lovat Dickson's book is the only evidence of the existence of such a diary. Lovat Dickson had yet to meet Richard, several months hence, and would have had to have been in possession of it *after* Richard's death in order to quote from it during the writing of his biography. The question is what happened to it after Lovat Dickson finished with it?

If Richard did keep a detailed day-to-day diary that was ultimately used as a basis for *The Last Enemy* then surely it would have been somewhat more accurate in its detail. My opinion is that Richard did keep a diary of sorts but that it actually only consisted of a number of loose pages of notes made during his recovery and that it was kept in order to record specific events and also satisfy his enthusiasm for writing.

Then came the day when his doctor agreed to let Richard out from the hospital, for short walks initially, but eventually he was allowed to stay out all day. His strength was returning; the care he had received had helped to put back some of the weight lost over the last few months. He had become a very thin and frail shadow of himself compared with his size and strength attained during the rowing trials for the Oxford rowing VIII a mere year and half before.

His walks took him into the locality where he could see London for himself. He savoured the sights and smells that initially he was hypersensitive to. He was used to the smells of the hospital wards, the ether, alcohol, fresh sterile lint dressings, hospital food, the warm and frequently stale air. Now he could take his time and taste the fresh air, smell the dampness of rain-soaked streets and feel the wind on his injured face. Sue, his personal nurse, prepared him for his first sojourn out into the Ravenscourt Park area. She got him dressed, placed cotton wool under his eyes, partly to protect and partly to stop his watering, lidless eyes from streaming tears down his face. She then gave him a pair of dark glasses, again to protect his sensitive eyes. The glasses must have also served to reduce the attention drawn to his injured eyes from the unsubtle gaze of members of the public. The burns received on his right hand were the most severe. They would always be a serious problem and the hand would have little useful function over the next two years. To protect the limb from inadvertent contact, causing excruciating pain, Sue placed Richard's right arm in an elevated sling so the hand could be guarded against his upper chest. And so he set forth, enjoying all that was outside in a positive frame of mind. As he took in all that was going on around him he believed his existence to be but a small part of the 'work of God'.

In actual fact Richard recorded this event in his diary after a trip to London sometime later, while he was a patient at East Grinstead. It was subsequently inserted in *The Last Enemy* prior to publication and edited to appear relevant to his time at The Masonic. The diary version appears later in the story.

It is interesting to compare his feelings towards the city with those of when he was a young boy. He used to hate the city, but he had learnt to appreciate the qualities of both the city and the countryside.

* * *

It was not long before he was once again enjoying the night-life of the better establishments in the West End, which he had enjoyed in the company of his university colleagues before the war. He did not see his disfigurement as something that should be hidden away. He had suffered those injuries fighting against the Germans. Dressed in his uniform with the 'wings' brevet on his tunic breast, all those that saw him would know how he had received his terrible injuries. I believe that when he went out he felt a certain amount of pride at their knowing he had fought and been injured in battle in the skies over England. His original opinion of aerial warfare, compared with that of the soldier, still existed.

Now and again Richard was able to take advantage of his new-found freedom and lunch at home with his mother who was working a full day with the Red Cross in the Prisoner of War Department. Very occasionally he would join his father for lunch at his club, if he could find the time for such a break from his work with the Sudan government. It was after one such lunch with his father that he met Bill Aitken, whom he had not seen since their days together at Old Sarum. Bill was still with Army Co-operation.

Over coffee they brought each other up-to-date with the news of their mutual friends. Bill was forced to admit that he had been wrong when he had assessed Frank Waldron and Nigel Bicknell as being of no use when it came down to fighting for the country. He had learnt that Nigel Bicknell had become a Blenheim pilot and been awarded the DFC. His squadron was on its way to attack a target in France when one engine cut out. Bicknell was able to reach and bomb the objective but was forced to ditch in the sea following the failure of the other engine during the return trip. In the icy water, he managed to support one of the surviving crew members for six hours before they were rescued. Having left the RAF, Frank Waldron eventually joined the Guards.

As the two parted Bill Aitken told Richard that of the 'ex-bad boys', he was the best example of a change for the better. Richard did not agree and told Bill that he was mistaken and that if anything he believed more strongly than ever in the ideas he had expressed when they were last together.

Bill had seen nothing of Richard since Old Sarum, therefore on what did he base his psychoanalysis? Knowing that Richard had been successful in combat and having been shot down and badly burned in the process would be sufficient, as he sat before him with his injuries evident. It is likely he had heard about Richard on the 'grapevine'. But at the time that Bill made his original assessment of the threesome, Richard was committed to becoming a pilot, with a preference for becoming specifically a fighter pilot; hardly the intentions of someone with the inclination to shirk combat, when faced with it. I believe that Richard reacted to this comment in his inimitable way. Not wanting to appear to conform. It could also be considered that he uses the situation to show that there has been a conscious improvement in his personality, and therefore he included a reaction that was intended to display such a change.

Nigel Bicknell's award of the DFC would add to Richard's frustration at a later date when so many of his colleagues had received awards. Despite his having shot down five enemy aircraft he had not received any recognition in this form, nor would he.

Meanwhile, Richard continued to visit Denise in her flat. Most evenings between tea-time and eight o'clock, when he was supposed to be returning to the ward in the Masonic, he stopped off on his way from his parents' flat to visit Denise. If the air-raid siren sounded then they would shelter in the basement where Richard would tell her stories or simply sleep, as he was still very weak. He was to her, one of a number of special friends. To Richard, she had come to mean everything. From his description of that first meeting, written some time later when his feelings for her had had time to develop, it is clear he had fallen in love with her. They spent hours talking together, entering into deep discussions on aspects of life. He wanted to shake her out of her solemnity, to take a fresh look at life, but with him as an integral part of it. It was in his nature to never let the opportunity of trying to win over the feelings of a beautiful young lady pass him by. But Denise was very special. Here was a beautiful woman with a wonderful personality who had a great strength of character and an indomitable spirit. Her Christian faith was strong and she knew where her future lay and remained steadfast and unrelenting. Richard tried to snap her out of her mourning by being brutally blunt. But Denise was aware of what he was trying to do and told him that he was only hurting himself. She told him that Peter and herself were united spiritually:

> Peter and I are extremely bound together . . . in spite of all your intellectual subter-
> fuges and attempts to hide behind the cry of self-realisation, you lay in hospital
> and saw Peter die as clearly as if you had been with him. You told me so yourself.

Clearly it meant a great deal to Denise in accepting a credible explanation for the circumstances of Peter's death that both Richard's and the official interpretation tallied. Richard would ultimately lose his fight to gain anything more from Denise than her friendship. It could even be considered that Richard implied in his book that there was more to their friendship than actually existed. All Denise may have ever wanted was friendship with Richard because he had been a close friend of Peter's, and to talk of him together would be therapeutic. There were only a few women that had the ability to control Richard, and not succumb to his charm. Denise was certainly one of them.

Denise held a deep affection for Richard, and today she still treasures her memories of their brief time together.

Richard yearned for Denise's love, and would continue to do so, possibly even up until the time of his death.

* * *

There has been a great deal of emphasis placed on the so-called change in Richard's personality during his recovery period; that he became an altogether nicer person. Some are of the opinion that this change did take place, some believe that it did not. What is obvious though is that he was still a young man, with a rapidly evolving personality, who was eagerly searching for knowledge. He was still uncertain of where his true beliefs and opinions lay in so many subjects, and had so many questions he wanted answering. Did he disregard religion or was there still a place for it in his life? Did he believe that his true position was in the company of the upper-class or did he feel most at home in the company of his fellow fighter pilots, regardless of their background? Why shouldn't he experience changes as life progresses and be affected by those in his life that have had the greatest influence on him. We all look for role models. Perhaps he saw such examples in Peter Pease, Colin, Noel, Rusty Rushmer, Stapme, Ras Berry, and Brian Carbury, to name just a few that we have become familiar with. But in the main they were those who were dear to him. Perhaps, as would be quite natural, just a little bit of each of these men's qualities rubbed off on Richard as his own personality developed: 'I could not feel that their experience was mine, that it could do more than touch me in passing.'

He gradually became aware of this, and that the loss of his friends, the sense of closeness, this affinity, must fade. This experience had been greatly heightened during this period by having been so ill, and by meeting Denise. There, at the core, was still the Richard that his close friends had always known, and were so fond of.

Richard was also becoming aware that his feelings towards fighting had changed.

* * *

In October 603 Squadron was re-equipped with the Spitfire Mark II, on 3 December it moved to Rochford and ten days later, on 13 December, 603 Squadron was finally pulled out of the front line and travelled north to Drem, North Berwick. By this time, the weary pilots believed that although the fighting continued in the south, the battle for Britain had been won. The squadron had been in action nearly every day for 65 days of the battle; only two other squadrons had been in action for a longer time during the same period. According to Richard, 24 had travelled south, and only eight had returned, which is not quite correct. Those who returned north with the squadron were: Denholm, Boulter, Stapleton, Berry, Carbury, Gilroy, Haig, Morton, Pinckney, Read, Ritchie, Sarre, Stewart-Clark and Stokoe, fourteen of the original pilots who had travelled south, less than four months before. Nine of the original squadron had been killed. This number does not include those killed who were posted to 603 once they were at Hornchurch.

On 29 November a dinner had been organised by the squadron to celebrate the destruction of their 100th enemy aircraft. The dinner was at the Dorchester and attended, by invitation, by the CO of Hornchurch, Group Captain Bouchier. During his speech he had the opportunity to make amends for his original, hasty, assessment of the squadron when it had first arrived at his beloved Hornchurch. Some time later he recorded these opinions:

> Memories come crowding in upon me, and from their store I give you this of 603. They were, I think, the greatest squadron of them all . . . No squadron was ever regarded more highly. No squadron ever went to war with such quiet grace, with so little fuss, or with more determination . . . 603 was composed of a collection of quiet and serious young men; men from the city desks of Edinburgh and the fields of the Lothians.

> Of George Denholm he recorded that 603: '. . . was led by one whose quiet
> personality wrapped his squadron round as with a cloak, and made of them by his
> concern for them and by his leadership and example a great and valiant
> squadron.'

During the early part of 1941, Colin Pinckney wrote to a Canadian guide whom he had
befriended during one of his summer vacations before the war, and summarised his part
in the Battle of Britain:

> At the end of August we moved down to Hornchurch, outside London, and then
> the fun started. I got one the second day, but was shot down myself and jumped
> out. I was away for three weeks, but once back it was a case of once bitten twice
> shy. I managed to get three more Huns and one Italian, besides hitting a few
> others, and when the squadron returned to Edinburgh just before Christmas we
> had collected 107 destroyed and confirmed, so the Old Country did its stuff in the
> Battle of Britain.

A few days before the squadron returned north Joan Stapleton gave birth to a son,
Michael, at her parents' home in Chislehurst.

In February 1941, the squadron moved from Drem back to its home base at
Turnhouse. By May it was back in the south of England where it remained until
November when it was once again sent north for a rest.

From those fine people in and around Edinburgh that have assisted with my research,
I was able to get some idea of and appreciate the terrible loss that the families and
community in general felt as a result of the loss of their 'sons'. It has been said that time
heals all wounds, but in this case the deep sorrow felt is still so very evident. The loss
of those local pilots, along with those that fought alongside them, is still felt almost as
deeply today as it was all those years ago, the only difference is that many of the nearest
and dearest have now come to the end of their own lives and have been reunited with
their kin folk.

No.603 Squadron finished the Battle of Britain as the top-scoring day fighter unit in
Fighter Command, shooting down more Me109s than any other squadron. No.609
Squadron, with whom Noel Agazarian was still serving, had achieved 48 confirmed
victories and could be assessed therefore as being the second most successful squadron
in the battle. Thus the top two squadrons were auxiliary squadrons, with a further three
in the top five, and five in the top ten. However, these statistics present an inaccurate
picture in that it would be an aberration to credit an auxiliary squadron specifically with
this achievement, as many non-auxiliary pilots had joined these squadrons by the start
of the battle and the number continued to increase as new pilots arrived to replace those
lost. Although there were exceptions, many of these non-auxiliary pilots had accounted
for a high number of their squadrons 'kills'. In the case of 603 Squadron Stapleton,
Carbury and Berry (although he was RAFVR) alone were credited with more than half
of those enemy aircraft shot down by the squadron. Nevertheless, the high number of
confirmed kills that 603 achieved and its 86% accuracy of claim rate made them by a
very wide margin the most successful squadron during this period, scoring more than
double the average of victories for units operating Spitfires. Bearing in mind that during
this protracted action the over-claim rate on both sides was massive, with the RAF over-
claiming at a rate of two to one, No.603 Squadron's accuracy of claims rate at 86%
confirmed was exceptional.

During the 32 days that the squadron was in action during the battle, initial claims
were for aircraft shot down during July while they were defending the north-east coast
of Scotland. The squadron claimed 67 victories with 57.8 confirmed, 47 of which were
Me109 fighters. During this period 30 of the squadron's aircraft were lost, thus giving a
credited victory/loss ratio of one 603 Spitfire for every 1.9 enemy aircraft destroyed.

Richard's own input during the seven-day period 28 August – 3 September, amounted
to 11 patrols flown. The average duration was one and-a-half hours, per patrol, and the

time flying combat patrols totalled sixteen and-a-half hours. During this time he accounted for five enemy aircraft destroyed, all Me109 fighters, with an additional two probably destroyed and one damaged.

It can be estimated that from the time Richard converted to Spitfires at Aston Down in June until the time he was shot down on 3 September, he had amassed a total of approximately 100 hours on Spitfires. It has been written that Richard was unofficially allowed to fly the Spitfire during his recovery period and that he accumulated a further 60 hours. Although he did have the occasional flight in a Magister or a Gull during his recovery, he never flew the Spitfire again.

Whilst 603 Squadron was the top-scoring Fighter Command unit during the Battle of Britain it should be remembered that many squadrons fought long and hard during the Battle of France, in the period leading to and during the Battle of Britain, and up until the end of the war. Nevertheless, the achievements of this small group of individuals that made up 603 Squadron were indeed outstanding, with George Denholm, 'Ras' Berry, 'Stapme' Stapleton, Jim Morton, 'Sheep' Gilroy and the brilliant Brian Carbury probably being the most effective pilots in the squadron, taking into consideration not just the high number of patrols flown, but also the number of victories they were credited with. They were outstanding aerial combatants.

While Richard was recovering in hospital, he tried to understand why those few should be so successful and indeed survive the battle while he and his contemporaries were either killed or maimed. His assessment is based on this small number and even then it is not really a fair assessment of the situation. Those in the squadron who did not survive the battle were from a mixture of backgrounds, including those who had attended university. Even on a wider scale it could not be said that individuals from a background similar to Richard's were more likely to become casualties than:

> . . . the tough practical men who had come up the hard way, who were not fighting this war for any philosophical principles or economic ideals; who, unlike the average Oxford undergraduate, were not flying for aesthetic reasons, but because of an instinctive knowledge that this was the job for which they were most suited . . . while their more intellectual comrades would, alas, in the main be killed. They might answer, if asked why they fought, 'To smash Hitler!' But instinctively, inarticulately, they too were fighting for the things Peter Pease had died to preserve.
>
> Was there perhaps a new race of Englishmen arising out of this war, a race of men bred by the war, a harmonious synthesis of the governing class and the great rest of England; that synthesis of disparate backgrounds and upbringings to be seen at its best in RAF squadrons? While they were now possessed of no other thought than to win the war, yet having won it, would they this time refuse to step aside and remain indifferent to the peace-time fate of the country, once again leave government to the old governing class? . . . Would they see to it that there arose from their fusion representatives, not of the old gang, deciding at Lady Cufuffle's that Henry should have the Foreign Office and George the Ministry of Food [note the Henry George connotation!], nor figureheads for an angry but ineffectual Labour Party, but true representatives of the new England that should emerge from this struggle . . . Could they unite on a policy of humanity and sense to arrive at the settlement of problems which six thousand years of civilisation had failed to solve?
>
> And even though they failed, was there an obligation for the more thinking of them to try to contribute 'their little drop', however small, to the betterment of mankind? Was there that obligation, was that the goal towards which all should strive who were left, strengthened and confirmed by those who had died?
>
> Or was it still possible for men to lead the egocentric life, to work out their own salvation without concern for the rest; could they simply look to themselves – or, more important, could I? I still thought so.

CHAPTER TWELVE

THE MAESTRO

November – December 1940

Richard's strength continued to return during this period of recuperation, and his body weight increased to something like that which was appropriate for someone of his height and age. He was now strong enough to undergo surgery to rectify the damage to his face and hands. He had now been in hospital for nearly three months. Ahead lay a period of almost two years filled with existing and new experimental techniques of skin grafting surgery, the recovery from which would be slow.

Archibald McIndoe had visited Richard during those first few days at the Masonic and he was due to call again at eleven o'clock one November morning at the end of 1940. Richard had got himself ready with assistance from his nurse and was bathed and shaved with fresh dressings on his hands well in advance of his arrival:

> The charge nurse ushered him in fussily. Of medium height, he was thick-set and the line of his jaw was square. Behind his horn-rimmed spectacles a pair of tired eyes regarded me speculatively.
>
> 'Well,' he said, 'you certainly made a thorough job of it, didn't you?'
>
> He started to undo the dressings on my hands and I noticed his fingers – blunt, capable, incisive. By now all the tannic acid had been removed from my face and hands. He took a scalpel and tapped lightly on something white showing through the red granulating knuckle of my right forefinger.
>
> 'Bone,' he remarked laconically.
>
> He looked at the badly contracted eyelids and the rapidly forming keloids, and pursed his lips.
>
> 'Four new eyelids, I'm afraid, but you're not ready for them yet. I want all this skin to soften up a lot first. How would you like to go to the south coast for a bit?'
>
> He mentioned the official RAF convalescent hospital on the south coast, generously supplied with golf courses, tennis and squash courts. But as I could not use my hands, and abhorred seaside resorts during winter, I wasn't very enthusiastic.

The home on the south coast to which Richard was reluctant to go was situated in the Grand Hotel, Torquay, overlooking the beach. Although he did not go on this occasion he would later spend time recuperating there in the future, time that he enjoyed. Instead, he asked if he could be sent to a private house in Sussex which had been offered by the wealthy owners as a convalescent home for those who were being treated at the nearby East Grinstead hospital. It was at Dutton Homestall and owned by A.J. 'Johnny' Dewar, the whisky magnate, and his wife Kathleen. Richard must have found out about it from the nursing staff at the Masonic or perhaps it was a suggestion from McIndoe himself during one of his visits. McIndoe agreed to send Richard there for a period prior to initial reconstructive surgery on his face. Before he departed from Richard's bedside, Richard asked him how long it would be before he would be able to fly again. During his first visit the same question had brought the reply of 'six months', which had depressed Richard. But on this occasion the reply was based on a secondary assessment of his injuries and came as no surprise: 'Next war for you: those hands are going to be something of a problem.'

Indeed his hands were definitely going to be a problem, most particularly the right, and would remain so, being a contributing factor in his death just over two years hence. McIndoe left to join Richard's mother for lunch. Two days later, on 20 November, Richard was driven down to Dutton Homestall, convalescent home for officers, only two miles from the Queen Victoria Hospital, East Grinstead; a distance that became known as the 'Whisky Mile' for obvious reasons.

* * *

Life was very comfortable indeed for Richard during the various occasions he spent at the Red Cross convalescent home at Dutton Homestall as he waited for the condition of his injuries to improve enough for McIndoe to start reconstructive surgery on his face and hands. The original and comparatively small section of the house had once been the shooting lodge of John O'Gaunt in the Ashdown Forest. Kathleen Dewar had seen a large Tudor mansion in Cheshire to which she had taken a liking to, and having had it dismantled brick by brick and beam by beam, it was reconstructed adjoining the original house at Dutton Homestall. The Dewars moved into the original small section and offered the remainder with its large halls and bedrooms to the Red Cross. The Dewars were able to accommodate twenty people in their home, as many as the main building of the East Grinstead hospital itself, and provide them with a high level of comfort with plenty of good food including butter and eggs from their small farming facility. There were also horses in the stables for those who were able to ride. The patients were allowed to come and go as they pleased. All but three of his fellow officers were Army; the other three, including himself, were all pilots. Richard described his arrival at the home:

> The house was rambling and attractive, and ideal for a convalescent home. I was
> greeted at the door by Matron and led in to tea.

Richard found the company of the Army officers rather unexciting but a little later the arrival of one RAF and one Fleet Air Arm pilot livened the atmosphere: 'By dinner time I was preparing to resign myself to a comfortable if not stimulating period of relaxation, when a couple of genial souls came rolling in very late and I met Colin Hodgkinson and Tony Tollemache.'

Later, during this first evening at Dutton Homestall, Richard noticed that when Colin got to his feet after dinner, he walked stiff-legged with a rolling movement of the right hip. He had been unaware that he had artificial 'tin' legs. Colin described the first time he met Richard: 'One evening after Tony and I had been drinking a few pints in the 'Blue Lantern' at Forest Row, we came back rather late to find a new inhabitant: a slender, curly haired young man whose mere attitude as he sat at the table gave an impression of extraordinary maturity – Richard Hillary.'

Colin Hodgkinson had been a trainee pilot in the Fleet Air Arm at Gravesend when, on 12 May 1939 he had been involved in a flying accident in which his legs were smashed.

While Colin was at Dutton Homestall, and Richard was still at the Masonic, another member of No.603 Squadron arrived at the home for a period of rest. This was Jim MacPhail, who had been shot down and burned and sent to East Grinstead for treatment. Colin Hodgkinson's attempts to return to flying had up to this moment included one flight in a Cygnet Moth. When Jim MacPhail arrived he was to help him further:

> John MacPhail [John was a middle name he sometimes went by] of 603
> Squadron, shot down and burnt in the Battle of Britain, found himself at Dutton
> Homestall at the beginning of November. Making, as usual, a dead set at anyone
> who had the slightest connection with the air, I told him my story. . . . John was
> sympathetic and arranged for me to have a flight with 16 Squadron, at Gatwick,
> an Army Co-operation Unit. I went up in a dual control Minor Moth, and this
> time felt much more confident and relaxed. I was immensely pleased with
> myself. My legs that day were in good condition, and the Moth flew obligingly.

> But my native caution told me that I must hurry slowly. A Cygnet and a Minor
> were first and satisfactory steps; the Spitfire was still a long way over the hill.

As his work progressed McIndoe found that not only was he spending much of his time
rebuilding the bodies of these injured airmen, he was also becoming intrigued and
somewhat annoyed by some of the bureaucratic rules that were to hinder his patients
during attempts to rebuild their lives. One such problem that he decided to confront was
the 'ninety-day rule' in the King's Regulations. The rule stated that if such an individual
did not return to duty after three months, he was invalided out of the service and would
receive a meagre disability pension from the Ministry of Pensions. It was an undignified
end for the youngsters that had, only a short while before, been the brave and chivalrous
aircrew that had been defending British airspace. Without hope these men could become
difficult. During his campaign against the 90-day rule McIndoe did a series of talks and
wrote a number of papers, one of which states:

> . . . from time immemorial an injured serviceman was given three months to
> return to duty. If, at the end of that time, he was still unfit he was invalided as
> useless and passed to one or other of the various civil or pension hospitals for
> further treatment. After this he was pensioned off for as small an amount as could
> be determined from the schedule of payments authorised for his particular
> disabilities. If the convalescence was a long one this system absolutely
> guaranteed that the man would arrive back in civilian life without hope, broken
> in spirit, bitter and disillusioned. He could also be in debt for, with invaliding, his
> service pay ceased and the eventual pension would not be settled for a long time.
> During this period he lived on charity.

Plastic surgery was a long drawn-out procedure and many of McIndoe's patients would
be with him for a very long time, some remaining in the hospital undergoing
reconstructive surgery for five years. McIndoe was therefore determined that this should
not happen to the young men who had come under his care. He had an ally in Kathleen
Dewar who knew many influential people. Another advantage was that McIndoe had
declined RAF rank when he had been 'recruited' by the services and was therefore able
to take steps that could otherwise have ended in disciplinary action.

> There are times in life [wrote McIndoe] when an approach 'through the usual
> channels' is sufficient to drive a way through rules and regulations. Here it was
> impossible, for no civil servant would dare to break King's Regulations. These
> would have to be altered before this problem could really be solved. Creating a
> precedent with a cast-iron case at a very high level seemed to me to be the best
> approach.

With the 90 days having elapsed, Colin Hodgkinson had by now been invalided out of
the service with a pension of £3 a week. This was the 'cast iron case' McIndoe used in
his attempt to have this ridiculous rule abolished. In fact it was through good fortune that
Colin had managed to persuade the authorities to allow him a period of convalescence
at Dutton Homestall, at the expense of the state, before returning to civilian life.
Otherwise he would not have met Archie McIndoe. McIndoe's recollections of his first
meeting with Colin Hodgkinson were recorded in *Faces From the Fire*, a biography of
McIndoe by Leonard Mosley:

> 'He was a red-headed thick-set figure precariously balanced on two artificial legs
> which were planted firmly apart and braced backwards to support his swaying
> body. His face was badly scarred. His eyes reflected the bitter desperation mixed
> with the wariness which betrayed a constant anxiety to maintain his balance. He
> kept within reach of a wall or a convenient chair. He was watching carefully and
> obviously had something to ask me. We moved into a corner and we talked.'
>   Hodgkinson made no bones about what he wanted. 'They've paid me off,' he

said, 'but I'm perfectly fit. I don't think it's fair to throw me out like this. I want you to help me to get back in the Navy.'

'Quite a proposition with those pins,' said McIndoe. 'How well do you walk on them?'

'Not too badly,' said Colin. 'It's coming gradually.'

'Well,' replied McIndoe, 'if you can only stop floundering around there might be something we could do.'

During this meeting McIndoe also noticed the extent of Colin's facial injuries. The reconstructive surgery that had already been carried out at Roehampton needed further work: 'You ought to come over to the hospital sometime. I'd like to fix up that eye for you.'

After the meeting he wrote:

> This was a great healthy bear of a chap and he was ideal for my purpose. With him I might drive a hole through the regulations and force the powers that be to reconstitute them. But first I had to have him under my wing, as one of my patients, so that I could fight for him.

McIndoe had Colin admitted to the Queen Victoria Cottage Hospital, where he carried out a minor operation to reduce the large disfiguring scar on his cheek and improve mobility of the facial muscles. The skin was opened again, and re-crocheted with the result that the scar was all but gone. The most important point was that Colin was now officially under Archie McIndoe's care and the surgeon began the fight to have him re-instated in the Fleet Air Arm.

As Colin worked hard at learning to walk efficiently on his tin-legs, McIndoe was busy telephoning and writing to the Admiralty in an attempt to get him back in the service. When Colin pestered McIndoe for an update on his efforts he replied: 'You get on with your walking and leave the admirals to me.'

Colin certainly created an impression on the others in Ward 3. Not one to keep to himself he quickly bored the others with constant talk of his intention to return to flying. Whenever McIndoe came on to the ward they would shout:

> For God's sake get the chap out of here! Give him back to the Jerries before he drives us crazy.

Initially, in the face of Air Ministry bureaucracy, McIndoe's battle was unsuccessful. But, one morning the secretary to the First Lord of the Admiralty, Sir Victor Warrender (later Lord Bruntisfield), arrived for a private luncheon at Dutton Homestall with McIndoe and Kathleen Dewar. During the lunch McIndoe spoke at length on behalf of the many young men that would later be faced with this desperate problem. A few days later Colin was summoned to the Admiralty by Sir Victor and there he underwent a medical and was required to fill in a number of forms. He returned to the convalescent home in Sussex where he tottered about the place expressing his unrest at the situation: 'Give it time, give it time,' said McIndoe, 'The penny is beginning to drop'.

So it had. At the beginning of November 1940 Colin received notification from the Lords of the Admiralty that he would be allowed to rejoin the Fleet Air Arm, and was posted to a naval air station in Cornwall. He was the first man to return to the service still drawing a pension for the very injury which had officially ended his career. The case had set a precedent. McIndoe would fight other battles against the 90-day rule before, finally, it was abolished by all the services.

Like Richard, Colin was also to record his experiences during this period.

How would his family and friends have reacted if he had been killed in an accident on returning to flying training, as was the case with Richard? Would the medical board have been blamed for passing him fit to resume flying, even though he had no legs? Would they just accept the fact that Colin was only doing that which he most wanted to do, despite the risks, of which there were many? Douglas Bader had, after all, successfully returned to flying and was an example to all that it was possible.

The work carried out by McIndoe on Richard and Geoffrey Page was with the knowledge that they were both keen to return to operational flying, and they had been party to the successful return to flying by Colin Hodgkinson. This indicated to them that it could be done. Whereas McIndoe had seen a successful return to flying by Page and Hodgkinson he would feel remorse at Richard's failure. In Richard's case his physical disabilities could not match his determination to succeed.

* * *

Tony Tollemache was a flying officer in the RAF with No.600 Squadron Auxiliary Air Force, when on 11 March 1940 the Blenheim Mark I which he was piloting crashed at RAF Manston. He was to be one of McIndoe's first Guinea Pigs at East Grinstead and was to play a very important part in Richard's life during his time there. In Tollemache he found an older, extroverted, eminently likeable man with an outstanding character and a reputation of being something of a jolly rogue. His severe injuries, disfigurement, and long periods on the 'slab' at East Grinstead did nothing to dent his rough sense of humour or his effervescent and gregarious personality, qualities I believe Richard admired in him. Tony became one of the best known characters in Ward 3. They became good friends and later Tollemache's mother would visit Richard when Tony was no longer at East Grinstead. In Tony Tollemache and Colin Hodgkinson Richard had found kindred spirits and they enjoyed their time together.

There was another person that Richard became attracted to at Dutton Homestall, and, not surprisingly, it was a young woman. Barbara Dewar was the daughter of their millionaire host and hostess. A 'society girl' of great beauty, the two were to get on well and enjoyed a short relationship during which, it has been said, they became engaged. The relationship ended amicably and Barbara Dewar later married Michael Astor of the wealthy family. Mary Booker, Richard's girlfriend during the last year of his life who has yet to enter the story, thought very highly of Michael Astor, who was a good friend of hers. Mary and Richard were guests at the grand society wedding, with Richard flying down from RAF Charterhall in order to attend, shortly before he was killed.

Unfortunately Barbara's mother, Kathleen, was witnessed displaying what was construed as an over-protective or jealous nature towards Richard, perhaps because she had also taken a liking to him. The situation did not improve, and culminated in a bitter exchange between Richard and Kathleen Dewar. The argument took place at Dutton Homestall in front of other patients and ultimately Richard was deeply hurt by the vicious verbal attack which I shall describe later, and, which was apparently unwarranted, spiteful and untrue. It could be perceived as inevitable that someone with Richard's personality would come up against somebody that would attempt to put him in his place; what is surprising is that it hadn't occurred earlier in his life, but this outburst was not appropriate. At that time, however, it is possible that Kathleen Dewar was venting anger for other more personal reasons.

* * *

In the summer of 1940 Archie McIndoe's work had come to the fore rather differently than he had intended when he was called upon to deal with an awful new kind of injury that became known as 'airmen's burn'.

The injury was caused when aircrew were trapped in their blazing aircraft long enough for the searing aviation fuel-fed flames to burn away their hair, faces and hands, together with a greater or lesser extent of the covered parts, depending on the protection offered by their clothing. These injuries occurred in a remarkably short space of time, sometimes merely seconds. The injuries caused agonising pain, gross disfigurement, and permanent disablement. Of the percentage of the 4500 airmen burnt during WWII, those who chose not to wear the appropriate clothing, particularly those who flew during the hot summer months of the Battle of Britain, received more extensive burns due to this lack of protection from the flames. They preferred to wear the minimum of their cotton shirts under the Mae West, appropriate only to their comfort while at dispersal, instead of donning the prescribed leather Irvin jacket and gloves which they found hot, cumbersome and claustrophobic. The long, arduous, painful job of rebuilding the looks, and attempts to re-establish the fried and mutilated hands of these young men into some kind of working order were experimental and involved previously untried techniques. Many of these techniques that were ultimately proven to work were initially frowned upon by the establishment, until such times as the support for them became overwhelming. These young men were well aware of the experimental work that was being carried out on their injuries, and it was they who named themselves the Guinea Pigs.

There was also the task of helping them to recover mentally as well as physically. Young, brave and fearless, as they fought against the German Luftwaffe, the flames took away their looks and placed a picture of sheer horror in their minds that would remain forever. A different battle had just begun. Whilst the possibility of death and injury had quite appropriately been given little consideration in order to apply themselves to the job at hand, what now lay ahead had been totally unforeseen. In some cases the after-effects of the physical and mental trauma were quite devastating, for the pilots were unable to face flying, and especially combat, without the sheer panic of once again being trapped in a flaming cockpit. Richard would be one of those who would later find he could no longer fly without experiencing moments of terror. He had discovered fear at its most disabling, the limits to which he could not have imagined in the exciting, heady days before he was shot down and burned. It was quite probable that he had lost his nerve.

When the air battles over the south of England started in earnest McIndoe did not wait for patients but toured many other hospitals in the area, looking for injured service personnel who were likely to need his particular skill in order to rebuild their bodies, and lives. Richard was one of those fortunate to have come under his care.

Richard was just one of many of McIndoe's patients but it would seem that they were drawn to one another, perhaps because each was attracted by their respective personalities. McIndoe saw Richard as a challenge both physically and mentally. He was aware of how good-looking Richard had been before his injuries and that he would find the adjustment to life ahead traumatic. He also became tolerant and understanding of the extremes of Richard's personality. In time McIndoe was aware that he had successfully rebuilt his face but his hands would continue to pose problems for some time to come. As Richard's psychological problems persisted he was willing to provide personal help in the form of counselling, helping him to come to terms with his feelings and emotions, to understand what was happening to those around him, physically and mentally and to acknowledge the changes taking place in his own personality. He was forever patient when the young, inquisitive existentialist bombarded him with questions.

Richard Hillary was not the first patient at East Grinstead to write about his experiences, but his book made the biggest impact of all both inside and outside the ward. He seemed to be intellectually more mature than the others, sardonic with an often sarcastic wit. Initially he made few friends and became the focus of ribald criticism from the rest of the ward. But before Richard died, the sight of him in his bright red pyjamas, long dressing gown (usually hung over his shoulders), varsity scarf (wound around his neck and hanging almost to the floor), and gold cigarette holder clenched between his teeth, making his appearance all the more disarming to the uninitiated, would forever be indelibly stamped on the memory of his fellow patients.

McIndoe described Richard as being a difficult patient with an alien character, acid wit and a supercilious attitude. Richard soon mellowed in the 'crew-room' atmosphere and befriended the great surgeon.

Archie McIndoe had been a plastic surgeon for 16 years by this time and had learnt to protect himself from the emotional trauma experienced when he was presented with a badly disfigured patient, be they child or adult. It was his style to show little or no sympathy but to offer hope by means of his professional skill as a surgeon. The patients were comforted by his confident and forthright manner. Years later when asked as to the reason for his success one of his staff said:

> I think one of the reasons was his complete lack of sympathy. He was, I think, a completely unsympathetic man. I once asked him what I should do about my wife, who had been concussed in a motor accident, and he said: 'Get her to a good doctor,' and though we had worked closely for years, he never even asked how it happened or expressed any sorrow. It was this lack of feeling, I believe, which made him such a success with the RAF boys. He could look at their terrible injuries quite dispassionately, with no pity and no feeling; and it helped them because it stopped them from feeling sorry for themselves and gave them confidence in his judgement, because they knew he wouldn't bother to encourage them just to cheer them up. They were just cases to him.

This was a total misunderstanding of Archie McIndoe. Any apparent dispassion was just a tool he used to hide his own personal feelings and at the same time motivate his mentally and physically wounded young patients to think along the most positive lines on their road to recovery, give them optimism and keep them cheerful. One minute they had been the proud and brave flower of England's youth, the next they were fried and whimpering. He was mending their minds as well as their bodies. With hindsight his powers of perception were astounding; this approach was exactly what was needed. If one needs an example of McIndoe's sympathy and understanding one needs to look no further than that which was expressed towards Richard Hillary, especially during their very last meeting when time was running out for Richard.

During an official memorandum McIndoe wrote of these young men:

> The impact of disfiguring injuries upon the young adult mentality is usually severe. The majority have been strong and healthy, and have given no consideration to illness or injury, nor to its possible future effects. They are usually unprepared mentally for the blow, so that for a period they may be psychically lost, depressed, morose, pessimistic, and thoroughly out of tune with their surroundings. It is difficult to gain their confidence or to convince them that they can be of use to the world. They believe that their former social status and facility of performance are at an end, that they are no longer marriageable, and must remain objects for well-meant but misguided pity.

To his close friend Edward 'Blackie' Blacksell, he put it more bluntly:

> Imagine how they feel, Blackie. On Friday night they are dancing in a nightclub with a beautiful girl and by Saturday afternoon they are a burned cinder. A fighter pilot can't help being vain because the girls all swarm round him like a honeypot. He can take his pick. Think what it must be like for that young man to go back into the same circle with his face burned to bits. One minute has changed him from a Don Juan into an object of pity – and it's too much to bear.

* * *

Because so many of his techniques were innovative and experimental, the pilots formed a club, initially to meet for a beer, a group that all shared the same problem and, as a unit, understood each other's plight. They named their club the Maxillonians after the fact that East Grinstead was officially a maxillo-facial unit for the treatment of jaw injuries. Initially the meetings were informal, with the club celebrating its first reunion after the Christmas of 1942, having about 60 old and new patients from Ward 3, with a number of high-ranking guests from the RAF at the dinner. The Maxillonians lasted about one year under that name, as it has been said that early in 1943 a burned airmen waiting on his trolley to be wheeled into yet another operation exclaimed: '. . . we're not fliers any more. We're nothing but a plastic surgeon's guinea pigs.'

Thus the The Guinea Pig Club was born, a title more befitting the atmosphere of the place and the attitude of its extroverted patients. It still exists today but the organisation was to ultimately don a far more important mantle. The club and the continuation of reconstructive surgery today are a memorial to Archibald McIndoe.

The work of the plastic surgeon was certainly resented in certain quarters. It was misunderstood as a luxury for the rich who wanted to pay large sums of money for improving their looks for professional or personal reasons. Thanks to his pioneering work McIndoe proved that it was surgical creative-art with miraculous qualities. McIndoe wrote:

> Eventually there comes the exciting moment when all the tissue required in the repair of an injured face is in position, all major contraction has been overcome and the patient has resolved his scars, softened his grafts, and is ready for trimming. The aim is to produce a face which in sum total is symmetrical in its separate parts, of good colour and texture and freely mobile, so that expression of mood is possible in all its infinite variety. It is not possible to construct a face from one destroyed of which the observer is unconscious, but it should not leave in his mind an impression of repulsion, and the patient himself should not be an object of remark or pity. Only then can the surgeon feel that his work has been faithfully done.

* * *

Initial surgery on Richard consisted of replacing his upper eyelids to preserve his sight. Whilst the most reliable method for reconstructing Richard's eyebrows would have been to use a temporal pedicle, for a fuller eyebrow, his were reconstructed using free grafts from the hair on his temple. McIndoe preferred the thinner skin of the temple as the hair follicles are nearer the surface. Initially a free graft from the temple looked good, but after a few weeks the norm was for most of the hair to fall out, with the likelihood of only one-third to a half growing back. The final result therefore was sparse, usually due to the fact that the transplanted bed is scarred, as was the case with Richard's left eyebrow.

In the case of Richard's hands, the scar contraction of the dorsal skin and fixation of the extensor tendons, together with the pull of the flexor tendons, drew each hand into the typical burn claw. With hyperextension of the hand joints, flexion of the finger joints and adduction of the thumb occurred. Once this had happened, which it did in Richard's case whilst his hands were under the tannic acid eschar, it is very difficult to correct. Capsultomies, tendon lengthenings, introduction of the necessary new skin, and months of physiotherapy and rehabilitation were required. But all this would only achieve a moderate return of the original function.

Initially, the crippling scar of his burned hands was excised. Flaps were turned to reconstruct the web bases of his fingers and scarred transverse ligaments of the metacarpal heads (the hand) are divided and a dermatome graft was applied to replace the lost tissue to the backs and palms of his hands. Richard's hands were treated with free grafts, but had his burns been deeper, pedicle grafts would have been required. To give some idea of the resultant disability to Richard's hands, the loss or partial loss of the thumb cripples the hand functions by 50%. His right thumb was almost useless.

Following this surgery, limited normal hand function was eventually regained enabling Richard to return to work. However, his failure to adhere to the advice of the physiotherapists meant that the use of his hands remained very limited.

Many injured pilots seriously considered an eventual return to flying and the war effort. It was with their support that the grafting of their burned hands was eagerly pursued by the surgeons. A sudden change of tactics by the Luftwaffe also created a demand for more RAF pilots to make up the depleted numbers and for those that were able, to return to operations as soon as possible. The priority of the surgeons, however, was to re-estabish as much function as possible, whatever the use.

The reconstructive surgery to Richard's lip was as a result of a small area burnt by the flames which would not heal properly. The resulting scar tissue became tight and stretched, a condition known as 'Irishman's Lip'. A free-graft was first applied across part of the upper lip, which took away his 'cupid's bow'. There is no evidence that he had the surgery to rectify this, but had he done so it would have consisted of having two edges of his lip, either side of the centred fixed point, lifted and sutured in two fixed curves, providing a shorter but wider 'bow'. The junction of the lip which has been lost by fire or as the result of a graft would not have imitated the normal lip curves.

The operation to replace Richard's eyelids was the first surgery carried out on him at East Grinstead by Archie McIndoe. It followed a visit by the eye specialist, the day after he arrived at Dutton Homestall:

> The following afternoon an eye specialist took a look at me: the pupil of my left eye, dilated by regular treatment with belladonna, interested him particularly.
>
> 'Can't close your eyes at all, can you?' he asked.
>
> 'No, sir,' I said.
>
> 'Well, we'll have to get some covering over that left eye or you'll never use it again.'

After a phone call to the nearby hospital he returned and told Richard:

> McIndoe is going to give you a new pair of top lids. I know your eyes are still infected, but we'll have to take that chance. You're to go in with Tollemache tomorrow.

This first visit to the Cottage Hospital on 22 November was not to Ward 3 but to the male ward in the main building called the Kindersley Ward. Richard's service record states that while at East Grinstead he was treated for the following:

> 1.) Burns of face, hands and legs received 3/9/40.
> 2.) Mastoid infection. Acute. 15/1/41.

An initial assessment of his being able to return to duties was made and recorded as: 'AE Bt. Fit: a) Doubtful. b) 6 months.' The first of the two categories states if Richard would be able to return to operational flying, while the second recommends the period of time that should pass before the next medical board.

It has been previously written that Richard went before two medical boards in an attempt to return to operational flying. What I have discovered, however, which gives an even clearer indication of how enthusiastic he was about returning to ops, is that he went before six medical boards, including the last on 12 November 1942, before finally being allowed to return to flying.

At the Masonic Richard had been the only patient with injuries received in action and had been spoiled by the nursing staff. Unused to hospital life he had mistakenly thought the high standard of care he received was usual. At Dutton Homestall the food had been exceptional and the accommodation was 'bordering on the luxurious'. His first experience of East Grinstead therefore came as a shock:

> It was one of several hundred Emergency Medical Service hospitals. Taken over by the Ministry of Health at the beginning of the war, these were nearly all small country-town hospitals in safe areas. Erected by subscription for the welfare of the district and run by committees of local publicity-loving figures in the community, they had been perfectly adequate for that purpose. They were not, however, geared for a war-time emergency; they were too small. To overcome this difficulty the Ministry of Health had supplied them with 'blisters' to accommodate the anticipated flow of troops. I heard of these 'blisters' and was vaguely aware that they were huts, but this hospital provided my first introduction to them.
>
> It was a fairly recent construction and of only one storey. There were two main wards: one reserved for women and filled with residents of the district; and

the other (eight beds) were for action casualties. Then there were the 'blisters'; a dental hut, and two others set at an angle to the main building.

Richard's reference to the 'publicity-loving figures' with its cynical inference, was rather scathing. By simply taking advantage of their prominent public profile these individuals were instrumental in alerting the general public to the much needed local facility, and assisting any subsequent fund raising campaigns that would be required to support it. In a letter to his wife, shortly before Richard's arrival, McIndoe wrote:

> We have been full to overflowing for the last six months and, at last, the committee and the good people of East Grinstead are beginning to appreciate some of the work done here. Two months ago a local resident stumped up £400 and after a considerable search we found what we wanted (an X-ray machine) and disposed of that. The next thing was enlarging the hospital and putting in massage departments, etc., etc. Well, a committee has been formed and money is being raised to do all I want. In addition, I have at long last secured the Dewars' equipment (the beds and other facilities at Dutton Homestall) and this goes into service next week. I have re-equipped two operating theatres and two wards . . . Now, it seems, if we can pay for things ourselves we can get almost anything we want and with the public inclined to help I think we can pull it off.

Having checked into the male ward, Richard and Tony Tollemache then went off to town for a drink and returned late, rather noisily and a little worse for wear. Stumbling through the ward they found their beds, situated next to each other, and began to get changed for bed. Opposite were two Hurricane pilots, one had received burns to his legs and a cage kept the bedding off the sensitive tissue, while the other had his eyes bandaged and was being fed by a nurse. Richard's humour took over:

> 'Is he blind?' I whispered to Tony.
> 'Blind?' he roared. 'Not half as blind as we are, I'll bet. No me boy. That's what your going to look like tomorrow when McIndoe's through with you.'

The nurse who had been feeding the Hurricane pilot confronted the noisy pair and warned them that their behaviour would not be well received by Sister Hall. This was Richard's first introduction to Sister Mary Rea, the Ward Charge Nurse.

Not only did Richard and Tony not let up but they took advantage of the opportunity to mock her Irish brogue. However, the situation was reversed when Sister Rea caught sight of Richard's red silk pyjamas which he was unpacking:

> 'It's the wrong address you're at with those passion pants,' she said.
> 'This is the hospital, not an English country house week-end.'
> 'Be off with you woman,' I said, and putting on the offending garments I climbed into bed and settled down to read.

Sister Mary Rea had come down from Bart's, since her predecessor was unable to cope with the rowdiness of the ward. Mary Rea was determined to succeed and allowed no nonsense from those in her charge. She later became theatre sister.

The next person to enter the ward was Sister Hall:

> 'Mr. Hillary, both you and Mr. Tollemache are to be operated on tomorrow morning. As you know, you should have been in earlier for preparation; now it will have to be done in the morning. I hope you will settle in here quickly; but I want it understood that in my ward I will tolerate no bad language and no rudeness to the nurses.'
> 'My dear sister,' I replied, 'I've no doubt that you will find me the mildest and most soft-spoken of men,' and sitting up in bed I bowed gravely from the waist. She gave me a hard look and walked through the ward.
> Tony waited until she was out of earshot. Then: 'A tough nut, but the best

nurse in the hospital,' he said. 'I don't advise you get on the wrong side of her.'

Shortly after the lights were put out McIndoe made a round of the ward followed by half a dozen assistants, mostly service doctors, who were training under him. 'You're first on the list, Tony,' he said, 'and you're second. By the looks of you both we'll need to use a stomach pump before we can give you any anaesthetic.'

He took a look at my eyes. 'They're still pretty mucky,' he said, 'but I think you'll find it a relief to have some eyelids on them.' He passed on through the ward and we settled down to sleep.

Richard and Tony Tollemache were awoken early the next morning and Taffy the Welsh orderly arrived and 'prepped' them for their operations. The surgery to replace Richard's upper eyelids would consist of two paper-thin patches of skin being pared off from the inside of his upper left arm. These grafts would then be wrapped around a wax mould into the correct shape before being stitched into place above his eyes. It was known as the 'Thiersch' graft after the pioneering surgeon who had developed the method. The 'prepping' consisted of sterilizing the area of skin to be used and completely shaving off any surrounding hair from the arm and armpit. The sterilized arm would then be loosely bound in a bandage.

Visually the first sight of these new eyelids was something of a shock for the patient. The amount of grafted skin used was necessarily excessive and gave the appearance of the individual having what became known as 'horse-blinkers' drooping down over the eyes like ruddy, sagging bags of skin. As the weeks went by and the patient convalesced, the grafts would settle down and shrink into place. Some further surgery would be necessary at a later date to trim the new eyelids more to shape, removing the excess flesh.

Tony Tollemache, as already mentioned, was an experienced patient at East Grinstead and his operation consisted of further surgery on his dreadful leg burns. As the charge nurse approached with the stretcher-trolley and their pre-operation injections the banter between Richard and Tony continued, probably hiding much in the way of pre-op nervousness:

> 'Bet you she's blunted the needle,' said Tony; 'and look at her hand; it's shaking like an aspen leaf.'
> 'Be quiet Mr. Tollemache, let's have less of your sauce now.'

Eventually they were subdued, injected with a relaxant and wheeled down to the operating theatre. Tony went first with Richard left behind to receive a stern telling-off from Sister Hall for being caught where he lay, high from the effects of the injection, puffing on a cigarette, oblivious to the fact that the curtain drawn around his bed did nothing to mask his misdemeanour!

Tony's prostrate form was wheeled back onto the ward and Richard was taken down to the theatre where the trio of McIndoe, Jill Mullins, McIndoe's theatre sister, and John Hunter, the anaesthetist, dressed from head to foot in surgical gowns, went about their work. McIndoe wore size eight gloves over his short, stubby, fingers but as he held the scalpel between thumb and forefinger he crooked his little finger, almost mockingly. He was once heard to say: 'The man with ladies' fingers is no surgeon'.

Hunter ushered Richard off into unconsciousness with one of many of his famous expressions: 'Well, good-bye . . .'

When Richard came round he could not see and his eyes had pads placed over them which were bandaged in place. Because he was unable to read, he talked instead, getting himself into trouble in the process. Tony had been looking out for him, but an opportunity arose that he just couldn't resist. Richard criticised the nursing staff and he hadn't been warned that Sister Hall was close by. With Richard stubbornly refusing to apologise he was moved to the all-glass covered balcony extension of the ward, away from Tony. As he went Richard fired a parting shot: 'You bloody bitch!'

Sister Hall left him alone with the final comment: 'And we'll have no bad language while I'm in charge here.'

A couple of days later Richard had the dressings removed from over his eyes and was able to see again. McIndoe commented on his workmanship: 'A couple of real horse blinkers you've got there.'

As the days passed the feeling of having these excessive bags of skin hanging dangling in front of his vision diminished as the tissue became accustomed to their presence and the muscles learnt to support the weight. In order to see, Richard had to tip his head backwards so he could peer from under them. It wasn't long before he was able to raise and lower his new upper eyelids at will. The recovery of the area of his arm from which the graft had been taken was more painful, with the removal of the dressings particularly unpleasant. It was during a bath that Sister Hall walked in as he was laboriously trying to soak the bandage from the sensitive area:

> 'Well really, Mister Hillary!' she said, and taking hold of it she gave a quick pull and ripped the whole thing off cleanly and painlessly.
>
> 'Christ!' I started involuntarily, but stopped myself and glanced apprehensively at Sister's face. She was smiling. Yes, there was no doubt about it, she was smiling. We said nothing, but from that moment on we understood each other.

Tony's graft had been a success too and after a few days the two men were allowed to leave the hospital on 16 December, for a period of convalescence at Dutton Homestall, before returning for further surgery on 7 January 1941.

McIndoe was keen that the burnt airmen in his care were taken out in public and he called for volunteers to partner the men during this phase of their recovery. It was all part of his greater plan for their re-integration in society although, intially, it was a move to re-establish their self-confidence. For the first trip out, McIndoe would only allow his patients into town for a few hours, where their physical appearance was accepted by the locals. Gradually they were allowed out on trips, to London lasting perhaps two or three days, and finally for more lengthy periods of rest and recuperation at home. On their return after such outings they were monitored for any signs of physical and psychological stress. The reaction to their being seen in public for the first time would vary, depending on the sensitivity of the individual. The open expression of pity shown in sympathy for them could be as damaging as any revulsion expressed, both verbally and by those that were forced to look or turn away at the sight of such injuries. Some would suffer psychological damage as a result of these reactions, others adopted an aggressive reaction as a protective shield.

Richard's first trips away from the cottage hospital were with a tall, wealthy and beautiful woman called Sheila Wickham. Sheila was one of identical twins who lived near RAF Biggin Hill in a large, spacious home called Redhouse. Sheila and her sister Moira responded to McIndoe's call for help in getting his disfigured patients out in public and Sheila was given the responsibility of looking after Richard. Sheila initially took him into East Grinstead and then to London where she insisted he travelled by bus in an attempt to re-establish his confidence.

Although the White Hart at Brasted is the better-known watering-hole for the Battle of Britain pilots from Biggin Hill, additionally Redhouse also became an open-house for pilots situated in the area, including Richard Hillary, Tony Tollemache and a number of the other Guinea Pigs. The sisters became known as the 'Glorious Twins' and there was a piano in the family home for sing-songs. A telephone line was installed so that the pilots could be contacted. They also made sure there was always a barrel of beer available just for their guests. In the homely atmosphere the pilots were able to relax away from the stress of combat.

As Richard left on his first outing, Sister Hall passed him what could be perceived as a kind peace offering. It was a package containing some brown make-up powder to tone-down and blend in the difference in colouring between his surviving facial skin and the new grafts on his damaged face. Even Sister Hall could not fail to become aware of, and fall for, his charm. Sheila recalled her memories of Richard:

> I used to visit the burnt boys at East Grinstead. I knew Geoffrey Page and Tony
> Tollemache but to me Dick was the bravest of them all.
>
> I took Dick out on his first trip, in fact when we arrived at East Grinstead it was
> the first time that any of them had been taken away from the hospital in this way.
> We tried to re-establish their self-confidence. On the first few trips Dick wore
> metal braces on his hands. After a number of trips into town I took him to London
> where I insisted he travelled by bus. Despite comments by a number of bitchy
> women he eventually regained his confidence and got used to being stared at.
>
> I also met Dick's mother who was a wonderful mother and a tough old girl.
> She told me that Dick was a much better person since he had been burnt than he
> had been while at Oxford. I don't think there was any change in his personality
> in the period after he had been burnt, he was always a charming person.

Richard subsequently ventured out with Denise who also ensured his spirit was maintained. She became, in her own words, his 'ghost-watcher'. He claimed it was her beauty that had diverted their eyes from him.

It was after one of Richard's trips out in public that he recorded his experiences in his diary. It was later included in *The Last Enemy*, but incorrectly used to describe his first venture out from the Masonic.

Whenever Richard went on leave to London he stayed with his parents in their flat at Knightsbridge Court and took every opportunity to take the short walk to visit Denise in Eaton Place. During her spare time she had knitted Richard a pair of woollen gloves, identical to a pair she had made for herself so that Richard did not feel that she had made them especially. She was by now a senior commander and a recruiting officer with the ATS. One of her duties was to visit girls schools in England and lecture on life in the ATS to those considering military service. Fine, upstanding and beautiful, she was a first class role model. In his diary Richard noted that together they would go out to lunch:

> It was a Dutch Sunday and for the Cabaret a young man rose and sang 'Yeomen
> of England', and then some song about the fleet which called for him to do a lot
> of 'Ho Ho Ho-ing' and 'Ha Ha Ha-ing' in a deep bass voice. After this a Dutch
> brass band fought a valiant battle with various national hymns and songs of
> victory.
>
> Denise said it reminded her of hours of agony spent on a hard bench at
> agricultural shows. Finally a lightly clad young lady from Bali performed some
> intricate dances, which the announcer was careful to assure us had a religious
> significance.

On other occasions:

> Had dinner at the Mirabel with Denise, Penny and John Davidson. Talked to
> Denise for hours: she has the gift of making one feel intelligent . . . Lunch with
> Denise at Scotts. She contrives somehow to look attractive in uniform. Suppose
> this is a necessity if one is a recruiting officer.

They also visited the evacuated London Zoo in Regents Park where they discussed the Darwinian Theory. One evening they went to the premiere of the film *The Battle of Britain*, produced by the American Frank Capra. Richard requested that Denise should not wear her uniform, but a brightly coloured outfit instead.

They would walk the streets. As they walked they talked, Richard trying to offer Denise comfort and understanding at the loss of Peter. Denise trying to help Richard come to terms with his burgeoning perspective on life. They occasionally argued, she the believer and he the hardcore cynic, about the influence of the beloved dead on those they leave behind. She quoted John Donne's *Devotions upon Emergent Occasions*, published in 1624, a copy of which had recently been given to her by a friend in an attempt to console her. Richard also quoted from this book in *The Last Enemy*. She quoted the famous passage in 'Meditation XVII' to illustrate to Richard man's involvement in mankind:

> No man is an island, entire of itself. Every man is a piece of the continent, a part of the main: if a clod be washed away by the sea; Europe is the less, as well as if a promontory were, as well as if a manor of thy friends; or thine own were. Any man's death diminishes me, because I am involved in mankind.

Richard and Denise provided ideal companionship for each other at this time, a time of almost nightly air raids. During these air raids it was not always possible for Richard to return to his parents' flat, so he stayed at Eaton Place, where they sheltered in the basement, sleeping on mattresses. As he set off on foot to hospital or Knightsbridge Court the next morning, Denise would leave for the War Office on her bike.

Denise was quite naturally, still experiencing terrible grief at the loss of Peter, but was trying to adjust to life without him. Her religious conviction allowed her to seek comfort in her faith and she, at one time, considered joining a convent after the war. Richard expressed his concern at such an idea. It is possible that by this time he had fallen in love with her, but the presence of Peter was still there between them. Richard wanted her to accept the fact that Peter was now dead and turn to him for love. It was not to be and as he recovered from the loss of his friend, the situation eventually began to irritate him. As with his other loves he craved her affection and had trouble accepting that, as far as Denise was concerned, their relationship would remain as it had been; just friends.

Richard summed up his feelings in his diary, quite beautifully:

> It was true that Peter was much in my thoughts, that I felt him somewhere near me, that he was in fact the touchstone of my sensibility at the moment. It was true that the mystical experience of his death was something which was outside my understanding, which had still to be assimilated, and yet, and yet . . . I could not help but feel that with the passage of time this sense of closeness, of affinity, must fade, that its very intensity was in part false, occasioned by being ill, and by meeting Denise so shortly afterwards; a Denise who was no mere shadow of Peter, but Peter's reincarnation; thus serving to keep the memory and the experience always before my eyes.

Two weeks later Richard returned after a '. . . short but very pleasant convalescence', for the next phase of his reconstructive surgery, two new lower eyelids. Tony Tollemache also returned for what was in his case, one last operation, for a new top eyelid:

> This time when the dressings were taken down I looked exactly like an orang-utan. McIndoe had pinched out two semi-circular ledges of skin under my eyes to allow for contraction of the new lids. What was not absorbed was to be sliced off when I came in for my next operation, a new upper lip. The relief, however, was enormous, for now I could close my eyes almost completely and did not sleep with them rolled up and the whites showing like a frightened Negro.

Every Tuesday and Thursday afternoon those that wished to go, were driven into East Grinstead to the cinema. After the film they waited in a nearby tea shop for the transport to arrive to take them back to the home. On the first trip two French servicemen went with the group. One had been a pilot in the French Air Force, the other was an army officer. As they sat in the tea shop the French pilot was approached by the waitress.

> *'Vous etes Francais?'* to which the pilot replied *'Oui, et vous?'*
> *'Dommage que je n'aille mieux. J'aimerais vous prouver que je vous trouve gentille.'* ('It's a shame I'm not feeling better, I would like to prove to you that I find you attractive.')
> To which the waitress replied, *'Faudrait aussi que je le veuille!'* ('Would I go

along with it?') The pilot finished by saying *'N'importe. J'aimerais toujours tenter la chance.'* ('Whatever, I always like to take a chance.')

A rather different approach to that which Richard would have tried. The French pilot used no subtlety, little charm, but it was, nevertheless, effective!

The atmosphere of the tea shop was something Richard found depressing and he made few further trips. He admits to being drained of any youthful exuberance and vitality but is assured by Tony that this would return in time. Their recent experiences both physical and mental had momentarily quashed such feelings.

On regular occasions Richard and Tony dined out together in a quality London restaurant. On one occasion after a splendid meal they sat like two elderly men, drinking brandy and smoking cigars, watching the pretty females as they danced with their partners. In the past they too would have been in similar company. But not on this occasion and they were thoroughly enjoying this new experience, which gave the two peace-of-mind knowing that such an existence, that of two elderly men, was not unenjoyable. It had been quite a while since the pair had relaxed in such an atmosphere and been able to enjoy the close contact of a woman with its associated sexual connotations. They were, however, reassured as the urge for such company returned to some extent. They were recovering their spirit and self confidence and savoured the experience.

It was during one of these visits to London that Richard and Tony went to see Rosa Lewis at the Cavendish Hotel. At the age of 66 she had recently suffered a stroke and had been admitted to hospital. On receipt of the bill she had discharged herself and promptly returned to work. Richard found her none the worse for wear, laughing and drinking her beloved drink, champagne. She greeted Richard:

> 'God, aren't you dead yet either, young Hillary? Come here and I'll tell you something. Don't ever die. In the last two weeks I've been right up to the gates of 'eaven and 'ell and they're both bloody!'

A few weeks later she was to survive when the hotel received a direct hit from a German bomb.

* * *

Despite periods of great discomfort, depression and boredom, this part of *The Last Enemy* comes across as terrific fun, both as an experience in real life for Richard and in its writing. Tony Tollemache has impressed him greatly, the feeling was mutual and they became great friends, albeit for a short time. The friendship was intense and seems to have been based on their getting through each day with as much outrageous behaviour as the hospital would tolerate. It was most certainly a means of escape from the physical and psychological burden that such people in their position would indeed suffer. It is a time in Richard's life when such a friendship was desperately needed. I think also that the older man really understood Richard's personality and was more tolerant of his extremes, unlike the younger, less experienced men on the ward.

Before he had been shot down Richard had been the dashing, handsome fighter pilot, with the piercing blue eyes, who went through life with a seemingly reckless abandon. He could charm almost any female that took his fancy. The initial surgery would have done nothing to bring back his recent good looks. In fact, before the newly grafted skin settled down and became more flexible, his face may well have appeared far worse than just prior to surgery. In time he would be able to move the facial muscles and exhibit at least some expression. The new grafts would have appeared taut on his face and paler than those which survived of his own skin. Nevertheless, his blue eyes stared from behind his mask of new flesh, and he was to charm still, and win the hearts of many young girls while he was at East Grinstead.

During his early days there Richard continued to scribble what has been referred to as his 'diary'. This period was also written in pencil and consisted of a number of loose pages of notes on his day-to-day thoughts and activities. It included a growing fascination for plastic surgery, and also contributed in part to his compilation of information which formed the framework for *The Last Enemy*. It seems to have been written in the forthright and honest manner that has become a familiar trait of Richard's, and which is shown in his assessment of himself as well as of those who feature around him. He questioned his fellow patients incessantly, demanding to know their feelings and opinions as they lay suffering, feeling sorry for themselves. To some it was seen more as an interrogation. The last thing they wanted to do was answer his tirade of questions, some too much to the point and others, too high-brow, which was typical of Richard. He was a nuisance and occasionally provoked annoyance: '"Oh, hang it up, for cripes sake, Hillary," and "Yeah, button up Buddy," would come from some American patient.'

* * *

On 12 August 1940 Pilot Officer Geoffrey Page had been shot down in flames over the Channel. He had managed to bale out of his flaming Hurricane but not before his face and hands had been badly burned. He was picked up by the same lifeboat that would rescue Richard 22 days later, taken to Margate General Hospital, and then moved to the burns unit at Queen Mary's Hospital, RAF Halton, Buckinghamshire:

> I looked down with watery eyes at my arms. From the elbows to the wrists the bare forearms were one seething mass of pus-filled boils. Then for the first time I noticed the hands themselves: from the wrist joints to the finger-tips they were blacker than any Negro's hands, but smaller in size than I ever remember them to be. I shared the VAD's horror until the sister said: 'That black stuff's only tannic acid. It's not the colour of your skin'.

Geoffrey Page underwent various treatments for his burns in the Queen Mary Hospital, RAF Halton, many of them experimental. During November 1940, he was visited by Archie McIndoe during one of the tours of his regional hospitals for patients who would require reconstructive surgery. Having been informed of any likely candidates, McIndoe went to see Page who later recounted in his book *Shot Down in Flames*:

> The visitor had dark hair parted in the middle and flat to the head, horn-rimmed spectacles, broad shoulders and a friendly, mischievous grin. His whole appearance was not unlike that of Harold Lloyd, the film comedian. Grasping a leather briefcase firmly inside a hand that would have done credit to a professional boxer, he advanced round to the left hand side of my bed and seated himself on an upright chair. Extracting a sheet of paper and pencil, he viewed me from over the top of his glasses. The words came out crisply.
> 'Hurricane or Spitfire?'
> 'Hurricane.'
> 'Header-tank?'
> I laughed. 'Yes. The wing tanks in my machine were self-sealing but some bright type forgot to treat the tank in front of the pilot.'
> His eyes twinkled. 'Just can't trust anyone, can you?'
> He didn't stay long and during his short visit the conversation was light-hearted and dealt with seemingly inconsequential details; was I wearing goggles and gloves, how long had I been in the water, and how soon afterwards was the tannic acid treatment given? The visitor rose and took a cheery farewell of me. He waved a large ham-fisted hand. 'Goodbye, young fellow, see you again.' Little did I realise how often this would be.

This was another occasion when McIndoe had left seething with rage at the damage that the tannic acid coating had caused, and that he was aware of the hardship ahead for Geoffrey Page. He wrote in his minute book: 'Damn and blast this tannic acid. It shouldn't be used. We've got to stop them using it.'

The Polish wing commander in charge of the burns unit at Halton was instructed to pick away the coating and apply saline dressings to the raw areas. Unfortunately, the damage had already been done to the young pilot's hands as he later recounted:

> Day by day my strength increased and with it the condition of my hands deteriorated. Fraction by fraction the tendons contracted, bending the fingers downwards until finally the tips were in contact with the palms. Added to this the delicate skin toughened by degrees until it had the texture of rhinoceros hide, at the same time webbing my fingers together until they were indistinguishable as separate units. The Polish surgeon watched impotently as the contractions continued. Then one morning he said: 'If your hands continue to form this thick scar tissue I'm afraid it will mean a series of skin-grafting operations. Are you prepared to try and prevent this?'
>
> 'What's the alternative?'
>
> 'We may be able to keep the skin soft by the use of hot molten baths, followed by massage.'
>
> The hot wax treatment commenced the same afternoon. The baths were a nightmare and the electric treatment was worse. And still the fingers curled inwards. It went on until the Polish surgeon confesed that it was no use.
>
> 'Your hands will have to be grafted,' he said. 'I will arrange for you to be sent to East Grinstead. To see Mr McIndoe.'

Page was taken by taxi to East Grinstead. His hand injuries were very similar to Richard's and he too would be spending quite some time at the Sussex Cottage Hospital. It had been three months since he had been shot down but despite the time lapse as he sat in the taxi he still felt sorry for himself, bitter, dejected and in pain from his injuries, wishing he had been killed rather than enduring the pain of the experimental treatment on his injuries. He had watched his fingers gradually curl inwards, towards the palms of his hands, totally useless. He resented having survived.

On his arrival at the East Grinstead hospital in this state of mind he was met by the kindly staff and the soft southern Irish brogue of Sister Cherry Hall. But his first introduction to those with whom he was to share a ward was far less comforting, for his first experience was of the callous wit and humour of the 'comedy duo' Tony Tollemache and Richard Hillary. Richard had recently undergone his first operation for two new upper eyelids. McIndoe was due to make a round of the wards and Page was told to unpack. He later recounted in *Shot Down in Flames*:

> Leading the way from her little office we passed through a door into the small bright ward. Large glass windows extending from floor to ceiling along the entire length of one wall let in a wealth of daylight. Outside, gently sloping lawns led down to the bright flower beds beyond.
>
> The peaceful garden scene was counterposed by a loud voice breaking the air.
>
> 'You stupid bastard, Richard . . . oooops, sorry, Sister.'
>
> 'Don't worry about Sister,' another voice replied. 'They're used to bastards in Ireland.'
>
> Sister Hall chose to ignore the sally. 'This is your bed, Mr. Page. I'll have a nurse help you unpack.' Without waiting she turned and left me.
>
> 'Let me give you a hand.'
>
> Turning from my struggles with the latch of my suitcase, I was confronted with the figure of a young man in his early twenties, bearing the livid red weals of fire about his forehead and eyes. A humorous mouth and twinkling eyes made the face very likeable at first sight. Deftly he opened the suitcase, talking as he did so.
>
> 'My name's Tollemache and that apology over there for an RAF officer is Hillary.'
>
> I glanced over in the direction indicated and received the shock of my life. Standing at the foot of a bed stood one of the queerest apparitions I have ever

seen. The tall figure was clad in a long, loose-fitting dressing gown that trailed to the floor. The head was thrown right back so that the owner appeared to be looking along the line of his nose. Where normally two eyes would be, were two large bloody red circles of raw skin. Horizontal slits in each showed that behind still lay the eyes. A pair of hands wrapped in large lint covers lay folded across his chest. Cigarette smoke curled up from the long holder clenched between the ghoul's teeth. The empty sleeves of the dressing gown hung limply, lending the apparition a sinister air. It evidently had a voice behind its mask. It was condescending in tone.

'Ah, another bloody cripple! Welcome to the home for the aged and infirm!' With that Richard Hillary limped painfully out of the ward.

Tony Tollemache laughed at the expression on my face.

'Most probably shook you a bit, his face I mean. Just had a new pair of eyelids grafted on and they look a bit odd for a day or two.'

I gulped. 'But they look raw and bleeding.'

Tollemache patted me on the shoulder. 'Only mercurochrome, old boy. It's a red antiseptic that looks a bit bloody, that's all.'

Left to my own devices, I felt lost and homesick like a small boy on his first day at boarding school. The ward was divided into three small sections by glass partitions that rose to shoulder height. In each section there were four beds. I noticed for the first time that, of the other three beds near my own, only one was occupied.

'Good afternoon,' I ventured cautiously to its occupant. Hillary's reception had been a trifling unnerving.

'Hello,' replied the youth in bed cheerfully. 'First time here?'

'Yes, it is.'

The other grinned. 'First two years are the worst. I'm Roy Lane.'

I introduced myself. Years later I was saddened to hear that Lane had been beheaded by the Japs after baling out of his aircraft. During the course of our conversation, Hillary's name was mentioned again.

'Don't let him get you down,' Roy Lane advised. 'He's a conceited young man with a sharp tongue and a large inferiority complex.'

'How can he be conceited with an inferiority complex?'

'Simple,' Lane answered. 'For years he's been told by his mother what a wonderful boy he is, but in the service he's had his backside kicked. Not surprising he's a bit mixed up.'

It was some weeks before I overcame my awe of Hillary.

Pilot Officer Roy Lane was from Southampton and joined No.43 Squadron at Tangmere on 13 July 1940. He was shot down during combat with He111s over Portsmouth on 26 August. His Hurricane crash-landed and in addition to wounds received he was badly burned. Lane was eventually transferred to East Grinstead from the West Sussex Hospital, Brighton, where he underwent extensive reconstructive surgery. On leaving hospital he went on a speaking tour of the factories, which may have been the basis for Richard deciding to attempt to do the same in America in June 1942. Lane was with the Merchant Ship Fighter Unit (MSFU) at Speke in 1942 and on 21 May 1942 he sailed from Iceland to set up and command the MSFU Pool at Archangel. He returned to the UK in November 1942 as pilot aboard the *Empire Moon*.

Lane was posted to India during late 1943 where he volunteered to go into Burma with the Chindits as air liaison officer to Brigadier Bernard Fergusson. When the Chindits arrived at their area of operation in Japanese-held territory they prepared an airstrip and a Hurricane was flown in for Lane to use. After a liaison trip to India he was returning to the strip when his Hurricane experienced engine trouble and he was forced to land in the jungle twenty miles east of the Chindwin River. Having managed to radio his position the RAF were able to drop supplies and information to him, but Lane was captured by the Japanese and is believed to have been beheaded by them on 20 June 1944. He is buried in Taukkyan War Cemetery, Rangoon, Burma. He was 24 years old.

* * *

It wasn't long after Geoffrey Page arrived at East Grinstead that McIndoe went to work on his hands, a procedure that Richard would later endure. The agony experienced after reconstructive surgery to the hands was immense. Page's first operation was to remove the scar tissue, and to take skin from his legs and graft it onto his hands. Post-operation, Page was in a great deal of pain. He was given pain killing injections and the nurses tended to the young pilot during his pain-wracked delirium, mopping his brow and reassuring him. Richard passed by the end of his bed. Page remembers the experience in his book:

> The prick of the needle was unfelt in the sea of pain. Soon my head stopped its senseless rolling and torture and disappeared over the horizon as the drug began its calming effect.
>
> Hillary paused at the end of the bed and stood silently watching what he thought was my unconscious body.
>
> 'You're not as tough as you try to make out, are you, Mr. Hillary?'
>
> There was something near to triumph in Sister Hall's voice.
>
> Quickly recovering from the surprise of being caught unawares, the tall figure gave a contemptuous snort. 'Bloody fool should have worn gloves.'
>
> She did not even bother to glance down. Hillary's hands were equally badly burned and for the same reason – no gloves.

Page lay in bed moaning and rolling his head as the suffering gradually wore him down:

> It was as if many nails were being hammered inexpertly into the fingers, then pincers would wrench the nails out, after which the hammering would start again. At the end of the fifth day – or was it the fifth year?

The morphine provided some respite. He was in tears of agony one day when McIndoe came on to the ward.

Assisted by Sister Hall, McIndoe removed Page's arm from its pillow support and proceeded to undo the crepe bandage and many other layers of dressing from his arm. The immense pressure that had been exerted on his arm by the tight sterile covering was suddenly relieved. The smell that reached their senses was that of putrefied flesh. McIndoe asked Sister Hall to fetch the saline arm bath. Despite the initial look of concern Page had noticed on McIndoe's face as he inspected his handiwork, when he looked up from inspecting his work he was grinning. As with all his patients, McIndoe endeavoured to explain his procedures and why it had been so painful. In *Shot Down in Flames* he recorded:

> 'You want to know what has been happening to you? As you know, your hand was completely covered in keloids – thick scaly scar tissue. Well, I stripped all that off from the knuckles almost to the wrist. In its place I put a paper-thin layer of skin taken from the inside of your thigh. We call that a theirsch graft. I sewed this skin graft into position – and in your case it took about sixty-five stitches and left long threads from some of them hanging out. After that I cut a dry sponge the exact shape of the grafted area, tied the hanging threads over it and knotted them.'

Page asked why:

> 'Well, you see the sponge was then moistened,' said McIndoe, 'This makes it swell. But the threads restrain it, so that it can only exert pressure against the hand, forcing the new skin against the raw surface. That way the two surfaces join together. It's the pressure that causes most of the pain, I'm afraid, and the

Top left: Edwyna and Michael Hillary. Photograph taken while Michael was on leave during WWI.

Top right: Portrait taken of Richard in his new school uniform prior to starting at prep school in Bedfordshire.

Bottom left: Richard, aged 9.

Bottom right: Frank McEachran, Richard's English teacher at Shrewsbury. Photograph taken during the latter part of his career.

NB: ALL PHOTOGRAPHS IN PICTURE SECTION ARE AUTHOR'S COLLECTION EXCEPT WHERE STATED.

Top left: Richard 1934/35, taken while he was attending Shrewsbury School.

Top right: On holiday at Rugely, Staffordshire, at the home of the Nelson-Edwards family. Richard points a .22 rifle at George Nelson-Edwards. Richard's own parents were in the Sudan.

Middle left: Accommodation at Trinity College, Oxford. During his time at Trinity, Richard is reputed to have climbed from one upper-storey window to another, using the ledge. The drop on this particular building is over twenty feet.

Bottom: Shrewsbury School – Churchill's Four on The River Severn. The Four went to Head of the River in 1937. Richard is third from right; George Nelson-Edwards is stroke.

Top left: Brothers-in-arms. Brian and Colin Pinckney circa 1937. Both loved shooting and fishing. When war came, one was killed after being shot down, the other was murdered.

Top right: Richard outside the boathouse with other members of the College Rowing VIII. Frank Waldron is to the left of Richard and was a 'Blue' with the Oxford VIII.

Bottom: Winners 'Head of the River Races' 1938 and 1939. Trinity College Rowing VIII. The team celebrates victory in going to the Head of the River. Richard is sixth from right, Frank Waldron far right.

Top: 'Practising in the frantic heat on the Danube. By the way whoever said it was blue must have been colour blind – It looks like the Thames by the docks.' Richard stroking a makeshift 'Oxford' VIII with Frank Waldron No.3.

(via The National Archives of Canada)

Bottom: 'Why we lost? Girls of the Hungarian rowing club.' Richard (8th from left), Frank Waldron (13th from left) with the rest of their crew. *(via The National Archives of Canada)*

Top: Oxford University Air Squadron. Summer Camp 1939. Richard: rear row, far left; George Nelson-Edwards: rear row, eighth from the left; Peter Howes: middle row, fourth from right; Michael Judd: middle row, far left; Squadron Leader Cracroft is holding on to the mascot with the CO, Wing Commander Hibbert, to his left.

Bottom left: Richard Hillary, Student Pilot OUAS. Photograph from Richard's file at the OUAS Headquarters.

Bottom right: Richard at Oxford, 1939.
(via The National Archives of Canada)

Top left: Richard, 1940. A portrait taken shortly after the award of his Wings brevet.
(via The National Archives of Canada)

Top right: Richard and Noel Agazarian, well wrapped-up against the cold and damp, outside the Sligachan Hotel, Isle of Skye – May 1940. *(via The National Archives of Canada)*

Bottom left and right: Flying Officer Noel le Chevalier 'Aggie' Agazarian. With No.609 Squadron at Warmwell during July 1940, and after the Battle (with Flight Lieutenant Frank Howell), by then sporting the 'Errol Flynn' moustache! (Note how much older he looks from the photograph taken just six months before.) *(The Chris Goss Collection)*

Top left: The 'Triangle of Friendship' from *The Last Enemy*. Colin Pinckney, Richard Hillary and Peter Pease, Old Sarum 1940.

Top right: Pilot Officer Peter Howes RAFVR, 1940.

Bottom left: Flying Officer A. Peter Pease RAFVR. A portrait painted posthumously by Sir Oswald Birley MC on behalf of the Pease family, which hangs in the home of Peter's young brother Sir Richard Pease. Richard Hillary posed for the artist.

Bottom right: '...the best looking man I've ever seen.' Pilot Officer Pease photographed after the award of his Wings brevet in 1938. Notice the absence of any 'VR' badges.

Top left: Spitfire Mk1, XT-M, L1021 'Sredni Vashtar', pictured at 'B' Flight dispersal, RAF Montrose, 1940. This is the only photograph of Richard's Spitfire in which he was shot down on August 29th. In the foreground is XT-K flown by Flying Officer Robin 'Bubble' Waterston and overhead is XT-R flown by Flying Officer 'Bolster' Boulter.

Top right: 'B' Flight No.603 Squadron RAF Montrose, July 1940. At dispersal behind the gun-butts, preparing for a patrol. Left to right: Flight Lieutenant Fred 'Rusty' Rushmer, Flying Officer Brian Carbury and Pilot Officer Noel 'Broody' Benson.

Above: 'Bill, Ken, Sheep, Black, Pat, George and Ian'. 'A' Flight No.603 (City of Edinburgh) Fighter Squadron, Turnhouse, October 1939.

Right: 'We wait to go.' 'Rusty' Rushmer and 'Bubble' Waterston. Although there was a seven-year age difference, these two were great friends and Rushmer was invited to tea with the Waterston family on a number of occasions. Officers' Mess, Turnhouse, August 1940.

O'Hara Greene Snell Skinner Perkins Stephens Downer Read Love

Foskett Lowes Ross Henderson Kerr Francis Jones Pickering Cardell

...ra Green Campbell Sharpe Goode Pollard Read,R.S. Reynolds Gosling Cruikshank

Tyler Gooderham Knowles Coleman Cobbe Stokoe Hanna Sellars Lake

Kingaby Egan Pearce Warn Buschegger Wills Godwin Chalmick

NO. 15 FLYING TRAINING SCHOOL,
LOSSIEMOUTH.
NO. 6 COURSE.

Top: No.6 Course, January 1940 at No.15 FTS, Lossiemouth. Bill Read (back row, third from right), Philip Cardell (fourth row, far right), Alfred Sarre (third row, far left) and Jack Stokoe (second row, fourth from right).

Bottom left: Flying Officer B.G. 'Stapme' Stapleton, DFC, RAF, pictured some time after the Battle of Britain.

Bottom centre: Pilot Officer 'Ras' Berry, Hornchurch 1940.

Bottom right: Richard on Loch Lee, Glen Esk, August 1940. Pilot Officer 'Stapme' Stapleton is firing into the bottom of the Luftwaffe dinghy as Richard attempts to escape the .22 gunfire. It was sixteen-year-old Billy Davie who told him to stop as he thought it a dangerous game. During this period, Richard tended to wear flying boots when he left the aerodrome and his casual shoes when flying.

Top left: Bubble fishing on Loch Lee, during one of the trips to Invermark and Tarfside.

Top right: Spitfire Mk.1, XT-M, X4277. Richard's Spitfire at dispersal on the southern edge of Hornchurch aerodrome, among Spitfires of No. 222 Squadron. It was photographed by Joe Crawshaw, a member of the No. 222 Squadron ground crew, on 1st September 1940. This is the only known photograph of the aircraft in which Richard was shot down three days later.

(via Mr. Joe Crawshaw)

Middle left: The *J.B. Proudfoot* Lifeboat and crew which rescued Richard from the North Sea on 3rd September 1940. Left to right: H. 'Goose' Parker (Bowman), Dennis 'Sinbad' Price (Signalman), T. Harman (2nd Cox), A. Lacey (2nd Mechanic), Edward 'Trunky' Park, DSM (Cox), Henry 'Mussel' Sandwell (Winch/launcher), A. 'Buller' Morris (Crew), E. Barrs (Mechanic with the *J.B. Proudfoot* relief boat), A. Ladd (crew), A.C. Robinson (Hon. Sec.). Following the rescue, a number of the crew visited Richard in hospital. Price and Sandwell later attended his memorial service.

Middle right: Denise. Denise Maxwell-Woosnam, ATS Commander, Peter Pease's fiancée and a friend of Richard Hillary and Colin Pinckney.

Above: The Maestro, Archibald McIndoe, after the war.

Top left: The original saline bath unit and medical team. The patient enjoys a cigarette before treatment begins.

Top right: Geoffrey Page (second from left) briefing pilots before the first operation sortie into Germany.

Left above and below: Colin Hodgkinson (taken shortly after his accident) and Tony Tollemache (taken some years after the war). Both became good friends of Richard during his time at the Queen Victoria Hospital, East Grinstead.

Above: 'Pip'. Pilot Officer Philip Cardell RAFVR, Hornchurch, September 1940. This photo, in which Pip is looking very tired, was taken at dispersal during the late afternoon, just a few days before his death. Spitfire XT-V, P9553, first saw service with 603 Squadron on 8th September. On 2nd October it was shot down over Croydon by a Me109 at 10.30am. Despite a gunshot wound to his leg, Pilot Officer Dexter managed to bail out, before the aircraft crashed in flames.

Top left: Richard 1942. By the time this photograph was taken the major reconstructive surgery to his face and hands was complete. Note how he instinctively holds his hands against and in front of his body, in order to protect them.

Top right: Barbara Dewar 1939. The photograph of a 'Society Girl'. John and Kathleen Dewar's daughter had a short relationship with Richard which ended amicably, though the mother resented the relationship. The message on the photograph needs no explanation: 'To my darling Richard, with all my love, Barbara, May 1941.'

(via The National Archives of Canada)

Bottom left: Lady Winifred Fortescue, author and friend of Richard's. Pictured after the war with her dog 'The Blackness'.

Bottom centre: Mary Booker.

Bottom right: Richard Hillary. This photograph was taken in 1941 by Talbots in New York at the request of Reynal and Hitchcock during preparations to publish Richard's book under its American title *Falling Through Space*. Inset: Portrait taken in 1940, before he was disfigured.

Top: 'Group Photograph, RAF Officers, Uxbridge, 1942'. Richard: back row, sixth from left. To his right is Group Captain Powell Sheddon, DSO, Battle of Britain pilot with 242 Squadron. He later went on to serve with Nos. 258, 96 and 29 Squadrons.

(via The National Archives of Canada)

Bottom left: Captain Michael Burn. He met Richard briefly one evening during 1942, before being captured a few days later during the raid on St. Nazaire. He spent the remainder of the war as a POW and a large part of his captivity was spent in Colditz. In 1947 he married Mary Booker and went on to

become a successful journalist, poet, playwright and author.

Bottom right: The pastel portrait of Richard by Eric Kennington. This copy of the original which is on display in the National Portrait Gallery, was produced by the artist at the request of Michael Hillary after Richard's death, and is kept at Trinity College, Oxford. Michael Hillary disliked the portrait. Richard's nose is too long and the artist created a far more pronounced 'cupid's bow' than actually existed. The scar tissue was also give a softer appearance.

Top left and right: On 14th September 1942, this photograph was taken at the Air Ministry to commemorate the second anniversary of the Battle of Britain. It has been said that Richard 'hid' behind his more exalted company because he had no medal ribbons, but neither did the warrant officer to the right. Left to right: S/L A.C. Bartley, DFC, (England); W/C D.F.B. Sheen, DFC and Bar, (Australia); W/C I.R. Gleed, DSO, DFC, (South Africa); S/L A.C. Deere, DFC, (New Zealand); Air Chief Marshal Sir Hugh Dowding, GCB, GCVO, CMB; F/O E.C. Henderson, MM, (Scotland); F/L R.H. Hillary, (England); W/C J.A. Kent, DFC, AFC, (Canada); W/C C.F.B. Kingcome, DFC, (England); S/L D.H. Watkins, DFC, (England); W/O R.H. Gretton, (England).

A number of photographs were taken proving that Richard's pose varied.

(via The National Archives of Canada)

Bottom: RAF Charterhall. Aerial view taken 23rd September 1942. There is much evidence of the recent building work. The clear area to the far left/centre of the photograph is the football pitch. Below it can be seen the wreckage of six aircraft, one of which has a wing missing. Prior to taking off on his last flight, Richard taxied his aircraft from dispersal (not shown), down the perimeter track from the top/centre of the photograph, to the end of the runway, seen in the bottom left hand corner of the photograph.

(RAF Museum, Hendon. P14348)

Top left: Course photograph of the pilots, No.54 OTU, RAF Charterhall, November 1942. The Pilots. Middle row, third from left is Andy Miller; fourth from the left is Sergeant Wilkinson. This photo clearly shows how much at home Richard was in the company of his fellow pilots, and very much the centre of attention. This was the last photo taken before he was killed.

Top right: Kenneth Wilfrid Young Fison (Sgt. Wilfred Fison RAFVR) – Hillary's R/O.

Bottom left: The Airfield Identification Beacon. Manned by airmen, it was while circling this mobile identification beacon that Richard lost control of the aircraft.   *(IWM)*

Bottom right: Flight Lieutenant (later Squadron Leader) Wilfred Handel 'Andy' Miller, DFC and Bar. A very successful night fighter pilot, Andy Miller was credited with eleven enemy aircraft destroyed. He was standing atdispersal waiting for Richard to land his aircraft, but instead witnessed the crash.

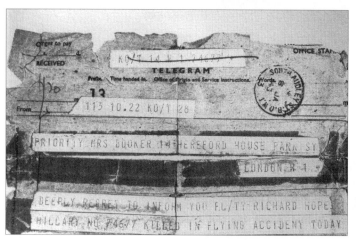

Top: The Bristol Blenheim Mk.V. Also known as the 'Five'. The name 'Bisley' had originally been allocated to the prototype of this model but was superceded by that of 'Blenheim V' before the prototype even flew. Only two prototypes were built, the first being AD657, with a forward fuselage designed for ground attack, the second being AD661 which was fitted with a fuselage designed for high altitude bombing. Production went ahead with the latter design only. The photograph shows a 'Five' fitted with the high altitude nose, the variant which Richard flew the night he was killed. The Blenheim V had a very short service life as its performance left much to be desired and as a consequence it was relegated to training use.

Middle left: The telegram informing Mary of Richard's death. 'Richard, I bow before this blackness of despair, this loneliness of night. The first of an eternity of nights...'

Middle right: Floral cross of red poppies on the crash-site. As can be seen, the original print was mounted in a display folder on the back of which was written the words: 'Where the Last Enemy was conquered.' The subject of this photograph would suggest that its owner was Richard's mother.

(via The National Archives of Canada)

Bottom: View of the crash-site today at Crunklaw Farm.

elastic bandage only adds to your misery. Hurts like hell, doesn't it? Ready for some more? Right. Stitch scissors Sister!'

McIndoe snipped through the remaining threads and slowly peeled away the blood-soaked sponge to reveal the grafted area. Page was expecting the worst:

> I remember looking at what was underneath and I went cold. All those days and nights of fiendish torture couldn't result in this – this stinking pulp of rotten flesh and oozing pus! It wasn't fair.

The initial sight that met his eyes was deceiving however. With a look of satisfaction McIndoe spoke to Sister Hall:

> Luckier than I thought. That's about a fifty per cent take, I think. get the hand into the bath. Let it soak for half an hour, then the usual dressings – plenty of sulphanilamid powder. The stitches can come out tomorrow.

He patted Page on the shoulder encouragingly and with a smile said: 'That's fine. Now we've got to get you fit for the next lot.'

Geoffrey Page had many more operations on his other hand and face ahead of him yet.

In July 1995 I spoke to him at length at his home in Oxfordshire about his memories of Richard Hillary while at East Grinstead Hospital. I had also arranged to meet Alex Tollemache there, Tony Tollemache's son. He had been keen to meet Geoffrey, the one time friend of his late father. Page recalls:

> Richard and I were the same age. Our hand injuries were almost exactly the same resulting in the same disability. We like so many other pilots had not been wearing our gloves.
>
> Although we were shot down over the Channel on different dates we were both picked up by the same lifeboat and taken to the Margate General Hospital. I was then taken to Halton near Aylesbury. It was while I was here that Archie McIndoe, then consultant-in-chief for plastic surgery to the RAF, chose me as a long term burns case. I was then sent to East Grinstead where I was to spend the next two years. Richard was to be chosen by McIndoe whilst on a tour of the Masonic, and for the same reasons.
>
> We were in a charming little ward with about ten beds, two pairs facing each other, either side. When I first went in Richard Hillary was lying on his bed and Tony Tollemache was standing by his. There seemed to be a love-hate war going on between Tony and Richard. They'd say incredible things to each other. All in fun, but much to the horror of the Irish nurse and sister. 'You can't be talking to me like that Mr. Tollemache, not in here.' And Richard used to say, 'Go and get stuffed!' It was that sort of level of conversation although they were two very intelligent men. Tony and Richard had this method of communicating which was based on straight-forward sarcasm. One tried to out-sarcasm the other, if there is such a word, I think it was their means of escape. Tony had very bad burns on his face and had to have a lot of work done which included new eyelids. His hands were not too bad, not as bad as mine and Richard's. His legs were very badly burnt however, and he was to have many problems with them.
>
> You could always tell when someone had plastic surgery. After they had a few drinks the grafted areas would become very red, and in Richard and Tony's cases they were red around the eyes!
>
> Richard's hands were like mine, very badly burned. In 1940 an unofficial order had gone out that you must wear gloves and you must wear your uniform jacket under your flying jacket. The burns cases were so much worse, some were burnt to death, because all that they wore was a cotton shirt. When the aircraft caught fire you only had a few seconds in which to get out. If you didn't get out

in that time you never would. There was an appalling number of hand burns. When I finally returned to flying I was always careful and put gloves on, in fact I had a pair specially made with zippers running down one side to enable me to put them on easily.

I met Richard's parents. That was quite a shock. His mother was an absolute tartar! When she came through the ward Richard's father followed dutifully three paces behind. He looked 'cheesed off'. I hope he found some happiness!

It took a few weeks for me to learn to overcome the awe I felt whilst in his company. He was an impressive figure, he was a tall young man, about six foot one. The first time that I met him was while I was talking to Tony Tollemache. Richard had just had a new set of eyelids grafted on. After such an operation in order to see you had to walk around with your head leaning right back, looking down your nose. This enabled you to see under these newly attached drooping bags of skin. The under-layer of muscle needed time to adjust and for the grafts to take and shrink. After which they would be trimmed during a subsequent operation.

Richard always used an enormous Noel Coward style cigarette holder and he used to smoke with this clenched between his teeth. The nurse would drape his silk dressing gown around his shoulders. He looked very dandy! He wandered around with his cigarette holder stuck between two of his crippled fingers looking around with his head tilted back. The fried Noel Coward look!

He was very confident. I think his view of his fellow human beings was that he looked down on them. Except, that is, for his women. I think he was alright but by withholding himself from the rest of mankind, I don't think the rest of mankind was in much of a position to judge him. His personality was such that it helped protect him from the trauma of his experiences. Unfortunately this did not endear him with his fellow sufferers.

Richard was no more mobile than I was and spent most of his time in bed. I had a few burns on my legs and a splinter from a cannon shell went through my calf. Richard limped painfully around the ward as a result of the skin removed from his legs to graft onto his hands. That was the most painful part.

The hand operations were actually carried out at East Grinstead during 1942.

Richard was required to wear an aluminium cast on the inside of each wrist and hand for a while, as I was also required to do. It was a casting with a curl. The curl was gradually straightened out by placing wadding between the hand and the brace, thus extending the fingers. Each night the nurse applied a little more wadding. It did not work as intended as each time they took the casting off the fingers, they returned to their original positions. I don't have a single finger that works properly.

We had our own overhead lamps which were switched on and off using a long cord which hung down from the ceiling. You could use your teeth or hand to operate the light, depending on how incapacitated you were. Richard was lying in bed, writing away like mad, and voices were coming out of the semi-darkness:

'Turn that bloody light out, Richard.'

We always had a stack of eggs in our bedside lockers and someone picked up an egg and threw one at Richard. All the others followed-up with some pretty wild shots but in the morning the wall behind was caked in egg. He pulled the top sheet up to protect himself but he did turn the light out!

The ligaments and tendons of their hands had been burnt and were shrivelling up as the surface tissue contracted. As they tightened, the fingers would slowly be drawn in towards the palm of the hands giving them the appearance of claws. The gadget to which Geoffrey Page refers was tried by McIndoe, not long after Richard arrived at East

Grinstead, in an attempt to halt the process. Richard noted in his diary that he was supposed to wear the device both day and night, but they proved to be uncomfortable bed companions. He confessed that every time he went to London he removed them. Richard was required to persevere with them during subsequent visits to convalescent homes after surgery in 1942. Unfortunately, the devices failed to work in the case of both Richard and Geoffrey Page.

Geoffrey Page continued with his recollections of the time he spent with Richard:

> We were in hospital for two or three months at a time. We could only have three operations maximum because of the dangers of the anaesthetic. So we were sent away to recuperate. Having said that, I was in a bed next to a chap called Peter Weeks who had been there three years, whereas I had been there for about a year and a half by that time.
>
> By then we had been in and out a lot. I helped form what is now known as the Guinea Pig Club and we still have an annual reunion. I go about once every three years. I don't know the majority of people that attend, as there had been so many patients by the end of the war that our particular time at East Grinstead did not coincide.
>
> Having been passed fit to fly, Richard would have learnt tricks that enabled him to fly an aircraft, as I did. The question was how effectively would he be able to fly an aircraft? We had several discussions about our returning to operational flying. His idea was to return as a night fighter pilot who could creep up on the enemy and blow them out of the sky. He was of the opinion that his hands would never be strong enough again to enable him to adequately and effectively control a Spitfire through tight evasive and attacking moves in the heat of combat.
>
> My idea was to do just that and go back doing what I had originally been trained to do, flying fighters in daylight. This was after all our only experience. I was ultimately proved to be right. Our discussions were always good natured and centred around the various degrees of difficulty associated with our returning to flying. We had many long conversations that were actually preparation for confrontation with the powers that be, and our attempt to persuade them that we were fit for a return to operational flying duties. Richard's intentions were far more fraught with danger. He had never flown a twin-engined aircraft and was unaware of the associated difficulties of flying one with his disabilities; they were heavier and harder to handle. I knew that with my hands I would not be able to handle such a situation with sufficient control. I stuck to my idea of returning to operations on what I knew best, flying fighters. Sadly for Richard, I won the argument when he was killed.

It is clear though that in time Richard also knew that he had been wrong to pursue his flying career in the way that he had chosen, and he was aware that he was in grave danger.

Geoffrey Page later told me that one of the motivating factors which had driven him to return as a fighter pilot, and which he hadn't declared to Richard, was a 'blood-lust'. He wanted to make the Germans pay for his suffering by shooting down one German for every operation he had endured. By the time he returned to operational flying he had been under the knife 15 times and his total eventually reached 17. By that time the emotions of the blood-lust had subsided into a tired declaration that it had all seemed so pointless.

Another interesting point is that unlike Richard, Geoffrey Page developed and undertook his own remedial therapy on his hands. Whether such treatment was suggested by the specialists at the hospital is unknown but likely. He acquired a rubber ball and spent hours exercising his gnarled and sensitive fingers as he lay in bed. Initially as he tried to squeeze the ball his withered ligaments, tendons and tender nerves screamed out in protest, the resulting pain causing tears to pour down the young airman's cheeks and leave his body bathed in sweat. Eventually, when endured, the agony became exquisite. As time went by the pain became less and the hands became stronger. The fact that Richard did not undertake such therapy to the lengths that Page

did is significant, especially when they later went before the medical board on the same
day in an attempt to return to flying.

Geoffrey Page continued:

> Like Richard, Tony wasn't a particularly close buddy of mine. Somehow though
> I liked him very much. He was an extremely nice man. He never went to the
> annual Guinea Pig get-togethers after the war.
>
> When I formed the club with five others it was really a drinking club for Ward
> 3. After an operation you were not able to get back into circulation for about three
> weeks. Boredom was our biggest problem and we decided to form this club. We
> held the first meeting in the gardener's hut.
>
> We made Johnny Dewar an honorary member as his contacts with the whisky
> world were eventually very useful.
>
> When the nastiness of the skin grafts was behind us and we were back in the
> real world, those of us that were able to look after themselves, were also able to
> look after others, such as the blind, who were unable to look after themselves.
> That worked very well indeed, and we eventually managed to get one of our
> members onto the board of the RAF Benevolent Fund. We therefore had a
> permanent sitting member there with the interests of the Guinea Pigs, and the
> money was put to good use.
>
> We were able to eliminate feeling sorry for ourselves. You only had to look
> around to see someone who was worse off than yourself. At the bottom of the
> ladder one usually found the most cheerful of them all. Blind, with hands burnt
> off, so Braille would not be an option.
>
> Godfrey Edmunds is mentioned by Richard in *The Last Enemy*. He was a
> great man and a great friend of mine. McIndoe said that he was the most badly
> burnt chap he had ever treated. He was so ill during the first few days after his
> crash the nurses were wishing he would die. He survived, and I have some lovely
> funny stories about him. He had this wonderfully vulgar sense of humour. I don't
> know if he did it on purpose or not, but he went back to his beloved South Africa
> and became a car salesman! You would think that anyone that saw him would run
> a mile. As it turned out he proved to be one of the best. He used to live in the
> village of Cockstand, which we used to pull his leg about.
>
> McIndoe grafted him two new eyebrows. Godfrey asked for them, but he had
> no scalp left from which to take a graft. Usually the graft for eyebrows etc would
> come from your scalp, but he had none left. McIndoe and Godfrey discussed this
> and the only donor area was his pubic hair. The eyebrows were therefore grafted
> from this area. Archie, Godfrey and I were having a few drinks somewhere and
> McIndoe asked Godfrey if he was pleased with his eyebrows. He replied, 'Yes
> Boss, but everytime I walk down the street and a pretty girl walks by my
> eyebrows start fluttering!' He also got married. One of his biggest regrets was
> that he was burnt on a training flight and not on ops. But most Guinea Pigs came
> into that category.

Godfrey Edmunds died four or five years before this interview.

In recent times Geoffrey Page has done a great deal of work for the Royal Air Force
Association (RAFA) and for the establishment of a Battle of Britain Memorial at Capel-
le-Ferne, near Folkestone, Kent.

In the early part of 1995, Geoffrey returned to East Grinstead for another operation
on some irritating scar tissue on his neck. It was the 43rd operation on his injuries since
that morning 60 years ago when he was shot down, and it wouldn't be the last.

CHAPTER THIRTEEN

WARD 3

December 1940 – May 1941

For Christmas 1940 the Dewars arranged a Christmas night party at Dutton Homestall, to keep the patients occupied during the festive period and serve as a distraction from their mental and physical discomfort. Kathleen Dewar was particularly active in relieving the boredom that the patients suffered from the enforced inactivity during the long periods of recovery. Frequently she would arrange for one of her friends and associates of stage and screen to visit her home and entertain the young men, raising their spirits and momentarily distracting them from their plight.

After Christmas Richard returned home for a few days, enjoying a very comfortable and luxurious lifestyle in comparison with Ward 3 at East Grinstead. He had managed to regain lost weight and was now back at twelve stone, the weight he had been before he was shot down. McIndoe, meanwhile, celebrated Christmas in the company of John Hunter and his wife:

> John has made a great study of cooking in the past 18 months and turns out a
> dashed good meal. He gets a diabetic triple ration in most things that matter and
> is thus able to go in for a good deal of fancy cooking denied to the rest of us.

By early January 1941 Richard was back at East Grinstead having the excess baggy skin removed from the grafted skin of his new lower eyelids. He was also to receive a graft on his upper lip. On his return to the hospital he was dismayed to learn that he was to be accommodated, not in the clean, spacious, sterility of the permanent male-only Kindersley Ward, but in one of the 'blisters'. This was the first time he was to stay in Ward 3.

Here Richard found that most of the injuries were deeper and more extensive than his own. The patients were lying around in different postures, some with hands attached to their stomachs, others with faces attached to their shoulders and some with their inner forearms attached to their foreheads with the arm crooked over the head.

Although he settled into the crew-room atmosphere of this smelly and necessarily very hot ward, with its wide ranging assortment of different personalities, he was unhappy with its lack of cleanliness.

Another badly wounded pilot had recently been moved from the Kindersley Ward into Ward 3. His first meeting with Richard was one that gave him great spirit in the face of overwhelming adversity and was an experience he never forgot. Pilot Officer George 'Ben' Bennions had been born in Burslem, Stoke-on-Trent in 1913 and had joined the RAF as a Halton 'Brat' in 1929. He was recommended for a cadetship at Cranwell and was given *ab initio* flying training. The cadetship did not occur, however, and he completed his flying training at 3 FTS Grantham in 1935, joining No.41 Squadron at Khormaksar, Aden, in January 1936.

Ben was still with No.41 Squadron flying Spitfires during the Battle of Britain and had received a commission in April 1940. He was in the thick of the action and between 28 July and 1 October 1940 he destroyed a total of 12 enemy aircraft with five more probables and five damaged. On 28 July he received damage to his own flaps which forced him to crash-land at Manston and after combat on 6 September he crash-landed at Rochford after his undercarriage collapsed. On the 11th Ben received a wound to his left heel caused by a shell splinter.

On 1 October, after shooting down his twelth Me109, he was himself shot down by 109s over Henfield, Sussex. His Spitfire X4559 crashed on Heatenthorn Farm, Alborne. He managed to bale out and landed at Dunstalls Farm. He had been grievously wounded during the combat when a cannon shell ripped into his cockpit and blew away part of his face including his left eye, leaving his brain exposed. The award of the DFC was gazetted on the day he was shot down. After initial treatment for his injuries in Horsham hospital in Sussex, Ben was transferred to nearby East Grinstead for reconstructive surgery which was carried out by McIndoe, and he became a founder member of the Guinea Pig Club.

After his recovery he was given an A2B non-operational category and only allowed to fly by day and with a passenger who could look out for him. In 1943 he was posted to North Africa where he became the liaision officer to an American fighter group which had recently been re-equipped with Spitfires. Ben later flew Spitfire patrols in Sicily but took no further part in combat. He received shrapnel wounds in October 1943 when the landing craft he was in at Ajaccio, Corsica, was sunk by enemy action.

Ben was released from the RAF in 1946 as a squadron leader and he became a school teacher. I had the great pleasure of meeting him at the last four Battle of Britain Fighter Association annual reunions at RAF Lakenheath, when he retold his memories of Richard. At 86 he looks marvellous.

Ben had been in Kindersley Ward when he had first arrived at East Grinstead and after initial surgery he was moved into Ward 3:

> I was feeling very sorry for myself and on the verge of tears as I shuffled towards my newly appointed bed in the ward that was to become my home for the near future. As I neared the bed I saw a figure sitting facing me at the other end of the ward. He was in a wheelchair, his hands were like claws, and his face and top lip had been terribly burned and signs of recent surgery were evident. He grabbed the wheels and set off towards me as fast as he could, his injured hands working hard at the task. I panicked, but just as he was about to hit me he swerved sharply to one side and came to a sudden halt. 'Here, have a chair, old man,' he said as he climbed out of the wheelchair and went off towards his own bed. I didn't know who he was at the time, he certainly wasn't famous then, but the experience had a profound effect on me. I sat on my bed and wept, such was my state of mind at that time. He showed such spirit in the face of such adversity. Despite his injuries he was able to lift himself out of the funk, that I now found myself in, and display such fortitude. He was the best example I saw and he helped me through the worst period, believing that there was always somebody worse off than me, and I never felt sorry for myself again.

The morning after his arrival Richard was first on the list for surgery. He was once again awoken by one of the orderlies who prepped him for his operation. In addition to having the excess skin removed from his lower eyelids, he was to have skin grafted from his arm onto his upper lip. They removed skin from the area on his shoulder between his vaccination scar and the feint scar from where the skin was removed which now formed his upper eyelids. At nine o'clock and feeling relaxed under the effects of the pre-op injection Richard was given another injection by the Sister and wheeled down to the operating theatre wearing his bright red silk pyjamas. 'For luck', as he put it. He was then anaesthetised by John Hunter.

Richard awoke blind once again and bandaged from forehead to lip. He was therefore only able to breathe through his mouth. Tony Tollemache and his mother came to visit him from three until four o'clock. Due to the discomfort from the surgery and the residual effects of the anaesthetic, Richard was still in a semi-stuporous state, feeling disassociated from what was going on around him. He was given injections to help relieve the pain and to aid sleep, although that was still filled with nightmares. He did not awaken fully until the next morning.

In the afternoon the doctors removed the dressings from his head, allowing him to see once again. The dressing on his lip was left in place, which inhibited his breathing to some degree. He was able to get to a mirror and survey the handiwork of the master surgeon. There were two sets of semi-circular stitches under each eye. In addition, McIndoe had taken advantage of the situation and raised Richard's right eyebrow in-line with his left and stitched it in place.

This last experience was documented in Richard's diary. It is different to what finally went to print in *The Last Enemy*. The most important point is that it would be reasonable to assume that this experience was jotted down soon after the events took place, and should perhaps be considered as reasonably accurate. Certainly, manipulation of the details would not have been necessary at this stage even if he was contemplating writing his book. This single diary extract appears in *The Last Enemy* having been divided into three separate sections during editing, with each aspect presented as being totally separate from one another, possibly to provide a consistent level of interest and detail throughout this period. These three sections consist of the operation to provide him with new upper eyelids, his description of Ward 3, and the operation to give him new lower lids and upper lip:

> *Jan 8.* Woken up early to have my arm prepared by one of the orderlies. I decided on my arm and not my leg as this will save me the bother of shaving my new upper lip . . .
>
> Ward 3 stands about fifty yards away from the main hospital building. It is a long, low hut, with a door at one end and twenty beds down each side. These are separated from each other by lockers and it is possible without much exertion to reach out and touch the man in the next bed. Towards the far end the lockers deteriorate into soap boxes. They comprise the furniture. Windows are let into the walls at regular intervals on each side; they are never open. Down the middle there is a table with a wireless on it, a stove, and a piano. On either side of the entrance passage are four lavatories and two bathrooms. This passage opens into the ward, where immediately on the left is the famous saline bath. Next to this in a curtained-off bed is a little girl of 15, terribly burnt by boiling sugar her first day in a factory. She screams fairly regularly and always before being lifted into the bath: her voice is thin and like that of a child of seven.
>
> As the time for her bath approaches there is a certain tension throughout the hut and suddenly everyone starts talking rather loudly and the wireless is turned up. For the rest, there is a blind man at the far end, learning Braille with the assistance of his wife, a squadron-leader, several pilot officers, a Czech, and sundry troops, unlikely to forget Dunkirk as quickly as most.
>
> McIndoe described the ward on Christmas Day as the most democratic in the country, made a passing reference to the mixed-bathing and praised the spirit which made the whole thing possible. I have yet to meet one down-hearted man amongst all these mutilated. Those with legs carry bottles for those without: men with charred hands condole with men disfigured.
>
> Someone newly burnt and dripping with pus will be placed in a bed next to a man with a day-old skin-graft. Neither complains: neither can.
>
> The predominant characteristic of the ward is the smell: it meets you at the door, a heavy pall; a mixture of bed-pans and old dressings.
>
> Sister gave me an injection at about nine o'clock and an hour later, wearing my red pyjamas for luck, I climbed on to the trolley and was wheeled across the fifty yards of open space to the hospital. There is something a little lowering about this journey on a cold morning. I reached the theatre, feeling quite emotionless, rather like a businessman arriving at his office. Doctor Hunter, vast and genial as ever, gave me my injection, shook me by the hand and wished me 'Good-bye'. A dark green curtain rose up my throat and I passed quietly away.

On coming round I realised that I was bandaged from forehead to lip and unable to breathe through my nose. At about 3 p.m. Mrs. Tollemache, Tony and Pamela Mills came to see me. I had by then developed a delicate froth on both lips and must have resembled a rather 'refined' stallion. They were very kind and talked to me quite normally. I'm afraid I replied very little as I needed my mouth to breathe with. They went about four. After that the day is a blur: a thin wailing scream, wireless playing 'each day is one day nearer', injections, a little singing, much laughter, and a voice saying, 'Naow, Charlie, you can't do it; naow Charlie, you can't do it; naow, Charlie, you can't do it.' After this, oblivion, thank God.

The young female patient to whom Richard refers was Joan. Taffy the RAF orderly refers to her earlier in the same chapter. Ward 3 was all male apart from Joan, who had been burnt on her head, face, arms and chest. She had been on the ward for a number of months lying bald and frightened in her bed, curtained off from the rest of the ward and conveniently situated next to the saline bath. The airmen had found her whimpering quelled their exuberance, and her screams unnerving whenever she had been carried to the bath. They were not unhappy to see her leave but presented her with a monogrammed silk scarf before she went. The ward was now all male.

The next day:

Jan 9. Woke early in a cold sweat after a nightmare in which my eyelids were sewn together and I was leading the squadron. Mrs. Tollemache came to see me in the afternoon, and in the evening Morley appeared and took the bandages off my eyes. I was left with a thick dressing across my upper lip which pressed against my nose, and two sets of semi-circular stitches under my eyes. I looked like an orang utang. Peering into a mirror I noticed that my right eyebrow had been lifted up a bit further to pair it off with the left. This was also stitched.

Later McIndoe came round with his Yes-men and peered anxiously at the scar under my right eye which was blue and swollen. He went on. There was comparatively little noise, but the ward stank and I was depressed.

By the time McIndoe had completed his tour of his patients Richard was instinctively aware that there was a problem. Disaster was about to strike, and this period at the hospital was to leave far from pleasant memories for Richard, and the other patients in Ward 3 at that time.

Despite McIndoe's efforts, burnt aircrew were still being sent from first-aid stations with their seared flesh covered in grease or coagulants, including tannic acid, and this, as he had gone to great lengths to point out, was a primary cause of infection. While the application of this treatment was to ease the victims' pain, it was coated on dirty skin and hair, sealing in bacteria against the raw wounds. The routines recommended by McIndoe were not being adhered to and as a result cross-infection was inevitable.

As the nurses went about their daily routines they too became aware of a far stronger odour than was usual on the ward. As they began to change the patients' dressings their worries were confirmed. The grafts were not taking, the wounds smelt and were suppurating. McIndoe came on to the ward. As he inspected the work of so many hours in theatre he now found himself removing the layers of stinking skin from the suppurating wounds and tossing them into a slop-pan. He was tired and angry. In response to his expletives Richard spoke: 'Welcome to the school, Archie!'

Any recent success was undone as grafts that had initially been successful began to come away. It was a terrible disappointment to both patient and staff and clearly something was amiss.

McIndoe and his staff at the hospital quickly realised that streptococcal infection was rife in the ward and that eight of his patients had contracted the infectious bug, one of whom was Richard. In a number of letters that he wrote during April 1942, while in Ward 3, Richard condemns the lack of hygiene. The fact that the infection had spread throughout this particular ward tends to make the likelihood of this being the case more credible. This was not the only time that streptococcal infection hit Ward 3. Very little has been made of this particular point over the years, owing mainly to a reluctance to say anything to the detriment of Archie McIndoe and the outstanding work he did at the hospital. Typically, Richard was not afraid to make his point known.

McIndoe and his doctors concluded that everything in the ward had been infected and ordered the evacuation. He gave instructions to Sister Hall who was concerned as Dewar Ward was already full:

'Any of them serious?' McIndoe asked.

Sister Hall confirmed that none were, and he continued: 'I want my boys washed down with anti-septic soap, dusted with M & B, and put across there before the night is out.'

Swabs were taken for analysis with the eight initially suspected of harbouring the infection immediately moved from Ward 3 to Dewar Ward chosen specifically for the purpose of isolation. Their new abode, endowed by the Dewar family and usually reserved for local women patients, was back in the main building and the facilities were far more comfortable than Ward 3. It was clean and tidy, and kept at a lower, more tolerable temperature. Headphones were available, hanging on the wall at the head of each bed.

This was a difficult time for McIndoe. The hospital was now extremely busy and certainly not designed for such an influx of casualties. He was spending long days in theatre and on the wards, while trying to solve the various administrative problems in the evenings. The infection in Ward 3 caused even more work and his wife was not making matters easy for him by nagging him in her letters to arrange for her and his daughters to be brought back to England from America. The strain was showing and when the resident doctors came *en masse* to argue with McIndoe over the use of Dewar Ward for the evacuation of his burns patients he waved authorisation from the hospital committee and confronted them over the delay in having them moved: 'If any more men lose their faces because of this delay, I'm bloody well going to report the lot of you to the BMA.'

Staff entering Dewar Ward were appropriately clad in sterile clothing of white masks, aprons and rubber gloves, which rendered them rather impersonal. These appointed staff set about clipping the hair of the patients close to the scalp. Their heads were then sterilised with medicated soap and then sprinkled with antiseptic M&B powder. They were not allowed to write letters and received no outside visits.

The problem with the virus was that their areas of recent and still-inflamed surgery were vulnerable. Streptococci bacteria set in, in some cases rendering the new grafts useless. They had to be removed and the swollen and infected wounds cleaned. The results of the swabs indicated that two of the eight did not have the infection. The names of the two were withheld.

Among Richard's fellow sufferers during this short but uncomfortable period were: Tom Gleave; Eric Lock; Maurice Mounsdon, one of Richard's friends from his days at Kinloss; a Czech sergeant pilot called Joseph Koukal and Bombardier 'Yorkie' Law who, referring to the many grafts he had, rather gruesomely suggested: 'When I get home I'm going to pull them all off for Christmas and give a quid to the first kid who can fit them back again.'

There was also a clever but disliked young Jewish boy by the name of Neft, who was to bear the brunt of their coarse and sometimes cruel humour for the period they were kept in isolation.

At 32, Tom Gleave, was one of the oldest pilots admitted to East Grinstead for reconstructive surgery. He was certainly the senior RAF officer present during Richard's time in Ward 3. He had joined the RAF in 1930 and was then already an experienced pilot. During 1934 he had been on loan to the Oxford University Air Squadron as an instructor.

On 2 June 1940 he took command of No. 253 Squadron at Kirton-in-Lindsey but on

9 August he was posted away to AOC 14 Group, although allowed to stay with the squadron until sent for. On 30 August he claimed five Me109s destroyed but was credited with one destroyed and four probably destroyed. (It later emerged that all five enemy aircraft were actually destroyed.) Squadron Leader H.M. Starr, CO of 253, was shot down and killed on the morning of 31 August and command once more reverted to Tom Gleave. Unfortunately at 13.00 hours on the same day, having already claimed a Ju88 destroyed and another probable, his Hurricane was hit by enemy fire and he was grievously burned before he was blown clear of his aircraft in an ensuing explosion. After landing safely by parachute he discovered just how badly burnt he was. His trousers had been burnt away save for the narrow strips under his harness:

> The skin on my right leg, from the top of the thigh to just above the ankle, had lifted and draped my leg like outsize plus-fours. My left leg was in a similar condition except that the left thigh was only scorched, thanks to the flames having been directed to my right side. Above each ankle I had a bracelet of unburnt skin: my socks, which were always wrinkled, had refused to burn properly and must have just smouldered. That my slacks should have burnt so easily is not surprising; oil mist percolates one's clothing, and I probably had enough on my person to lubricate a battleship. My service gloves were almost burnt off, and the skin from my wrists and hands hung down like paper bags. The under side of my right arm and elbow were burnt and so was my face and neck. I could see all right, although it felt like looking through slits in a mass of swollen skin, and I came to the conclusion that the services of a doctor were necessary.

With his face and hands covered in a hard shell of tannic acid Tom Gleave spent the next few weeks in dreadful agony as the burns covered with tannic acid had gone septic. He was initially admitted to Orpington Hospital before being moved to East Grinstead for reconstructive surgery. The journey to the Sussex cottage hospital was particularly painful in his memory as the orderlies had dressed him in his RAF uniform and this chaffed the exposed, suppurating flesh. As described by many burns victims, the pain was exquisite.

By the time he was admitted to Ward 3, Tom Gleave had had the same dressings on for three days, after initial attempts to remove them at the previous hospital had done considerable damage. He was immersed in the saline bath and the relief was bliss and remained in his memory for the rest of his life. Gleave watched the old bandages gradually float free as the bath unit staff made notes on his burns. He lay there for half an hour during which time one of the RAF orderlies said: It's a good job you kept your hand on it when it happened, Squadron Leader. Your marital prospects are perfect.'

His burns were dressed with an invention of McIndoe's, large pieces of gauze soaked in Vaseline and antiseptics to prevent it from sticking to his flesh. He was put to bed and every two hours throughout the night the nurse would come and pull back the sheet and pour water over his tender burnt flesh with a shower of salt water from a watering-can with a rose on the end. This initiative was introduced as a result of the effect landing in the sea had on burns, compared with those pilots who had parachuted onto dry land. Gleave recalled meeting McIndoe for the first time in Leonard Mosley's book, *Faces From the Fire*:

> One day the Maestro toured the ward and I met him for the first time. He stood over me looking at me through those horn-rimmed spectacles with a clear candid gaze I have never seen in the eyes of any other man. It gave one immediate strength. You had an instinctive feeling that this man was not going to fool you. He weighed up my face, and then said that the first facial grafts I needed were eyelids, top and bottom. My burns were healing rapidly. I could see new skin every time I was put in the bath – or 'the Spa' as we named it. But the Maestro thought the process could be speeded up. 'We will pinch-graft the two large patches on your leg,' he said, 'and give you two top eyelids first. Your eyes will

be covered for a week.' He paused and his eyes twinkled. 'You won't like it, but it's worth it.'

Tom Gleave had total faith in McIndoe and developed enormous respect, affection and gratitude that was never to diminish over the years:

> It was just the way he said it. I believed it. I felt like a shipwrecked man who has been floating around in the sea for hours when a lifeboat suddenly comes by.

McIndoe had carried out a great deal of work on Tom Gleave by the time the infection struck in Ward 3. Both patient and surgeon were greatly distressed over the loss of so much of the grafted skin. The tube pedicle from Gleave's shaven head to form a new nose was suppurating and came away and a graft stitched over an exposed nerve on his temple which had been causing excrutiating pain also failed and the suffering began again.

Tom Gleave was a fine pilot and a kind gentleman who held the respect of all around him. When the Guinea Pig Club was formed on 20 July 1941, he was voted onto the committee as Vice President.

* * *

Pilot Officer Eric Lock was 20 years old and had joined No. 41 Squadron at Hornchurch in August 1940. Known as 'sawn-off' due to his short stature, he was an outstanding pilot who claimed twenty enemy aircraft destroyed between 15 August and 17 November, the day on which he was shot down and wounded in the right arm and both legs. He crash-landed on Martlesham Heath, but was unable to move due to his injuries. Lock remained in his cockpit until he was found by two soldiers who carried him for two miles on a stretcher hastily constructed using their rifles and coats. He was hospitalised until May 1941 during which time he had 15 operations to remove shell splinters from his body. On 3 August 1941, while flying as a flight commander with 611 Squadron, he dived to strafe German soldiers on a road near Calais and was not seen again.

Pilot Officer Maurice 'Mark' Mounsdon had joined No.56 Squadron at North Weald on 3 June 1940. With a number of claims to his credit he was shot down by enemy fighters over Colchester on 31 August, and spent the next nine months in various hospitals including East Grinstead. His memories of his wartime experiences are 'as clear as if it had been yesterday' and he recalls:

> From Kinloss I went to Meir where I met Geoffrey Page. Together we were destined to serve in 56 Squadron and we used to go about together. We were posted to the squadron on the same day. We were at Meir for about ten days when the postings came through and the adjutant, or whoever it was, said, 'You and Page, No.66 Squadron.' We left separately, as I had a car and wanted to pick it up and take it with me to my new squadron. We got to 66 Squadron the next day and we'd been there nearly two weeks, undertaking flying training on Spitfires, when the military police arrived to arrest us as deserters. We'd been sent to the wrong squadron, they had wrongly told us 66 instead of 56! The CO of 66 said, 'I trained these boys and I want to keep them,' and contacted the Ministry. He was unsuccessful and we had to go. We drove down separately to 56 Squadron at North Weald the same day but the squadron wasn't there, it was up at RAF Digby. There were a couple of brand new Hurricanes recently delivered to the squadron, so we took them up there.
>
> I was shot down on 31 August. We were scrambled at about eight in the morning. We had been sleeping at dispersal so we could get airborne as quickly as possible. There was only eight or nine of us left at that time, we weren't a full squadron by now, due to losses. We took off and were told to orbit Colchester at 20,000 feet and sure enough we saw the bomber formation coming in. We could

also see fighters above us. We made a quarter attack on the bomber formation, but we weren't very well placed, although that's no criticism of the leader. It just happened.

We made an attack and I got one in my sights and gave him a good blasting before we were through the formation. It was as I was regaining altitude and turning to initiate a second attack that I was hit. I was caught out in only a split second, as I was frantically looking around the whole time for the German fighters. I just happened to glance to the starboard side and when I glanced back at my port side there was a yellow nosed 109 coming at me. I can't remember if I saw him first or he hit me first. Cannon shells smashed into the left side of my Hurricane and I received a lot of shrapnel splinters in my thigh and leg before the same 109, or possibly another, hit the gravity tank and I was instantly in an inferno. I was sitting in the blast from a blow lamp, so I scrambled out just as fast as I could. In doing so I tore the RT cable from the plug which remained in the set.

I landed by parachute at Great Dunmow where I saw the skin on my hands hanging off in what appeared to be shreds of tissue paper. Some pieces of shrapnel removed from my leg were under half an inch long, but small as they were they still do a devil of a lot of damage. I also had a great many more splinters, some of which still show up on X-rays. My leather flying helmet and frayed RT lead were discarded at the time but later returned to me.

After I was shot down I was in a civilian hospital for eleven weeks, then the RAF picked me up, took me to Halton where I met Geoffrey Page again. McIndoe came to Halton, saw a lot of people and picked out the ones he thought he could do something for and I went to East Grinstead just after Christmas, in January 1941. On admission they took a number of colour photographs of my injuries, to record progress accurately, I suppose. Of all the nurses, Sister Meally was the one I remember most vividly from my time in Ward 3.

I remember the occasion when I met Richard Hillary again at East Grinstead, in fact I remember it as if it were yesterday. I was in Ward 3, in the bed next to Tom Gleave and opposite was Eric Lock. I went in and out of East Grinstead a good few times because they'd do a bit of work and then either send you on leave or back to the RAF station. I remember coming back to Ward 3 after one such period away and I recognised Hillary in the bed opposite. He was all bandaged up after having had his eyelids done. I went over to him and said, 'Hello, Richard,' but he wasn't quite sure who I was and I said, 'It's Mark Mounsdon.' All through my days with the RAF I was always called Mark, instead of Maurice, but I have no idea why! Richard said, 'What are you doing here?' and I said, 'The same as you.' We were in and out of hospital together for about the next six months, or the first part of 1941 anyway. We got on well together. After this period I didn't see much of him as I was sent to the officers' convalescent home in Torquay and I rather lost touch with him. Tollemache was also in at this time.

Hillary was never, ever, an unpleasant person. I think any suggestion that he was a shit is totally wrong, people are fond of criticising if they can, especially if they can make some money out of it. It is total rubbish to suggest he was any worse behaved than the rest of us. I dare say as undergraduates they got under one another's skin, of that I wouldn't be surprised at all, and by his own admission he was unco-operative. If you are like that then you are bound to have a few people criticise you but I regard that as being behaviour typical of an undergraduate. Since the war, whenever I have chatted with those who also knew Richard, they never, ever, said anything to his detriment. We were all suffering. The pain was terrible and had we not been so young many of us would have probably not survived. But suffer we did and complain we all occasionally did, Richard no more than the rest of us, although he was prone to speaking his mind when perhaps he should have said nothing.

In response to criticism levelled at Richard's behaviour on the ward, I have to say that things didn't happen very often and one has to consider that some of its inhabitants were in a pretty rough condition and would sometimes get a bit emotional. I remember once feeling so low I just burst into tears. We were stressed, and if Hillary was accused of such behaviour then you could say that of pretty well everyone else at some time or another. I suppose you could criticise the hospital a little because it was very happy go lucky, and this is on record. You can read any book on the Guinea Pig Club and this comes through very clearly. However, I think that the regime was a good thing, for the type of patients we were.

As soon as they could get us out and down to the pub they did. We used to call a taxi and even though some would be in plaster and had to be practically levered into the vehicle, they were got there. Although in that respect it perhaps went a bit too far on occasion.

Girls used to come and go in the ward, and not all to see Richard. I remember he took great pleasure in telling me of his adventures when he returned very drunk after taking a young girl up to London.

I thought that *The Last Enemy* was a good record of the time but didn't expect all the details to be accurate.

As a young man I took a lot of photographs. I always had a small camera with me at Kinloss and I took a lot of photographs about the place, including many pictures of Hillary and the aircraft. I kept them with me when I went to North Weald. There the mess was overflowing and a number of Nissen huts were erected, where, in one of which, I had a room. At that time we were spending half the day at our forward airfield at Rochford when, on 24 August, we heard that North Weald had been bombed. We flew back in the evening just as it was getting dark. I looked out as we flew over and much had been razed to the ground including my accommodation. I had nothing but the clothes I was wearing and my collection of photographs was all lost. Fortunately my little camera, which was a very good quality Zeiss, had been left at dispersal and safe. The only item I managed to salvage from the ashes was my tobacco tin in which I kept a set of cuff-links. It was an extensive collection of photographs including many of Hillary which, I feel sure, would have appeared in many books over the years!

I wanted to stay in the RAF after the war but because of my injuries I couldn't get a full A1b flying category, only a limited flying category, and so I left. I would have stayed in otherwise. In my opinion it was quite wrong for Hillary to be allowed back to flying. His hands were not capable of doing the job. McIndoe knew this and did the right thing in writing to the medical officer at Charterhall in an attempt to have him taken off flying. But as we know the letter wasn't read in time. What further compounded his problems was the fact that he shouldn't have been allowed to fly that particular, awkward, aircraft, especially night flying. I often have the suspicion that the senior staff at Charterhall didn't like him very much, they allowed him to continue despite his obvious problems.

The only way I would have been able to fly a Spitfire or a Hurricane again would have been the occasional flight under the 'old pals act'. I flew a Hurricane when one was delivered to Airwork at Marshall's, Cambridge, and I persuaded them to let me test it. Which was fun, of course. Hillary, like me, managed to get a light aircraft flying category but should have never been allowed to fly anything else and my situation puts that into a little more perspective. My legs received second and third degree burns as well as severe shrapnel wounds. I had the same facial injuries as Hillary as I had also not been wearing my goggles, and underwent the same reconstructive surgery. However, my hands were not as badly burnt as Hillary's and he still received an A1b flying category, which leads me to believe he really must have had some pretty influential friends.

I was posted back to Strike Headquarters, back at North Weald, and eventually ended up with Operations Group 'B' in the operations room. I used to fly around in the station 'Maggy' [Magister] and taxi people here and there. When I finally finished with East Grinstead I said I wanted to go back to flying, they said that as I only had a limited flying category I was to go to training command on light aircraft. So I went to 22 EFTS, at Marshall's, Cambridge. I did an instructor's course on Tiger Moths and Magisters. They kept me there on the instructor staff and we taught ATA pilots and all sorts of others. I had by then been promoted to flight lieutenant and they sent me to Booker as a flight commander where I remained for eighteen months.

I read about Richard's death in a newspaper. I thought the Battle of Britain was great, as far as I was concerned. I had a marvellous time. When you are that age and in a Hurricane or a Spitfire squadron you didn't want to do anything else. I joined because I wanted to be a fighter pilot, it was what so many of us opted to do in the war and for the same reasons.

With his technical training Maurice Mounsdon finished the war with 8303 Disarmament Wing in Germany with instructions to locate anything of importance in German industry. This involved the liberation of a few aircraft and cars and allowed the unit, consisting of about three squadrons, to search all sorts of areas including underground factories and munitions works for rockets, bombs and jet engines, anything of interest.

Unable to get an A1b flying category Maurice returned to GEC after the war, where he remained until retirement. He is still an active member of the Guinea Pig Club and has recently joined the No.56 Squadron Association. It is certainly interesting to compare his injuries and subsequent attempts to return to operational flying with Richard

* * *

The Czechoslovakian sergeant pilot Josef Koukal was of No.310 Squadron based at Duxford. Koukal had been with the Squadron since July 1940. On 7 September he had been shot down over the Thames estuary. By the time he managed to bale out of his flaming Hurricane his clothing was on fire and he had been terribly burned. As he had been flying at an altitude of 22,000 feet he decided to delay opening his parachute in an attempt to extinguish his burning clothing. At 11,000 feet he opened it having achieved his objective. Unfortunately, on landing his clothing burst into flames again and he suffered seventy percent burns to his body. A local man saved the Czech pilot's life when he rushed to his aid, as he lay writhing in agony on the ground, and extinguished the flames. Josef Koukal became one of the founder members of the Guinea Pig Club. In 1972 he returned to England when the crash site of his Hurricane was excavated, and was also introduced to the wife of the man who had saved his life.

* * *

As they waited in anticipation, there were signs that the infection was taking a hold on some of the occupants of the quarantined ward. McIndoe referred to the streptococci as: 'Those lousy, evil smelling bugs!'

Still Richard used his sarcasm and sometimes cruel wit to escape from what was becoming inevitable:

> On the second day Neft's face began to suppurate and a small colony of streptococci settled on the Squadron Leader's nose. The rest of us waited grimly. Neft showed a tendency to complain, which caused Eric Lock to point out that some of us had been fighting the war with real bullets and would be infinitely grateful for his silence.
>
> On the third day in our new quarters the smell of the bandage under my nose became so powerful that I took to dosing it liberally with eau-de-cologne. I have since been unable to repress a feeling of nausea whenever at a party or in company I have caught a whiff of this scent . . . the Squadron Leader was too ill to complain, but Eric Lock was vociferous and the rest of us sullen. A somewhat

grim sense of humour helped us to pass the day, punctuated by half-hours during which Neft was an object of rather cruel mockery. He had been a pork butcher before the war and of quite moderate means, but he made the mistake of mentioning this fact and adding that foul-mouthed talk amused him not at all. From that moment Yorkie Law, our bombardier, gave him no peace and plied him with anecdotes which even curled what was left of my hair. By the evening Neft had retired completely under his bed-clothes, taking his suppurating face with him.

Eric Lock, Yorkie Law and Richard were loud and foul-mouthed, using the unfortunate and necessarily 'faceless' staff as a target for their sometimes ruthless comments. They were nevertheless grateful for their presence as they were not allowed visitors. During this time Tony Tollemache appeared at the window to wish Richard farewell. Tony was returning to basic duties and was posted to Hornchurch.

During the middle of January 1941 Richard awoke with a painful earache. An ear, nose and throat doctor, visiting East Grinstead to attend a plastic surgery course run by McIndoe, was in the hospital and after examining him diagnosed mastoiditis and prescribed Prontosil: 'I slept fitfully, aided in my wakefulness by the pain in my ear, Eric's snores, and the groans of the Squadron Leader [Gleave].'

It had been eight days since his surgery to provide him with a new top lip and to trim his new lower eyelids. The time came on lunchtime on the eighth day for the bandages to be removed from these new grafts. A blessed relief in Richard's opinion. The odour of the eau-de-cologne was no longer serving as a masking agent for the smell coming from the dressing. Richard's description of his discomfort is very damning; he regarded it as the job of the staff to change the dressings frequently enough to avoid such an occurrence. The dressings were peeled away, and the stitches removed from the upper eyelids and his new upper lip. Richard described the state of his lip as having recovered from the burns to the point whereby he only had two scars on it; the condition of his lip at this time is just visible in a photograph taken at this time. His new lip was surveyed by the doctors with satisfaction but when Richard asked for a mirror:

> It was a blow to my vanity: the new upper lip was dead white, and thinner than its predecessor.
>
> In point of fact it was a surgical masterpiece, but I was not in the mood to appreciate it. I fear I was not very gracious. The lip was duly painted with mercurochrome, and the doctors departed. The relief at having the bandages removed was enormous, but I still could not blow my nose for fear that I should blow the graft away. I took a bath and soaked the bandage off the arm from which my lip had been taken. This was a painful process lasting three-quarters of an hour, at the end of which time was revealed a deep narrow scar, neatly stitched. Sister then removed the stitches.

Unfortunately this procedure was a little premature as the two sides of the wound came apart, much to the fascination of the others in the ward who were well enough to have a look!

The operation to replace part of his upper lip left him without a 'cupid's bow'. He never talked about this, but a number of people who knew him mentioned it when I interviewed them about Richard. It was something that certainly bothered him. When he smiled the grafted top lip grew taut and was seen by some as actually quite disarming. This can be confirmed to some extent in the group photograph taken at the 1942 Anniversary of the Battle of Britain dinner. Although in exalted company, he was by that time famous for his best-seller and had become a national hero. The smile failed to come across as quite the expression it was intended but rather, with the drawing back of the top lip to reveal the teeth, as something of a sneer. His eyes however, compensated, always conveying the truth of the expression.

It has been said that one of his last minor operations was when McIndoe agreed to provide him with a cupid's bow. Such an operation did not take place. The last photograph taken of Richard was in late November 1942. He only had a few brief spells of leave in the interim before his death and underwent no surgery. The misunderstanding may come from the portrait of Richard drawn by Eric Kennington in 1942. This pastel portrait shows him with a cupid's bow. This I believe was due to the angle from which Kennington viewed his subject. The shape of Richard's lip after surgery left the hint of a cupid's bow, but far wider and with little emphasis. The side-on view created the impression that the 'bow' was far more pronounced than it actually was. Perhaps both artist and sitter were aware of this and the angle was deliberate.

That night, following the removal of the dressing from his lip, Richard was unable to sleep due to the continuous throbbing pain from his ear infection: 'At about two o'clock I got up and started pacing the ward.' Yet again he had little consideration for his fellow sufferers:

> A night nurse ordered me back to bed. I invited her to go to hell with considerable vigour, but I felt no better. She called me a wicked ungrateful boy and I fear that I called her a cow. I finally returned to bed and attempted to read until morning.

By morning he felt far worse, both from the effects of the infection and the Prontosil, medication notorious for causing nausea and giving an alarming grey hue to the skin.

The ear, nose and throat specialist provided a clinic at the hospital every Friday and Richard was sent to the out-patient department the next time he called:

> February 17th was a Friday . . . . It was arranged for me to see him, and putting on my dressing gown, I walked along to the Out-patients' department. His manner was reassuring. He felt behind my ear and inquired if it pained me. I replied that it did. That being so he regretted the necessity, but he must operate within half an hour for what appeared to be a most unpleasant mastoid.

On one of the few occasions that Richard provides a specific date in *The Last Enemy*, he is incorrect. Unless he broke with normal routine, the ear, nose and throat (ENT) specialist visited the hospital every Friday. In fact 17 February was a Monday and by this time the infection had gone and he had been moved back to Dutton Homestall to convalesce. His diary confirms this point. The 17th incidentally was the day on which John Boulter was fatally injured at RAF Drem with No.603 Squadron.

With the ENT specialist's decision made, Richard was transferred to the glass extension in Sister Hall's ward at his own request.

The operation to remove the mastoid from his ear took place in the 'Horsebox,' the name given to the emergency theatre. McIndoe was already hard at work in the main theatre. The operation did not proceed until Richard had changed into his lucky red silk pyjamas!

It was not the end of the problem for Richard however, as infection had already set in and his weakened body fought for some time to recover from the effects. The nurses in Sister Hall's ward took care of him. Morphine was again administered to reduce the pain, sending him once again into a sea of pain-filled, drug-induced, delirium. The streptococcus had also infected his new lip:

> I remember being in worse pain than at any time since my crash. After the plastic surgery I felt no discomfort, but now with the continuous throbbing agony in my head I thought that I must soon go mad. I would listen with dread for the footsteps of the doctors, knowing that the time was come for my dressings, for the piercing of the hole behind my ear with a thin steel probe to keep it open for draining, a sensation that made me contract within myself at the mere touch of the probe on the skin.

Once again he was to lose valuable weight as his temperature gradually returned to normal. The effects of this relapse caused his weight to drop from twelve to nine stone.

A dramatic and alarming loss.

It was while Richard was recovering in Sister Hall's ward, that a 2,500lb bomb landed close to the hospital, but did not explode. The patients had heard it come down, and Geoffrey Page had recognised the sound of the aircraft's engines as belonging to a Junkers Ju88. He later wrote:

> Raising my head from the pillow my ears followed the path of the machine as it growled across the night sky. Steadily the uneven beat grew louder and I knew that it would pass directly over the hospital. As the whistle of the falling bomb commenced, the horrors of sound created during the first few days in Margate after being shot down came back vividly. Pain and self-pity, hatred and revenge are subjugated in the blind terror that rose in my throat as the projectile screamed earthwards.
>
> Even if movement had been possible, it was all over too soon. The bomb struck the ground a few yards beyond the large plate glass windows. The one-storied building shook violently and the blackout curtains flapped inwards.
>
> I lay there with my eyes and muscles screwed up tightly, waiting for the explosion that had not occurred. Hardly had I relaxed than the sleeping figures about me awoke and the night nurse came hurrying to the ward, her flashlight playing dancing patterns about the walls and ceilings. Her high-pitched voice contrasted oddly with the sleepy male voices that plied her with questions.
>
> 'Nothing to worry about . . . nothing to worry about...just a small air raid.'
>
> My laugh rang out bitterly. 'It may be a small air raid, but there's a bloody great unexploded bomb a few yards away.'
>
> No one thought of going back to sleep that night. Within the hour air raid wardens, rescue squads and bomb disposal experts had taken a look at the situation and advised the same thing. The ward was to be evacuated.

Richard had also heard the bomb falling to earth, but was at this time in such pain for a moment he had hoped that it would put him out of his agony. He found himself in tears of anger and disappointment on realising that he was still alive. In actual fact it was thought necessary to evacuate the whole hospital and move the patients along the 'Whisky Mile' to Dutton Homestall.

McIndoe examined Richard and decided, in consultation with the bomb disposal squad, that to move him in his current condition held a greater risk than the chances of the bomb exploding. But he couldn't be left in the ward surrounded by so many panes of glass and the easy alternative location of the huts was decided upon.

Incensed at the idea of being moved to the hot, smelly huts, Richard let his feelings be known to McIndoe's assistant who had arrived in the ward to make arrangements to have him moved:

> Wild horses, I said, would not drag me back to that garbage-can of human refuse. If anyone laid a finger on my bed I would get up and start to walk to London. I preferred to die in the open rather than return to that stinking kitchen of fried flesh. I had come into the hospital with two scars on my upper lip: now I had a lip that was pox-ridden and an ear with enough infection in it to kill a regiment. There was only one thing to be said for the British medical profession: it started where the Luftwaffe left off. An outburst to which I now confess with shame, but which at the time relieved my feelings considerably.

It was Sister Hall who pulled out all the stops for Richard. "'I think perhaps he should stay here in his present state, sir," she said. "I'll see if I can fix up something."'

Proof that Richard was indeed happy with the spirited atmosphere in Ward 3, but very unhappy with conditions. McIndoe's chief assistant was Percy Jayes, another outstanding surgeon in the hospital who was fast becoming an authority on reconstructive surgery to the hands.

Sister Hall suggested to the somewhat harassed doctor that she would take the problem off his hands. The doctor was only too relieved and left the ward: '"Well, Mr. Hillary," she said, "quite like old times," and went off to see what she could arrange.'

One of the hospital consulting rooms was hastily converted into a ward for Richard with sand bags placed strategically to protect the bed, and he was moved into it. Geoffrey Page and the other patients were by now settled into the luxurious comfort of the Dewars' home at Dutton Homestall.

Word reached McIndoe that Richard was finding things very difficult and ultimately making life somewhat awkward for the staff that he held in such high regard. Putting a few minutes aside in what was by this time an exceptionally busy schedule he walked into Richard's new ward and, still dressed in his operating robes, sat down on the end of Richard's bed:

> He talked to me for some time – of the difficulties of running a unit such as this, of the inevitable trials and set-backs which must somehow be met. He knew, he said, that I had had a tough break, but I must try not to let it get me down. I noticed that he looked tired, dead tired, and remembered that he had been operating all day. I felt a little ashamed.

The next day Edwyna Hillary and Denise Maxwell-Woosnam drove down from London to visit Richard. On seeing his mother Richard was alarmed at the effect his latest bout of ill health had had on her. His obvious weight loss and the effects of the Prontosil did not lessen the worry she felt on initially seeing him in this state. Both she and Denise later told Richard that they thought he was 'on his way out':

> Poor Mother. The crash, the sea, the hospital, the operations – she had weathered them all magnificently. But this last shock was almost too much. She did not look very well.

It should also be considered Edwyna was in her sixtieth year and still working at this time.

The bomb was eventually defused and removed from the site. The other patients were brought back from Dutton Homestall. Richard was moved back into the main ward, his favourite, and there made a full recovery.

By this time McIndoe was working to the point of exhaustion, doing between nine and 11 operations a day. He was suffering from a stomach disorder, at this time undiagnosed, but thought to be an ulcer and was also having problems with his right hand, the surgeon's hand that had, under such expert control, done so much good. In the spring he would finally take a break to relax and recover, when he stayed in a cottage near Rye where he indulged in some rough-shooting. The long-distance relationship with his wife was by now becoming strained. They had been apart for quite a while. There were also unfortunate rumours that McIndoe had been seen in the company of other women, which did not help matters. In June 1941 after another intensive period of work he went alone for another short break to the Port Sonachan Hotel on Loch Awe in Argyll. He wrote: 'I have set about making every minute count in the matter of getting fit again in the shortest possible space.' He walked, fished with a local ghillie and took full advantage of the complete solitude.´

By contrast he was by then spending more and more time with the men on Ward 3, not only was he working with them, he was also relaxing in the same company. He would often lead a sing-song on the piano in Ward 3. He was also a familiar face at the Whitehall restaurant in the town, drinking with his patients (although his drinks consisted of a small measure of gin heavily watered down, by the obliging but descreet landlord, to avoid aggravating his stomach problem). The patients of Ward 3 held McIndoe in the highest esteem, he was 'the Maestro'. His surgical reconstructive skill, his approach to the psychological problems and the all round care shown by his team gave them genuine hope for the future. They had great faith in him and put their future in his capable hands. In many ways they worshipped him, and over the years were never to waver in this opinion.

McIndoe also gave a number of parties at his home, Millfield Cottage. Jill Mullins acted as hostess and a few faces were regularly in attendance at such functions including Edward 'Blackie' Blacksell, who was becoming a close friend of McIndoe's, Geoffrey Page and Richard Hillary. By this time romance had blossomed between Geoffrey Page and Jill Mullins, which lasted beyond his discharge from hospital and finally ended two years later after he had returned to operational flying. The disappointment of the break-up did not end there for Page as Jill Mullins died tragically of a brain haemorrhage en-route to South Africa with her newly wedded husband. She was buried at sea. Geoffrey Page later married Pauline Bruce, daughter of the distinguished actor Nigel Bruce.

On a number of occasions Richard came to visit McIndoe at his cottage during his time off. They enjoyed lengthy discussion and, ever the existentialist, Richard picked McIndoe's brain for responses to some of the many questions the young pilot was desperate to find answers to. Richard fascinated McIndoe and he later recalled:

> He is obsessed with death and keeps asking me whether I know when it's coming to a patient. I tell him I know, but they don't. This doesn't seem to comfort him. He is a strange bloke. The boys in the ward don't like him. He has a sharp tongue and an intellectual approach which gets them on the raw. He mixed them up so much recently that they bombarded him with their precious egg ration and this quietened him down for a time. But like all of his type, he bobbed up again.

His attitude to Geoffrey Page was different. Page was a quiet-spoken and gentle young man who showed vulnerability, but beneath there was a determined will that interested McIndoe and he warmed to him as if he was a son. Of Page he wrote:

> The bloody fool wants to fly again. He'll never be able to do it, of course. But fancy thinking of it, after all he's been through!

The tremendous bravery shown by Godfrey Edmunds during his time at East Grinstead cannot be understated, and Richard was clearly affected, considering his own persistent complaining in the face of adversity. Shortly after the incident with the unexploded bomb Edmunds was re-admitted for further surgery and placed in the bed next to Richard's. This move could conceivably have been contrived in order to show Richard how insignificant his own injuries were compared with Edmunds.

Godfrey Edmunds was from South Africa and was the worst burnt pilot in the RAF to survive. He had been taking off on his first solo flight in a Hampden when he put a wing in. The bomber flipped onto its back and burst into flames. Edmunds had remained trapped inverted in the cockpit for several minutes before he was freed. Little of his body had remained untouched by the flames. For months he lay on the brink of death, suppurating, burnt beyond recognition. McIndoe performed emergency surgery but then left Edmunds to recover enough before he operated again.

After nine months Edmunds recovered enough to spend some time away from the hospital. When he returned to undergo the first of many operations to rebuild his burnt features, he met Richard. In one of the excerpts from his 'diary' written at that time he describes his memories of Edmunds. These notes were later used when writing his book:

> Edmunds' operation today. Both lids and lips done at one session. He soon came round after they brought him back and seemed as cheerful as ever, though three-quarters of his face is covered with bandages. He has the worst burnt face I have ever seen and has been here off and on for a year already. His courage is amazing and makes me very ashamed.

Richard was clearly impressed by Edmunds' fortitude and cheerfulness in the face of such adversity, particularly as his own disfigurement was far less than Edmunds'. Even when Edmunds' new right eyelid became infected with streptococcus and had to be removed and thrown away his spirit did not seem to dwindle. It had been McIndoe's first eyelid failure and it was unfortunate that the patient was Edmunds. Richard later wrote in *The Last Enemy*:

> I could not but marvel at his self-control and unruffled good manners. I remembered a few of my own recent outbursts and felt rather small.
>
> Here was this twenty-six year old South African with no ties in this country, no mere boy with his whole life to make, terribly injured without even the satisfaction of having been in action. Sometimes he behaved as though he had been almost guilty not to have been shot down, as though he were in hospital under false pretences; but if ever a pilot deserved a medal it was he. He read little, was not musical, yet somehow he carried on. How? What was it that gave not only him but all these men the courage to go on and fight their way back to life? Was it in some way bound up with the consciousness of death? This was a subject which fascinated me and I had discussed with McIndoe. Did people know when they were about to die? He maintained that they did not, having seen over two-hundred go, none of them conscious that their last moment had come. He admitted that in some cases people might have a premonition of death, but in the cases of terrible physical injury he would say never. Their physical and mental conditions were not on a different plane: the first weakened the second (if I report them accurately), and there was neither consciousness of great pain nor realisation of the finality of physical disintegration.

Richard's own grafts had been infected by the streptococcus:

> I knew well enough, meanwhile, that sheer anger had pulled me through my mastoid complication. But what of the men who, after the first instinctive fight to live, after surviving the original physical shock, went on fighting to live, cheerfully aware that for them there was only a half-life? The blind and the utterly maimed – what of them? Their mental state could not remain in the same dazed condition after their bodies began to heal. Where did they get their courage to go on?
>
> It worried me all day. Finally I decided that the will to live must be instinctive and in no way related to courage. This nicely resolved any suspicion that I might recently have behaved rather worse than any of the others, might have caused unnecessary trouble and confusion.

Richard spent many evenings at McIndoe's cottage discussing this matter over a drink and answering his many questions on the subject. He did not arrive at his conclusions overnight as suggested.

* * *

On 15 February 1941 Richard was moved once again to the officers' convalescent home at Dutton Homestall to recover his strength. On the same day, Kathleen Dewar had arranged for her friend, Lady Winifred Fortescue, to visit the home for lunch. Lady Fortescue was at this time an eminent authoress with a number of books to her credit whom Kathleen Dewar had invited to her home in order to meet Richard and in particular to offer him guidance with his writing ambition. Kathleen Dewar had felt it necessary to exaggerate Richard's familiarity with her books.

Lady Fortescue recalled the occasion in her book *Beauty for Ashes*:

> I had an invitation to luncheon one day from the friend at East Grinstead. . . . She told me that one of the young airmen, who was being treated by the 'wizard' plastic surgeon for terrible injuries, was very anxious to meet me. 'To meet me?' I echoed. 'Do I know him?' 'No, but he has read your books. He wants to write and doesn't know how to begin; he wants to talk to you,' she replied. In general I refused social invitations, but this was one that must be fulfilled, and I accepted it at once. . . .

Lady Winifred Fortescue was the elder daughter of the Reverend Howard Beech. It was her first book *Perfume From Provence* that brought her almost immediate fame and is still in print today. Published in 1935 it told of the life Lady Fortescue and her military historian husband Sir John enjoyed in Provence.

Her second book *Sunset House* told of their reclamation of an old stone farmhouse on a steep hillside in the Alpes Maritimes that Lady Fortescue lived in after the death of her husband.

Sir John had suffered from repeated ill health, and having recently recovered from a bout of pneumonia he died in a Cannes hospital from an almost gangrenous abscess on his appendix – peritonitis. The couple were devoted to each other and Lady Fortescue was naturally beside herself with grief.

After this tragedy she began to write about her life in full, in particular her meeting and subsequent marriage to Sir John. In *There's Rosemary, There's Rue*, published in 1939, she tells of her first meeting with the man she would later marry and their first home together in Windsor Castle during the reign of King George V and Queen Mary.

In 1941 she wrote the appropriately titled *Trampled Lilies*, which told of the many thousands of French soldiers who tramped past her home in the Alpes Maritimes who had been called up from their homes at short notice. The need for accommodation for French Army officers was thrust upon her and she responded with typical selflessness. In fact she became so concerned about the plight of the humble *poilu* that she and a friend 'Mademoiselle', busied themselves trying to find food and shelter for them. As a result of their efforts, a number of *Foyers* were set up all over Provence where the mobilised men could rest and enjoy some recreation.

As the German army advanced, Calais fell and Lady Fortescue realised she was about to become trapped in France, as an enemy alien. Thus began her mad dash across France to Brittany where she managed to escape on one of the last boats to leave France for England.

She settled in a rented cottage called Many Waters, situated in a beautiful, isolated valley in Sussex. It was while she was here that she met Richard and later wrote about their brief friendship in her book *Beauty for Ashes*, published in 1948. Her memories of the event vary somewhat from those recorded by Richard and later published by Lovat Dickson as an extract of Richard's diary.

After a journey which very nearly resulted in a traffic accident with an Army lorry Lady Fortescue arrived at Dutton Homestall, where she was introduced to the assembled guests. She recalled meeting Richard:

> With his back to the room, silhouetted against a sunlit window, stood the tall lithe figure of a young man. He was talking to our host, who turned to me and said as I approached: 'Lady Fortescue, this is Richard Hillary, who was so anxious to meet you.'
>
> During the war one had been inured to bearing the sight of tragic disfigurements, but this beautiful boy – for one could see that he had been beautiful – his figure, his hands, his fair wavy hair – those blazing blue eyes still were. But his face had only just been grafted – eyelids had been added which were dead white in a bronzed face and held in place by a talc frame, half a lip had been added – the same dead white – one arm braced upon a kind of tennis-racket contrivance with loops on the rounded frame to straighten crooked fingers immersed too long in tannic acid. The other hand with some fingers burned off.
>
> He wheeled towards me, and stood with his gallant head thrown back and the bright sunlight shining full upon that marred face, the burning blue eyes, streaming from strain, staring defiantly into mine.
>
> 'Look well at me,' they seemed to say. 'But damn you, don't you *dare* to pity me.' I was being tested. Thank God I passed that test.

Lady Fortescue sat with Richard during lunch. She longed to help him with his cutlery but resisted the temptation and he managed, albeit clumsily. Although Kathleen Dewar had introduced Lady Fortescue to Richard hoping she might be able to assist with his ambition to write, the circumstances were not conducive for such a discussion and Lady Fortescue invited Richard to Many Waters and he accepted. On her return home she marked the date on her calendar but believed that Richard would forget or find some other distraction.

On the day in question, a fortnight later, Lady Fortescue gave her maid the afternoon off. She was engaged to an RAF pilot and the sight of Richard's disfigurement might be too much for her. Kathleen Dewar dropped Richard off at the lodge gates of the country cottage, on her way to a committee meeting. Lady Fortescue recalled:

> Precisely at four p.m. the front door was smartly rapped by the old Sussex horse-shoe I had fixed there, and I ran downstairs to open it. Outside stood a tall figure muffled in an overcoat of Air Force blue. Richard Hillary!
>
> 'Oh, I am glad you remembered!' I cried eagerly. 'I was terrified you would have forgotten!' he replied.
>
> 'Well we *didn't*, did we?' I said, welcoming him into my little hall and, having realised his savage resolve to be independent, not offering to help him to take off his overcoat.

Lady Fortescue's shyness quickly disappeared as she made tea and Richard toasted bread over an open fire. After tea the two moved upstairs to Lady Fortescue's writing studio where a fire glowed in the grate. Richard found the tranquillity appealing:

> For years I've been looking for the Circles of Peace. This is the centre of the Circles of Peace.

Richard later refers to the Circles of Peace while on holiday in Wales with Mary Booker.

He slumped into an armchair and recounted his wartime experiences, being shot down and the suffering he had endured in various hospitals. He spoke of his mother:

> 'I fear the first sight of me after the smash must have been a bit of a shock to my mother, for I was rather a mess, but she didn't show it, bless her – she's rather an extraordinary person, my mother; I can treat her like a contemporary, and even if she can't approve the things I say or do, at any rate she never fails to see the other fellow's point of view. No, she *never* fails. She's got vision – and she can hit out from the shoulder.' He chuckled to himself gently. 'I was rather nice to look at once, and I suppose getting a bit uppish and spoiled. She told me in hospital that perhaps this accident had saved me from becoming a cad.'

Richard believed he could write at Many Waters, away from the noise of gramophone records and the chatter of the other patients at Dutton Homestall, 'the monkey house at the Zoo'. She recalled the conversation:

> 'No one could do serious work there. I do want to write. Somehow I feel I've got to write – but what about? How? When and where?'
>
> 'Write about all the things you've been telling me,' I said urgently; 'all that and more. You made me see it all too vividly that I can never forget some of that horror. If you write that story only half as well as you told it, your book will be read all over the world.'
>
> 'If I speak the truth about lots of things I'd be shot out of the Service, and certainly never admitted into another hospital,' he chortled.

Richard is referring mainly to his comments about the lack of cleanliness at East Grinstead, details of which were never published in his book, but his concerns were expressed in no uncertain terms in his letters at that time. Lady Fortescue continued with her memories of Richard with his frank confession:

> 'I'm the enfant terrible wherever I'm sent. I'm a damned nuisance too, because

I'm a rebel at heart, and I refuse to keep silly rules. If I want to go out and enjoy myself, why shouldn't I go? If I want a drink – lots of drinks – why shouldn't I have 'em? I'm certain of one thing – that repressions and inhibitions and rules and regulations and red tape never did anyone any good. I believe in the liberty of the individual.' He gave me a wicked twinkling look to see how I was taking all this, and observing the elevated right eyebrow and a mocking light in the eye, observed:

'You and my mother must get together. You'd understand each other. And I say, if I give you the address of someone, and she writes to you, I wonder if you'd ask her down here to stay with you. It's just what she needs – this place and you. I'm worried about her. She's talking of shutting herself up in a convent and becoming a nun – just because she's had a bad time – she'll tell you all about it when she comes, I'm sure of that.' He scribbled a name and address on my writing pad, muttering as he did so. 'What a waste! What a nun!'

'Do you think she will write to me?' I asked. 'I'd love to have her here.'

'Yes, she will,' he said emphatically. But Denise never did.

Richard returned to Dutton Homestall by taxi at six. Lady Fortescue offered Richard the use of her cottage whenever he sought the quiet, to think over his book or to make notes. She wrote:

'Even if I'm out with The Blackness you can always let yourself in, because the key lives under the flat stone near the front door. You'll find an abundance of scribbling paper, pencils and writing paraphernalia on my desk if you want to write, and your own comfortable chair if you want to think things out. The fire is always laid ready to be lit, and it would be the cosiest thing in the world if on returning from a walk in the woods I saw smoke curling from my chimney!' I assured him. He promised to come whenever he could, but again I wondered whether he would. The young may have long, long thoughts, but they often have short memories. Still, he had remembered to come to-day. Nevertheless it was with joy in the weeks which followed that sometimes, as The Blackness [her black Labrador] and I returned from his riot in the woods, I did see smoke rising from my chimney from a fire lit by Richard Hillary.

A few months later, Lady Fortescue received a message from Richard asking her to telephone. She recalled:

His voice answered me, rather breathless for some reason which soon proved to be excitement.

'I've got a job! I've *got a job*!' he almost shouted.

'Oh Richard! What? Where? When?' I eagerly asked him.

'I'm dying to tell you all about it – the real you and not just a ghost-voice on this infernal though useful machine. Can I come to tea to-day?'

'Of course. Lovely! Get here as soon as you can. I'm thrilled!' I answered, then hung up the receiver. But he never came. It grew later and later, but still no Richard, only one of the gardeners' children with yet another telephone message saying that he had been called away for an appointment with Lord Beaverbrook, and if not too late afterwards would come to see me on his way back.

Lord Beaverbrook? Something to do with the new job, no doubt. Ministry of Information? A newspaper king too. Probably Richard was to work for him – writing of a sort, but not of the kind about which he dreamed. Still, all writing is valuable experience, and even journalism teaches concentration – only so many words to a column, and space very precious. I had done it, and I knew. I longed for Richard's arrival, and when hope of it faded with the daylight, I hoped for a telephone message or a letter; but nothing came. A dead and depressing silence for days, for weeks, for months.

I never saw him again.

Richard had brought light to the life of a quite wonderful woman and her apparently
lonely existence. She had been immediately aware of his qualities. Many Waters had
provided him with a much needed escape from the rowdy atmosphere of the hospital and
convalescent home of the Dewars. It was a quite perfect environment with an equally
suitable and easy-going companion in Lady Winifred Fortescue. How she had longed for
him to call again, leaving us feeling sorry for her when Richard failed to show for that
last meeting.

Richard had also recorded their first meeting in his own diary. The details vary:

> *Feb 15.* Asked who was coming to lunch and was told Lady Fortescue. Cursed
> myself for not having read any of her books, but need not have worried, as she
> showed no desire to talk about them. Asked her whether she wrote in longhand
> or dictated. She said 'longhand and in pencil so as I can rub out mistakes'. I have
> not the concentration to write in longhand and find that one's thoughts run too
> quickly for one's pen; yet feel that if I dictate to a short-hand typist I shan't be
> able to think of a thing to say. L.F. tells me she has taken a delightful cottage,
> surrounded by small pools fed by waterfalls. Has called it Many Waters and
> asked me to go and see her there. . . .

> *Feb 27.* For the last few days I have been unable to concentrate on anything,
> but today Miss Wagg motored me out to see Lady Fortescue, and as I had hoped,
> I was not disappointed.

> She has taken the most delightful cottage, set in an enchanted valley of
> trees and waterfalls and approached by a single precipitous path. Slithering
> my way through the wet leaves, I came half-way down to a gate marked 'private',
> beyond which in the distance I could see a large red stucco house. For a moment
> my heart sank, then, remembering *Perfume from Provence* [which he had read
> by this time], I breathed again. The authoress of that book . . .? No, it just
> wasn't possible.

> I walked on; and round the next bend I found my reward. Like proud
> courtiers, streams of cascading water poured down from the wooded hills, to
> subside in respectful homage in the quiet pools around the cottage. It was
> enchanting; and no mere trick of light and shade for I could not have chosen a
> more miserable day for my visit, with a thin driving rain blowing across the hills,
> and a white mist hanging over the water.

> I rang the bell, in some fear that the good lady had forgotten; but the door
> opened, and she welcomed me like an old friend. First I was shown the cottage
> which should be priceless for the view from the bedroom alone, and then we
> made our own tea, toasting buns at the fire.

> I asked Lady Fortescue if she had heard Hilaire Belloc's epigram:

> > The devil, having nothing else to do,
> > Tempted my Lady Fortescue.
> > My Lady, tempted by a private whim,
> > To his extreme annoyance, tempted him.

[Richard had adapted Hilaire Belloc to use 'My Lady Fortescue'.]
She sat back, stretched out her legs (clad in blue slacks) and roared with laughter;
from which I gathered that the answer was 'No'. After this she talked; of the
lovely house which she and her husband had built together in Provence; of his
death and how she tried to live there alone, but could not; and how she rebuilt
'Sunset House'; of her leaving France after Calais fell and taking this cottage 'to
be alone to lick her wounds'.

As she talked of Provence her face grew animated and it was not long before I
found myself upstairs in the midst of a pile of photographs; views of the house, of
their bergerie up in the Alps, to which they escaped when the Midi became too hot;
of their carpets of narcissi; of magic-scented tobacco plant bursting in fertile

abundance everywhere; and finally of the sky in the Alps, lowering and heavy before a storm, and fleeced with white streaks of trailing glory in the ensuing peace.

It seemed but five minutes since my arrival when the bell rang, and there stood the estimable Mr. Baker, perspiring but triumphant, with talk of cars and imminent gas lectures, and so, very regretfully, I said 'Goodbye', but not before being asked to come again 'very soon'.

Richard returned to Many Waters on a number of occasions. They both took turns to talk freely in each other's company, both benefiting from the therapy. Despite the age difference (Lady Fortescue was 53 at this time) they were kindred spirits and the beautiful setting made for a perfect place for him to continue his recovery.

With the success of her books Lady Fortescue gained many fans both in England and France. Her narratives, written in a simple way, reflect a spontaneity, enthusiasm, happiness and sympathy. They still sell well today.

In 1945 she moved back to Sunset House [its real name was Fort Escu], at Opio, Provence, where she wrote the aforementioned *Beauty for Ashes*. She died there on 9 April 1951, aged only 64. She was a warm-hearted and generous person who, always aware of their needs, cared greatly for those around her. It was appropriate that someone who wrote of her real-life experiences in such a vivid way should offer advice to Richard.

* * *

In March 1941 Richard was invited to a 'guest night' at RAF Hornchurch by Tony Tollemache. It had been a month since Tony had returned to administrative duties, and he provided an opportunity for Richard to return to the station at which he had served with 603 Squadron seven months before. Unfortunately, it was an unpleasant experience for Richard. Although back in a familiar environment, the faces of the pilots and ground crews were unfamiliar, and he found the station was haunted by the memory of his fallen friends. Nevertheless, during the evening, he fought his way into the spirit of the occasion finally retiring to Tony's bed. The next morning he awoke to find an abusive note hanging over his head and Tony asleep, stretched out on the sofa.

It was this event that left Richard keen to get in touch again with some of his old friends from his Oxford days and he invited twenty of them to his parents' home for drinks. With the ego that Richard possessed, it could be construed as having been his intention to invite former university colleagues as a display of extroversion; the wounded Battle of Britain fighter pilot ace the centre of attention amongst his friends. After a while he left the party and walked the streets as he pondered his feelings. He realised that he had lost touch with his friends and had little in common with them anymore. He was living in the past and should be looking to the future. Those friends that had come to mean so much to him were now dead and at this time he felt very alone. The exception was Colin Pinckney, who was still alive but based abroad with his squadron. Perhaps only the companionship of friends who had shared his own experiences could have aided his psychological recovery adding emphasis to his developing yearning to return to a crew-room atmosphere.

The major work in the reconstruction of Richard's face was now complete but there were still a number of painful operations that had to be endured in order to repair his hands. A number of smaller operations would also be required to 'tidy up' some of the earlier work and to rectify any resulting problems. As he walked out in public, tall and proud in his RAF uniform, initially he would not attract any undue attention. But as people drew near they would see his face under the shadow of the peak of his service cap. The people of East Grinstead had grown used to the sight of the injured pilot, but in the streets of London he would attract the attention of those less prepared.

Richard still had a full head of hair. But there was much skin on his face that was new. The grafts that were drawn over his facial bone structure were pink and shiny, with the edges of each graft clearly visible. He had no eyelashes, and his eyebrows were pieces of scalp grafted from within the hairline at his temple. His lower lip had been undamaged and was still full, but the graft on his top lip was stretched, far paler in colour, and appeared taut, especially when he smiled. Under his clothing the tender scars on his shoulder from the surgical removal of Thiersch grafts were still visible.

* * *

While at East Grinstead Richard began to write about his experiences in a little more detail, to turn his diary into a book, a book on his life thus far. By March 1941 he had completed the 'Proem' in rough form. A year later this book would be published in America by Reynal and Hitchcock under the title of *Falling Through Space*. In June 1942 it would be published in Great Britain by Macmillan Publishing as *The Last Enemy*.

While at East Grinstead he had met an influential lady by the name of Patricia Hollander who had been carrying out some useful work at the hospital as a librarian, and who believed that Richard had a gift for writing and that he had a significant story to tell. During a BBC radio interview she later recalled: 'He had a naturally arrogant walk, his gestures were naturally arrogant, everything he did was arrogant.'

Pat Hollander telephoned a friend and the editor-in-charge at Macmillan, Rache Lovat Dickson, and arranged an appointment for Richard to present his idea for a book.

When he first met Richard in 1941, Lovat Dickson was 38 and had achieved a high level of success in business; apart from their initial meetings, he came to realise that they had much in common. Much that he learned of the scarred young man before him reminded him of himself. Unfortunately, one aspect of Richard's experience that Lovat Dickson did not possess was that of the fighter pilot and Richard bore the scars of battle. Lovat Dickson would have relished the opportunity to have done the same and would gladly have fought for his adopted country in defence of its people. Sadly for him he was too old and his 'service' consisted of joining the American Home Guard in London. He later wrote: 'In age I was halfway between these youthful warriors and the elderly who could never be called upon to fight.'

In his biography of Richard, published in 1950, Lovat Dickson wrote about this first meeting with Richard at Macmillan & Co in St Martin's Street, London. It was a cold wintry day and as he entered the warmth of the publishing house the wind left Richard's face red and his eyes watering profusely, a condition his friends had become used to since he had been shot down:

> I knew from Pat Hollander's description, when she spoke to me on the telephone, making the appointment, that he was mutilated, but I was shocked by first glimpse of him by the ravages which the flames had made. It was a cold afternoon in March. The sharp wind had whipped colour into his face, but under the new skin it did not glow: it pressed against the thin surface, as though only the crushed lines of the patches held it on, and a touch, a rough movement, might release it. It looked very painful, and the lidless eyes, which had had no protection against the wind, were watering; it was as though at a moment before he had had an accident, and the anguish was still being felt. All this was sensed as he stood in the doorway and I greeted Pat Hollander.
>
> Then, as she introduced me to him, I found myself fixed by a pair of blue eyes in which a strange light glowed, a light which gave me the quick impression of being fed by an amusement which could only just be contained. I found myself smiling in return, and the first embarrassment of our meeting was over.
>
> Patricia Hollander explained that Richard wanted to write a book of his experiences, and that he had already written the first chapter, which he would like to read to me. A publisher naturally shies away from having scraps of work read to him; I therefore urged him to leave the manuscript, and said that I would get in touch with him as soon as possible. But the blue eyes were fixed on me, and the bright smile was playing about those shapeless lips, and I found myself yielding, as I was to do on so many occasions later.

I did not hear him read the first few lines because I was watching his thin skeletal fingers, horribly raw in colour, without nails and permanently bent, gripping the pages. He did not read well. He was shy, and the nervousness underneath his domineering manner made the skin on his face flush, so that all the marks of the burns stood out like weals. It was a terrifying sight, but not a horrible one.

And underneath the bad reading, overcoming the distraction of the burns, were the words of the first chapter of *The Last Enemy*. It was first-class reporting. The chapter is all action, and to describe action well is something which young authors find very difficult. But nobody could have done this description better. Obviously if he could write the whole book in this way it was going to be important; and to Richard, who was perspiring with the effort of his reading, and very red in the face, I said that if he could write a few more chapters and bring them back I thought we might make a contract. I told him that lots of people had the faculty of writing, but not many had the necessary perseverance. I told him that if he would write half a dozen chapters to prove that, we could then make a contract for a book. That was all he wanted.

My last vision of the boy as he left my room was of a mocking smile, though whether he mocked me, the process of publishing, or the lady who had brought him to me, I could not tell. He had disturbed the room and upset my complacency, and what I fidgeted with as my daily task seemed for a moment or two futile in comparison with what he had done. Fancy trying to write, I thought, after that scaring experience, and while still suffering pain. But he had looked both persistent and restless. I had an idea that he would go on with what he had set himself to do, and I had a feeling that he might, as they say, really pull it off.

In his diary Richard wrote:

> To London with Pat Hollander who very kindly took me to see Lovat Dickson at Macmillan's, to whom in some trepidation I read extracts from the book. He listened with patience, and while not effusive was encouraging: he could not of course judge a whole book on extracts, but how long would I take to finish it? Having no idea I said three months, and we left quite optimistic to have a very long drink.

In his 1950 biography of Richard, it would appear that Lovat Dickson deliberately softened his interpretation of the events of this meeting in order to present himself as being more sympathetic, patient and friendly. What Richard did and what he himself had allowed were not the done thing; he should have gone through an agent who would have presented a finished, typed, manuscript to him for consideration. Although Lovat Dickson did interview young would-be authors of the Battle of Britain, pilots and researchers alike, it is hard to believe that the editor-in-charge of one of the world's largest publishing companies would be overly willing to sit and listen to the first jottings of a young man being read aloud to him without showing some disdain. I believe that he felt compelled to sit back in his chair and listen to Richard reading from his manuscript, perhaps embarrassed at his predicament, unable to bring himself to tell the disfigured hero opposite that this really was not the way he conducted business. In time he came to appreciate the fact that Richard could indeed write.

In his initial letters to Lovat Dickson Richard quite naturally maintains a level of formality. This he later dropped as he got to know his publisher. Michael Burn, who came to know Lovat Dickson in the years after Richard's death and to whom I shall refer later, believed that Lovat Dickson later made more of his friendship with him than there really had been.

In 1960, Lovat Dickson published the first volume of his memoirs entitled *The Ante-Room*. Three years later he published the second volume entitled *The House of Words* in which he once again writes of his first meeting with Richard. There is a significant difference between this piece and that which was included in his biography of Richard thirteen years earlier. The section in *House of Words* is much longer, includes greater detail, and is written in an honest and forthright way. He reveals his true feelings during that meeting with Richard, although he exaggerates Richard's injuries. Nevertheless, with this second interpretation of events I think we are now able to appreciate what that meeting had been like.

Richard could now apply himself to the task of writing his story. He had an objective for the near future and an assignment as a writer, his chosen vocation.

Richard's book was to become a best-seller almost overnight and its author a national celebrity. Without the success of the book Richard would have just numbered among many heroic Battle of Britain fighter pilots. With the book and his untimely death came the legend.

* * *

During late May, early June 1941, Richard received news that another of his closest friends had been killed. Noel Agazarian.

The last time the two had seen each other was exactly a year before, during their conversion training to Spitfires. Noel had become a brilliant pilot with Yorkshire's 609 'West Riding' Squadron, having joined Blue Section on 8 July 1940 at Warmwell from No.5 OTU at Aston Down, while Richard had been posted to 603 Squadron.

During the early part of 1941 Frank Ziegler, the incoming intelligence officer (IO), remembers his first meeting with Noel as he was being shown round by the outgoing IO:

> Next moment the flap of a small marquee opened and, followed by derisive shouts from within, two bodies wearing Mae Wests precipitated themselves into the open and lay struggling on the muddy grass. Others followed more leisurely, and we all watched until they had finished.
>
> 'This is Aggie,' said the IO, indicating the larger body as it regained the vertical. 'The other one's Novo.'
>
> 'Officers of the West Riding squadron,' added the one called Aggie. 'I'm half Armenian, half French, and Novo's a dirty old Pole. How do you do.'
>
> He was a tall powerfully built young man – he had been a boxing blue at Oxford – with a small Errol Flynn moustache and a soft honeyed voice with just the right tinge of foreign intonation to make it irresistible to girls. His real name was Noel Agazarian. The other, Nowierski, was slightly bald and much older – he was thirty-four. He wore the DFC ribbon and looked tough and experienced.

This episode confirms Richard's assessment of Noel in that he was highly competitive, preferring the physical challenge that he had experienced while on holiday in Skye earlier that same year. A few moments after these introductions a squadron section was scrambled. Noel stood with Frank Ziegler as the Spitfires took off and Ziegler later recalled in his history of 609 Squadron:

> 'Like birds aren't they?' said Aggie, answering my thought. 'However long I fly, I shall never tire of watching Spits take to the air.' Sadly, fate had ordained that he wasn't to fly or watch much longer.
>
> 'How do they know what to do?' I asked him. The IO had long since disappeared, and I feared I might already be on duty when they returned.
>
> 'Operations will give 'em a vector. Steer one-eight-zero, fifty bandits approaching Weymouth, angels twenty – I don't think! It's probably only a bogey. Times aren't what they were. Scramble, scramble – and never a sausage.'
>
> I gathered there had not been a combat since Christmas, and that the pilots were 'browned off' at having to observe a state of Readiness all day, punctuated with eventless patrols. For it was much the same team which had been accustomed, not long before, to being 'scrambled' sometimes two and three times a day as a whole squadron to combat the hordes of Dorniers, Junkers, Heinkels

and Messerschmitts in one of the vital battles of history. These survivors of 'The Few' did not yet know that they and their dead comrades had already won the day. Such was their morale that they appeared actually to have enjoyed it, and were expecting and hoping that, as soon as weather permitted, it would recommence. Meanwhile, they resembled restless race-horses.

Most restless horse in the stables was Aggie, in the cockpit of whose beloved Spitfire I had been seated for the last half-hour while he, standing on the wing, explained the mysteries of the numerous buttons, levers and dials. He had, he told me, already applied for a posting to North Africa, where Wavell's campaign against the Italian army momentarily provided the war's sole military news. Within a couple of weeks he was gone, and soon afterwards was killed.

Aggie took exercise by wrestling with anyone he could provoke, including the temporary IO. One evening, after some of the squadron had returned from a house-warming party in the new WAAF Officers' Mess, Novo the Pole was found to have gone to bed and bolted his door. Aggie disapproved.

'Come on, Novo, open up! We want you!'

Silence from within.

'Open up, you Polish bastard, I say!'

Still no reply.

'Right!'

Entering the cubicle opposite to get a run, Aggie hurled his powerful frame three times against the slender obstacle. At the third impact it splintered and Aggie was inside. Then, not having fixed the next part of the programme, he was suddenly sheepish, especially when Novo, putting aside the letter he had been writing, rose from his bed, found a screwdriver, and without a word disappeared. Presently he returned carrying a door from 152 Squadron's corridor. This he substituted for his own, fixed the broken door where it had come from without waking the occupant, and returning to bed with a polite 'Good-night,' he resumed his letter, leaving Aggie speechless with defeat.

Noel scored his first victory on 11 August 1940 when he destroyed a Me110. The squadron had been vectored onto a major attack on the docks, oil tanks, barracks and gas works in Weymouth and Portland. No.609 Squadron was ordered to attack the fighters while No.152 Squadron attacked the bomber force. The next day Noel was getting ready to go on 24 hours' leave when he was called to readiness and immediately afterwards scrambled. The squadron encountered an orbiting circle of eighty Me110s and attacked. Noel claimed one of the twin-engined Messerschmitts damaged during this patrol and may have been credited with a Me110 destroyed or 'probable' during the afternoon patrol. His promotion to flying officer was promulgated on 14 August 1940.

He shared in the destruction of a Me110 on 25 August. On 7 September Noel's aircraft was hit by return fire, probably from a Dornier Do17:

> Three of us attacked the last Do17's . . . As I broke away beneath I could see fire coming down at me at an angle of 80 degrees.

He went on to attack a formation of Heinkel He111s: '. . . but a bullet had gone through my oil sump and I force-landed at White Waltham.'

On 15 September he shared a Do17 and on the 25th he shared in the destruction of a He111. The following day, he claimed a Me109 destroyed and on the 27th he destroyed a Me110 which was seen to plunge into the sea off the south coast from Warmwell.

On 30 September he was acting as 'weaver' for the squadron when five Me109s approached from behind. He turned to confront them, they dived away but he had lost the squadron. He then carried out an attack on the rearmost of a number of homeward bound Heinkel He111s. He hit the starboard engine of one, which produced a lot of black smoke. He unfortunately came off worse when he was hit by the 'highly concentrated' return fire from the bombers. The glycol system of Noel's Spitfire had been shot away and he force-landed back at Warmwell. He was flying Spitfire R6915 which now hangs spectacularly in the Imperial War Museum in London. It was credited with five enemy aircraft destroyed and three damaged.

On 15 October 1940, while flying as Blue 2, Noel shot down a Me109E north-west of Southampton. It crashed in flames. This successful attack was carried out after a bullet had pierced the canopy just above his head.

Noel shared in the destruction of a Me110 and a Dornier Do17 on 2 December 1940, near Thorney Island.

He was posted to the Middle East during early February 1941 and joined No.274 Squadron on 6 April at Amriya, Libya, in the Western Desert. He shot down a Me109 over Tobruk on 1 May. On 16 May he was himself shot down and killed when 274 Squadron were intercepted by Me109s over Cyrenaica whilst en route to, or returning from, a patrol to strafe enemy convoys at Gambut. Noel was buried in the Knightsbridge War Cemetery, Acroma, Libya. He was 24.

Noel's total claims amounted to five or six destroyed with three shared destroyed, four and one shared damaged. It was generally considered unfortunate that the 'dashing and fearless' Noel Agazarian was not awarded the DFC for his contribution in helping to win the Battle of Britain. I believe that to be an understatement and there were others like him.

In *The Last Enemy*, Richard recalls being told of Noel's death by his mother during one of her trips down from London to see him at East Grinstead while he was still recovering from his mastoid infection. It was devastating news:

> At first I did not believe it. Not Noel. It couldn't happen to him. Then I realised
> it must be true. That left only me – the last of the long-haired boys. I was horrified
> to find that I felt no emotion at all.

His words do express emotion, regardless of this final comment, but emotion quelled by his own poor state of health. Colin Pinckney was still alive at this time and could be considered to be one of the long-haired boys. Within the time span of *The Last Enemy* Noel was indeed the last of this group to die.

In actual fact Richard's infection of the mastoid was during January; he therefore would not have heard about Noel's death during this time as it was another two months before he was killed. He may well have received the news under the same circumstances but during a stay at the hospital for follow-up surgery. Another inconsistency is that in *The Last Enemy* he expresses a period of melancholy after Noel's death, in which he mentions the first intimation of spring and crocuses bursting out of the ground, although Noel was killed in May 1941.

During this troubled period he would try to keep himself occupied with long walks through the local streets:

> Walked all the way up Piccadilly, going into each bar until I reached the circus
> ... Drank too much and stayed up too late ... 3.00 a.m. What a failure I am, and
> how I am wasting my life.

It was possibly his meandering through the London streets and the scenes he witnessed that gave him the idea for the fictional last chapter in *The Last Enemy* entitled 'I See They Got You Too', set in bomb-torn London with its ulterior motive of indicating to the reader that he had by this time altered his conviction towards the war and not become the kind of jingoist he apparently despised. Without the belief that a transformation of sorts had taken place in him, Richard may not have written *The Last Enemy* and we would not have been able to enjoy all that is good in it.

*   *   *

By the time that Richard left hospital to start working once again, he was of the personal opinion that he had gone through a great psychological ordeal but had managed to remain unchanged. He was still egotistical and his reasons for fighting the Germans were the same as when he first decided to join the RAFVR, despite so much in-depth analysis of both his views and those of his closest friends. His psychoanalysis had also been of fighter pilots he had known at East Grinstead. He questioned many on their initial reasons for fighting and their attitude towards the war following their own first hand experience.

However, the short period of ultimate excitement experienced in combat, the horror of having been shot down twice in a few days, the agony he had suffered initially from his burns but later from the operations, the skin grafts, the mastoid infection and the slow drawn-out periods of rehabilitation and his mental turmoil had changed his character.

After surgery he had initially looked worse than he had once his burnt skin had started to recover. The grafted skin on his face was beginning to soften and blend in just a little more with his surviving facial tissue. This allowed him the ability to express himself in a more familiar manner using facial expressions, something that had been absent since he was first burnt. This was apart from that expression which he had still been able to convey with his eyes. It would not be long before his friends and family were aware that all the surgery had been worthwhile as his face appeared to have improved to the point whereby his injuries would no longer be as evident.

Bett Westmacott recalled the effect his appearance had on her at that time:

> His face, despite these ghastly scars, and they were ghastly, was one of the most arresting I have ever seen. Before that nobody would have looked at him, he was just another pretty boy. Since his injuries he was completely unforgettable.

During this period his personality had softened. He had felt humbled by those that had been injured to a far greater extent than he and showed far greater courage in the face of such adversity. He had become aware that his own complaining must have appeared selfish and inconsiderate under those circumstances. He realised that he was better off keeping quiet, although at times his temper certainly got the better of him.

He became a sympathetic listener, particularly if he was to glean information for his analysis of the other fighter pilot patients. He admired their courage and fortitude, their ability to tolerate such pain and live with apparently such limited hope for their future, bearing in mind the extent of their particular injuries, lost hands, legs, eyesight and faces. This he admired enormously but felt an overwhelming curiosity to discover from where they mustered such fortitude. He was aware that he was in the company of an outstanding group of individuals, the company he would later miss when he moved on to administrative duties.

Some of his fellow patients were also aware of the change in Richard and when he met colleagues whom he had not seen since he had been shot down some of them were quick to note the change in his character. Whatever, the main aspects of his character remained.

According to *The Last Enemy* shortly after returning to work at the end of May 1941, Richard received a letter from his pacifist friend from his Oxford days, David Rutter. Rutter explains that he had read the notice about Noel in the newspaper and asks Richard if he could visit him at his home in Norfolk. This Richard duly does.

Richard goes on to say that had not seen David Rutter since the celebration, in the bar at the Cavendish, on the occasion of his and Noel's commission in the RAFVR. Rutter had joined them for a drink. In comparison with his two Oxford colleagues, he had just had his first appeal as a conscientious objector turned down.

Richard tells us that almost a year had passed since they had last met and David Rutter was married and working on the land in Norfolk. Richard took two days' leave, one to spend in Norfolk, the other to allow him a night out in London and visit his parents. To Richard the letter came as an opportunity to justify the decision by him and his colleagues to go to war, and to confirm who had made the right choice.

On arrival in the arable farming community of their Norfolk village home, Richard discovers that Rutter had been constantly analysing his decision to become a conscientious objector and had finally decided that he had been wrong to follow this particular course of action. Richard recalled that his friend was a broken man.

As previously mentioned, I have been unable to confirm the existence of David Rutter or whether Richard had changed the name, as pacifists weren't popular at that time. Therefore, if the name was not a pseudonym and he did not exist, Richard may have invented such a character as part of his plan to present the change in his feelings towards fighting in a different light than that of the jingoist. In presenting this character to us, perhaps he was also trying to put across the justification for the pain and suffering he had endured. Had his experiences and the deaths of his dearest friends all been worthwhile? With hindsight, we now know that the Battle of Britain was indeed of enormous significance and that, had it been lost, Great Britain had been expecting to be invaded by the Germans. At the time of Richard's own assessment he was able to appreciate the magnitude of the valiant effort made by the Royal Air Force fighter pilots. In time he would learn to accept and appreciate the sacrifice made by Peter Pease, Peter Howes, Noel Agazarian, Colin Pinckney and all other aircrew as a tragic loss to the nation, but also as being a necessary part of the conflict.

* * *

Richard was keen to continue writing, but the urge to fly again was growing within him. He also looked forward to mixing with those individuals in whose company he felt most at home, the fighter pilots. His brief time with 603 Squadron had given him immense pleasure and he knew he could regain his happiness back in such company. Unfortunately, things did not work out quite as he hoped.

While medically he was graded unfit for flying duties and officially he was still convalescing, Richard was keen to get back to work.

CHAPTER FOURTEEN

AMERICA/THE WRITING OF *THE LAST ENEMY*

June 1941 – November 1942

During May 1941, Richard had gone along to see Mr Alfred Duff Cooper at the Ministry of Information with a plan to which he had recently been giving a great deal of thought. He had first mentioned this idea to Archie McIndoe while at East Grinstead and McIndoe had thought it a good idea. It involved visiting the USA on a tour of industrial sites and talking to the workers about the war effort and their part in it. Richard later described it as being: '. . . to try to make something living out of a job of putting nuts and bolts into an airframe.'

Duff Cooper, a retiring but exceedingly honest man (later 1st Viscount Norwich), and Sir Walter Monckton at the Ministry of Information were quick to see the possibilities in such a trip but were also aware of possible disadvantages. The purpose of the Ministry of Information was propaganda, but they could never be seen to be actively engaged in it. The USA was still not in the war at this stage.

McIndoe thought it was a morale-boosting idea for Richard, but he was concerned about Richard's appearance. He wrote to his wife in America: 'I have still a lot of work to do on him, I don't think it does justice to our work to show him off at this stage.' McIndoe was, however, keen about persuading America to join the war effort and his letters to his wife Adonia urged her to tell the Americans, in her broadcasts, of the conditions in Britain in the hope that they could be persuaded to join Britain in its fight.

Richard's usual level of enthusiasm and zeal was quite hard to quell and the staff at the Ministry of Information were indeed tempted to allow such a plan to go ahead.

He was still in the RAF and therefore only the Air Ministry could give the go-ahead. With the advantages in mind, and perhaps with a discreet hint from official quarters who were also aware that something may be gained from such a venture, the Air Ministry gave Richard permission to travel to Washington DC, where he would be attached to the Air Mission. Officially he was posted to No.1 Depot on 22 May 1941, with the status, 'pilot supernumerary non-effective sick' changed to an 'administrative supernumerary for duty as a lecturer whilst detached to Air Attaché in Washington'.

Richard attended RAF Hornchurch on 4 June 1941 but prior to this he had been discharged from Dutton Homestall for a period of leave effective from 17 May and returned home to his parents' flat in Knightsbridge Court.

He spent his time relaxing, socialising and, after his meeting with Lovat Dickson, felt motivated towards writing his book. The task was not an easy one and the pressure was now there to produce the finished manuscript. The condition of his hands only allowed him to write for short periods at a time and still only with his left hand, although he did eventually learn to use his right hand again. He tried to use a dictaphone but was unable to construct what he had to say in a satisfactory way. Even though he had the time, he was finding writing difficult and, as he was prone to do, he started to lose confidence in his ability to produce a completed manuscript. He wrote:

> . . . it won't come, and I can't help feeling it will always be like this. I've never done anything, and I'm beginning to wonder if I ever shall . . . I'm a sham, gracefully doing nothing and being witty to visitors, and I know it, that's the awful part of it.

To Richard his writing was important as was his urgent need to return to the war effort. Writing was something he had in mind as a future career, and he needed to feel that he was doing something of value. Not that he hadn't sacrificed enough already.

Richard sailed to America in convoy onboard the MV *Britannic*. En route the escort was detached to hunt the infamous German battleship *Bismarck*. This was reported in the national papers back in Britain and Richard was one of the passengers who provided an account of the event. He arrived in New York during the third week of June and cabled his mother to confirm his safe arrival.

In his absence his Personnel Occurrence Report (POR) continued to be the responsibility of the administrative department at RAF Hornchurch and was updated on the 4 June and 9 July 1941.

When Richard told McIndoe that his plan had been given the go-ahead McIndoe wrote once again to his wife to confirm the news and to inform her of the date when Richard intended passing through New York. Once again McIndoe expressed concern that he still had to finish the work on Richard's face and his American colleagues may have looked critically at his crude first attempts. However, his patchwork face and disabled hands may have influenced the Americans just as much as any speeches.

As the first of the British war wounded to visit the States, Richard was greeted by the American media at a small press conference held in the Plaza Hotel, New York, the morning after his arrival. He was excited by their positive response, published in the newspapers the next morning. He had received a good press from the New York reporters but things started to go wrong when he went to Washington. Sir Gerald Campbell, Minister at the British Embassy in Washington, approved the speeches he had prepared but expressed dismay at Richard's appearance. He feared that the women, whose clubs he was about to visit, would take one look at him and express their concern, saying: 'We don't want our boys to die for Britain.'

The mid-Western states would certainly be against him, as enthusiasm for the war had declined since the Battle of Britain and the Blitz. Sir Gerald Campbell therefore decided that Richard's speeches *would* be delivered, but in the form of a pamphlet and a series of recordings which would be broadcast over the networks. He was also allowed to write anonymous agency copy for the British Press Service for distribution to American newspapers, who were largely uninterested. Richard wrote an article for *Harpers Magazine*, but it was rejected. Always vain about his looks, the decision to prevent Richard from speaking in public was a quite dreadful disappointment, and his only comfort at that time was from the kindness and hospitality of his American hosts.

In response, Richard managed to muster some influential support for his appearing in public to deliver his message personally. These people included several chiefs of aircraft production, a number of diplomats: '... and all the women with whom I came into contact.'

With such backing he confronted the ambassador himself, Lord Halifax. His move had been pre-empted. Sir Gerald Campbell had managed to gain support from the secretary of state, Sumner Welles, who put the case to President Roosevelt himself, but from the 'mutilated airman angle'. The response from the White House was that it would be a 'psychological error' for Richard to appear on public platforms. Nevertheless, Lord Halifax still went to the president to plead Richard's case, stating that it had been unfairly presented. This attempt to persuade Sir Gerald Campbell also failed and to compound matters further an article appeared in a Washington newspaper at this time suggesting: '... the presence here of Flight Lieutenant Hillary is not as good propaganda as the British think.'

It was suggested that American men might indeed work harder as a result of hearing first hand from a pilot who had used the tools they were making, but the other side of the argument was that the unceasing work of trying to get America into the war may be, to some extent, undone by seeing the awful results of battle.

For Richard's ego and self esteem this experience had been devastating. He had fought so long and hard to rebuild his life after such a disastrous experience, and was now desperate to achieve success with this fresh challenge. He had re-established a reasonable level of self-confidence, found a new aspect of his career and bravely ventured out without letting the reaction of the public to his injuries affect him. His pride and self-esteem had allowed him to grow used to those who turned their heads away at the sight of his face. But that was in London, an area currently deeply affected by the war and whose people were, in the main, used to such sights and familiar with the causes of such injuries. Although his injuries had softened considerably by the time he arrived in the States, his appearance was something that the populus was not used to.

This was a terrible knock-back that he had probably not fully recovered from, even by the time he was killed. In a spirited response, however, Richard made light of the rebuff in his first letter home to his parents, dramatising himself as an international incident: 'Shall Hillary appear?'

June 30th 1941

Dearests,

I had hoped that my first letter to you would have been one of sensational success but alas that is not how things turned out.

The first day was full of promise; twenty-five reporters and camera-men in the Plaza Hotel and a most satisfactory Press the next morning, which seemed to please the powers that be. I then went to Washington where I met the Minister at our Embassy. My pre-arrival publicity had been unfortunate as the story had got around the Embassy that a badly mutilated airman was coming out to talk to the chaps. Had the cable read 'operational pilot coming out to lecture' all would have been well. But naturally enough everyone said that this was a psychological error at this moment. The Minister read my story, approved of it, but felt that I was on no account to be allowed to go around the factories as I should be unable to avoid lecturing to women's clubs. The situation right now is so tricky over here and there has been such a falling off in enthusiasm for the war, especially among the women and in the middle-west, that he felt that the showing of my face to the women of America would have entirely the opposite effect from what we had hoped. I pointed out that I had no desire to speak to the women of America anyway, but he seemed to think it impossible to avoid and was eager for me to produce my speech as a pamphlet and to do radio talks. This I was not a bit keen on doing, for I felt that if I ever was to talk to the factory workers they might as well have the whole thing fresh. The radio talks could come later. With this idea in view I took a plane up to New York to see Col. Donovan. He gave me lunch, together with several chiefs of aircraft production who were all in favour of the idea and said that the whole thing could be arranged without any publicity. I should be flown down, and a plane would be ready to fly me off again as soon as I had spoken. As I was going down in a purely technical capacity, I should not be at liberty to speak to anybody but technicians in the unlikely event of the story getting out.

Fortified by this news I flew back to Washington and within the next few days managed to convince Casey, the Australian Minister, Rex Benson and his wife, the Military Attaché, Beaumont Nesbitt, the Air Attaché, George Pirie, the American Air Attaché to London, Scanion, our Press Attaché, Childs, and all the American women with whom I came in contact. This I thought formidable enought armament with which to go to the Ambassador. That night I dined with him and the Lady Halifax and the next day saw him alone for half an hour. Unfortunately, the nigger was already in the woodpile. The case had been put to him from the Minister's angle; he had put it up to Sumner Welles, who in turn wrote a letter about it to the President from the mutilated airman angle. A certain Mrs Clark, who is pro-British and quite useful, also, I gather from Bill Donovan, saw the President and suggested it was a bad thing. Naturally enough, the reply came back from the White House, 'psychological error'. Halifax having seen me said he regretted that the whole affair had gone to the President in that light and that he had a perfectly open mind on the question, merely not wishing to take any step which at this moment could have the faintest chance of back-firing.

The Air Attaché had an alternative plan, that I should make a tour of the army air-fields, gain experience, possibly speaking a little on my way back up the West coast. Even this plan, however, has now been tabooed. As you may well imagine, all this has driven me nearly crazy, though I have so far managed to appear agreeable to everyone.

But two days ago was nearly the last straw. An article appeared in a Washington paper (though only in a gossip column) that made the 'I told you so' brigade hop with joy. It went like this:

'That the presence in Washington of Flight Lt. Hillary . . . is not good propaganda as the British may think. In the great battle over England Hillary's plane was shot down in flames and he landed by parachute – with face and hands horribly burned. A plastic surgeon fixed his face temporarily, but he is still badly scarred. He takes it beautifully; laughs and jokes about it, telling what a pretty boy he 'used to be'. No doubt he shows how well the British 'can take it', but all American mothers who see him, even in high society, murmur: 'Heavens. It might be my son!' I heard a few of them say that last Thursday at the Sterling ball. Lt. Hillary makes these women realise that war is a thing of suffering and distress and not the carnival for which they have been preparing.'

The dawn however is I think at last breaking, for after the last attempt to keep me quiet failed, I sat down and wrote a series of articles about England for the British Press Service. They liked them and, subject to the approval of the head of the Information Service, I am to continue writing them and to do some broadcasts together with producing my speech as a pamphlet.

The last effort to keep me quiet consisted of having me sent to Boston to see a plastic surgeon called Quesanzian with a view to six weeks of operation. He was perfectly charming, but said that he had orders to keep me there, so I hopped a plane and came straight back to New York, thus prolonging the Status Quo.

In Washington I have been staying with Mrs. Raymond Lee whose husband is Military Attaché in London. She is quite one of the most delightful women I have ever met and gave me every assistance in Washington. In New York I am staying with Eddie Warburg and his wife who have made me feel like one of the family. Eddie has given me his office in Rockefeller Plaza to write in till things get settled and Mary has introduced me to just about everyone in New York, both woeful and diverting.

The American attitude to the war is pretty difficult to guess as no two people think the same and everyone talks about it all the time. However, I hope and feel that it is the momentary shivering on the bank of the winter bather waiting for someone to push him in.

In some ways the reasons behind not allowing Richard to go ahead with his plan were realistic. But it was the manner in which he failed that caused so much unhappiness for him, including the last attempt of 'political hospitalisation'. In his letter he was happy to quote the compliments the reporter paid him when he sings his praises. His egoism was still profoundly dominant. But he had been hurt, attention had been drawn once again to the same injuries which he had been trying to come to terms with. The boyish looks were gone and what was left was nowhere near as attractive, yet still had great appeal based on his ability to convey his charm.

In many ways Richard had been fortunate, in that he had yet again been introduced to so many prominent and influential figures. Not influential enough to persuade those that had blocked his public speaking, but enough to ensure that his recovery continued while he enjoyed luxurious hospitality and an above average lifestyle in the company of one of the richest men in America at that time, Edward Warburg.

It must have taken a great deal of effort for the authorities to dampen Richard's enthusiasm for his plan. Such was his strength of character and determination to do that which he believed in.

In his office in the Rockefeller Plaza he was appointed a secretary, Miss Levine, who typed his manuscript. Richard had initially been given a dictaphone on which to record his book. Bearing in mind the difficulty he had writing, this was thought be an end to that problem. Unfortunately, when the wax cylinders were taken to the stenographers they delared that they couldn't understand a word that he had said. So Richard wrote it out by hand for Miss Levine to type up. Yet again there was a problem; Miss Levine could not read his handwriting and he had to dictate the text to her! Nevertheless, Richard committed himself wholeheartedly to completing his book, using his diary notes and the scripts from his broadcasts as the basis for the next chapters.

At this time Richard made the acquaintance of Antoine de St-Exupéry through his translator Lewis Galantière, who was possibly more interested in getting Richard's book published in the same house as St Exupéry's. St-Exupéry was also a fighter pilot who had been in the French Air Force during WWII and had gone into temporary exile in New York after the fall of France. He was a clumsy man with a shambling gait whose flying career had been marked by frequent crashes. His prewar books *Vol de Nuit* and *Terre des Hommes* had made him world famous with great critical acclaim.

Like Richard, St Exupéry had an ability to write about his experiences in a way that was appealing. His book about his wartime exploits before the fall of France, *Pilote de Guerre (Flight to Arras)*, was published in 1942 on the same day as *Falling Through Space (The Last Enemy)*, and has much in common with Richard's own story. Set in May 1940, it tells of his experiences and of the comradeship in his squadron, 22/3, and of his fight to overcome overwhelming odds which finally ends in defeat; a defeat that St Exupéry refused to accept. Like Richard, St Exupéry had also been wounded. While Richard wrote about his squadron in victory, St Exupéry wrote of defeat. Over a champagne luncheon the older St Exupéry had offered to write a preface for *Falling Through Space*.

It is possible that St Exupéry generated a disquiet in Richard that somehow deepened into a sense of guilt that he had been shot down too soon, and that more would be demanded of him. He knew his part in the war was not over and that once again he would risk his life, mainly because he now realised that his reason for fighting had changed. He now wanted to honour his fallen friends. This was despite his having already done his share and having ensured the memory of their generation and their sacrifice was recorded in his book. Michael Hillary believed that the meeting with St Exupéry was decisive in making his son return to operational flying and certain passages in *Flight to Arras* are suggestive:

> War is not the acceptance of danger. It is not the acceptance of combat. For the combatant it is at certain moments the pure and simple acceptance of death.

St Exupéry also shared Richard's reasons for becoming a fighter pilot:

> Up here at any rate death is clean. A death of flame and ice! Of sun and sky and flame and ice. But below! That digestion stewing in slime . . .

Ask almost any fighter pilot why he chose that method of fighting, however, and the answer is nearly always the same.

Later St Exupéry returned to work with the Air Force. This he did in the North African theatre where he rejoined the survivors of his squadron. Here he managed to persuade the American general, under whose command his squadron was operating, to allow him to return to operational flying duties. At least ten years older than the regulation flying age, St Exupéry flew operational sorties over occupied France. He was killed while flying a P38 Lightning, and the circumstances of his death are to this day tinged with mystery and, like Richard, his memory has passed into the realms of legend.

By the time of St Exupéry's death, Richard had already been killed. As a writer, Richard's encounter with St Exupéry had been significant.

It is interesting to contemplate the possibility that St Exupéry discussed his intention to return to operational flying with Richard, and thus strengthened Richard's own resolve to return to fight the war in the air.

Another French pilot, Jules Roy, later compared Richard with St Exupéry stating that:

> His [Richard's] entire 'adventure' had been confined to war. Yet his days of active service were few, and comprises only fourteen pages of the two-hundred and twenty [One hundred and eighty three in the paperback]. He has a born writers gift for describing fact with laconic but intense detachment. It brings his text alive. The chronicle of spiritual development runs throughout.

Not only did Edward Warburg set a room aside in which Richard could write his book, he also introduced him to yet another influential associate and personal friend, Eugene Reynal. Gene Reynal was the senior partner in the New York publishers, Reynal and Hitchcock. Richard was very fortunate indeed that both Edward Warburg and Lewis Galantière either believed, or were convinced by Richard, that he could indeed write and that he had a story which was worth telling. He was also fortunate in that Edward Warburg telephoned Gene Reynal asking him to come and advise Richard about the writing of such a book. Gene Reynal later wrote to Lovat Dickson with his memories of that first meeting:

> Richard was the first person I had seen who had been injured in the war and I remember well the first impact of his disfiguration upon on me. Needless to say I was attracted to Richard as a person immediately. We spent a long and happy afternoon together exploring the whole problem. He had with him four or five pages which he had written describing his being shot down in the air which was all at that time that he had set down on paper. I was greatly moved by it and told him that if he could write an entire book with the same insight and gift for handling language that was shown in these few pages I thought he would have a book of the utmost importance and one which would do him great credit. We gave him a contract immediately and through many conversations the pattern for the book as a whole was evolved. He was in and out of my house a great deal that summer while he was writing it and he also received a good deal of help and advice from Lewis Gallantiere who had also taken a great shine to him. Lewis had translated several of Saint Exupery's books and given Saint-Ex a good deal of help in the shaping of them.

Galantière was impressed by Richard's book, despite there being so little written at this time, and was instrumental in confirming the potential of the project to Gene Reynal. A contract was signed in early August 1941 with a three-month deadline for completion of the manuscript. It was at this time that Richard moved out of the Warburgs' appartment in New York, into one of his own.

The joint experience of these three men undoubtedly contributed towards the quality of the finished manuscript, which was outstanding from one so young and with so little experience.

*   *   *

Richard had received both adverse and positive media attention. Out of sympathy, friendship, a genuine attraction to him, and admiration for all that he had endured and achieved, the Warburg family and Mrs Jeanette Lee offered Richard kindness and friendship. They treated him as one of their own family. Richard's comfort at this difficult time also came from the kindness and hospitality of the American people in general.

Mrs Jeanette Lee was the wife of the American military attaché in London and she offered to accommodate Richard during his stay in Washington. Contrary to the spirit he exhibited in his letters home, when Mrs Lee met him in Washington she found him to be extremely nervous and depressed. He saw himself once again as being a failure. She noticed how easily he became tired and how weak his hands were. She had troublesome door knobs in her house adjusted to enable them to be opened with the minimum of effort. The two were to become very good friends for the duration of his stay with her in her home at Georgetown, situated just outside Washington DC. She wrote: 'I tried to explain that the shock to American women would be caused not by the sight of him, but by the idea . . . these emotions might just be the beginning of what we in America would have to learn.'

Richard felt cruelly humiliated by the whole experience. Here was he trying to re-integrate into society, the boyish looks replaced by disfigurement, but he was receiving just the sort of reaction he had been so determined to avoid. Richard also got on very well with Mrs Lee's eight-year-old daughter. Mrs Lee later recorded: 'He loved to take his meal with her and tell her fairy stories.' It was his first opportunity to express his skill as a raconteur since the hayloft with the eager young children at Tarfside.

Whilst the British Embassy had agreed to have Richard make a number of recordings for broadcast over the network radio system, under an RAF directive he had to remain anonymous. The recordings were produced on vinyl disc and made in the studios of the National Broadcasting Company (NBC), at Radio City, New York on 11, 14 and 19 July and 2 and 9 August 1941.

During the first recording Richard talked about his sentiments surrounding the beginning of *The Last Enemy*, his philosophy on the war, Tony Tollemache and a man known only as 'John', a classics scholar whom he had known at Oxford and who had chosen pacifism when his colleagues had gone to war. John's wife had witnessed her husband's gradual loss of self-confidence in himself as a consequence of his beliefs and he ultimately realised he had been wrong in choosing to be a pacifist. In *The Last Enemy*, Richard calls this character David Rutter.

Whilst all the recordings were edited to some degree prior to broadcast by NBC, it would seem that this first recording was never broadcast, possibly because of the sensitive nature of Richard's reference to the beliefs of 'John'. The other recordings were about periods of action in which Richard had been involved during the Battle of Britain.

At this time his writing had not received its final polish prior to publication, which it later received under the guidance of Gene Reynal and Lewis Gallantière. The listener can, however, get an idea of Richard's initial style and his voice has an air of mournful weariness about it and sounds like that of a middle-aged man, not a 22-year-old.

The response to the broadcasts from the American listeners was heartening and brought him a great deal of fan-mail which added to his feeling of well-being in his new environment. NBC offered congratulations to Richard on the success of the broadcasts with the possibility of his making futher recordings.

After Richard's death, Michael Hillary acquired a set of the discs from NBC. He subsequently loaned them to the BBC and on 15 February 1949, the Corporation was granted permission by NBC to copy them. It was either the wish of Michael Hillary or NBC, however, that only specific sections, amounting to 24 minutes, 14 seconds, were copied for filing in the BBC Sound Archive.

It is interesting to note that the recordings were made a few weeks after he started writing in earnest, in the facility he had been given in the Rockefeller Plaza. Having signed a contract, he now had a deadline to meet and was making good progress. He was now doing what he had always believed he was good at, despite occasional lapses in confidence during some of the darker periods of his recovery.

Richard's daily routine mainly involved writing, with his evenings occupied with functions at which he never failed to gain the attention of the most attractive women present. He lived a quality lifestyle in the company of Americans who offered Richard kindness as well as the benefit of their hospitality during his stay. They described him as exuding:

. . . gaiety and humour, youthful charm mingled with an early maturity; an enjoyment of beauty, music and good living; a delight in excelling, whether in an argument or in a game; kindness; and carelessness about money. He also had a biting tongue, particularly on the subject of bureaucracies.

He made many friends and continued to be outstandingly successful in attracting the most beautiful members of the fairer sex. It was Mary Warburg who said that she thought Richard's success with women compensated for his disappointment about his speaking tour:

It was not my opinion, nor anyone else's who knew Richard, that the women of America couldn't take it; he would have charmed them all once he began speaking . . . he made one feel perfectly natural, although his scars in those days were quite red and very noticeable. I was only upset when I cut his finger nails. They were thick, and all but two deeply imbedded, and the burned skin pulled his fingers down into a clenched position.

At the parties he sometimes appeared slightly aloof to his hostesses and quite often withdrew quietly from the attention he attracted. He was still pondering his future, much the same as at the party at his parents' flat when had invited some of his old associates from Oxford. He withdrew when he no longer felt comfortable in their company.

During his stay in New York, the daughter of Gene Reynal introduced Richard to Merle Oberon, an actress who would, even by today's standards, be placed in the bracket of 'superstar'. It was written that she:

. . . immediately felt an overpowering sympathy and warmth towards him. She herself had known what it was to see her face destroyed; she knew in the essence of her being the pain of loss of looks which only a beautiful human being can know. And she had been lucky; she had regained her looks, with only slight scars left behind to mark the torment of her ordeal.

The affair between Richard and Merle Oberon was fun-filled and passionate, with a great emphasis on sex. They found an overwhelming sexual desire for each other, and it was common knowledge that the relationship was based on this. With a deadline to be met with his publisher, however, Richard still managed to continue a hectic social life and an affair.

During this period there occurred the possibility of Richard becoming the technical director to Alex Korda; even though he was having an affair with his wife at the time.

Merle Oberon was an actress who had starred in films made in London and Hollywood, and was up there with the very best at this time. She was 30 years old and rich and famous when she met Richard, and was well on her way to becoming a celebrated hostess and friend of many well known people.

Merle had received facial injuries in England on 16 March 1937 when her Rolls-Royce which was being driven by her chauffeur Digby, crashed in Carburton Street in London. Merle was badly cut over her left eye and ear when she was thrown forward from her seat in the back, and was treated in the Middlesex Hospital where her wounds were stitched.

In *Merle, A Biography of Merle Oberon* by Charles Higham and Roy Moseley, Tessa Michaels of United Artists, who was Merle's publicity agent, recalled the relationship between Merle and Richard:

Merle was overwhelmed by desire for Hillary. He brought out the frustrated maternal element in her nature as well as the healing element she had inherited from her mother, who had worked as a nurse. She wanted to give Hillary back a sense of his lost manhood; that he could still be attractive to a woman of great allure. She knew that by reawakening his dampened and suppressed sexual fires she could give him back his virility and self-confidence. Her keen instinct told her that, without her really knowing, Hillary had withdrawn from sexual contact with women following his crash and that women must have shrunk from him in horror at the idea of embracing his tortured and charred flesh. Tessa says: 'Merle told me she knew he was very much a man, still, and had such a great, good heart, that she could breathe her power, her strength into him. It was a beautiful thing for her to do.'

One day at the Hotel Sherry-Netherland, Merle drew Tessa aside and instructed her to clear away all appointments, everything, even war work, for two full weeks, which she could devote to Hillary utterly. Alex was in England, but there must be no gossip and Tessa in her role of press agent must make absolutely sure that not a soul among the columnists and gossip-mongers obtained even a hint of what she was planning. Tessa proved to be a tower of strength in the matter.

Merle spent nights with Hillary at a hideaway apartment in the Ritz Towers. From what she said later to Tessa, it is clear that she restored Hillary's virility; that he obtained intense pleasure from her body. Her fineness of spirit overcame what must have been an agony in seeing his naked flesh. Hers was a true heroism, a true expression of total romaticism. Hillary's biographer and intimate friend, Lovat Dickson, a London publisher says today:

Merle was just what Richard needed at the time. You must remember that Richard was still very attractive, even with his terribly injured face and hands, that his eyes could still twinkle. And Merle helped him to laugh and have fun. She gave him laughter – he always said, and he had many women, that their affair was not heavy and major, but it was lighthearted, cheerful and it took his mind off that dreadful thing Lord Halifax had done to him: that upright monster of rectitude with his straight back and rolled umbrella who had lost a great war hero his chance to talk to the assembly workers.

Richard had enjoyed a number of brief sexual relationships since he had been injured and clearly he had been lacking none of his charm and sexual prowess at this time. It certainly gives the story a romantic angle, instead of the rather sleazy feel that the affair between an older married woman, famous actress and nymphomaniac, hiding away for days at a time with a young RAF officer, would naturally attract. Merle Oberon's biographers wrote:

She and Richard had much in common apart from their shared disfigurement, the experience that made them resemble the hero and heroine of the Enchanted Cottage. They had both undergone plastic surgery and could talk about that; they both loved England, and Merle could overcome his bitterness with their shared patriotism; they both loved the Warburgs and the Reynals. According to Dickson, Richard was a frenzied, driving lover, and we already know Merle's intense sex-drive; there is no doubt that their night together was ecstatically abandoned and fulfilling.

During those weeks with Merle, Hillary was inspired to the poetic beauty of his book, *The Last Enemy*, much of which he wrote in her presence. He would show her passages in it, and with her vibrant love of poetry, her romantic nature, she would respond with suggestions and deeply felt praise. Simultaneously, she poured all her radio earnings from performances in New York into the newly-developed fund for the United Services Organisation which was being put together at the time as a basis for troop entertainment.

It was a painful separation when Richard returned to England that autumn. But he must, he told Merle, get back into the Royal Air Force, and she, fearful of what would happen, became nervous and tried to dissuade him. She knew it was futile since he longed to serve his country and now that he had been denied his chance by Lord Halifax, he must assuredly return to the air. Back in England, the Royal Air Force leaders knew that it was a risk giving this man with his maimed hands and impaired eyesight one of their extremely rare and valued aircraft to fly.

But they could not deny him the opportunity; and he went into special training for the injured in manipulating the joystick and observing enemy or friendly signals.

The aircraft were in short supply, but not rare. It was experienced pilots that they were desperately in need of:

> His letters to Merle disappeared in a fire in 1960, whereas those to his English girlfriend Mary have been preserved. It would be correct to assume that his correspondence to Merle was of a similar character: filled, despite his condition, with the lust and joys of youth. Knowing her character, it is easy to see that she would have responded in kind. She longed to travel to England to join him. On a windy afternoon in 1960 at her home in Bel Air, sparks from a chimney set fire to the roof. The house was well ablaze by the time it was brought to Merle's attention. The fire was a disaster and a large amount of her valuable and most personal belongings were lost, including her treasured and irreplaceable love letters from Richard.
>
> But she had to stay, to keep working on the isolationist factions. She succeeded in raising a hundred thousand dollars for war charities by selling one kiss a night for sixteen nights at several thousand dollars a kiss. She said later, 'Kissing strange men is awful. Some frightened me so much that I cheated by giving them a quick peck even though they had paid thousands for the chance. When one man mounted the platform and moved towards me, I was so scared I hid behind Bob Hope.'

Following Richard's death, Michael Hillary discovered the bundle of love letters from Merle Oberon amongst his son's possessions. He burnt them.

* * *

At this time Duff Cooper at the Ministry of Information, cabled Sir Archibald Sinclair, the Liberal air minister in Churchill's wartime government, for his blessing on Richard's activities.

While in New York, Richard encountered a contemporary, Mr R. Wilkinson, who later recalled that Richard was troubled by the heat and unable to perspire through the layers of grafted skin.

Richard had sent a telegram to Archie McIndoe asking him to sanction further surgery on him by Dr Jerome Webster. In an earlier letter home, Richard told his parents of this intention:

> I have been to see Dr Webster in New York, who is reputedly America's foremost plastic surgeon, and he is quite prepared to operate on me in a couple of months, should the government decide that it is necessary. Have now had a bar put on the signing of my name to any newspaper articles, pamphlets, broadcasts, etc.

On receiving this letter, Richard's father was concerned that his son was going to be treated by anyone other than Archie McIndoe and, in an attempt to put his mind at ease, decided to write to him. Mary Warburg also wrote to Edwyna Hillary to put her mind at rest.

On 6 September 1941, Richard sent a cable to his parents confirming that surgery to the fingers of his left had been successful. By 8 September he was back in hospital for further surgery and had completed a quarter of the manuscript for *Falling Through Space*. Richard later wrote to McIndoe about the latest operation:

> I have to confess that I persuaded Webster considerably against his will, to do a graft over the bridge of my nose between my eyes. I did this partly as a sop to official Washington which, as you know, had been yammering for me to have my face done and partly because there has been some contraction of my left lower lid. My face is actually improved but as our officials here have such a bee in their bonnet about it, I doubt if they could ever be persuaded to notice the face unless

> I had some little job done.

The lower eyelid had actually been trimmed back too soon at East Grinstead. The slow process of contraction had still been occurring and as a result the lid had become taut and uncomfortable. More surgery would be required later in an attempt to rectify this problem. The graft carried out by Dr Webster on the bridge of Richard's nose, reduced its natural curve noticeably.

In a letter to McIndoe written shortly before he left America, Richard told of his initial treatment by the Ministry. McIndoe was furious and termed it: 'The official botch-up'. In response to Richard's humiliation he wrote to the authorities in Washington, using such expletives as 'goats' and 'stupid baboons' to emphasise his comments.

By this time Dr Webster had operated on Richard in New York. In addition to the graft over the bridge of his nose, the surgeon attempted to improve the condition of the eyelids and brow of his left eye. Richard also included details of this in his letter. In reply McIndoe wrote:

> They've made a bloody awful mess of that eye. You'd better come back to the ward and I'll put it right for you.

McIndoe was anxious to have Richard back in his care once again, both physically and mentally. The experience further added to the bond between these two individuals.

On 8 November, Richard wrote to his parents, from the home of Mrs Carola Rothschild, informing them that the manuscript was nearly ready, for publication on 6 February 1942. That night he went to the opening performance of *Blithe Spirit* by Noel Coward, accompanied by Edward and Mary Warburg and Merle Oberon.

When the manuscript was finished Richard gave it to Gene Reynal, who subsequently provided him with a set of galley proofs (the book in continuous form without page numbers), which he brought with him to England when he returned in November 1941. Richard's time in America had been productive. He had enjoyed a busy and flamboyant social life in the company of many who had cared for him. He had written home regularly and even sent food parcels to his parents and Denise. On returning home he was quick to write and express his gratitude to those who had looked after him; he was to remain in touch with the Warburgs and Jeanette Lee until his death.

He had written his story in a remarkably short period of time, leading one to believe that the long periods of contemplation about his own experiences, as well as those of his colleagues had been justified; even if his enquiring nature had at times irritated the less understanding of those who had shared his company at East Grinstead.

The book was written out of a fierce compulsion to tell his own story and that of those held most dear to him who had ultimately given all in the fight, commitment that he strove so desperately to appreciate and understand in comparison with his own input. It is also clear however, that in writing his story he took deliberate liberties with the truth.

It was the Air Ministry who demanded that Richard return to Britain, for Richard might well have been tempted to stay on in America. He had grown to love and appreciate those around him and he longed to explore the country outside New York and Washington DC. He admired their straightforward attitude, they did not mess with words and said what they felt. He found their inquisitive and restless nature gained an immediate response from his own. His attraction to America may well have been due to his earlier influence by the writing of Henry George and his attempts at radical reform there.

While in America he had conversations with the young of the draft age; some of this contact had been established as a result of the fan-mail he received after his radio broadcasts. He described their sentiments as identical to those of our own young men just before the war:

> They thought the world was their oyster, and the war to be fought so they could gain experience of life. They, as we before them, have the inestimable advantage of not going forward waving flags, only to come back cynical and disillusioned. We were cynical and disillusioned before it started. Our so-called Lost

Generation found itself quickly enough, and I have no doubt that the Americans
will have the same experience. The only difference I can see is, that when we held
a debate, even on pacifism, we had some difficulty in taking ourselves seriously;
the younger Americans, never.

The American generosity and kindness had been offered openly. Those around him had
also shown a confidence in his ability to write his own story. Richard would later
consider a posting back to America.

* * *

On his return to Britain in November 1941, Richard took the galley proofs for his book
to Lovat Dickson at Macmillan. He was relishing the opportunity to surprise Lovat
Dickson not only with his manuscript but also with the news that he had already signed
a contract for its publication. In 1963 in the second volume of his autobiography *The
House of Words*, Lovat Dickson recalled the meeting:

> One evening in October 1941, when I was on the point of leaving the office, my
> secretary came to say that Flight Lieutenant Richard Hillary was downstairs to
> see me. The memory of that burnt face, those fleshless fingers, and the outline of
> that superb bold young figure came back to me. The office was about to close,
> and I longed to get home, but like a well-trained hound I sank back, recalling that
> vivid first chapter he had read me six months before. What now? Had he come to
> read me an equally vivid Chapter Two? To circumvent this, but prompted by that
> urge never to discourage anyone who might write anything, I ran downstairs to
> interview him in those leather stalls where visitors to Macmillan's have been
> interviewed since the building was first put up nearly seventy years ago. There
> he sat, hunched in his RAF greatcoat, his cap by his side, looking just as I had
> remembered him. What a good-looking youth! A figure and head out of fifth-
> century Greece with a twentieth-century grin fixed on it, worn like a mask at a
> masquerade. That grin was so derisory that it occurred to me to wonder what he
> saw, looking at me through his mask. A petulant, fussy, tired looking middle-aged
> civilian in striped trousers and a black coat, ready to give the official brush-off to
> an importunate writer? And yet a spark was ignited between us as we stood there,
> so different in age, so unlike in appearance, for a moment regarding each other.
> Across the generation separating us a signal of some kind wavered like the
> leaping of an electric spark. I knew I was to be stuck with this man for life; he
> knew the same. What we did not know was how little time was left. For better or
> worse, in sickness and in health; these unspoken vows are as strictly kept
> between publisher and author as between husband and wife.
> 'Glad to see you again, Hillary. How is the book coming?'
> 'Here it is. You told me to come back when I'd finished it.'
> From the bench on which he had been sitting, he pulled forth an untidy mass
> of galley proofs, and laughed at me. Richard knew quite well what he was doing,
> making this pompous old bastard snap out of his complacency; he was getting a
> lot of pleasure from this moment, and all sorts of unworthy thoughts were
> flashing through my mind. Six months ago he had written one chapter. Now,
> incredibly, there was a finished book. It had been accepted by an American
> publisher, and the type had been set. Had somebody written it for him? The
> Americans were not yet in the war, but they were our undeclared allies, and RAF
> heroes were very much admired there. Had an American publisher taken this
> book simply because it was by one of these heroes? I saw that it was called
> Falling Through Space, and I didn't think that was a very good title. And said so,
> while I was wondering what to say next.
> 'Well, you think of a better one,' Richard said cheerfully. 'Isn't that part of a
> publisher's job?'

'Yes, if we take the book. How did you get it finished so quickly?'

A grimace of recollected pain passed over his ravaged face...

Within a few days he was back at the office, wanting to know what we had decided. 'It takes at least three weeks for a manuscript to be considered,' I said severely. 'Why do you think yours should have priority before others waiting in the queue?'

'Because, if you are going to publish it, I want to get it out quickly while I'm still alive.'

As a matter of fact, we decided within ten days to publish it. This was not a book that had to go to readers. There could be no doubt at all about the quality of this work. It was not just an account of a pilot's experiences in the Battle of Britain, and that is why the American title was so inept. The active training for the battle and the battle itself takes up only half the book. The most important and interesting part is the second half, which tells how a spoilt young man who had gone into the war *pour le sport*, who had mocked at everything, not least at himself and his own class, came in the end humbly to accept humanity.

It was ready for publication in June 1942, in spite of Richard's certainty that we had lost the printed sheets between the printers and the binders, that something was bound to go awry: he knew that I was determined at all costs to prevent the book from appearing! It had been chosen by The Book Society, and we managed to allocate enough paper for 15,000 copies. It was very well received on publication . . . Within a few weeks we had sold every copy. Time after time we went back to press, but we could never produce enough to meet the demand.

During this second meeting Richard's forthright nature is met with a certain amount of firmness from Lovat Dickson, and determination to show who is in charge. Richard could have easily taken his book to another publishing house if he thought his treatment by Lovat Dickson was unsatisfactory. It had been a challenge in proving to Lovat Dickson that he could finish the book, and a book worthy of publication. Richard is aware, as Lovat Dickson struggles to impress upon him, that there is a tried and tested system in place for the processing of such a manuscript, Richard knows that the book is good enough to be accepted and the young man taunts the experienced older man with that self confidence.

Lovat Dickson thought it incredible that Richard had completed the book in the six months since the two had last met, 'Had somebody written it for him?' he had thought and had asked Richard 'How did you get it finished so quickly?' This incredulity seemed to diminish when he realised that Richard had been working on the manuscript full-time. He had also had a great deal of help from the Warburg family and his New York publisher.

On signing a contract with Macmillan's, Richard received £25, half of the total advance.

Richard adopted Lovat Dickson as his private publisher and took every opportunity to visit him at work. Lovat Dickson admired much of what he saw in Richard and there is also a certain amount of envy of his achievements. Despite the relationship between publisher and writer generally being a fragile one, the two became friends.

Lovat Dickson was also an excellent contact as he knew so many celebrities and influential people that Richard would be eager to meet in order to help confirm his status in society.

At this time it is possible to believe that there was a certain amount of acceptance by Richard that he was not going to become an operational pilot again. What tends to contradict this are the repeated appearances in front of medical boards of the CME. These alone express enthusiasm for a return to operational flying. In the interim he took the necessary steps to find a wartime career on the staff of the RAF. When the war was over he knew what he wanted to do, little further consideration was needed.

He underwent a period of convalescence from November 1941 until January 1942 when he was sent to the staff college at Gerrards Cross, Buckinghamshire. Between the end of October and early November he took up an offer of introduction from Merle Oberon to a close friend of hers in London. Her name was Mary Booker. It had been Merle's intention that Mary look after Richard, not that they should fall in love, but Richard and Mary began a relationship that was to last until the time of his death. Richard telephoned the number on the letter and arranged to call by her home one evening.

CHAPTER FIFTEEN

MARY

Mary Walter had been born in Petropolis, Brazil, near Rio de Janeiro on 10 March 1897. She was 44 when she met Richard. Her father was Charles Hamilton Walter, who was a wealthy merchant trader between Britain and Brazil. Her mother was Ada Yeats, a first cousin to the two brothers W.B. Yeats the poet, and the painter Jack Yeats. Her father was a collector and connoisseur who possessed an appreciation and extensive knowledge for beautiful things. It was from her father that Mary also developed this trait. The family were Catholics. Like Richard, she came to England as a child and it was here she began her schooling. Her father died in 1912 and her mother married again during World War I.

On 23 January 1918 at the age of 20, Mary married Henry Booker at Brompton Oratory. She had two daughters by him and they were both grown up by the time Richard entered her life.

In the early thirties, despite trying very hard to make her marriage work, Mary obtained a civil divorce from her husband, but she continued to care very deeply and practically for her daughters.

She was a woman of outstanding beauty who possessed an aura of charisma that rendered her unforgettable in the eyes of those around her. Her closest friend was Deirdre Hart-Davis, who wrote of Mary:

> No other friend has been to me what she was. Through all the years she never failed me for even a minute. Her warmth and generosity, her spontaneous response to humour and delight as well as to other people's joys and sorrows was like a limitless well. She never counted the cost to herself, and she also had a wonderful innocence.

While photographs, sculptures and portraits show something of her beauty, to see it in the flesh was the opportunity to fully appreciate her deep attraction. Her eyes were deep hazel. Richard described her mouth as so perfect, she might have had some surgery done to it. She had not. She wore little make-up and possessed a head of hair that she described as 'a challenging rampage'. In her early twenties her hair started to go white, two streaks of silver-white that rose back from her forehead like rams horns, which was a not uncommon occurrence in someone so dark. She had a fine figure, slim and of medium height. She walked with a light spring in her step.

In her youth Mary had been a 'society beauty', much feted, and photographed regularly at pageants and charity balls, dressed perhaps as a Venetian or Marie Antoinette. She was later embarrassed by these photographs and, thinking them nonsensical, hid them away. Despite being aware of her beauty she did not like being shown off. This only served to enhance her attractiveness to others. At a function she could enter a room full of guests and gain the attention of everyone present. Of her looks, dress sense, modesty and charisma, Mary once said: 'This is power. . . I must be careful of it.'

Mary was certainly above the average level of intelligence that one would associate with a young society girl. She had read a great deal but was not an intellectual. She once told Richard: 'You are more intellectual than I am, but I'm far more intelligent.'

Mary was considered conventional and liked to shop at Harrods. Richard said that she saved one the trouble of defining the word 'good'. She was a very kind person and Rosie Kerr, a mutual friend of both Richard and Mary, once said: 'She was very very good… so selfless, loving, so terribly good to me . . . so very understanding and wise . . . made no lethal remarks, would never have blamed anybody, and never boasted . . .'

She spent little on clothes, but what she did wear looked good on her. A gossip writer in the thirties once wrote of her ability to wear clothes saying that she could wear a salad-bowl on her head or around her neck and make it look part of a *grande toilette*.

But not everyone was charmed by Mary. Some found her artificial and thought a manipulative nature was hidden beneath an apparent lack of interest in material things. Some found her references to 'love' and the 'spirit' embarrassing.

After she was divorced from her husband, Mary tried to support herself and her daughters. Her husband had become very possessive during their marriage and afterwards Mary valued her independence. She tried working in the film industry through Alexander Korda, but she was too reticent and failed. It was her reticence and her sheltered life that Richard was to pick up on.

Along with two friends, Peter Lindsay and Edward Hutton, she went into the business of interior design. She was a success. With Peter Lindsay she restored two quarrymen's cottages in North Wales one of which she kept, initially as a holiday home and later as a more permanent residence. Mary later took Richard to this hideaway to escape from their busy social lifestyle that seemed to plague them towards the end of his life.

In the years after her divorce she was not much courted. She could have easily found a partner but it was not what she wanted. She valued her friends greatly, and in particular most of her closest friends were female.

At the beginning of the war she was a nurse, but that did not last. She subsequently turned a job down with the Ministry of Supply.

After Richard's death she became the London manager for Miles aircraft, but during their relationship, although it is known that she worked, it is not known what job she had. Mary had many influential friends. Something else that Richard was able to use to his advantage. She had friends in the Foreign Office, she had friends among the French, some of whom, as members of the Special Operation Executive (SOE), were parachuted into occupied France. Admiral John Godfrey, Director of Naval Intelligence since 1939, said to be the model for 'M' in Ian Fleming's James Bond books, admired Mary greatly. It is possible to consider that she may have undertaken some sort of secret work, especially when it has proven so difficult to find out what work she did undertake. She was extremely discreet. But in the opinion of her friend Rosie Kerr, it is most unlikely. She also had many friends amongst the American journalists in London.

During the Blitz she had a lucky escape when the house she shared with lodgers received a direct hit while she was out. Many of her possessions were destroyed but no one was hurt.

Mary kept a diary and it showed that she lived a hectic social life. She had a great many friends, to which she gave generously of her time, even when she lacked time to herself. When Richard entered her life, she had been on her own for a very long time. Her busy lifestyle and many close friends only made up in part for the hours of solitude. She was alone both physically and spiritually. The relationship did not come easily to her after being alone for so long. But after a period of adjustment she fell in love with him and was committed to the relationship. Eventually, her social life was an imposition on their relationship and they craved privacy.

Her reticence is hard to accept when one reads the many letters she wrote to Richard during their relationship. As Michael Burn, who married Mary in 1947, wrote in his book *Mary and Richard*:

> People often spoke of her reticence, of her serenity. Serenity was probably always there in her expression. . . but passage after passage in her letters appears to contradict it. Over and over again she is, as Richard is also, insisting on anything

but reticence between the two of them when alone; far from serene; far from being a woman to whom things came easily. One finds her torn by anxiety when he is in hospital; trying not to telephone; exasperated by his arrogance and badgering; passionate in his company; hardly able to bear his absences; jealous of others and of the air; frightened by the strength of their love; furious with the futility of her as well as his social life and their lack of privacy; insecure; sometimes exhausted; and near despair at her inability, as their crisis approached, to give him peace and to be ordinary, to transfer herself into (using RAF slang) the easy-going, 'Wizard, jolly good show' class.

One answer of course is that the impression given so far is the impression she gave quite naturally, to friends, to company, to people she loved, but was not in love with, and in the letters (that she wrote to Richard), she is in love. The lightening had struck, out of the blue, before she had had time to instal, as she was well able to, a lightening conductor. She becomes, as he is, someone to whom it is all or nothing.

But that is not the only answer. The serenity is still there, deep down, and springing not only from her religious faith. It springs also from brief but unshaken visions of a shared and perfect understanding between them; and also, whenever those visions failed, from a self-discipline which over many years had weaned her from caprice, and given her a truly extraordinary power of detachment, so that she could view their few rows as 'idiotic'; could steel herself, though hating it, to go away for weeks; could treat jealousy lightly; and could consider both herself and him sometimes with amusement and wit, sometimes merely 'with great interest'. It enables her to stand aside and look on them as some god might, who 'had chosen us as the two people most spoilt and in need of character-building, and . . . thrown us together to show us undreamed-of possibilities of happiness and then put in the way just the sort of obstacles most frustrating to our particular natures. Just to see if we could take it, or destroy the gift'; or, 'as though some humorously-minded chemist had thought fit to take two cool still fluids and gently pour them into the same cauldron to watch the result . . .'

From experience she knows the potency of this detachment to destroy; and in their most crucial exchange of all, when she asks him to revert to friendship, to their initial relationship, is amazed and reconciled to find from his reply that he is not only aware of his potency, but possesses it, and is equally scared of it himself. Thus, though she lived from the heart, she had a strongly controlling mind and will, was both romantic and classical; one of those whose light is confined to a small space only among people, an unrecorded place in time, but which is nonetheless both true sunlight and true moonlight, capable in other circumstances of warming and illuminating a great landscape.

I should like readers to imagine her exercising one of the rarest of her rare endowments: listening. Mary with her disillusion about the goodness of human beings way back in the past, long since mastered, and grown tolerant; Richard with his very recent disillusion about their unimportance to him conveniently exploded into a book, but not yet by any means conquered in himself.

Mary and Richard embarked on a short, eventful, tumultuous relationship that ended when he was killed. It is hard to say whether, had he lived, they would have ceased to be lovers or continued together. At one stage, just prior to his return to flying, the love affair had all but come to an end, but, by the time of his death it had found a new high. Either way, I believe they would have remained close friends for many years to come.

They were good for each other. Mary's social life and associates, to which she had come to rely on so heavily over the years, were perfect for Richard at the time. Eventually, they both tired of this lifestyle and yearned to escape; he to the 'crew room' atmosphere of the RAF stations; she to the privacy of a home uncluttered with regular callers from her social set and with time to relax. Both wanted time alone together. Despite being able to move in such a social environment with infinite ease and having many true friends there, the two were not in their true element in what the gossip-writers refer to as London 'society'. They looked to the future together. Later they became desperate to escape to a place of their own and they looked to each other for the means to achieve this. Richard wrote of: 'That appalling London existence', and with irony of 'the Claridge front'.

Having returned to flying, following the period in which his book was published and a time in which he was much feted, he wrote to Mary from RAF Charterhall stating: '. . . my London period sapped my will'.

In response Mary wrote of the same people in the same surroundings:

> I am in a prison of soft hands, so much more difficult to escape from than the barbed wire variety. I have a strange faith in you . . . that you will get me out.

The two admitted they were spoilt, but neither was selfish. Although the attraction was physical the story of Mary and Richard is indeed a wartime love story but they looked to the future together, to a time after the war.

Mary was certainly not one of Richard's many conquests. She remained in control of the relationship and maintained Richard's interest, even if it meant threatening to end their association. She always held something back, and that was necessary in order to maintain his attention; she was the older, experienced woman with the busy social calendar and impressive list of friends whom Richard would enjoy meeting. When out together in public they made an attractive and appealing couple. The young, dashing RAF pilot, scarred as a result of being in combat during the Battle of Britain, and Mary the middle-aged beauty feted by so many of society's males.

*   *   *

On a December evening in 1941 Mary met Richard for the first time when she returned to her third floor flat at 14 Hereford House, Park Street, situated only a few hundred yards from Marble Arch and Knightsbridge Court where Richard's parents lived. As she walked through Hyde Park she noticed that the blackout was not fully drawn in her living room allowing a chink of light to shine out into the night sky. As Vera her housemaid was the only one in and unlikely to be using the living room, she wondered who it was that had decided to pay her a visit.

Dutifully, Vera met Mary at the door and informed her that a young man was waiting to see her and had been there for some time. As recalled in *Mary and Richard*, she entered the living room:

> He lay sprawled out and fast asleep in the largest armchair. From the table behind him the light shone on his fair hair. In RAF uniform, the top button carelessly undone, his legs straddled out before him, he looked oddly alert in spite of his deep sleep. His closed eyes, widely spaced, were without eyelashes. Sparse irregular eyebrows and discoloured skin on a broad intellectual forehead told of terrible burns. Above the wide humorous mouth a small nose tilted with similar humour. His hands, hanging limply over the arms of the chair, bore traces of beauty, despite the fact that the fingers of both were drawn up like the claws of a bird.

Richard slowly opened his eyes and saw Mary, now sitting in a chair opposite, regarding him thoughtfully. He jumped to his feet instantly, feeling somewhat embarrassed at having made himself so at home in a stranger's living room. She noticed how tall and slim he was as he stood before her. Mary laughed at his predicament and smiled, putting him at ease. The look of embarrassment changed to that of 'impish charm'.

They talked for an hour, during which time Richard passed on messages from Merle Oberon. He also spoke of his abortive mission to the US; the kindness and hospitality of those American people whom he spent time with; his book and its imminent publication in the States and acceptence for publication in the UK by Macmillan. He also spoke of having been shot down; of the time spent in hospital; his disabled hands and of the failure of initial attempts to re-establish their use. Mary described the way he spoke to her as having: '. . . a pose of nonchalance, and a slightly aggressive attitude to life', underneath she was aware of 'a sensitivity which must have caused him a degree of mental suffering far beyond the physical torment of those months after his rescue from the sea.'

As he left Richard asked Mary if she would have dinner with him one evening, adding: 'I suppose one can dine in public in London?'

She noticed a look of uncertainty in his eyes and agreed, adding that she badly needed cheering up. As he left, Mary noticed that he cocked his hat at an incredibly rakish angle before departing.

The charm and deliberate display of vulnerability initially gained Mary's sympathy. He was certainly prepared to dine out in public if he so desired, as he had already done long before their meeting. He had spent time socialising in London during his rehabilitation and was out most evenings while in the US. Mary's diary also revealed:

> Behind a facade of great ease of manner there lurked a hint of shyness which revoked any impression he might otherwise have created of over-confidence. Only twice during that first evening did he reveal anything of himself. Once, when he spoke of his reception by our Ministry on the other side, when it came out in short, abrupt sentences, delivered rather aggressively. The hurt has gone deep, I thought. Then again when he left, asking me if I would dine one night. I was about to reply with conventional politeness when I was suddenly aware that his eyes were on my face with an intensity of waiting; waiting for a sign of hesitation in my acceptance.

Mary accepted and their friendship began, during which Richard wrote to her incessantly sending letters and poetry declaring his love. Mary wrote keenly, in response. Three evenings later Richard telephoned Mary and asked to see her: 'I feel incredibly low and confused. May I come round?' He did and duly seated himself in the same armchair.

He wasted no time in confiding in her as to his dilemma. What was he to do with his life next? He had been offered a place on a course at the RAF staff college with the opportunity of a new wartime job, but away from flying. He had to decide if he wished to attend this course and therefore follow this particular avenue. He attended the regular medical boards with the hope that he would eventually be allowed back to operational flying while the country was still at war. He still required more corrective surgery on his face and, more importantly, if he wanted to return to flying, his hands. He was reliant on further surgery on his hands, without it the opportunity of flying again was practically non-exisitent. They were in very poor condition. He could not make up his mind whether to return to East Grinstead immediately or wait until he had completed the course. If there was a chance of getting back to operational flying duties he wanted to make progress in that direction as soon as possible and not waste time on a staff training course with the likelihood of being stuck behind a desk for the rest of the war.

It is clear that while Richard was in this dilemma, had the authorities made it absolutely clear that his operational flying days were over, he might well have accepted this and progressed with a staff job in mind. His strength of character and determination were allowed to dominate those in authority with a weaker disposition. This is with the benefit of hindsight, as others who had perhaps lost their legs or an arm, or had burns to face and hands, like Richard, had successfully returned to flying duties.

Mary found him moody, depressed and frustrated. Regardless of the subject matter he always returned to talk about his position in relation to the war. His original plan had been to fight the war as a fighter pilot and with the war won he planned to write. He had started successfully. Since he had been shot down his plans were in disarray. He had to reassess and make a decision. He loved writing, had belief in his ability, and still saw his future in his talent as a writer. At this time this was his only positive aspiration. But, in the meantime, he still wanted to do more for the war effort as a pilot in the RAF; not from behind a desk. Mary noticed in him a real passion for living, a great spirit mixed with moments of moodiness and self absorption.

Richard remained on leave until the New Year and regularly visited Mary at her flat. She came to look forward to finding him there when she returned from work. According to the mood she found him in: '. . . they would either play a lazy ping-pong with ideas, or start sparring with a ruthlessness which at times reached a white heat of antagonism.'

The existentialist was much in evidence in Mary's company. He bombarded her with questions on a variety of different subjects, pushing for her opinion, in conflict with her reticence. Richard was straightforward and lacking in self-consciousness, which disarmed her completely. Mary found that despite her reticence she began to answer in the same forthright manner. This was all so new to her. Richard flattered her with the intense interest he showed in her and stimulated her with his attitude, humour, and talent for words. They were well matched. Michael Burn wrote:

> Richard liked to tease her and try to goad her out of what he termed the still detachment of her mind, accusing her of not daring to face unpalatable truths, of viewing human beings through pink veils of illusion. He would not rest until he had provoked her out of her calm into furious indignation, as he always succeeded in doing. He would then laugh gleefully, and proceed to take endless pains to charm her back to harmony by being absurdly funny and insisting on taking her out to dance. . . . She was old enough to impart an experience of life he considered of value to him, and not too old for him to enjoy taking her out.

The relationship developed and they grew to know one another so well that the ideal conditions for companionship existed between them '. . . having everything in common mentally, and expecting nothing emotionally'. Since Richard took a healthy interest in sex, he discussed it openly with Mary and with total detachment. He told her that when he was a boy at school, he always took special care when crossing the street because he lived in constant fear of being run over before he had his first experience of sex. Michael Burn wrote:

> With great delicacy and charm, and above all with that lightness of touch which was so characteristic of him, he informed her about all his love affairs, starting at the age of sixteen, and announced that he had never been really in love the whole of his life. 'No one has ever captured my mind, and I've never wanted them to. I want to be free to do the things I have in mind to do. Even during my first affair, with a girl of twenty-two, I wasn't blinded by the romance. I saw things straight. I shall always see things straight.' He laughed when she retorted that the charm of youth, as she had always understood it, was that the young always believed themselves to be totally in love, and she considered what he was saying to be not only sad but hideously cold-blooded. This attitude was altogether too romantic for him.

He spoke of Merle in the warmest of terms and with equal detachment. Mary remarked that he did not speak like a young man in love, to which he replied: 'Oh, I love her. No one could help it.' But then repeated that he was not in love with her, and never had been.

Mary suggested that he was perhaps incapable of falling in love. In reply he claimed that he did not want to fall in love until he was ready for it and that he would resist until he felt it was right. He had been concerned that although he enjoyed a highly sexual relationship with Merle, she may have asked him to marry her, which was highly unlikely. He was determined to gain more experience of life and women before getting married. He also wanted to establish himself in his chosen career before getting married. By this he meant writing. He spoke of the possibility of travelling abroad as a journalist:

> 'I've got to travel', he said, 'I've got to learn, and make a career. I've got to learn

to take care of myself before I can take on the responsibility of someone else.'

Mary offered Richard argument and the advice of an older person. She told him that these things didn't wait on time and that he should be aware that he may be taken unawares. She also wrote that she believed Richard knew what it was like to be in love and that such love would come naturally when he was confronted with something stronger than himself.

He continued to display a cool, steadfast exterior with an air of detachment that threatened to isolate himself from his true feelings. However, this inner belief that Richard possessed could not be shaken by outside influence. This strength was in stark contrast to the sudden loss of confidence that occurred intermittently when confronted with the obstacles in life. It is very unlikely that Richard had not fallen in love with Merle Oberon, but their parting had been inevitable from the start. Their relationship had been intense but casual and when Richard returned to England it was possible that they intended taking up where they left off at some future meeting, making the separation to some extent easier.

* * *

On 8 December 1941 America finally entered the war and on the same day Richard wrote a letter to Mrs Jeanette Lee in Georgetown to thank her for all her help during his stay:

> When I came to you I was practically at the end of my tether . . . I regret so much that I left before the war finally broke out in the Pacific. The American reaction is something I would have given a great deal to see. The let-down feeling after coming from America to this London, now suffering all the inconvenience of war without any of the excitement, is very depressing, and I cannot face going into hospital again . . . I have applied to do some reporting for the RAF in the Middle East.

It is clear that after his awful initial experience in America he derived a great deal of pleasure from his time there.

* * *

On 24 December 1941 Richard wrote to Lovat Dickson from his parents' flat in Sloane Street, in response to his request that Richard should prepare a piece on himself for the front flap of the dust-jacket for his book, but to appear as if written by another:

> Dear Lovat Dickson,
>
> Taking you at your word and casting shame to the winds, I enclose the following blurb which you can cut and minimise to your heart's content:
>
> 'RH is a young man who was still up at Oxford at the outbreak of war. He had hoped eventually to become a foreign correspondent, an ambition which everybody reading this book will have no doubt that he will achieve. This is his first book and with it he has set himself a high standard, but one which he will doubtless maintain. Here is a writer who happened to be a pilot, not a pilot who happened to write a book. It is no mere record of fighting experiences; it tells not only how but why the youth of this country went to war, tracing with an ease and clarity of style that is admirable the transition from a left-wing Oxford egocentricity to a spirit which from August to October last year drove the enemy from these shores.
>
> Starting at Oxford before the war the author takes us through the Battle of Britain and his months in hospital to the final dramatic climax of a blitz on London.
>
> By turns humorous and tragic, it is an essentially human document and the book which everyone knew must come out of the Air Force.'
>
> If you can do better I shall be only too delighted as I have now to go back to hospital until after Christmas when I will get in touch with you again.
>
> Yours sincerely
> Richard Hillary

Very few changes were made by Lovat Dickson and this piece appeared on the front flap of the dust-jacket. It is outrageously conceited in its frankness, but the honesty of his comments is typical of Richard. What actually appeared on the dust-cover was:

> This book not only provides a very vivid narrative of war service in the RAF, but gives a clear picture of how the pilot is affected mentally and spiritually by his adventures. Richard Hillary is a young man who, at the outbreak of war, was still up at Oxford. He had hopes of eventually becoming a foreign correspondent, an ambition which everyone reading this book will have no doubt that he is fitted to achieve. With this, his first book, he has set himself a high standard. It offers evidence that here is a writer who happened to be a pilot; not a pilot who happened to write a book. It is no mere record of fighting experiences; it tells not only how, but why the youth of this country went to war, tracing with an ease and clarity of style that is admirable the transition of a young Englishman from being a left-wing Oxford egocentric to the attainment of that spirit which from August to October of 1940 drove the invader from our shores.
>
> Starting at Oxford before the war, the author takes us through the Battle of Britain and his six months in hospital, to the final dramatic climax of a Blitz on London. By turn humorous and tragic, it is an essentially human document and the book which everyone knew must one day come out of the Air Force.

For the rear flap of the dust-jacket Richard provided the following piece:

> Richard Hillary was born in Sydney, Australia, in 1919. He came to England after the last war with his father, who was in the Australian Treasury. In 1931 he went to Shrewsbury, and in 1937 to Trinity College, Oxford. He was at Oxford when the war broke out and, with other members of the Oxford RAFVR, was immediately called to duty. Since he was shot down in the Battle of Britain, much of his time has been spent in hospital, but he has also been to America on special duties, and it was there that this book was completed. He is now back in active service, though the slow and painful convalescence from the very severe burns he encountered on his last fight means that he is still to return to hospital for further operations and treatment from time to time.

On 27 December 1941 Richard attended a medical board at East Grinstead. His fitness was assessed as being: 'a) Doubtful. b) ? months. Next board: as required.'

Another letter sent to Lovat Dickson from Knightsbridge Court might have been sent from hospital or home. It read:

> Dear Dickson,
>   Herewith the photograph – I imagine it can be copied. The dedication I would like is: For DMW.
>
>   Yours sincerely,
>   Richard Hillary.
>
> P.S. Are we having a plain cover?

The dedication, DMW, stood for Denise Maxwell-Woosnam.

It is interesting to note that Richard drops the 'Lovat' and simply refers to his publisher as 'Dickson', perhaps an attempt to maintain an appropriate level of formality between writer and publisher.

The photograph that he enclosed was the black and white portrait taken in America showing him in civilian clothes. The photograph was 'touched-up' by Macmillan before it was included in the book, in an attempt to reduce the harsh appearance of the scar tissue. Richard was not fully supportive of such a move, since perhaps it carried echoes of his treatment in New York.

A response to Richard's enquiry came in the next mailing when Lovat Dickson enclosed a sample of the dust-jacket.

* * *

On 5 January 1942 Richard attended the RAF staff college at Gerrard's Cross, Buckinghamshire, not far from his parents' rural retreat. He was a pupil on technical training War
Course No.21, on completion of which he was entitled to wear the symbol 'WSA'.

The course had an intense schedule and ran from 08.00 am until 10.00 pm each day,
apparently without a break, Monday to Saturday. It left Richard 'completely exhausted'.
His confidence fluctuated continuously during this period and he was concerned that his
reputation for plain speaking, unconventional views and facetiousness would catch up
with him and counter the image of the scarred Battle of Britain 'ace'. He was also keen
for the publication of his book to occur before the end of the course to, according to
Richard, prevent his companions 'thinking me entirely imbecile'. The real reason for
wanting this was more likely ego related: his adventures would now be in print!

The next letter Richard wrote to his publisher was dated 6 January 1942 and written
on 36 Knightsbridge Court notepaper. It is the day after his course was due to start and
he was in the habit of taking letter writing materials with him when he went away:

> Dear Dickson,
>
> Thank you for the cover – I too like it and I think a more naturalistic
> representation of the bird (an albatross by the way) would be an improvement.
>
> My only criticism is that it is rather similar to the cover of 'Fighter Pilot' but
> perhaps that doesn't matter.
>
> I don't know whether the photograph is my copyright or not. I merely had it
> taken by Talbots in New York and I know that Requal [*sic*] and Hitchcock have
> used it. If you think its good enough I won't bother to have another taken.
>
> The book came out in America on Friday and according to the half dozen
> cables I have had the reviews are excellent, so that is encouraging. It is unfortu-
> nate that they have a different title for otherwise they might have helped the sales.
>
> Sorry I forgot to tell you the address.
>
> > Yours sincerely,
> > Richard Hillary.

The book cover was a pale blue with a bird, its wings spread, appearing at first glance
to be the RAF eagle, which was what the publishers intended. But the neck and beak are
too long and, as Richard notes, it is actually an albatross, a waterbird. There are a
number of diagonal lines running the length of the cover in the same white shade as the
title. *Fighter Pilot* by Paul Richey had a dark blue cover with the RAF wings in the
middle of the cover. Both covers are particularly bland in appearance. The photograph
supplied by Richard, taken by Talbots, was adequate and used by Macmillan.

Mary and Richard wrote incessantly to each other during this period, and at any time
during the relationship when they were separated. They got together at weekends. None
of Mary's letters to Richard during this early uncommitted part of their relationship has
survived, and only three of his from January in which he wrote about the course and
those around him, as well as himself and Mary, who was the overwhelming new interest
in his life. In one letter he wrote of a Squadron Leader 'of fairly new copy' in his billet,
and, as was his trait, he was quick to produce a thumbnail sketch and target his beliefs
for ridicule. Much as he had done with Peter Pease:

> The Squadron Leader gets up at 5.30 and meditates, from time to time putting
> down the odd gin. The Ten Commandments apparently are a good basis, but
> do not go far enough. I protested that they went too far, that Moses was an
> amiable old gentleman putting up a memo to the Almighty with a view to
> getting a spot of order, when that withered old sourpuss Aaron had to go and
> put his oar in. Looking around at the high jinks among the youth and beauty,
> and completely forgetting that he had been young himself once, he was filled
> with terrific self-righteousness and kept pestering Moses to put in a clause or

two against natural inclinations. Finally, as one always does when one is pestered too long, the old man agreed, and the result thousands of years later is people like friend (the Squadron Leader) meditating at crack of dawn on a misconception. He was not convinced and retired to bed, saying that 'Sometimes there were times for plain talking and sometimes there were not,' – a portentous statement, the exact application of which still eludes me. Work continues to pile up, but not enough to make me forget how much I miss you, and look forward to seeing you at the weekend . . . You are very elusive, but I am cantering determinedly behind . . .

Richard and Mary spend the weekend together. On 11 January Richard wrote from staff college to his friend Edward Warburg in New York:

After this staff course I may come out on the Staff in Washington if Bill Thornton (the Air Attaché) will have me. If not, I'm going back to hospital to get medically fit again. I shall fly again. This I think will be possible. I have no intention of taking an office job at the Air Ministry. What do you think of the future of Anglo-American relations now? My view is that above all 'the people are a myth' – that to worry about the Lancashire miner and the Middle Western farmer getting together is a complete waste of time. Why not have two dozen experts who know both countries travelling backwards and forwards to get a united war effort, and half a dozen economists to arrange a post-war system whereby your boys don't grab all the European markets and in your capacity of creditor nation expect us to give you all our trade when we can't afford it? I think we should have a set currency price level and exchange control etc etc etc . . .

Richard wrote that he had been so deep in thought about Mary that he had walked into:

. . . the business end of a sentry's rifle, and was compelled for a moment to focus my mind on worldly things. Do not, darling, I beseech you, pucker your lovely brows at this levity, for it is not what it seems but cloaking lightly the agitated palpitations of a bewildered heart!. . .

Were I Mr Beverly Nichols, and I had any suede shoes, and were there any daffodils, I would now trip lightly outside and dance among them for sheer joy of living. Thwarted by all three factors, I will now content myself with a stoup of port in the Mess, a slightly smug expression being the only visible sign that inwardly I am hugging myself with joyful anticipation. All my love to you.

The excitement of a new relationship, the infatuation, the joy of something so fresh in his life is quite overwhelming. For Mary too, this was something to bring her a new happiness. Here was a young, good-looking man who was attracted to her, someone so different from all the others that had shown interest in her.

In the third and last surviving letter to Mary from this period, dated Wednesday 26 January, Richard looks forward to a weekend away together in the country where they will stay with mutual friends: '. . . more than anything I can remember for years.'

He suggests that he takes advantage of his disfigurement during the train journey: '. . . to pull all manner of hideous faces, so that we may have a compartment to ourselves.'

Unfortunately, there were a number of other guests at the country retreat and Richard had to leave early to return to the staff college on the Sunday afternoon, unhappy at not having had the privacy he had longed for with Mary.

On 2 February, two days after their weekend away, Richard wrote to Mary. In his letter he declared his feelings for her:

My darling,

. . . I suppose it is surprising how little we have said about our feelings for one another, and for me everything happened so naturally it was not necessary.

But Mary, I love you . . . It must be love when one feels suddenly that one is no longer self-sufficient, that someone else is more important, and that it is only when with her that one is happy. For me that in itself is an entirely new experience, and one by which I am still a little bewildered.

What your feelings are, Mary dear, I can only guess. That you should feel just as I do would be too much to hope, for I am not really arrogant enough to assume it. For I know very well there must be several men who, to a greater or lesser extent, fill a place in that very warm heart of yours. But of course, when I write that 'it is too much to hope for', I am only deceiving myself, for I do hope, oh so much, that you should, and once or twice I have almost persuaded myself that it's true.

Richard had continued to write letters to Merle after he had returned to England, although it was during this period, in which he missed female companionship, that he met and fell for Mary. She filled the gap in his life and perhaps he did the same for her, although she did not immediately fall for him. Mary also wanted Richard to let Merle know of their affair, thus confirming that the previous relationship was not going to be rekindled at a later date.

Richard continued:

Oh, Mary, I am doing this so badly, and I know that it is only now that I'm getting to the real crux of the matter.

That is, what you think, which is going to depend finally on how much you care, or whether you believe as I do that this is the most important thing for two people (or rather, specifically for us). For I must admit, although in this instance I think we are clear, even if we were not, I don't think I should be able to stop. For this reason, perhaps oddly, I want to make you happy. Probably you imagine that to be only natural, but I'm afraid that I have always been so selfish that for me it is something quite new.

Richard

Over the next six weeks, until the conclusion of the course at the staff college Richard continued to write to Mary and declare his love for her. He also telephoned her regularly when time did not allow him to write. Later, Richard also had Mary's name and address included, along with that of his father, as next of kin on his service record.

Richard arranged a cocktail party at his parents' flat at Knightsbridge Court, and it was at this function that his parents met Mary for the first time. Their friendship would last for the rest of their lives.

* * *

During the latter part of February 1942 Richard was devastated by the news that his dear friend Colin Pinckney had been killed. In a letter to Mary Booker, dated Sunday 1 March 1942, while still at the staff college, Richard expresses his feelings:

I am writing this just before going to bed and I feel a little sick, for I heard today that Colin Pinckney has been killed flying in Singapore. You do not know him, but you will, and I hope like him, when you read the book. His death makes an apt postscript and it raises in my mind yet again the question which I have put in the book and attempted to answer, of what is the responsibility of the man who is left. I say man and not men, for I am now the last. It is odd that I who always gave least should be the one who remains. Why, I wonder? Do you remember the quotation from which Hans Habe has taken his title? 'A thousand shall fall at thy side, and ten thousand at thy right hand; but it shall not come nigh thee.'

Tomorrow I shall go forward again, but tonight I have my head turned over my shoulder a little. And that is why I come to you, Mary, as I suppose I always shall.

In December 1940 Colin had been posted to 243 Squadron in Singapore. Richard had last seen Colin when he had called by Denise's flat in Eaton Place with the news of his posting. Richard had expressed an overwhelming feeling of foreboding, but failed in his attempt to talk his friend out of going.

Colin saw action during the initial attack on Rangoon by the Japanese in December 1941, where records show he flew Brewster Buffalo F2A-2s W8190 and W8191. It was thought that he made two claims for enemy aircraft destroyed during this time, but this now appears not to be the case.

Colin wrote home after his first engagement with the enemy:

> The Jap Air Force is competent and inefficient at the same time. If we have the strength we can easily deal with them. I was not very lucky myself, as the Japanese fighters picked me as their target and chased me down and round the paddy fields and pagodas for what seemed like half an hour. Fortunately they were damned bad shots. I was not able to be particularly offensive myself. The squadron is doing well, though we don't get the publicity given to the Americans.

On 23 January 1942 he was shot down and killed by 50th Sentai Ki27s while flying Buffalo W8239. In the company of another Buffalo they had been engaged by a large number of enemy fighters. To avoid combat with such a superior force both RAF aircraft dived through the cloud, but when the other friendly aircraft pulled out, its pilot had lost sight of Colin's aircraft and the enemy. A few minutes later he saw something burning on the ground.

Reports from eyewitnesses on the ground state that an aircraft was seen to crash in that locality, but it was so far away that it was impossible to identify it. The only other light thrown on his death was a report that a nurse in a Pegu hospital had seen his body brought in. This report was unconfirmed and Colin's body was never recovered. Army Liaison Officer O.D. Gallagher wrote to Colin's father:

> The New Zealanders in his flight had a great respect and liking for him. You no doubt know of the aptitude Dominion men have to criticise Englishmen (I am South African). Well, I can tell you that the New Zealanders' dealings with 'Pinker' gave them a new idea about the Englishman.

Mr Perrett, a lecturer from Colin's time at Cambridge, offered this insight:

> When, after baling out in the Battle of Britain, he could not use a 12-bore gun, he came down here and stayed with me, desperate to get a tramp through the fen with some sort of gun. He had a 4.10 and with that he managed to get several pheasants, though he could not use one arm.

The award of the DFC was Gazetted on 8 May 1942 and the citation credits Colin with four victories. He actually destroyed four with three probables, two damaged and one destroyed on the ground. Mrs Bingham-Wallace, wife of his fellow pilot, said of him:

> Colin was at our house in Rangoon the day before he was killed, the first rest he had had for weeks, and I recall now how Mummie and I tried to persuade him to take a rest for a few days; he looked so tired, and I feel if only he hadn't been so overworked he would have been here with us today. However, he was greatly admired for his devotion to duty, and I know from experience how greatly he was loved and respected by all his men. All I can say is I hope my small son Colin will grow up as charming as his namesake.

Squadron Leader Brandt, DFC, wrote of Colin:

> I admired above all else his complete sang-froid, and his wonderful self-control even after the most nerve-racking events. I remember so well his casual accounts of the many times he spent fighting off enemy fighters who at the time were so much more manoeuverable than we were, and of the time when a bomb landed not two feet away from his slit trench.
>
> On one occasion I know that he and probably only one other could have been

so successful in fighting off the number of fighters that were attacking him at the time.

It was a great blow to us all when he failed to return from an interception, particularly as we were able to get so few details of his last sortie.

He was a fine leader, and I don't think I can put it better than to say that although I was some years his senior in the RAF, I fully expected him to eventually assume command of the squadron, and I would have been proud to have served under him.

There are memorials to Colin at St Neots, Eton, Trinity College, Cambridge, Hungerford, Charlton-cum-Rushnall, and together with the other Battle of Britain pilots, in Westminster Abbey.

Richard had lost all his closest friends, and could now be perceived as being the last of the Long Haired Boys and the sole survivor of the Triangle of Friendship, but in his eyes he had achieved little in comparison with his dead friends. Colin had been a successful pilot and had received the DFC. Surely the opportunity for a similar achievement was a major factor that drove Richard to return to operational flying, at any cost?

* * *

On 4 February 1942 Richard went before No.1 Central Medical Board in Hammersmith and was assessed as being At BL; still not the A1B which was required in order for him to return to operational flying. He was re-admitted to East Grinstead on 10 April with no prognosis. The next board would be on discharge from East Grinstead.

On 11 February Richard wrote once again to Lovat Dickson regarding the publication of his book. The letter was headed 'RAF Staff College, Gerrard's Cross' and read:

> Dear Dickson,
> Herewith the jacket covers. I am just sending off the final lot of corrected galleys. Have you any idea yet when we shall come out?
>
> Yours sincerely,
> Richard Hillary.

On 7 March he had lunch with Brigadier Charles Haydon, a regular Irish Guards officer, who was then in charge of the Commandos on Lord Louis Mountbatten's staff. The object of the meeting was to 'pick his brains on Air Superiority', for an appreciation he was writing as part of the course at the staff college. The opportunity was no coincidence in that Charles Haydon was Mary Booker's first cousin and another useful contact.

The meeting was beneficial to Richard who was then keen to exploit the possibilities of a staff career before the urge to return to flying overwhelmed him. Haydon took to him and although his injuries would limit his use he considered using Richard who would accompany the raids and, assuming he came back, would then report for the newspapers about them. If such a job was forthcoming, lodgings of his own would be provided in London. The prospect of this job surfaces time after time in his letters to Mary. The possibility of having his own place to which Mary and he could retreat must have offered him some peace of mind from the torment of their 'lack of privacy'. The prospect of writing for a living also motivates Richard and he begins to write more intensely. He had recently been lacking in confidence and was aware of his failings; which were those of most beginners. He had written a little during his holiday to Wales and around this time he finishes a short story and has planned two others; exercises in the macabre that the writer Eric Linklater later persuaded him to drop and stick to 'the straight lines of reality'.

* * *

Of his meeting with Charles Haydon, Richard wrote to Mary:

> I was not feeling too well. I went all peculiar-like once or twice during lunch and,

> on dropping my good host at Whitehall, instead of leaping out, opening doors,
> saluting, and what not, just sat back in a corner, nodding vaguely and feeling very
> sick indeed. Then on the way back [to Knightsbridge Court] I quietly passed out,
> much to the annoyance of the cabby, who had to pick me out at this end.

Back at college he was again unwell the following Monday and wrote to Mary from his
sick-bed:

> . . . this afternoon I began to feel rather ill, and, choosing the top of the stairs to
> have a dizzy fit, came rocketing down to the bottom and twisted my ankle . . .
> I now feel quite well again, and intend to do nothing until I see Archie.

In a letter dated 18th March, Richard apologised to Mary for feeling sick during his
lunch with Brigadier Charles Haydon, and also wrote: 'I have hopes that I shall be able
to hand you the first copy of the book in this country'.

Towards the end of the course he had to decide where he would like to work on the
staff of the RAF. Initially he requested a posting back to the States. It was his intention
to return there, not so much for the friendship of its inhabitants but to establish more
useful contacts for after the war and to collect material for another book. This
application was refused; his commandant stating that he had already been there and that
he should be given more responsibility. His application to travel to the States and train
American pilots was also refused, but this one was on medical grounds. The
commandant at Gerrard's Cross was a great help and sympathetic to Richard's
intentions, but he did not want him to fly again and advised him regarding a career on
the ground. He had suggested a position with Air Staff India or in Command Operations
under Brigadier Charles Haydon. Prior to Richard's meeting with Charles Haydon the
commandant put a good word in for him.

On publication of Richard's book in America, he had received many telegrams of
congratulations from his friends including: Mary and Edward Warburg, Jeanette Lee,
Carola Rothschild and Raymond Hitchcock, who wrote: '. . . initial reviews prominent
and favourable, all auspices promising.'

A short while later his friends in America sent him cuttings from the newspaper
reviews. The *New York Times*, *Sun*, *New Yorker*, *Herald Tribune* and the *Boston Herald*
all sang its praises. It was chosen as Book of the Month, coincidentally alongside his
boyhood inspiration John Steinbeck's *The Moon Is Down*. An abridged version was
produced for the *Reader's Digest*. It was quoted from and highly recommended. Mary
Warburg wrote to Richard:

> All the Australian pilots here have read it. They started by disliking it, then
> couldn't put it down, because it made them so mad, then couldn't put it down
> because they loved it so. It has had the most enormous success . . .

From February through to July, Richard continued to receive letters from America with
such comments as: 'You have what it takes!' and 'I shall try to do something worthy of
the inspiration you have given me.'

And from a member of the teaching staff of a US college:

> . . . It will make an indelible mark on some of the boys in our college who are
> just as smug and self-satisfied as Richard Hillary was . . . before. Keep up your
> writing – today you are worth a dozen pre-war Richard Hillary's.

In a letter to Richard, dated 18 March, Lovat Dickson described the American reviews
as 'admirable'. Such success would also be forthcoming in Britain, but it brought
Richard little peace of mind.

On the same day, using Knightsbridge Court headed notepaper, Richard wrote again
to Lovat Dickson:

> Dear Lovat Dickson,
>   I enclose the American reviews which look as though they may be quite

useful. I shall be at the Staff College until 28th March after which 26 Rutland Court SW3, KEN 3545 will find me. May I have these cuttings back when you have finished with them, please, as I have no others?

When I finish at the Staff College I'm going to Wales for a week and on April 10th I go once again to hospital.

Yours sincerely,
Richard Hillary.

On 29 March 1942, Michael and Edwyna Hillary moved from 36 Knightsbridge Court, Sloane Street to 26 Rutland Court, Rutland Gate. The same day, Richard wrote to aplogise to Miss Levine in New York: '. . . I was extremely upset that for some reason, best known to themselves, the publishers had omitted not only the dedication but also the thanks to various Americans and especially to you and Mr Warburg. I am very upset.'

Miss Levine had typed Richard's manuscript. He also asked her to send on to him a number of items of clothing, including his old dinner jacket and tails he had left behind when he left.

* * *

On Monday 1 August 1942, Squadron Leader George Nelson-Edwards, now commanding 93 Squadron, was instructed to move his squadron to RAF Valley in Anglesey for a week's armament practice camp. During a game of snooker he was surprised to receive a call from an old chum:

> At about midday the Steward interrupted me in the middle of a break to say there was a call for me from Headquarters Fighter Command, Stanmore. This was nothing unusual, Command was continually calling up to ask when we would fly back to Andreas. As I grabbed the receiver, I immediately recognised a familiar voice from the past.
>
> 'Hello Hal, is that you?'
>
> 'Hello, Dick,' I countered, 'how on earth did you track me down here of all places?'
>
> 'Hal, can you come down to Stanmore? I can't explain on the phone. Perhaps you could pop down during your embarkation leave. I've something to discuss with you.'
>
> 'So you've heard we are due for overseas then?'
>
> 'Of course, I've been in on the planning. It won't take up much of your time when you're in town saying your goodbyes.'
>
> 'OK, Dick, but why this 'volte face'?' I asked.
>
> 'Look, Hal, I'll explain it all when I see you. Please accept that I must talk to you before you vanish abroad.'
>
> 'Very well,' I replied. 'I'll call you as soon as I get my leave sorted out.'
>
> 'OK, Hal, see you soon. So long.' He rang off.
>
> My thoughts were working overtime. What in heaven's name did Dick Hillary want to discuss with me? Our relationship had long since gone downhill. Even before we came up to Oxford it was on the decline. Dick had made it perfectly clear that he didn't want to know me, so what for Christ's sake did he want from me now? He had written a brilliant book, had got himself a new set of affluent friends, I wasn't in the same league anymore. It had to be something very important indeed to prompt him to ask me for a hearing.

On 9 August he led the squadron back to the Isle of Man, and in early September they flew to Kingscliffe, a satellite of Wittering, where they became part of 324 Wing in the new Tactical Air Force, as they prepared for an unknown overseas destination. George took ten days embarkation leave from 8 October and caught a train to London to see 'Pan', his wife and ex-Windmill Theatre head show-girl, Pamela Nelson-Edwards (nee Davidson). During this leave, he decided to take Richard up on his invitation:

I was still puzzling over Dick Hillary's strange request, so one morning I took the Underground to Stanmore, arriving at Headquarters Fighter Command around eleven o'clock. I soon found Dick's office, which he was sharing with another Staff Officer, only to be told that he was away on the south coast near Brighton, busy making an air sea rescue film. It was a wasted journey. There was no possible chance of a second trip to Stanmore, I had no idea when, if ever, I would see Dick again.

On the evening of 27 March 1942 the staff course finished and Richard wrote in his diary, expressing a marked change in his emotions and attitude towards a future career:

Today marked the end of a three month course at the RAF Staff College, three months of fairly intensive, and in the main interesting work. True, when asked for comments on the course, I submitted a paper referring to "the mouldy hand of Andover tradition which still appears to have a stranglehold on a College which surely at this moment should have as its aim the production of officers with initiative rather than resignation; with practical ability rather than academic precision", – but in reality I have learnt much and been agreeably surprised at the tolerance of the DS (Directing Staff), for my facetiousness, which from past experience I know to have been often resented. Most of the Air Staff have been down to lecture, and we have had several excellent speakers, but the two best, Hildred of BOAC, and Harris of the TOC, demonstrated that a lifetime in the Service is not conducive to eloquence.

Staff work of some competence is, of course, essential if we are to win the war; and if it is to be one's appalling fate never to fly again, but to use one's brain and be responsible for the lives of others, then I think the course is as good as one could want. But it has proved to me that I can never be a Staff Officer. I am no organiser: but they have made a brave attempt.

I wish to Heaven I knew whether Archie's next operation will make me fit for flying again and whether, if it does, with this course behind me, they will allow me to function again. The Commandant, of course, does not wish me to fly, and asked me in the event of my having to work on the ground, what I should like to do, and what suggestions I had made to DPS at the Air Ministry. I said, 'To return to America,' but he did not agree. He thought that having already been once, what I now needed was responsibility. Air Staff India or Combined Operations here were his suggestions. 'Think it over', he said and passed on. I did: for three hours I walked up and down and thought it over; and I knew he was right. I had thought that this sort of problem was over for me, but I was wrong. When I analysed it I had to admit that enchanted though I am with America and the Americans, and eager as I was to do a real job of work this time, it was the possibility of collecting material for another book, of making contacts for after the war, that really made me plump for America.

Having decided this I felt much better. I should very much like to work under Charles Haydon in Combined Ops., but I fear I should have little to do with his side except from the drudge's point of view. I wonder how many other officers on this course are selecting jobs with an eye for the future. A depressing number, I fear.

On the night of 27/28 March 1942, the same night on which Richard finished his course at the staff college, Michael Burn, later to become Mary's husband, was captured during the Combined Operations raid on St Nazaire.

Michael Clive Burn had fought in the Norwegian campaign in 1940, and was serving as a captain in No.2 Commando when he entered her life. One evening during October 1941, while on leave in London from military training at Speen Bridge, Scotland, he had seen Mary at a London night-club and was impressed by her beauty. The next day he fulfilled an earlier invitation to attend the flat of his commanding officer where, much to his surprise, the door was answered by Mary. They talked for a while, but Mary was unaware of the impression she had had on Captain Burn; he felt that: '. . . she must be far beyond my reach; everyone must be in love with her'.

Shortly after this meeting, before he had a chance to see her again, his leave came to an end and he returned to Scotland to continue training. Two months later Richard was introduced to Mary and their relationship began.

Following his capture at St Nazaire, Michael Burn was kept in a number of camps, and eventually incarcerated as a prisoner of war in Colditz where he remained until the end of the war. While in Colditz he wrote a novel, *Yes, Farewell*, based on life there which was published in 1946. He dedicated the book to Mary and Richard.

On release he tracked Mary down and on 27 March 1947, they were married. In 1953 he published *Poems to Mary*.

* * *

In the days following the official dinner to mark the end of the staff course, Richard went to another celebration at a friend's house before attending a sitting for a portrait by Oswald Birley MC, although Richard was not the subject. The portrait was a posthumous painting of Peter Pease for which Richard provided the body on which the artist could base his work.

I think it is safe to assume that Richard received a far more acceptable report from the college than he had during his earlier flying training. The earlier youthful belligerence had now been replaced by experience both practical and psychological. While he received quite damning reports during his flying training I have found nothing of that nature concerning his time at the staff college. When you consider Richard's background, education and experience, in addition to the fact that he enjoyed the course work, it is evident that he had a very real future as a staff officer, and could have progressed through the ranks to attain a quite senior position, had he wished to. He had the strength of character and determination to get what he wanted. However, in the face of more senior rank and experience, he would have had to learn to obey. Keeping his mouth shut was something that he never got used to.

This diary extract is very revealing and vital in assessing his attitude towards being permanently grounded. At this time, having found the course both interesting and enjoyable, he knew he could put his talents to good use. It had inspired him to find an alternative career. He was actually considering this option rather than returning to flying. Based on this information he was prepared to accept that his injuries were too serious and that he should put all his effort into providing a worthwhile input into the war effort, but from the ground.

A few weeks later Richard included the following passage in a letter to Mary:

> What is the particular quality of the Air Force? I find it hard to analyse. I suppose it is true that before the war, whereas the Army and Navy each had a separate mentality – the result of tradition – the Air Force had none. It still has none, but it has something else which sets its members very distinctly apart from the other Services. To say that it is an ethereal quality is both whimsical and untrue, yet I can think of no better word. It is something, some knowledge, not understood if you like, which can only be born of the combined humility and supreme self-confidence which every combat pilot feels. Perhaps in the end it is this. Any human being lies closer to the unseen than any organisation, but as an organisation the Air Force leaves more scope for the human being as such than any other. And yet if they do feel this thing, it must be unconsciously, for they themselves are strangely disappointing. Too often the theme is sublime, but in the attainment of it something is lacking. Will the time come in the days of peace as Mr Harrison asks 'when they will conquer something more than fear?'

In another letter to Mary written as the course came to an end Richard wrote:

> I made a long speech to Macmillans' production manager today, but it looks as though we cannot hope for publication before the end of April.
>
> I hated so much to leave you this time, and I could not even see you at the

window, so I had to content myself with the hope that I was in your heart –
anyhow for the time it took me to cross the Park.

Are you working very hard with your Warships Week?

Don't please charm too many people, because I shall be jealous, even though
it is only general charm you are dispensing.

I am wondering how you liked the book, and I am hoping that you did, for
your criticism means more to me than all the others, because you are the only
person who can know what she's talking about.

With two weeks' leave between the end of his staff course and a return to East Grinstead
for further surgery, Mary and Richard travelled to North Wales to stay in Tan-y-
Clogwyn, her holiday cottage at Llanfrothen, near the Croesor stream. Mary described
this time together as the 'immortal holiday'. She wrote: '. . . in such happiness as neither
had dreamed possible.'

During this two week period she discovered how different Richard was away from
the pressures of his studies and worries about his future. The couple found total
relaxation together, walking during the day in the splendid rural setting, talking and
planning for the future as they lay by the fireside of the cosy cottage in the evenings after
dark. While lying on the grass watching a light aircraft peform basic aerobatic
manoeuvres in the blue skies overhead the couple described the white rings of vapour
left by the performance as 'Circles of Peace' at a time when war seemed far away. Mary
declared her love for Richard and they were united in their feelings for one another in a
brief, happy, humorous and carefree time in which any concerns were dispelled as they
discovered more about each other. Mary wrote:

> His sensitiveness was greatly increased by his accident, which made him terribly
> conscious of his appearance. He seldom passed a mirror without making a face
> at himself, or without putting his hat at some comic angle to raise a laugh. He was
> terrified of being hurt or made unhappy and put up a strong barrier of
> invulnerability. He would also take great trouble not to hurt others; and if he had
> found that he had offended, would go to great lengths to put the matter right . . .
> No, he was not a good hater, for as soon as an outburst of fury had died down, he
> felt that it was not worth while. [This aspect of his sensitivity was certainly to be
> brought to the fore with the row with Kathleen Dewar.] All the same he never
> forgot and in the case of a wrong done to a friend did not forgive . . . His gay
> spirit and sense of humour enjoyed a ridiculous situation... equally enjoyed a joke
> against himself . . . had an irresistible desire to break up a pompous situation or
> deflate a pompous person . . . sarcastic and ironic, with a keen appreciation of
> intellectual wit, but fully aware that this was not his genre . . . His insatiable love
> of discussion would lead him to turn any gathering into a cauldron. Then
> suddenly he would turn the whole thing into a joke against himself in such a
> disarming way that no one could bear him ill-will. His gift of comedy got him
> into awkward situations, from which he extricated himself with a lightness of
> touch that took away one's breath . . .

Back at his parents' flat in London he wrote in his diary:

> Perfectly glorious holiday . . . rained most of the time, but went for long walks,
> wrote a little, and became very domesticated doing the cooking and fetching
> coals. Returned completely refreshed.

On 6 April Richard was officially posted to No.1 RAF Depot as a supernumerary P.P.
Staff Duties and Air Ministry Operations for further technical training. (On 7 June
however he was still there as a supernumerary.)

In a letter to Mary dated 10 April 1942, the day he was due to re-attend East
Grinstead, he wrote:

> Your very lovely letter arrived this morning, and I have read and re-read it with

a full heart and a deep gratitude that this morning has been granted us.

Those few days in the country, I can say quite honestly, are the happiest I have ever spent. We seem, my darling, so dangerously complementary the one to the other that with each day a separate existence seems more unbearable.

Wales already seems an impossibly lovely dream – waking to hear you singing as you pottered about downstairs, wanting you so badly that at times I felt almost ill; walking with you on the hills, your hair caught by the wind and your face impossibly beautiful; laughing together. . . and the knowledge that for those few enchanted days we would be together and nothing could separate us.

Their mutual happiness peaked at this point and their lives together were never to be as carefree again.

When Richard was re-admitted to the Queen Victoria Hospital he was still hoping that further surgery on his hands would enable him to return to operational flying duties. He therefore put great faith in Archie McIndoe. Richard was also to have work done on his left eyebrow and lower left eyelid.

By early 1942, more than 250 burned airmen had passed through the hospital, and most had come under the care of Archie McIndoe while the others had been treated by other talented surgeons on his team. Many were to remain hospitalised for a considerable time. Regular return visits were also required for the majority, for the remaining years of their lives.

In his first letter to Mary since returning to the Queen Victoria Cottage Hospital he expressed fury against his old antagonist Kathleen Dewar. In the chapter entitled 'The Beauty Shop' Richard, true to form, had written about the hospital but made mention of its shortcomings and was concerned that she might take advantage of her influential friends to have publication of the book stopped in Britain:

> The Maxillo Facial Unit
> Queen Victoria Cottage Hospital
> East Grinstead
>
> 15th April 1942
>
> Darling Mary,
>
> I have just read your letter and I'm on the trolley waiting to go in. It promises to be quite a party except that I have one spot on my nose, so they may not touch that . . .
>
> I'm afraid I'm really worried about [Kathleen] having a copy of the book sent her from America. Pray God it does not arrive before May 1st, because she will do all in her power to stop the publication (in Britain), 'in the name of the Hospital'.
>
> I feel so helpless now. If only I could get hold of Rache Lovat Dickson or a lawyer or something – there is nothing you can do.
>
> I fear I'm being rather silly, but that woman is EVIL.
>
> I love you,
> Richard

Richard managed to charm Kathleen Dewar's secretary into holding back any parcels coming from America (in case they might contain his book) until 1 May. He also thanked Mary for forwarding a letter from Merle Oberon which also contained the press cuttings of the American reviews of *Falling Through Space*.

The post operation recovery was very painful and Richard became depressed at the inactivity and helplessness of his situation, and matters were made worse as the streptococci infection once again infected this latest surgery. When the dressings were removed from his eyes he discovered that McIndoe had provided a fresh graft to the upper eyelid of the left eye, instead of the lower which, as photographs show, was an obvious cause for concern. On 19 April he wrote:

In hospital
In bed
In anger!

My darling,

Your two adorable letters have been the only bright spot for the last few days.

The bug has now spread to my eyebrow graft, where it is doing its work. I suppose I should accept this as all in the game, but I cannot. I know it is due to negligence and the inevitable carelessness which results from too much familiarity with filth. I do not particularly care for myself, but if the eyelid falls off it falls off. I don't expect anyone here to understand that, but its true.

One of Mac's minions asked me if I was not 'browned off'. I said, 'No.' A year ago I should have been very angry to have come in perfectly healthy, to have the wrong eye-lid grafted, and to be presented free with a streptococcus. Now I am resigned and find it fairly humorous. He of course thought I was being sarcastic, which I was, but I meant it. At the time it infuriates me that the patients sit here with a dumb acceptance of things going wrong.

I know Archie does a magnificent job (although even if he didn't, they wouldn't notice), but the wards are full of infection even now.

Humanity is irony from the neck up. I guess that's the first thing you've got to realise, if you want to fight for it. You'll get nothing out of it, and if you don't find virtue being its own reward sufficient, you have to be human enough to be amused by it, otherwise God help you.

As you see, I am in grave danger of returning to my belief in the survival of the fittest. ME, R.H.H., and to Hell with the rest of the snivelling half-witted bums that surround me.

I'm the split personality you think me all right, but it's not the poet that's uppermost.

I'll champion lost causes after this war. I'll write and I'll make people listen, but I'll make damn sure the sponsoring of them takes me to the top.

I was wrong when I wrote in my book that the mass of humanity leaves me cold. It doesn't – it infuriates me.

For example: I know (don't ask me how) that if I could get back to flying, I wouldn't get shot down again. I'd go on knocking Germans out of the sky until I was one of the country's heroes, covered with medals and written to by soft old women. But I wouldn't be doing it for them. I would be doing it for the sheer lust of killing to get something out of myself. It's no good, Mary. I don't want to fool you. I just don't believe what I wrote in that book – sometimes I do. I meant it when I wrote it, but now I don't. It's only when I'm with you that all the tenseness, the anger goes out from me and I'm at peace. And you know, God bless you, how long it sometimes takes you.

Richard's condemnation of the hospital hygiene was not made public by himself or Lovat Dickson in his biography of Richard's life. It is, however, damning in comparison with that which has been written over the years since the war, where the work carried out at the small cottage hospital received nothing but praise.

As we know, Richard was never one to hide his feelings, under any circumstances, and his biting humour and sarcasm comes through in the previous letter. Also, in one paragraph he shows great determination to succeed as a writer after the war; and in the next, a determination to fight again while the war continues, to shoot down more Germans, gain further fame as a fighter pilot and receive medals for his achievements. Perhaps, his enthusiasm for returning for the last reason would have been quelled, had he, not inappropriately, been awarded the DFC for his achievements prior to being shot down. Richard gives the impression of being a man with a great deal of anger bottled up inside; looking for a means of release through writing or fighting. He also expresses doubts about being successful in his attempt to return to operational flying.

His concern that *The Last Enemy* contains personal opinions that he no longer believes to be the case, comes as no surprise. At the time of writing he was a young man with a rapidly evolving personality and character; an existentialist who was always searching for answers that would ultimately affect his beliefs. It took a strong character to admit that his original beliefs had changed.

On Monday 20 April Richard celebrated his 23rd birthday. He wrote to Mary who was due to visit him in hospital on the Wednesday:

> Today and tomorrow will pass for me all too slowly. But on Wednesday I shall
> be happy. Do you really think you can stay over for the night?

Preparation for his book continued with some initial delay caused by the process of censorship by the RAF, but there was further delay as well.

On the 24th, while in hospital at East Grinstead, Richard replied to Daniel Macmillan's letter which informed him that the The Book Society had chosen *The Last Enemy* as their 'book of the month' for June. But to ensure his book would be The Book Society's choice, publication would have to be postponed until that particular month:

> Dear Mr Macmillan,
>   Thank you for your letter of 22nd April. I am naturally delighted that the Book
> Society want the book for June and I certainly agree to the proposal, although I
> am a little disappointed that it will not come out until 19th June.
>
>   Yours sincerely,
>   Richard Hillary.

Richard received further accolades when news spread of The Book Society's decision. Lovat Dickson immediately wrote to offer his congratulations and arranged for Richard to sign 200 copies of his *The Last Enemy* for The Book Society. A number of these were subsequently sent to friends of Richard, at his request.

In another letter to Lovat Dickson, written at East Grinstead, Richard expressed his consternation that the publication date for his book had been put back:

> Dear Rache,
>   Thank you for your note in spite of the bad news. I wonder if you would mind
> very much sending a copy to Mrs Booker at 2A Albion Gate, Hyde Park who
> knows one of the *Evening Standard* staff who is eager to read it.
>   I have had two fingers on my left hand broken and my left eyebrow and eyelid
> grafted. However, I hope to be up and about again within a week. They have not
> bandaged both my eyes so I can still scan the papers every day for the smell of a
> notice.
>
>   Yours ever,
>   Richard.

The letter was signed in pencil. This was the first time that Richard referred to Lovat Dickson in writing by his first name and the 'yours sincerely' was dropped in favour of 'yours ever'.

I believe that Richard has somewhat overstated the surgery on his hand as I can find no medical reason for two of his fingers to be 'broken' as part of the reconstructive procedure. Perhaps he is referring to further work on the tendons in an attempt to straighten out the fingers.

The work on the left eyelid was corrective. After the initial surgery the eye area had become uncomfortable as a result of contraction. The problem associated with the visual and practical aspects of the left eye and eyebrow continued until his death.

During this period at East Grinstead Richard was once again in the company of familiar faces. He was as unpopular as always and annoyed those around him whom he referred to as 'baby boys'. The publication of his book during this period apparently brought little in the way of praise from his fellow patients on the ward, possibly out of envy but more likely as a reaction to his personality. Why offer praise to one whose ego was already so inflated? He knew his book was good. Nevertheless, they couldn't help but be impressed.

* * *

A new friendship developed during this latest visit to East Grinstead. Rosemary Kerr was slightly older than Richard and known to all her friends as Rosie. She was the daughter of Admiral Kerr and, coincidentally, a close friend of Mary Booker. She had been seriously injured in an appalling car accident a few months earlier in which she had sustained horrific injuries. Her face had been smashed and the skull was fractured in seven places. Archie McIndoe had begun the slow job of rebuilding her looks. Initially Rosie had suffered great pain, suspended in traction above the bed, her nose had gone and there was a hook in her mouth. The pain was so great that she wished to die. Mary went to visit her at the hospital on many occasions. Eventually, as Rosie's injuries began to heal and McIndoe's surgical mastery came to fruition, she decided to stay on and join the nursing staff and ultimately became great friends with McIndoe and Richard. Thus developed a 'quadrangle' of friendship between Rosie Kerr, Mary Booker, Archie McIndoe and Richard Hillary.

Rosie's initial introduction to the existence of Richard Hillary was when he telephoned his ex-girlfriend Barbara Dewar at Dutton Homestall, while she was in the company of her mother and Rosie Kerr. In *Mary and Richard*, according to Michael Burn, after the call Barbara left the room and the vindictive Kathleen Dewar described Richard as:

> . . . a picture of an impossibly conceited youth, using the glamour of his injuries and the Battle of Britain to augment his attractions and get on; a picture of someone so scheming and unpleasant that Rosie expected Mephistopheles.

But when Rosie Kerr met Richard for the first time: 'Instead, this rather jolly creature came in.' A deep friendship later blossomed between Rosie and Richard.

Richard spent 25 April with Mary. After travelling back to East Grinstead the next day he wrote to her:

> I hated so much leaving you yesterday, and very nearly changed my mind and missed the train. It was lucky that I didn't, because when I got back my eye was in a pretty bad state, and today I am feeling a bit low. The eyebrow promises to be a great success, however, and the stiches come out of my hand tomorrow, so with any luck I shall be on a few days leave before my next incarceration. If only my eye would heal I could come tomorrow.

Another of Richard's companions at East Grinstead at this time was once again Geoffrey Page. One evening the two discussed the possibility of returning to operational flying. By now Geoffrey had endured eleven operations and he had just returned from a weekend with McIndoe at the surgeon's flat in Chelsea. Page was still smarting from having been told by him that he could forget about a return to flying: 'There are no buts.' McIndoe had said with anger in his voice. 'You've done your stuff, and now the other silly sods can get on with it.' Page later wrote:

> For the first time I realised how deeply he was affected by the useless death and injuries sustained by all the young men.

Later that evening, back in bed at East Grinstead, Page still felt the disappointment of facing the future without operational flying. Earlier, Richard had given him a copy of *The Last Enemy*, and was eager for his opinion. Page recalls:

> He walked over from his bed to mine and put a copy of it on my bed saying:
>   'I've finished my book, Geoffrey, do you want to read it?' I said I would but that it would take a bit of time. Everytime I wanted to turn a page I had to bellow for the nurse!

That evening, after his meeting with McIndoe, Richard stolled over to Page again. *In Shot Down in Flames* Page recalls:

> 'How are you enjoying it?' The words interrupted my train of thought and with difficulty I brought myself back from the incredible thoughts that discharge from the hospital brought to mind.
>
> "Oh, the book!' I glanced at his copy of *The Last Enemy*, lying on the blankets. Hillary had an unconcerned air about him but I knew that my criticism was awaited eagerly.
>
> 'I think it's beautifully written, Richard. In fact I'm surprised a supercilious bastard like you could produce something like this.' Hillary grinned.
>
> 'However, there's just one thing I don't quite understand.' The author was now alert and tense.
>
> 'You write,' I continued, 'of your being an irresponsible, conceited young undergraduate before the war, then, as a result of your wounds you change, and presto, here you are, a different person.' I shook my head before continuing.
>
> 'In my opinion, you're still as bloody conceited as ever.' The grin returned to Hillary's face.
>
> 'Perhaps you're right. Anyway that's the way I felt when I wrote it.' I changed the subject.
>
> 'I'm being discharged from here after my next op.'
>
> 'Lucky man, any plans?'
>
> 'Yes, I have plans. I'm going back on flying duties.' My companion whistled softly in surprise.
>
> 'You too, eh?' It was my turn to be surprised.
>
> 'Don't tell me you're going back flying as well, Richard?'
>
> 'Certainly, but no more of this bloody day fighter nonsense.' I raised my only remaining eyebrow questioningly.
>
> 'Night fighters – that's the answer, my boy.' Richard leaned forward confidently. 'If you get in a dog-fight by day, one's hands might not be able to cope with the lightning speed of the situation. Whereas at night, you creep up behind the target, take your time and shoot the bastard down.'
>
> I was silent for a while, digesting his words. Finally I worked my shoulders around as if to shift a load on my back.
>
> 'I don't think I agree,' I stated thoughtfully. 'You see, Richard, we know the day fighting game and we know how to fly Spitfires. With a night fighter aircraft you've got a much heavier machine to handle and in the darkness –'
>
> Hillary broke in: 'Don't agree!' I did not reply at once and when I did it was on a different tack.
>
> 'Funny you should want to fly again as well. I'm scared stiff at the idea, but I'm even more frightened of what people will say if I don't go back.' Hillary nodded in agreement.
>
> 'I think that sums up my feelings as well.'

This comment is crucial when examing the motivating forces behind Richard's fatal decision to return to flying. Geoffrey Page continued:

> He rose from the bed and pushed back a straggle of long hair from over his ear.
>
> 'There is of course,' he added with a twinkle in his eye, 'the small business of getting passed as fit for flying duties by the RAF medical board.'

At the earliest opportunity the two pilots went to see McIndoe, but received a fierce rebuttal from the surgeon: 'You haven't got a hope in hell of getting back.'

Page persevered: 'I don't see why the medical boys should turn me down. I feel fit and I'm certain my hands will cope with an aeroplane.'

'Not only do I not approve of it, the Air Force won't let it happen,' McIndoe replied. 'How can you expect them to let injured persons like yourselves back into a squadron?

It might have a bad affect on the morale of the other pilots.' [The point Ras Berry had been faced with when Richard visited him at Fairlop.]

'But what about armless and legless types?' said Page.

'Not the same thing,' said McIndoe. 'I'm sorry, it's a cruel thing to say, but I'm pretty certain that's the way the Central Medical Establishment would look at it.'

Geoffrey Page had, however, formed a close friendship with Jill Mullins, McIndoe's assistant. They had been to London together on several occasions for an evening out and their relationship was to blossom. He was also able to confide in her:

> Dismally I told her what Archie had said. She looked at me with those large, sympathetic eyes and put a soothing hand on my arm. The real reason, she told me, was that McIndoe felt that both I and Hillary had done our fair share and that now the fighting should be left to someone else. The story of the Central Medical Establishment's reaction was just an excuse to hide the surgeon's true feelings.

Page passed on this information to Richard and a week later they held a private conference and agreed on a course of action. Page later wrote:

> Although we differed in viewpoint, between the merits of day and night fighters, we were of one accord that Archie McIndoe should be badgered until he gave his support to our ambitions. After weeks of propaganda and nagging, the surgeon finally threw up his hands in mock disgust.
>
> 'If you're determined to kill yourselves, go ahead, only don't blame me.'
>
> Like a couple of happy schoolboys we went off to celebrate.

McIndoe provided each of them with a letter to the president of the Central Medical Establishment, Air Commodore Stanford Cade, who happened to be an old medical friend of the surgeon's, clearing them both for a medical exam by the board.

Geoffrey Page went before a medical board at the headquarters of the RAF Central Medical Establishment, Kelvin House, Cleveland Street, London. Air Commodore Cade made the final decision on the results of the medical findings.

On 15 May 1942 Richard also attended a medical board at Queen Mary's Hospital, RAF Halton, Buckinghamshire. Air Commodore Cade was also presiding and assessed him as being A2hBh; still short of the required A1B for a return to operational flying. This category did, however, provide medical clearance to fly. The following comments were added to his service record: '1) Light aircraft only. 2) Daylight. Return to unit: No prognosis.'

Air Commodore Cade also made the final assessment of Richard after his medical board in November 1942 when he was finally passed fit to fly.

On returning to East Grinstead Geoffrey Page shared his news with Richard: 'I'm back, I'm back! They're letting me fly again!' Richard replied:

'Congratulations. Let us hope they don't kill you off too soon.'

At this time McIndoe remembers Richard as being: '. . . a very unhappy young man.'

He decided to slip away to his parents' home at Rutland Gate. The imminent publication of his book at this time served as a useful distraction from the disappointment of his failure to regain his operational flying category. Whereas his friends were managing to return to operational flying, Richard's highly competitive nature caused him to perceive himself as a failure, at a time when any knock-back was more deeply felt, and he was not prepared to give up the challenge.

A short while after, Geoffrey Page reported for duty with No.3 Anti-Aircraft Co-operation Unit at Cardiff Municipal Airport. Three months later, having proved that he could fly single-engined light aircraft, he appeared before another medical board and was passed A1B, the highest category obtainable, and returned to flying Spitfires, this time at Martlesham Heath. He went on to achieve that which Richard had so desperately sought; further success as a fighter pilot, acclaim for his achievements, appropriate awards and the satisfaction that he had 'done his bit' in the conflict. It begs the question, why wasn't Richard asked to prove himself over a three month period as Page had been required to do? Instead he was sent straight to a night fighter training unit, flying twin-engine aircraft. This point puts the difficulties that Richard had to overcome into perspective.

The date of the next board was initially scheduled for 12 November 1942. However, Richard went before further boards at East Grinstead on 18 June and 6 July 1942 and made further progress when he was classified as At Bt.

* * *

The publication of *The Last Enemy* brought a number of uncomfortable moments for McIndoe. It has been written that the wartime edition of the book included no mention of his name. This was not the case and he wrote about the book in a letter to his wife Adonia in America:

> Hillary's book has just burst upon the public here and has caused me some
> amount of embarrassment. I got an American copy from him and read it the other
> day. No real harm in it but you know what my colleagues are and how they hate
> public references to anyone else.

Richard returned to East Grinstead for further painful reconstructive surgery on his hands. During this time McIndoe was aware that, despite Richard's apparent contentment, he still had one desire left and that was to return to operational flying and damn everybody. At the end of March he wrote in his diary: 'I wish to Heaven I knew whether Archie's next operation will make me fit for flying again, and whether, if it does, they will allow me to function again.'

On this return to hospital he learnt that subsequent visits would be required and in the letter to Mary written on his 23rd birthday he stresses again the urge to return to flying; an intention he had earlier seemed to have dismissed:

> I shall have to come back here if I am to become operationally fit; and even if I
> am finally passed, it will be a good six months before I am back again with a
> Squadron – all rather depressing.

Richard's relationship with Mary was going through a difficult period. As she wrote after their return from holiday together in Wales:

> He went into hospital and difficulties began to appear. Friends had come to share
> my flat, which meant that it was no longer mine.

The friends numbered three, a married couple and a relative of theirs, and were long-time acquaintances of Mary's. They paid rent to stay with her and even when she became aware of the effect it was having on Richard, was loth to let her friends down. The lack of privacy tormented Richard; when he called on her he wanted her to himself and not to have to disguise his true feelings under a subterfuge of friendly banter. Mary wrote:

> Richard had to make up his mind what he was going to do when he left hospital.
> What he needed at that time was to be able to come in and sit by the hour and
> talk, as he had been in the habit of doing. He got such nerves about the lack of
> privacy in the flat, that it amounted to a phobia.

Richard was driven into frenzies over the lack of privacy and for weeks the matter dominated his correspondence to Mary. She would not let Richard stay overnight at her flat, wishing to maintain her sense of discretion. This meant that time together for the couple was difficult to arrange with nowhere private at their disposal. The social and moral objections to their relationship, at this period, were also much more forcible than today and descretion was required, as there were many who would generate gossip, some out of jealousy. Mary's children had also to be protected from any possible over-exposure of their love affair.

Michael and Edwyna Hillary were unperturbed over their son's relationship with a woman so many years his senior. They in no way disapproved and quickly came to love

Mary. After Richard's death they supported each other.

On Mary's birthday in 1958, 16 years later, Michael Hillary wrote to her:

> Many are born, and live and die, without leaving an imprint on the sands of time. You on the other hand are a continuous source of inspiration . . . and a constant paean of thanksgiving goes up for the happy event that brought you into the world.

With Richard in this state of mind a serious confrontation was never far away. Such an argument occurred just prior to a letter he wrote to Mary on 21 May from East Grinstead. Richard had just had the fearful row with Kathleen Dewar during which she had accused him of taking advantage of his situation to get on in life and called him a coward to his face, in front of a number of other patients, including Geoffrey Page. Amongst other things, she had accused him of being afraid to go back and fight; and Richard had lost his temper. However, Kathleen Dewar's outburst of fury may have been as a consequence of her having discovered that during their relationship Richard and her daughter Barbara had used McIndoe's office at East Grinstead in which to spend time alone. This apparently occurred with the maestro's full knowledge, which may have further added to her anger and was perhaps seen by her as a betrayal of all the kindness and hospitality she had shown towards Richard. He telephoned Mary and recounted the incident to her, and then later wrote:

> Tomorrow I come to London until Monday, when I return here for a new arm splint for my hands, then go to Torquay for a fortnight. I will tell you all about the strife and turmoil when I see you, but as always you are right. By losing my temper I put myself in the wrong, and said things which though true were better left unsaid and I should have realised this . . . and kept my sense of humour. [McIndoe had also been present and actually pointed out to Richard that Kathleen had been out of control of herself.]
>
> I felt quite sick afterwards and had to ring you up at once . . . I feel completely drained of vitality and long only to be with you.
>
> There is so much beauty in the world that it seems quite pointless to let oneself be dragged down by pettiness like this. I must not let it happen again . . .

Sadly Richard did let it happen again; this time with Mary.

The effect Kathleen Dewar's comments had on Richard was profound and he became somewhat paranoid that she would attempt to put him down further. The matter aggrieved him right up to his death.

The causes of his aggressiveness towards almost anything included: the untidiness of the man in the bed next to his; pent-up feelings of dissatisfaction with his own lot; the many painful operations; uncertainty about his future, and his bouts of depression and wavering self-confidence. This state of mind eventually wore Mary down during one of his visits to her flat in London, reducing her to tears.

On 27 May 1942 Richard was admitted to the RAF Officers convalescent home in Torquay for a two week period of rest before further surgery, this time to re-establish his lower eyelid in addition to further crucial work on his hands. Richard kept himself pretty much to himself while there and prepared himself for what he called his 'squalid little job' on the staff. He read and wrote a great deal, regardless of his having to wear the aluminium racks on his hands in the continued attempt to straighten out his fingers.

Mary wrote to Richard on the same day he departed for Torquay, apologising for having broken down and showing a lack of understanding as to his true plight. This was the first of the bundle letters which have survived, written by Mary to Richard, and discovered by Michael Burn after her death. According to him the letters show her in moods not at all typical. Richard kept these letters and later, while at RAF Charterhall, he decided to send them back to Mary for safe-keeping. Although Richard was able to physically relax at Torquay he found no peace of mind to the many aspects of life that troubled him at this time. He was unsure what the future held for him. He was agitated by his strength of feelings for Mary and their strong sexual appetites were frustrated by the time they spent apart. Mary wrote:

> Be happy darling in Torquay, and don't worry about anything. Just concentrate
> on getting well. You have been through a difficult and nervy time, but I feel that
> it is all behind you, and with your new job (Combined Operations) you will feel
> happier and more settled in your soul. Apart from this you and I must make a
> perfect life – a world of our own framed in a frame of peace. We have all the
> qualities – dependence with independence; attachment with detachment; together
> yet apart – and with all this we share the gift of laughter, the quick communion
> of the mind and the sudden ecstasy of passion and desire which rises up between
> us and shuts out the world of reason. All this we have and more, and as I write I
> hold my breath not daring to believe it.
>
> Goodnight, my love. I see you sleeping next to that very untidy man, but I will
> put out the light and in the darkness I will hold you close.
>
> I love you,
Mary.

During the coming period the two write incessantly to each other. Their love letters
continue to express and analyse the infatuation and deep feelings they have for each
other; and their determination to overcome all to ensure that their relationship will get
back to its previously ecstatic state. While Mary urges Richard to take full advantage of
this two week post-operative recovery period by the coast, a bout of ill-health continues
to affect her own well-being. It does not, however, curtail her hectic social life, which
concerns Richard in his absense:

> Please, darling, get well too. Don't stay out too late and don't see so many people.
> You see, I pretend to think of your health, but I suppose you think I'm jealous –
> well, you're quite right. I *am*. I love you so much that it hurts.

On the evening of 27 May, Richard had dinner with friends at Shaldon, just north of
Torquay on the south shore of the Teign estuary, whom he had not seen since the start of
hostilities. Sadly, he found he no longer had anything in common with them.

The next day he wrote: 'I feel so helpless all this way from you when you are ill and
I should be by your side to love and cherish you back to health.'

This is the period in which Richard attempted to use a typewriter, with the tender ends
of his right hand protected by what he called 'extensions'. He also wrote to his publisher:

> Dear Rache,
>
> . . . This is my first effort on a typewriter so you must be indulgent with my
> mistakes. I am using two false fingers on my right hand which I can detach when
> I am finished.
>
> I agree with you that the two you have chosen are the best; the others are
> intolerable. I do suggest however that you should ask to have a look at the
> original proofs and see whether the scars are so bad that it is necessary to remove
> every line and all trace of character.
>
> I really only care for one of the two you like; B, the least full-faced of the two.
> I will ask my mother to send them back to you tomorrow – see you on the first.
>
> Yours ever,
Richard.

Chas Frizell, who had been on the same course as Richard at Kinloss, was also
convalescing at Torquay at this time and remembers spending time with him there:

> He had just returned from writing his book in America. He had been sent
> there by the RAF as a sort of ambassador to encourage the lease-lend factory
> workers to 'sling the nuts and bolts a little faster.' These were his exact words. He
> told me that because he had looked so much like a 'gargoyle' his efforts proved
> to be somewhat counter productive, the reaction of the American mothers whom

he addressed was, 'if this is what happens to young men in war, we want no part of it.'

While at Torquay he also told me that he was trying to get back to flying. I had the feeling that he was not really keen on it but wanted to remain in the limelight, perhaps 'ardent for some desperate glory.' In good conscience he could have enjoyed a comfortable Staff job, and I remember advising him against going back to flying. Even at Kinloss, Dicky never gave me the impression that he was really that keen and confident about flying.

I found Chas Frizell's memories raised many interesting points. Did Richard write his book as an alternate means of impressing upon the Americans the importance of their input into the war effort at that time, and was he advised by others? Chas was yet another who advised Richard against a return to flying. He quotes Richard as being 'ardent for some desperate glory', and that, in his opinion, it was not for the love of flying that he contemplated a return to operations but to achieve further success. He had already been accepted on to the staff of the RAF.

* * *

Lovat Dickson sent a copy of *The Last Enemy* to another author who was published by Macmillan. This was Eric Linklater, a Scotsman who was an experienced writer with more than twenty books to his credit. Richard and Eric Linklater would later become good friends for the final period of Richard's short life. In response to the gift of the book Linklater wrote to Lovat Dickson on 2 June:

> I have never thanked you for Hillary's Last Enemy. It is very good indeed; excellent description, an extremely interesting story of a mind in growth and most moving. I read a good part of it in a train, and was much embarrassed when – in a crowded carriage – I found myself weeping. But I think I would have been ashamed of myself if I hadn't wept. Because if one isn't moved by bravery like that, why God damn it, one's mind is as good as dead. Thank you very much; and if Hillary has the normal liking for being congratulated, do tell him how much I have admired a fine peice of work, both literary and otherwise.

Perhaps, as a veteran of the trenches of World War I, Linklater's emotional reaction to *The Last Enemy* was heightened by acts of bravery that he had witnessed personally, and his frank opinion of the book was not one he shared with Richard.

Whilst apart Richard and Mary continued to write of their deep feelings for each other. However, whenever they met things never went according to their plans. While desperate for each other's company when apart, for one reason or another the atmosphere became fraught once they were together. Richard arranged to meet Mary at the party arranged by Lovat Dickson. On 3 June she wrote:

> I wonder why our hours so blissful and so treasured, always turn out not as expected – never as planned in our minds. To begin with you are never in the mood that I had arranged for you to be in . . . As viewed from the point of view of an outsider (very difficult) we are the most extraordinary couple that ever loved. There is no getting away from it, we are both still afraid of being hurt. We seem to watch each other with slightly bristling fur and at the least sign from the other up it goes like a streak of lightning. Too highly sexed to stand the wear and tear of artificial society, I suppose, for in Wales we lost none of the excitement, cut off in paradise from the rest of humanity.

On 4 June Richard wrote another letter to Lovat Dickson headed: RAF Hospital, Torquay:

> Dear Rache,
> Thank you for your very excellent party – I almost succeeded in drinking my cold away.
> I enclose the three letters, and if you will kindly have them addressed and

despatched together with the books I shall feel that I have done (my possible beneficiary) duty in the right quarters.

Do you agree with me that the photographs are colourless and could be improved? I agree about Australian serialisation, thanks very much.

Yours ever,
Richard.

Another, more minor reason for the delay in publication was due to the fact that Richard was intermittently required to return to hospital for further surgery and not, therefore, readily available. Meetings with the publishers at St Martin's Street were infrequent and on one occasion Lovat Dickson bumped into Richard at a party at the magnificent mansion of Woolworth heiress Barbara Hutton in Regent's Park. Richard had attended functions at the house regularly, as many young men and women who were already in the forces or were about to join up, gathered there. This particular party was thrown by Morley Kennerley of the publishers Faber and Faber. He and his wife Jean were living in the house at the time. Faber and Faber were currently an up-and-coming publishers, as opposed to the older established and conservative firm of Macmillan. Richard took this opportunity to exercise his wit in the company of the two publishers, with Lovat Dickson, not without annoyance, bearing the brunt of his cutting humour. He took the opportunity to pretend that the delay in having his book published was due to Macmillan having lost his manuscript, and that amongst the many books that Macmillan published, his own small offering was insignificant. Jean Morley joined forces with Richard to tease Lovat Dickson. Nevertheless, the humour did not hide Richard's genuine concern. Despite his faith in Macmillan he was becoming impatient, and it was not in Richard's character to hide his feelings.

In response to Mary's letter of 3 June Richard wrote on the 5th expressing his reasons for his moodiness at their meetings:

It is true that we still hold back from one another, but for me it is no longer from fear of being hurt, but from an exasperation that amounts at times to frenzy at the people who surround us, kind and amiable, but cutting us as surely through our private life as a plough through a field, inexorably, furrow after furrow, till I feel I must scream.

And then finally we are alone; but by then it is no longer any good. O darling when I have my flat, I'm sure we shall be happy again, free from a thousand pettifogging little worries . . . it will be like falling in love all over again . . .

Darling get well soon and don't hold back from me. I do love you most deeply and hate to see those moments of doubt in your eyes, though often enough it is my fault.

On 14 June Richard went to Adastral House to see his friend Squadron Leader Hector Bolitho. Bolitho served as an intelligence officer throughout the Second World War and was also a writer and edited the *RAF Journal*. He recorded in his diary:

Richard Hillary came to my office this morning, with a copy of his book, *The Last Enemy*, published by Macmillans. He wrote in it, 'For Hector, whose studied imbecility among the bouncing brasshats is so refreshing. Affectionately, Richard'.

The affection has not come without tribulation.

Some six months have passed since I first met him; when Air Vice-Marshal Colyer summoned me to his office one morning, early in January, and said, 'In the next room is a young pilot you can help. He has been badly burned and you may get a shock when you see him and shake his hand'. Then – 'He wishes to write and his first book had already been accepted in America'.

Richard Hillary came into the room and, for a moment, I held his parched, burned fingers in mine. He had been shot down in September 1940 and, for the better part of a year, he had endured continuous skin grafting, and operations, in the hospital at East Grinstead. But his exceptional good looks still shone out, from the mask of grafted skin. When the Air Vice-Marshal told me what to expect, I had steeled myself not to show any sign of surprise and to be all sympathy. But I have never known a mutilated man less in search of pity. All the stimulus and valour came from him – and the will that gave shape to our conversation. He was aggressive and certain of himself, as a writer rather than a warrior.

Richard was justified in protecting himself with all the defences he could muster. From the long months of operations at East Grinstead, he had been sent to Washington, in June 1941, to lecture to the Americans. It had been a sad blunder, for the sight of his wounds and burned skin was not likely to encourage mothers and wives to send their men into the perils of battle. His valour during this time must have been incredible; out of his inward alarm grew the pride that shows now, in his defiant blue eyes. Only another writer can appreciate the fortitude with which he sat at a desk, during this unhappy venture, to finish the book he had begun in his bed at East Grinstead.

I am fond of him, and we have become friends, but we argue frequently, and his frankness is sometimes startling. The second time he came to Adastral House he brought me two articles. 'You can have one of these for the *RAF Journal*,' he said. Then – 'But I want to sell the other one'.

I sent the article to Mr Edward Hulton, by hand, hoping to have good news for Richard as soon as possible. I had described the circumstances to Edward Hulton in a letter, to hasten his decision. Within three hours he telephoned me; he said that he would be delighted to use the article in *World Review*, and pay twelve guineas.

I called Richard immediately, with the encouraging news. All he said was, 'Good! Couldn't you push him up to fifteen?'

As compensation for his long pain, he began to enjoy the first glow of literary success. It was delightful to watch him with a copy of the American edition of his book, or the proofs of the English edition, which was being nursed through Maxmillans [*sic*] by Lovat Dickson, who became his Maecenas from then on.

Richard Hillary has told his story in *The Last Enemy* with such sensitiveness and talent that it would be silly for me to add any more. But I must write of an episode that followed a bristling argument one morning, when he tried to hustle me into an opinion I would not accept. We became quite angry, over our glasses of sherry, and then silent. After a minute or two he said, 'Oh, by the way, I think you ought to dine and meet my publisher. He may be of some help to you'.

The victory was his. When I said, 'Of course,' he answered, 'All right, Claridges tomorrow, at seven-thirty'.

Richard attended another medical board at East Grinstead on 15 June, but made no progress on his previous medical when he was again classified At Bt. He expressed his disappointment during a telephone call to his mother:

They're going to make me an office boy. They refuse to let me fly.

Richard was discharged from the Torquay convalescent facility on 18 June 1942 and granted a period of sick leave from the 19th until the 30th when he returned to London to await a posting to the Air Ministry.

CHAPTER SIXTEEN

THE LAST ENEMY

Richard's book was finally published on 19 June 1942. It was an immediate success and Richard received accolades from friends, family, service colleagues and public alike. He was suddenly inundated with invitations to attend functions all over the country, and was even contacted by the Society for Psychical Research seeking verification and evidence of his experiences when he had 'seen Peter shot down'.

In response to Richard's dedication of the book to: 'DMW', Denise later wrote:

> Did ever a more unworthy person struggle to do justice to a greater compliment. I don't think so.

During a BBC broadcast sometime after the publication of *The Last Enemy*, Sir Desmond MacCarthy said:

> A war book which made a deep impression when it came out and is destined to live. It will, I think, become a classic.

Elizabeth Bowen wrote for *The Tatler*:

> *The Last Enemy* is what I have deliberately called 'literature', because it contains not only the outer story of Mr. Hillary's experiences (as an undergraduate, as a pilot in training, as a pilot in action, as a casualty, as a patient in a hospital for plastic surgery), but the inner story of his adaption to them . . . Every page of *The Last Enemy* shows that he would have been a writer under any circumstances . . . As a self-portrait, it has been executed with a detachment and lack of sentiment so rare that they cannot be admired enough.

From *The Times Literary Supplement*:

> This is a book of war aims in which the act of aiming a Spitfire at the enemy is only incidental; if anyone is still unconvinced that this war is a war of ideas over the secret places of the human spirit, he will find a proof here. Mr. Hillary's enemy is hardly at all the one he met in the air. The last enemy of his title is drawn from 1 Cor. XV. 26, but even that is not a very precise definition. It is not death, but rather the evil of negation of life ingrown in self, which engages Mr. Hillary as he hunts himself through the fortunes of this striking discourse.

From *John O'London's Weekly*:

> A book it would be difficult to overpraise. . . . No more human document has come out of the war.

The novelist Storm Jameson, who had been introduced to Richard by Lovat Dickson, wrote:

> You've written the best book of this or the last war. I've managed a fair share of physical agony in my life, and I've never seen it written about with your – it seems natural – power to make one word or phrase do the work of fifty. I guess now there's nothing you can't look to be able to do in writing.

The letter was described by Richard as 'enchanting' but it was somewhat embarrassing in its humility. In contrast V.S. Pritchett wrote a review which appeared in the *New Statesman*, saying:

> Mr Hillary conveys the impression that he likes the spectacle of himself believing, and not that he believes . . . he remains egocentric, busily self-conscious in defiance and remorse.

A view shared by Richard's colleague and fellow pilot at East Grinstead, Geoffrey Page.

The change in Richard, as expressed in his book, had occurred but not in the manner described. It had been a lengthy, gradual change and he had concocted such an outcome in order to bring the story to a successful conclusion.

He had written his book in order to honour the memory of his friends but at the same time celebrate those in his squadron who had achieved great success: Brian Carbury, Ras Berry and Stapme Stapleton, men he believed were from an inferior social class, but whom he still held in the highest regard. He had written: 'If I could do this thing, if I could tell a little of the lives of these men, I would have justified, at least in some measure, my right to fellowship with my dead, and to the friendship of those with courage and steadfastness who were still living and would go on fighting . . .'

It is a shame that he neglects to mention the efforts of others, such as Jim Morton, John Boulter and Sheep Gilroy who had also achieved success.

In the period since he had been shot down he missed their company. He felt that he had been less of a human being than Peter Pease and less of a combat pilot than Carbury, Stapleton and Berry but in telling their story and becoming famous in the process he had done nothing to endear himself to them. When once he had been accepted by them and had mixed well, now he was away from their environment and comradeship and even perhaps guilty of 'shooting a line'.

After his book was published he wrote in his diary:

> One must write sincere books. One's emotions afterwards may be those of an old tart counting her money the morning after; but at the time one must mean everything one says.

It had originally been Macmillan's intention to produce an initial first edition print of 10,000 copies. But in response to The Book Society making it their choice for 'book of the month', the print number increased to 20,000, causing an inevitable delay. Macmillan, however, only managed to allocate enough paper from their wartime allowance for an initial print of 15,000 copies. Richard's jibe to Lovat Dickson was that this was a ruse because Macmillan had lost the manuscript between printer and binder, therefore requiring it to be printed again. This formed the basis for the humour at the Kennerleys' party with Lovat Dickson the obvious victim. In America *Falling Through Space* was in its fourth edition, bringing the total run to 9,000.

When Richard called at Lovat Dickson's office he expressed an interest in the publishing process and business in general. He talked about his determination to become a writer and outlined a number of themes that he had in mind for when he had the time to commit them to paper. It is interesting that Lovat Dickson advised him not to follow them up, but to write about his experiences. He also thought that to introduce Richard to other writers in the Macmillan 'stable' who were masters of their craft, might well provide guidance. This was at a time when Richard's own lack of self confidence returned. Mary wrote that he longed to romanticise and on such occasions his only help was a streak of sentimentality, which he depised. He wrote:

> I know I am not a great writer. I can write good prose, and I have a certain feeling and some wit, but the feeling is not strong. . . . I am lazy all through. I shall never write anything until I have cured myself of this.

On 19 June Richard wrote a letter to Lovat Dickson confirming that he had written three letters in reply to complaints about some aspects of the book, and was awaiting a response.

Richard received a letter of complaint from one of the nurses at East Grinstead. Being awakened early each morning by Nurse Mary Courtney offering a cup of tea did not agree with him and his unpleasant remarks offended the hard working Irish nurse, and her anger had to be quelled by her superior, Sister Hall. It was agreed that Richard would not receive tea, and therefore not be awakened. In return Nurse Courtney would no longer have to endure outbursts from Richard. Unfortunately, she took offence to Richard's interpretation of these events when published in his book and felt compelled to write to him from the Queen Victoria Hospital, expressing her unhappiness at how the events had been depicted:

> I am still much troubled by the reference in your book to me as part of the hospital staff. If it were merely a personal matter I would be ready to laugh with you at what you term a joke, but many who have read the book have not thought it funny and do read it as a definite reflection on what is to me an honourable profession.
>
> I don't want to be either narrow-minded or tiresome but I must ask you to have the reference deleted from the second printing. Naturally the publishers will have seen to it that all personal references such as this stop short of libel. Nevertheless I consider it detrimental and certainly cannot forego your humour at my expense.
>
> Yours faithfully
> M. Courtney

From his parents' home at 26 Rutland Gate, Richard subsequently wrote to Rache Lovat Dickson at Macmillan, enclosing the letter from Nurse Courtney:

> 9th July 1942
>
> Dear Rache,
>
> I enclose the letter. I have written to the good woman, explaining that no slight was intended and apologising if I have caused her any pain. I have told her that I have requested you to remove the offending passage and that you will write to tell her what action you propose to take.
>
> I suggest changing 'Courtney' to a 'staff nurse' throughout, and merely telling her that the passage will be altered. Do you agree?
>
> Yours sincerely
> Richard

The offending passage was not removed and no changes were made to subsequent editions and reprints.

Richard's personality was certainly likely to upset somebody sooner or later, and this seems to be a case in point.

Only five years had passed since he had returned the copy of John Steinbeck's *Of Mice and Men* to his English teacher, Frank McEachran, at Shrewsbury, and told him that he wanted to become a writer. In the words of Lovat Dickson, in response to the success of *The Last Enemy*:

> . . . he had 'arrived' with this one book, and I was uncommonly proud of him. All his life he had loved discussion and disputation. He had it now, with minds as lively as his and much more experienced.

By this he meant Linklater, Arthur Koestler and the like. Koestler was by now famous for his book *Darkness at Noon*. There is no doubt that Lovat Dickson derived great satisfaction from being in the same company as these three authors from his same stable, listening intently to their various discussions on subjects that fascinated him. As well as admiration, there must have also been a certain amount of envy. All three had talent that he admired, and they all bore the scars, mental and/or physical, of having fought or at least been present in a combat zone. Perhaps he would have liked to have been allowed to fight, survive, and now while sitting in their company, be accepted as one of their number.

By September *The Last Enemy* was in its third print. *Reader's Digest* had also decided to publish an abridged version of the book. Following the publication of the book, Lovat Dickson had arranged for Richard to attend Hatchards bookshop in order to sign copies. Apart from the task he carried out for The Book Society, this was his first book-signing promotion and he was impressed by the number of people who queued for his signature.

On the same day as his book had been published Richard celebrated by having dinner with Denise Maxwell-Woosnam. A misunderstanding between Richard and Mary over the arrangements for that evening culminated in a argument referred to by Mary as having reached a 'climax at Victoria Station'. Unfortunately, she had thought Richard would be dining with her and not Denise. Mary wrote to Richard during the evening after this latest exchange:

> There is no doubt but that we are not only too exaggerated in our individual make-up, but also we are too exaggeratedly alike . . . Both of us are drifting further and further apart in a dense fog of obstinacy born of too much sensitiveness and much too much pride. Ever since that moment of parting I have not been able to think of you as apart from myself, but only of 'us' as one colossally absurd person.

From late June until October the tension in the relationship between Mary and Richard became intolerable. Amongst the many words of affection and longing in his letters to Mary at this time Richard's own mental turmoil, caused by his continuous, almost manic, self-scrutiny appears and he is afraid that through his 'off-handedness' and 'working out of frustrations' he will lose Mary, this despite her 'Oh so sweetness and understanding'. The tension mounts and the inevitable looms – can he continue as things are or does he opt for a 'complete break'?

During the time that they had been together Mary had provided so much support for Richard; through the pain of his many operations, the uncertainty about the future, and the periods of depression and loss of self confidence. She had been there for him to love and feel loved, encourage him to write, to discuss the future. Her spirit, like his, was indomitable but she was far more tolerant and wiser seeing 'humanity as it is, and still loves it'. Now, with their happy times together in Wales seemingly so long ago, she decided that she had to detach herself from what had now become a burden; for the sake of her own well-being.

Michael Burn likened the relationship at this stage to: 'Two high-tension cables endeavouring to touch without exploding.'

Mary and Richard had not enjoyed any great periods of happiness together since their 'escape' to North Wales, and with no real news on the job in Combined Operations, and its accompanying accommodation, their lack of privacy continued to be a discerning factor. Richard still talked of writing but his second spell at East Grinstead became crucial; if the surgery was successful then he would return to operational flying, until then he was frustrated. It seemed to be just a matter of time before either Richard or Mary, or both together, would make a decision to end the relationship. Perhaps if they had been able to meet in the privacy of their own flat the relationship would have been less tumultuous. With Richard's temperament it was doubtful. He seemed to be fazed, or allowed himself to become fazed, by the merest concern. Unfortunately, he had many serious matters to worry about, including the one to decide his immediate working future.

When Richard and Mary met on Sunday 21 June, the tension she felt from Richard, and consequently herself, became intolerable and just three days after the publication of Richard's book Mary decided that despite her deep love for Richard she could stand it no more, and left with a friend to stay in Dorset.

Mrs Dorothy Toye (nicknamed 'Mac' to Mary), a lifelong friend, had earlier extended an invitation to stay at a cottage at Little Woolgarstone near Corfe Castle which was owned by a couple of homosexual professional singers who had divided the last 13 years of their lives between their English country home and America. Mary described them as 'fairies'. They also acted as housekeepers to their guests.

The traditional grey stone cottage with its thatched roof was sub-let by the 'fairies' to Mary's GP, a Hungarian, who had offered the cottage to Mrs Toye as a getaway. It was the ideal location for the two women to escape urban life and many of its attendant problems. Richard became insensed with jealousy when Mary wrote telling of a visit by the heterosexual doctor.

On the morning of 22 June, the ladies left London for a three week stay in the country, 'thinking it might make things easier for him'. Earlier that same morning she received a telegram from Richard and in reply she wrote him two letters.

> I was thinking last night before I went to sleep how, when we first knew each other, we used to talk and discuss everything under the sun. I thought to myself that you had been through an experience from which you needed me or somebody like me to help you to readjust your life. I realise now how far this was from the truth, as it turns out. In reality it seems to me that in your life everything has always gone the way you wanted and that suddenly the path is strewn with thorns, and I, who could give you peace within and happiness and moments of ecstasy all rolled into one, seem to be the cause, at the same time, of those thorns in the path of your happiness.
>
> It is as though the gods had chosen us as the two people most spoilt and in need of character-building, and to have thrown us together to show us undreamed-of possibilities of happiness and then put in the way just the sort of obstacles most frustrating to our particular natures. Just to see if we could take it, or destroy the gift.
>
> And so I am here to gather strength in the thought of you, away from that crazy passion that your presence evokes, and which unfulfilled threatens to destroy the gift. Please write and tell me that you think I am right, as I hate so much being away from you . . .

From his parents' flat on 23 June Richard wrote his reply:

> . . . Somewhere, somehow there must be an answer that is not a frustration or a complete break, but I'm damned if I can see what it is. Anyhow darling, have peace in the sun . . . I feel you beside me all the time you're away, and as when we're together in the flesh we are never alone, this spiritual awareness is really more satisfactory.

Richard continued to call at Mary's flat in case the mail brought confirmation of a job at Combined Operations, but he reported to her that there was 'still no news'.

He was also asked to write an article during this period. The uncertainty about his future role in the war coupled with that of his relationship with Mary and the belief that she had deserted him was driving him to the point of desperation; were Combined Operations going to take him on, or was he going to direct all effort towards a return to flying? In a letter dated 25 June, Richard wrote:

> I miss you most frightfully and am sick to death of everyone. We can of course do nothing until some decision is forthcoming, but at night I have nightmares and wake in a cold sweat. Why do you do this to me? Tomorrow I . . . end my London season chez Colebox (Lady Colefax, hostess and interior designer). A fitting conclusion I feel.
>
> If Combined Operations do finally decide that Hillary is invaluable on the Claridges front, I shall move into the flat at once and never to stir save to come to you . . .

> When I am settled I shan't behave so badly. I love you very dearly. Please bear
> with me.

From this last paragraph it would seem that Richard thinks that Mary is on the brink of
ending the relationship; something that he is unused to. He also had an appointment with
the BBC that same day. As an enthusiastic publicist for his own book, keen to put forward
his own ideas, Richard worked closely with Lovat Dickson over the coming months.

On Thursday 25 June therefore, Richard attended BBC Broadcasting House, Portland
Place, to record an interview conducted by J.W. MacAlpine. It was No.11 in the series
'Meet the People' and was broadcast in the North American Service three days later at
14.00-1415 hours on Sunday the 28th.

The interview recording is 11 minutes 15 seconds long and was, in the main, scripted,
with the occasional ad lib. The talk included details of his time at Shrewsbury and
Oxford and of his combat experiences, but latterly he quotes from his article, published
in the June edition of the *RAF Journal* (No.19), entitled 'The Pilot and Peace'. In the
article given by Richard to Hector Bolitho on 14 June, he attempts to draw a mystical
distinction between pilots and the rest of humanity and highlight the difficulties faced
by RAF pilots in adjusting to a peacetime existence. In the August edition of the *RAF
Journal* (No.21, 8 August 1942), Leonard Taylor, editor of the *Air Training Corps
Gazette*, and a very experienced officer, was critical of the article and very capably
explained away the concerns expressed by Richard as: '. . . merely the age-old problem
of the soldier returning from the wars . . .'.

Richard's voice sounds like that of a much older man.

The BBC Sound Archive maintain a copy of this interview and the subject notes
include the following details:

> **Side 1.** (3 minutes 35 seconds). His early individualism and dislike of
> 'systems' which led him to join the University Air Squadron, hoping to fight the
> war as an individual. In the squadron, one could remain an individual, though
> within a system.
>
> **Side 2.** (3 minutes 33 seconds). Realised it could not be run except by
> 'system'. His personal experience of battle: shot down in sea, blinded and burnt
> and thought death certain.
>
> **Side 3.** (4 minutes 7 seconds). His rescue and recovery; settled down to Staff
> job. Reflection on post-war resettlement of pilots and others – problem of the
> individual and the system will recur. Favours exchange of technicians and pilots
> with other countries.

Extracts from the transcription of the recording read:

> **RH:** . . .but when I left Shrewsbury I went to Trinity College, Oxford, in 1937,
> where I was expected to go on rowing. I didn't particularly object to this at first
> because that was the road that would lead to the Sudan or some other Empire job.
> **JM:** Still following in the system laid down for you eh?
> **RH:** Yes, but as soon as I got to rowing in one of the university shows it seemed
> too much of a good thing, it seemed to demand my entire time and energy.
> **JM:** . . .and you were getting lazy perhaps [laughing].
> **RH:** Yes, possibly [laughing]. I hated having to plan life on a program, you know,
> training all day, no time to myself.
> **RH:** After Munich we knew we'd have to fight in it, and we knew in a sense that
> we had right on our side, but we thought the war could have been avoided but for
> the bungling of incompetent old statesmen. But we had a sort of lack of ability to
> take ourselves seriously, or anyone else.
> **JM:** Still rebelling against system eh?
> **RH:** Yes, I suppose so. I think that's why I joined the University Air Squadron.
> When the war came I wanted to be able to fight it with as little authority and as
> much individuality as possible – you know, individual combat . . . we soon

realised how extremely youthful the idea was that you must break away from the system to realise yourself. The idea that all or any system by its very nature was bad. You see, a squadron couldn't be run without a system and the system couldn't be run without individuals – whether they were Poles, Czechs, bankers or bakers they had to work alone, and yet together, and they had a chance to fulfil themselves and at the same time a sense of corporate responsibility, or to put it another way, we found something to fight for.

JM: What about the flying itself?

RH: Well, I remember my surprise when I shot down my first German – you know, pressing the button and the feeling 'great heavens, it works!'

JM: And how about nerves?

RH: Well you're scared beforehand, all right, you know. It's like the 'before the race feeling' in rowing, and when you're going up before contact with the enemy you feel rather queasy. But you get great satisfaction from seeing the other pilots. You look out and you see Bill on the right and John on the left and so on, and it gives you a feeling of security and then when the fight begins you've no time to be afraid.

JM: I see you were in the Battle of Britain for three months and then you were shot down. I'd like you to tell the Americans that story, Hillary.

RH: Must I really? I'm getting a bit tired of it.

JM: I wish you would.

RH: Well, um, it was like this. It was a bright sunny day, the squadron commander had been warned by the ground controller that at least 80 enemy raiders were approaching very high. We ran into them some miles out to sea, coming straight on for us and they had considerable advantage of height. When we got close to them, we saw they were yellow-nosed Messerschmitt 109s, which were reportedly with crack German squadrons. I should have been extremely grateful for an order to make off rapidly at that moment, but our orders were to break 'em up. In point of fact, they broke us up.

JM: You were outnumbered?

RH: Yes, I'm afraid we were. They came straight down and at odds of ten-to-one it's not surprising. It became quite impossible to keep formation, it was immediately a question of each man for himself. All of us, and we were eight, were attempting to gain height before making an attack. The whole sky was just a mass of twisting machines and tracer bullets. One moment it seemed impossible not to run into about half a dozen planes ahead and the next the sky appeared to be quite clear. I managed to get my sights on one plane, quite close I remember, and I gave him a short burst. At that moment I had the stick knocked out of my hand because, instead of breaking away, I'd hung on and tried to shoot him down. I was hit from dead astern by a cannon shell and the whole machine just went straight up in flames.

JM: And then what?

RH: Well, I remember trying to push the hood back and then I don't remember anything until I found myself falling through the air. I pulled the ripcord of my parachute, completely automatically I suppose, and came down in the sea. I could see that my hands were very badly burned and by the feel of my face I imagined that was too and when I couldn't see my hands anymore I knew I had gone blind.

JM: What chances did you think you had then?

RH: Well, in the time that I was in the sea, I became certain that I was going to die and that nobody had seen me come down, and I thought I might as well hurry things along a bit by letting the air out of my life-jacket. And in point of fact, although I succeeded in doing that I couldn't go down because my parachute was holding me up. I don't think I was particularly afraid of the actual fact of death, the way in which I was to go I was absolutely horrified with, certainly. But it's easy enough to dramatise death afterwards, in point of fact when you're about to die your emotions are lowered as your physical condition – your mind is probably working all right, in fact I'm sure it is but it's working in low gear, you don't really feel what's going on . . . But I'm now resigned to going in to a staff appointment within the next week or so.

JM: That must be a big problem for a fighter pilot, settling down to a quieter job like a staff appointment?

RH: Yes, I'm afraid it will be. I've been thinking a lot about it.

JM: It'll be even a bigger problem after the war, I should think, a problem for all fighter pilots . . .

RH: Well yes that is a problem. They found themselves in one system, in a life, well just about the most exciting life that any schoolboy could dream of. But even suppose they are prepared to accept an existence of bowler hats, rolled umbrella and eight-thirty to town, what sort of office job would they be suited for? They know what it means to live, but will they know how?

JM: I see, it's a sort of a gap between a fighter pilot's life and the humdrum existence of telephones and appointments and things like that?

RH: Yes, exactly, you can see it in most of the pilots I know. Their experience is so specialised and somehow when they meet men with quite different experience they often feel they have nothing to say to them. You see, the pilot has no experience of their world and is usually completely unpolitically minded, and so he likes to get back to the squadron and be among his own people, with their 'slang' and their 'shop' and their action and not words and I think he is probably a disappointment to the people he meets. To some he may seem uneducated, lacking in social graces, limited to words like 'wizard' and 'div' when he wants to express his feelings, you know what I mean.

JM: I'd scarcely say that you are inarticulate Hillary, if I may say.

RH: Well, maybe not. But the problem's still there.

Having fulfilled this contract, Richard was paid four Guineas (half-fee); the balance went to the Air Ministry.

The same day, Richard received a missive from Sammy Stockton, a contemporary from Richard's days at Trinity and fellow oarsman in the College VIII, who reminded Richard that he *hadn't* rowed at Bad Ems during the summer trip of 1939, as implied in the book.

The next day he took the opportunity to escape the city life and travelled to Lady Sylvia Combe's cottage at Lingfield, Surrey. Richard resented the fact that Mary seemed to be adjusting to life without him at her country retreat, although in every letter Mary had expressed her unhappiness at being away from him. Perhaps he sought to make Mary feel uncomfortable by taking a similar break. His companion for the week-long break was Rosie Kerr who was taking a few days to convalesce away from the ward at East Grinstead. At this time Rosie had recently undergone major reconstructive surgery to rebuild her face, and looks.

Richard spent his time at the country retreat answering questions about his book and 'mumbling'; a word he used to describe his conversations with both Denise and Rosie. The couple were a good match and communicated well together. Rosie was nearer Richard's own age than Mary and they had both been patients at East Grinstead on and off for the past two years and shared the same experiences. Rather than feeling distant to Richard's complaints about the hospital Rosie was at one with his cynicism and sympathetic to his moans about the hospital and the staff. She still saw him as that 'rather jolly creature'. There was nothing but friendship between the couple. During the visits after her terrible crash Mary had given Rosie back the will to live and they were to remain devoted to each other. From Yew Tree Cottage at Lingfield, Richard wrote to Mary and the couple continued to write about their respective daily activities, at length. On 26 June he wrote:

Our fate was still undecided today, but Charles [Brigadier Charles Haydon] is pressing for a decision over the week-end. Today they said they 'were going to give the matter their consideration', and I have told Charles that, if by Monday there is no decision, then I go to the Air Ministry and ask what the hell they do want me to do. He agrees . . .

It is almost as if Richard is trying to influence the powers-that-be by saying that unless he is given a role within Combined Ops then he will return to flying, with its inherent dangers, and damn the consequences.

On the 30th Mary wrote to Richard:

. . . since no decision has been reached, and you have to go into hospital anyway, it is really best that we do not just meet once in unsatisfactory circumstances, and then have to separate again. It would just be an agonising strain and fray our nerves to bits again. So as things are it is perhaps best so, and since I feel I cannot be in London without you I would rather stay here, where I am so alone and with you in spirit.

Richard expressed an excessive level of jealousy over the visit to the cottage by its owner (Mary's Hungarian doctor) perhaps made all the more worse by his concern that their relationship was unsalvageable. The next few letters and telephone conversations contain little else but Richard's rantings and Mary trying to reassure him that there is nothing going on between the two of them.

I awoke this morning with the feel that you had gone from me; there was no contact. All the way up in the bus I felt that something was wrong and then I got your letter, I did not like it.

. . . I have to be in hospital this evening . . . I feel sick and alone. I am afraid I am too dependent on you. But I love you. I need you quite horribly.

Before his operation Richard sent Mary a telegram:

WRITE.HOSPITAL STOP A LITTLE HURT AND VERY UNHAPPY BUT I SUPPOSE ITS ALRIGHT LETTER FOLLOWS LOVE RICHARD

Mary had managed to reassure Richard that the visit by the doctor was nothing to be concerned about.

His period of sick leave was extended from 1 July, when he once again went under the knife, until the 20th. This latest operation was Richard's final operation, the outcome of which determined a possible return to flying. On this day Mary wrote a letter to Richard in an attempt to reassure him after his last dour missive:

It is absolute Hell knowing that you are being operated on to-day, and that I do not know how you are, only that you are unhappy and feel yourself alone. I too feel empty and sick at heart. Why should it be like this? I am trying my best to be grown up about this time away, to look upon it as a cure . . . Write and tell me that you are no longer unhappy and no longer feel alone. I will never again go away from you like this. It is too hard, and life seems so terribly short to be thus cut in half.

In the remaining time that the couple had together, Mary was never to leave Richard again in this way; for it was Richard who was to leave to begin his training for night-fighting. It was a time when the same old pangs of loneliness, homesickness and being apart from loved ones would return. Apart from flying, Richard's only outlet was through his contact with Mary, through their love letters.

I cannot help but think that if Mary's suffering was as hard as she makes out in her letters to Richard then why did she tolerate the situation as it was, or was she desperately hoping that this was the only chance of finding a cure; that by the time she returned Richard would have received news of a post at Combined Operations and their new life together would be assured? If not, then surely her only course of action was to end the relationship. Her letters at times seem to indicate a reluctance to return, despite her longing to see him again, for fear of a reoccurrence of what had gone on before.

On 2 July Richard wrote a letter to Mary from his hospital bed at East Grinstead, a first attempt at writing following surgery to his lower left eyelid and hands:

> . . . your Wednesday letter arrived. It made me happy again . . . Stupid, isn't it. But all seemed so unlike you . . . not to tell me, I mean (about Dr T coming to the cottage).
>
> I don't feel very well as I am full of M&B, but I gather from Rosie, who watched it, that the operation was a great success. She tells me that my lower lid lay for about half an hour on my stomach, ere McIndoe seemed to remember it, when he stitched it on again.
>
> I slept all yesterday – knocked cold by Dr Hunter – for apparently on coming back from the theatre I terrified the wits out of the ward sister. She had visions of 'Author of Hospital show-up dies in ward'. For some reason or other I could not get my breath, coughed violently, went purple in the face and caused general alarm and despondency. After getting me on my side and making generous use of the oxygen cylinder, things improved however and anyway here I am. I'm rather sorry I missed it all.
>
> Long letter from H.G. Wells today of which I cannot understand a word – also one from female pacifist shaken by the book. My God I never thought I'd get pushed into a corner with the 'unliteriots'.
>
> Last night I had a series of most peculiar half-waking dreams mostly concerning you. One often has that feeling when one knows one is dreaming and yet remains conscious. Last night the process was reversed. The reality was the dream and consciousness though present was weak – most peculiar [This, I believe, had also been the case when Richard 'saw' Peter Pease die.]

On 3 July Richard wrote to Mary:

> The only lovely dream I had – a dream all heart – was one in which I came to you in hospital. Your eyes were bandaged. I took you in my arms and kissed your lips and told you that my great desire was to make you happy. You turned to me and with your lips against my cheek you murmured, 'Stay by me. Stay by me.' I woke to find the day already there and lay still to recapture the beauty of the dream, but it had gone and I could sleep no more.

Mary and Richard became determined to find 'somewhere of their own'; a basis for their future together. Unfortunately, their lack of success in an age when so many couples under the age of 30 were to spend months and even years on waiting lists for homes was sure to put strain on a relationship. While many gain solace from the fact that sooner or later they will eventually find a home together, Richard remains impatient. His stubbornness to accept the lack of privacy, perhaps at not being able to have Mary to himself was described by her as: '. . . his inability to compromise, even for a time, creating a bitter resentment in him, which threatened to turn on me.'

Perhaps Richard resented the fact that Mary had allowed friends to lodge with her without due consideration. In the process, she was negating the only private place the two could meet. Now there was nowhere. Could it also be that Richard actually believed that time was running out for him and that he wished to spend that which was left alone with Mary.

By the time Mary managed to find them a home, it was too late; the inexorable roller-coaster ride was coming to an end.

* * *

Soon after publication Richard wrote a letter to Macmillan from his parents' flat at Rutland Gate, in response to receipt of the outstanding balance of £25, payable on publication of his book; fifty percent of the advance agreed:

Dear Mr Macmillan,

 Thank you for your letter and the £25 which arrived safely.

 The book has certainly suffered prolonged birth pangs, but not long enough I hope to upset the sales too badly.

Yours sincerely,
Richard Hillary

It was during the period following Richard's discharge from hospital that Lovat Dickson followed up his earlier advice to provide him with guidance for his future writing endeavours, by introducing him to Eric Linklater.

One night the three went out to the Savile Club, in Sackville Street, Piccadilly. After a meal they retired to the roof garden on a midsummer's evening where they sat facing westward over the rooftops to Mayfair. The atmosphere was relaxed and informal. Eric asked Richard to tell him more of the plots for three short stories he was intending to write; one of which he had developed around the time of his trip to Wales with Mary, the other two were still in the early planning stage. To both men the plots were undistinguished exercises in the macabre, but interesting in that they indicated how enthusiastically his mind was searching for originality of form and presentation; he was still so young, however, and lacking the experience that was needed to write on subjects in an authoritative way. His first idea was to tell the story of a jealous child throwing another through the porthole of a ship. The second told of a wife as she watched her husband, whom she hated, about to have a fatal accident which she could see impending, but of which she would not warn him. The third story was even more macabre. It told of a man who frightened himself to death. Lovat Dickson had earlier suggested to Richard that he forget these ideas and stick to writing about his experiences. Eric Linklater sat and listened impassively until Richard had finished, and then set about dissuading him in earnest.

The Last Enemy had been written in an authoritative way. As his life progressed and he gained more experience, Richard would be able to write about more subjects in this manner, but until such times he was advised to continue in the same vein as he had begun, 'the straight lines of reality'.

It would seem that he paid heed to what Eric Linklater had suggested to him, in that he began to contemplate a follow-up to *The Last Enemy* based on his experiences since.

Richard had a number of things in common with Eric Linklater. They were both seriously injured due to wartime action, and they both had an outstanding talent for writing from personal experience. Perhaps Linklater saw in Richard his own youthful enthusiasm of 20 years previously and wanted to offer guidance, based on his own experience, in order for Richard to benefit and follow a successful career.

* * *

Lovat Dickson introduced Richard to other members of literary society whose work he admired including Storm Jameson (later Dr Jameson) president of P.E.N. International Association of Poets, Playwrights, Editors, Essayists and Novelists, from 1939 to 1944, in succession to, among others, H.G. Wells and J.B. Priestley. Storm Jameson was from Whitby in Yorkshire and she became successful after gaining early success as an author with a first-class degree in English at Leeds University. Lovat Dickson had introduced Richard to Elizabeth Bowen, who wrote of Richard's book:

> A remarkable piece of literature. Every page shows that he would have been a writer under any circumstances.

The other successful writer whom Lovat Dickson introduced to Richard at this time was Arthur Koestler. Of Czech and Russian ancestry, Koestler was once described as 'a phenomenon which only the first half of this century could have produced'. Political, scientific and social conditions are now such that no group of situations is likely to recur to give an embryo writer the experience Koestler had during the first 35 years of his life. As Linklater had suggested to Richard, Koestler also wrote about his experiences.

At one time Koestler was vice-president of the Voluntary Euthanasia Society and it was his attitude towards suicide that allowed him later to consider so freely the possibility that Richard's death might have been suicide. Such comments, however, were to cause Richard's friends and relatives a great deal of anger and upset. To this day the suggestion by Koestler that Richard decided to end his life is spurned by Richard's contemporaries and any reference to Koestler is met with disdain.

* * *

On 6 July 1942 Richard was once again classified as AtBt following a medical board at East Grinstead. He was also granted another 14 days' sick leave.

In a letter to Richard, dated 10 July, Patricia Hollander, who had been responsible for introducing him to Lovat Dickson, gave her impression of *The Last Enemy*:

> I preferred to think that the incidents of the children and the dying woman were highly coloured fiction: you as a cross between 'Whistler's Mother' and the canine nurse in Peter Pan was more than I could bear. It seemed more probable that you would have relieved the children of their sweets and/or drunk the woman's brandy. And in spite of this I wept . . . Bless you my lamb and good luck in whatever it is or whoever it is you are going to do now. My fond love – Pat.

* * *

On 13th, Richard was posted to Fighter Command as a supernumerary. He was given the job of re-writing and re-codifying the secret Pilot's Order Book and lodged nearby at the RAF Officers' Mess No.2, The Cedars, Stanmore Common:

> . . . and issuing it as a Command Publication. This entails reading through some 4000 orders, deciding what is obsolete and what is relevant – re-type the whole bloody lot – collect everything under an appropriate heading – to be decided upon by me! and plan, yes plan! the lay-out of the whole thing. The Pilot's Order Book is the thing every pilot has to sign as understanding the rules and regulations that apply locally. And I have to standardise the whole bloody lot. I suppose this is secret, so say nothing. It's certainly secret to me.

From his letters we may deduce that Richard was enjoying himself in that he felt he was doing something useful. Mockingly, but at the same time with affection, he wrote of his immediate superior at Stanmore:

> . . . very charming and a complete Hollywood version of the English silly ass.
> 'Good show, old boy, good show!'
> 'Wizard!'
> 'Terrific, old boy!'
> and so we go on all day. I'm catching the habit myself.

It was while Richard was serving at Bentley Priory that he befriended Wing Commander O.H. 'Dirty' Watkins, who became a close friend and colleague while he was at Fighter Command HQ. After Richard's death, Wing Commander Watkins contributed an obituary on Richard's life, to Air Ministry Bulletin No.8923, which was publicised on the Air Ministry News Service.

While at Bentley Priory, Richard also met the commander-in-chief (C-in-C) of Fighter Command, Air Marshal William Sholto Douglas, who was ultimately responsible for Richard's return to flying.

In a letter to Mary dated 21 July Richard wrote about how he had contrived to get a meeting with Sholto Douglas:

> . . . John Simpson, a friend of mine here in Operations, dined with the C in C, gave him my book to read, and told him that I wanted to go into Combined Operations. SD., after reading it, sent for him and asked to see me when I arrived. I meet him tomorrow at 11 am. He has agreed that in two months time I shall go to Combined Op as a Squadron Leader . . .

Richard's original intention had been to prompt a move to Combined Ops, and not a return to flying, and he greeted the news with scepticism. He had already been kept waiting too long. In a letter to Mary written the next day Richard included no mention of the meeting with Sholto Douglas:

> . . . two months is not too long, assuming always it is only two months. One never knows with these slippy narks.

Tragically, after such a frustrating wait, the post at Combined Ops suddenly ceased to be an option. He had placed so much hope on this particular plan for his future; the official reason Richard was given was that he had been through the RAF staff college and must therefore remain at the disposal of the RAF, although, Richard at first held one particular man to blame. In a letter to Mary written shortly after arriving at RAF Charterhall in November 1942 Richard wrote:

> I must hand it to ---- He has certainly done his work well. This is the worst organised, over-little-Caesared, and most disagreeably-peopled station that you can imagine . . .

A few days later he once again mentioned the officer concerned but softened his view:

> On one point I'm thinking that I have not been quite fair. Old ----. Certainly he did the mischief about Combined Operations, but I really was exaggerating when I suggested that he wanted to write me off. In fact he could not have chosen to send me anywhere else but here . . .

After a seemingly interminable wait, not unusual for those familiar with the ways of the Air Ministry, his career move was gone and with it the chance of having his own flat to which he and Mary could retreat for privacy. He had been so impatient, but also enthusiatic and desperate for a fresh challenge while the war was still being fought. He also saw his plan as a means to salvage his relationship with Mary. Now, in Richard's absence, Mary began to look in earnest for a new home, initially for both of them.

On the same day as he had written to Mary about John Simpson (21 July), and in order to collect information for the Order Book on which he was working, Richard took advantage of his flying category (light aircraft only/daylight) to fly a Vega Gull to RAF Fairlop, the satellite airfield for Hornchurch. Tony Tollemache, who was back flying by this time, accompanied Richard on this trip and was probably a source of support as this was Richard's first attempt at controlling an aircraft with his disabled hands. It was at Fairlop that he met 'Ras' Berry, whom he had not seen for nearly two years, and who was by now a squadron leader and the CO of the multi-national No.81 Squadron taking part in fighter sweeps over Europe. Ras had not seen Richard since he had been burnt and only remembered him as very handsome.

Richard expressed a keenness to meet the pilots in his squadron, but Ras had to make the unpleasant and difficult decision of refusing him in case his terrible scars might have a demoralising effect on certain new members of his flock. He did not actually tell him his reasons but hastily ushered him off to the bar saying: 'Let's get a drink Richard'.

He later reflected on that decision in an interview:

> He was so utterly brave, I have never seen so badly burned a chap anxious to get back in the air again. I had got to know him well at Montrose and at Hornchurch, but when I saw him and what he wanted to do I couldn't give him the help. He was so badly burned around the face and hands I think that one or two of my young lads would have felt it very difficult to stomach that. I could be wrong but I felt that at the time. He didn't take any offence at that. But he was a man of great courage and got night flying again and unfortunately he had a crash and that was that, poor old Dick. He was an outstanding man and certainly very good with the pen. His book, *The Last Enemy*, endeared him in the hearts of the Scottish folk, although he was not a Scot.

Richard wrote of the trip to Fairlop: 'It was great to be up again.'

Richard's work allowed him to fly on more than one occasion during that period. Prior to another flight he telephoned Mary, who happened to be at Beaconsfield with his parents, to inform them that he would be flying over the house shortly and to look out for him. They later waved at him from the garden as he went over. After one of those flights he telephoned Mary to tell her about his adventures and that he had come close to having two accidents. However, his mention of that brush with danger alarmed her and on the same day she wrote:

> My heart fell three feet into space this evening when you said you had almost had two accidents in your plane today – and then to tell me that you had no one to show off to. I have never seen you show off to anyone but yourself, and that you do constantly and get a jolly good kick out of it too. I find it endearing when you have both feet on the ground, but not when you are away from me – not when you are up in the sky. Please promise me not.

Richard was invigorated by the flying, it was a real boost to his morale and he had once again sampled that which he missed, the crew-room atmosphere and camaraderie; as once he had enjoyed the bump-suppers at Oxford, the pub crawls to Limehouse while at East Grinstead, and the drinking sessions with Tony Tollemache. While he felt that his work and that of all at Fighter Command were of importance to the war effort, he was sensing that he could become an active participant in the air war again.

Richard and Mary spent the day together in London on 24 July and in the evening they attended a party. In the absence of her tenants he spent the night and left the next morning, discreetly leaving a note for Mary on the hall table. Richard remained apart from the other guests; they were not the company he sought. He was tired of the company he had been keeping in the period prior to, and after, the publication of his book. He had once again sampled the pleasure of being back with other aircrew at an aerodrome and was now aware that was where his immediate happiness lay:

> . . . it was hard to believe my waking eyes this morning when I saw a letter from you on the hall table [wrote Mary]. So few words, and yet it brought back the man I write my letters to.

On 2 August she wrote: 'I am mad to get something fixed up soon and have an oasis to fly to where I can see you and talk to you in a world that belongs to us.' Once again she finished the letter: 'Think of me darling especially in the air, so that I do not have the feeling of being left behind.'

It is interesting that when Richard was wretched with the lack of privacy just a few months before, it seems that Mary was not prepared to take steps to attempt to improve the situation; only now does she show the enthusiasm to find them a place of their own, at a time when she thinks she will lose Richard's attention to flying.

On boring days Richard wrote to Mary, telling her the words she wanted to hear. On days when he was busy or flying the distraction was too great and Mary was left feeling he no longer needed her. Richard's social life took its toll and in a letter written on 2 August from No.2 Officers' Mess, The Cedars, Stanmore Common he confesses:

> I feel rather depressed to-night. It is my own fault for not being firm about these drinking sessions.
>
> I had lunch with Cavalcanti [the film director, Alberto Cavalcanti] – the meal prepared by his mother, a charming old lady, and what a cook! She spoke French, and I found mine had become very ropey.
>
> Cavalcanti is very anxious to make the picture [*The Last Enemy*] . . . He wants me anyhow to help him make a documentary about Air-Sea Rescue. I don't know whether to ask for the time off or not.

Cavalcanti was indeed keen to make a film of *The Last Enemy*. His colleagues, Richard wrote, thought it too pacifistic and compared it to Journey's End, a play by Sherriff which had exposed the disgrace and comradeship of war through fear, barbarity, and boredom of the trenches in World War I. He wrote to Mary: 'My God, I never thought I should be pushed into a corner with the militarists.'

Mary wrote of Richard after the war: '. . . he hated war more bitterly than any young man I have met.'

Cavalcanti shelved any plans he had to make a film of his book until after the war. Instead, he asked Richard if he would consider helping him with the making of a short film about the Sea Rescue Services. Ealing Studios subsequently wrote to him about it. As Richard's publishers, Macmillan successfully negotiated the rights to the sea rescue script.

* * *

After dinner with Mary on the evening of 4 August, Richard travelled to Cliveden on the river Thames at Taplow in Berkshire, for a weekend with Lord and Lady Astor. In its heyday this great house was the home to three dukes, an earl, a prince and, by 1942, the mega-rich Astors. In more recent times, it was the backdrop to the Profumo scandal. Today it is a hotel, and widely regarded as one of the finest in the United Kingdom.

George Bernard Shaw and his wife were among the guests. In his letter to Mary, Richard wrote:

> America was represented by Bullitt, and a large genial and slightly odorous female by name Miss Bonnet, who took endless flashlight photographs. She has covered every war front and been practically lynched twice. Now she is off to Sweden. The only hope that I could have offered her was to reassure her that she would not be raped. I resisted the temptation . . .

Little appeared in his letter about his meeting with Bernard Shaw which is surprising as Bernard Shaw was present at Henry George's first address in London, sixty years previously. He, like Richard, thought George a great man. Shaw wrote: 'Hearing him had fired me to enlist . . . as a soldier in the Liberative War of Humanity'.

In a letter written by Mary to Richard on Wednesday, 12 August 1942, she mentions that, prior to him telephoning her that evening, he had flown a Spitfire again for the first time in two years. In the same letter she expresses concern at the same problems the two were experiencing with the incompatibility of their lifestyles and their relationship:

> . . . You ask me if it was you, or the state of my life, which got me so down over the weekend.
>
> Between us alone there is nothing but happiness, but the fact that we can never be alone together becomes at times so distorting that I am capable of imagining anything. In this you can help me not at all. You seem to have no power (or is it inclination?) to reassure me at such times. On Friday I put down the receiver on our conversation in sudden despair. A note; a telegram; a postcard just saying – darling don't be silly – would have brought me through the tunnel. Instead you left me in silence and went off gaily to your weekend . ..
>
> I have no sad resignation in my make-up. Automatically my blood turns to stormy petrol, and my heart closes down with the thought that you do not care, and that therefore it is not a thing worth while.

Flying the Spitfire again would indeed be an appropriate progression from flying the Gull and the Master which were training aircraft in which another pilot could be relied upon in the event he couldn't cope. Apart from the mention Mary makes in this letter to Richard there is no evidence that he ever flew the Spitfire again after having been shot down on 3 September 1940, as such a flight would not have been officially authorised and would have only been allowed under the 'old boys agreement'. One would think that the thrill of flying the Spitfire again would have caused him to dismiss the idea of a return to night flying in favour of daylight operations (by now the Mark V was in use but who's to say which mark would have been made available for such a flight). His approach to Sholto Douglas might have been with this in mind.

It was during this time that Sholto Douglas agreed to see Richard again and the outcome of this meeting was that he gave Richard his word that if the board passed him fit to fly he would also sanction his return to operational flying. The challenge was there, before him, and hard to resist over a staff job, which could be used as a last resort if he failed. In 1966 Sholto Douglas published his memoirs *Years of Command* in which he reflects on the opportunity he gave to Richard to return to flying. It is another example of the extraordinary influence Richard held over those around him, regardless of rank, in that 24 years later Sholto Douglas (by then Marshal of the Royal Air Force Lord Douglas of Kirtleside) felt compelled to write two pages about Richard in his memoirs:

> Richard Hillary was typical of the intellectual who becomes a fighter pilot. That in itself sounds formidable enough, because the qualities of both must produce in a man obsessively strong traits of individuality. By the time that he arrived at Bentley Priory, the whole force and expression of Hillary's character had become rather excessively individualistic. It was known that he was exceptionally talented and highly-strung. That was clear enough from a reading of his remarkable book *The Last Enemy*, which had been published only a few months before. He had also been a handsome young man; but by then his face was disfigured with scars, and his hands were like claws. But it was not his physical disability that caused him to have what appeared to many to be a chip on his shoulder. He was much too intelligent for that. I found him charming, forthright, and with a tart sense of humour. My liking for him might have been because I have always preferred that a man should have some bite in his character.
>
> In Hillary's case there was some inner devil goading him on which none of us could really quite understand. He never spoke about it, but the result of that goading was to be seen in his manner. From the moment that he arrived at my Headquarters he started nagging at everybody about being allowed to return to operational flying. He had been through a hard and trying time, and many people went out of their way to help him; but Hillary simply could not reconcile himself to having to stay on the ground. He spoke to me several times about getting back to flying, and each time I told him that I simply could not recommend it. But he kept pestering me, and in the end I gave in with a rather foolish suggestion.
>
> 'If you can get the doctors to pass you,' I told him, 'you can go back on ops.'
>
> I said that because I felt quite certain that the doctors would never pass him fit for any sort of operational flying. But I had not counted on Hillary's pertinacity and persuasiveness; and one day he appeared in my office triumphantly waving a favourable medical report, and he called upon me to live up to my promise. I felt in honour bound to keep that promise even though I believed that, for all that the doctors might say, he was not fit for operational flying. But I did tell him that I considered that it would be impossible for him to go back to single-seater day fighters, and that instead he should go to an Operational Training Unit with a view to becoming a night fighter pilot, in which the flying was not as rough and tumble as it was in the day fighters.
>
> My proposal was accepted gratefully enough, although I sensed that Hillary was a little disappointed, and he went off to a night Operational Training Unit, with plans at the back of his mind about possibly joining Max Aitken's squadron. I heard nothing more until there came the news of his death in a crash at night early in 1943. I had only just left Fighter Command when it happened, and I was on my way overseas.
>
> There have been many times when, in thinking about what happened, I have reproached myself for having allowed Richard Hillary to win me over. I should never have made him that promise. Perhaps in doing what he did he found something of whatever it was that he was looking for. But there was an additional feature about his death that has always troubled me. There has never been a full explanation of the reason for the crash in which this talented young man died.

That was sad enough; but in it the young navigator who was training with Hillary was also killed. That adds to my own feeling of regret about having allowed Hillary, through a rash promise on my part, to have his own way.

It is interesting to consider that Richard seemed to express disappointment at Sholto Douglas' recommendation that he could go back to flying, but on twin-engined night fighters, as we were led to believe this is what he intended to do. Perhaps, by now, his intentions had changed and he had approached the C-in-C with a return to a Spitfire squadron in mind, as Geoffrey Page had done.

Owing to her busy social life Mary referred to her lack time to herself or alone with Richard as 'cluttering'. During one of these engagements Mary dined with Admiral Godfrey and a well-known writer. Later, an American journalist arrived with a number of other friends and insisted they should all sit on the floor and play a game with matchboxes. The conversation became 'so incredibly silly' Mary rose to leave and the writer also took the opportunity to escape and escorted Mary home. On the way home he said of Richard, 'I like that one'.

On 19 August Richard wrote to Daniel Macmillan:

> Dear Mr Macmillan,
>   Thank you for your letter and the very welcome cheque. I am indeed glad that the book is going well, and am doing my best to respond to Lovat Dickson's urgings by producing another.
>   Yours sincerely,
>   Richard Hillary

Richard summarised his idea for a follow-up to *The Last Enemy* to the novelist Charles Morgan. The title Richard had chosen was *Dispersal Point* and Morgan liked the idea. He mentions to Mary that he is making progress with a number of short stories, those which Linklater had recommended he abandon. However, it would seem that all these ideas were never put down on paper and remained in his head up until his death.

On 1 September he confessed:

> I am in a black depression and must make some decision what I am going to do very shortly. I haven't written anything for a year.

The fact of the matter was that Richard was not unhappy working on the staff, doing something contributory to the war effort; but while the war was still being fought there was the underlying urge to return to action. Whether it was as a result of the row with Kathleen Dewar in conjunction with a number of other reasons is not known for sure, but it must have been contributory. Although Richard could gain satisfaction from his work at Fighter Command and with furthering his writing career, he still wanted to play a part in actually fighting the war. He wanted to get back to flying, not because he loved flying, but because he wanted to justify his survival in the air battle over Britain in which most of his friends had perished; to justify the fame he had gained as an author; to dispel his feelings of being a bit of a 'sham'.

By mid-August Richard was pre-occupied with work and his extra-curricular attempts to return to flying; the subject of anecdotes from those that knew him at HQ Fighter Command. The relationship between Richard and Mary was stagnant and rather than the continuous declaration of affection for one another the letters were full of more practical matters, in particular the hunt for accommodation. His quest to fly again was now very much on a personal level. Instead of relying on others he persevered alone. Two years down the road from the time he had singularly decided to join the RAF as a fighter pilot where he would be:

> . . . as free from outside interference as possible (and have) total responsibility for his own fate. One either kills or is killed, and it's damned exciting.

The excitement of that period was long over; he had not been killed, but, contrary to his declaration, he had been maimed. Now he was once again in the position of determining his immediate future in the war. He had to overcome the medical board but with the promise from Sholto Douglas he was fortified and even in the event of further failure he would at least be able to move on knowing he had exhausted all avenues and could not be accused of not trying.

On 24 August, a further unease burdened Mary. Merle Oberon returned from America.

Prior to his departure from America, according to Richard, he had meant to end the relationship, but had not. Mary worked herself into quite a nervous state in anticipation of the effect Merle would have on Richard if the two were to meet again. On the same day as Merle arrived in the UK Mary wrote to Richard:

> . . . just at this moment I need your presence more than I have ever needed anybody or anything in my life. It was only when the telephone bell rang that I realised fully the tension of nerves and the sickness of heart that had hung like a cloud over my day.
>
> With the circumstances reversed, you would have felt rather rocky about me!
>
> Darling please don't go away from me. It makes me feel so terribly sad. You think I don't care enough about all this. I hate it more than you could possibly imagine . . .

Mary also expressed concern that Richard had previously intimated that he would not necessarily take the earliest opportunity to inform Merle that their affair was at an end and that he and Mary were now having a relationship, simply because Merle was of a more tempestuous nature and Mary would be able to cope better emotionally with the situation as it was. Richard acted in this way out of weakness and while he treated the matter light-heartedly, Mary found the situation very unpleasant.

Merle was now over here as part of an entertainment troupe organised to perform on behalf of the British and American armed forces in Britain. She had told her friend Patricia Morison, a singer and actress in the troupe, that she: '. . . would be leaving for the whole weekend [28-30 August], that she wanted to give him [Richard] two days and nights of complete happiness.'

Richard's letters to Mary indicated that things turned out to the contrary, although he was hardly likely to tell her the true course of events if they had been as Merle had intended.

Neither Richard nor Mary had told Merle of their affair, and so it was simply a question of Richard seeing Merle to let her know that there would be no question of their resuming their relationship.

Knowing of his intentions to see Merle again, Mary took herself away to Tan-y-clogwyn, her cottage in North Wales. It must have been quite harrowing for her knowing Richard was with her close friend and his former lover.

On 29 August, she wrote:

> . . . This coming here without you just now is playing strange tricks with time and memory. I find you here in the cottage; I hear your voice and in spite of the blazing sunshine I expect to see you come in at the gate in that absurd black sou'wester . . . and yet you are missing all the time, and with the need of you I no longer have the content which before has never failed me. It is nearly five months since we came here together. Yet with the charm of every detail imprinted on my memory it seems like yesterday.

On her return to London his letter was waiting, but it told of a series of events that was clearly in contrast with that told by the biographers of Merle Oberon. According to them, Patricia Morison recalled that Richard was given 'two days and nights of bliss'. If we believe Merle's declaration to Patricia Morison and that happened, then Richard presents a much different version of events to Mary, perhaps because, as things turned out, he was able to establish beyond any doubt that his relationship with Merle Oberon was over, although they remained good friends. On 1 September from No.2 Mess, The Cedars, Stanmore he wrote:

As you know, Merle wanted me to dine with her on Sunday, but seeing very little future in it, I determined to ring her up from here, saying that I was in Peterborough and would not be back.

I had meanwhile however written to her and explained fairly clearly that I felt we should really call it a day. I did this as nicely as I could, and she rang me up yesterday to say that she quite understood, and to thank me for the letter. She was very good about it. I think now we will find that everything is settled.

Could it be that Richard concocted this letter in order to hide what really happened? He knew that anything other than this explanation would be unsatisfactory to Mary.

What should be considered is that Merle Oberon's biographers also refer to a meal she had with Richard before dashing off for their weekend together and this meeting was witnessed by Patricia Morison. To believe this version of events would make Richard's story a fabrication and, if so, it is a wonder that Mary didn't find out the truth, particularly as Mary and Merle met on numerous occasions during her brief stay in London and continued to write to each other for some year's after Richard's death.

Prior to the weekend with Richard, Merle had said to Patricia Morison: 'I have an appointment with someone. I want you to meet him.' Her biographers wrote:

They went together to an inn, an ancient structure with low ceilings where a crowd of servicemen were drinking. They waited at a table; suddenly, Merle glanced up and saw a tall figure in Air Force uniform appear in the doorway. It was Richard Hillary.

Theirs was a joyous reunion. Patricia Morison said:

'I'm afraid I may have shown my shock at his appearance. There was no face. The hands were twisted into claws. But the voice was magnetic and irresistible and the physique was big and impressive. Something came through the horrifying twisted flesh: a quality of warmth and fineness of character. Merle greeted him with incredible tenderness.'

All through lunch at the inn, Merle was exquisitely sensitive, pretending she didn't notice Hillary's desperate efforts to cope with a knife and fork.

It was during a brief interval when Richard left the room, that Merle told Pat that she and Richard would be leaving for the weekend and she wanted to give him two days and nights of complete happiness. Patricia Morison continued:

When Merle returned from the weekend, it was obvious that she had achieved her purpose. But Hillary was in love with another woman, an English girl named Mary Booker, and he could not commit himself to Merle; nor, as Korda's wife, could she commit herself to him. Their romance was doomed; there could be no chance of permanence and it is not entirely certain whether, had they been free, they would have entered into a long-term relationship. They were restless spirits both: it was part of their empathy that they had this wildness in common.

If we are to believe this version of events then Richard lied to Mary. He did finish the affair, but only after one last fling. Richard's version would have been intended to soften the blow for Mary, but his actions would still have been deplorable. Richard was to see more of Merle at social gatherings before she returned to America.

Richard mentioned to Mary, early in their relationship, that Merle might want to marry him. There is no evidence to suggest that Merle had any intention of marrying Richard, although her own marriage was all but over by this time.

* * *

On Wednesday 2 September 1942 Mary dined with Richard. This was their first meeting after her trip to North Wales and Richard's possible liaison with Merle.

In a letter to Mary written on 5 September from the mess at Stanmore, after they had had lunch together, Richard explains that he had been trying to regain his fitness:

> This evening I played squash and in doing so discovered the real reason for my
> inability to concentrate on anything. It is simply that I am completely out of
> condition. After two games I had to sit down, I felt so sick.

Another experience that Richard had found disheartening. As a result of his injuries, the
confinement, and the effect of the medication, particularly the anaesthetic given prior to
the many operations, his condition had obviously suffered since those days during which
he strove to make the Oxford First VIII.

With his posting at Fighter Command HQ nearing the end he offered hope to Mary
that he might be permanently in London: '. . . and then you will be able to come and give
me inspiration.'

By 10 September his request for temporary release from the RAF in order to assist
with the making of the sea rescue documentary was confirmed, and he awaited the
arrival of a replacement:

> Then darling we may really be together, and I will spoil you as badly as you
> spoiled me. But you it cannot hurt; me, it has nearly ruined.

Richard once again blamed Mary and never lived up to his promises to her once he was
in her company.

During August and September Richard and Mary met on only a dozen occasions and
those closest to him, including Mary, were left unaware of his ongoing efforts to return
to flying; those that his decision could hurt the most. Mary's busy 'cluttered' life
continued to keep her occupied. In the main almost every evening was spent with those
dearest to her: her mother, who lived just outside London, her new grandchild, old
friends, Dorothy Toye, Rosie Kerr, Gerry Morel, who had been dropped in France and
returned terribly injured, Mary's Hungarian doctor, her school friend Kitty Bruce,
Edward Hulton, David or Michael Astor, and the Director of Naval Intelligence. A new
name entered her life: F.G. Miles FRAeS, the former pilot and now aircraft designer and
manufacturer to which he gave his name, was to later find Mary employment in his
company. Miles' wife was Mrs M.F.M. 'Blossom' Miles née Robertson, daughter of the
actor Sir Johnston Forbes Robertson. She had gained a degree in aerodynamics and
eloped with Miles. One other friend that has to be mentioned is the Reverend Monsignor
John Gabriel Vance MA, DPhil, who was Mary's friend and spiritual counsellor. They
spent many hours in pleasant discussion as she had done with Richard, but this
conversation was on a different plain. It was with him that she prepared for a return to
life alone, back in solitude.

* * *

By September *The Last Enemy* had been reprinted three times. Boots the Chemist, who, in
those days, ran a large circulating library, had taken 1,000 copies of *The Last Enemy*,
which was a record for a first book. It was emerging as a classic of the war, even though
a number of other Battle of Britain survivors had also written and had their own stories
published. While these books were full of hard-hitting action, drama and excitement in
which the reader was introduced to the true nature of their bravery and sacrifice, Richard's
book told more of the build-up to the battle and the period after. He introduced the reader
to his friends and, one by one, they were killed, leaving just himself to tell of his agony
and recrimination at being the only survivor. Like so many other aircrew and civilians he
suffered the now recognised 'survivor syndrome': 'Why have I been saved?' This was
what made it stand out.

* * *

The success of his book initially gratified him, but as time went by his friends noticed
that he was withdrawing into himself more and more. His feelings of pride and
satisfaction at the overwhelming demand for his book were tempered by his memories
of his dead friends. He was continually depressed by the thought that he had done so

little in comparison, yet he was now reaping the benefits of telling of his, and their, part in the Battle. Why had it been he that had survived to record their epitaph and make a lot of money when he believed he had done so little? He wanted to do more, to achieve a greater affinity with the public for his combat achievements as a fighter pilot, thus justifying his present status.

The facts show, however, that Richard shot down more enemy aircraft than all but one of his closest friends. Only Noel Agazarian was to shoot down a greater number of enemy aircraft, but he achieved a total of seven over a much longer period on operations. Richard shot down five enemy aircraft, with three more probables, in just 11 patrols with a total flying time of sixteen and a half hours.

Once again, Richard was going through a period of self-doubt. Had he been something of a fraud in telling the story when the others were no longer around to question and thereby confirm that which he had written as being the truth? If he truly felt this way, then surely that should be construed as guilt? He knew that some of what he had written had been invented by himself while other true events were twisted and dissected for maximum impact to the readership. He may well have invented and changed even more, but it is now almost impossible to confirm this. His deep feelings for Peter Pease, Colin Pinckney and Noel Agazarian were genuine and mutual. There is no doubt that the loss of all of his fellow 603 Squadron pilots was deeply felt, but the loss of these closer friends caused a deeper emotional upset. Richard had decided to tell his story and the sacrifice made by his contemporaries. With this purpose now at a close, the story was being read by many who were in awe of his courage and determination, and perhaps even his ideals. The effect is still great on the readership to this day; one cannot help but feel admiration for all that he went through. But to Richard it is clear that it was the others who deserved the praise, those that were dead and those that were in his squadron and still fighting, and not he.

While his squadron continued to fight, the conflict never left his mind and he wrestled with the decision that had to be made, to return to fight, or to remain on the staff and to write after the war. The latter would not give him peace of mind and he was faced with the possibility of the war ending with his part having not been played out. With the former he was aware that the possibility of his being killed existed. The long period of contemplation caused a noticeable change in his personality. His friends were aware of these changes and the cause, for it was with them that he had initially tried to reason and gain reassurance that whatever choice he made, it could be justified. He became withdrawn and moody and the romantic and humorous side of Richard was quelled during this period of indecision.

* * *

Sometime after the publication of his book Richard paid a visit to the operations room at Romford, (Ops No.1). The operations block at Hornchurch had been so badly damaged during the attacks by the Luftwaffe that it had to be moved to the Masonic Hall in Western Road in order to keep the station operational. Corporal Joy Caldwell was on duty that day and remembers the visit by the tall, well-spoken pilot with the facial scaring:

> I didn't know who he was at the time but during our conversation he passed me a copy of the book he had written and said 'Read this'. It was signed on the fly sheet. He was chatty and very charming. What has stood out in my memory of him over the years, however, were his claw-like hands.

* * *

On 15 September 1942, Richard attended the Battle of Britain Anniversary Dinner in London. Here he met for the first time Wing Commander Max Aitken, CO of No.68 Squadron, a night-fighter unit equipped with Blenheims. During the conversation Aitken suggested that Richard telephone him if he was passed fit by the medical board. The suggestion was enticing to Richard and an opportunity he was looking for.

The press were present to take a number of informal photographs of a group of eleven Battle of Britain personalities in the company of Sir Hugh Dowding. In the photographs that are available from that occasion Richard can be seen both smiling, and looking serious. It has been said that by standing behind the others Richard is deliberately 'hiding' the fact that he hasn't any medal ribbons on his tunic; although Johnnie Kent makes room for him in one shot and his lack of awards is there to be seen by all.

On 13 September 1942 he completed his duty with Fighter Command at Bentley Priory and between the period of 14 September to 15 November 1942 he was officially on detached duty from the RAF whilst working on the Sea Rescue film for the RAF. Entitled *For Those in Peril*, it was produced by Michael Balcon and directed by Charles Crichton. It was filmed at Ealing Studios and on location off the south coast where actual Sea Rescue launches of the RAF and their crews were used to produce authentic sea and action shots. Those same rescue launches had by that time plucked six British and 11 American aircrew from the sea after they had baled out of their stricken aircraft.

Richard wrote the script which was in turn read and approved at HQ Fighter Command, Bentley Priory, by his friends 'Dirty' Watkins and 'Laddie' Lucas who freely admitted they had no experience of approving scripts. The accompanying letter to Richard said:

> . . . it appears very good with a nice turn of humour here and there. You might
> draw some criticism from your changes of weather but be sure they don't give
> you a choppy sea during a thick fog.

With the script written, Richard went to the coast to supervise the shooting of the film at his own request, which he did conscientiously and well although the director, Charles Crichton, found him: '. . . not particularly keen on a small propaganda job.' Especially when it included conferences with Government officials from the Air Ministry, Admiralty and the Ministry of Information, the last of which had treated him so disgracefully in America and he was no doubt still nursing a fierce grudge.

Richard mentioned that he thought of this work a useful test and talked of using it to get further leave in which he could write another book. Initially he produced the story from which the script was written. The stars of the documentary were David Farrar, Ralph Michael, Robert Wyndham, John Slater and John Batten. I have included it here as another example of his writing:

> Rawlings hadn't much use for himself that summer evening. He had seen better
> and brighter railway stations. Beyond the dreary looking hall, the town looked as
> though it could do with a good wash.
>
> And, high in the sky, smoke trails marked the passage of many aircraft. He
> wouldn't have minded so much if it hadn't been for the aircraft, he told himself.
>
> Going out on a job somewhere that he couldn't do, he supposed; wasn't
> allowed to do because there was something wrong with his blasted tummy so that
> he couldn't stand height.
>
> 'You'll be wanting the Air-Sea Rescue lot,' said the porter. 'They'll be down
> at the harbour, except Mr. Murray. He'll be on his way up. He comes for his
> paper... you'll not be the only one, I'm thinking.'
>
> 'Only what?'
>
> 'Only one in the Air Force who wanted to fly and found himself going to sea...
> Here's Mr. Murray now.'
>
> The sight of the short, stocky figure that was Mr. Murray didn't help. For a
> start, he was 'oldish', getting on for 40, Rawlings reckoned, much too old ever to
> have thought of flying.
>
> The soft voice that said 'I'm Murray. Glad to have you with us,' didn't help.
> It was too satisfied that the job its owner did mattered, and Rawlings wasn't sure
> that the job did. Or that there was any kick in it.
>
> He said so ten minutes later over a pint of beer as half a dozen Air Force

fellows with wings and decorations burst into the hotel Murray had taken him to.

'Oh! we have our moments, you know.' Murray's voice was still quiet and patient.

'Maybe, but I envy those fellows.'

'You needn't . . . They don't look so glamorous shivering in a rubber dinghy. And a cannon shell can make just as bad a hole in you in a launch as it can in a Spitfire.'

'Hell, but I flew in civil life.'

'And I had 20 years in big ships. I wanted to go back . . . but what's it matter so long as you've got a job to do.'

'Bushy' Leverett hadn't a chance with the Boston once the engine was hit. He had been low enough coming out of France as it was. When the flak he thought he had left behind found him his only hope was that he could get down on the water before he caught fire.

That he managed it surprised him. That he and his crew of two got into the dinghy before the machine sank was a bigger shock. He hadn't expected it.

If it wasn't for the blasted fog and the bit of flak that had got George life would be grand.

It wasn't as if they hadn't been going in. There were enough Spitfires about to report them fifty times over. The only thing to do was to wait and trust to luck and God and try to patch George up . . .

A Spitfire fixed the position, and the controller who set the rescue organisation going didn't like it. The dinghy was too far over towards the French coast for him to be happy.

It was slap in the middle of a minefield.

Still, he ordered Murray and Rawlings out and Naval craft and the Walrus in case the boats couldn't get in, and Spitfires as escort.

'It's funny, you know, 'Bushy,' . . . I've always dreamt I should die through being shot in the back.'

'Shut up, George. You weren't. It got you in the chest.'

'It won't matter where if they don't come soon. What's that? It's them . . . Help. Help.'

'Shut up, you fool.'

'It's a launch, 'Bushy.' It's a launch. Can't you hear it?'

'Yes. But whose? Keep quiet. Remember where you are. Which side of the Channel. Thank God there's a fog.'

'*Achtung minen*,' said a voice somewhere in the fog.

The Walrus found the dinghy first when the fog cleared. The pilot waved cheerily as he passed over 'Bushy' Leverett's head the second time, waved in answer to 'Bushy's' frantic signallings which he took for gestures of joy.

They weren't. But the pilot was never to know. As he touched down he touched off a mine. A great column of water shot high in the air. Fragments of the Walrus fell round the dinghy.

And a couple of miles away to the north and to the south the crews of two launches saw the explosion, one crew British and one German.

Leverett brought back the most comprehensive picture of what happened next, though Rawlings was never to forget that rescue launches 'have their moments.'

Leverett had a grandstand view, though it was some minutes before he knew that anything was happening.

He was too busy keeping the dinghy clear of mines.

Murray's launch was hit first. The German's had the longer-range guns. But it was only the wheelhouse that splintered and neither Murray nor Rawlings paid much attention.

The next thing 'Bushy' knew was that it wasn't just a scrap between a couple of boats but that the whole sea seemed to be full of them and that the dinghy was just the ball in the middle of the field for which every player was making.

A British launch caught a packet in its engine that stopped it and set it on fire, while a moment later black smoke billowed from a German boat as British naval craft with heavier guns heaved into the picture and began firing shells.

When the German saw the British naval craft getting uncomfortably close they called it a day and made back for France, but Leverett and his crew had no sooner been picked up by Murray than shore guns began firing at them.

How they got out from under the guns through the minefield Leverett never quite knew. But get out they did, with Rawlings in the bow dodging mines and in a final attack as they got clear from a low-diving Focke Wulfe spitting cannon shells.

One of the shells got Murray before the escorting Spitfires were down low enough to get the F.W. and the party was over. Except that Leverett didn't like a victory roll a Spitfire pilot did.

'Don't be so cocky,' he said. 'You've got a cushy job. You ought to try this for a day.'

Rawlings was inclined to agree.

From this script we can see that Richard called upon his own experiences as a fighter pilot who, having been shot down, endured an insufferable wait before being rescued. As Eric Linklater advised, Richard should stick to writing about his own experiences, for which he clearly had a talent, and avoid writing about that which he knew little.

Richard received a letter from Lovat Dickson. Enclosed was a cheque for £250 from Ealing on account, for the script. Lovat Dickson also mentioned the possibility of Richard doing a talk at a Foyles (book shop) literary luncheon.

* * *

While Richard was away Mary attended a party on 18 September as her busy social life continued:

'Practically the whole party met this morning at the Ritz before lunch . . . your name was bandied about with the rest . . . At any rate they all seemed to agree on one point and that was your hideously bad manners.

You will be glad to hear that Merle has taken your hint about the bedroom hair and is doing it as she used to do. Consequently she really looks lovely again, and at least five years younger.

She told me the other day that the only thing for you would be to fall madly in love with some glorious woman – you need a good influence in your life, it seems. I thought to myself that what you need and what you want are conflicting elements in your life [Merle did not know the extent of the relationship between Richard and Mary and if she was told, it wasn't until sometime after his death.]

By 25 September, Richard was back at his parents' flat at Rutland Court. Merle stopped by to see him. In one of his frankest and most moving letters to Mary he wrote:

It is now half past six, and the day seems to have gone very slowly. I have sat and sat and thought, but with little result so far. Merle came along, as you know, and was really very sweet. Otherwise the day has been gray. You have been much in my thoughts, and sitting alone I realise how badly you spoil me.

This script is really the big test. If I cannot do that, then I certainly do not feel justified in asking time off for the book. Have a good week-end, my sweet, but take me with you, and bless you for your wonderful long-suffering.

Was Richard concerned about the success of the script for the Sea Rescue project or, since his conversation with Cavalcanti, was he contemplating writing the screen play for *The Last Enemy*?

Richard had dinner with Mary that night, took her roses and stayed over at her flat. During the meal they discussed their past problems and how the possibility of having their own place together still meant a great deal. Mary wrote in a long letter started on the evening of the 25th:

> ... You say in your letters that I spoil you. I am quite aware of it, and I am equally aware that I encourage your self-centredness by being fascinated and occasionally amazed by its enormity. The unique experience of loving someone who is more interested in himself than he is in ME, is one that I find absorbing. When I think that I might have died without experiencing this salutary phenomenon, I go cold all over. The moment for you to go cold all over will come when I suddenly tire of it – when the novelty wears off.
>
> Doubtless you will be too nippy to let this happen. The technique of surprise is the one best employed with a woman of my spirit. I assure you that no one who hadn't a colossal core of self-confidence could swallow you whole with such delight.
>
> The question of unselfishness is a different one. What you think is my unselfishness is very often pure selfishness. You arrive to fetch me for dinner in a feeeelthy mood of drink and literary frustration – Determined to have a disagreeable evening. My fighting spirit is up at once. I immediately call into play all my feminine instincts, which automatically play the role most suited to enable me to enjoy my dinner. The fact that I do usually enjoy my dinner feeds my ego. Q.E.D. Finally you end up by making love to me with all the passion and tenderness that matches mine.
>
> Deep down I know that I could always count on you in matters of 'epic' unselfishness. I believe that, if I rang you up in tears and begged you to come round at once – even if it was before breakfast – I believe you would rush madly across the Park.
>
> Think it over, and give me a straight answer one of these days.
>
> I have been thinking very much about you in your work on the script and willing you to give it birth. With your originality of ideas and positive genius for expressing them in vivid language, I have not the slightest doubt that it will emerge with the same alive quality that characterises everything you write. Someone once defined genius as 'seeing everything anew', and, whereas I do not go so far as to say you are a genius, I do think you have a new and original view of life, and of expressing yourself. This makes it impossible for anyone to help you, except by inspiring you with faith in your own achievement. This I do, with all my heart, adding the advice of discipline of the mind to work to time.

This letter really does give the impression that Mary was on the verge of terminating the relationship, but her love and desire for him prevented her from actually severing the last tenuous cord. Mary still referred to their visit to Wales as the purest period in their time together.

It was during this period that he successfully applied for another medical board, without telling Archie McIndoe.

On 28 September Richard wrote to Walter Goetz of the Political Intelligence Department of the Foreign Office, as recommended by Arthur Koestler, enclosing an article for *Die Andere Seite* and published in German, in London. For this he re-hashed the fictional air-raid at the end of *The Last Enemy*, but added a passage involving the arrival of two German pilots at East Grinstead:

> ... The one so badly wounded that he died without regaining consciousness; the other, burned and in need of morphia, stretched on the casualty table, sheer naked terror beneath the braggart facade of this Nazi bravado; indeed a terror that was a very part of that Nazi teaching. For he believed that he was to be killed. It was for that reason that I, being able to speak German, had been summoned. And

when, taking the needle from the surgeon, I came up to him, he cried out and
drew away. For surely here was a man, himself a victim of the Luftwaffe, to
whom had been granted the privilege of finishing him off.

It took me ten minutes to convince him that we intended him no harm. Slowly
the terror left his face, and such was his exhaustion that tears of relief ran down
his face. For a moment he looked what he was, a simple, probably kind-hearted
boy, caught up in a system which he would never understand, and now lost,
wounded and alone, amongst a people he had been taught to hate, bewildered to
find himself not tortured, not killed like a dog, but taken in, cared for, and nursed,
like any other human being.

The next day, Richard was elected onto the membership of the Savile Club, where
several of his associates were already members.

In between jobs Richard had a busy social life responding to invitations, living the
part of the scarred fighter pilot and successful author. But he felt that all he was doing
was leading nowhere and he needed to focus on an objective far more fulfilling. Despite
Mary's encouragement, he lacked mental discipline, was lazy, was not furthering any
writing career he had in mind for after the war, and he offloaded his emotional concerns,
'innermost problems', on Mary. It seems by now that the only option left to him that
would give him peace-of-mind was a return to operational flying, something he was not
so eager to discuss with her, however.

* * *

It was about this time that Eric Linklater introduced Richard to the artist and sculptor
Eric Kennington. Kennington had just finished a series of officially commissioned
portraits of RAF personnel including a number of well-known fighter pilots that have
since appeared in various publications. The two immediately became friends.

Kennington had been one of T.E. Lawrence's (of Arabia) closest friends. Although,
they had both witnessed the horrors of the First World War, they had served in different
units. After the war Kennington painted a portrait of Lawrence which has remained quite
possibly the best produced. The portrait was requested by Lawrence 'primarily to help
him learn himself'.

During this troubled period of his life Richard asked Kennington to do the same for
him. Kennington asked Richard for a fee of £30 and Lovat Dickson duly offered Richard
ten guineas to: '. . . give us (Macmillan) the right to reproduce it when we require to do
so in connection with sales of the book.'

This was assuming that Richard would gain copyright of the portrait on completion.

Perhaps Richard thought that as he was returning to flying, with its inherent risks, he
wished to leave such a portrait to his friends and loved ones in the event of his being
killed? On arrival at Kennington's farm Richard said: 'I can learn here how not to play
a part – and I've a decision to make.'

Homer House and Eric Kennington provided another refuge as had Lady Fortescue
at Many Waters in which Richard could be himself.

He travelled to Homer House for a number of sittings during a two day period
towards the end of September. It would appear that during this difficult time for Richard,
Eric Kennington provided an escape, someone to confide in, and ultimately he made his
decision to return to flying while in the artist's company. As a result, Kennington was
devastated by the news of Richard's death, feeling a great burden of responsibility.

The portrait was produced in fairly quick time. When it was completed Richard
stared at it and said: 'I've got a face.'

* * *

Lovat Dickson wrote: 'Kennington had made no attempt to minimise the damage, beyond
placing him in a strong light which emphasised the main form rather than the colour.'

Of the people I have met that knew Richard, there are mixed feelings about the
portrait presenting him as unnecessarily stern, perhaps defiant; a trait of Kennington's

portrait work of RAF pilots. As described by Michael Burn: 'His portraits of the RAF, executed in spare forceful strokes, have the girdered, iron-jawed, slightly unnatural look of men who have subdued their weaknesses.' Michael Hillary wrote that Kennington had: '. . . failed to get the likeness.' It is more likely that the look on Richard's face was simply because he was staring out of a window into daylight. Kennington painted all of his pilot subjects with a serious expression. The severity of Richard's scar tissue has been 'softened' by the artist and his 'cupid's bow' enhanced which is contrary to Lovat Dickson's comments. Kennington was accustomed to drawing (in the case of the portraits he produced of RAF pilots, he used pastels) men trained for war and after Richard's death, Kennington told Mary in a letter: 'I like the race of men – if they are rough, tough workers – not so much those that sit at desks.'

Kennington talked as he painted, mainly about T.E. Lawrence and Richard sat listening intently. The two had much in common. The artist lent Richard his copy of Lawrence's book *The Mint*, as yet unpublished, which at this time really only consisted of a mass of notes compiled by Lawrence during his time as an aircraftman in the RAF, and originally destined for a book that Lawrence had intended to write: 'one of the rare manuscript copies of the original unexpurgated script' and not 'the emasculated pallid edition that was published in 1955.'

The book told of Lawrence's attempt to escape from world renown. In 1922, in a state of near mental collapse, he changed his name and joined the RAF as AC1 Ross, initially being posted to the depot at RAF Uxbridge and then to RAF Cranwell (where Lawrence found some happiness) before transferring to the Tank Corps at Bovingdon.

This work influenced Richard greatly at a time when he was pondering his future. Richard later wrote, just before he was killed: 'It was reading 'The Mint' that decided me to return'.

Like Lawrence, Richard saw himself as someone who also wished to re-discover himself among 'ordinary people'. As Lawrence had meant the squaddies and mechanics at Uxbridge and Cranwell, Richard meant men like those that he had known before he had been shot down. However, Lawrence attempted to find anonymity amongst the minor ranks of the RAF whereas Richard enjoyed being the centre of attention, aware that those around him were familiar with his achievements as a Battle of Britain fighter pilot, author and national celebrity.

Richard was many years younger than Lawrence when he decided to return to flying, and instead of attempting to remain anonymous Richard was a pilot who signed for the responsibility of taking up an aircraft, of which he was prepared to take charge, with one other crew member.

The pastel portrait of Richard by Eric Kennington, signed in red pastel 'EHK 42', shows him with his battledress deliberately left open revealing its red silk lining. (This jacket was probably the one he was wearing the night he died.)

Later, Michael Hillary asked Kennington to reproduce two copies of the portrait of Richard and arranged for one to go to Trinity College, Oxford, and the other to Shrewsbury School. Kennington produced one and invoiced Michael Hillary for £30, but stated in his accompanying letter that he had no energy for a repeat of the portrait and would be taking a complete break from art. Michael Hillary informed H.H. Hardy, Richard's former headmaster at Shrewsbury, that a portrait would probably not now be forthcoming.

Richard left his portrait to Mary, who lent it to Michael and Edwyna Hillary for the remainder of their lives. The portrait passed by the wish of all concerned to the National Portrait Gallery, where it remains today, hanging above the portrait of Sir Archibald McIndoe.

It was while he was sitting for Eric Kennington that Mary decided that Richard was becoming too remote from her and she was no longer prepared to accept the tensions of the relationship. Richard received the letter from Mary, while he was sitting for Kennington, calling an end to their relationship:

Darling, I don't know when I shall see you, and anyway it would be impossible to say – I'm better off writing.

It is just that I feel miles away. I don't feel that I know you any more. When you ring up I have nothing to say, because I feel we know so little about each other's background, that there would be too much to explain.

I realise that I've been nervous and restless and not happy for quite some time. I don't seem to belong anywhere, as I am no use to you in serious matters, and cannot ever give you that carefree relaxation in contrast to hard work, and I'm no good at fitting into that middle pigeonhole.

If I had never known those moments of oneness so startling and unlike anything else I have ever experienced, I would have written this letter before. But I know I can't go forward having to look back to recapture an illusion.

I suppose we are neither of us big enough to have survived all the difficulties. I would rather just be friends with no kind of responsibility or expectation from either of us to the other. Surprising though it may seem, on the face of things, I too have work which relies on tremendous concentration, and of late I've been fuzzy-minded. My mind wanders about in restlessness, and I find no inner peace to get me through the outer chaos.

I feel I'm explaining badly, but if I did not expect so much that you are not able to give me, I would not burden you, and I myself would be less unhappy.

All this has nothing to do with your going away, seeing other people who can help you in all you want to achieve in life. All this is right.

I cannot write any more. I know you will understand that it is not my love that has failed.

This letter seemed to drain the strain from the relationship as from this moment on the couple seemed to get on better than at anytime since their trip to Wales. I believe that when faced with the future without each other to turn to, they began to appreciate afresh the value of each other's company. Regardless of this 'dismissal', the love letters continued almost as if nothing had been said. Perhaps Richard could not accept the consequences and, as he wittered on, Mary's love for him did not allow her to snap him into reality as she herself did not really wish to lose him.

A letter from Richard arrived before Mary had completed her letter of dismissal:

Darling,

I have quite lost my heart to Kennington. He has the most extraordinary personal magnetism of anyone I have met – a great man I think. Certainly his sculpture of Lawrence is a masterpiece. His farm is so restful, that I feel the life in me stirring and the writing is beginning to come.

I return to-morrow until Thursday to sit for him. He is no longer with the RAF, so it must be a private arrangement. He is being very reasonable however.

Now I really shall have something to leave you. As soon as it is done, I will make my will and set my family's mind at rest.

All Love
Richard

To her original letter Mary added:

Your letter arrived this morning. I had looked forward to it so much, so I read it through four times to try to place it. Finally I find it in the letter of a man to the woman he has been married to for 17 years, and is in the habit of writing to every day! I never achieved being married so long, so I feel that my heart is at the bottom of the sea.

It shows my darling how far away you are from me. There is no blame, but I am right in what I say at the beginning of this letter. You and I must never pretend. I know that as friends we are perfect for each other. But I must have a little time to adjust the heart, which you always complained was too big anyway.

Mary

Richard's reply came at once, dated 6 October 1942, written without preparation and in places therefore it reads confusedly. Nevertheless, he expresses immense honesty, maturity and strength from one so young:

It was a shock, though not entirely unexpected.

You're right, of course, and the deficiency has been mine. It's not that I love you any less; in spite of this I feel you a very part of me. It is not even a question of being big enough to rise above the difficulties. The difficulties have become a very part of us; they have made the present situation intolerable, because, by their very nature, they have made all spiritual and mental contact – except through the act of love – impossible. I should have seen this before: a purely physical relationship is a thing which could never be for us, and yet almost – by the very fact of our only contact being physical – we are suffering from an animal frustration. Yet these difficulties are transitory, they cannot destroy us. We are too big for that.

As you say, we must never pretend. I never have. My letters reflect my mood exactly. You are there. It is on you that I depend, but at the moment contact is impossible. This letter must seem ordinary enough, and yet I strain to be a part of you as I write it. I am not much good at straining.

I must give all of myself or nothing. Before I met you, it was always nothing. I had so little to give, and I did not want to waste it. (No, that's wrong. I had a lot to give but not then.) Now I cannot give you everything – so I give you nothing. It is quite simple. At this moment I can give nothing to anyone. It is bad and yet it gives one power – immense power, and that's bad too. If I took a woman now (other than you) I think I would destroy her – for though when confronted by small things, I am lost – chaotic – inside I'm frozen, hard, but powerful. Is this nonsense? I don't know. This is not a premeditated letter so there must be something here of what I'm trying to say.

It's funny that I should get your letter after three days of such peace sitting in that room of Kennington's which is not Kennington's but Lawrence's really – not only because of all L's things there – I felt such a wonderful surge of peace and potential creation as I have never felt before. Kennington knew it I think. He has an uncanny second vision – you can see it in his portraits – they are all of the subjects as they may be in five years time. I just sat there and let his words flow over me. He remarked on it finally. 'Funny', he said, 'you sit there and hand over your mind for me to play with and yet you have the power – not I.'

I was really distressed at leaving. Had I been able to stay – something would have happened – something good. More I cannot say.

But enough of this! It is irrelevant – or is it? No I think not.

I can make nothing of this letter. (You perhaps will) and yet in some way it seems an explanation – an explanation of why we can never talk now. It is those circles of peace again. They must return – they must. We are too important to each other to fail.

I will not apologise – or say I have treated you badly. I have not. It would be in some curious way an insult to say so – insult to you I mean.

In three weeks this triviality comes to an end. Then what? A momentous decision I know. And yet it does not affect me. I shall go back I think. I can rationalise no further. I must let instinct decide. Maybe it is for this that I have withdrawn into myself. I don't know.

This I do know – you are right. We cannot play down to circumstances. We must accept them – forget them, and wait. Need it be long?

It would seem that Richard also wanted to end the relationship. But once alone, at Charterhall, he needed Mary. He missed her love and sex. But while he craved for her attention at that time, the relationship would still have continued to fail in other circumstances.

On 7 October, after his two days with Kennington and the day after his reply to Mary's letter, he wrote to the artist from his parents' flat:

> Dear Kennington,
>
> Two immensely important days: thank you for them. Lawrence, I wonder, or you? T.E. to some extent certainly, for The Mint helped me to clear up something that had been worrying me for months. To fly again or not? I had got to the stage when I could rationalise no longer, but relied on instinct to tell me when the time came.
>
> The answer I can see now is simple. Does one wish to write for power – or success – call it what you will, or because one has something to give? Again I have despised these men I have lived with in messes – pilots too – despised them above all drunk, and have felt a longing to get away from them and think. But Lawrence is right. Companionship such as this must depend largely on trivialities (the wrong word), ordinary things is perhaps better...
>
> But it was not all T.E. There were moments when I wished you would not speak of him; he got in the way. How glad I am that I have nothing to hide from you . . . I can almost find it in me to pity those poor unfortunates at the Air Ministry.
>
> Forgive this letter: it is not saying what I intend. (I can almost imagine Buchman looking over my shoulder and rubbing his hands.) It is simply that for those two days no one was being 'clever' and the issues for once were almost simple.
>
> I appreciate your doing the portrait very much. I also like it. Whether it's 'good' or not, I suppose we'd better leave to Kenneth Clark and posterity.
>
> Yours sincerely
> Richard Hillary

And there we have it, the reason for his return to flying. The companionship, rough mess games and bouts of heavy drinking that he had once spurned and had again witnessed recently in the mess during his course at the staff college at Gerrard's Cross; but on this latest occasion he had actually taken part, and thoroughly enjoyed himself.

A brief letter from Richard to Mary, written after he had seen her, dated and headed, '8th October, 26 Rutland Court', quite possibly in Mary's own hand, reads:

> My Darling,
>
> Something has gone wrong with my eyesight and I am retiring to bed, but I want you to know that my last thoughts are of you, that I love you, and that when I saw you to-night my heart turned over.
>
> Richard

Was this a ploy to gain her attention or did Richard have a problem with his vision? It was known that since he had been injured he suffered from severe headaches, possibly migraine. During a previous attack of dizziness he had fallen down a flight of stairs. Putting these afflictions together leads one to consider the possibility of such problems occurring after his return to flying; possibly contributing towards the difficulties encountered and ultimately his death.

In a letter written by Mary to Richard on 9 October in response to his long letter of the 6th she wrote:

> Thank you for writing as you did. It is a wonderful letter, and no one but you could have written it.
>
> As I read it, all my generosity of heart opened up again and brought you back to me, and nearer than you have been for months past. No other letter could have given me back my faith in you. I wrote my letter in the light vein that we are wont

> to do, but in my heart I had ceased to understand or even want to understand. I just wanted to get away and be alone, as I was before you came.

Despite Mary's letter of dismissal clearly neither Richard nor Mary wanted to end the relationship. Richard admitted, 'I must give all of myself or nothing' and in the current circumstances he could not do that. Mary was delighted to receive a letter from Richard which did anything but suggest their affair was over. Neither could they face the possibility of life without having each other to turn to. The return to loneliness would have been more than they could bear. Mary revelled in the fresh start they were now enjoying; perhaps it was her desperate hope that she would achieve that when she wrote the letter rather than enduring further heartbreak. Of that change in their relationship, Michael Burn wrote:

> That interchange of letters between 5 and 9 October is the most remarkable of the correspondence. It broke through the ice that had been forming around the relationship, into a warmth that had almost been lost, and led the two of them on in mutual understanding.

Mary felt uneasy about Kennington perhaps because of the fact that Richard preferred to be with him and did little to disguise the pleasure he derived from this experience. She may also have been concerned that Richard may have discussed their relationship with the artist. Her suspicions were perhaps to some extent justified when, after his death, Kennington wrote of Richard:

> . . . he could be a shrewd, hard judge of people, shredding them mercilessly – sometimes scurrilously, but who could reprove? When in a thoroughly naughty mood, as he swung his loose limbs and side-glanced with very bright eyes, so much younger than the surrounding made-up face, he was an irresistible child . . .
>
> Too critical, too truculent, and too assured, was the verdict of some of our household. I defended him against these charges (of which he was aware), saying he would probably use others for a time to rid himself of a load of suffering . . .

In his will, when disposing of the portrait Richard described it as being by: '. . . the only complete man I know.'

On 11 October Richard wrote to Mary from his parents' flat:

> . . . I am now very nearly at the end of the tunnel: my decision is as good as made. Thursday, in fact, will be the nature of Ave atque Vale to the literary world. Eric Linklater is still at me (I dine with him and Peter Flemings on Monday), but even him I have half convinced.
>
> Saturday to Fighter Command with the script and to make arrangements for the nature of my return . . .

Richard referred to attempts by Eric Linklater to dissuade him from flying again, which had obviously failed. Richard also mentioned delivering his finished script for the Sea Rescue film to Headquarters Fighter Command and to further pester the authorities about allowing him to fly again.

In Richard's letter to Mary dated 13 October he wrote:

> Darling, please don't get too cold or go too far away. I have no right to ask it of you, but in a little while now I shall be all right. I have a decision to make and I want to make it quite alone – and try to be honest with myself about my reasons. In three weeks time I shall know the answer . ..
>
> . . . I am off to dinner with Rache [Lovat Dickson] after a hectic day at the studio [supervising the making of *For Those in Peril*]. We are certainly working against time.
>
> Think of me a little my darling. I feel you very near to me. Is that illusion? I'm sure I'd know if you shut yourself right off.

It would seem obvious, and in running with his ongoing thoughts, that this reference to 'I have a decision to make' is to his return to operational flying, but according Mary this reference is nothing to do with the RAF, but an honest admission from Richard that he wanted to take full advantage of his liberty. A few days after the letter arrived Mary expressed her own opinion of what this comment meant in one of her diary entries:

> . . . he rang up to say he wanted to see me. He came and told me he felt he wanted to make love to someone else; that he was puzzled and disturbed by having such a feeling, when he was only really happy when he was with me . . .

Michael Burn later wrote: 'Her typescript breaks off here, at the bottom of the page, with no page following.'

Were the foundations of this relationship really sound, or was it just a question of time before Richard, free to carry on in the manner he was used to, would fall for another? Was Mary just allowing him to continue simply to keep him for as long a possible? It is a coincidence that *the* decision that he had to make alone is without doubt whether or not to return to flying

Around this time Mary introduced Richard to her friend and confidant Monsignor John Vance. Vance had read *The Last Enemy* and knew a great deal about Richard through Mary; but he had never met him. The occasion was a dinner party and the next morning Vance wrote down his initial impressions of Richard. Vance later prepared a biography about Richard's life, which was never published, mainly due to the adverse reaction to it by Denise and Michael and Edwyna Hillary. It is clear, however, that after Richard was killed he added to this initial piece, and then included it in the manuscript of his biography. He later sent this lengthy passage to Mary:

> As he walked into the room, I was struck by his stature and bearing. He walked with great alertness and yet there was something in his poise and footfall that indicated a 'brake' on his forward movement. He was undecided about something of moment or had made a difficult or, perhaps, reluctant decision. (In point of fact, though I did not know it, he had just decided to return to the Air Force.) It was emphatically not the bearing of a young man who strode 'breast forward' into life. Later, as he strode down Piccadilly after dinner, I caught the lightness of his step, the rhythm of his movements and a certain 'huddled-togetherness' of bearing. He was, I thought, seeking comfort within, and finding none . . .
>
> On listening to his voice I recorded the impression of a vibrant personality, strong in passion, violent in determination, concentrated in self-determination and sensitive to a degree – not only for himself but, it might also be, for others. There was a plaintive note, when he spoke softly, which told of great power to experience inner pain and anguish. It sounded as if he were accustomed to question himself and his own purposes, unduly perhaps, and perhaps mercilessly. It had a gentleness, a modulation and a note of compassion unusual in youth; it was the voice of one who had suffered in body and mind keenly and terribly. To me it was a most appealing voice.

Aspects of this passage were written after Richard had been killed – with the benefit of hindsight and a greater knowledge than that gleaned at a single dinner party.

Apart from a letter of farewell written by Mary during the dreadfully distressing period immediately after news had reached her of Richard's death, no letters from her to Richard have survived after October, when the last exchange took place.

Although Richard continued to telephone Mary every night, between the 11th and the 22nd the couple only met twice, and that was by chance. While Mary continued with her busy social life Richard finished 'the trivialities' and prepared for the impending medical board; willing to give his best performance in order to leave the Air Commodore no choice but to pass him A1B. On the 17th Richard wrote: 'I shall go back, I think.'

The hesitation leads one to believe he could still have been persuaded not to return to flying, or to accept a 'no' from the medical board. By the 21st the 'I think' had become 'I am sure'.

On 19 October whilst suffering from a bout of melancholia and nostalgia Mary wrote to Richard:

> I tell myself this, and still it all crowds in on me that I cannot be of any use to you – that I cannot be with you to share your gaiety or your depressions . . . I just feel I am, as regards you, a failure.
>
> All this bores you at present, I know. You don't want to be bothered with emotions. Quite right. I'm bored too now I've written it down. But we did say we would tell each other what we felt.
>
> Don't you have your ups and downs? Are you always so sure, calm, and serene about everything as you seem? Have you really achieved such power of detachment, that you never feel even a sadness at this separation? Did you feel no quickening of the heart when you saw me the other day? [At Yvonne Hamilton's] Were my jet black nails the only thing you noticed?
>
> When you've thought up some good answers to these questions, I would like to know the rock-bottom truth. The answers to perfectly *idiotic* questions are always so interesting.

* * *

As a result of the success of his book, Richard was invited to speak at a Foyle's Literary Luncheon. Book shop owner Christina Foyle had started her monthly literary luncheons in 1930 at the age of 19. Until recently, they took place in the Grosvenor Hotel and over the years attracted many distinguished speakers, including J.B. Priestley, George Bernard Shaw, and A.A. Milne. Christina Foyle died on 10 June 1999, aged 88, after nearly seven decades of such literary luncheons.

The invitation to speak would be the only occasion at which Richard would have a captive audience, the likes of which he had hoped to address in America, and for which he had been deemed too badly scarred for such a job. Lovat Dickson was aware of the opportunity to enhance the commercial success of the book and prompted Richard to accept. 'What's in it for the old crook?' Richard had asked Lovat Dickson, who replied:

> Well, nothing for me, Richard. We can sell the book without these adventitious aids. But people would like to see you. You've stirred their curiosity and wonder. This is the Humanity for whom you are writing. Talk to them about your service life. Many of them have sons or young relatives in the Air Force. Tell them what it is like being there.

Richard agreed and went away to write his speech.

This was exactly the situation he had prepared for when he went to America the previous year, and had been so badly treated by officialdom. This time there was no hesitation in allowing him to stand before an audience that may have had relatives that were facing the daily risk of similar injury and disfigurement in defence of the country.

Lovat Dickson was worried by Richard's casual approach to the speech. He had declined his publisher's offer to check the draft copy before the day in question, leaving him concerned at the uncensored content:

> Wouldn't he like me to read it over first? No. He wouldn't forget to turn up on time? He wouldn't. He wasn't going to say something outrageous? He wasn't. He wasn't nervous? No.

Lovat Dickson arranged for Eric Linklater and Denise Maxwell-Woosnam to join them for the lunch. The three men gathered in his office at 11.45, with Richard the last to arrive.

They then met Denise for a quiet drink together before they left Richard at the top table while they found their seats elsewhere in the room at Grosvenor House. Mary,

Michael and Edwyna Hillary were also present along with a few other members of the
armed forces, indicated by their uniforms. The memories Denise recalls of the occasion
rather contradict Lovat Dickson's attempt to keep Richard's head clear from the effects
of alcohol.

Lovat Dickson was nervous and sat in air of tenseness, in anticipation of the content
of Richard's speech and how it would be accepted by the audience. The young author
did not let his publisher down, to Lovat Dickson's enormous relief.

The following is a passage from the address given by Richard at Foyle's Literary
Luncheon on Thursday, 22 October 1942, reproduced in the publication *John
O'London's Weekly* and in *The Spectator* on 15 January 1943.

The subject had surprised Lovat Dickson, and Richard's young, clear voice echoed
around the crowded room. The audience sat listening intently in the stillness.

Richard's talk was entitled 'Where Do We Go From Here?' and was published in *The
Spectator* under the heading 'The Artist and Fascism'. He began by defining the artist,
scientist and truly religious as examples of what he believed to be the greatest bulwarks
a country could have in the fight against Fascism and Hitler. Richard stated that by their
inherent individualism they would never yield to the totalitarian forces and ideology of
Fascism but would fight 'for their own small circle of friends' and for civil liberty.

He used the analogy of a prewar art critic turned wartime RAF pilot who, finding
himself bored by a drunken garrulous medical officer in the mess, is himself equally
boring to the medical man. They both fail to see each other's sensibilities and yet neither
would become fascists. Each is far too individual ever to succumb to the dictatorial
philosophy of the Fascists:

> I suggest that the man is perhaps representative of all of us, of the subconscious
> of all of us anyway, of all of us whose art is not a thing big enough of itself but
> simply a means to power. Let us remember two things: one, that Fascism is not a
> national creed but a state of mind; two, that all those that love power more than
> people will go Fascist if and when Fascism is a majority movement. Finally, let
> us not go around and look at our friends and say, 'Oh, he will be a Nazi.' Let us
> rather ask ourselves – what is my position? And if we can answer that question
> fairly, then I think that that itself is a not inconsiderable war aim, and if, after
> having looked into our hearts and seen the danger, we can honestly say it is
> alright when the day comes, I shall feel then we shall have a spiritual armour
> which, come what may, will see us through to the end.

The end of Richard's speech was evidently greeted with warm applause from his
audience.

The following evening Richard dined with Mary. After leaving her he returned home.
The next day he replied to her 'questionnaire' written on the 19th. Perhaps something
had happened during the evening of the 23rd to prompt this parody of the hard,
impersonal side of his character:

> I don't know about *rock-bottom truth*, but here are your answers.
>
> Q. Do I ever have ups and downs?
> A. Yes.
> Q. Am I always so sure, calm, and serene about everything as I seem?
> A. Yes.
> Q. Have I achieved such power of detachment, that I never feel sadness at
>   this separation?
> A. No.
> Q. Did I feel a quickening of the heart when I saw you at Yvonne's?
> A. Yes.
> Q. Were your jet black nails the only thing I noticed?
> A. No.
> Q. If you were much in my thoughts over the week-end, what did I think?

> A. Where is she? What is she doing? What is she wearing? What is she
> thinking? What do I care?
> All of which answers are superfluous after Friday night.

What had happened that night to prompt Richard to reply to Mary's letter of the 19th in such an uncompromising way? Whatever it was they were together again for the rest of the weekend. On Tuesday 27 Mary wrote Richard a romantic letter:

> Whenever that inevitable antagonism rises up between us, when you are at your
> most unbearable Bassington, and I most maddening, so that you long to beat me,
> I shall remember and hug the memory to my secret heart. This is my answer.
>   My darling, I take your head between my hands and kiss your lips.

There is a radiance about this letter that has been missing from Mary's letters to Richard for quite some time. What had occurred that had made her feel so happy and seemingly contented? Had Richard committed himself to Mary in a way that was genuinely reassuring to her after all she had put up with from him? Perhaps he had simply assured her of his love for her. Certainly as the roller-coaster ride nears its inexorable end their relationship seems to have reached an all-time high. They were together again that evening and in her diary against Friday, 30 October, Mary wrote of that day: 'Dine Richard. Miracle.' The word 'miracle' is, during his lifetime, the last word written about their relationship in Mary's handwriting that has survived. Only five weeks earlier she had written to him that: 'the very memory of the few occasions I saw real happiness in your face strikes me each time in wonderment, as though a miracle had happened.'

They spent much time together during November, with little in the way of interruption, either by friends calling or either of them going out to social functions. For the last few weeks Richard had been aware of what his immediate future held and knowing that allowed him to relax and enjoy life with a more positive outlook and peace of mind. He no longer lacked confidence about his immediate working future, his work on the staff of the RAF and input on the Sea Rescue film script proved that. Although, in attending yet another medical board with the intention of being passed fit with an A1B category for operational flying, he faced failure, in that event he was prepared to continue with his staff appointments. After the war he would write. It is clear that he had derived pleasure from his recent work and I believe he would have accepted failure at the medical board and returned to staff work with the Air Ministry in addition to any other writing work. The latter he hoped would help build a future in writing after the war.

* * *

Richard's feeling of individualism had now been re-kindled and he remained free from outside interference as he pestered the authorities at Bentley Priory in his attempt to regain operational flying status. Sholto Douglas had given him the challenge, foolishly, and he had risen to it. He had attended many medical boards and on this, the seventh and last, he knew well what they expected. It may also have been the case that by now they were only too aware of his determination to fly again and passed him as a result of his overwhelming enthusiasm and strength of will. After all, there was a war to fight.

During this time Richard withdrew into himself in preparation, and when questioned by his friends, Arthur Koestler and in particular Eric Linklater, on the merits of a return to operations, he could not be dissuaded. Despite their depth of feeling for him, they could not have done more, even though they knew a return to flying would be fraught with danger:

> ... when we opposed him, he withdrew behind a bitter mocking mask, and turned
> the subject aside with a joke ... He became moody and truculent ... spiritually
> frozen ... as if his closest friends were not to be trusted ...

... and the sinister words: 'Something bigger than us was at work on this boy; some power had seized him, which never entered our calm and negligible lives.'

According to Michael Burn, it would not have been in Mary's nature to openly attempt to dissuade Richard from that which she knew to be so important to him. The only suggestion of an expression of her personal opinion was in a letter to Richard when she mentions that she was bound to be 'with Linklater'. In a letter to Mary written on 19 November from RAF Charterhall, Richard thanked her for not questioning his decision as his mother had also done.

Finally, on 12 November, Richard's period of indecision was brought to an end when he went before the Central Medical Board at Kelvin House for the final time and was classified A1B – Return to Unit (RTU). He had not told Archie McIndoe that he was going, which he should have done. It was his own decision and he didn't want anyone else to try and dissuade him or perhaps in the case of McIndoe, influence the board.

When one tries to apportion blame on the medical board it should be appreciated that Air Commodore Stanford Cade was responsible for making the final decision on his case, as he had with so many others that had gone before. The case of Geoffrey Page is very illuminating as he had been able to persuade the president to allow him to return to operational flying, even after he had been told he could not. It must be assumed that Richard adopted the same determined attitude. While there are no details of Richard's board we can appreciate what he had to endure from that which Geoffrey Page recorded of his own earlier experiences in his book *Shot Down in Flames*:

> Central Medical Establishment occupied two floors of a dingy building lying in the shadows of one of London's largest hospitals, the Middlesex. A large waiting room filled rapidly early each morning as a horde of young men, almost all with aircrew brevets, invaded the cloistered atmosphere. Magazines that had been thumbed through a thousand times littered the large table in the centre of the room. A huge, unattractive clock on the whitewashed walls loudly ticked away the minutes of bored waiting. As wild animals in a cage, so these men looked out of place and confined in this atmosphere. Theirs was a world of white clouds and blue sky, of green grassy airfields and wooden dispersal huts.
>
> 'Flying Officer Page, please!'
>
> The medical orderly's voice rang out and temporarily silenced the tick-tock of the clock. A few heads looked up from their magazines as I rose to my feet and left the room. Following my guide I was led into an office marked 'Adjutant'. Behind the desk sat a sallow faced administrative officer. Picking up a file he glanced up, 'Page?' I nodded. The eyes returned to the open file. Quickly the adjutant read through the case history.
>
> '– third degree burns, hands, face and legs; gun-shot wound, left leg.' He put down the file and looked up again. 'You should get your bowler hat without any trouble.'
>
> I felt my heart sinking.
>
> 'I've come here to get a flying category, not to be invalided out.'
>
> The adjutant snorted deprecatingly.
>
> 'Forget about it, you haven't a chance.' He indicated the door.
>
> 'You still have to undergo a full medical examination for us to discharge you. They'll call you from the waiting room.'
>
> With a sick feeling in the pit of my stomach, I returned to my seat.
>
> An hour passed before I was called again, and then only to provide a urine specimen for analysis. Another dragging hour passed, during which time a steady stream passed in and out of the room as their names were called. My gloom deepened as the memory of the adjutant's words bored cruelly deeper and deeper into my mind. The administrative officer was relegated to a position of hatred alongside the Germans in my thoughts. Finally my name was called again and this time the medical examination began in earnest.
>
> Blood pressures were taken, columns of mercury blown up and held by lung pressure, reflex muscles tapped, and blindfolded one-legged tests carried out.

Examinations by the ear, nose and throat specialist followed. With one ear blocked whispered words floated across the room for me to repeat. Tuning forks hummed, tonsils and nasal passages were looked at. Then to the eye doctor. A darkened room – flashing red lights and diagonal bars. A pencil light played into each eye. After that came the colour blindness tests and the inevitable reading of the letter chart with one eye closed.

Another long, interminable wait until I was told to come back after lunch.

Sick with worry and anticipation, I left the sandwich I had ordered in a nearby pub untouched. How had I fared with the various doctors, I wondered? And if they invalided me from the service, what then? I felt fit enough to fly, so why not let me? All this red tape when I was obviously one hundred percent fit. I caught sight of the pitying expressions of the two bar-maids as they discussed my injuries. Obviously they did not think I looked one hundred percent fit. I fled from the pub.

Again my name was called. This was it, the final summing up by the President of the medical board, and then the verdict. Respectfully the medical orderly tapped on the glass door of the Air Commodore's office. He opened it on hearing the muffled summons.

'Flying Officer Page, Sir.'

The grey-haired man nodded from behind the desk without looking up.

'Have a seat, Page. I won't keep you a moment.' The door closed behind the departing orderly, and I sat tensely on the edge of the chair as the President continued to record his findings on paper of the previous examinee. With a flourish he signed his name and placed the file aside before reaching for my documents. Carefully he read through the findings of the various specialists.

'Hmm –' He looked up thoughtfully. 'Apart from your injuries you seem fit enough, Page. What would you like us to do, invalid you out or give you a limited category?'

'Limited in what way, Sir?'

'Oh, fit for ground duties in the United Kingdom only.'

I swallowed hard. I disliked the use of falsehoods, but I knew that this was a critical moment in my life.

'Well, actually Sir, what I'm after is a flying category. You see,' I added hastily as I saw a frown appear on the doctor's face. 'I managed to get some unofficial flying recently through a friend of mine in one of the squadrons.'

Both of us knew I was lying.

'Grip my hands.'

I stood and leaned across the desk grasping the President's hands in my own. Every ounce of physical and nervous energy I possessed was concentrated into my two maimed hands as I forced them to tighten their grip. Months of hard work with the rubber ball stood me in good stead. The Air Commodore raised his eyebrows again, this time in surprise.

'More strength in those than I imagined possible, Page.' He picked up his pen and commenced to write.

'I am passing you fit for non-operational single-engine aircraft only. At the end of three months you will be boarded again, and if you've coped all right, we'll give you an operational category.' I passed through the door in a dream.

'Oh, and Page.'

'Yes, Sir?'

'Good luck, and don't let me down.'

The two elderly women stopped and stared after the figure of the young RAF pilot as he half ran down the street, tears of joy pouring down his cheeks.

'Poor boy,' said the skinny one. 'He must have heard some bad news – so young too!'

By now, Richard had endured the same procedure on seven occasions and also sat opposite the Air Commodore for final assessment of the medical results. Richard's hands were nowhere near as strong as Geoffrey Page's, mainly because he had not been carrying out the same very necessary rehabilitation exercises with a rubber ball. His left eye was also still troubling him. But Richard possessed greater interpersonal skills; he knew how to get his own way. When faced with the same decision, to have him grounded, he also managed to persuade the president to re-establish his flying category. Air Commodore Cade would certainly have had his reservations about letting Richard fly again, but this was a busy medical man, not a typical service disciplinarian, and he wanted to allow these young men every opportunity, particularly when the likes of Richard and Geoffrey exhibited such determination in wanting to return to flying. Page was successful and did not let the president down.

Unfortunately, Richard's physical and mental state did not match up to the demands he asked of himself and the consequences were tragic. Like Richard, Page was also scared at the prospect of failure but he was both physically and mentally in better shape to face the challenge and, of course, chose an easier route by returning to the single-engine aircraft he was already familiar with. It is unfortunate that Air Commodore Cade did not afford Richard the same three month restriction as he had placed on Page, until such times as he too could prove himself fit to fly operationally.

On 15 November 1942 Richard was finally passed fit for flying duties and posted to No.54 OTU for operational training. After the medical he saw his friend Pat Hollander who recalled:

> When he went up [to the Medical Board], this quite elderly doctor said: 'Well, do you want to go back flying?', and he [Richard] said [to Pat Hollander]: 'What was I supposed to say? No I don't, I dread it?' He said: 'Yes, I do'. 'OK, you've passed,' said the doctor.

He now knew where his immediate future lay. This decision was against all reasonable logic, but under these specific circumstances. Richard had shown the determination to succeed. His strength of character, his charisma, self confidence and over-bearing persona had perhaps taken its toll on the medical board members. Others with similar injuries had successfully returned to operations. It has been argued that he should not have been allowed to go back to flying. Perhaps it was the specific flying duties for which he volunteered that ultimately led to his death. Geoffrey Page had made the correct decision, albeit with hindsight. Richard may well have survived had the president of the medical board refused to allow him to return to operational flying training, but can he really be blamed when others had been successful and when confronted by such a persuasive individual? Maybe they were of the opinion that such spirit should be tapped and utilised to help win the war, or that it could be damaging to the individual to decline in the face of such overwhelming determination. In Richard's case the authorities had been wrong to send him back to fly, bearing in mind his disabilities. What made it worse, unknown to the authorities obviously, was that the aircraft he would fly were clapped-out, ex-operational, and twin-engined. His death, therefore, could have been averted but it was to some degree his own doing.

According to Rosie Kerr, Richard had been not at all confident that he would get through the medical and, alternatively, was terribly worried because he knew that to be passed A1B would be a desperate blow for his mother. The medical was unusually brief and he was soon back. He had been asked few questions and it had been left to him to convince them whether he was up to the task of operational flying. By the condition of his hands there-and then they could see he was not. He told the board he was and he was passed fit. During the recording of her memories Rosie was asked:

> 'Was he jubilant?'
> 'No,' she replied. 'Not jubilant. Not at all jubilant.'

Clearly, Richard is worried as he has to break the news to someone he loves dearly and will be subjected to yet more worry, his mother. He would also be apprehensive; after all his effort he has now been passed fit to fly and his mind is focusing on the trials and tribulations that lie ahead for him with the hope in the back of his mind that he could later join Max Aitken's squadron.

Having been classified medically fit for flying Richard had to get permission from the commander-in-chief Fighter Command, Air Vice-Marshal Sholto Douglas, but as he had previously given Richard his word that if he was passed fit to fly, he would also grant his permission and sanction a return to operational flying. A rather foolhardy promise on his part, as it was in Sholto Douglas' remit to have simply said no and put an end to the matter and not relied on the doctors. Suggesting that he return to night flying was based on the need to avoid daytime combat flying with disabled hands, without due consideration to the problems he would face flying a twin-engined aircraft, a quite unbelievable error on his part.

There were two trains of thought, for and against a return to flying. Lovat Dickson wrote, considering the options:

> The Royal Air Force is an enlightened Service . . . and had, I think rightly, conceived the view that young men desperately injured who craved to go back to fight again should, if it were at all possible, be allowed to do so; that it was better to lose a plane and the man, though this would not necessarily be the outcome, than have a nervous frustrated psychological case, not injured enough to be discharged, carrying on a ground job, and infecting with his disillusionment and despair all the others.

The other view was that of Rosie Kerr, who expressed dismay and astonishment, on behalf of his friends, at his being passed A1B fit:

> Incomprehensible. He was not fit. They had only to say, once and for all, that they could not afford to lose more planes, let alone two lives, his and his radio-observer's, and reject him. After a few weeks he would have accepted it, and found something else. Incomprehensible!

Her comments, written many years after Richard's death, were based on her own tragic experiences when, during February 1942, her fiancée, a Free French Air Force pilot with eighteen 'kills' to his credit, Commandant Jacques-Henri Schloesing, had been shot down and badly burned. The French Resistance nursed him back to good health and helped him to escape to England where he was treated at East Grinstead. After D-Day he was determined to return to operational flying and was killed on the day Paris was liberated. Two French generals had visited Rosie's mother to ask if she could get Rosie to dissuade him. This Rosie refused to do. It was not for her to do, but for those in authority. Mary had held back from attempting to dissuade Richard and had merely expressed her opinion on the matter, 'I find myself with Linklater.' Her moving letter of farewell, written after Richard had been killed while she was in the pits of despair, shows just how much she had held back.

Feeling somewhat melancholy Richard considered the immediate future with a positive plan in place. He also had to break the news to his friends and family. One of the first that he spoke to was Eric Linklater. In response to the news Linklater replied: 'And now you're happy I suppose?'

Richard replied: 'Damned unhappy, I haven't told my Mother yet.'

Eric Linklater later wrote:

> I remember very clearly the night when I discovered that I could try no more to dislodge him from his resolution for fear that happened. In his character – in his mind, his spirit, his personality – there was quality like something with a sharpened edge and a fine surface, and I was suddenly frightened that my argument would dull the edge or tarnish the surface. And that is the sober truth of it.

By trying too hard to dissuade Richard they faced the risk of alienating him, and losing his friendship if he were to later hold them responsible for a decision he regretted. While the medical board were responsible for passing him fit to fly it should be considered that they had passed a number of other 'disabled' pilots fit to once again resume operational flying. Although they must shoulder some of the blame, what if he had successfully returned to flying single engine-fighters regardless of the eventual outcome? We then have to consider once again Sholto Douglas' part in the tragedy.

Lovat Dickson recalls hearing the news:

> What did we all feel, hearing that he had taken this irrevocable step? Knowing that it meant almost certain death we should have made outraged protest to the authorities, brought every influence to bear to countermand so insane a decision. But we were under the spell of Richard's personality. Something bigger than we was at work in this boy; some power had seized him which had never entered our calm and negligible lives . . . I felt a sinking of the heart when he told me the news, and must indeed have looked woebegone, for he attempted to cheer me up.
>
> 'I'll get a book out of it, Rache, and you'll make a hell of a lot of money, and be thankful.'
>
> But like Eric (Linklater) I could not attempt to dissuade him. The decision was made; anything I might have said would have sounded cautious and middle-aged, and to be contrived towards my firm's commercial interests. I could only say, 'You fool, Richard, God help you,' and be brisk with an enquiry as to when he was to leave, and what his address would be.

Opinions had varied about whether Richard should return to flying amongst those that knew him. Linklater, we know, avoided putting his case too strongly, afraid to alienate Richard. Mary was, like his mother, afraid that some harm would come but did not try to dissuade him, possibly for the same reason as Linklater. Denise Maxwell-Woosnam was among those who had agreed with his intentions and encouraged a return to action, but had no idea that he would be flying cumbersome, poorly maintained, twin-engined light-bombers.

On the afternoon of 15 November he went home and told his mother the news, that he would be returning to flying. On the 19th he wrote to Mary from Rutland Court:

> Mary darling,
>
> I can't find it in my heart to write much at the moment, but I want you to know that I am grateful to you. I know my instinct is right about this thing and you have never questioned my decision. Bless you for that.
>
> I say very little, but though you upbraid me for it I think you know well enough that you are the one person who means anything to me.
>
> Just keep faith and I shall be all right and when I come through, which I know I shall – it will be gain – not loss.
>
> I love you with all my heart.
>
> Richard

That night, he sat down alone at a desk in the writing room of the Oxford and Cambridge University Club, placed his drink on the table, turned on the reading lamp and wrote to his mother:

> Mother Darling,
>
> I just want to say thank you for always having faith, for not questioning my decision, for never betraying that you feel unhappy and, above all, for your unfailing sense of humour.
>
> We do not often speak together about it and for this and many other things I am so deeply grateful. I know what you think of my going back and if I were outside looking on I would agree with you. Yet I am glad that the decision has been left to me. One can go on arguing the thing out rationally ad nauseam. I can write, I am more useful on the ground, I only want to go back so that people may

say 'Well done!' and to get a medal. I am frightened of going back, I only want to make a name, and so forth and so on.

Finally one must listen to one's instinct, and the time will come when I shall know that my instinct was right and my reason wrong. You must try not to worry about me and have the same faith I have that I shall be all right, for I know it. It may be that ---- has the inside information to which he pretends and that I am to be given something else to do. It may be that a thousand things will happen. I do not know. But that it will be alright, I do know. So please try not to be unhappy and lonesome . . . I should not be at peace if I did not go back. Afterwards it will bear fruit and I shall write.

There are very few things to which one can cling in this comic war. To see straight and know where one is heading is perhaps the most important of all.

God bless you always.
Richard

Richard also wrote to his new commanding officer enclosing Mary's name and address, requesting that if he was killed a telegram should be sent to her four hours before one was sent to his mother. This would then give Mary the chance to get to Edwyna and break the news to her before the formal Air Ministry telegram arrived. Richard then wrote his will. Sadly this was unwitnessed and apart from his bequest to Mary of the Eric Kennington portrait, he also requested the following:

To Mary I also leave £20 that she may give a dinner for me to which she will invite Michael and Barbara Astor [Richard's ex-girlfriend], Denise Maxwell-Woosnam, Eric Linklater, and Rache Lovat Dickson.

To Tony Tollemache, I leave my gold watch.

To Merle Oberon (Lady Korda), I leave my gold aeroplane clip.

To my mother I leave my everlasting love and gratitude . . .

I want no one to go into mourning for me.

As to whether I am buried or cremated – it is immaterial to me, but as the flames have had one try I suggest they might get their man in the end.

I want no one to feel sorry for me. In an age where no one can make a decision that is not dictated from above, it was left to me to make the most important decision of all. I am eternally grateful to the stupidity of those who left me that decision. In my life I had a few friends. I learnt a little wisdom and a little patience. What more could a man ask for?

He left the club at midnight and returned home to his parents' flat where he chatted with his mother about the events of the day before going to bed.

Richard received a letter from the station intelligence officer at RAF Hornchurch, dated 21 November 1942, asking him to complete a personal combat report for: 'Your claim of one Me109 destroyed on 3 September 1940, between 09.15 and 10.30 hours.'

This was required by Group who were compiling the combat statistics for the period of the Battle of Britain.

Richard's copy of this letter was not found among his personal effects, and was assumed to have been destroyed.

On the evening of 23 November, Richard had dinner alone with Mary in her new flat. Her furniture had only been moved in that day and it was her first night in the home she had hoped for since the spring. Some stability was re-established in her life. The home where: 'what he (Richard) needed was to be able to come in and sit by the hour and talk,' and where 'he will read all through our meals and afterwards too.' It was all coming right; but too late.

Richard reported for duty to No.54 OTU RAF Charterhall on 24 November 1942. There would be one final entry on his service record. His letters to Mary continue from here, but hers have not survived.

CHAPTER SEVENTEEN

RETURN TO FLYING

24 November 1942

I heard the sighs of men
That have no skill to speak of their distress
No, nor the will, a voice I know
And this time I must go

Wilfred Owen

RAF Charterhall is situated in the Scottish Borders, a short distance east of Greenlaw on the B6460. The land for the airfield at Charterhall was requisitioned from the Trotter family, local farming landowners whose family home was originally named 'Charter Hall'. This gave rise to the occasional modern-day mis-spelling of the name of the airfield. From as far back as 1840, the house with its adjoining land has been called 'Charterhall'.

Prior to Richard's arrival it had only recently begun operational flying training and was home to No.54 Night Fighter Operational Training Unit (OTU) which had been formed at Church Fenton, Yorkshire, on 25 November 1940 with Wing Commander W.K. Beisiegel in charge. Beisiegel was a Canadian and an experienced fighter pilot, but according to many veterans he was not a popular CO at Charterhall.

The Air Ministry had urgently required the airfield at Church Fenton for use as a fighter station for the defence of Leeds and so on 1 April 1942 an advanced party from the unit moved into Charterhall in preparation for the arrival of the main body between 2 and 7 May. Despite the base being far from completed, the buildings were handed over on the 10th. Course No.21 (pilots) and Course No.19 (radar operators/observers, R/Os) arrived on 12 May and flying training began from Charterhall and its satellite airfield at Winfield, situated to the east, on the 13th.

Charterhall does not conjure up many pleasant memories for those who served, or trained there. The countryside was undoubtedly beautiful during the months when the weather was kind, but the winter months could be particularly severe. Like any airfield it is open to the elements.

Charterhall was the most widely dispersed RAF station ever. Most of the accommodation was at least a mile from the main entrance, thus making it an especially long walk from dispersal on the south side of the airfield. Because of the lack of transport and shortage of fuel, bicycles were issued as the main source of transport. It was not uncommon for an individual to step outside a classroom after a lecture only to find someone had taken his bike. It then became necessary to grab the nearest one available in order to avoid a long walk. Therefore, when it came to handing in their bike it invariably had a different serial number to the one originally issued! If there were no bikes available, they had to walk. Richard never used a bike, possibly because of his hands. If transport failed to turn up, or there was not a colleague available who could have given him a lift, he walked.

'A' Squadron was situated on the north-east corner of the airfield, and this was where Richard spent the first part of his course. Many of the airmen and aircrews remember the arduous cycle ride to and from the airfield, which they undertook several times a day, or night. On a freezing cold winter's night, after a particularly unpleasant training flight, chilled to the bone, a long way from home and missing one's family and wondering if you were yet to become one of the many accident statistics, one can start to appreciate the reason for Charterhall's reputation for being a miserable place.

While many of the airmen were initially living in tents the officers were more comfortable in permanent accommodation which had been completed in time. Even if they were still short of internal fittings.

Richard was billeted in single-storey accommodation on site No 1, one of six dispersed sites situated on farmland to the west of the airfield. These sites included accommodation for officers, sergeants and airmen alike and were reached via tracks leading off either side of the B6460 Greenlaw road, the farthest being Richard's over a mile and a half from the main entrance. The huts were either nissen style or constructed of either wood, cement rendered brick or concrete block. The last two types had corrugated asbestos sheet roofing. In addition to the male accommodation, there was a separate site for the officers, sergeants and airwomen of the WAAF. Although ablutions were provided on the same site as the billets, the officers' bath house was actually next to the mess, making the task of bathing very impractical. Today there is little to identify the sites, apart from a single nissen hut and the narrow paths which lead off the main road to the now empty farmland areas where once there were a great many billets.

Richard's batman was George Head. George and a number of his fellow batmen including Jack Paris met in the airmen's mess and talked amongst themselves about their respective charges. They thought highly of Richard. Jack Paris recalled:

> His injuries were shocking, but whenever I walked past and saluted him, he always gave me a smile.

On the airfield 54 OTU was dispersed in three flights, A, B, and C, and were situated around the perimeter track with their aircraft parked on hard standings near the flight offices. The buildings at the airfield dispersal sites were of the cement rendered brick and concrete type, with corrugated asbestos roofs. Close by were also situated blister hangars in which maintenance work could be carried out under shelter. These hump-backed hangars were open at either end. They could be sealed with large canvas screens but these were usually damaged and ineffective. All of the buildings were camouflaged in black and green paint, thus softening their somewhat stark appearance into something that was necessarily drab.

The main domestic area of the airfield, including the watch office and tower (later called the Air Traffic Control Tower, ATC), was situated on a noticeable incline, over-looking the runways, dispersal areas and blister hangars on the slope below (100m/ASL: Above Sea Level). The highest point was Charterhall Wood, a pine forest further up the slope to the rear of the domestic area, on the other side of the B6460 from the main entrance (128m/ASL). A ridge of high ground from Charterhall Wood (128m/ASL) across to Mount Pleasant (105m/ASL) was situated between the watch tower and the lower lying ground on the north-east side where Richard's aircraft crashed (70m/ASL). This is relevant information when assessing the eyewitness reports from staff in the watch tower.

* * *

By March 1941 MkIV Airborne Interception (AI) apparatus had been installed in all night fighter squadrons in Fighter Command, with five of the six Blenheim squadrons converting to the Beaufighter. The number of enemy aircraft losses increased as the number of RAF stations equipped with Ground Control Interception (GCI), operating in conjunction with aircraft with MkIV AI, also increased. Only three enemy aircraft had been shot down in January 1941 but in May of the same year 96 were shot down, although not all to the combination of GCI and AI. It was the success of this GCI/AI combination that paved the way ahead for the young trainee pilots and radar operators of No.54 OTU at Charterhall.

During the move from Church Fenton, four ground AI training units were moved by road to Charterhall under armed guard, such was the level of secrecy surrounding AI at the time.

Charterhall also had six Link Trainers and a Night Visual Trainer situated in purpose-built huts on the instructional site close to the main entrance. Such a large number was entirely appropriate when considering the amount of instrument flying that was to be undertaken by the student pilots and Richard took full advantage of this facility when flying was cancelled owing to inclement weather. Later, when partnered with Wilfrid Fison, his radio/observer (R/O), they would go to the Link Trainer for practice together.

A mobile Airfield Identification Beacon (AIB) unit was driven out from the station each evening and established in a position two and a half miles to the north-east of the airfield. This portable unit with its flashing white light had its own generator and was mounted on the back of a lorry. It provided the pilots with a means of locating the proximity of their airfield, and during night-fighter exercises was used by the controller to maintain an aircraft in a waiting position pending involvement in the exercise. It was also possible to warn the aircrews of enemy night-fighter activity by turning off the flashing white light and replacing it with a triangle of red lights. The pilots would not attempt to land until the red lights were replaced by the flashing white, signalling that it was safe to do so.

* * *

No.54 OTU used an assortment of aircraft for training including the Airspeed Oxford with dual control, side by side pilot/student configuration, for initial conversion; Lysanders for target towing over the North Sea range; Blenheim Mks I, IV and V; and the Beaufighter MkIIf. Most of Richard's flying was on the Blenheim MkV.

Last of the Blenheim aircraft types to enter RAF service, the Blenheim V was otherwise known as 'The Five' but also mistakenly referred to as the 'Bisley'. Before the prototypes of this design were completed the specification was revised and thus the name 'Blenheim V' superseded that of 'Bisley'. The service life of the Blenheim V was destined to be short, as with a maximum speed of 230 mph, the aircraft was decidedly underpowered.

It served in the Middle and Far East but when the units equipped with the Blenheim V reached Italy, losses were such that they were hurriedly re-equipped. Many 'Fives' were converted for use as dual-control trainers and were amongst the first RAF aircraft to employ two-stage amber night simulation filters, which were flown by Fighter Command operational training units.

* * *

The day before his course was due to begin, Richard left Kings Cross on a train bound for Berwick-on-Tweed. Michael Hillary had taken him to the station where they exchanged farewells. As usual Richard's father had shown no gesture of physical affection or kind words but then re-appeared with a packet of cigarettes which he pushed gently into his son's hand, before once again leaving. He had been determined to make some effort to convey his feelings to his son, but had found it difficult.

For Richard it had been yet another 'boarding school' farewell, which is something that, as parents get older and relinquish time with their youngsters, the children find harder, not easier, to accept.

On reaching Berwick, Richard changed trains for Reston, a small village further up the north-east coast, one mile west of the A1 on the Newcastle to Edinburgh line. Here he dismounted and waited at the tiny, rural station with its single building (which exists today as a private house) and single wooden platform, for the connection which ran on a single gauge rail track stopping at Duns, Greenlaw and Earlston. This service was abandoned after the flood of 1948, when bridges and sections of the track were washed away. The route taken by the local railway through the Border landscape is still evident today.

En route the train passed a station called Marchmont, which consisted of only a small platform. This was practically adjacent to the airfield but one and a half miles to the north-west, across the shallow valley of Blackadder Water. This small station was used to unload equipment and stores sent by rail. Some airmen also chose to leave the train here.

Dismounting at Greenlaw, Richard and his colleagues were given a lift in an RAF van, which arrived after half an hour to take them the three and a half miles to RAF Charterhall.

Richard's company en route had usually consisted of officers and NCOs alike, some of whom were already established at Charterhall and had been on leave; others were like him, due to begin training on the next course which began the following day. They were full of trepidation, for the reputation of the unit was well known.

* * *

The Borders during wintertime can appear very cold and desolate. Charterhall became a very different experience for Richard; he had been accustomed to RAF stations where the facilities were in close proximity to the airfield. His comfortable social life at home would also have contributed to the difficult transition. Richard would also have felt apprehensive at what lay ahead and homesick. He had gone to a great deal of trouble to persuade the authorities that he was fit to resume flying duties, he was now under pressure to succeed.

On that return to training he would also have been less likely to have called upon his fellow students for assistance with his classroom studies, as he had with Noel Agazarian and Peter Howes at RAF Kinloss three years previously. In the past he had been in the company of friends at the same stage of training as himself, but now he was a Battle of Britain hero and national celebrity, as a result of his book. He would not have been keen to show his failings on that occasion. It would have also been the case with his physical disabilities, but he was unable to hide those.

He soon settled into the routine and started to appreciate once again the comradeship of his fellow student pilots. Andy Miller became friends with Richard during their time together on the course and recalls:

> Due to the success of his book Dick was more of a celebrity to the locals than if he had a clutch of DFCs and DSOs.
>
> He never mentioned anything about his love-life to me and he wouldn't as I was a sergeant and he was a Flight Lieutenant, but we became good friends, and in general we chatted about flying and his previous flying experiences which involved great trauma, loss of friends and, of course, his own terrible injuries. He was a big brother figure to me in a way. We became friends even though I was a sergeant at the time, because he was that sort of character, he would mix with the NCOs as much as he would with the others, perhaps more so, he didn't care what they thought. We all called him Dick.
>
> Our course thought very highly of this Battle of Britain hero, which is what we saw him as being. He got on well with all of us, he wasn't a quiet person, he chatted openly, laughed and joked. All the stories of his arrogance and selfishness are all balls.

* * *

Shortly after arriving at Charterhall in November 1942, the three squadrons of No.54 OTU were allocated their dispersal sites. 'A' was the conversion squadron, flying principally the Airspeed Oxford and Blenheims; 'B' was the intermediate squadron, on Blenheims and Beaufighter IIfs. On successful completion of these two stages the students progressed to the 'C', advanced squadron, which was based at Winfield and specialised in AI flying, air to air, and air to ground firing, in Beaufighters.

Richard may well have felt somewhat of an outsider on his course because generally the pilots came from No.12 AFU Grantham, Lincolnshire, where they had been taught on Oxfords and Blenheims, and had therefore been together for some time. Prior to the AFU course many of these pilots had qualified as pilots on training courses in America and Canada. The R/Os came from No.62 OTU, RAF Usworth, County Durham, where they had been taught to use the MkIV AI, installed in Avro Ansons which served as flying classrooms. The AI course lasted six weeks and the total flying time averaged 65 hours. Radio interception, chasing and finding exercises amounted to about eight hours. It was a common sight in the Northumberland skies to see one Anson following another as the students learnt how to use their equipment. In point of fact most of the Anson pilots at 62 OTU then applied to go to 54 OTU to take the night flying pilots' course there. Most had learnt how to use blind flying aids (BABS), and accrued valuable night flying experience while at Melton Mowbray.

During the first ten days after Richard arrived at Charterhall he undertook classroom lectures and conversion flying, initially with an instructor in a dual controlled Airspeed Oxford. He then progressed to the Blenheim V with the instructor demonstrating the characteristics of the aircraft, with Richard next to him in the cockpit, before eventually climbing out of the aircraft and leaving him to fly a 'circuit and bump' solo. Richard had flown light aircraft on numerous occasions during his work on the staff of the RAF, but this must have been a very difficult period of adjustment for him, from single-seat fighters to the cumbersome twin-engine bomber. The first few flights must have made Richard realise just how difficult the task ahead would be, and he was yet to fly at night, of which his experience, once again, was negligible.

The R/Os arrived at the station sometime towards the end of that period and initially the only time that they spent in the company of the pilots would have been during off-duty hours. This was less likely to occur if the pilot was an officer and the R/O a sergeant. 'Crewing-up' was then organised and, whenever possible, pilots were paired with a like-minded R/O with similar interests. In the main the training staff carried out this part of their job exceptionally well. Some outstanding partnerships developed, and those that survived the training went on to forge a formidable operational night fighter team. Some remained together for the duration of the war.

Once paired up, time together was during off-duty hours as the pilots had still to complete their conversion training. In the meantime the R/Os would be getting extra ground radar training and navigation training on the only De Havilland Dominie that the unit had on strength.

By the time Richard arrived at Charterhall the final building work had been completed by the contractors. The hardstandings, hangar lighting and the Drem lighting were the last major tasks to be finished. The flying figures for the previous month of October showed a marked increase in the previous month's figures: 2,288 hours of flying (618 being at night), with nine aircraft involved in accidents and three aircrew killed. During the last eight months of 1942, in which Charterhall had been open, there had been 97 crashes resulting in 17 deaths. These accidents generally fell into five categories:

1) Pilot inexperience when converting to a new type. This was particularly the case when converting to the Beaufighter IIf, which did not have dual controls; therefore the student stood behind the instructor while he demonstrated the characteristics of the aircraft before the student took over.

2) Much of the flying was carried out at night, requiring many hours of instrument flying.

Night navigation by the R/Os involved the taking of 'fixes' on radar beacons, and as they too were under training, errors were inevitably made.

3) Many of the aircraft were in a semi-dilapidated condition and often obsolete operational types relegated for training purposes. Spares were in short supply with mechanical failure commonplace.

4) There were the typical servicing difficulties associated with a wartime airfield and essential maintenance was carried out at dispersal, in the open, with the ground crew and aircraft at the mercy of the weather. Often temporary measures were taken until the aircraft could be replaced, which was unlikely, so it was simply a matter of keeping a dilapidated aircraft flying for as long as possible. The electronics and instruments were affected by condensation and there was always a shortage of spares.

5) The urgent need for new crews meant that the training course had been devised and developed as a rapid and intensive programme which provided operational crews as quickly as possible. RAF training had then, as it does today, a reputation for being of a

high standard. Nevertheless, the courses were very short compared with peacetime practice.

The following list was gleaned from accident reports that involved aircraft from Charterhall and Winfield and shows a variety of causes:

Mid-air collision between two aircraft flown by students.
Ground collision.
Taxiing accident.
Controls locked on landing (technical fault).
Crash from height due to icing.
Engine failure.
a/c swung on landing/take-off (occasionally resulting in collision with other static aircraft).
Flew into high ground.
Flew into tree on take-off.
Heavy landing.
u/c accidentally retracted during take-off.
Burst tyre resulting in crash.
a/c undershot due to flap failure.
Loss of control in storm.
Overshot due to technical failure.
Low flying accident.
Belly landing due to undercarriage failure.
a/c stall and crash.
a/c stalled and bounced on take-off resulting in cartwheel.
Aborted take-off.
Undercarriage collapse.
Rudder and elevator jammed.
a/c struck tree while landing.
a/c spun in due to loss of control.
a/c landing, collided with static a/c being refuelled on ground (ground crew killed).
a/c ran out of fuel.
a/c and crew reported 'missing' while carrying out exercises out to sea.
Ground collision.
Glycol fumes in cockpit.
Failure of electrical systems.
Loss of control over sea (icing suspected).
Pilot selected 'flaps up' instead of undercarriage and crashed half a mile from aerodrome during circuit and bumps.
a/c dived into sea.
Ground loop.
a/c rolled three times due to poor instrument flying but landed safely.
High speed crashes.

There were also a number of accidents during gunnery practice over the North Sea ranges during the last part of the course ie, 'Lysander towing drogue hit in the spats by cannon fire'; 'a/c flew into drogue towing cable'; and 'explosion in cannon breach'. Richard had not progressed to this stage of training by the time he was killed.

In some cases it was not possible to confirm the exact cause of the accident, as was the case with Richard's crash, because assessment often relied heavily on supposition. But analysis of other accident reports does allow us to narrow down the cause by comparing the common denominators. It is therefore possible to place the cause of Richard's accident under one or more of the common causes, with a number of additional problems that were definitely known ie. loss of control due to either/or insufficient attention paid to instruments, icing of the control surfaces, an unknown technical failure, inexperience of night flying, flying post-operational twin-engine aircraft and hampered by student disability, as in Richard's case.

The unit received a new influx of one course per month with three courses underway at any one time. As Richard arrived ready for the start of his course on 24 November, Course No.23 was being posted having just reached completion of its training. November had been the worst month for flying accidents since the arrival of the unit at the Borders' airfield in May of that year. Despite autumnal weather conditions, 2,243 flying hours had been achieved with 554 flown at night. Unfortunately, eight aircrew had lost their lives.

The first accident after Richard arrived had been on 9 December, when a Blenheim I flew into a wood at Johnstonebridge, Dumfries, during a cross-country flight. The emergency crews were alerted when the aircraft became overdue and the now familiar feelings of foreboding were experienced in the stomachs of many of those on duty at the time. The wreckage of the aircraft was found with the body of the pilot, having been thrown out on impact, lying nearby.

By the end of 1942 No.54 OTU had amassed a total of 25,584 hours' flying time, with 17,448 by day and 8,136 by night. The pilot input had been 296 with an output of 227; the equivalent of roughly ten squadrons. It is also interesting to note that almost seven aircrew per month were taken off courses, or chose to leave of their own volition. Had Richard decided to quit, then he would have been far from the only one inclined to take such action, but his determination to succeed was greater; as was his stubbornness at not being seen to fail by all that knew him. Perhaps the sight of individuals opting off courses made him all the more determined to remain and succeed, regardless of the difficulties. The risk he was taking was clear to see, aircrew were regularly being killed, the unit had gained a nationwide reputation, albeit within the service, for its accident statistics, and his options were only too clear to him. Go home and join the staff, stay and face the likelihood of death, or survive the course to become operational with the reward of more success as a pilot, and a 'few putty medals', which is what he wanted. Latterly, the risk of death merely meant that he could join his dead friends.

* * *

With an emotional parting from his mother, and the terrible feeling of loneliness and homesickness, Richard had found the journey to Charterhall akin to returning to boarding school, as he had done on so many occasions.

On arrival at Charterhall he was given a letter thoughtfully sent by Mary to coincide with his arrival. As a child he had cried himself to sleep at night with his face buried in the pillow. As a man, he would immerse himself in letter writing to his family and friends. But later in the evening he was once more overcome with trepidation at what lay ahead.

The following letters were all written to Mary during 25 November 1942:

> Officers Mess,
> RAF Station Charterhall,
> Near Duns,
> Berwickshire
> a million miles from anywhere

> My Darling,
>   Your letter greeted me on my arrival very late in the evening. I crept away with it to my wooden hut two miles away from the Mess and read it. Then I cried myself to sleep . . . until I remembered old ----, and then I had to laugh . . .
>   I am stealing odd moments between marching – yes , marching – to and from lectures to write this, so it will be very incoherent. I will do better tonight when I get back to my hut.
>   At the moment I am filled with overmastering depression.
>   Later that day he added:
>   We have just had the list of fatal casualties in the last few weeks read out to us as a warning – very encouraging.

I now have a suspicion that I am sitting in a room reserved for instructors – they are of no senior rank, but they look at me oddly.

This is indeed a queer place for journey's end and yet in a way it is good. It is so utterly bare and without human contact that one must at last be self-sufficient. That is the best way to go.

But I wish you were here. I shall write to-night, all night if I cannot sleep. Now it's impossible.

I love you

R.

And that night he wrote:

I feel like a Hollywood gangster hero, who voluntarily walking back into the gaol hears the prison gates clang to behind him for the last time.

First the journey. I left Kings Cross at 10 am and arrived foodless at Berwick about 6 pm – strangely touched by a last gesture of my father, who, after bidding me goodbye, came back with a packet of cigarettes. I avoided thought all the way up by reading right through Hesketh Pearson's life of GBS [George Bernard Shaw].

At Berwick night had fallen and the platform was cold, but the train to Reston arrived after ten minutes. In the compartment were a couple of youngsters, fresh from training school and eager to get on the course. It was largely to get back into communion with these that I made up my mind to return in the first place – but I felt outside, or rather not so much outside, but as though I was back again two years, and though somewhat the same they were less fine than those I knew then.

. . . At Reston we changed again and I went to a compartment by myself, and watching the sparks fly by I felt very low and in need of you.

Finally at Greenlaw we all decanted, and after half an hour a van trundled us the five miles into the camp. It is perhaps the camp more than anything which is likely to break me.

The sleeping huts are dispersed over a distance of a couple of miles. My room has no fire, coal being scarce [They were actually allowed one bucket of coal per day]. The walls are horribly damp. All this I could bear if it were not that in the mess – such as it is – there is no chance of ever being alone, and yet I am alone all the time. This is the end of the world; ---- a cad and a bully, and the ground staff deadbeats who can get in nowhere else.

The whole almosphere is the one I dread most – emptiness – Do you remember the line in my book about Sunday lunch at Shrewsbury – the bars on the windows, the boys crouching dispiritedly over plates of cold trifle. This is the same.

They have told me that as I am a Flight Lieutenant I need not march to lectures with the others. Kindly meant, but it puts me still further from them. Not that I'm aloof. I think they like me well enough, considering me rather a droll fellow who may save them some 'bullshit'. (They consist of six officers and ten sergeant pilots.)

The telephone in the Mess – the only one I can get at – is in full view of everyone . . . The baths, which have no plugs, are in a separate building, though I don't see why this should worry me, as I shall never have the rapid organising power to fit one in.

The worst moment was an armament lecture – an exact repetition of one we had at Kinloss. I kept expecting to look up and see Noel [Agazarian] beside me, instead of which there was a pinched little boy who picked his nose.

All day my eyes have pricked with tears, and now at last in the privacy of my room I have been weeping like a child for an hour. Why? Is it fear? I have not yet seen an aeroplane and I know not yet whether the night will terrify me or not. Is it just the atmosphere? Very largely, I know. But perhaps this is what they mean in the Air Force by 'lack of moral fibre'. I have often wondered. Maybe this is what happens when a man's nerve goes. And yet I am not consciously frightened of anything, merely unutterably wretched and missing you most frightfully.

This is an awfully egotistical letter, and not much of a showing on my first day. But suddenly I know that I should have listened to advice and not come back.

Phyllis Bottome said that it was only Nazis who forced themselves to do things and that that way was unnatural for me. I should like to believe her now, but perhaps that is a mere bleat of fear. Certainly my London period must have sapped my will, but I did not think I would break as quickly as this. And yet it is so largely the surroundings and the sense of being trapped, and knowing, almost for certain, that I shall not pass out of here till Max [Aitken] has left the Squadron or until it has gone overseas – and then knowing no one any longer in Fighter Command. [Prophetic words. Max Aitken was posted to HQ, Eastern Mediterranean, Fighter Tactics Branch early in 1943, well before the date Richard was due to complete his course.]

I have been looking through the scant library here and coming across T E Lawrence's letters [*The Mint*], I took the book out and, believe it or not, opened it at this page: Garnett speaking about Lawrence wanting to get back to the RAF:

'Since the period at Uxbridge had been a time of great suffering, when he was continually on the verge of breakdown, one wonders whether his will had not become greater than his intelligence. . . .' [Richard left out the centre section of this passage]:

'Such a predominance of will was Lawrence's chief danger. It shows itself frequently in his treatment of his body, on which all his life he was apt to impose quite unfair strains, often of a stupid character. For example, he neglected a broken arm in 1926 and so made a less than satisfactory recovery, just as he had gone back to work in his class with a broken leg in 1904... The courage of the boy too proud to make a fuss is something we admire; in an educated man it is ridiculous and a sign of abnormality.'

Richard continues with his letter:

And yet am I now to go crawling to them on my knees, snivelling to be let out?

They already regard me askance – 'Done no twin engined stuff? Only six hours at night? Are you sure you want to go into night fighters? Don't forget it isn't only your life, but your air gunner's.' A damnably cruel but true point.

Perhaps they're right – perhaps it is the night which is subconsciously too much. I know I'm not frightened of flying by day.

Perhaps it is merely the fear of being so much alone – a bitter pill, when I always thought I liked it so much, but the total lack of human contact is awful – they are machines, not men. At Fighter Command they were people. One could talk to them and like them.

I spoke to Dirty Watkins at Headquarters Fighter Command. How surprised he'd have been if he knew how I hated to let him go. He is prepared to fly me to Northolt on Saturday [for the wedding] if I can get half-way – a miracle if I can get permission or a plane, but I will try.

In response to a 'charming' missive from the 'evil' Kathleen Dewar, Richard added:

I sometimes wonder, had she not called me a coward – oh well, one can't go on rationalising for ever.

Please excuse the pencil, but I can find no pen and must go ten miles to buy one.

Rache and Koestler are both in on some scheme – both very secretive about it, for getting me out to do something 'soon'. What the devil do they mean? If I get through this three months, and am then dragged out, I think I shall break up altogether. If they know something, why don't they tell me? . . .

Forgive this long and (yes, I believe it's true) self-pitying epistle, but I feel much happier for having written it, and for having you to send it to. Don't be ashamed of me if you can help it, my darling.

I shall think of you in your new surroundings and hope to dream of you.

I love you so very much that at moments I think my heart will break. You are everything that is not here – warmth, humanity, humour, and intelligence.

I thought I might write an amusing book here. Perhaps I yet shall, if I can ever be alone, but what escapism it will be.

Good night. God bless you. You are very near to me and the tears are over.

Richard

The 'cad' and 'bully' to which Richard referred is Group Captain Beisiegel, the station commanding officer.

Richard changed as his overwhelming feelings of homesickness gradually subsided and he recognised some of the same qualities in his new companions that he had seen in his old friends. The heavy atmosphere lifted as he became used to his new surroundings, companions and looked forward to the flying training that lay ahead. The self-pity in his letter writing also diminished. The answer to the question posed about Lovat Dickson and Koestler is that they didn't want to be on the receiving end of Richard's wrath, and lose his friendship, if they were to succeed, which had been the deterrent in the first instance but now, in his absence, they would try harder.

The wedding to which Richard referred was that of Michael Astor to Barbara, his ex-girlfriend and daughter of Kathleen and Johnny Dewar. The 'miracle' he asked for, in the form of leave and a light aircraft, was granted and Richard flew south for what was a wartime 'society' wedding in Mayfair. The reception was held in Grosvenor Street with the bride dressed in a 'gown of heavy ivory satin with a bouquet of white lilies, gardenias, and stephanotis'. Richard was re-united with Mary and amongst the many guests Richard found himself in the company of some of his dearest friends including Rosie Kerr with her rebuilt face and the master behind the work on both hers and Richard's face, Archie McIndoe. According to Rosie Kerr it was during the reception that Richard told McIndoe of his current mental condition; that he had 'lost his nerve'. Such a meeting did occur with McIndoe, as McIndoe's biographer was able to confirm from his papers, and he was horrified at Richard's state of mind. But it is most likely that this meeting occurred about a fortnight after the wedding.

Richard had dinner with Mary that evening and flew back to Charterhall the next day.

Mary was still seeing her old friends. Sadly, there is no record of her thoughts and feelings at this time because her letters were destroyed at Charterhall – no record of what she felt when she opened Richard's pencil-written letters; of the icy, windy weather; the obsolete poorly maintained aircraft; his weak, troublesome, disabled, hands and the frequency of his agonising headaches and dizzy fits. We can only guess. We do know that each time Richard left her she returned to her flat and wept.

Mary was there for Richard, offering her love and support through this period. She gave him confidence and was witness to the change in him, a change that was 'out of recognition', according to their mutual friend Rosie Kerr, who believed that Mary would have changed him even more had he lived.

Officers Mess
Charter Hall
near Duns, Berwickshire
Tel. No. Coldstream 134-135
Sunday 29th November

My darling,

Such a very wonderful letter. I will make the promise that IF I get the chance to really do something, then I will take my friends' advice (to give up operational flying).

It was like some extraordinary dream to see you again so soon, and to have you again in my arms. Never have I felt so close to you, nor felt the need of you more . . .

Please excuse the scrawl, but I am just off to bed – as my fire has not been lit
– a proper letter tomorrow.

I shall dream of you.

R.

P.S. You spoil me outrageously.

After the Astor's wedding, Richard took the opportunity to hold Mary in his arms; a
chance which had arisen sooner than he had hoped.

Richard's next few letters to Mary show how depressed he was at that time by the
poor weather and living conditions, particularly compared with the lifestyle he had been
used to.

On 30 November Richard wrote again to Mary. In her previous letter she suggested
that Richard write his daily letters to her in the form of a narrative that he could perhaps
use later as the basis for a book; this I believe he did instead of keeping a daily journal,
which his father believed was destroyed along with his other papers by the station effects
officer. There is also the possibility that Richard complied with this suggestion by Mary
in order to prevent valuable information being lost if he were to be killed – in the manner
that actually occurred. It was standard practice, as I shall mention later, and he may have
been aware of it. I do not believe, as I have mentioned before, that he was *expecting* to
be killed:

I will take your advice, darling, in that I will make notes – not of a book, but in
diary form, and I will write them to you. But to-day I cannot start properly. I am
too weary and again very low. For I have a splitting headache; my teeth are
chattering and I fear I am in for a chill. And yet I must fight this, for if I go to bed
now I shall have to drop a course and I shall still not have flown. I expect to start
tomorrow. Any more of the nerviness of this waiting will be calamitous.

After a morning of lectures, and a wonderful letter from you, written before
the wedding, I set off for 'A' Squadron, already unable to move my eyes without
feeling as though I had been hit by a hammer . . .

The wind was very bitter on my hands and face, and I arrived chilled to the
marrow. (This wind has a peculiar quality – it bores into your very soul.) All
afternoon I sat there, and having brought no book I could only brood. Then at
5.30 I climbed out of my flying kit and walked the 35 mins back to sick quarters,
where with much mystery and hand-waving the Station M.O. produced two
aspirin and vanished off somewhere to play bridge.

My eyeballs are aching, so I must turn in, for I must not pack up tomorrow.

First, however, thank you for buying such a lovely present in my name. I hope
you are being truthful about the price.

Second, I love you dearly.

Third, to-night has been a near thing, but it has not ended in tears.

R.

On the same day, 30 November 1942, Richard wrote to Lovat Dickson on headed
notepaper from the mess at RAF Charterhall. With a frank honesty and clearly suffering
from homesickness Richard indicated that he was more aware than ever of what he was
up against. His fortitude showed how determined he was to overcome adversity and
return to operational flying. It also shows how Geoffrey Page had made the correct
choice when, while at East Grinstead, the two had sat and discussed their future as pilots:

Dear Rache,

I have had a letter from Mrs Wagg, an old lady in East Grinstead, enclosing
one from Lady Campbell, wife of the British Minister in Portugal. Unfortunately
at the moment I have mislaid it, but he wants the book translated into Portuguese
and is eager to know what steps to take. What do we do?

This spot is so desolate and utterly lacking in human contact that the first two days nearly broke me. It is scarcely the spot for a spoilt egocentric brat of tottering morale like myself – the first thing they did was to read out the list of fatal casualties on the previous course, 12 in all, as a warning!

However, I must persevere though the learning to conquer these heavy twin-engined brutes is proving something of a problem for my hands.

Write to me now and again that I may have some contact with the world of books. Writing here is out of the question; there is the privacy of a regimented concentration camp.

Dismally but determinedly,
Richard

Richard wrote back to Miss Wagg (not Mrs as Richard states in his letter), who was the sister of Alfred Wagg, first treasurer of the Guinea Pig Club:

Dear Miss Wagg,

I am here for three months 'hard', learning to be a night fighter. When I say 'hard' I mean it, not only the camp which is understandable, but also the effort of re-orientating oneself to two years ago. Still, I'm glad I've made the decision. I'm happier for it – as long as I can do the job. I'm finding this night stuff devilishly difficult.

On 3 December Richard wrote to Mary with the news that he had started flying, albeit an assessment flight with his instructor and flight commander at Charterhall, Flight Lieutenant Benson. Benson was the same rank as Richard and had also been a fighter pilot in the Battle of Britain. Since then he had become a night-fighter ace and had arrived at Charterhall on 27 October for a period on instructional duties. His navigator Lewis Brandon had also been sent to Charterhall to instruct the R/Os. Benson's part in this story is significant. Richard wrote of his first flight with him:

Much better to-day, for I have finally flown; with no particular distinction and only dual, nevertheless I have flown. My greatest difficulty is taxi-ing these heavy brutes. I find that I have not the strength in my right thumb to work the brakes, so I am to have an extension fitted to the brake lever.

My headache is still with me, but better. If only I could lay my hands on a car, life would be quite tolerable. The evenings here, with the snow-dusted mountains pale under an orange sky, are very lovely.

Richard's flight was in an Airspeed Oxford.

It is from this passage that we realise that Charterhall and the surrounding area is not the 'forgotten man's last stop' but a place of outstanding beauty. The image given by Richard was based on his assessment made soon after he arrived, when feeling very homesick and suffering the discomforts of the region's seasonally inclement weather in conjunction with the basic standard of his accommodation. Certainly the opposite to what he had been used to recently. He goes on:

Were it not that one's chattering teeth force one to walk on, it would be time well spent just to sit on the aerodrome and look across the great stillness. For it is still; the roar of machines taking off and landing only seemed to emphasise it.

It's curious psychologically that I have only to step into an aeroplane, that monstrous thing of iron and steel just waiting for the chance to get me down, and all fear goes. I am at peace again.

Not that this course is going to be easy. It is so utterly different from day fighting – no question of 'There they are, let's have a go', but very cold, calculating, and scientific. One must acquire a quite different temperament and learn that one's greatest enemy is one Isaac Newton.

A letter from you to-day with the criticism of Gerald Heard. As you say, hardly the answer to my problem.

Tomorrow the CO has ordained a station parade in the morning, to make quite sure of wasting time and to give himself the pleasure of telling some of us (me without doubt) to get our hair cut.

You ask me to have faith, darling. Yes, but faith in what? 'That things will be all right,' you say. Depends what you mean by 'all right'. If you mean faith that some miracle will happen, and I shall be ordered to some job which I can not only do well, but enjoy, then I say no. It is bad to have that faith, and undermining. If you mean faith that I have done the right thing in coming back, then yes. But if you mean faith that I shall survive, then again no. If this thing plays to its logical conclusion, there is no reason why I should survive. After a few hours flying, my instinct will tell me that I shall survive, while my reason will tell me that I shall not – and this time reason will be right.

It may be of course that I shall come through, but it does not do to think so. I came back not expecting to come through – it was a very part of my decision to come back, and suddenly to see a pink spectacled light through all that darkness would be merely hedging the bet.

How self-consciously priggish that sounds! However, I mean it. I am so unhappy that you went back after I had gone and wept. As you wrote it, I had the picture vividly clear, and I was not there to comfort you.

No more to-night as I must sleep – with your picture by my side.

R.

Richard repeated some aspects of this letter when he wrote to Arthur Koestler on 2nd December:

... Being a rather selfish fellow, however, what is of far more interest to me is how to keep the extremely bitter cold not only from petrifying the burnt skin on my hands and face, but from prying into my very soul... I suppose the atmosphere brought to the surface the subconscious dread of dying up here, at night and in the cold ...

... As before, the more I fly the more my instinct will tell me that I shall get through, while my reason telling me that I shall not, will grow fainter.

But this time my reason will be right. I know too much not to doubt it ...

The next day Richard wrote to Koestler again:

One can rationalise for ever and one's reason finally tells one that it is madness, but it is one's instinct to which one listens.

When I was still waffling I read The Mint, T. E. Lawrence's unpublished agony in the Air Force, describing his first period at Uxbridge as an Air Force A.C.2. This, I confess, influenced me strongly, as it was what I was looking for. As much as anything I came back for that, and yet ...

The 'logical conclusion' would have been for Richard to have been turned down by the medical board and he would never have arrived at Charterhall. Having been passed fit to fly, the parameters had changed and the 'logical conclusion' would have been for those responsible at Charterhall to have taken Richard off the course; others had gone the same way. The longer he was allowed to stay on the course the 'logical conclusion' loomed of Richard becoming yet another fatality statistic, and in that respect he was right. Richard liked to think he could make it through the course, but all things considered he knew that he was up against extreme odds. It took courage for him to persevere, but in this case perhaps it would have taken a greater display of courage to actually quit the course.

Following his first flight, Richard's letter writing changed completely, becoming lighter, with the tone changing for the better. He was in circumstances and surroundings and with men that he felt comfortable with. His self-confidence returned and he was once again the extrovert and the centre of attention amongst those with whom he was training. His attitude towards his survival also became more optimistic, as he had probably hoped it would.

Richard wrote Mary a second letter on 3 December, elated at having successfully flown solo, in daylight. Up until that time, he had amassed 2 hours 40 minutes flying 'dual' with his instructor during both day and night exercises:

> My darling,
>   The morning started badly; bitterly cold, a long walk over to flights, and an indifferent dual performance on a Blenheim [Remember that Richard had been a difficult student pilot]. Then this afternoon something clicked. My instructor climbed out and in an over-casual voice said, 'O.K., off you go. Just time for a couple of circuits and bumps,' and I was on my own.
>   Round I go, twice without mishap, and I am exhilarated as after my first solo three years ago. I saunter into the mess, my battledress carelessly undone, and a voice calls out, 'So you made it.' Pilots cluster round: they have been watching. 'I saw you take off.' 'Very nice landing.' – 'The old ace back on the job again.' So they are human after all. I feel a new-old warmth beginning to course through me; the potion is already at work.
>   I pick up a newspaper – Beveridge Report? Oh, the fellow is thinking about after the war: we'll probably all be dead anyway. Let's find out what Jane's doing in the *Daily Mirror*. We turn the page: we comment on her legs, and I look more closely at the faces around me. I am happy. [I was able to confirm from those who were at Charterhall with Richard, that this is accurate – In the eyes of many of the students he was the experienced ace of the Battle of Britain, and they did make the effort to watch him fly. He thrived on the attention and, as can be deduced from this paragraph, Richard's confidence was returning.]
>   We wander into dinner and afterwards we crowd round the fire, order beers, more beers, and talk shop. Time passes. Am I bored? A little, but only a very little, for to-morrow I shall be up again. This morning I was thinking seriously of asking for a transfer to a day OTU – Spitfires again – easy to handle, people I know. Now I'm off on a new adventure.
>   That was to-day darling – that and your letter. So you're turning into a miracle worker now, along with everything else. I refuse resolutely to believe it: there must be something you cannot do. And be warned – here I am beginning to settle in – here, funnily enough – if I only had time I could write, whereas in London I could not . . .

Mary mentioned in one of her letters that she had been attempting to find Richard employment, perhaps with Miles Aircraft, with whom she would later work. The last three lines of this letter is in response to this.

From this letter we can perhaps see how Richard was intending to write about his adventures since *The Last Enemy*. His state-of-mind had totally changed and he was giving all the credit to Mary and her efforts to keep him motivated and his spirits high. He even admitted having considered reverting to Geoffrey Page's idea of returning to daylight operational flying in the aircraft he was most familiar with – the Spitfire. I believe that was not the first time he had considered this option.

Richard's version of events concerning his flying that day differs significantly from that of his instructor, Flight Lieutenant Benson. In a letter to his wife after Richard's death Benson included comments which he repeated in 1987 shortly before his death:

> I sent him off solo and it was terrible. I gave him further instructions and then he challenged me to stand behind him whilst he flew and tell him what he did wrong. I did. He nearly killed us both. But somehow we eventually got it sorted out and he got the hang of it. He thought a lot of me for that.

While at Charterhall Richard amassed a total of 16 hours and 35 minutes flying solo, both night and day, up until his death.

* * *

During December, Richard received three letters from his publisher. A Christmas reprint of *The Last Enemy* had been considered but ultimately did not occur, sales of the fifth impression were going well, enquiries from America regarding two short stories promised by Richard, and confirmation that his name would come up for election at the Garrick Club on 7 January 1943; the eve of his death.

Mary found her new home too large for her to live in alone and took in a lodger, 'one of those distinguished Americans who used to write admiring books about Britain'. But Richard was no longer jealous, he was flying again and happier. He also behaved in a more forgiving manner towards Kathleen Dewar. He was proving to her that he was no coward.

Richard's two greatest interests were flying and writing. Of his writing, we have seen much lately in the form of his letters. Now, the two merge once again bringing him an increased level of excitement, anticipation and pleasure. His flying had previously provided the basis for a best-selling book. Perhaps it would provide the same again.

During the first episode he had nearly died in combat. The level of danger had once again risen to something comparable, if not, in excess of the danger previously experienced during the Battle of Britain. But the danger did not come from the enemy this time, but from the weather, the aircraft, the night and Richard's own weak, disabled hands. He was soon to experience absolute terror; that which would only become sheer in that tiny moment in time when the pilot realises that he has done all he can to recover his aircraft and is going to die. Richard's previous brush with death had revealed new limits of fear often not anticipated when one is so young and reckless. But once experienced the fear is always there, lurking, waiting to come to the fore when the individual is again faced with, or anticipates, another dangerous situation. It is this fear that Richard refers to as his 'loss of nerve'. In the meantime Mary continued to write, offering encouragement and motivation for him to continue writing his narratives to her.

Richard's confidence and enthusiasm continued to grow as he progressed into the course and this was reflected in his letters to Mary. In her last missive, Mary told Richard that she had invited his mother to her new flat:

Charter Hall
7.12.42

> A sixty mile an hour gale has been blowing all day with a cloud base of 600 feet, so flying has indeed been a battle with the elements. Taxi-ing round the perimeter track develops into a fierce tussle between pilot and machine. One wrestles with the wheel as though forty thousand Gremlins were blowing on the rudder and tail-fin. In doing so I took most of the skin off one hand, and as a result I'm in a lowering temper.

The next day Richard wrote to Jeanette Lee, one of those who had cared for him while he was in America:

> Dear Jeanette,
>   I have at last managed to get back to flying, and after three months in this wilderness I shall be a fully fledged night fighter and go to a squadron. Reason and my friends told me it was madness to return, but in London I felt out of touch and though I am half-way through a new book I listened to my instinct and not my reason, with the result that here I am. My hands caused some trouble at first with these heavy machines, but now I'm settling in and enjoying myself.
>   The general situation is better, especially for us in the RAF. What a difference from this time two years ago!
>   This is the forgotten man's last stop. We expect to be snowed up shortly, which will put an end to flying. Then I tremble to think what will happen, for flying is the only thing that keeps one sane. Write and tell me your news, Jeanette dear. I'm very cut off here.

Clearly, Richard had come to be very fond of Jeanette Lee during his stay. 'Half-way through a new book' was an exaggeration. The plan was in his head and his daily activities, feelings and descriptions were recorded in his letters to Mary and intended as the basis of the main content. Despite Charterhall being 'the forgotten man's last stop', Richard was happier, as long as he could continue flying, otherwise he would sit, brood and lose confidence.

The same day he wrote to Mary Warburg, another of his hostesses in America, and exaggerated again about his progress with a new book:

> . . . I'm pretty scared and my hands give me quite a lot of bother, but anyhow I am back.
>
> In London I was well into a new book and had written the script for a picture to be filmed next month and yet I felt more and more out of touch with reality – and here I am, learning to get pleasure from ordinary people and ordinary things again.
>
> It's a little hard learning to go to school again after three years – it makes one very nostalgic for all those, now dead, who trained with me, yet I'm beginning to enjoy myself and the old glow is returning . . .
>
> Apart from the intense cold and driving winds, it is difficult to keep clean as some maniac seems to delight in stealing the bath plugs!
>
> The news generally is encouraging at last, especially for us in the RAF. What a difference from two years ago. Now finally it looks as if its our turn.
>
> My love life, now suspended, has been for the last year one of quiet domesticity, slippers by the fire, etc. – a great and pleasant change, though a sign of advancing years, I fear . . .

This last paragraph is quite astonishing, intended perhaps to create a specific image in the mind of Mrs Warburg or an expression of what he himself would have found ideal.

The reference to the situation being better in the RAF than it had been two years previously appears in both letters and refers to the fact that the RAF was, by that time, carrying out offensive operations against the enemy, instead of defensive as had been the case with his own flying experience.

In response to a letter Richard wrote to Eric Linklater at his home in Scotland, he received a reply dated 8 December:

> It's bloody, isn't it? I loathe discomfort – little wooden huts – cold weather – Spartan sanitation and early rising – and people. How I sympathise with you . . .
>
> . . . In the last war I behaved with much the same sort of high-minded lunacy as you are showing now. My whole desire and single effort were to get to France: I did and the next thing that happened was that I was sitting up to the knees in mud in a shell hole in Passchendaele – You turn your back upon the loveliness and old brandy of a modish existence to seek the magnificence of combat in the upper air with Orion for your only neighbour and find instead the muted squalor and the populous bleakness of an RAF hutted camp . . .
>
> . . . I put my nose into a work entitled *The Last Enemy* the other day. It's all right. First impressions were amply confirmed. The author is truly a writer, and he has no need to worry. When a new subject is ready and ripe in his mind he will sit down and write again, no matter where he is. He is, I imagine, a superior person (in the Confucian sense) for I find that he shows a very decent and distinguished reticence when describing his worst and most excrutiating sufferings – but makes a hell of a row about a draughty hut, boredom, and cold water. Superior persons are ill-at-ease with anything but the best of everything: Including pain . . .

Richard had mentioned Eric Kennington in his letter:

> . . . You said he was a great man – I think you're wrong. He is a Good man. That is so rare a state that I am not surprised at your perplexity when meeting it, and your constant failure to classify it.

> Now just you be careful in those horrible airplanes and don't go up too high
> or come down too quickly.

On 10 December Richard wrote to Mary again, his letter writing taken over by his experiences; less waxing lyrical to Mary about his feelings for her and more of the narrative writing about his adventures. He was, at last, back in the flow; his writing and flying had taken over:

> I was on second detail and had to do a cross-country. This entailed working out
> a course on the computator before taking to the air; a feat quite beyond the
> mathematical imbecility of my brain. Fortunately three others were on the same
> exercise, so I left it to one of them, a young fellow called Smithson, a serious-
> minded youth, without much originality; but, like all the others, perfectly capable
> of understanding the (to me) impossible intricacies of a computator.
>   'You are a clot,' he said cheerfully, and did his best to show me how it was done.
>   As soon as I was airborne I folded my map and stuck it away: it was about as
> much use as a sick headache and for an hour and a half I flew the three legs of
> the journey on my instruments in unbroken cloud, grey, damp and clawing. It's a
> curious sensation to be flying like that, unable to see anything, confined in that
> small space with only the monotonous voice of the ground control to remind you
> of the existence of another human being. I find it intensely interesting.

This flight took place on 9 December. On landing, Richard was told that 'Smithson' (actually Pilot Officer K.J.D. Rawlins) had been killed when his Blenheim MkIf crashed into a wood at Johnstone Bridge, Dumfries, and burnt out.

Richard goes on to explain the nonchalant behaviour exhibited by experienced aircrew after such an event:

> Koestler has a theory for this. He believes there are two planes of existence,
> which he calls the 'vie tragique' and the 'vie triviale'. Usually we move on the
> plane of the 'vie triviale', but occasionally, in moments of elation, danger, etc.,
> we find ourselves transferred to the plane of the 'vie tragique', with its un-
> commonsense cosmic perspective.

Back in the service life he had been missing, Richard was enjoying himself. He continued to progress satisfactorily and was happier than he had been prior to making the decision to return to flying.

In his letters Richard's writing exudes an air of excitement, of anticipation for the day ahead, the thrill of the challenge and the satisfaction at keeping pace with the demanding course requirements – the enjoyment of flying, his existential analysis of all that is going on around him and his philosophical acceptance of the bad with all that is good. He exhibited the writing style that Eric Linklater and Lovat Dickson knew would be his strongest point if he were to pursue a career as a writer after the war, writing about his own experiences in life.

As time went by Richard experienced an increase in the number of headaches he suffered. The symptoms described in his letters, extreme pain and visual disturbance, are akin to migraine. On 14 December Richard wrote to Mary:

> My darling,
>   The most agonising headache, so I'm off to bed. I'll write to-morrow . . .

The next letter to have survived, assuming that there were others in the interim period, was written after his Christmas leave. It is believed to have been during this period that, having travelled home to London, Richard met Archie McIndoe.

It has been written that the two met at the Astor wedding (which they did, but as I have already mentioned, a discussion about his mental condition most probably did not take place then), or that they ran into each other in London while Richard was on leave during December. But Richard had actually contacted McIndoe beforehand and arranged to meet him. The two went off to Richard's club for a drink. There he confessed his nerve was gone and he had to get off the course. McIndoe later wrote:

> I have always been certain that he knew what the end would be. Three weeks before his time he came to see me and said that unless he could be shifted from night flying he could not last out much longer. But he stipulated that the course on which he was flying should not be interrupted lest someone should say he was afraid to continue. The idea was that he should return to East Grinstead for another operation. Disturbed by this news and impressed by the passive way in which he gave it, I wrote immediately to his station medical officer. Richard was suffering from the common complaint where his body would not tolerate what his mind could contemplate. His nervous system had not brought his physical responses under control.

On returning to East Grinstead McIndoe wrote a letter to the medical officer at RAF Charterhall. It was dated 17 December 1942:

Re: Flight Lieutenant Richard Hillary.

Dear Sir,

> This officer has, as you know, had a long series of plastic operations for the repair of severe burns of the face and hands. I saw him the other day and was impressed by the fact that his left eye did not appear to be standing up to the strain of night flying as might be expected, a fact of which Hillary is aware but which I think he is loath to admit.

> As you know, he is a very able young writer, and I feel very strongly that flying under these conditions can only end in one way. This would be a great pity. He unfortunately was boarded by the Central Medical Establishment before I knew that he was going, and I am afraid he brought great pressure to bear to get back to operative work. I have in fact more to do to his face, and particularly his lower left eyelid, which will necessitate his attendance at East Grinstead in the future, and I would therefore be glad if you would arrange for his return to me at an early date.

> In the meantime I do feel if you could with discretion restrain him from further flying, it might save him from a very serious accident. After I have dealt with his eye, I can reopen the matter with the CME, and a more satisfactory disposal could be made for him.

> Would you be so good as to treat this letter as private and confidential to yourself? The feelings of these young men are very apt to be hurt in relation to this vexed question of operative work following an injury. I feel however there is a strong case here for intervention.

Yours faithfully
Archibald H McIndoe
Consultant Plastic Surgeon RAF.

Unfortunately, the medical officer at Charterhall was on leave for three weeks and because the envelope was marked 'private and confidential' the contents were not attended to by other members of the medical staff and it remained on his desk unopened.

In a letter written at Charterhall, Richard tells of a day trip to Edinburgh, home of 603 Squadron. It would seem that the letter was written to a girl he met or already knew in Scotland's capital; perhaps from his time with the Edinburgh squadron:

Dear Faery Queen,

> Thank you for helping me to escape Witches Wood for one day in Wonderland.

> We duly left Edinburgh at 10.30 (ie: 22.30) but thanks to our drivers extremely hazy idea of navigation we did not get back until three o'clock in the morning. The journey back I found very interesting after our talk on officers

mixing with men etc. I was in charge of our bus, filled entirely with Sergeant Pilots, happily drunk after their days outing, and naturally singing, loudly, discordantly, obscenely and with great enthusiasm. Five miles out of Edinburgh I discovered we had a WAAF onboard, getting a lift back to camp. Should I stop the dirty songs? I decided not; she should not lawfully have been on the bus, and she must have known what to expect. I have no doubt her ears were red if we could have seen in the general murk.

Question: Would the Wing Commander agree with me.

The weather today has been so bad there has been no flying, so I still don't know if I shall get home for Christmas. If I can't get away I shall ring you up and throw myself upon your mercy for one day. Please excuse the scrawl but I'm writing at dispersal by candle light, all the lights have fused.

Yours sincerely,
Richard Hillary

During the Christmas leave Richard stayed with his parents. On the first evening he had dinner with Mary. The following evening he visited Denise Maxwell-Woosnam at Eaton Place. Her brother was with her and the three had a drink and Richard stayed to supper with them. To those present, Richard did not appear depressed, but dispassionate and fatalistic and several times repeated that he had found the key to life. He talked as though he had become a spectator of life.

At midnight Richard requested that Denise, who had been wearing her khaki uniform, change into her loveliest outfit. After some protest she overcame her shyness and modesty and duly obliged. He stayed silent for a while towards the end of his visit, thanked Denise for her hospitality and said goodbye to her for the last time.

On Christmas Eve, Mary and Richard had dinner in the company of Arthur Koestler. On Christmas Day, Richard remained at home with his parents and Mary spent that time with her mother and family. Edwyna Hillary later recorded that her son had said to her:

If I should die before you, Mother, do not mourn. Go on being bright and gay. I have enjoyed my life, and I know all the answers.

His father wrote of Richard at this time:

We were impressed by the fundamental change in him. Beneath his usual gay manner he was quieter and seemed suddenly to have grown from boyhood into a man . . . It was evident he was in a disturbed state of mind on his last leave. He and I sat in the same sitting-room for about half an hour without saying a word to each other, by which time the strain had become almost unbearable. I was aching to say, 'There was a time when you brought all your troubles to me, old man. Can you not do so now?' Whether from a natural reluctance to intrude upon his privacy or for some other reason I do not know, but the words did not come from me. At that time I did not know that his crippled hands were making it almost impossible for him to fly bombers. If I had spoken he might have told me, and it is possible that I could have done something about it. On the other hand, he might have resented the interference. Whatever the outcome might have been it will be my eternal regret that I did not invite him to confide in me.

This passage is tinged with regret at not having made the effort to communicate more openly with his son, thus making the most of their time together. Michael Hillary, like Linklater, did not want to take action in order to perhaps prevent Richard losing his life unnecessarily, for fear of an angry reaction. Believing that there was the possibility he might be successful can be the only argument in favour of such a decision; with hindsight it is absurd that more was not done and his parents and friends must have been tormented by guilt at not having tried harder.

During the evening on Christmas Day, Mary and Richard had dinner with Brigadier Charles Haydon and his wife and one or two other friends.

It was during this trip home that Richard met Colin Hodgkinson, his friend from his time at East Grinstead. In his autobiography, published in 1957, Hodgkinson recalls the chance encounter in Piccadilly when Richard took him to his club in Sackville Street. At the end of the meeting they rose to leave. Hodgkinson wrote:

> Surprisingly he held out his hand.
> 'Goodbye Colin, I don't think I'll see you again.'
> 'Why?' I asked. 'We might run into each other.'
> 'No,' he said, smiling with his twisted lips, 'I don't think I'm to last it out.'

The publication of Hodgkinson's assessment of Richard's remarks had unfortunate consequences. Richard made similar fatalistic comments to an associate from his time at HQ, Fighter Command, Squadron Leader 'Laddy' Lucas DFC, whom he had also met during the same leave. Richard's parting words had 'haunted' him for many years after his death.

On Boxing Day morning Richard returned to Charterhall for the last time.

The following day Richard wrote to Mary. He had had a thoroughly enjoyable Christmas and there was little evidence of the awful pangs of wretched homesickness that had overwhelmed him when he had first arrived. There now seems to be an air of contentment and anticipation with what lay ahead. He also expresses enthusiasm for including further narrative and to rectify his long-standing fault of not answering questions which she had asked during the more troubled part of their relationship and which he had been reluctant to answer in his letters to her:

> Darling,
> Coming up in the train I pondered over how you spoiled me. It's really terrible and I must not accept it as a matter of course.
> I was so happy over Christmas; thank you for it.
> To-night somehow I cannot write, so I'm not going to try. Tomorrow however I shall produce a screed. I shall also take to answering your letters as my New Year's resolution.
> Thank you for such a wonderful Christmas present also.
> A small boy's letter, but to-night I feel spent.
>
> I love you,
> R.

Richard was unable to write his 'screed' for some days. The course work and the flying had taken over.

He had yet to fly at night. Before progressing to night flying the student night flying pilots were given a short period of artificial night flying, or sodium training, during daylight. Day was turned into night by fitting dark coloured filters to the cockpit windows and the pilots' goggles, a method used for many years in the film and TV industry, in the form of a dark blue filter placed over the camera lens, a convenient method of avoiding having to wait for night time, and was referred to in the profession as 'Day for Night'. Take-off and landings were practised using sodium flare-path lighting, which was particularly bright and could still be seen through the filters, simulating night time runway lights. With this phase of his training complete, Richard was paired up with an R/O, in Richard's case Sergeant Wilfrid Fison described by the station medical officer as: '. . . a very special observer, an old Cambridge Blue, of a temperament just calculated to suit Hillary, and the prospects were that they would make a good pair.'

Richard's next letter was written on 30 December and was the kind of letter Mary had suggested he write; a detailed narrative that he could later turn into another book:

> There has been no moment at all in which to write or think in the last few days, for we are flying night and day. And yet somehow I must get all this down, these three months, even if it's only notes and impressions so that it may not be wasted. As long as you don't mind it scrappy, disjointed, and rambling, I will send it all

to you, and then maybe some day I shall have peace and time to put it together.

Richard goes on to describe the Boxing Night dance and the parade the morning after his arrival back in the Borders. Having endured the previous day's long arduous journey back to Charterhall, 'the forgotten man's last stop', there was a formal parade of the whole station in one of the hangars with a speech delivered by Group Captain Beisiegel, the CO. The speech was treated with disdain:

> We march down and we form up and we wait – the whole station – stiff, frozen, until all feeling goes from my fingers – twenty minutes before the G.C. arrives, heaves himself out of his car and waddles forward to inspect us. He takes an hour to do this – the parade has no other function, and I stand squeezing my toes in my shoes, seeing how long I can stand absolutely motionless. The one nonsense – the other beneficial self-discipline derived from the nonsense. An ambulance is drawn up opposite the lines of men – our line outside the hangar – standing on what yesterday was a sea of mud – now frozen solid. Why the ambulance? I soon remember. Two airmen, green in the face, are escorted over to it. Nobody moves but the Padre and the Liaison Major – God forbid, no prayers – they walk up and down, up and down. The G.C. and his staff are somewhere behind. I hear a female voice say No.8 Squadron attention, so I know that he must be near the end. Everyone is called to attention and he speaks. I cannot hear what he says, but it is something to do with Christmas being over; shoulders to the wheel, etc.
>
> Finally it is over. 'Fall out officers,' he calls out. We are pupils and it should not apply to our Squadron. I walk off – pushing the others before me. He eyes me but can say nothing. We salute and then march away – stamping our feet, waving our arms, fearing the moment when circulation will return.

On 1 January 1943 Wing Commander W.K. Beisiegel left RAF Charterhall and took command of No.57 (Spitfire) OTU at RAF Eshott, which had recently moved there from Hawarden. In exchange the station commander at RAF Eshott, Group Captain Rupert H.A. Leigh, took command at Charterhall on the same day. Both men were fighter pilots, and Leigh had commanded 66 Squadron during the Battle of Britain. Beisiegel had commanded 616 Squadron from September 1939 until May 1940. One interesting aspect of Leigh's career is that on 18 October 1939, while a flight commander at Central Flying School, Upavon, he tested Douglas Bader when the legless aviator was trying to get back on flying duties.

Under Beisiegel's command, morale had been low, which was not surprising considering the accident record, and it was hoped that Rupert Leigh could rectify that. Certainly there was a marked improvement in the level of morale after he arrived.

Later that evening Richard was on the night flying detail:

> There will be no ground crews to service my aircraft, but those four of us who are on night flying detail must do a night flying test, so we get our aircraft and fly it round the aerodrome once each – the others starting it up.
>
> I go first, in a Blenheim. I have never flown one before, always having been put in 5's (Bisleys) in A Squadron to save my hands. The Bisleys have a switch to shut the gills – the Blenheims a wheel somewhat behind the pilot that needs about 50 turns.
>
> The Bisleys have a simple lever up and down to raise and lower the undercarriage. The Blenheims have a catch out from the handle, which must be pushed in with the thumb, before the undercarriage can be pulled up. [Much the same as a car handbrake of that period.] No one has ever shown me the cockpit, but I think I can manage, and take off. I find I cannot reach the catch with my thumb. Ground Control calls up. 'Hullo One Zero Two your undercarriage is still down.' It is indeed and I cannot be bothered to answer [This last comment is worth bearing in mind when assessing the reports written after Richard's final flight, as he may well have chosen to once again ignore ground control when

spoken to by radio telephone]. I have let go of the stick and am wrestling with the lever with both hands. It will not budge. I curse and sweat blood, but it will not come up, so I land again, very dispirited.

My Squadron Commander comes up. 'Can't cope, old boy. Too bad.' Genially: 'We'll have to throw you off this course. No Bisleys in this squadron.' Finally he arranges for someone to go up and pull it up for me, until I get on Beaufighters, which I shall find simpler.

Why did the squadron commander allow Richard to continue when his problems were starting to come to the fore? That had been the opportunity to have taken him aside, tell him that in light of this recent problem and the fact that the Beaufighter would be even harder to fly he should be removed from the course. He did actually tell him that he would have to be 'thrown off the course', but he does not take this action. Possibly, he succumbed to Richard's reputation, charm and strength of character, as others had. He relented and allowed him to continue; he would die nine days hence. Richard's narrative to Mary continues:

In the afternoon I go with my Radio Observer for an hour on the Link Trainer. This is really the only flying I enjoy here, because it is warm.

At 4.30 we go down again. Night flying begins at 5. A 50 mile an hour wind is blowing from the North, and some light snow is falling.

Then begins the worst part – the getting ready. No blithe leaping in and taking off as in a Spitfire.

My R.O. and I go into the locker room and he helps me. First I take off my shoes and stand on my coat while he winds my Irving [sic: 'Irvin'] suit trousers, leather and fur-lined, around me, pulling and heaving on the zips. Next my boots – over the trousers and again zip, zip [Among so many other things, Richard could not manage zippers either]. Now the Irving coat. I struggle into it and tighten the belt around me while he buttons me into my Mae West. Now maps in one boot top and torch in the other. Gloves – these take a little time because of my hands. Finally, helmet R.T. connection and about a mile of oxygen tubing. I stand up breathless but triumphant, and waddle towards the door. He, too, like an advertisement for Michelin Tyres, waddles beside.

'Hi! stop. Wait!'

I halt; surely I cannot have forgotten anything? But yes – my parachute! I sling it over my shoulder and we go into the flight office.

My instructor greets me – 'Sorry, old boy, all scrubbed for the moment – bad forecast.'

My R.O. and I look at each other. Then we sit down slowly and beg a cigarette. Our own are buried away beneath the layers of what almost amounts to our skin.

But finally we may go. I sign the authorisation book, sign for my colour card and we go out. I buckle on my parachute – tight fit with all this on – and my R.O. gives me a leg up. I scramble along to the hatch – which is locked. I call out to an airman who must crawl up inside and undo it. Inevitably he says, 'Fuck,' before disappearing from view, but he gets it to open and I wallow in – my R.O. following, for on this trip he is to sit beside me and work the U/C [undercarriage].

I settle into my bucket seat and together we dig around for the straps. Yesterday's mud has caked hard on – good, at least I shan't get filthy for once. An airman shouts from the darkness outside 'Petrol on!' Damn them. 'No, not yet.' Why can't they have a little patience? The straps will not meet. We try to lengthen them, hitting our hands and fumbling with the torch I have pulled out of my boot. But they are fully stretched. Oh well, by now I really don't care. If we do a crash landing, we do a crash landing. If I go through the windscreen, I go through the windscreen. I switch on the petrol. 'Petrol on.' I plug in my R/T and by slewing sideways in the seat and feeling behind me find the oxygen plug. My

R.O. tells me he cannot find his. I switch on the torch. There is none. He must do without. I switch off the torch and turn on the ignition.

'Contact starboard!'

It must be deemed therefore that Richard was willing to fly without proper final preparation before take-off. The risk that Wilfrid Fison might suffer as a result of not having oxygen available did not exist as the flight was to consist only of a low altitude circuit and bump but oxygen masks should have been worn at all times during night flying. Richard's honest depiction of these events indicates that he is flustered by the airman's premature call but, unwilling to call a halt to proceedings until such times as he was happy that his seat belt could be fastened and that Fison did have oxygen available thus putting him in the proper frame of mind for the flight, he struggled on:

I strain my eyes through the shoddy unclean perspex, but I can see neither the fitter nor his torch, only the night, starry but very dark, and, light against that darkness, furtive clouds hustled before the wind and clutching on to the cockpit hood he puts his head in out of the wind.

'Scrubbed again, sir,' he says hoarsely, 'switch her off,' and clambering out stiffly we walk back to the crew room.

'Sorry, old boy, been put to sixty minutes.' The O/C night flying fingers his lower lip apologetically, and goes on – 'Afraid we'll have to sleep here. There's a gale warning at the moment and 60 below freezing at 10,000 feet, but they expect it to clear up about 3 am. If you'll get out of your gear I'm getting some transport and we'll go and get some supper.'

Six pilots and their R.O.'s climb aboard (transport) and we rattle round to the night-flying canteen and get some hot sausages and tea.

W. [Wilfrid Fison] (my R.O.) settles down beside me, and asks me if I'm going to hear the gramophone concert in the RT hut the following night.

'They're playing Beethoven's Fifth,' he adds.

Opposite us sits George, a plug-ugly likeable young Australian animal, and his R.O. – also Australian. George butts in.

'Just like Pommie to waste his time listening to that fuckin' Beethoven – waste o' time, that's all.'

'Why, George?' I ask.

The long thin mouth, close up under a long square nose, splits up into the half-moon that I can never be sure is a smirk or a scowl.

'Fuckin' old Hillary,' he says with the greatest good will. 'Want an argument, do yer? Well, I know a good tune when I hear one . . . Got an ear for music – but to sit there hearing why a lot of instruments make that noise just because your grandparents tell yer it's good – get fucked.'

W., leans across to me. 'You know, if I ever had any doubts about the Darwinian theory, George has settled them.'

George's little pig eyes move restlessly between us; there is a frown of suspicion on his forehead.

'Come on, George, you old . . .' I say. 'What about your argument? What do you mean by good music?'

George's brow clears. He puts back his head and cackles. 'Fuckin' Pommies,' he says, and then he tells me about music.

Suddenly I felt quite exhausted. I wasn't trying to be funny or even to get a rise out of George, as W. loves to do, but I was quite suddenly unutterably weary of it and merely wished to eat.

'OK, George,' I said. 'You win, I can't argue with you.'

George looked suspicious again. 'Too fuckin' clever for me, that's what you think, isn't it? Too fuckin' civilised. Well, my father kept a Hotel. What do you think of that?' His face is pushed close to mine. Oh dear, oh dear, oh dear. How did I get pushed into this corner?

'Probably the man who made his money by pinching our bloody sheep and sending us broke when we had a station,' I say. It's all right, George is happy again.

Richard's grandfather on his father's side, Thomas Hillary, had emigrated from England to Australia to be a sheep farmer. The business had failed. George continued:

'Boy, what wouldn't I give to be surfing right now on Bondi Beach instead of sitting here fuckin' freezing.'

His R.O. breaks in, his eyes alight. 'Yeah, shaggin' in the hot sun, with no clothes on, getting freckles on your arse.'

We all shout with laughter and bang the table. Peace is permanently restored.

'You know,' says George, 'I like you, Hillary – in spite of all that bull.'

I think what an ideal crew George and his R.O. make, and I mentally raise my hat to the Wing Commander. I also ponder Koestler's theory that l'espoir de la fraternite is always a wild goose chase unless one is tight or physically exhausted in a crowd – as after long marches.

To-night I am almost convinced he is right, but he must not be – for it was for that reason that I returned.

We finished our meal and were driven back in the truck to the crew room at Dispersal where we laid out some blankets, piled up the fire and turned in; the wind howling and whistling outside and the door bursting open and banging continuously. All the others asleep, so I had to shut it. Woke once and looked at my watch – 6 o'clock – I can still hear the wind and I am not sorry. At 7 o'clock we are shouted at and woken up. Transportation is ready to take us up to the mess. We must have breakfast and be down again at 8.30.

The night is over. The day begins. Snowing heavily. Bitterly cold.

I love you
R.

This letter contained Richard's first mention of the radio/observer, appointed to fly with him from the beginning of January, 1943. Kenneth Wilfrid Young Fison BA, ACA, RAFVR [who preferred to be called by his first middle name] was, at 37, 14 years older than Richard and married to Joyce. They had two children; eight-year-old Geoffrey (today, the Reverend Geoffrey Fison BA, Ret'd) and a younger daughter Susan. His father was Kenneth Fison, retired by this time. His mother was Winifred.

Born in Seaford in 1905, Fison had been educated at William Hulme School, Manchester, Marlborough College and Clare College, Cambridge, where he took an honours degree in Modern Languages. As a member of the great Cambridge hockey team of the late twenties, he was awarded a blue in 1927 when he played in the Cambridge XI against Oxford in a team that was to beat Oxford at Beckenham four years in succession. Described as a brilliant wing forward he played for the Beckenham Hockey Club for a number of years. His brother, Robert Y. Fison, also played in the 1927 side and went on to play for the England international XI fifteen times. He also captained the side.

Qualifying as a chartered accountant, Fison later joined the business of Messrs. Young and Rochester, shirt manufacturers, and became a director and secretary. He served as head warden of an ARP post in Bermondsey during the greater part of the London blitz, but had to give up these duties when his firm moved to Ledbury. He joined the RAF as a radio observer in December 1941. At the time of joining he recorded in his diary the words of Edmund Burke: 'When Bad Men combine, the good must associate; else will they fall one by one, an unpitied sacrifice in a contemptible struggle.'

Partnering Fison with Richard was a shrewd move on the part of the staff at Charterhall. The two got on extremely well and a close friendship quickly developed, this despite Fison being an NCO. Fison was intelligent, kind and soft spoken and in the company of Richard he tended to allow his more extroverted officer pilot to dominate proceedings. Fison had arrived later than the other R/Os for the final stages of his training. Both navigator and pilot seemed to share a mutual understanding of each other's failings, and Fison's letters home to his wife suggested nothing to indicate that Richard and he had been inappropriately paired up. Joyce Fison was aware of Richard's fame as an author, but also his disability and accepted it.

There now occurred a down-turn in Richard's attitude towards flying and in his own self confidence. He was starting to experience insurmountable difficulties with night flying. He was aware that the situation was becoming serious and he was once again losing belief in his ability. If he failed to overcome those problems then he would not progress any further. As a result of the slowing in his progress he started to fall behind the other pilots on the course. The Battle of Britain hero, the survivor, the ace, who was the centre of attention, a situation he revelled in and which gave him confidence and motivation, may have started to gain their attention for the wrong reasons.

The Blenheim Mark I was almost impossible for Richard to fly due to the layout of certain controls. On the Blenheim I the gills were closed by means of a handwheel situated to the rear/right of the pilot seat which had to be rotated many times by hand – on the 'Five' there was a switch. The undercarriage on the Blenheim I was operated using a lever with a locking catch which had to be depressed – again, the 'Five' had a switch. Richard was unable to operate either of these with only the use of the thumb on his right hand, as if things weren't difficult enough. Richard therefore found the layout of the controls on the Blenheim V far more suitable. As there was no pre-requisite for him to progress onto the Mark I before training on the Beaufighter could begin, Richard was allowed to continue flying this type until he was able to progress to the Beaufighter.

In part of a 3 December letter to Mary he wrote:

> Yesterday I got as far as the cockpit of a Beaufighter before flying was cancelled owing to weather – the nearest I have got yet. As soon as I can fly a Beau I am going over to the third leg of this course and do all the rest of my training on Beau's, for although it is a much more powerful aircraft the cockpit layout is much easier for my hands.

On inspection of the instrument layout in the Beaufighter IIf, Richard had been enthusiastic; the ergonomics of those particular controls was the same as the Blenheim V. Unbeknown to Richard the difficulties that he experienced when flying the Blenheim I, were nothing compared with the handling problems he would have faced if he had progressed onto the Beaufighter IIf, towards the end of part 'B' of the course, and in order to progress to part 'C' he would have been required to accumulate five hours' flying time on type.

The Bristol Aeroplane Company factory had received several direct hits during a raid on Bristol resulting in the hold-up of production on the Hercules engines. Such was the demand for Beaufighters at that time, a temporary measure was introduced – the installation of Rolls-Royce Merlin engines in the Beaufighter IIf. The Beaufighter I, with Hercules engines, proved to be a tough, reliable aircraft, albeit rather clumsy. The MkIIf with the Merlin engines became a little underpowered for its extremely heavy weight. This, no doubt, contributed to the cause of some of the accidents at 'Slaughter 'all'. A significant difference between the MkIIf and the MkVIf, which began arriving in September 1943, apart from the increased power in the radial engines, was the pronounced swing to port on take-off. The Beaufighter IIf, with its Rolls-Royce Merlin engines, swung to starboard, while the Beaufighter VIf, with its Bristol Hercules engines, swung to port. In order to counteract that swing the correcting throttle was moved in advance of the other throttle by $3/4$ of an inch, up to 80-90mph and then the swing could be held with the rudder. The pilot then brought the throttle parallel, ready to 'un-stick' at 120mph.

The other difference with the Beaufighter IIf was that owing to its being under-powered the ten ton aircraft had a gliding angle of 45 degrees. The Beaufighter VIf had more power and fully feathered airscrews. The experienced pilots found them a delight to fly. However, the inexperienced student pilot found the swing a problem resulting in a large number of accidents. These statistics contributed greatly to the unfortunate reputation it had gained, and were never to improve.

There is little doubt that, had Richard reached this stage, he would have been incapable of flying that aircraft and would have had to quit, face being taken off the course, or die trying to succeed.

Avoiding an accident had been a near thing, and he *had* to master the Blenheim V and then the Beaufighter in order to progress on to the last part of the course at Winfield which involved only Beaufighters.

The thumb and forefinger on his left hand, the only digits that functioned, enabled him to work the throttles backwards and forwards, these controls being conveniently situated on the left of the aircraft cockpit. Otherwise, he might not have been able to fly twin-engined aircraft at all, as he had only the use of the thumb on his right hand. Consider also that his hands were both encumbered with several pairs of gloves. It is tragic when you consider that Geoffrey Page had successfully returned to operational flying by then and, as he had discussed with Richard while East Grinstead, was flying Spitfires. Richard's hand disability was almost exactly the same as that of Geoffrey Page. While Richard may not have been able to control the Spitfire adequately in combat, the lighter, easier to control fighter would have definitely been a better choice in which to try to return to operational flying.

As I have already mentioned, no dual control Beaufighters were ever built and conversion at Charterhall from the Blenheim consisted of the student standing behind the instructor, who would carry out a series of 'circuits and bumps', with a demonstration of stalls with wheels up and down, before handing control over to the student.

The instructors were well aware that his difficulties were in the extreme, that there was little chance he would progress on to Beaufighters and that it was only a matter of time before he had an accident. But tragically they still let him fly. He had had enough; was aware that the risk had become too great, with the likelihood of survival being slim, and with absolutely no hope of progressing any further on the course. He had tried hard, against overwhelming odds, exhibiting great courage, but as the course progressed he began to founder. As Richard secretly awaited confirmation that McIndoe had used his influence to have him taken off the course for medical reasons, he continued the subterfuge.

* * *

On New Year's Eve Richard attended the gramophone concert to which Wilfrid Fison had referred during the previous evening. It was held in the speech/broadcasting hut on the instructional site.

Following the recital, Richard stepped out into the darkness and driving wind, the smell of pine strong in the air. With the collar of his RAF greatcoat raised for protection from the elements, he tramped through the fresh, light flurries of snow the three quarters of a mile along the Greenlaw road to the officers' mess. There, a New Year's Eve Dance was under way. A number of local dignitaries had been invited.

During the party Richard was introduced to Mrs Mariora Swinton and her 16-year-old son John (later Major General Sir John Swinton, KCVO, OBE). Mrs Swinton was at that time married to Lieutenant Colonel (subsequently Brigadier) A.H.C. Swinton. Sir John recalls:

> Our host was Group Captain Beisiegel. My mother told me that she remembered
> the occasion well, that she found Hillary most attractive – despite his disfigure-
> ment – and that she asked him to come over for a meal. His answer was that he
> would certainly do so 'once I have mastered the control of this beastly aircraft'.

On 1 January 1943 Richard wrote to Mary recording his own memories of this period:

> Darling,
>   Another year is past – a year in which I have written little and done nothing
> that can be measured in objective terms, but for me a great year. I had you and I
> grew up. 1942 was ours, and with all the horrors that occurred all over the world

nothing can make me anything but grateful to it for what it granted to me. I thought we must founder, but we did not, only grew ever more strong. I only hope that 1943 will allow me to put into action the personality which now, (thanks largely to you) is me, be it good or bad.

The evening before last I thought that the great snow had begun. As night fell, down it came – driven across this bleak wilderness by a vicious wind.

In this letter Richard gives an account of the recital in the R/T training hut, given by the same officer who was responsible for the destruction of Richard's surviving papers and letters from Mary and his other friends, after his death:

It was my first visit. [To the classical music recital. There had been regular such gatherings by enthusiasts on the base] Outside the beating of the snow, unutterably dreary across the camp against the huts: inside, another world – a breath of lost civilisation. My first impression was of breaking in on a private family party. About thirty people, mostly airmen and WAAF's – curiously enough no pilots – and all with a knowledge and appreciation of music to which I doubt if I shall ever be able to pretend. (My 1st visit – their 17th.)

Flying Officer How, the R/T speech officer, who gives the programme, is an old gentleman of upright carriage, protruding ears and an academic manner – ex-choirmaster – music teacher and voice trainer. Each work is carefully explained – we are told what to listen for – the undertones 'like this' – he plays a couple of bars, 'and now this' – two more. He reads from a marked passage in some book, and the snow and the aerodrome are forgotten.

Programme.

Wilhelm Tell	Rossini
Meistersinger	Wagner
5th Symphony	Beethoven
Karelia	Sibelius

His explanations are above my head, but I listen as eager to learn and accept his authority, as I am unwilling and disinclined when he tries to standardise my R/T patter and voice control by day. Now he is at home – the master. Before he was uncertain – trying to teach me my job.

Richard's letter of 1 January continues with a response to Mary's mention of beauty and about orientation in her last letter:

I reject appreciation of the beautiful if you mean it in the purely aesthetic sense, for whether beauty – aesthetic beauty – is of any but selfish value is a moot point. But if you mean it in the sense of Plato's 'Beauty is the splendour of Truth' then I agree.

What in terms of action has the well orientated man got that anyone else has not? Creative Imagination and all that follows from it, eg production of an intellectual theory which reorganises understanding and opens new vistas before the mind's eye; the production of an original and significant work of art; the production of a personal relationship which drives both individuals to greater integrity; the production of vitalising social changes.

But more of this to-morrow – I must to bed as I am flying to-morrow day and night.

My love and prayers that together we may achieve something great in 1943.

R.

It is interesting to note Richard's reference to prayer. He has suggested on previous occasions that he is not religious.

It is when one reads Richard's narratives to Mary that his potential for further writing, after the war, is realised. Had he survived and continued to write about his experiences I believe there would have been many more publications. On 3 January Richard wrote to his mother:

There are moments, far too many, when you make my heart turn over, and I am filled with such unutterable tenderness for you and all you have done for me, that in my happiness I feel quite sad . . . in the last two years I have made many mistakes, but I have gained a little wisdom and living up here seems to point to it rather than lessen it. For I try to live now on the principle, 'I live this day as my last.' Here it is not difficult. I can summarise my tiny drops of wisdom quite easily. The first is:

I have not the right to make any man small in his own image; and the second is:

Time is very short, and there are a great many people in the world. Therefore of these people I shall try to know only half a dozen. But them I shall love and never deceive.

Richard also wrote to Mary on this day. It was the last of his long descriptive narratives written to her before his death in which he once again provided a detailed description of one of his night flying training flights. Together with his other narratives, the substance and style for another book that would never be finished. Richard also wrote about fellow Guinea Pig Bill Simpson's new book, *One of Our Pilots is Safe*, and paid it a fitting tribute. As with *The Last Enemy*, Bill Simpson's book was well-written and told of a more harrowing experience than that which Richard had endured, for his injuries had been far more destructive. Bill Simpson and Richard had met at the officers' convalescent home at Torquay when Richard had read his manuscript and helped him to find a publisher:

Charter Hall
3rd January 1942 (Sunday)

. . . Simpson's book I see is going very well, but I do not grudge its success. About all the others which have been well received I have felt a petty exasperation – due largely to having written nothing further myself. And yet I know that they are people who happened to be watching an accident with a camera in their hands and thus got a good picture, while I am a professional cameraman and will always – on the rare occasions when I use my camera – get a good picture. They will never do it again. Is this arrogance on my part? Certainly the exasperation is because I am beginning to fear that either through force of circumstances or lack of concentration I am rapidly becoming an amateur myself.

S. on the other hand has suffered so much, and has emerged with so little bitterness that I am genuinely glad of his success. I do not mean by this that I think that anyone who has an inclination to write, and passes through a time of great physical and mental suffering, will write necessarily better than before. That happened to me; but to apply it as a general rule seems to me as a sceptic as logically unsound as the man who has a deep emotional experience in which he feels a great love of humanity and feels himself a part of the universe, and deduces from his own personal experiences that therefore there must be an all loving God. I accept the experience, but I reject its inference.

Or to take it further. Most really religious (say rather than spiritual) people have suffered terribly during the process of their own self-mastery; but to infer from that that suffering is a necessary and beneficial thing imposed on mankind by an all seeing Deity seems to me nonsense. As well say 'God made the wind to fill the sails of ships.'

But I am rambling.

Yesterday I got as far as the cockpit of a Beaufighter before flying was cancelled owing to weather – the nearest I have got yet. As soon as I can fly a Beau I am to go over to the 3rd leg of this course and do all the rest of my training on Beaus, for although it is a much more powerful aircraft the cockpit lay-out is much easier for my hands.

In the evening the weather cleared and I was on first detail night flying. My Squadron Commander had arranged for me to fly a Bisley from A Squadron, as

frankly I'm scared stiff of the old Blenheims at night – you can't even see your
instruments – and also as I was to do a height test the cold would have been too
much for me – quite apart from fighting with the undercarriage.

From this we can appreciate the consideration shown to Richard by his squadron
commander and the instructors. He couldn't manage the Blenheim MkI, so they allowed
him to continue flying the MkV. His progress could have been brought to a halt there
and then. He was so close to progressing on to the final part of the course, but in truth,
so far. While the Blenheim I was obsolete and his mastering it could be discounted as a
necessary part of his training, the Beaufighter posed even greater problems. Perhaps if
he had flown the 'Beau' that night he would have finally decided that further attempts
would be futile and quit the course; or still died trying. Richard's letter continues:

It was bitterly cold but clear and starry. W. and I clambered into all our equipment
and were driven over to A Squadron to pick up No.238 (Blenheim V, BA238). We
only had to try two other A/C before getting the right one in the dark, so were in
not too bad a temper. As there was nothing for him to do on a height test W. sat
up in front with me. We plugged in our oxygen and turned it on full, squeezing
the tubes to see if it was coming through.

Mine seemed OK – his also. We taxied out – always a nightmare to me as I
cannot reach the brake – and last night a 40 m.p.h. cross wind. The serviceability
rate of these A/C is so low that I always marvel whenever we leave the ground at
all. Of course at any other unit we wouldn't – they would put every aeroplane
unserviceable at once – this had been proved by aircraft from here – diverted to
another aerodrome, being refused permission to take off again.

But anything goes here and off we went. As soon as we were off the ground,
I knew there was something wrong. The old monster started plunging away to
starboard. We flashed a torch through the filthy perspex to see if the gills had not
shut, but they seemed O.K. so I continued. (I wonder if W. knows just how
terrified I am at night? I hope not.) Then we started to climb. At 10,000 ft the
pitch control of the port engine jammed. At 19,000 ft I was waffling about at 100
m.p.h. with the outside temperature 50 below. Then the R.T. packed up (I could
receive from the ground but not transmit).

I told W. to get a homing. I listened to him calling up. His voice very drowsy.
Oh God, he's going to pass out. Down I pushed the nose, down until I thought
my ears would crack – all the time hearing ground control giving us homing
vectors and W. repeating them, slowly, happily and quite wrong.

I should of course have kept a mental note of the courses we were flying, but
having so much else to do I had left it to W. What if the R.T. packs up altogether?
A moment later it did so. A feeling oddly enough of resignation – not panic. Then
I saw it, – the flare path, way below us. We were all right. I came down slowly,
feeling very sick (my own supply of oxygen cannot have been very good) and
started to reflash my navigation lights at 1,000 ft. Nothing happened. Why the
Hell can't they answer? I glanced again at my instruments. 11,000 ft! What a fool
– mustn't get drowsy. That might have led to disaster – a quick circuit at what I
took to be 1,000 ft; turn on nicely over the East Funnel of lights at 800 ft – wheels
down, flaps down, throttle back, down to 100 ft. Why no chance light? – and then
the stall. Too late I realise what has happened. We are not at 100 ft but at 10,000
ft and all the time the plane is spinning and spinning.

Well that's what might have been. Another lesson learned. [An insight into
what may have happened during his last flight. The letter continues]:
I lose more height and when I really am at 800 ft start flashing my navigation
lights. A green lamp flashes back. I can land. I turn to W. and put up my thumb.
He grins back, quite unaware that he was nearly out. (He has great confidence in
me! If he did but know!)

Round the circuit and down with my wheels – a flood of light comes on where the ground crew have not put strips over the undercarriage positive indicator lights. I am quite blinded, but W. gets down on his knees and holds his hand over the glare.

We are coming in – Hell of a cross wind – we're drifting badly. I straighten up over the runway, throttle back, we're still going like a crab. Then the wheels touch and we are down. As I turn off the runway I can feel the sweat running down inside my Irving suit and my hands are trembling. Climbing out I put my foot gingerly to the ground. Oh how welcome it is. Solid earth beneath my feet.

In the air twice I had promised myself that if I got down I should go to the Wing Commander and say that I'd had enough. Already the mere thought of it amused me. What was for supper? That occupied the first place in my mind.

We staggered back to the crew room, weighed down by our parachutes, fears forgotten, chattering and laughing.

We were met by the Officer i/C Night Flying, the M.O. and an ambulance.

'What happened? Are you all right?'

'Yes,' I said, 'My R.T. packed up and Fison was answering for me. He doesn't know the patter – that's all. Actually his supply was a little short, I think.'

'Oh, that's what happened. We thought you'd had it.'

Grinning with relief they sent off the ambulance and offered us a cigarette. I took one from the M.O. wondering what he'd think if he knew how nearly I had made use of that ambulance, said that I was ill, sick at altitude, anything. Nobody could blame me. There was still time. W. helped me out of my kit, I relit my cigarette and we walked over to night supper.

Then no transport – somebody had boobed again and so the long weary, cold walk up to the mess. Time, midnight.

Outside I bade W. goodnight (how much rather that he were allowed in our mess than some of the dregs) and walked in for a moment before going to bed.

A party was going on. I could hear a piano playing, and a huge barrel of beer frothed past, carried by four drunken clowns. I collected some letters from my locker and turned to go out to my room, but one of them saw me – my Flight Commander.

'What ho, Hil! How did it go?'

I told him. He answered quite soberly.

'Christ, old boy. Shaky do, eh? I wouldn't fly one of these Blenheims at night for any price – I tried it once – shook me to the tits – Can't even see the instruments and fuck all outside. Oh, it's a grand life we lead here old boy. To-morrow you'll have all that and your engine'll cut too just for full measure, and if you prang they'll say it was your fault. Come on in. Someone's birthday – good excuse for getting pissed – only thing to do here.' [How prophetic the Squadron Commander's words would be a couple of nights hence; Richard's death was attributed to 'pilot error'.]

He took me by the arm, but pleading tiredness I slipped away – put my calling time of 7.15 on my door, climbed into my night-pullovers and socks and then into bed.

Well darling, that was yesterday – illegible, unrevised, and very hurried, but I hope you understand it.

All hope of getting on with the book has vanished for the moment. Flying, or rather waiting to fly night and day; at the moment I am writing this with my feet too hot in front of the writing room fire [in the mess] and the back of my neck freezing from the inevitable draught. Night flying has been put to 60 minutes as a snow storm is expected. I am on second detail – normally nine o'clock, but to-night I imagine we shall not get off before midnight – down about 3 am – God willing.

Your letters to keep me sane my darling – and both 'masks' now look down on me in bed. The second will not fit the frames alas. What a pity about the cottage. If you do see anything you might let me know and we can have fun imagining how it might be if we could only have managed it.

Max [Aitken] I hear will be leaving the Squadron very shortly, but who will
take his place I know not.

Write soon.

You will fly beside me.

R.

Undoubtedly, even without the malfunctions, the previous flight was still a difficult one
and certainly there were many technical failures during those exercises. His nerve would
seem to have gone and the admission of this to Mary and his ability to conceal it from
Fison is evidence of his strong will. He is permanently in anticipation of it all going
wrong. The flight was fraught with risk and the trauma he experienced as a result was
real and not so easily shaken off as he inferred once he was back on the ground. Gripped
with terror during the flight but with feelings of responsibility towards Wilfrid Fison he
battled on to maintain physical and mental control. At that moment he had had enough,
but back on the ground he just postponed his resignation from the course, perhaps for
just *one* more day. But with that decision, time had finally run out. He would not
progress any further on that course, he was not physically capable. If his nerve had not
been broken, then it is close to breaking. The authorities were wrong to let him continue;
he was wrong not to call it a day, particularly with Wilfrid Fison onboard. Richard was
aware of his failings, he concealed them from Fison who had great faith in his
experience and ability. He had a right to know. In persevering Richard knew he was
gambling with his R/O's life by that stage, but simply disregarded this point as he
continued to battle against overwhelming odds, instead of resigning and attempting to
return to operations by another means. But no, he had too much to lose, his ego could
not take such a knock.

Nevertheless, at this stage the bonding with Wilfrid Fison was complete. Had they
survived they may well have enhanced their friendship, as so many night fighter teams
did. Surely it would only be a matter of time before Fison would be granted a
commission and the two could share each other's company in the mess.

On Monday 4 January 1943, Richard wrote again to Mary:

Darling,

Not writing to-day as am off to bed. Flew last night till 4 am. Lovely machine
– everything working, she just purred. I'm quite sure aeroplanes are human. The
one before was determined to get me.

I'm hoping desperately to get down towards the end of the month.

Love you
R.

Following the near disaster in the Blenheim I, Richard had flown the 'Five' on this flight.

During the first week of January the station medical officer returned from leave and
opened the letter he found on his desk marked 'private and confidential' from Archibald
McIndoe, dated 17 December, 1942. In his reply, written on 7 January 1943, just a few
hours before Richard was killed, the squadron leader MO wrote to McIndoe:

Dear Mr McIndoe,

Thank you for your letter of the 17th inst. about Flight Lieutenant Hillary. I
am sorry to have delayed replying but I have been away from the unit. Until I had
returned I haven't had the opportunity of checking up the points you raised.

I find Flight Lieutenant Hillary difficult to deal with, as any indication that his
condition was not progressing as it should would result in him immediately
withholding his own personal feelings.

Without indicating that I had had a personal letter from you, I asked him how
things were going. I suggested that his left eye looked a little irritated but he
insisted it was better than it was before he came to this unit, a matter, of course,
on which I have no information.

I may have imagined it, but I think there was a certain caution exercised to prevent me from finding out Hillary's real view.

I agree with you that intervention is suitable in such a case, but I am also sure that Hillary's self-respect is an enormous obstacle. He is due to go to London about the 19th of this month, and promised to call on you while in London. I did not tell him you had specifically desired it, but I said it was only fair to the surgeon who had devoted so much time and trouble to effect a cure to let him check up from time to time and see how things are going. I will remind him when I see him making preparations to go off and hope that this will meet with your approval.

During January Richard had been expected to attend a party for the Guinea Pigs, at East Grinstead. The guest of honour at the event was Air Marshal T.L. Leigh-Mallory, AOC Fighter Command.

CHAPTER EIGHTEEN

THE DEATH OF RICHARD HILLARY/THE LAST FLIGHT

RAF Charterhall
7/8 January 1943

I stopped and looked up into the night. They were there somewhere, all of them around me; dead perhaps, but not gone. Through Peter they had spoken to me, not once, but often. I had heard and shrugged my shoulders; I had gone my way unheeding, not bitter, either on their account or mine, but in some curious way suspended, blind, lifeless, as they could never be.

Not so the Berrys, the Stapletons, the Carburys. Again instinct had served. They hadn't even the need of a Peter. They had felt their universe, not rationalised it. Each time they had climbed into their machines and took off into combat, they were paying instinctive tribute to their comrades who were dead. Not so those men in hospital. They, too, knew, knew that their discomforts, their suffering, were as nothing if they could but get back, and should they never get back they knew their silence was their role.

Richard Hillary, *The Last Enemy*

* * *

Richard's friendship had not only developed with Fison but with the other trainee pilots on his course. As an experienced Battle of Britain pilot, he was regarded with a certain amount of awe by these young men and comradeship was mutually offered by Richard in return. He was back in the crewroom atmosphere that he had been craving for so long. He was the centre of attention. Of superior intellect to quite possibly all but Fison, he was well aware of this and enjoyed such a position.

On the morning of 7 January 1943, Richard probably stayed in bed until quite late, recovering from the late night before. He got up and carried out his ablutions before starting the long walk down to the mess for lunch. His flying detail indicated that he was not due to fly until quite late into that night and it is likely that he spent the time in the classroom, writing letters or perhaps at the Link Trainer with Fison.

Richard's squadron was dispersed on the northern edge of the airfield, a lengthy walking distance of more than a mile from the mess, which he would have walked if unable to cadge a lift from a passing vehicle. Those that had been detailed to fly during the early part of the evening were busy climbing in and out of their flying clothing with the sound of engines accelerating and decelerating outside, as the training aircraft flew in and out of the aerodrome. Richard and Wilfrid Fison began the laborious task of kitting up, Fison giving vital assistance to his pilot who we know struggled to don the cold weather attire, and along with the other members of the squadron on the same flying detail, stayed in the warm until their time came to fly.

Richard and his R/O had also to consider that the aircraft they would be flying was BA194, the Blenheim V of 'A' Squadron that Richard had been allowed to use on previous exercises. It was infinitely easier for him to fly than the Blenheim I but it was situated at 'A' Flight dispersal, further around the perimeter track to the east. Additional time would have to be allowed in order for them to walk or be driven to their aircraft, locate the correct numbered aircraft in the dark, warm-up and carry out pre-flight checks and taxi to the appropriate take-off point by the designated time.

The weather was unpleasant with low cloud and sleet, driven almost horizontal by the wind, stinging the faces of those that ventured outside. The Irvin suits provided the best protection from the cold both outside and in the confines of the aircraft. Even if the heater was working, the draughty aircraft soon reduced the effectiveness of these once the airflow outside increased.

Richard took off for an altitude test early in the evening of the 7th. Any problems that Richard and his R/O came up against on this flight went unrecorded, but from his letters to Mary, which describe frequent malfunctions and difficulties, it was likely that the flight didn't go totally without a hitch. Nevertheless, he landed the aircraft safely and he and Fison waddled the distance back to the dispersal hut of 'B' Squadron. In the locker room they removed their flying clothing which, in addition to his battledress uniform, consisted of parachute, Mae West, leather flying helmet with oxygen mask including attached RT lead and oxygen hose, scarf, three pairs of gloves, flying boots, a sheepskin jacket and leggings (the last two items are known as the Irvin suit). All zippers had to be fastened by Fison because of the state of Richard's hands. All this was in addition to their uniform underneath.

They then relaxed with a cigarette and a hot drink. At 09.30 Richard spoke to Mary on the telephone in the mess and he told her that he had completed one night-training flight and would be making a second after midnight. It was during this period, sitting by the stove in the briefing room, enjoying the unity with his fellow aircrew, that one pilot, a Polish trainee, noticed Richard looked: 'tired, strained, and very red about the eye', although this tells us very little as we know that Richard's left eye was a problem and that they were all tired and strained.

Richard and Fison then travelled round to the night-flying canteen with Sergeant Andy Miller, his R/O, Sergeant F.C. Stone (later Flying Officer Stone DFC and Bar), and the two other crews who would also be flying later. There they had a supper of hot sausages and tea, before returning and kitting-up for the second flight of the night. All four crews would be flying in pairs on a radar/fighter interception exercise. After the pre-flight briefing they walked out to their respective aircraft and took off once again.

Miller and Sergeant Stone – a massive 16 stone, 36-year-old, former police officer from Birkenhead – took off with the other crews as Richard and Fison clambered into their Blenheim V for the last time. The crews had been paired up during the pre-flight briefing. One aircraft would act as an enemy aircraft while the other attempted to track it down by liaising initially with the Ground Control Interception (GCI) unit and then take over using their on-board radar units. The GCI was limited in its range, sometimes to as little as two-to-three miles, and it was the job of the ground controller to vector the night fighter to the right position and height to allow the R/O to pick up the contact on his AI unit. The R/O then gave instructions to his pilot to bring the aircraft just below and behind the contact until the pilot achieved a visual sighting. The pilot then manoeuvred his aircraft into position before opening fire.

The GCI was able to assist only one aircraft at a time in locating an 'enemy' aircraft, leaving other aircraft to stooge around for a while. Ordinarily this was another reason why Richard and his fellow pilots would be instructed to orbit the flashing light of the Airfield Identification Beacon (AIB) and await instructions.

Having carried out this exercise the crew would then change places allowing the other crew to do an interception, before the GCI operator would offer his assistance to another two aircraft. In addition to the pilots and R/Os some of the GCI operators were also under training in the use of their specialised equipment.

Problems began for Miller almost immediately after take-off:

> We took off along the larger 1600 yard runway from west to east. Although full throttle would have been standard practice it was noticeable that the aircraft had come un-stuck from the runway much later than usual. The leading edges and control surfaces of my aircraft were iced-up and as a result I had a great deal of

trouble getting off the runway, needing all available power to get the aircraft into the air.

After a few minutes of being airborne I found I could no longer handle the aircraft and felt I was rapidly losing control. I instructed air traffic control: '. . . there is something wrong with this aeroplane. I'm not sure what.' Ice was not such a known thing in those days. I then aborted the flight. This I proceeded to do and despite a general lack of handling experience regarding icing-up and flying this particular aircraft, I kept the air-speed at about 140 knots, a higher speed than usual. This was necessary because the ice on the aeroplane would reduce the airspeed, possibly to that of the stalling speed of the aircraft, normally 130 knots, and this could mean disaster with the aircraft spinning in. As this new stalling speed was now an unknown denominator I kept the revs up.

Andy Miller's aircraft touched down and in order to stop the Blenheim before he ran out of tarmac he decided to steer it off the runway onto the thick muddy surface of the airfield. This helped slow the aircraft down at a greater rate than if he had stayed on the runway.

With the sweat running down his back inside the heavy flying apparel he taxied to dispersal and with his R/O climbed out from the cockpit feeling incredibly relieved at their narrow escape. They walked towards the welcoming warmth of the dispersal hut:

In the meantime Dick had gone up. When we got back the other two pilots and navigators had landed and we were standing outside the dispersal crew room and decided to wait and watch him land, knowing it was Dick Hillary up there. He was flying around, over the beacon to the north-east, we couldn't see him, only hear him.

The cloud cover was sweeping low over the airfield at a height of 600-700 feet driven by the wind. There was only the occasional break and, slightly higher, at 1,000 feet was a further complete layer of cloud.

The ground controller spoke to Richard on the radio/telephone and had told him to circle the flashing beacon. He then asked him: 'Are you happy?'

To which Richard answered: 'Moderately. I am continuing to orbit.'

Andy Miller explains this less than confident reply from Richard:

By that time, with the aircraft foundering, he was probably shitting himself! When Dick replied that he was 'moderately OK and continuing to orbit', the aircraft was probably handling far worse than usual with the ice on it and that was why he wasn't 'perfectly OK'. He probably thought: 'What does that silly bastard want when I'm trying to fly this aircraft.'

I feel certain that this explains Dick's reason for saying what he did.

Richard was orbiting, waiting for a decision to be made regarding a 'partner' for the exercise. Flight Lieutenant Benson, in the watch tower monitoring the situation, wrote later:

I must have overestimated him because I liked him and admired him for what he'd been through. He wasn't happy, so we recalled him.

When he was spoken to again a few minutes later there was no reply.

Back at 'B' Squadron dispersal Miller noticed the sound of the engines increase rapidly to a high pitched whine:

. . . which lasted no more than six or seven seconds and then there was a terrible crash. He'd gone up into cloud where his aircraft picked up even more ice on the control surfaces and the aircraft stalled and in he went. From where we were standing we could see the flash of the fuel ignition reflected on the underside of the low cloud.

The aircraft would have been hard to handle by an experienced pilot, even using a bit of flap to counter the drag of the ice, but once the control started to slip away from him his hands would have become practically useless. The stories about his eyes and his inability to concentrate on his instruments were all rubbish. Had I been aware of the accident report at the time I would certainly have argued against it.

Yes, he had lost control of the aircraft, but because of the ice. He was a Spitfire pilot and not experienced with these sort of aircraft and conditions. He was used to blue skies with little instrument and bad weather flying. I think in that situation he was probably no more experienced than I was, but I had the full use of both hands, he didn't. It was much more difficult for him to handle the situation and once the aircraft started to become uncontrollable, that would, in my opinion, be the end. The initial point of loss of control was when the forward speed dropped below the point at which a stall would occurr, which was, with the ice on the wings, about 130 knots. When I had come in earlier we were able to get down to about 130 because I put down a bit of flap, which gave a bit more lift. If you were more experienced and found you were losing speed, you could put a bit of flap down to give more lift in that situation. But this required experience he didn't have.

Having considered the details of my interview with Andy Miller and his explanation for the crash, Geoffrey Page made his own assessment and agreed that this was the probable cause of the crash: 'That makes sense, the ice would cause the stall and the aircraft would commence to spin dive.'

* * *

During his first flight that night Andy Miller's reaction had been purely instinctive in saving his own life and that of his R/O Stone. Whether Richard had the experience or not, his hands may have rendered him unable to take the required remedial action.

Flight Lieutenant Benson recalled the crash: 'I was watching his navigation lights, and he spiralled straight in from a thousand feet.'

'Ben' Benson may have heard the final descent of the Blenheim and its impact with the ground, but he would have seen nothing. No navigation lights were used, the cloud cover was complete and the field of view was partially obscured by high ground and woodland.

Andy Miller's recollections continue:

We had so little experience flying Blenheims. I had only been flying the type for about a month. Two or three weeks later we changed to Beaufighters when, after a total of only one hour and five minutes of standing behind an instructor as he flew, I was sent off solo.

We had problems as a result of the age and poor mechanical state of the aircraft. The Bisley was quite a good aircraft and we thought it was better than the Blenheim I. On the Bisley you had variable pitch propellers, which gave us more control, whereas on the Blenheim you only had two positions – Fine and Coarse pitch.

The Bisley was heavier and had a great big nose thus reducing the visibility, particularly while taxiing. Because of the nose sticking out it wasn't until you got the tail off the ground that visibility improved. I also think the engines on the Bisley were better. In the Blenheim I you were closer to the nose, which was like a glass-house, and you could see out clearly.

Dick couldn't fly the Blenheim I. The tendons on his right hand had been fried and had contracted, therefore only his right thumb was of any real use. His left hand was slightly better in that the thumb and forefinger were OK and the other three fingers were curled in towards the palm like the unusable fingers on his right hand. The throttles were situated on the left hand side as you sat in the cockpit of the Bisley. On take-off there was so much torque with the Bisley and Blenheim I you had to lead with the port engine, pushing the port engine throttle ahead of the starboard, therefore keeping the aircraft straight. Dick could in fact wiggle the throttle levers. Stabbing them to go forward and pulling them back by hooking his finger around the lever.

You did not have enough airflow over the elevators and rudders to give you the control at this stage and so you manipulated the throttles therefore providing enough power to each engine to ensure that the attitude of the aircraft was reasonably level. It wasn't until you got the tail up that you really got any rudder control.

Dick was doomed to go from bad to worse. No matter what he thought the outcome would be with the hope of joining Max Aitken on Beaufighters. The Beaufighter, which Dick would have had to have mastered in order to complete the course consisted of the Mark I and II. The Mark I had the Hercules engines, providing about 1,400 brake horse-power and the Mark II had the Merlins which gave about 800-900 brake horse-power. Most of the Beaufighters at Charterhall were Mark II's and they were very difficult to keep in the air on only one engine. Both Marks were unstable. As already mentioned, on take-off you had to manipulate the throttles to compensate for the yaw to port. If you pushed the steering column slightly forward during this, the aircraft would sink back down again and you needed to pull her up again to prevent disaster. You went along rising and falling until you gained enough height.

It wasn't until we got the Mark VI (September 1943), with the di-hedral tailplane, that the aircraft became more stable. The controls became heavier but the attitude of the aircraft was straighter on take-off and didn't require the pilot to compensate for the yaw to port.

If Dick had managed to progress onto Beaufighters he would have been killed anyway. Especially on the Mark II. If anything had gone wrong he would have been even less likely to have been able to control the Beaufighter than the Blenheim I or the Bisley.

Nobody in the Air Traffic Control tower could see his aircraft. It was a pitch black bloody night, we took off through a ceiling of broken cloud at about 600-700 feet, at most, and then through a complete layer of cloud at 1,000 feet. There was no way they could see him, there was also the high ground between the airfield and the crash site. I was in the best position to see what little there was to see.

He wasn't orbiting the visual beacon because he would have had to have been too low to see it. We had AI on-board and a radar beacon on the station, so he would pick that up on radar and orbit the area. Dick was at an altitude of about 2,000-3,000 feet when he started to go down, and the whole descent only took a matter of seconds. That was too high to have seen the flashing beacon. For any pilot to have seen the beacon that night they would have had to have flown below the cloud base of 600-700 feet, which was too low, particularly in that terrain.

The pilots also had to calibrate their altimeters for the height of their aerodrome above sea level. It is possible that some failed to do that.

Although Andy refers to the 'Bisley' as being the aircraft flown by Richard, it was in fact the Blenheim V. The prototype of the Blenheim V was named the Bisley, but long before it went into production many changes had been made to the original design and the name Bisley had by then been superseded by Blenheim V. Apart from the single prototype, no Bisleys were ever produced.

In response to the accident statistics from Charterhall Andy Miller told me:

At the time I had no idea that the accident statistics were as bad as they were. We knew the rate was high by the frequent occurrences, and by the nickname given to the aerodrome. It scared the bloody life out of me then, without knowing the full picture!

The authorities were quick to apportion blame on the pilot. Not the poorly maintained, obsolete aircraft. In those days we carried out no external checks on the aircraft. No braces were used for the rudders and ailerons. These were marked

with flags and you went around removing the flags and checking the movement.
There were none at Charterhall.

* * *

The reflection of the flash on the low cloud signalled the fiery impact of Richard's
aircraft with the earth two miles to the north-east of the airfield. The direction of the final
descent of the Blenheim was north-west to south-east when it crashed in a field (783506,
Ordnance Survey – Landranger Map 74) at Crunklaw Farm, owned at the time by the
Elliott family. It had struck at the bottom of a small hill, next to a bend in Howe Burn,
some 500 yards from the farmhouse and 500 yards in the opposite direction from the
Reston to Greenlaw railway line. It had struck the ground at a shallow angle, but steep
enough for the nose and engines to plough in and turn the aircraft on to its back. The fuel
tanks ruptured on impact and the wreckage exploded in flames. A great deal of the
aircraft broke away and careered ahead of the bulk of the wreckage. The debris field
measured about one hundred yards and ended at a tributary stream from Howe Burn, at
the base of a hill to the south of the field.

George Frizzel, a shepherd at Crunklaw Farm for 32 years, lived with his family in a
rented cottage close to the main farmhouse. The reconstruction at the beginning of this
book is from his memories of that night. His eldest son Bill, home on leave at the time
from training with the Horse Guards, had been the first at the scene with his father. On
first approaching the site, it was immediately evident that the crash had been of
sufficient magnitude to negate any possibility of survivors. The fierce flames had
prevented them getting close enough to pull the bodies clear. The one crew member that
had been visible gave George the impression that he had been in the process of baling
out when the aircraft crashed, simply by the position it was in – hanging out of the
wreckage. This opinion was given some credibility when it was recorded by another
witness, possibly an airman from RAF Charterhall, that the parachute on this victim, had
been opened. Perhaps, having lost control of the aircraft, Richard had ordered Fison to
bale out while he struggled to keep the aircraft aloft.

In the meantime, George Frizzel's youngest son, Jimmy, who had been awakened by
the sound of the crash and anxious to see what had happened had got dressed, dashed out
of the house and across to the burning wreckage. On seeing his son running across the
field his father reacted by shouting to his eldest son: 'Get that boy away from the flames'.

A short time after, the crash rescue team arrived and took charge. The station
ambulance followed and took the bodies back to the mortuary at RAF Charterhall where
they were stripped of their clothing and personal effects. Richard's gold cigarette case,
with its inscription and his initials, was found on his body. It had been damaged. The
flames had reached everything else in his pockets. It has been said that owing to the lack
of human remains, Richard's coffin was filled with sand. That is not true.

Richard and Wilfrid Fison were certified dead by Keith A Houghton-Thomas MB, ChB,
the cause of death was recorded as being:

Due to War Operations –
a) Shock.
b) Multiple Injuries.
c) Burns.

The death certificates were signed by LACW M. Munro, RAF No.437287, 'informant'
from RAF Charterhall, and the local registrar at Edrom, J. P. Wilson.

George Frizzel handed the watch he had found to the local police. He had been able
to identify its owner from the backplate which had been inscribed.

The next day Bill Frizzel re-visited the site with his life long friend, Jim Renton, who
worked out of neighbouring Middlefield Farm. They sat on a sluice gate on Howe Burn,
wrapped up against the conditions, and pondered over the events of the previous night.
The two were to remain friends for the remainder of their lives and their respective
deaths occurred just weeks apart. According to the version of events given by Jim

Renton, he had been in the company of Bill Frizzel and his father on the night of the crash, and had also run towards the burning wreckage. His testimony states that while George Frizzel approached from one direction, they approached from another but were beaten back by the flames. They used the shelter of Howe Burn in order to get closer and see if there were any survivors. Through the flames they saw George and between them the figure of one of the crew prostrate on the ground. From their shelter they leapt up, ran across to the body and, with help from George, managed to pull the body clear. Unfortunately, the individual was beyond help.

Later that day, George Frizzel brought his youngest son Jimmy to visit the site. When the initial cordon around the wreckage had been lifted, a number of small items were removed by those who were aware of the pilot's identity and wanted a souvenir. It is not known what happened to the remains of the aircraft; in some cases crash wreckage was simply buried on-site, in most cases it was removed to the airfield.

Back at the aerodrome Andy Miller and the other crew members were naturally shocked and dashed into the dispersal hut to telephone the watch tower for confirmation that the pilot had in fact been Richard.

Miller was devastated. After having removed his flying clothing he went back to his billet and wrote a brief letter to his mother and father informing them of what he had seen:

> Dear Mom and Pop,
>
> Dick Hillary was killed early Friday morning, and as I saw it done I feel pretty badly about it. We had supper together that night before going up. I had been up once, and was detailed to go up again, but as I got severe icing I returned to base. In the meantime Hillary had gone up. All at once, as I was about to change, I heard a whine and terrific crash. I said, 'Christ, I hope that isn't Hillary'. I ran to the officer. He rushed out – (had) telephoned 102 (who) had not answered. My God, it was Hillary.
>
> I hope you will excuse this short note, but I don't feel like writing any more.
>
> Your loving son,
> Handel

Andy Miller's mother later telephoned Richard's parents, expressing her own sorrow at the loss.

* * *

It has been mentioned that Richard had been instructed to 'orbit the flashing beacon', the mobile AIB, which was situated two and a half miles to the north-east of the airfield just off the B6460 between Bogend and Mount Pleasant (801495 Ordnance Survey – Landranger Map 74). The crew, led by NCO Bernard Beadle (whose wife transmitted the telegram informing Mary and Michael and Edwyna Hillary of Richard's death), *were* operating the beacon that night, but the cloud was too low and the cover complete. Despite Beadle's testimony that he could see Richard's aircraft as it orbited the site, according to Andy Miller it would have been impossible to do so once Richard and Fison had climbed through the second layer and were therefore either orbiting in the general area or using their onboard radar unit to maintain contact with the airfield radar beacon. They maintained an orbiting pattern that roughly corresponded to that which they would have flown had the beacon been visible. This is what Miller had intended to do before he abandoned his second flight. Today, a tree at the isolated site bears several sets of initials carved into the bark long ago, perhaps by some of the beacon unit operators.

During an altitude test exercise Fison usually sat up front in the cockpit with Richard. If he had operated his AI set, as required to do, during that last flight, he would have been aft when the crash occurred. They were due to carry out a radar/fighter interception exercise and he would have needed to have been in position at that time. The R/O's position offered no means of strapping in, and after the crash, one member of the crew was found partially clear of the wreckage, while the other remained strapped in their seat. It is possible that it was Richard still in his seat while Fison, having not been strapped in, was thrown on impact.

News of Richard's death soon reached the local residents. Whenever news reached nearby Chirnside School that another aircraft from Charterhall had crashed the children would run around the playground shouting 'a plane's crashed!' The pilots had often used the white walls of the school, on a prominent position atop a hill, as a landmark on approaching the aerodrome from Berwick.

The deaths of Richard and Wilfrid Fison brought the total number of accidents at RAF 'Slaughter'all', since May 1942, a period of 235 days, to 49, and the total number of fatalities to nineteen. By the end of the war there had been an accident at Charterhall approximately every four and a half days, and a fatality approximately every thirteen.

* * *

Over the years, Flight Lieutenant 'Andy' Miller DFC and Bar, RAF (Retired), has never had any doubt that Richard lost control of the aircraft as a result of ice, which had formed on the control surfaces. We have no reason to doubt his memories and opinions, which have not altered in 50 years. He may have been inexperienced at the time but he went on to become an outstanding night fighter pilot, putting his flying expertise to good use in his post war years. He retired after 13 years service with the RAF.

Squadron Leader Lewis Brandon DSO, DFC and Bar, a highly successful operational night fighter radar operator and instructor at Charterhall while Richard was there, expressed his own opinion as to the cause of the crash. He believed that Richard lost control of the aircraft but cites his weak, disabled hands as the cause of the crash. This opinion is also shared by his good friend and pilot during their three and a half years together on operational duties, the late Wing Commander James Gillies 'Ben' Benson DSO, DFC and Bar. Benson was Richard's instructor and the Duty Officer i/c night flying (responsible for providing technical experience in the watch tower) the night he died.

Brandon recalled Benson's interpretation of the crash:

> As Hillary's aircraft turned to port, I believe he allowed the port wing to drop a little too far, the aircraft started to lose forward speed and began to fall into a spiral descent to port. Richard in the meantime had initially tried to right the aircraft but the condition and weakness of his hands prohibited him from doing this. He was unable to recover from his gradual descent to port which followed a spiralling pattern. Within seconds the situation deteriorated, as did the chances of him being able to correct the attitude of the aircraft . . . The explosion lit-up the entire countryside.

Lewis Brandon confirmed they did *not* fly with lights on and is of the opinion that the aircraft flipped onto its back before hitting the ground. This impression may arise from the fact that the wreckage was upside down when viewed later the same day. Nobody could see the attitude of the aircraft while it was airborne. He recalled that if the pilots were unable to see the beacon whilst airborne, they would have maintained an orbiting position in roughly the right area, and not worried about being too exact. It would have only been for a few minutes until their partner on the night fighter exercise had also become airborne.

Richard would have battled with the control column right until the end. Perhaps he had managed to level the aircraft, seconds before impact, as the shallow angle of impact suggests.

A number of others that I have spoken to, also expressed their opinion, including the late Sergeant Jack Wilkinson who was also on the same course as Richard and Andy Miller, and appears in the pilots' group photograph. His opinion as to the cause of the crash is similar to those of Lewis Brandon and 'Ben' Benson, but he also believed that the 'clapped-out' condition of the aircraft was a contributing factor. Like Lewis Brandon, Jack Wilkinson was not at the airfield that night.

Peter Crane was a member of the ground crew staff at RAF Charterhall. He recalled:

I was one of the last people to speak to the pilot Richard Hillary and his navigator Sergeant Fison before their fatal accident. I was duty wireless mechanic that night and had to repair a minor radio fault just before his aircraft took off. I recall clambering along the wing to get in the cockpit.

There was a marked difference between these two: Hillary with his terrible injuries and determination to overcome all odds and Fison, one of the few NCOs on the course, a dapper, friendly man, content to remain in the shadow of his extrovert partner.

In the early hours, a few miles from the aerodrome, the Bisley plummeted, giving neither occupant any chance to bale out. At the time I shared the view that Hillary's death had been inevitable and was sad for Sergeant Fison and his family that he became just another statistic. I recall him with respect when I browse through Hillary's autobiography *The Last Enemy*.

Peter Crane's statement raises the possibility that Richard did not reply to the ground controller in the final instance because his radio may have, once again, gone unserviceable.

* * *

Of all of them, Andy Miller was probably in the best position, and an active witness, to the final weeks, days, hours, and minutes of Richard's life. Only Richard himself knew what went on during the final seconds.

If we believe the accident report that Richard simply flew lower and lower until he hit the ground because he did not pay sufficient attention to his instruments – which were, after all, poorly lit – the personal views that I have included here would be incorrect.

* * *

Richard's instructions to the commanding officer at Charterhall were respected and later that morning Mary was informed of his death by telegram:

PRIORITY MRS BOOKER 14 HEREFORD HOUSE PARK ST LONDON W1 DEEPLY REGRET TO INFORM YOU FLT/LT RICHARD HOPE HILLARY NO 74677 KILLED IN FLYING ACCIDENT TODAY

Approximately four hours later, a similar telegram was sent to his mother, and during the interim period Mary made haste to be with Edwyna when the news reached her. That had been Richard's plan in the event of his death and it worked out the way he intended. Edwyna Hillary was working with the Red Cross at St James's Palace when she saw Mary enter the room. According to Michael Burn:

> . . . before she had spoken, she came towards her and said, 'Is it Richard?' Mary took her home, and stayed with her and Richard's father during that day. That evening Rosie Kerr, on twenty-four hour leave from East Grinstead, was having dinner at a London restaurant. A young man was going around the tables, asking people, 'Have you heard? Richard Hillary's been killed.' Rosie heard him and collapsed.

Archie McIndoe was both devastated and infuriated on hearing the news of Richard's death. He knew that this was not the way he would have chosen to die. It was squalid and unnecessary. His anger was inflamed further when he received a letter from the squadron leader medical officer at Charterhall, dated 11 January 1943, in which he wrote:

> Dear Mr McIndoe,
> No doubt you will be aware of the tragic fulfilment of your fears in connection with F/Lt Hillary. He and his observer were killed in an accident at 01.37 hours on 8.1.43 less than 24 hours after I wrote to you. Unfortunately Hillary had been given a special observer, an old Cambridge Blue, with temperament just calcu-lated to suit Hillary and the prospects were that they would make a good pair.

The mental conflict in Hillary's mind must have been great, because with his past 'incident' the risk of flying must have been so much more real to him. I think he was determined that his will should rule his mind. It shows what strength of character he had, but what an obstacle that is to understanding existing between patient and doctor. It is easy to be wise after the event but with Hillary insisting that there was nothing the matter with him and a Medical Board less than two months before, I could not put him off flying arbitrarily and I had hoped by the 19th of January you would have been able to give me the necessary assistance to do so. He was in London about Xmas but I imagine he did not call and see you.

This accident has distressed us all here considerably and though Hillary's reputation has caused much public attention, the loss of the observer is one the country cannot well afford either.

The letter was signed by the squadron leader medical officer. In response McIndoe made only one remark about the letter that was recorded: 'By God, the fellow's passing the buck.'

He did not reply to the letter but instead wrote to Michael and Edwyna Hillary. At no time had they held McIndoe responsible for the death of their son.

Mary and Edwyna shared a mutual belief in spiritualism and communication with the dead. This was just one of many facets of their relationship, but at this time one which helped to unite and console the two ladies in their grief. Mary went home from the Hillarys' flat to her own, and that night wrote Richard this goodbye, the last letter from the brown paper envelope that Michael Burn had found. It gives an insight into Mary's spiritual beliefs:

8.1.43

Richard, I bow before this blackness of despair, this loneliness of night. The first of an eternity of nights. I feel your spirit stretching forth to me, from out the stars, through all of this world's tears I see your face trying with infinite compassion of understanding to comfort me. But you must let me cry. These tears held back with all the courage that lay between us these last months can no longer be held back.

You once wrote, 'I had a sudden vision of what life would be without you. It was like a shadow passing across the sun.' That same shadow has passed across my sun. You who were my light have gone from me into light itself. Help me to share that light with you in spirit as we shared everything together here in life. I must achieve this. I must not be desolate. You will help me, I know. I must find a new selfless happiness in the knowledge that your search for those circles of peace is now ended, that your desires are fulfilled beyond the dreams of our imagination. I must not grieve that it had to be thus without me. I must overcome these black waves of the never any more. I cannot believe it. The realisation comes only in sudden spasms as daggers in the heart. I see no life without the joy your presence gave me – the sound of your voice, the touch of your hands, your laughter, and the tenderness of your complete understanding of me. I am alone as I was before you came. Alone yet not alone, for your spirit is all about me in these rooms which held our happiness. So near I hold my breath and yet so far beyond my human longing as to break my heart. I seem to see you smile with an infinity of wisdom and I strain to think only of you who have stepped gloriously out of all this sadness into eternity. You have left me rich in the memory of completeness and fulfilment of love and with much to do in honour of that memory.

My darling I will do my best and if I fail in the small things of this earth it will be because I no longer belong down here, but always 'fly beside you'.

The next telegram to reach Richard's parents was from Group Captain Leigh at Charterhall, requesting confirmation of the funeral arrangements. A full RAF funeral at Charterhall was offered, if required, but they requested that Richard's remains be returned to them for cremation. It is likely that Michael and Edwyna Hillary felt bitterness towards the RAF having let their son return to flying, and decided they wanted him back under their control and away from those they held responsible for his death.

The coffin was transported by train; leaving Berwick at 09.16 and arriving at Kings Cross at 23.47 on 9 January. A telegram had been sent to inform Michael and Edwyna of the intended time of arrival in London. It received an escort of RAF airmen from Charterhall, with Squadron Leader Arbon and Flight Lieutenant Gregory in charge.

Four days later Richard's mother wrote to Mary, in response to a letter she had just received from her:

> Mary my sweet,
>   What can I say to you that could possibly help you? You see darling, I have not the gift of expressing myself which was Dick's in such full measure.
>   You and your loving friendship to me in these dark hours have been more than wonderful and now we have to help one another – you are the family and the only young part left of it now.
>   I love you very dearly, you were so much, so very much more than loved by Richard.
>   . . . he will always be very near you, watching you. Our home is your home always, you will forever be an honoured member of the family.

At this time Michael and Edwyna Hillary were inundated with letters of sympathy from friends, relatives and the many admirers that had heard their son's radio broadcasts or read his book.

* * *

During the BBC news bulletin at 9 o'clock on Saturday, 9 January, it was announced that: 'Richard Hope Hillary, Royal Air Force Flight Lieutenant and Battle of Britain hero, has died on active service.'

The Times carried the announcement that Richard had been 'killed on active service' in its late edition on the same day and that of the death of Fison in the late edition on Monday, the 11th. Both the BBC and *The Times* were inaccurate, for as we know they were killed whilst training.

Most major newspapers carried the announcement of Richard's death the day after he was killed. Those that did not, certainly featured the news over the following few days. Each referred to his book and included details of his education at Shrewsbury and Oxford, the University Air Squadron and having been shot down during the Battle of Britain. Often they quoted from *The Last Enemy*. They wrote of his slow recovery and finally his own insistence on returning to flying. Until all the details were available, some reporters continued to mistakenly refer to Richard as having been killed on 'active service'.

Most papers included similar quotes from friends:

> He was one of the first Battle of Britain pilots to be shot down. His face and hands were terribly burned, and while in and out of hospital for months his one ambition was to return to operational flying. He overcame every obstacle, saying to his friends that he wanted to take an active not passive part in the war. His first book telling the story of a fighter pilot in the Battle of Britain, was a best seller, and it also had a successful sale in America. He talked about writing a second book, and was working on the background.

Such interest from the media confirmed his national celebrity status as a result of the success of his book. The reports in the English papers were generally quite accurate, although over-dramatised in parts.

The official announcement from the Air Ministry of Richard's death read:

9.1.43 – No.28

Air Ministry News Service   Air Ministry Bulletin No.8923

F/Lt. Richard Hope Hillary, author of "The Last Enemy", who was shot down in the Battle of Britain and was badly burned, has been killed.

He was passed medically fit for flying some time ago and at the time of his death he was flying with F/Sgt. Kenneth Wilfred Young Fison, who was also killed.

Wing Commander O. H. Watkins, DFC., who was a close friend and colleague of Flt.Lt. Hillary when he was at Fighter Command Headquarters on special duties said today:

'Hillary was desperately keen to get back to flying and I know he was delighted when he was passed medically fit. Although he was very interested in working on a script for our Air Sea Rescue film, he was really impatient to get it completed and begin a refresher course of training. Hillary was the type of pilot I'd always be glad to have flying with me.'

Richard Hillary became famous for his book published last June in which he told a moving, yet dispassionate story of his months in hospital after being shot down in the Battle of Britain.

He was badly burned about the face, body and hands, but surgical skill and Hillary's own fortitude eventually enabled him to leave hospital long enough to go to America on special duties (where he wrote his book), and, later, to resume flying.

He had been in and out of hospital ever since September 3, 1940, the day on which he was shot down. This month he was to have attended a party for the 'few' – Battle of Britain pilots who have had features and limbs 'remade' by plastic surgery – at their convalescent home at East Grinstead. Air Marshal T. L. Leigh-Mallory, C.B., D.S.O., Fighter Command A.O.C. in C. is to be present.

Born in Sydney, Australia, in 1919, he came to England after the last war with his father who was at the Australian Treasury.

In 1931, he went to Shrewsbury and in 1937 to Trinity College. His flying career began at Oxford where he was a member of the University Air Squadron.

He was still at Oxford when war broke out and he was immediately called up. In October 1939 he was commissioned pilot officer.

After a period of operational training he was eventually posted to No.603 (City of Edinburgh) Squadron in July 1940, when the squadron was operating from a Scottish base. The squadron was moved south in August and immediately plunged into the Battle of Britain, shooting down 14 enemy aircraft in fierce battles over south-eastern England on August 31.

Hillary was shot down on September 3 – the first anniversary of the outbreak of war. The German airforce was continuing its attempts to batter the air defences on south-east England, chief objectives being our forward fighter bases.

The first wave of enemy aircraft came in shortly before 10 a.m. the bulk of the 250 raiders flying in to make a two pronged attack north and south of the Thames.

Eight aircraft of the City of Edinburgh Squadron took off from Hornchurch and when over Manston at 22,000 feet sighted six Dornier 17's flying in 'V' formation with six Me.109's at the same height and twelve more slightly above. A dogfight with the Messerschmitts followed. At least two of the Me's and one of the bombers were shot down.

It was in this fight that Hillary's aircraft was hit. He was trapped in the blazing cockpit but managed to struggle free and bale out, being picked up from the sea by a lifeboat and taken to Margate Hospital suffering from shock and severe burns.

There, began the long series of surgical operations, convalescence and more surgical operations described in his book.

Last summer Hillary was for a time at the R.A.F. Staff College and was then posted to Fighter Command Headquarters on special duties. For six weeks he was loaned for work on the script of an Air Sea Rescue film and when that was complete he passed his medical board as fit for flying duties and was posted towards the end of November.

He had dubbed himself 'the last of the long haired boys' in his book, for he was the sole survivor of his little coterie of Oxford undergraduates who came into the R.A.F. at the outbreak of war.

It was typical of Hillary that he should choose the title of his book from 1st Corinthians XV.26 – 'The last enemy that shall be destroyed is death'.

Those who knew Hillary, knew him as a clever conversationalist, modest, and very much interested in writing.

Hillary's father now lives at Knightsbridge, S.W.

* * *

During the Battle of Britain and the entire Second World War citizens of Edinburgh scanned the newspapers for news of their squadron, although later in the war, few local lads remained. There had been great success, but also terrible grief suffered by those folk who had lost members of their own family, grief that is, naturally, deeply felt to this day. There had also been great sadness for those lost, who were not from the area but had been fighting with the Scottish Squadron. On 11 January the Edinburgh newspaper, *The Scotsman*, announced Richard's death with a poignant article headed: 'Last of the Long-Haired Boys.'

* * *

As already stated, Squadron Leader Arbon and Flight Lieutenant Gregory were the officers in charge of the escort of Richard's remains on their journey south from the mortuary at RAF Charterhall to the crematorium at Golders Green, where he was cremated on Tuesday 12 January 1943. In attendance were the escort, Richard's parents and a number of Richard's friends, or their representatives. These included: Mary Booker, Rache Lovat Dickson, Mrs Charles Haydon, Major Eric Linklater, the Reverend Arthur Malin, Mrs Geoffrey Toye and Denise Maxwell-Woosnam.

The funeral service for Kenneth Wilfrid Young Fison was held the next day, 13 January, at 15.00 hours at St Peter's Church, Blatchington, Seaford, Sussex. His wife Joyce, mother Winifred and father Kenneth, were present, along with other members of his family. Lord Buckmaster, a close friend of Wilfrid Fison, wrote:

> His home life, with a devoted wife and two small children, was of the happiest; at 37 there was no call for him to seek the most dangerous of all ways in which to serve his country. Yet he renounced all those things that other men hold most dear and too old to be a pilot, chose to be an observer for those flying our night fighters. At his age the road was not an easy one, but he never faltered in his purpose. The difficulty of close and continuous association with those but half his age, the red tape and routine, the dull and dreary phases of initial training, none of these held the power to defeat him. Buoyant in spirit was he, bubbling with enthusiasm also for any task to which he set his hand. What a pleasure it was to talk with him; whatever the subject – training in the RAF, the welfare of workers in his factory, post-war reconstruction – he brought to bear on it the full force of a keen and active mind, with an outlook always optimistic and essentially humane. It was not indeed possible to meet him without feeling better for it. So vital was he that hard it is to realise one will no longer meet him in a friendly visit to one's own house or anothers, or by chance in the ordinary walks of life. Yet something surely of that valiant spirit still survives amongst us here, since his selfless example remains a beacon light shining through the mist of self-interest in which our sense of duty is so often shrouded.

Also on this day, following her telephone call of condolence to Edwyna Hillary, Ruby Miller wrote to Richard's mother, enclosing the letter she had received from her own son which informed her of Richard's death:

> My boy, Sergeant Pilot Handel Miller, was your boy's bed-mate at Charterhall. When he came home on leave a few days before Xmas he talked of no-one else

but your boy – so great was his admiration of him. His fiancee bought *The Last Enemy* for his Xmas box, and he took it back for the author to autograph . . .

. . . Now my dear I know its not going to be easy, but keep your chin up in triumph even as he would wish it – you know what he said – 'I was not afraid' – 'The Lord Gaveth and the Lord Taketh Away', 'Blessed be the name of the Lord' – a mother is ever from the moment she gives life to her child called upon to sacrifice. You had him and loved him for 20 years, during those years he had accomplished more glory and triumph than many of us do in 70 years.

Andy Miller was not Richard's 'bed-mate', but his mother may have mistakenly got this impression if Andy had told her he was billeted on the same site as Richard. Eight months later, Edwyna Hillary returned Ruby Miller's gesture when Andy went missing over Heligoland, Holland.

* * *

The news of the death of Richard Hillary had been a source of grief to the many who had known him and to the thousands who had known him only through his book. It was in response to that reaction by the nation that a service was arranged to allow those who wished to honour one of 'The Few' to do so.

According to an article published by the journalist Mr William Hickey:

Normally the RAF discourages individual commemoration of fliers who are killed.

The case of Flight Lieutenant Richard Hillary is exceptional. Many thousands of Britons and Americans have been moved by his remarkable book. . . . There is to be a memorial service on Monday at St Martins-in-the-Fields at 12.30.

The service was held on 25 January and was conducted by the Reverend W.H. Elliott, Precentor of the Chapel. The day before he told a reporter from the *Sunday Chronicle*:

I am deeply grateful to have been asked to conduct this memorial service for one of our gallant airmen. There must be many more people who would be glad of the opportunity of paying tribute to our heroes in the Fighting Forces who so gallantly sacrificed their lives.

I think it would be widely appreciated if more of these Services were held.

The Reverend Eric Loveday and Richard's uncle, the Reverend Arthur H.M. Hope, also took part in the service.

Michael and Edwyna Hillary sat at the front with the Air Ministry representative, Air Commodore P.F. Fullard, Lady Douglas (representing Air Chief Marshal Sir Sholto Douglas), and Lord and Lady Desborough.

Three hymns were sung: 'All Creatures of Our God and King', 'Abide With Me' and 'I Vow to Thee My Country'. The psalm chosen was the beautiful 91st, which it has been said, '. . . crystallised all that Richard believed in'. The lesson was appropriate: I Corinthians, Chapter 15, Verse 26: 'The last enemy that shall be destroyed is death.'

It was reported that some 1,500 people went to pay their respects and owing to the lack of room some stood at the back of the church. It did not go unnoticed that, dressed in their blue fisherman's jerseys and reefer jackets, Dennis 'Sinbad' Price and the grey-haired Henry 'Mussel' Sandwell, two members of the Margate lifeboat crew who had rescued Richard from the North Sea in September 1940, were amongst the congregation. They had travelled to London in order to pay their last respects to the young man they had once saved from certain death.

One journalist wrote of the setting for Richard's memorial service:

No church appeals more to London sentiment than that of St Martins-in-the-Field. The now absurd rusticity of the name and the central position (poised, as Francis Thompson might have said, between Heaven and Charing Cross), the combination of Gibb's serene classic architecture with a warm democratic tradition, and its service as refuge for the bodies and souls of all distressed, have

endeared St Martin's to very many. In its own way it is as national as Nelson's
column and the National Gallery. There, only too often, do we bid farewell to
many great national figures.

On the same day, a short while before the memorial service was due to begin, a Boston
III of No.605 Squadron, which had flown up from its base at Ford, took off from RAF
Hunsdon, Hertfordshire. The pilot was Flight Lieutenant Mike Olley, onboard was the
commanding officer of the squadron at that time, Wing Commander 'Uncle' George
Denholm, Richard's former CO of 603 Squadron. Their 'mission' was to fly over the
approximate spot where Richard had landed in the sea on 3 September 1940, and, while
the memorial service was in progress, scatter his ashes over the waves of the North Sea.

The name of 'Flight Lieutenant Richard Hope Hillary RAF(VR)', was added to the
memorial at Golders Green Crematorium, Hendon, Middlesex, by the Imperial War
Graves Commission (IWGC).

* * *

In March 1943, Mr W Elliot of Gavinton, near Duns, the brother of the owner of
Crunklaw Farm, wrote to Edwyna Hillary and Joyce Fison informing them that he had
designed a memorial: 'To the two gay and gallant airmen who lost their lives on his
brother's farm.'

The memorial was in the form of an illustrated leaflet made by hand and featuring the
words:

> To the memory of Richard Hope Hillary and his navigator W. F. Fison who both
> met their death together and thus conquered 'The Last Enemy' leaving behind a
> noble example for us to strive to follow.

His life, – what was it?
Ah, who knows!
T'was just a visit
I suppose.
Joy and Sorrow
For a day;
Then tomorrow
he's away.

Youth, this morning;
Manhood, noon;
Came the warning –
Death so soon;
Hear his voice
From out the blue. . . .
'Happy Landings –
Wait for you'.

Edwyna Hillary and Joyce Fison were each sent one of these tributes and the response
from Edwyna Hillary reflected the reaction of both mothers:

> My dear Mr Elliot,
>   Thank you so much for the most charming memorial you so kindly sent to us
> which you designed to our son. We shall value your tribute to his memory all our
> lives. We are so glad to know the name of the farm where he met his death –
> Crunklaw – a beautiful sounding name. Some day we should like so much to
> meet you, your brother and sister-in-law. Would it bother you to write to tell me
> the hour at which the accident occurred and how your brother found my son's
> body. Death I hope and pray was instantaneous. I would treasure any detail
> however small your brother could tell you, – my heart aches to know all details.
>   We have ordered a photo to be done for you – I regret it is not a very recent
> one, as this one was taken during 'The Battle of Britain' but as soon as it is finished

we will both sign it and will feel happy and honoured for you to have one.

Our son was home at Xmas he was so happy to be back on the active list and to be flying again. His death has left a tremendous blank in our lives, he was so gay and gallant and such a wonderful son, we therefore have such delightful memories of our times together and these can never be taken away.

Thank you again from the bottom of my heart for your memorial, your sympathy, and your loving thought that inspired you to write to us.

Some time after Richard's death, at a time when Michael and Edwyna Hillary thought they would be able to cope, the couple travelled to RAF Charterhall at the invitation of the station commander, Group Captain Rupert Leigh, who had done much to assist the family in matters concerning his station. Perhaps it had been Edwyna's spiritual beliefs that lured her to the site, or simply the couple had felt compelled to see where their son had died, in an attempt to come to terms with their loss.

Prior to their visit, the Hillarys had written to the Elliots, the then owners of Crunklaw Farm, requesting permission to visit the site. Having received their full support, arrangements were made and they duly headed for the Scottish Borders. From the airfield they drove to the farmhouse at Crunklaw Farm and, leaving the car, walked down the track to visit the site of Richard and Wilfrid Fison's death. The field still showed very obvious signs of the crash. The couple were left alone for a while before returning to the farmhouse where they were offered the gracious hospitality of the farmer and his wife. They were then taken back to Charterhall before returning to London. Edwyna's spiritual beliefs ensured that Richard was still in her presence, for the rest of her life.

A short while after the accident, a large floral tribute in the shape of a cross decorated with artificial poppies appeared amongst the burnt grass, oil, and churned soil of the crash site. Its origin is unknown but it is possible that the cross may have been placed there by representatives from RAF Charterhall, at the request of Richard's parents and loved ones. Filed in the Lovat Dickson Collection in the National Archives of Canada is a photograph of the floral tribute at the crash site, taken during the spring or summertime of 1943. The photograph is a copy of the original which was kept in a presentation folder. Written in pencil on the back of the folder is the moving epitaph: 'Where the Last Enemy was conquered.'

The photograph may have been taken by Mr W. Elliot on behalf of Edwyna Hillary or by Richard's parents during their visit to the site. In the photograph the floral tribute appears to have been out in the open for some time and the leaves on the trees indicates that the photo was taken in the spring, at the earliest.

In her letter of thanks for the memorial, Joyce Fison sought Mr Elliot's assistance for a visit to the crash site she had in mind. In reply to her letter he wrote:

> I was pleased to have your letter and also glad to hear that my small attempt had given you a little consolation in your very hard trial. I am only sorry that the tribute was not more in keeping with the sacrifice which your gallant husband made for his country. He certainly has been one of the best and one the Nation will be proud of in the days that are yet to be.
>
> As requested I have got a guide to Berwickshire which may interest you and on the map I have marked various places which have a certain connection with the accident and it may help you to actually locate the scene etc.
>
> My hobby used to be photography but I regret to say that I have had to give it up as I cannot get materials although I have been requested to do a little for the war office . . . but the war office has to have every plate accounted for and but for that I might have taken one of the actual scene of the accident, but you can take it from me it was a most peaceful part of the country and that your husband and Hillary died before they felt pain . . .

Included with the letter were a number of photographs of Crunklaw Farm taken before the war.

In October 1943 Joyce Fison received a commemorative edition of *The Last Enemy* from Richard's parents. Written inside were the words:

> Inscribed for Joyce Fison
> whose gallant husband made
> the supreme sacrifice with
> the son of
> Michael Hillary
> and
> Edwyna Hillary
> parents of the author
> 25.10.43

Joyce Fison suffered further tragedy when her daughter Susan, along with her two young sons, were killed in an air-crash whilst returning to England after visiting her in Guernsey.

* * *

For some years after, 'Hillary's Field', as it became known by the locals, remained scarred by the damage caused by the flames, fuel and oil. Indentations left by the engines and the smell of oil persisted for as long as it was used as grazing land. When it was eventually ploughed for arable or cereal crops, nothing grew on the site where the engines had lain. In 1964 Mrs Sheila Romanes, a local historian whose husband served in the RAF and briefly flew from Charterhall, took her eight-year-old son George to tea with the Darling family, who had taken over ownership of Crunklaw Farm from the Elliots. She took him down to the crash site, which he insisted she show him. Even after 21 years the impressions left by the two engines were still visible and a couple of tiny items of wreckage were still about. Young George returned to his mother in triumph, he had found a small peice of wreckage as a souvenir and still has it today. There is still a small area about the size of one of the engines, where little grows, but generally there is nothing visible today to indicate the tragedy that occurred.

* * *

An investigation into the accident had begun immediately after the crash. The operational record book (ORB) for RAF Charterhall and RAF Winfield (satellite):

> 8.1.43: The weather was only fair and little flying done. There was an accident at night when a Blenheim flying from Charterhall on a training flight crashed and burnt out. The cause could not be ascertained. The pilot Flight Lieutenant Hillary and his Navigator/Radio, 1336052 Sergeant Fison K W, were both killed.

At the Air Accident Board of Enquiry at Charterhall it was found that the flight had been properly authorised and the weather suitable for such an exercise.

Bernard Beadle, the NCO in charge of the beacon, was called to give his evidence. He stated that he had seen Richard's aircraft descend out of the cloud, turning to the left (port), with the navigation lights on. The aircraft lost height moderately quickly, but not in a steep dive, and eventually struck the ground. Richard had already spoken his last words on the radio/telephone prior to this part of the descent.

Group Captain Leigh stated: 'From the above evidence, therefore, I attribute this unfortunate accident to loss of control on the part of the pilot while orbiting.'

The report included details of the hours Richard had accumulated in his log, since he had arrived at Charterhall:

> 20.00 on the Link Trainer
> 3.00 sodium
> 2.40 dual – day and night
> 16.35 solo – day and night
>
> Nearly all on Bisley.

It is interesting that the aircraft was again referred to as a 'Bisley' when its correct name was the Blenheim V.

In response to the findings, Group Captain Leigh then added: 'I feel that the tendency which I have experienced myself, of ex-single seater day pilots to rely on external visual aids when night flying as opposed to reliance and confidence in instruments, has no small bearing on this accident.'

All other witnesses on the night were aircrew and stated that Richard's navigation lights were turned *off*. Therefore Beadle would have not been able to see anything of an aircraft descending from low cloud on a pitch-black night. Additionally, there was no mention of an audible anomaly with the pitch of the engines. The station commander based his findings on flawed evidence. The Inspectorate of Flight Safety (RAF) Aircraft Accident Record Card (A.M. Form 1180) on Richard's crash contained the following details:

Accident Report.

Date:	8th January 1943
Unit:	54 OTU
Group:	81
Signal:	AT946
Aircraft Type and Mark:	Blenheim V 25, BA194, E
Engine Type and Mark:	Mercury 15, 182233 E and 185983 E
File:	G17679
Place:	Middlefield Farm, near Duns
County:	Berwickshire
Name and Unit:	Hillary R.H.
Rank:	F/Lt
No:	74677
Casualty:	Killed
Control Lost:	Possibly
	Definitely **X**
	Instruments **X**
	Lost
	Navigation
	Petrol
Weather:	Vis:LT.
	Rep
	All **X**
	Ice
Fire:	Air
	Ground **X**
Errors:	Any **X**
	Error **X**
	Airmen
	Care
	Gr.Care
Stage:	Flight **X**
	Take off
	Taxi
	Static
	Final Descent **X**
Duty and History:	Training
Solo	
Total:	422 ILCG
Type:	28 ACF

Night
Total:	15	PSFI
Type:	12	EOK
Instrument:	13	UOK
Link:	21	AOK

Report:

Aircraft spiralled into ground whilst orbiting flashing beacon. Fire on impact. Officer Commanding assume pilot paid insufficient attention to the instruments whilst orbiting. Station Commander concurs. Pilot lost height gradually. Cloud base 2,000 feet with 10/10 cloud.

Instructor:

[Flight Lieutenant Benson] Due to pilot losing control of his a/c whilst orbiting the beacon in cloud.

The weather reports show that conditions, although difficult and unpleasant, had not been exceptionally severe for the region, and had not warranted the cancellation of flying, but the cold, cloudy sky was unfriendly, and occasional wind-driven sleet was sweeping across the airfield unchecked. The cloud ceiling was confirmed at 10/10, but at 2,000 feet, which is not correct.

The Blenheim may have initially lost height gradually, but the pitch of the engines increased to a high-pitch whine, witnessed by aircrew and the civilian witness, George Frizzel, as it dived into the ground (although George Frizzel stated that the engines were 'making a very funny sound'). There was no gradual loss of height, unperceived by its pilot.

I believe the inaccurate assumption as to the cause of the crash was due to the fact that, apart from the statement by Benson, the squadron commander and station commander did not witness any part of the last flight of Richard Hillary and Wilfrid Fison, and relied upon reports to knit together their interpretation of events, as required. But the information they received was both limited and unreliable, and did not include the testimony of those such as Andy Miller who had been in the best position on the airfield to see.

At this stage I would like to include information from the *World War II Pilot's Handbook* and the chapter entitled 'Stall':

> A stall caused by ice is not the same as a normal stall.
>
> It occurs at a higher speed preceded by a noticeable, sloppiness of the controls. The aircraft does not break cleanly. Gradual transition from normal flight, through heavy mushy flight, to the full stall.
>
> The aircraft will fall off one wing or the other depending on the individual characteristics of the aircraft.
>
> As stalling speed in straight and level flight increases because of ice accretion, it increases even more in banks.

I think that this passage adds credibility to the theory that Richard's crash was caused by ice, based on the information available from those that were present.

It is possible that with so many crashes occurring at Charterhall 'pilot error' was a politically favourable outcome of this enquiry.

The question over the R/T from the ground controller, 'Are you happy?' was part of the training routine in which the pilot, turning gently to port, would keep the beacon approximately half-a-mile off his port wing and make a series of circles. Richard's answer, 'Moderately. I am continuing to orbit', was his honest admission of discomfort.

Aware that he was having trouble controlling the aircraft, Benson had ordered Richard to land. The accident report confirms this, in part, as it states that the accident occurred during the 'final descent'. It is interesting to ponder the possibility that Benson did not act just on the word 'moderately', but that there had been further communication between Richard and the tower, confirming that he was indeed in trouble. Nevertheless, the final communication from the tower was met with silence.

A number of years ago, in response to a particular route of enquiry, I received a phone call from a former World War II pilot who claimed that he knew the female R/T operator who had been on duty in the watch tower on the night of 7/8 January. The caller informed me that the experience had affected her so much that, over the years, she had only ever been able to confide in him. Her version of events stated that there *had* been further communication with the tower and it had resulted in Benson taking over the R/T set to recall Richard after he had ignored the female operator's instruction to return to the airfield and land. As Richard struggled to control his aircraft he was apparently angry, crying, and expressing fears that he was being recalled to be finally thrown off the course, and would rather die trying.

No further contact with the caller has been possible, but if this story is true then it displays no more than a reckless determination to overcome the difficulties, not a suicide attempt.

* * *

Blame for his death should therefore be directed at those responsible for allowing him to return to flying training; the medical board, Air Marshal William Sholto Douglas and perhaps certain individuals at Charterhall. The fact that he had been a determined, strong-willed character and could be very influential when up against those of a weaker disposition is not a valid counter-argument against such a bad decision.

* * *

Flying Officer How, the R/T speech officer who had given the gramophone recital in the R/T hut on New Year's Eve, was also the effects officer for the Courts of Adjustment. Richard had spoken of How with affection in his letter to Mary written the day following the recital.

After he had died it had been How's duty to go to Richard's accommodation and remove his personal belongings for return home to the next of kin. Richard had written the name and address of his father as next of kin on his service record, Air Ministry Forms 543 and 1406, when he had first joined up.

In Richard's room Flying Officer How found a considerable number of personal effects, enough to fill more than one large trunk. Amongst his mass of uniforms, casual clothing and toiletries was his reading matter which included: *The Oxford Book of Prose*, the novels of Dostoevsky, Bernard Shaw, *Introducing James Joyce*, *Saints and Revolutionaries*, *War and Peace*, *Planisphere of Air Navigation Stars*, and *The Mint*.

Amongst Richard's effects were also: the typed script of a short story he had written entitled: 'The Voyage Back', nine sheets of his diary from 27.3.42 until 10.4.42, seven pages of a manuscript in pencil, and Richard's last will and testament. There was a typewritten record of all letters and telegrams he had sent between 1 June and 31 December, 1941, and his gold aeroplane clip. The sum of 6d was also found and 'placed to the credit of the estate'.

With all these items the effects officer placed the silver cigarette case which had been found on Richard's body and, although damaged, had survived the flames, unlike the other items found in his pockets. At this stage Richard's gold watch did not number among his effects.

As Flying Officer How perused Richard's papers he came across letters sent to him by Mary that he had not returned to her for safe keeping; he also found letters from other friends of Richard including those from Rosie Kerr. In his letters to Mary, Richard had made a number of scathing comments about Charterhall and in particular the station commander (Beisiegel). Flying Officer How may have come across Mary's response to these comments and similar comments in Richard's jottings. In referring to the love letters from 'Mrs Mary Booker', 'apparently written by a married girl', he decided to destroy all of Richard's papers, thinking that he was doing the right thing for all concerned. But it was a dreadful error on his part.

Flying Officer How then wrote to Michael Hillary confirming despatch of his son's effects to the Central Depository, RAF Colnbrook, Middlesex. This was the start of a great deal of correspondence between Richard's parents and the Commanding Officer at RAF Charterhall, over the matter of his personal effects. The letters were always polite but to the point.

Michael Hillary travelled to Colnbrook in person to demand his son's belongings (perhaps an example of the growing anger and bitterness he felt towards those he felt responsible for his son's death). The officer in charge handed them over without the required 'Court Grant', but on returning home Michael discovered that certain items were missing. He forthwith wrote to Group Captain Leigh at Charterhall requesting the immediate despatch of Richard's gold watch, wallet (which included papers of sentimental value to Denise), fountain pen, letters and a recent manuscript. Thus it was here that the legend that the RAF destroyed Richard's manuscript and war diaries began.

A short while later Edwyna Hillary also requested the return of Richard's battledress with red silk lining. Richard had been wearing his battledress under his Irvin jacket and it had been badly burnt in the crash. In a letter dated 28 February, Group Captain Leigh, explained, rather prudently, that it had been 'destroyed in the crash'.

In response to Michael Hillary's letter about the 'missing' items, Group Captain Leigh informed him that the 'smashed' remains of the watch had been brought to the station by the local police on 22 February. It had been 'found in the vicinity on the crash'. It was sent to Colnbrook the next day. The wallet was found on Richard's body, but 'consisted of only charred remains and was therefore destroyed'. The fountain pen, maroon Kashmir scarf (a gift from Mary), and letters, were presumed 'destroyed by fire'. Nothing was found of a manuscript. The station commander informed Michael Hillary that he had personally chosen Flying Officer How for the task, as he was a: '. . . thorough, reliable and scrupulous officer, and I have the utmost trust in his powers and ability.'

In order to avoid causing further pain to the next-of-kin, Flying Officer How had sought the advice of the station medical officer before a decision was made concerning what should, and what should not be returned. In response to this judgement Group Captain Leigh stated in his letter to Michael Hillary: 'I would be worse than a fool if I countenanced articles of this nature being forwarded to next-of-kin.'

Of the items that had been returned, Michael Hillary gave his son's uniforms, greatcoat and service cap to a friend and colleague whom Richard had met at staff college.

Although Richard's will had not been witnessed and he therefore died intestate, the letters of administration were granted to his father who passed them to Frank Moss, Michael Hillary's solicitor, who dealt with the matter, and who later became the solicitor for the Richard Hillary Trust. By confirming the authenticity of the paperwork and the handwriting, he was able to handle Richard's assets more or less as he had requested:

> To Mary Booker I also leave £20 that she may give a dinner for me to which she
> will invite Michael and Barbara Astor, Denise Maxwell-Woosnam, Eric Linklater
> and Rache Lovat Dickson.

Richard also left his painting by Kennington to Mary.

Michael Hillary applied for Richard's financial assets through His Majesty's High Court of Justice, and on 16 April he was granted £1,290.

There was a dinner in Richard's honour, to which Michael and Edwyna Hillary and Mary invited the guests Richard had suggested. This dinner became an annual event and went on for many years. Michael Burn married Mary in 1947, and he too became great friends of the Hillarys.

It is not known if Merle Oberon received the gold aeroplane clip, as Richard had wanted. Richard also left £500 in war bonds in his parents' safe at their flat.

Tony Tollemache was serving at RAF Wick, Scotland, as this time. In a letter dated 20 March, written in response to a letter from Michael Hillary, informing him of the bequeathal of Richard's gold watch, he wrote: 'I suggest we leave it at Colnbrook for the present . . . I'll make some arrangements when I am next on leave . . .' It is not known if he ever collected the watch.

During March there was a belated discovery by the RAF that Richard had held a service issue .45 revolver, and Michael Hillary received a letter asking that, if it were found, it should be returned.

The letter sent to Richard by the station intelligence officer (SIO) at RAF Hornchurch on 21 November 1942, was never found and was probably destroyed by Flying Officer How. After Richard's death, Michael Hillary wrote to the SIO, requesting details of his son's total score and mentioned the fact that he had not been awarded the DFC, which is said to have rankled. In a reply, dated 4 March 1943, he was informed that Richard had been credited with: five enemy aircraft destroyed, two probably destroyed and one damaged.

On Saturday, 7 March, the station commander at Charterhall, Group Captain Rupert Leigh, travelled to London to speak with Michael and Edwyna Hillary personally about their son's death. The couple had heard a number of disturbing rumours that their son may have taken his own life, and by providing them with all details, no matter how upsetting, Group Captain Leigh sought to dispel these harmful and dreadfully upsetting rumours.

On 8 March 1943, from his home in Rutland Court, Michael Hillary – described as a warm-hearted, upright and straight-spoken man from whom his son had gained much of his independence – wrote to Richard's commanding officer at RAF Charterhall:

> Dear Group Captain Leigh,
>
> I want to thank you most sincerely on behalf of my wife and myself for your very great kindness and thoughtfulness in coming personally to explain to us the circumstances of our son's death. I bitterly resent those circumstances. One braces oneself to meet the hazards of action against the enemy, but finds it very difficult to accept the senseless waste of a valuable life in training. However, our minds are now at rest, and we can disregard any rumours that reach us. The truth, however gruesome, is preferable to the uncertainty in which we have been living.
>
> The position in regard to the letters and papers which were burnt is not satisfactory, and I am writing to say some of the things I had to leave unsaid in the short time available on Saturday.
>
> I do not question the motives of your Effects Officer, but the wisdom and prudence of his actions are open to grave doubt. His mistaken zeal in his attempts to save pain has dealt us perhaps the blow next hardest to our son's death, for, apart from the indignity of his and others' inquisitorial examination of our son's letters and papers, we have been irrevocably prevented from knowing our son's last thoughts and state of mind in the last days of his life. To anyone not entirely devoid of the finer feelings and perceptions, the destruction of his correspondence because of some quite unimportant letters from women suggests the sort of callous act that springs from a form of moral righteousness that does incalculable harm.
>
> Being the man you are, I quite understand your readiness to support your Effects Officer's actions; but it does seem to me that, in exercising moral censorship of my son's affairs, he gratuitously usurped a private right that no amount of blessing by you can extenuate or justify, especially when the censorship was exercised with a rigidity of mind which apparently did not admit of any discretion, and a criterion was applied that was surely more suitable for a Girl's Sunday School than a fighting service. I could understand indiscreet letters not being sent to a young wife; but my son was not married, and the fact that he had a father was either overlooked, or his father was not considered competent to decide the moral issues involved. I maintain it was for me, and not your Effects Officer, to decide upon the disposal of my son's letters and papers; and I should have thought the obvious course would have been to seal these up and send them to me by Squadron Leader Gregory, when he accompanied the body.

Having expressed these views, I should not wish to pursue the matter further. My son is dead, and nothing else matters. And I loathe publicity. But you will appreciate that other people are concerned, whose interests are of a different kind; and they have already made it abundantly clear that they are profoundly dissatisfied with the position. It is common knowledge that my son was engaged in the preparation for the background of another book, and several people had seen what he had already written, and were aware of what he was writing. The letters to him from some of these people were, at his request, written in narrative form with a view to incorporation in a publication at a later date. Most of these people are closely associated with literature and the press and, with all respect to your Effects Officer, flatly refuse to believe his statement that Richard had written nothing at Charter Hall. On the contrary, they know that he wrote a daily journal; and part of that journal, written up to the 4th January, is in the possession of one of his friends. They know too that some of the matter he had written was derogatory to the administration of the RAF Station at Charter Hall, and would at once conclude that the material was destroyed with a view to the suppression of damaging criticism.

Almost daily I am told of letters that were written to my son and were not returned; and only this morning I received a letter from the Chief Intelligence Officer at Hornchurch, stating that he wrote to Richard on 6th November. I enclose a copy of this letter. It was not returned and was presumably one of those destroyed.

Ever since Richard's death the press have been trying to obtain information as to what he had left of written material, and two at least of the leading London papers have made offers to buy this material for publication. So far they have been told that the effects have not been delivered. Now they have to be told that there are no literary effects, and I shall have to ask my son's publishers, who dealt with these matters for my son, both to close off these enquiries, and in addition not to expect any material for the Memoir which they have already commissioned two popular authors, Eric Linklater and Arthur Koestler, to write.

It is all very disturbing. Like my son, the letters have been uselessly and unnecessarily destroyed, and nothing can bring them back. It is only another instance of the mischief and harm that can be done by well-intentioned stupidity and moral righteousness, and a lack of courage to face criticism.

I am sorry to have had to write at such length, but I wanted you to know the position. All I ask personally is that I may be allowed to forget the whole painful episode as quickly as possible, and for that reason I shall not expect a reply to this letter.

Yours sincerely
Michael Hillary

In a letter to Mary, Richard had admitted the fact that he hadn't written anything for a year; his plan for a follow-up to *The Last Enemy* was in his head. Asking his friends to write their letters to him in narrative form was also foundation for his plan. Clearly, his plans were well under way, but the manuscript was unwritten. Flying Officer How later confirmed that he had found nothing that remotely resembled a manuscript. The sadness felt by his friends, determined to see his surviving work published, was met with this news, and some found it hard to accept.

Richard's sporadic, occasional, daily jottings up to 4 January were apparently loaned to Lovat Dickson and later published in his own biography of Richard; these have not been seen since. The admission by Michael Hillary that only 'part of that journal' had been found, adds credibility to my theory that there was no actual 'diary'. The only other record of his activities had been in his letters to Mary. Not only did he ask for his friends to write to him in narrative form but he also wrote to Mary in the same way. Linklater and Koestler, with pens at the ready, had already been commissioned to write an essay each for a memoir on Richard to which Lovat Dickson and Phyllis Bottome would also contribute.

On 8 March, Michael Hillary wrote to Lovat Dickson, enclosing copies of his letters to the Charterhall station commander concerning the 'missing' papers; he informed him that the existence of a manuscript was now 'doubtful' and that there was no diary. Lovat Dickson had all there was. There would be no further material.

Also on Sunday, 8 March, Eric Kennington paid the Hillarys a visit. He had produced a painting, *The Heart of England*, which he offered as a tribute to Richard and had discussed the matter with Edwyna Hillary. Later that day he wrote to Mary, whom Edwyna had put in charge of distribution of prints, and expressed his views:

> . . . She was suffering from a foul blow received the day before. No doubt it will strike you too. They burnt his letters and Mss. For myself I feel a strange resentment against that destruction. I know so well the stage and players where the tragedy was carried out, having lived on numerous stations, and have seen the pain (though not so severe) that such callousness causes.

The matter of the destruction of Richard's papers was even brought up in Parliament. On 7 April Mrs Cazalet Keir, member of parliament for East Islington, asked the Secretary of State for Air, Sir Archibald Sinclair, through the Speaker: '. . . whether it is the usual practice of the Ministry to destroy after their death, letters and personal papers belonging to officers and other ranks killed on service?' Sir Archibald Sinclair replied:

> No, sir. The normal practice is to hold the private books and papers of deceased personnel in safe custody until they can be handed over to the person entitled to receive them.

Mrs Cazalet Keir then asked: 'Is it a fact that under the regulations no station commander has the right to destroy any private letters or papers?'

Sir Archibald Sinclair responded: 'Yes, sir. That is so.'

* * *

In 1980, Gordon Watkins, a senior producer at the BBC, was considering making a documentary based on Mary and Richard's letters. During his research he managed to trace Richard's CO at RAF Charterhall, Rupert Leigh, who was by that time a retired air commodore, and wrote to him regarding the destruction of Richard's papers and letters. In November of that year, Mr Watkins received a lengthy and helpful letter in response:

> . . . a word about the duty of Courts of Adjustment and therefore of an Effects Officer. Apart from the duties implied by the title it is an unwritten law in the three Services and strictly adhered to, that the Effects Officer should destroy any letters, papers, correspondence etc., which might cause pain to next of kin, relations, etc.

Some letters had been found among Richard's belongings which:

> had obviously been written to him by a married girl . . . They could have caused shock or pain to the parents (or to some parents) – who could tell? Not least, the girl concerned could have been put in a very tricky position.

Flying Officer How therefore thought he was doing the right thing in destroying them. It is supposition, but conceivable, that the letters from a 'married girl' included some that had not been written by Mary, and that Flying Officer How discovered letters of a intimate nature from another married woman.

Regarding any notes which could be construed as a manuscript, Air Commodore Leigh wrote: '. . . the Effects Officer had searched everywhere and there was no trace and I believed him.'

During the sixties, Air Commodore Leigh had met Flying Officer How again and he included important information from that meeting in the same letter:

> He had returned to the Guildhall School of Music after the war and had just retired . . . I said we were both now out of the service and could talk quite freely. I told him I'd often wondered what had happened to that Ms. Once again he swore he had never found it and knew nothing about it. And once again I believed him with complete confidence.

CHAPTER NINETEEN

TRIBUTES

Air Chief Marshal Sir Christopher Foxley Norris GCB, DSO, OBE, RAF (Retired)

In 1995 Sir Christopher recalled his memories of Richard Hillary at Oxford:

> He was conceited, but had every right to be, he was good-looking, clever, dashing and bumptious. But the people around him at that time did not hate him for what he was. If they did hate him, it was for personal reasons. Much has been exaggerated over the years.
>
> When *The Last Enemy* was published I thought it was a very good book and I wrote and told him so. I received a reply which said: 'Thank you for your kind words about my book. I am surprised to find you among my admirers. It fooled you too!' He then went on to say that he had made up a lot of it, and referred to it as a 'novel' rather than an auto-biography. It was the book that created the legend, had he not written it then he would simply be known as a Battle of Britain fighter pilot.

Wing Commander Geoffrey Page DFC and Bar, RAF (Retired)

I asked Geoffrey if Richard would ever have mellowed with time, to which he replied:

> I still have a very strong impression of Richard. I thought he was a conceited young bastard. I thought he was someone you couldn't get that close to. Maybe he did have his chums, but he really did attract the girls. They came rushing.
>
> I certainly do not believe that he was a 'shit' as has been mentioned in recent times. That, I believe, is a modern day statement, and not one made by anyone that knew him in those days. Nevertheless, he had a very supercilious attitude, and at times he was almost reclusive in his manner.

Squadron Leader Lewis Brandon DSO, DFC and Bar, RAF (Retired)

In 1961 Squadron Leader Lewis Brandon wrote:

> I lived in the same mess as Hillary for over two months and to me, as to several other instructors there, it seemed inevitable that he would crash eventually. His physical disabilities caused by the terrible burns he had received were such that he was not really capable of flying an operational aircraft.
>
> His disabilities were far worse than people were aware. It has been written that despite his injuries his hands were still strong, which was rubbish. His fingers became very sore and the hands were not strong. He struggled to fly the aircraft due to this lack of strength and the sensitivity of his fingers. The cold also added to his discomfort.
>
> I used to eat with him in the mess and I would watch him try to hold his cutlery. He would pick up the knife with his right hand and close the fingers around it with his left hand, slowly and laboriously. He would then pick up his fork and, using his right hand, push the fingers closed around the handle. He couldn't just let them go either, he had to force his fingers open again. It was a memory I have kept of him for all these years. He should never have been allowed to fly an aeroplane no matter how persistent he had been.

Sergeant Pilot Jack Wilkinson

Jack Wilkinson recalled:

> The story of Hillary having had his navigation lights on was a myth.
>
> It seemed to me that nobody could get that close to him. He was aloof. When he spoke to you he gave the impression that his thoughts were elsewhere. The only thing I shared with him was the crew-room where he spent most of the time writing his letters home. I believe that no one got close to him.
>
> I remember that Richard Hillary could be so very charming, when it suited him. He could also be cynical and fairly ruthless. His detestation of Charterhall mellowed considerably once he began flying again.

Group Captain George Denholm DFC

George Denholm had kept in touch with Richard, up until his death. He recalled:

> Richard was an extraordinarily troubled individual with such a determination to carry out his purpose. So many people attempted to dissuade him from going back to flying. Of course it is easy for us to say it now, but fancy going back to flying a Blenheim round the daunting heights of the Scottish hills!
>
> I was the one who scattered his ashes over the Channel. He well deserved a very special interment.

Rache Lovat Dickson

> In fact, I knew that he would die. Not I alone, but friends such as Eric Linklater, Arthur Koestler, Storm Jameson and Elizabeth Bowen, writers to whom I had introduced him. They had accepted him and come to feel deeply about him; he seemed to symbolise what we, as writers, were always finding just beyond our reach: the nobility of human character. To all of us, conferring together, it seemed a wanton waste that Richard should go back into the war: this time he would almost certainly die.

George Nelson-Edwards

It was while he was out in North Africa that George was informed by a war correspondent by the name of Jack Profumo, who was paying the wing a visit with another correspondent, Randolph Churchill, that Richard had been killed. Later having returned to England, and now working at the new Combined Operations HQ at No.1A Richmond Terrace London, as an air planner, he decided to pay a visit to the Cavendish Hotel:

> One beautiful spring day I took an extra hour off during the lunch break to go and visit Rosa Lewis at the Cavendish Hotel in Jermyn Street. I hadn't seen her since my Oxford days. The puzzle of Dick Hillary's phone call to me at RAF Valley, Anglesey, shortly before I departed on 'Operation Torch', was still niggling me. It occurred to me there might be an outside chance of Rosa throwing some light on the mystery. On enquiring at Reception I was told she was in and would be pleased to see me.
>
> Rosa had a small private office at the far end of the Hall where she sat amidst piles of letters, documents and invoices, accumulating in untidy heaps on the top of a very large ornate Victorian style bureau. The walls were obscured by hundreds of photographs and pictures dating from the pre-World War One days to the present time. She remembered me all right, which flattered me, because she had never known me quite so well as the others. I couldn't afford to stay there every weekend.
>
> Entering the 'Holy of Holies' I spotted almost at once a large photograph of Dick standing out amidst a glut of pictures.
>
> 'I've come to pick your brains, Rosa.'

'What is it, dearie? What do you want to know?'

I told her the story of how Dick had tracked me down in North Wales saying he had something very important to discuss with me; how I had missed seeing him when I went down to Fighter Command, Stanmore, and how, within a few days, I was on the high seas heading for an unknown destination.

'Ah, Dick!' she sighed 'I was very fond of that boy. Though I loved all the boys, of course, he was without doubt one of my favourites. What a tragedy!'

'Yes, indeed it was,' I replied. 'Can you remember when you last saw him?'

'Oh dear me now, when was it? I think sometime during last summer before he went back to flying. Foolish boy, he should never have done it.'

'Did he say anything about wanting to contact some of his old school and Oxford friends?'

'I can't say for sure, duckie, it was quite a long time ago you see, although I do seem to remember he said he had some scheme afoot. I couldn't say for the life of me what it was though. Have a Champagne Cocktail with me, luvvie, just for 'old times' sake.'

After a few minutes an elderly waiter, whom I thought I recognised from the old days, entered with a silver tray on which were two tall familiar goblets containing Rosa's favourite beverage.

'To Dick, the dear boy, wherever he may be now.'

Our glasses clinked. Rosa was far away, my request for information long forgotten. After a few minutes I thanked her for the drink and sadly stepped out into the sunlight on Jermyn Street. The next time I saw the hotel, the old Cavendish had been demolished and replaced by a large modern structure which somehow dispelled all the happy memories of the past. I never saw Rosa again.

In February 1945 George Nelson-Edwards was taken ill and admitted to Hallam Street Hospital with jaundice, which would end his wartime operational flying career. While he was in hospital he noticed a lady wheeling a trolley through the ward with books and magazines; it was Richard's mother Edwyna Hillary whom George had not seen since he had stayed with them at Shirley Cottage in 1937. She recognised him at once and they had a conversation about the 'old-days' and how Richard and he had drifted apart. Richard had seemed to not want to know him anymore after they had gone to Oxford:

> I told her about the unexpected telephone call he had made to me in North Wales, when 93 Squadron was fog-bound at RAF Valley. He asked me as a matter of urgency, to see him prior to our departure overseas on 'Operation Torch'. I told her how I turned up one morning at HQ Fighter Command, only to find that he was away making an air sea rescue film down at Brighton. Mrs Hillary was intrigued by my story, but just as puzzled as I was. What was it that Dick was so anxious to see me about? During the last few months of his short life, she told me, he was working on a new book. She thought that this might have had something to do with it. Well, maybe so, but it was pure speculation, and a mystery it will remain forever. I promised to visit the Hillarys at the first opportunity after leaving hospital. Regrettably, it turned out that I never did.

For the next 51 years George Nelson-Edwards never ceased to wonder what it was that Richard was so concerned about. Intrigue turned to frustration over the years, and on one occasion he even turned to a ouija board in the hope that he could find an answer. Such action he thought was a little stupid, but as Air Chief Marshal Sir Hugh Dowding, head of Fighter Command, had reputedly used one on several occasions he felt justified in his actions, but as expected it did not give him an answer.

Sir Archibald McIndoe

The following is an extract from an article entitled 'Valiant For Truth,' by Sir Archibald McIndoe, which appeared in the *Guinea Pig Club Magazine*:

This is a story which could have been multiplied many times in the RAF. Richard Hillary, however, was not like other men. During his short, tumultuous life he made the most outstanding literary contribution of the war in any service. His book, *The Last Enemy*, will stand not only as a work of art, but because it gave significance and deep meaning to the lives of thousands of young men, less articulate than himself, who in an age of doubt and near despair could still their inner fears and questionings with nothing but blind courage.

The station medical officer was away on leave, and my unofficial letter marked 'private' lay on his desk unopened for two weeks. On the night he returned and before he could take action, Richard Hillary met his Enemy face to face. The wheel had come full circle and no-one could stop its remorseless swing.

I often think of him in that last moment – his crippled hands fighting for control of his spinning plane – the cold sweat pouring from his body, the screaming crescendo of the engines, his patchwork face frozen in that mocking twisted smile, his eyes at last gleaming with the supreme knowledge he had so painfully sought and had so short a time to comprehend.

Colin Hodgkinson

Perhaps my and Tony's [Tollemache] rather rowdy, extroverted attitude set off in a way that appealed to him his own inward self dissection. Others found him superior and offensive, maddeningly 'odd'. I thought him a courteous, if astringent, companion and an inspiring personality by the nature of his stoicism. Stoicism was the order of the day at East Grinstead, but Hillary's had an intellectual quality which I found fascinating. In a way he never suspected, my brief meeting with him did me a great service.

In this extract from his memoirs, Colin Hodgkinson went on to express his belief that Richard took his own life.

Merle Oberon

Merle Oberon had kept in touch with Richard right up until his death. Her biographers described her reaction to the news that Richard had been killed:

The death was a shocking blow to Merle. She left work for several days and remained in seclusion, hysterical and inconsolable. There is no doubt that Hillary had touched her more deeply than any man; that he had worked his way through the vanities and self-satisfactions of the star in Merle and brought out the tenderness, givingness and impassioned romanticism that lay at the heart of her nature and represented the best part of that nature.

Chas Frizell

On balance, I retain fond memories of him. His presence enriched my life at Kinloss, and although 'age will not weary him, nor the years condemn' I rather regret that he is no longer around, at least in this world. I was saddened by his death not only for personal reasons, but because he had the talent to write, and I thought after the war he would have been cynical and courageous enough to have exposed any travesties of history, of which there are legion. As has been observed, the first casualty of war is always the truth.

Lady Winifred Fortescue

Lady Fortescue heard of Richard's death whilst on holiday in Devon. She wrote to Edwyna Hillary to express her own grief and during the following months the two of them remained in touch. In her book *Beauty for Ashes*, she recalled:

Often during those months in Devon, in the quiet of the woods or when driving to some public engagement, and always when one of our aeroplanes roared through the sky, I thought of Richard Hillary and wondered what had become of him. His silence saddened me, but I felt that whatever happened to either of us we should always be friends, for we had understood each other instantly and perfectly. I had become suddenly so busy, rushing from place to place, that I had no time to write letters. Richard was probably busier still. It was at any rate comforting to have seen him last in much better condition, with no dread repetition of a surgical operation hanging immediately over him. Those last joyous words to me, 'I've got a job! I've *got a job*!' comforted me then so much.

Eric Linklater

Linklater who, whilst reading of Richard's courage in *The Last Enemy*, had been moved to tears wrote:

> But no one in the smallest degree encouraged him to fly: his friends pleaded that he would not, fellow-officers tried brusquely to dissuade him, and at Fighter Command his early applications were regarded with disfavour. But he had made up his mind.
>
> It was a remarkable mind. It was a growing mind – which in itself is not unremarkable – and it curiously contained, with the ebullience and vigour of youth, a sudden maturity and even fragments of that serenity which, though it is never common, is most often found in people more than thrice his age. He would glow, at times, with the delicious excitement of youth still making fresh discoveries every day: but he had also a quality of detachment that allowed him to savour both his own and contrary opinion. He would talk, now and then, like a three-quarter running with the ball in his hands; then listen like a priest in a Chinese temple, smiling. When serenity is camp-fellow with the vigour of youth, the mind that houses them can be formidable in its resolution.
>
> But what gave him his determination? – His nature was complex, so the answer cannot be simple, but this should be remembered: he was a pilot who had lived, for a little season of intensified perception, in the thin bright air that is twenty-thousand feet above the earth. In a man whose mind is deeply imaginative and equally capable of delight, flying must leave a hunger that nothing else can feed. Few of us know the sensation of handling a Spitfire to the altitude of the sky, but we have all seen pilots, in the enormous air summer of a day, drawing their patterns of exuberant delight: whatever the sensation may be, it must include a very joyous enlargement of the spirit. So there is what to think of when looking for an answer: in Dick's mind there was the flavour of an old delight. There was also a romantic image.
>
> I see Dick's gaiety and his high seriousness, alike and equal, as two aspects of his gallantry. Gallantry was born in him, but in the swift maturing of the war it acquired a new shape. It became a dedicated gallantry.
>
> I can find no other explanation of the unconditional imperative that sent him, so resolute and so unhappy, into that wintry sky. That he also carried, like a love-locket, a romantic image of himself as a fighter-pilot, does not invalidate the dedication, though it made his acceptance of it a little easier. It suggested the way by which he was to prove himself both 'croyant et pratiquant'.

Robin C. Hope

Robin Hope was Richard's first cousin and his closest surviving relative in Britain. During my research he provided information and recalled his memories of Richard:

> Dick, as he was always known in the family, came to stay with us at Egmanton from time to time. He was a regular visitor at the rectory (which he called the Recarage) while he was at Shrewsbury. When we moved to the Perivale Rectory

this also became a welcoming centre for all the family, whether from Australia, or on leave from postings abroad, as well as the friends of my brother and me. Visitors returned again and again. Richard used to spend the Christmas holidays with us because at that time it was impossible for him to get from England to Khartoum and back during a public school Christmas holiday. He, like other members of the family, spent a few days at the Rectory at other times.

Dick and I were first cousins and we got along all right, but we were never close. I was a few years older than he was so we only coincided at Oxford during my fourth year. We did not meet then until at the end of the Trinity Term of 1938, he was at the same party at Headington as my fiancée and I. He came over to us saying, 'I must meet my soon-to-be new cousin', and made himself very pleasant to us both, as he knew very well how to do. I got married soon after Munich and went to India where I remained for the whole of the war, so that was my last meeting with Dick and it left a good taste in my mouth.

Dick womanised in a large way and he never had any problems doing so with his good looks. He was very pleasant and very proud of himself. There is no doubt that he changed after he had been shot down. A friend of mine, and contemporary of Dick's, Michael Foxley-Norris, brother of Sir Christopher, told me recently that he thought Dick was not a nice person. But I have to say to any such comment that I really knew Dick and disagreed.

Michael Foxley-Norris had been at Trinity with Richard and had also been in the Oxford UAS. He, like Richard, was also a good oarsman and although a contemporary of Richard's, he was not a friend.

Robin Hope passed away in March 1999.

* * *

On hearing the news of Richard's death, the friends that he had made during his stay in America wrote to his parents. These included all the rich, intelligent and generous women who had taken him in, during his time there. Mrs Carola Warburg Rothschild wrote of him:

> No one who ever knew him can forget his luminous quality. The star-dust that was his portion has left a glow, which guides us towards the ideals for which he gave his life.

Mrs Jeanette Lee recalled how well he had got on with her daughter. Two years after Richard's death the American Air Marshal Collyer wrote to Mrs Lee and wondered if Richard would 'still have been great', had there been no war. In reply she wrote: 'I cannot answer that question, I only know that the influence he had on all of us was great.'

Richard's secretary, Miss Levine, who typed his manuscript while in New York, had anticipated being involved in the typing of the sequel. She wrote of him after his death:

> He was too anxious to return to flying, and when he walked out of the office, I told Mr Warburg I had a feeling we would never see him again... he always gave me the feeling of someone living on borrowed time, as if he had been granted a short reprieve from the grave . . .

* * *

After Richard's death Lovat Dickson borrowed Richard's letters from Mary and had copies typed. His intention was to use them in a memorial work – a commemorative biography – that was being contemplated at the time (he sent a set of copies to Michael Hillary). Originally, it had been intended that a volume of letters and 'unpublished manuscripts' would be produced, but as this material was not forthcoming, it was proposed that Lovat Dickson, Arthur Koestler, Eric Linklater and Phyllis Bottome each contribute an essay to a memorial volume.

Eric Linklater wrote a piece entitled 'The Numbered Days', which was subsequently revised for the 1947 publication of his book of essays *The Art of Adventure*; he had already written a biographical note for the special commemorative edition of *The Last Enemy*, published in April 1943, which included a colour reproduction of the Kennington portrait of Richard.

However, the essay by Koestler did not meet with the approval of Michael and Edwyna Hillary, Denise Maxwell-Woosnam, Lovat Dickson and Eric Linklater, who all disliked the piece and his questionable use of Richard's letters to Mary – originally provided for background only – which, Linklater wrote: 'sank it'.

Koestler called on Mary two days after Richard's death and again a short while after, when she introduced him to Richard's parents. He had expressed considerable interest in any work that Richard may have left behind.

By the end of January, when the copying of the letters was complete, Mary gave permission for Koestler and Linklater to use them on the clear understanding that they were used for background only. In April 1943, three months after Richard's death, Koestler published an article in *Horizon* entitled 'Birth of a Myth', later re-published in 1945 in the collection *The Yogi and the Commissar and other Essays*. It was the first of a number of essays about Richard to be published after his death. According to Koestler, Richard was a new kind of hero who was not motivated by conventional ideas of patriotism or masculinity.

During the writing of his essay Koestler apparently 'misunderstood' the request from Mary and actually quoted from about a fifth of the letters and always selectively in order to fit a thesis. His thesis describes the development or 'crystallisation' of the myth of Richard Hillary; a myth that does not exist.

Koestler's inclusion of Richard's letters signified the end of the possibility of a commemorative biography.

Lovat Dickson later explained that Koestler and Linklater went about the writing of their essays under the misapprehension that the letters were to be included. The first real signs of trouble over the publication of the letters appeared in a letter from Mary to Lovat Dickson when she wrote of a, 'misunderstanding about the *reading of*, as opposed to the *quotation from* the letters'.

Linklater was able to rectify the problem before his own essay was published.

It is known that Koestler's essay caused great upset to Richard's family and friends with the aforementioned suggestion of suicide. But the following passage also caused great pain:

> Richard Hillary was burnt thrice. After the first time they brought him back and patched him up and made him a new face. It was wasted, for the second time his body was charred to coal. But to make quite sure that the pattern was fulfilled, it was his wish to be cremated; so they burned him a third time, on the 12th January, 1943, in Golders Green; and the coal became ashes and the ashes were scattered into the sea . . .

Later, Lovat Dickson criticised the ten-page essay by Phyllis Bottome entitled: 'Richard Hillary and the RAF' – in which she offers her opinion on Richard's relationships with Anne Mackenzie, Denise Maxwell-Woosnam and Mary Booker. An extract was later published in the *The Spectator* on 15 October 1943, minus the comments on Anne, Denise and Mary at the request of Denise and Richard's parents, entitled 'Serpent-Doves'.

In December 1943, Mary wrote to Michael Hillary in response to his request for an explanation as to why his son's letters had appeared in Koestler's essay, despite her instructions to the contrary, informing him that, according to Lovat Dickson, they had written their essays: 'with the understanding clearly in their minds that the letters were to be included'. It is possible that, as far as Richard's parents were concerned, the situation was exacerbated by the emergence of his love-letters to Anne Mackenzie, his former girlfriend from his Oxford days.

Lovat Dickson wrote to Michael Hillary stating that Koestler may have gone too far in his use of the letters. In December 1943, Linklater remained perplexed about the commemorative biography – particularly in light of Koestler's essay and the reaction to it – and persuaded Lovat Dickson to 'mark time'.

In March 1945, Phyllis Bottome – who was the second cousin of Peter Pease – subsequently abandoned her intention to write a biography of Richard, because of the 'strain on the minds and nerves of his parents' who, 'simply can't give a biographer a free-hand.' She had been keen to include Richard's letters because, according to her, they showed tremendous psychological development in one year; the early letters were full of the joy of life, in contrast to the later ones when 'his days were numbered'.

Michael Hillary wrote to Lovat Dickson accepting that the commemorative biography now seemed impossible. In reply Lovat Dickson confirmed this and the matter was closed. Linklater's excellent essay was completed and published. Lovat Dickson's biography on Richard's life was published seven years after his death.

* * *

Meanwhile, Pat Hollander, who had originally introduced Richard to Lovat Dickson, had written a play about Richard entitled *The Lost Generation*, which she had completed within three weeks of Richard's death. In February, she was contacted by Michael and Edwyna Hillary who, having read the script, were adamantly opposed to it being staged, the main reason being their wish to avoid further grief. Correspondence continued between these two parties and, as neither was willing to compromise, their relationhip deteriorated and the Hillarys chose to distance themselves from their son's former colleague. Arrangements were then made for Michael and Edwyna to see the play, now called *The True Glory*, either privately before its opening in London, or during its run in the provinces, after which Michael Hillary wrote that he found some parts 'highly objectionable'.

By 1949 the Hillarys were living in a flat in Clarewood Court, London; from here Michael Hillary wrote to the Lord Chamberlain, who was responsible for the licensing of plays, in a last-ditch effort to prevent the play from opening in the capital. Amongst other things, Richard's parents were unhappy with the depiction of certain characters in the play, including that of his mother. The Lord Chamberlain was unable to support the Hillarys' case and the play opened at the Garrick Theatre. It was heralded as the World War II equivalent of *Journey's End*.

* * *

In 1944 John Middleton Murry, the critic and outspoken pacifist, published an essay 'Richard Hillary' in his magazine *Adelphi*; it was later re-published in *Looking Before and After*, one of the first publications of the pacifist *Sheppard Press*, which Murry helped to found. Murry was more explicit than Koestler as he pursued the suicide theory, albeit with a vaguely religious undertone. He had even less evidence than Koestler; and it should be seriously considered that he had none at all.

Murry had read *The Last Enemy*, but had never met Richard or corresponded with him. He had never consulted anyone that had known him, read any of his letters or studied any relevant documents. He relied totally on the fragments of Richard's letters included in Koestler's essay. However, Murry was a critic of repute and a good writer who might convince someone that knew nothing on the subject.

* * *

By October 1948, Lovat Dickson was planning a biography on Richard. Unlike Koestler, he made every effort to ensure that his book would conform with the wishes of Richard's parents and the end product was to their liking. Denise had kindly loaned him her diary for reference.

Initially he wrote to Michael Hillary, outlining his book and aim. In the same letter he also raised the possibility of *The Last Enemy* being published by Pan Books in paperback, while the hardback was still in print. As it turned out, it was 1956 before Pan published the book; a review of *The Last Enemy* by J.B. Priestley, written after initial publication, was included at the front of the book. In November 1949, Michael Hillary read Lovat Dickson's manuscript and corrected and cut any aspects, factual or otherwise, he thought necessary.

Rache Lovat Dickson's *Richard Hillary – A Life* was published by Macmillan in 1950, and is the only previous full biography published on Richard. From the Memorial to Andrew Comyn Irvine at Shrewsbury School Lovat Dickson quotes:

> They are Most Rightly Reputed
> Valiant, Who Though They Perfectly
> Apprehend Both What is Dangerous and
> What is Easie, are Never the More
> Thereby Diverted From Adventuring

Lovat Dickson was described by Michael Burn, who knew him, as 'a kind and able man, devoted to Richard's memory'. The book gave an account of Richard's life that was useful in that it provided information on Richard's early life, but it contained many inaccuracies and a number of points which, inadvertently, caused upset to relatives. For example, Lovat Dickson's interpretation of the hospitality offered by the Hope family during Richard's visits, both before and after his schooling, fell short of the warm, welcoming environment that was always available to him.

Where the essays of Koestler and Murry contained an excess of analysis, Lovat Dickson's suffered from a lack of it. It is too hagiograhic; he finds no fault in his subject – the young hero who had practically forced his manuscript upon him nine years before – but this was perhaps because Lovat Dickson sought approval of his manuscript from, among others, Richard's parents, which resulted in most criticism being removed before publication (all comments by Frank McEachran, Richard's English teacher at Shrewsbury, were excised from the final draft). He quoted from Richard's letters and chose mainly from those which had been written at Charterhall describing the grim existence and the ordeal of the night flying. (In some cases Lovat Dickson failed to reproduce Richard's letters accurately. This was another point which motivated Michael Burn to put the record straight when he included the same letters in *Mary and Richard*.) Lovat Dickson decided against using Mary's letters and therefore details of the love affair are given little space, an obvious gap in the continuity. Had the story of their love been told in more detail it might have curtailed any suggestion that their affair had been unhappy. Nevertheless, this book put right the work of Koestler and Murry, and Lovat Dickson donated some of the royalties to the Richard Hillary Memorial Trust.

In 1953 Admiral Andre Jubelin wrote a 42 page preface for a translation into French of *The Last Enemy*, which he called a masterpiece and places Richard as a literary meteor alongside the French prodigy Raymond Radiquet, who was born in 1903 and died when he was 20. Radiquet wrote *Le Diable au Corps* when he was just 17. The Admiral speculated in his preface that Richard, the romantic hero in his own book, might well become to English literature what Benjamin Constant's *Adolphe* and Stendhal's *Julien Sorel* are to French. He had no doubt that Richard felt he had a mission to his dead comrades: 'How extraordinary that out of that diminutive band of fighter pilots, there should have arisen one young man, able to immortalise not only them but a gigantic battle on which past all question hung the future of the world.'

* * *

In 1946, the Trinity College Rowing VIII retained the Head of the River title at Oxford. The then Captain of the Boats, Philip Landon, wrote to Michael Hillary:

> Dick's name and fame are, of course, well-known to all our rowing men; and Trinity will never forget the great services that he gave to us in those triumphant and happy years, 1938-39. How glad he would have been if he had been here to share our pride and success of this post-war VIII in retaining the position which he, as stroke, won for us!

* * *

The influence of Richard's book was far reaching. A society called The Association of Combatant Writers, comprising those who had fought in the French resistance, had met in Paris since the war to pay homage to a writer who had fallen in battle. On 20 May 1950, it was Richard's turn. Michael and Edwyna Hillary were among the many distinguished guests for what was a very moving ceremony. Although those in attendance only knew Richard through his book, Richard's parents sat amongst many who had also shown great courage in the war and listened to speeches from the president of the Association, Monsieur Pierre Chanlaine; the British ambassador, Sir Oliver Harvey; General de Larminat, Mlle Jeanne Bortel of the Comedie Française, and the Marquis Amodo. Pierre Chanlaine gave the following speech: 'We who have fought without weakening because we loved our country, and because we could not bear to live without that precious thing, liberty, we render deeply-felt homage to this young comrade, killed at the age of 22, in the full flowering of his talent.'

The British ambassador for France then rose and gave his speech:

> The youth of our two countries is tormented by fundamental questions, in a manner which I think is without precedent in history. In particular, war is no longer the simple thing it appeared to be a few generations ago; but with you as with us, a new testing. I do not think there is any more moving spectacle in the whole of history than that of the courage filled with doubt of our age – the spectacle of the young people of our two profoundly civilised countries, who have never hesitated to look their doubts in the face and go into action. That is why *The Last Enemy*, like Saint-Exupéry's *War-time Pilot*, is a book which will always be read. [The title *War-time Pilot*, as mentioned here, is a literal translation from the French *Pilote de Guerre*. The book was re-titled *Flight to Arras* for publication in America.]

The last to speak was General Larminat. He spoke of those soldiers he had known:

> Valiant, strong, skilful, such among them was this young prince of the mind and of the heart, Richard Hillary. He chose that form of combat which was most obvious, most direct, and applied to it his strength, his enthusiasm and his clear-mindedness. In it he served his country well, for it he suffered the acutest pain without complaint, he blithely faced a heroic death.

* * *

In 1953, Michael and Edwyna Hillary set up the Richard Hillary Trust Fund at Trinity College, Oxford. The fund was initially intended to provide an annual award for up-and-coming writers and poets within the College, as chosen by the Trustees. Soon after, it was extended to include students from all colleges at Oxford. The first selection committee consisted of a number of 'elders': Lovat Dickson, Eric Linklater, Arthur Koestler and Mary Booker; with Bill Aitken, Godfrey Carter, Lady Titchbourne and Denise Maxwell-Woosnam.

To some degree it suffered during the early days after conception. Eric Linklater had earlier expressed concern and warned of the pretentiousness of a Memorial Fund until the market value of Richard's book was proven.

In 1965, the Trustees announced the creation of the Richard Hillary Memorial Prize and their intention to make it a national award. A prize of £400 was awarded for a contribution of original, imaginative literature, prose or poetry, published or written in the preceding calendar year. The prize was open to men and women of British Commonwealth citizenship of 30 years of age or under.

During the early days, Michael Hillary worked hard to establish the Trust. He later handed over the reigns to the Trustees at Trinity, in whose capable hands it remains to this day. Michael Astor, the first chairman, later wrote:

> Richard used to talk about a book he wanted to write one day about politics; by which he meant (as he stated) the need for society to reduce the role of politics

and politicians to a minimum. The true voice of the romantic, the artist, of all who find ourselves agnostics without a party we can believe in (much). Here, I imagine, he was trying to find his own position rather than prescribe anything in particular for society as a whole.

The Richard Hillary Trust is a well organised and prestigious annual awards scheme for promising writers and poets. It was intended to perpetuate the memory of Michael and Edwyna Hillary's son and only child. The publication of Michael Burn's *Mary and Richard* in 1988 brought renewed interest.

* * *

The suggestion that Richard may have committed suicide is something that has been considered by some, but totally discounted by the vast majority. It is a theory born of early rumours and from Arthur Koestler in particular, but also suggested by Colin Hodgkinson with the publication of his autobiography in 1957, which the newspapers latched on to. The theory was perpetuated in more recent times by the biographers of Merle Oberon. Quite naturally, such publicity caused those that were close to Richard a great deal of upset.

The upset to Richard's parents by the initial suggestion was quelled in part after the personal visit by Richard's station commander at Charterhall, Group Captain Rupert Leigh. It had also caused many of his contemporaries unease prompting the following remarks:

> 'He would not have taken the life of his R/O in addition to his own'; If he was going to kill himself then he could have done it earlier on in the course [Section 'A', conversion to type] while he was still undergoing solo flying training'; 'His demeanour at the time did not show any outward signs of someone that was contemplating suicide.'

Unfortunately, what cannot be said with *absolute* certainty is that he didn't kill himself. My belief is the common one, that he did not, and that he would have fought until that last moment to regain control of his stricken aircraft. He had known all along that his fight to regain operational status was going to be a mighty task. More so, in his case, because of his crippled hands. He had agreed with Geoffrey Page's comments at East Grinstead: 'I'm scared stiff of the idea, but I'm even more frightened of what people might say if I don't go back.'

The situation became worse as he found the night flying experience 'terrifying'. The strain had become too much.

There had been a number of incidents that could have, in Richard's opinion, resulted in an accident. What skill he possessed was pushed to the absolute limit, of that there is no doubt. The resulting physical and mental strain took its toll. While faced with the possibility of an accident, I do not believe that he actually *knew* he was going to die as has been mentioned by too many. He knew he was taking a very great risk, all things considered, but to him it was a great challenge, and he dearly wanted to succeed – although, sadly, that determination to succeed, seemed to include a willingness to risk the life of his R/O in the process.

The records show that Charterhall lost an alarming number of aircrew and aircraft. In an attempt to avoid carelessness and obtain the utmost in commitment and concentration from the new induction, Richard and his group had been given the current accident statistics on arrival at the RAF station. I also believe that because the number of losses had become alarming and the establishment was getting a bad reputation, attempts to blame the student pilots more than the standard of the machinery were already underway in order to avoid the situation coming under serious scrutiny. Where the definite cause of an accident was unavailable, there seemed to be a need to complete the accident reports stating that the pilots were to blame, based in many cases, on nothing more than supposition.

Richard quite possibly lost his nerve, which was his own opinion. He had discovered new limits to his fear brought about by his terrifying experience when he had been shot down. Although, he had secretly initiated a plan to have himself 'removed' from the course, in the meantime he was still willing to fight on and hopefully achieve his objective. He didn't want the other trainees to know he had 'lost his nerve', particularly bearing in mind the light in which he was held. He still wanted to succeed. He was bright, intelligent, courageous, determined, reckless, but not stupid. It was the little hope that he still had that motivated him to continue, despite the odds of an accident occurring. While he still had that hope, he continued on the course. His declaration, to his closest friends and family, that the threat of death existed, was an example of his honesty. He wanted them to be aware of the risks: 'I don't think I'm to last it out.' The suggestion that he knew he was going to die does, however, play its part in the development of the legend.

Richard's attempt at suicide, while floating in the North Sea, is no basis to assume that he would have tried again. This piece, like others, may have also been invented by Richard for his book, in order to enhance the drama. In which case this, as an example for a later attempt at suicide, is without foundation.

Richard did suffer moments of black despair. His relationship with Mary was frustrating for them both at times, but not a reason for suicide, particularly as it was going well at the time of his death. The prospect, however, of failing in his attempt to return to operational flying was daunting, and became increasingly difficult to face as the course progressed.

Richard did not kill himself, because he had plans and had expressed hope for his future. He was also responsible for the life of Wilfrid Fison. His service colleagues and contemporaries are also firmly of this opinion.

Colin Hogkinson never again commented on the suggestion he had made in his book, even when the matter was raised with him. Perhaps, when he wrote his book he had not realised how such a statement could be sensationalised by a journalist in need of a story. He passed away at his home in the Dordogne, in September 1996.

* * *

On 12 May 1957, a letter was published in response to Robert Pitman's piece in the *Express*. Wing Commander F. Kalinowsky, who had seen Richard in the briefing room, prior to his last flight, disputed the suicide theory and gave his account of the crash:

> I have the simple and unquestionable answer to the alleged mystery of Richard Hillary's fatal crash. I was one of the few eye-witnesses.
>
> I had been only a few days in No.54 OTU and had not met Hillary personally, but I had seen him twice on the airdrome (*sic*). On the night of the crash, I had come with my pilot Flying Officer Zykun to the dispersal hut and there was Hillary, standing alone by the stove. He looked tired and depressed.
>
> I said good evening and my pilot, who knew Hillary, asked: 'What, flying again?' He explained later to me that Hillary was tired of night flying and flew too often.
>
> We watched him take off at the end of the runway. Hillary's plane climbed rather steeply, and at some two hundred feet one engine spluttered and died.
>
> My pilot said to me: 'Did you hear that? His engine packed up.' Then Hillary's plane dived and crashed.
>
> Later we discussed Hillary's crash and came to the conclusion that the tragedy was due to the pilot's lack of experience in flying a twin engined plane and that he was over-tired. Any suggestion that Hillary wanted to die in this way – and take with him another man – is preposterous.

He wrote to Edwyna Hillary endorsing this last point and she responded gratefully.

If Wing Commander Kalinowsky did witness a crash at Charterhall, and there were many, then it certainly was not that of Richard's aircraft. Andy Miller added:

> The trouble with passing on such information is that after fifty years many people

that read it believe it as being fact, particularly if the information appears repeatedly in books, but is actually uncorroborated. I know my information is accurate because I documented most of the details at the time.

Dick did not show any outward signs that he was unhappy and the redness around the eye, as seen by another Polish sergeant who saw him that night, was nothing new. His left eyelid drooped and the inside of the lower lid was open to the elements. If he had been out in the wind then it would get irritated.

I believe that the suggestion that Richard killed himself would have perpetuated in certain quarters, regardless of what Koestler and Hodgkinson had written, although they drew unnecessary public attention to the idea and offended the relatives of Richard and Wilfred Fison in the process. Although Joyce Fison was aware of Richard's disability, she did not hold him or the authorites to blame for her husband's death. When the rumours emerged suggesting that Richard may have committed suicide, she found the suggestion very distressing and discounted them totally.

As long as doubt existed as to the cause of the crash that killed Richard, all causes are open to consideration; and some may choose the suicide theory. But in quoting Richard I would like to try bring the matter to a close. In his letters to Mary he wrote:

> . . . it is you and you alone who mean anything to me; and that anything is more than the whole world . . . For me a great year. I had you and I grew up.

and:

> Somehow I must get all this down . . . and then maybe I shall have peace and time to put it all together,' and 'I only hope that 1943 will allow me to put into practice the personality which (thanks largely to you) is me . . .

Michael Hillary declined to appear on a BBC radio programme about Richard because Arthur Koestler had also been invited, and he held him responsible for the suicide/murder theory. Indeed the Hillarys never forgave him for suggesting such a thing and he was never invited to their annual get-together.

*　*　*

On the 25th anniversary of the Battle of Britain Michael Hillary was asked to write something about his son. Mary helped by recording her memories of Richard during that last Christmas leave together:

> The main point, which I remember vividly, was the change in his attitude from that of his previous leave for Michael Astor's wedding.
>
> At that time he knew that various people of authority were pulling strings to get him grounded, and this somehow seemed to prevent him from making the effort to integrate himself with the life of community up there. It had been a shock to him when he first arrived, to find none of the same spirit of comradeship with his fellow men that had existed with all his friends in the past. They naturally treated him as someone special, someone whom they regarded with respect as being one of the original Battle of Britain 'heroes'. This threw him back, and gave him a feeling of being alone in a place where human warmth and friendship were essential to combat the bleak isolation of it all.
>
> As time went on, a change took place.
>
> 1. Richard gained confidence in overcoming the disabilities, which at first he had thought we would never overcome.
>
> 2. He found a bond of friendship, first with Fison, his radio observer, and then with his fellow pilots, who showed genuine pleasure and friendly interest in his achievements against such heavy odds.
>
> All this added up to the change in him when he came down the last time. It seemed to me that he had accepted the fact that he would have to go through with it. Facing this decision had aged him in maturity. He was much quieter. He didn't want to meet people, excepting those he was most fond of – Denise, Tony – . He

gave the impression that he wanted them to be clear regarding his devotion and the value of all they had given him of themselves, so that there should be no hurt or misunderstanding. He spoke to me of the importance of this on several occasions, always adding, 'But I need never explain anything to you.'

If he didn't see much of you and Edwyna it was because it was too sad, and he thought you would see through his facade – for there is no doubt about it, that he was convinced that he wouldn't come through. I did all I could not to let him know I guessed this, and we talked of the future. That he would fight physically for life is undeniable. He talked of its fulness, and how he felt more fitted than ever to try to make a fresh start, with the new confidence and strength he felt within himself; beneath it all I felt he had lost hope that he would ever be given the chance.

He wanted our letters, edited by him, to be published [thus contradicting any suggestion that Mary didn't want such personal letters read by others, (unless she was specifically referring to his recent narratives sent from Charterhall) and removing any concern of Michael Burn's that his wife's love-letters should not have been published in his book], and talked of ideas for other things he hoped to write about, but he knew I knew, and underlying it all our hearts were heavy.

He talked a good deal about you and Edwyna – saying that he didn't want you to find a telegram on the mat. I didn't know then that he had made arrangements with his CO that I should have the telegram four hours ahead, so that I should perhaps be of some help in breaking the news if the worst should happen. Whatever happens, what is written must be so worded that there is no hint of that suicide which is so utterly false. He was gay and always full of hope for the future and had everything to live for. But he was calm and ready for anything that came which would put an end to it all . . .

I believe that some of this assessment by Mary was perhaps not actually the case.

The reason for Richard's quiet mood may have simply been due to fatigue and having to readjust to life at home with all its comforts. The flying, the aerodrome, his aircrew colleagues and the practical lessons themselves were still prominent in his mind, such had been his physical and mental input. As he had needed a period of adjustment on arriving at Charterhall for the first time, he now needed the same in order for him to relax and for those that knew him to see him as he had been before he left. Unfortunately, the leave was too short for him to readjust.

* * *

The Hillarys lived a quiet life, were happy and unsentimental. Although devoted to their son's memory, they were careful not to appear too proud. They remained in contact with Richard's friends who had survived the war – every member of the Trinity VIII Richard stroked to the head of the river in 1938 had been either wounded or killed in the war.

On 19 April 1959, on the eve of what would have been Richard's 40th birthday, Edwyna Hillary reminisced about the last summer holiday they had spent together: 'They all knew the war was coming.' She said. 'I'm glad he had that last summer.'

Edwyna Hillary died at home at Clarewood Court, Marylebone, on 11 November 1966, aged 85. Seven months before, not far from her Clarewood Court home, she had been involved in a road traffic accident when she was knocked down by what was thought to be an army lorry. Although she died from ailments pertaining to old age, she never recovered from the trauma of the accident and, having been nursed by her husband through the last months of her life, she passed away.

Michael Hillary remarried on 7 March 1974 aged 88 and the remaining years of his life were happy. His new wife was Christina Bladon, who had been a close friend of the Hillarys for many years and had known Richard – although she was not particularly fond of him and her memories are uncomplimentary.

Even after Edwyna's death, Mary and Michael Burn remained close friends with Michael Hillary. Colonel Michael Hillary died on 23 October 1976, at the Middlesex

Hospital, aged 90, and he and Edwyna are buried together in the East London cemetery.

Denise married Geoffrey Patterson. She remains in touch with Sir Richard Pease, Peter's younger brother, and still remembers Richard's kindness to her.

After 27 years of blissful marriage to Michael Burn, Mary died unexpectedly following what was thought would be a routine visit to a London hospital on 10 August 1974.

During a desperate period of mourning Michael Burn took out a package he knew contained newspaper cuttings, 20 years of minutes from the Richard Hillary Trust, correspondence between Eric Kennington and Richard, letters to Mary from Michael and Edwyna Hillary sent after his death, and the originals of 61 letters from Richard to Mary, covering practically the whole of 1942 and ending on 4 January 1943, four days before his death. In addition Michael Burn came across an old brown envelope containing 31 manuscript letters from Mary written during the same period as his had been to her. Richard had returned them for safe keeping. These were the physical memories of his late wife's past love affair with Richard Hillary.

Michael Burn began to read this trove of valuable and much cherished information he knew existed but had felt no urge to read during her lifetime, although Mary had suggested that he do so and that he should perhaps even consider writing about Richard in the future. Many had suggested to Mary that she write about her relationship with Richard, but she did not. Perhaps it was fate that within an hour of starting to read this material Michael Burn felt the overwhelming compulsion to record the love affair between his late wife and Richard Hillary. He also believed that was what Mary hoped would occur and the letters were therefore deliberately left by her to be 'discovered'.

Having filed each item in order for Mary's and Richard's family to peruse, years later Michael Burn realised that should he die the story would go untold. He therefore decided to incorporate the letters in a book. He was also concerned when he discovered: '. . . with a good deal of amazement how diseased a record of the printed word to date presents of Richard.'

*   *   *

The subject of Richard being awarded the Distinguished Flying Cross (DFC) for his success in combat has been broached on a number of occasions. For his period of service he would have been entitled to receive the 1939-45 Star with Battle of Britain Clasp, Defence Medal and War Medal, had he survived the war, for they had not been gazetted at the time of his death. In the years since his death the next-of-kin was entitled to apply for them. But Richard was not awarded the DFC, which has been said to have been presented after having achieved five or more kills. Officially the award was given '...for exceptional valour, courage and devotion to duty whilst flying in active operations against the enemy'. Richard had certainly accomplished this criterion by the time he was shot down, although his period in combat was short, and the fact that he did not receive the DFC was disappointing to Richard – although he made no specific mention of it. It certainly caused his parents great consternation in the years after his death. Many people that I have spoken to believe he should have received this award. During World War II 20,354 DFCs with 1,550 first bars and 42 second bars were presented making it the most numerous award for gallantry of that conflict. However, it should be remembered that a great many pilots who fought in the Battle of Britain could also consider themselves unfortunate not to have received the DFC for their achievements.

*   *   *

The legend of Richard Hillary has developed out of the public's fascination for him. Prior to his return to flying, his book had made him a celebrity, and his voice was heard on the radio – a voice that was of a man who, at that time, was held in awe by so many. By 1959 *The Last Enemy* had sold 360,000 copies in the English edition alone and been translated into every European language. It was particularly successful in Germany.

In the years since World War II the fascination with Richard Hillary has continued with a number of radio plays that have been broadcast. On 10 September 1954,

Associated Rediffusion broadcast a 90-minute version of *The Last Enemy*, which had been adapted as a play for television by Barbara Harper and Peter Graham Scott. The part of Richard was played by Peter Murray. The external shots were filmed at Dunsford airfield, and the program was a great success.

In 1991, London Weekend Television broadcast *A Perfect Hero* starring Nigel Havers. It was based on the fictional book *The Long Haired Boy* by Christopher Matthews who based the story loosely on Richard Hillary.

* * *

Had Richard Hillary survived the war there is little doubt that the 'legend' would not exist, for it was his book and subsequent death at such a young age that established this. However, he would still be a national figure. He would have continued to write, of that we can be reasonably sure:

> I had meant to go on to a squadron and write the real RAF and make it a book –
> a book, I mean. It is the biggest subject I have ever seen, and I thought I could
> get it, because I felt it so keenly . . .

He was determined to do so, indicating his intentions with an outspoken procociousness from a very early age. He then wrote his bestselling book just five years later and, up until the time of his death, he was as determined as ever to develop a career as a writer. He also had a publisher and other experienced authors in support of his talent and endeavours. Koestler reckoned that with the 'bourgeois' novel becoming exhausted and less popular there was a niche developing for a new breed of writer to take over from the cultured middle-class humanist. The adventurer, revolutionary and the airman who lived life dangerously and provided an insight for the reader. Richard may have found a place among them.

To those around him Richard had matured in a very short time as a result of his experience in the war. While there were a number of fighter pilots who gained fame for their achievements during the Battle of Britain, they seldom received public acclaim for their post-war careers, be it in the RAF during peacetime or while following a career in civilian life. Some remained in the limelight due to the publication of biographies, autobiographies and other works that highlighted their wartime achievements. While Richard was unhappy with what little he had achieved during his time as a fighter pilot, he would, I believe, have continued to gain public recognition as a writer and over the years gain further acclaim to that which he had received as a result of *The Last Enemy*.

Richard's log book has been lost. It was not returned to his family with his other possessions after his death and leads one to wonder if it was taken as a souvenir. Perhaps as an 'official document', the authorities exercised their right to keep it. Nevertheless, no one has ever come across it.

Referring to other sources, I have been able to establish that Richard flew a total of approximately 422 hours up until the time of his death. He flew the following aircraft types: The twin-engined Airspeed Oxford and the Bristol Blenheim Mks I & V; and the single-engined de Havilland Tiger Moth; the Hawker Hind, Hart, Audax and Hector; the Avro Tutor; the North American Harvard; the Miles Magister and Master; the Percival Gull; the Westland Lysander and Supermarine Spitfire MkIa. Of the total hours' flying time approximately 100 of these were flying Spitfires. He had flown 15 hours at night and 12 on instruments.

The places where Richard lived, was educated, trained and served with the RAF, and was hospitalised, all exist today. Hawnes School in Bedfordshire is now the headquarters of a religious cult, the airfield at Hornchurch is now a country park – the site previously occupied by hangars is now a housing estate and the streets are named after many of the pilots who flew from there during the Battle of Britain. Unfortunately, 'Hilary Road' has been spelt incorrectly.

The airfield at Charterhall still exists, but only as a relic of its wartime training purpose. At the end of October 1945 54 OTU had returned to Yorkshire whence it had originally come from in May 1942. From 20 May 1942 to 31 May 1945 the unit had a pupil input of 1,053 and an output of 882 qualified crews, enough to man over 30 squadrons. There had been 336 accidents, resulting in 84 fatalities (the total number of fatalities includes accidents which resulted in the death of both aircrew and ground crew at Charterhall and its satellite, at Winfield). The unit had, however, flown 91,860 hours, of which 65,774 were by day and 26,086 were by night, which was an average of over three flying hours to every elapsed hour. In simple terms the unit had an average of three aircraft flying continuously, day and night, for over three years. It is this outstanding achievement that must be remembered when assessing the high number of losses, one fatality for every 1,106 hours flown. The unit's excellent performance had also been achieved while the staff, air and ground crews had to endure primitive conditions at what was after all a temporary airfield.

*   *   *

Richard Hillary, a man like so many others in the war, died having barely entered adulthood. The difference was that he was destined to leave his mark on this world. In *The Last Enemy* he told the story of what he and his friends and fellow pilots had done, and their various reasons for doing it. He felt he had no choice but to 'finish the job' that Peter Pease, Colin Pinckney, Noel Agazarian and Peter Howes had set out to do. He had miraculously survived being shot down at 10.40 on 3 September, 1940. Maybe a higher power had decided that he would not die that day and live in order to tell his story and that of his friends who had died. With the task complete he himself was then taken at 01.37 on 8 January, 1943. Perhaps it had been fate that he had been chosen, the one gifted with the pen, to survive long enough to bring to the public the story of bravery and suffering that he and others had endured. It has often been said to me during my research that this had been his purpose.

Richard could be temperamental, and appear to be superior and arrogant, but after he was shot down he mellowed to some degree. He was without doubt a womaniser and he tended to speak his mind, regardless of what others thought. During my research his fellow pilots mostly had good things to say about him, however. He was a fine combat pilot and a charming person. He was a romantic with a vulnerable, sensitive side to his nature and perhaps his memory will now be held in its true perspective.

After his death, Richard's Aunt Beryl (Malin) wrote:

> He soared into the blue vault of heaven, sometimes tormented, but sometimes buoyantly happy and free as the air through which he raced. He was surrounded by peace. I think at such a moment he looked again into the face of death with a smile on his lips, master of his own soul.

'I just couldn't recover her once she started to go in.' The apparition before me paused momentarily, then spoke for the last time.

'I must go now; my friends are waiting'. As he turned and started to walk away I noticed another man, similarly attired, standing at his right elbow a few feet behind. As my apparition walked away his partner paused facing me, then dutifully turned and joined his colleague. As they walked they were joined by more, their footfalls silent on the rugged, gravel-strewn surface of the perimeter track. I had the feeling I knew them all. The mist swirled and cleared; they were gone.

I returned to my car. The night was bitter and I had been standing for what seemed an age, but I felt no cold. As I climbed into my car and closed the door I felt an overwhelming excitement tinged with sadness, and curiously satisfied that my quest was at an end. The car clock showed 23.15.

NO.603 (CITY OF EDINBURGH) SQUADRON

The following is a history of 603 Squadron up to the time that Richard Hillary joined them with a brief insight into the unit's activities until it was disbanded in 1957.

The Auxiliary Air Force was founded in 1924 to be a corps d'élite of young men who wished to serve their country. The long-term plan was for twenty Auxiliary squadrons, the first being No.602 (City of Glasgow) Squadron founded on 12 September 1925.

> The Auxiliary Air Force squadrons were to be raised and maintained by the County Territorial Associations and manned by locally recruited part-time personnel, with only a small number of regulars as permanent staff and a non-regular CO, the idea being that the regular staff would maintain the aircraft in between the visits made by the part-time pilots.

No.603 (City of Edinburgh) Squadron Royal Auxiliary Air Force (RAuxAF) was formed at Turnhouse on 14 October 1925, under Squadron Leader J.A. McKelvie AFC, with Flight Lieutenant C. R. Keary as his adjutant. A squadron town HQ was established at 25 Learmouth Terrace, Edinburgh and there was a good response when recruiting started.

Initially the Squadron was equipped with the two-seater De Havilland DH 9A bombers and the Avro 504K and by July 1926 consisted of three officers and 55 airmen. By December 1928 the strength had increased to seventeen officers and 155 airmen. Flight Lieutenant Keary left and was replaced by the distinguished first world war aviator Flight Lieutenant H S P Walmsley, MC, DFC. The 603 Squadron pilots were known as 'weekend airmen' because they did much of their flying at the weekends in addition to ground training. When free from their regular vocations, which were varied to say the least, they got together at the aerodrome.

In March 1930 they were re-equipped with the Wapiti; the Hart in February 1934; the Hind in February 1938; the Gloster Gladiator MkI in March 1939 and finally Spitfire MkIs from 14 September 1939.

In 1931 Squadron Leader H.R. Murray-Philipson assumed command and at its annual Summer Camp in 1933, at RAF Manston, Kent, 603 Squadron logged 613 flying hours, more than any other AAF unit. Squadron Leader Geordie Nigel Douglas-Hamilton assumed command in 1934 and that summer the squadron, flying Hawker Harts, thrilled the crowds at the Empire Air Display.

* * *

The squadron was re-equipped with the Hawker Hind light bomber in February 1938 and in April came a new CO, Squadron Leader Ernest Hildebrand Stevens, known by squadron members as 'Steve' or, more famously, 'The Count'. He was to remain as CO of 603 right up until 5 June 1940, when he was posted 'supernumerary non-effective' sick owing to a recurring shoulder problem. From 3 to 7 July, Squadron Leader Stevens' duties consisted of liaising with the other airfields on the east coast, Prestwick, Perth, Leuchars, Arbroath, Dyce and Montrose, in preparation for his new role as a controller. At the time of Richard's arrival he was visiting Montrose and Dyce. He was eventually posted to No.11(F) Group as a controller. In his place Flight Lieutenant George Denholm was promoted to acting squadron leader and took command of 603 Squadron.

On 15 April 1938, 603 took over the administration of RAF Turnhouse following the closure of Station HQ, and on 24 October the squadron was transferred from No.6 (Auxiliary) Group in the Bomber Command to No.13(F) Group (initially No.12 Group) to become a fighter unit after thirteen years as a bomber squadron; the first in Scotland. This required an extensive period of internal reorganisation within the squadron. For one thing it had to shed all its air gunners. During WWII Turnhouse was used as sector control for strikes on enemy shipping and for the interception of enemy raiders in the north.

On 15 April 1939, flying the recently requisitioned Gladiators of No.54 (F) Squadron, 603 provided an impressive display when Air Chief Marshal Sir Hugh Dowding GCB, GCVO, CMG, Air Officer Commanding, Fighter Command, came to present the Lord Esher trophy to 603 as the best all-round AAF squadron of 1938.

Less than a year later on 16 October 1939, 603 shot down the first enemy aircraft over this country since the Great War, and with 602 (City of Glasgow) Fighter Squadron, shot down the first enemy raider onto British soil, on 28 October. On 23 August 1939, 603 Squadron was embodied into the RAF. At that time it consisted of 23 officers, 19 NCOs and 97 other ranks.

The two flights consisted of the following pilots:

'A' Flight (Station Flight): Flight Lieutenants Pat Gifford and George Denholm, and Flying Officers H. Ken Macdonald, J.A.B. Somerville, Pilot Officers Ian S. Ritchie, Jim S. Morton and George K. Gilroy.

'B' Flight: Flight Lieutenant Ivone Kirkpatrick, Flying Officers Fred W. Rushmer, J. Laurie G. Cunningham, Geoffrey T. Wynne-Powell, Robin McGregor Waterston, and Pilot Officers Charles D. Peel and Graham C. Hunter.

The first war patrol was flown on 5 September 1939, by Flight Lieutenant George L. Denholm and on 14 September the squadron received the first of the new Spitfire Mk I, to replace the existing Gladiator Is, and training began in earnest at nearby RAF Grangemouth.

At 17.45 hours on 1 October 1939, during a period of intense practice flying on the Spitfire by the pilots of 603, Flying Officer J.A.B. 'Hamish' Somerville, flying Spitfire L1047, was killed when Spitfire L1059, flown by Pilot Officer Jim 'Black' Morton, landed on his aircraft while he was taxiing at Grangemouth.

On 7th October Pilot Officer Graham Hunter was seriously injured when he crashed on the edge of the runway while landing at Turnhouse in hazy conditions.

* * *

By November 1940 the squadron had shot down its 100th enemy aircraft and engaged Mussolini's Regia Aeronautica when it attempted to join forces with the Luftwaffe in cross-Channel sorties. In December 1940, following the vital part 603 played in the Battle of Britain, 603 Squadron returned to Scotland, where they completed many coastal and convoy patrols before moving back to Hornchurch in May 1941, as part of the Hornchurch Wing. During the summer of 1940, they had carried out *defensive* patrols, during their second period they carried out *offensive* fighter sweeps and bomber escorts over France. Flying the Mark Va, supplemented by the Vb in August, they continued in this role until they returned to Scotland in December 1941.

In April 1942, the squadron pilots and aircraft, by that time the Spitfire MkVc, were loaded onboard the US aircraft carrier USS *Wasp* and taken within range of Malta. On the 20th the aircraft took off for the island where, without their regular ground crews, they carried out defensive duties adding a further 61½ kills to their tally. Meanwhile, in June the 603 ground crews had been sent by sea to the Middle East, spending the rest of the year without aircraft.

On 3 August, the pilots of 603 became the nucleus of No.229 Squadron. On 1 February 1943, the squadron was reformed together with its ground crews from Cyprus as a maritime strike unit in the Middle East equipped with Beaufighter Mks I, VI, X, and XI, with which it operated most successfully from North Africa (Gambut 3) on anti-shipping strikes in the Mediterranean and the Aegean. During this time 603 pioneered the use of rocket projectiles in this theatre of war. Throughout the remainder of 1943 and much of 1944, these operations were carried out with great vigour and more than 50 vessels were sunk and several German aircraft were shot down during what were essentially anti-shipping operations. The unit was disbanded on 26 December 1944. The ground party returned to Britain by sea.

On 10 January 1945, No.229 Squadron, which had by then also returned to Britain, was renumbered to No.603 and from RAF Coltishall, flying the Spitfire MkXVIe, the unit provided escort for Beaufighters on anti-shipping strikes and attacks on V2 launch sites on the continent. By that time the squadron had claimed some 250 victories in total, 58 during the Battle of Britain and 171 before their departure to Malta in 1942.

In late April 1945, the squadron moved home to RAF Turnhouse, and was at Drem when the war ended when two white Ju52 transport planes landed with a number of high-ranking German officers onboard. They had come to sign the surrender of Nazi occupied Norway. Wing Commander George Denholm had overseen the procedures in Norway while Group Captain

Stevens was the senior British officer present in Scotland. A table from one of the billets was used for the signing which took place in the middle of the airfield with a number of the squadron pilots looking on.

* * *

On 15 August 1945, 603 Squadron was disbanded but reformed again on 10 May 1946. On 16 December 1947, King George VI gave permission for use of the 'Royal' prefix for all Auxiliary Air Force squadrons. No.603 (City of Edinburgh) Fighter Squadron, Royal Auxiliary Air Force, chosen as 'The Queen's Squadron' in 1955, was disbanded on 10 March 1957, whilst equipped with the DH Vampire FB5 at RAF Turnhouse.

On 1 October 1999, No.2 (City of Edinburgh) Maritime Unit was renumbered No.603 (City of Edinburgh) Squadron, Royal Auxiliary Air Force, forty-two years and seven months after it was disbanded. This announcement brought an extra big smile to the faces of the veteran members of the squadron who had gathered at East Fortune on 16 October 1999, to celebrate the occasion of the 60th Anniversary of the German raid on the Naval shipping in the Forth.

SOME BIOGRAPHIES

Lord David Douglas-Hamilton

The family connection with 603 is worth noting. David Douglas-Hamilton was the youngest of four brothers and their service in the Royal Air Force was unique in its history. Before the war they were all professional flying instructors and all went on to become squadron commanders.

Douglas had been the Scottish Middleweight Champion and in 1933, while serving as a member of parliament, had become the first pilot to fly over Mount Everest. By 1935 Douglas was commanding 602 (City of Glasgow) Auxiliary Air Force Bomber Squadron.

Malcolm, the second eldest, entered the RAF through Cranwell, where he trained with Douglas Bader.

As a squadron leader, Geordie N. Douglas-Hamilton was CO of 603 Squadron at Turnhouse for four years, from 1934 until 1938.

Lord David had initially been at St Andrews University before moving to Balliol College, Oxford. Here he continued the tradition of his brothers by excelling at boxing. He became the captain of the University Boxing Team, winning most of his fights by knockout, taking full advantage of his height of 6 feet 4 inches. He was also a Scottish heavyweight international boxer. David carried the flag of St Andrews at the Empire Games of 1934, held in London. In October 1938 Lord David married Prunella Stack and they had two sons.

By the time war was declared, he had amassed a great many flying hours and was a competent instructor. However, much to his irritation, he still had to undergo the full training program.

Meantime his other brothers had been serving elsewhere. Douglas was now a controller with 11 Group and was sent to France on 17 May 1940, by Air Chief Marshal Dowding in order to liaise with the fighter squadrons operating there. He used a Miles Magister while there and for that was mentioned in despatches. Geordie had become chief intelligence officer of Fighter Command at the Headquarters at Bentley Priory, where he worked closely with the commander-in-chief. Malcolm was training Greek air force pilots in Salisbury, Rhodesia.

Unfortunately and to his bitter disappointment, on completion of training, Lord David was given an instructor role at Netheravon, with the acting rank of flight lieutenant. While there he kept busy by organising exhibition boxing with the former English heavyweight champion, Freddy Mills.

At last in 1941 Lord David was posted to an OTU and then in the summer of 1941 to command 603 Squadron in Malta where his first operational mission took place on 27 November 1941. With the squadron he established a reputation as an outstanding leader and pilot.

By October 1943 Lord David was a wing commander flying high-risk reconnaissance missions with No.544 Squadron, equipped with the Mosquito, from RAF Benson. His navigator was Philip Gatehouse. On the morning of 2 August 1944 Lord David took off on his 31st mission with the unit. The Allies were going to invade Southern France and they needed information about German fortifications, anti-aircraft positions, and airfields from Southern to Central France; Lord David's specific target area was from Nice to St Dizier, a larger area than they had ever covered before.

Badly shot-up by anti-aircraft fire Lord David managed to nurse his aircraft over the Channel and reached the outskirts of Didcot. The aircraft was flying on only one engine and Gatehouse was believed to be seriously wounded, even dead. Crash crews were at the ready as the Mosquito approached the airfield and eyewitnesses reported seeing one undercarriage leg down and in the process of being retracted in preparation for a belly landing. The other engine suddenly cut out and the aircraft fell away from its approach, hit some trees and crashed. Having nursed the damaged aircraft all the way home, Lord David was killed along with his navigator.

Michael Judd

Michael Judd, Richard's colleague from his Oxford days, was born in Sutton Scotney, near Winchester, Hampshire, on 19 September 1917. He learned to fly with the Oxford University Air Squadron and on completion of his initial training he joined the RAFVR. On 16 November 1937, he was one of the first group to receive commissions in the RAFVR. Judd was called up at the outbreak of war and in October 1939 he was sent to No.7 Flying Training School (FTS), Peterborough. Having qualified as a pilot on 1 December he was immediately promoted to flying officer. He completed his training at Peterborough on 29 January 1940, and in March he was posted to No.1 Air Armaments School, Manby, as a staff pilot. In May he attended Central Flying School (CFS) on an instructors' course and in June he qualified as an instructor on intermediate training aircraft and was posted to No.8 FTS at Montrose. The following month Richard was posted to 'B' Flight, 603 Squadron, detached at Montrose at that time, and the two were reunited.

In November 1940, Judd was promoted to flight lieutenant. He remained at Montrose until September 1941, when he was posted as an instructor to No.73 Operational Training Unit at Sheik Othman, Aden. During mid December 1941, he was sent to Area Headquarters (AHQ), Western Desert and at the end of the month he was finally sent to an operational unit, No.238 Squadron, flying Hurricanes, where he was a flight commander. He then served briefly with No.33 Squadron. On 1 January 1942, it was announced that Michael Judd had been awarded the Air Force Cross (AFC), for his work in training. On 24 February he was slightly wounded in combat.

From 5 April until 23 July 1942, Judd led No.250 Squadron when he was posted to 239 Wing. He returned to 250 Squadron in early September which he led until 23 November, when he was posted away due to illness. On recovery he served briefly at AHQ, East Africa and in January 1943 he was promoted to acting wing commander and was attached to the RAF delegation in Washington, USA. Early in 1944 he returned to the UK and briefly served with 83 Group Support Unit (GSU), before taking over No.15 (F) Wing as wing commander flying. He left to join No.22 Sector HQ in May before joining No.143 Wing in July. He transferred to No.121 Wing on 31 October and on 22 January 1945 he was promoted to acting group captain, joining Main HQ, 2nd Tactical Air Force (TAF). On 20 September he received an air efficiency award.

He was released on 13 November 1945, with six enemy aircraft destroyed, three damaged, and one damaged on the ground, to his credit. On 1 January 1946, he was mentioned in despatches. Michael Judd finally relinquished his commission in the RAFVR on 1 July 1959, retaining the rank of group captain.

The Agazarians

The Agazarian family, whose home was in Knightsbridge, London, sacrificed a great deal in the fight against the Nazis. While Noel was flying with No.609 Squadron, an older brother Flight Lieutenant Jack Agazarian RAFVR was seconded from the RAF and joined the Special Operations Executive (SOE). After being trained as a wireless operator Jack and his wife Francine were returned to France to work with the resistance under the command of Major Francis Suttill DSO and his operation code-named 'Prosper'. After a chance encounter with two Germans, posing as Dutch agents, involved in counter-espionage he and his wife were brought back to England by Lysander aircraft for a rest. Their situation had been compromised. Suttill's organisation was to suffer during the next period. Early in the war he had 30 agents working for him, by 1943 he had literally hundreds. During 1943 the Germans had infiltrated Prosper and many agents and those connected with them were arrested by the Gestapo. Many were tortured and executed, and Suttill himself was captured on 24 June 1943. Just prior to this Jack had been called back from his leave earlier than had been intended. Owing to a shortage of newly trained wireless operators he was asked to return to France despite the fact that he had been pulled out of a very dangerous situation only a few weeks before. Jack was returned by a Lysander of 161 Squadron and after only one week in Paris, on this his second mission, he investigated an address known to be suspect and was captured. He heroically resisted brutal torture under interrogation, was imprisoned for the next year and a half before he was executed by firing squad at Flossenburg, near the German-Czech border, six weeks before the end of the war. The following appeared in *The Times* on 15 May 1971:

> In Memoriam, Agazarian. – Murdered – Jack Charles Stanmore. 29th March 1945. Flossenberg (sic). F/Lt., Royal Air Force, V.R., Noel Le Chavalier, killed in action, 16th May, 1941, Cyrenaica, F/O Royal Air Force V.R. Detur Gloria Soli Deo.

Following her work with McIndoe at East Grinstead, Monique Agazarian, sister of Noel and Jack, was also attached to RAF Uxbridge. She then joined the Air Transport Auxiliary (ATA). Monique was one of the few women actually taught to fly by the ATA, as most held peacetime licences. She was a gifted pilot and one of her contemporaries was Amy Johnson, the pre-war record breaker.

One of the first aircraft she was required to deliver was the Spitfire and her latter-day memories express her enthusiasm for the fighter:

> Spitfires really were delightful to fly, you just thought what you wanted to do and it did it. . . . The first time I rolled I was quite nervous. But it turned over so sweetly. . . . You really were part of the machine. . . . I had a glorious time.

At the end of the war 'Aggie' 'beat-up' her parents' Knightsbridge home in a Naval Seafire 47. This typified the Agazarians' irrepressible spirit. After the war Monique participated in a number of civil aviation business ventures. She died in 1992, aged 72.

Chas Frizell

After his training at Kinloss Chas Frizell went to an OTU after which, on 17 May 1940, he was posted to 257 Squadron at Hendon with only four hours' experience on Spitfires. At that time 257 Squadron were equipped with Hurricanes and he had to convert as did a number of newly trained pilots when they joined their first squadron. On 15 August he had to bale out of his aircraft after it caught fire during a routine patrol. On 15 September 1940 he was badly injured in a car accident along with his friend and fellow pilot Jimmy Cochrane at Martlesham Heath when fellow squadron member Bob Stanford Tuck drove into the back of their car. Frizell received severe facial injuries, a badly damaged knee and severe concussion which caused a permanent memory loss of details about the crash itself. Along with Cochrane, he was hospitalised for three months during which time they were sent to Torquay to recuperate. Afterwards Frizell returned to FTS, this time as an instructor. He met Richard again at Torquay while he was attending a medical exam to see if he was fit to return to operational flying. He did not fly again operationally until March 1942 when he joined No.91 Squadron. He later served with 124 and 152 Squadrons. He remained in the RAF until 1946 when he was released as a squadron leader and returned to Canada to live.

Sir Christopher Foxley-Norris

Born on 16 March 1917, Christopher Foxley-Norris (later Air Chief Marshal Sir Christopher Foxley-Norris CB, GCB, KCB, DSO, OBE), had been educated at Winchester and Trinity College, Oxford, where he read Greats. It was here that he first met Richard Hillary. Sir Christopher also learnt to fly with the Oxford UAS and was commissioned in the RAFVR in December 1938. In 1939 he won a Harmsworth Scholarship to the Middle Temple.

In early 1939 Sir Christopher was called up and posted to 9 FTS, Hullavington. From there he was sent to No.1 School Army Co-operation, Old Sarum where, as a pilot officer, he passed out from War Course No.5 with an exam mark of 85.1%, one of the highest marks ever achieved. From Old Sarum he was posted to 13 Squadron in Douai in France.

Back in England following the fall of France, Sir Christopher volunteered for Fighter Command and was posted to 5 OTU, Aston Down in August where he converted to Hurricanes. On 27 September 1940 he joined 3 Squadron at Turnhouse and moved to 615 Squadron at Northolt on 19 November.

On 26 February 1941, Sir Christopher was bounced by 109s and shot down in flames. He baled out and landed near Ashridge, Kent, where he was greeted by hostile locals. Sir Christopher was posted to Central Flying School, Upavon in June 1941, where he underwent an instructors course and from there he was sent to 10 FTS, Ternhill. He later instructed in Canada on the Commonwealth Air Training Scheme. In early February 1943, he was sent to Ferry Command to fly Hudsons on transatlantic missions. By mid-1943 he was with 143 Squadron at North Coates flying Beaufighters on anti-shipping duties, as a flight commander. Following acquittal from a court-martial for an alleged breach of security, Sir Christopher was posted to 252 Squadron in the Middle East where he remained until 23 September 1944, when he took over command of 603 Squadron in North Africa. On returning to the UK during early 1945, he was given command of 143 Squadron which was then part of the Banff Mosquito Strike Wing. He was awarded the DSO on 25 September 1945.

Sir Christopher enjoyed a long and distinguished post-war career during which he held various appointments and commands before retiring on 22 April 1974 as an Air Chief Marshal. On 2 January 1956 he was made an OBE, a CB (1966), a KCB (1969) and a GCB (1973). He became Chairman of the Battle of Britain Fighter Association in 1978 and was at one time CO of Oxford UAS at Manor Road.

Ronald Adam

As the controller at RAF Hornchurch during Richard's time there, Adam left an indelible mark on the pilots who flew from the airfield. The smooth distinguished tone of his voice, issuing instructions to squadrons in concise and calming manner, became almost legendary with the highly stressed Hornchurch pilots who were playing their part in the Battle of Britain.

He became an outstanding contributor to the British film industry in a career which had begun in 1936, but his tall figure and distinguished demeanour guaranteed him many 'character' roles after the war in films such as: *'Q' Planes, The Lion Has Wings, Song of Freedom, Escape to Danger, Angels One-Five, The Lavender Hill Mob, Captain Horatio Hornblower R.N., The Million Pound Note, The Man Who Never Was, Reach for the Sky.*

Ronald Adams (*sic*) was born in Bromyard, Worcestershire on 31 December 1896 and educated at University College, London. On 2 December 1914, at the age of 17, he was commissioned in the 15th Reserve Battalion of the Middlesex Regiment as a temporary second lieutenant. He later transferred to the Royal Flying Corps where he qualified as an observer before moving on to pilot training. He served with No.18 Squadron and flew Camels with No.44 Squadron before joining No.73 Squadron in France.

On 7 April 1918, Adams was very possibly the 78th victim of the 'Red Baron' (the 'kill' was actually credited to Kirchstein) near Hill 104, north of Villers-Bretonneux. Richthofen's report reads:

> I was observing, and noted that a Kette (three) of German planes pursuing an English
> plane was being attacked from the rear. I dashed to their aid and attacked an English
> plane. After putting myself behind him several times, the adversary fell. The plane
> crashed into the ground and I saw that it smashed to pieces.

Adams survived and was taken prisoner. Having sustained serious injuries in the crash he spent the next eight months in various hospitals and prison camps before he was finally repatriated on 17 December 1918.

After the war Adams qualified as a chartered accountant but found his life lacked excitement and moved into theatre management. He took on the Embassy Theatre in London and moved into the acting profession itself. It was at this time that he changed his name, dropping the 's' at the end of the surname.

Having joined the RAF at the start of WWII, he undertook several appointments, including fighter controller at RAF Hornchurch during the Battle of Britain. By the end of the war he had attained the rank of wing commander. He was married twice. The first, to Tanzi Cutana Barozzi, was dissolved, the second was to Allyne Dorothy Franks. He lived in Surbiton, Surrey, until his death on 28 March 1979 at the age of 83. Whilst Ronnie Adam is fondly remembered by aircrew and ground crew who served at Hornchurch during the Battle of Britain, he was always quick to dismiss his own input rather modestly as 'nothing special'.

Eric Bode

In piecing together the career of the Luftwaffe pilot credited with shooting down Richard Hillary, it became clear that much relevant paperwork had been lost or destroyed during the war years. I found that dates often clashed with others, a not uncommon occurence with service records.

After the war, records were compiled by the German authorities using available surviving documents. A date indicating an apparent posting may in fact be the first available date found on a document up until that time. For example Bode was with II/JG26 on 3 September 1940. The first available document proving he was with II/JG26 is a casualty list which he signed on 19 September 1940 giving his rank as *Hauptmann* and *Gruppe Kommandeur*. Thus his record has been completed noting his rank and posting to the squadron as being 16 days after he shot down Richard!

Erich Bode had been born in Magdeburg on 25 July 1909 and had reached the age of 31 by the time the Battle of Britain occurred, which was old for a fighter pilot. He had been a pilot in the Rekalamestaffel Mitteldeutschland in 1934. It is possible that he served in Spain with the Legion Condor in the Spanish Civil War. It is known that he was a *Leutnant* with *Luftgaukommando III* from 27 September 1939 and from 10 of November 1939 he was with *Generalkommando I. Fliegerkorps/Konigsberg*. He later became *Staffeloffizier* in 4/JG26 before the Second World War.

On 25 July 1940, he succeeded the large, powerfully built Hauptmann Karl Ebbighausen as *Kapitan* of the 4th *Staffel*. He later succeeded Ebbighausen as *Kommandeur* of the Second *Gruppe* when he was killed in action on 16 of August. His body was never recovered. Ebbighausen was the third Second *Gruppe Kommandeur* to be killed in three months. Bode's rank of *Hauptmann* and position were officially recorded as being on 19 September 1940.

Bode's third and last 'kill' occurred on 3 October 1940. He lost his command the same day, quite possibly as part of the plans of Major Adolf Galland, *Geschwader Kommandeur*, to replace many of the older, pre-war *Kommandeurs* of JG26 with a new influx of more youthful enthusiasm. They had been excellent officers in peacetime but they did not all prove themselves to be the best leaders in combat. By the end of October all eight JG26 *Kommandeur* had been replaced by younger men. Galland later stated that this move was one of the main contributing factors in the success of JG26. Bode's replacement was Hauptmann Walter Adolf from III/JG27 who took over command on 4 October.

From 2 May 1941 Bode was with the *Generalkommando Ia Operation* and attained the position of *Chief Division (IV)*. On 1 October 1941 he was promoted to *Major*. From 15 November 1941 he was with *7th Jagd Division Ia* and on 8 January 1942 was with *Generalkommando Air 2 Division*. On 25 June 1943, Bode was posted to the *3rd Jagd Division Ia* and on 16 January 1944 he was posted to the *2nd Jadg Division Ia*. He was promoted to *Oberstleutnant* on 1 June 1944. On 19 July 1944 he was posted to *XII Flieger Korps*. On 13 July 1944 he was on the *Flieger Reserve OKL* and *Generalkommando II Flieger Korps*. From 21 August 1944 he was with the *Luftwaffe Flieger Staff Ia, Generalkommando I Flieger Korps*. By 15 February 1945, Bode was in charge of *Generalkommando IX Flieger Korps (7)* and *Flieger Corps*, Chief of Staff by 7 April 1945.

Bode survived the war and died on 11 December 1991 in the parish of Seehausen am Staffel See, close to where he was born. He was 82.

Bill Aitken

Following his chance meeting with Richard, Aitken was posted from Army Co-operation to fly Spitfires. He was seriously injured whilst force-landing his aircraft, after it had been hit during combat. After the war he went into politics and became the member of parliament for Bury St Edmunds. He had two children Jonathan and Maria.

Sir William Aitken MP died suddenly in 1964, leaving Lady Aitken to bring up her two children. Her immediate grief was made worse by the massive death duties that were demanded of her. As a result she had to sell the family moated home in Suffolk.

Jonathan Aitken became a successful businessman, journalist, author and politician before being imprisoned in 1999 for perjury and perverting the course of justice. Maria Aitken, a well-known actress, also came up against the law as a result of her use of controlled drugs.

Archibald McIndoe

Archibald Hector McIndoe was born on 4 May 1904 in Dunedin, New Zealand. His grandfather emigrated from Scotland in 1859. Powerfully built, thick-set, extroverted by nature and a keen sportsman, the young McIndoe showed excessive drive and ambition in becoming a specialist in the field of medicine. At the age of 23 and after five years at the Otago Medical School he opted for an internship at the Waikato Hospital at Hamilton on the North Island. But he soon came to realise that what was perceived by him to be the boredom of being involved in general practice was something that he would be unable to tolerate. Before his year at Waikato Hospital was complete he received notification that he had been put forward as a candidate for a three year scholarship at the Mayo Clinic, a medical foundation of repute attached to the University of Minnesota, USA. Dr William Mayo, with his brother Charles, had made advances in stomach surgery in the Mayo Clinic, which had gained international renown. McIndoe initially failed to gain a place and on seeing his disappointment Will Mayo granted him an extra scholarship. One criterion for the scholarship was that he was single. McIndoe was in fact married but had kept this secret in order to secure a place. Now he had to leave for America without his wife Adonia. It was a painful parting but she was fully supportive and understanding of his ambition to be a successful surgeon. He would not see her again for over a year. In Rochester, at the Mayo Clinic, McIndoe initially gained a degree in pathology before progressing to developing a very promising career as an abdominal surgeon, on one occasion being cited as: '. . . . one of the ablest men the Mayo Foundation ever developed'.

He gained a degree as Master of Surgery at Minnesota University. In 1929 he received a Travel Award and chose to travel to England where he was to visit several hospitals; it was a busman's holiday. With his wife and young daughter he was unimpressed with England but was to meet a truly great surgeon whose reputation was firmly established in the USA, and from whom he was to draw several parallels with himself. This was Lord Moynihan, president of the Royal College of Surgeons. Moynihan managed to persuade McIndoe to leave America and come to work in England with assurances that there was work for a man of his skill. The assurances were forthcoming, jobs weren't and McIndoe's commitment met with terrible disappointment. He had a wife who was expecting another baby and a three-year-old daughter, but no means of support. McIndoe decided to meet a cousin he had never seen, Sir Harold Gillies. Gillies had been born, also in Dunedin, New Zealand, on 17 June 1882. His father was a Scotsman who had emigrated and in time Gillies returned to Britain, to study medicine at Cambridge University.

He made a name for himself as a great plastic surgeon and also had a private practice in Harley Street. He was to become the greatest influence on McIndoe's career and life. The qualifications gained in the USA and the reputation of the Mayo Clinic counted for very little in the closed-shop atmosphere of British surgery and McIndoe had to study for an English fellowship with the Royal College of Surgeons before he could hope to compete for work. However, before he gained this qualification, Gillies managed to use his influence to get him employment through Philip Manson-Bahr as a lecturer on tropical diseases at the Hospital for Tropical Diseases, ahead of far more qualified competition. But the work was boring and the achievements of Harold Gillies as a plastic surgeon became a source of great fascination to McIndoe and he eventually turned to the art of 'skinning and grafting' in the 1930s when Gillies offered him a partnership in his practice. Thus one of the most famous partnerships in plastic surgery was formed.

Initially, McIndoe was carrying out operations to remove scars, reduce the size of pendulous breasts, to improve hairlips, cleft palates and reshape noses at the Harley Street practice, making the ugly beautiful. Even before the war he had gained a reputation for his work. Generally, people are of the opinion that plastic surgery is a modern day development, but such work started many hundreds of years ago with some evidence to indicate that it began as far back as the Stone Age! But it was WWI that created an overwhelming need for such work to begin in earnest by many surgeons including Sir Charles Valadier, who helped rebuild and re-establish function to the bullet or shrapnel-shattered faces of the soldiers in the trenches. It was fascinating how he could remove a piece of rib or thigh and implant it in the jaw as a replacement. As a captain in the Royal Army Medical Corps (RAMC), Harold Gillies had seen the surgeon at work. Interested in the repair of wounded faces, he had also watched French surgeon Morestin at work while on leave in Paris and it was these experiences that had shaped his own enthusiasm to become a plastic surgeon. Ultimately, he was sent back to England to organise a plastic and jaw repair unit and pioneer his new speciality. He joined a small experimental unit, under Sir William Arbuthnut Lane, at Aldershot specially set up to deal with the appalling injuries received by soldiers in the Battle of the Somme, and he worked ceaselessly to improve his knowledge of plastic surgery. Gillies himself was to become one of the innovators, and it has been said that he was the 'modern father of plastic surgery', who devised many outstanding reconstructive procedures including the tube pedicle graft and the onlay eyelid graft. By WWII he was the chief civilian consultant to the British military forces and had organised plastic units both home and abroad. He was knighted for his work during WWI and after.

By the outbreak of WWII the partnership had ended. McIndoe's work was now able to stand on its own, as Gillies himself put it: '. . . . the tail was beginning to wag the dog'.

McIndoe and Gillies had argued frequently and a rift had developed that was never to fully heal. The war would have separated them anyway, but McIndoe had served an apprenticeship under a master and had himself become a plastic surgeon of repute, learning many new techniques unique to Gillies. One aspect had been how to use the latest equipment like the Dermatome. The Dermatome was a machine that consisted of a drum with a razor-sharp blade designed to remove a piece of skin, thick to wafer-thin, and to any shape, in a planing action, for grafting onto a damaged area of up to ten inches in length and more than four inches in width. It was fast and versatile. He also learnt to apply Gillies' approach: time, patience, planning and technique.

The work of a plastic surgeon is enormously meticulous and painstaking with fine cutting, grafting and stitching. In addition, a high level of creativity is required to sculpt the flesh and bone, rebuilding something functional and aesthetically acceptable from an area of destroyed looks and functions, be it a face or a pair of hands.

McIndoe knew that with the possibility of war his skills would be required by the nation and he had prepared himself. If war had not been declared he knew he would have been able to retire within ten years. He had now become wealthy, a far cry from his status when he and his family had arrived from America, more than 15 years before, to live in a damp basement flat with no source of income. He now drove a Rolls-Royce, had a share in a Harley Street practice of repute and enjoyed holidays all over Europe.

McIndoe was made consultant surgeon to the RAF in 1939 but was not keen, however, to accept the rank of a wing commander in the RAF, which accompanied the position. He believed those in authority would have control over him as they were of a higher rank and he wished to retain total autonomy.

He attended a meeting with Sir Harold Gillies and Sir William Kelsey-Fry, pioneer of plastic dental surgery to decide upon appropriate sites for plastic surgery units around the country in the event of war. McIndoe's headquarters were to be at the Queen Victoria Hospital, East Grinstead, with Barts being declined as the other option. There were only four full-time plastic surgeons in the country at this time, McIndoe, Gillies, T. Pomfret Kilner and Rainsford Mowlem, who was also a New Zealander and in partnership with Gillies and McIndoe. Kilner went to the Ministry of Pensions unit at Roehampton, Gillies took over a rambling mansion called Rooksdown House, near Basingstoke, Mowlem went to St Albans and McIndoe to East Grinstead.

Initially, McIndoe travelled to East Grinstead with the nucleus of his senior staff to inspect their new place of work, and assessed the facility as being ideal. The Queen Victoria Cottage Hospital at East Grinstead, which had opened in 1936, was a very small unit at this time with a twelve bed ward for men, similar for women, six beds for children and six private wards. A wooden hut was in process of being constructed, known as a 'blister' and annexed to the main complex. This had been ordered along with two similar huts after the Munich crisis. It was called Ward 3 and would become the temporary home of the Guinea Pig patients. Ward 3 smelt of creosote, had a concrete floor, a wooden shell, and an interior colour scheme of cream and brown. There were three pot-bellied stoves situated at intervals along the centre of the ward. The beds were regulation and the bedside lockers were frail, providing the only space between the beds. Less than an arm's length: 'Bit of a shock, still we can tart it up a bit.' McIndoe commented.

Those who witnessed the visit remember a stocky, thick-set, powerful figure, of medium height, slightly craggy features with a square jaw and brown eyes behind round tortoiseshell specs. He was apparently seen by some as neither a very subtle nor very sensitive man, somewhat abrupt in manner and with a piercing gaze. His accent was colonial with its slightly chopped vowels and his voice decisive in its terse, pointed sentences. The staff had no idea then that this man would make the town and the hospital famous for the work he was about to undertake there. Within five years of the end of the war East Grinstead had become the most renowned centre for plastic surgery in the country and had grown accordingly, with many new buildings having been added to the original structures. This included the large, well equipped Canadian wing.

McIndoe built a powerful team at East Grinstead with Jill Mullins as theatre sister and John Hunter as anaesthetist. He had met and worked with them both at St Andrews Hospital, Dollis Hill; at the Hospital for Tropical Medicine and at Bart's. The relationship between the three of them had blossomed. They were each specialists in their own field and had a great deal to offer.

Jill Mullins was a beautiful red-headed theatre sister with excellent interpersonal skills, a quiet, firm manner and total commitment to her work. She also adored McIndoe.

John Hunter, a large rotund Oliver Hardy-like individual in appearance with puffy lips and a double chin, was an ebullient character of whom McIndoe later wrote: 'I couldn't have accomplished what I have done without his help. I've seen no one to touch him as an anaesthetist.'

Hunter was an outstanding anaesthetist and surgeons and anaesthetists agree that he was one of the best children's anaesthetists in the world. He was more popular than McIndoe amongst the Guinea Pigs, with his catch-phrases of: 'Just a little prick,' and 'goodbye', before they drifted off into unconsciousness. One of his patients later wrote of him: 'The rotund figure in its white theatre gown looked more like a pork butcher to me than an anaesthetist'. Another commented:

> Above the paunch was a friendly face consisting of chubbly cheeks, double chin,
> rimless glasses, a small moustache and a few wisps of hair which failed to hide his

baldness. 'I'm John Hunter, better known as The Gasworks,' he said. 'Which reminds
me, have you heard the story of the girl called Virginia –' And he launched into a
ribald story. As the rabelaisian details rolled out he continued his preparations. he
massaged my arm in the direction of my elbow and then said: 'Just a little prick, if
you'll pardon the expression.'

The three provided much diversity in temperament; McIndoe tough but to some degree
sentimental; Jill Mullins, who could communicate with anyone from any walk of life, and John
Hunter, friendly and jovial.

Many more trips followed before McIndoe finally established the unit, getting to know the staff
and putting in place procedures and practices. The hospital staff were unfamiliar with plastic
surgery. McIndoe taught them the history, and lectured on pedicles, thin, medium and full-
thickness grafts, bone transplants and post-operative care, which was more important in plastic
work than any other form of surgery. A bad dressing might put at risk the whole operation. A
withering graft not noticed quickly enough might undo several months of surgical repair.

Above all, McIndoe stressed that his staff must gain the sympathy of the patient. In gross
deformity the mind is just as crippled as the body. The plastic surgery nurse must have the
understanding and insight into the patient's mental problems. The nurses were impressed not only
by the dynamic approach to the new work at the hospital, but also by the informality of the new
boss and the atmosphere he wished to establish. The new surgical team finally made the move
from Bart's to East Grinstead.

During this period of waiting McIndoe arranged to have his family evacuated to America,
sending them to stay with his old friends at the Mayo Clinic, Rochester, NY, while he bought a
cottage called Millfield, near to the hospital in Sussex. He still stayed at his Chelsea flat
intermittently until later in the war. The parting was long and painful for the family, as the many
letters between them reflected. Adonia wanted to return to be with her husband. McIndoe was
determined that she remain out of harm's way.

A week after moving his team to East Grinstead, McIndoe instructed the Office of Works to re-
decorate Ward 3 in pastel shades of green and pink in order to make it less depressing for the
patients. The brown and cream had vanished, the iron beds and camp beds were put into store and
replaced with wooden beds borrowed from the Gordon Hospital in Vauxhall Bridge Road, and
chintz curtains were hung at the windows.

By the time of the Battle of Britain McIndoe was 38 years of age. Few of the plastic surgeons
deployed around the south of England could have predicted the number of patients with burns who
filled the wards and demanded the very highest of skill to rebuild their bodies. During the aerial
combat of WWII 4,500 Allied airmen: '. . . had the bark knocked off them' as McIndoe put it.

Eighty percent of these were burnt on the face and hands. As McIndoe described their injuries:

> A pilot is hurled like a blazing torch from his plane and sustains burns of the exposed
> parts of his body, or his plane crashes and he is enveloped in flame, lying unconscious
> against red-hot material. He sustains deep burns of the exposed parts of his body,
> together with a greater or less extent of burning of the covered parts, depending on the
> efficiency of the protective material.

Goggles were kept raised on the forehead or occasionally hung on the instrument panel. In panic,
when hit, some ripped off their oxygen masks. Thus, for one reason or another, face, hands and
scalp were exposed. More than 200 of those pilots who required reconstructive surgery at East
Grinstead were 'faceless ones', with hideous 'mask' burns which had taken all the skin on their
faces away. Each of these men had between 10 and 50 operations ahead of them and an average
period in hospital of three years, including periods of convalescence.

The first 50 were moved to East Grinstead from the emergency units. Amongst these were
Geoffrey Page, Tom Gleave and Paul Hart, the aviation pioneer, who had to have his whole face
rebuilt after crashing on a Welsh hillside.

With this initial influx of wounded came no less than 16 different accents, including Canadian,
Australian, American and Czechoslovakian. Ward 3 was definitely not the 'Beauty Shop' that
Richard describes in his book, and that was his intention. It was very hot and smelly but within
there developed an atmosphere of comradeship and extroverted bravado that gave those men hope.
There was always somebody worse off than them.

Once the young pilots had been fighting high over southern England, now the flower of

England's youth lay in agony, scorched and suppurating, hovering between life and death. Initially the priority was to save their lives; the process of making them whole again would come later, if they survived. McIndoe realised that many of these young men were receiving the wrong treatment for their burns. Service medical officers and first-aid staff were spraying the burnt areas with tannic acid and painting gentian violet on the charred eyelids. The process formed a sticky crust and the familiar keloid scarring which made skin grafting almost impossible.

McIndoe provided a surgical, mental and emotional approach. The pilots believed him when he assured them of his intention when he outlined what reconstructive surgery (as McIndoe preferred to call it), he had in store for them. As well as a new nose, lips, eyelids and working hands, he gave them hope at times when they felt utter desperation. As he once wrote:

> It is my practice to describe to the patient the scheme to be followed, announce the exact number of operations it will entail, how many weeks and months will be spent in the hospital and how much time will be required out of hospital to recuperate, what the patient should do during these off periods, and finally, the approximate date when the face will be completed. Only then can his confidence and above all his intelligent interest be maintained, for assuming that in addition a pair of badly burned hands must be restored the total period of incapacity may be four years.

He was honest and forthright with his patients. He allowed them to exploit what mobility they had and not remain confined to their beds. They were allowed into the town, regardless of the reaction of a few members of the public who may have been horrified by their appearance. It was all part of the rebuilding process. They were taught to live with their injuries. Friends and relatives were taught the same, and one day they could look forward to the prospect of being able to live, love and enjoy life to the full once again. He gave them hope for the future, and the chance to get back into the air, even with tin legs, claw-like hands and smashed faces. As a result of this work McIndoe became another hero of the Battle of Britain.

McIndoe also began preparing the local townsfolk for having burnt and disabled soldiers, sailors and airmen wandering in their midst. It was imperative that he gained their support. He initially gave informal lectures and talks on the work he was undertaking at East Grinstead, and later football and cricket matches were organised against local teams. His intention was to lessen the shock when his disfigured patients were allowed to wander into town, and for them to ultimately adopt friends and acquaintances in the local community whose companionship and acceptance of their injuries would provide a suitable stepping stone for the re-integration of his patients back into society. He told them:

> I've got to have your help. These men are human beings and must not be treated or even looked at as abnormal. Take them into the pubs and buy them a drink. Or into your homes. Talk to them. After all, there's nothing the matter with them that a little kindness and understanding won't cure.

The hospital had brought the reality of war home to the occupants of this small Sussex town and its many wealthy inhabitants. The sight of these men wandering into town, some in wheelchairs, was unusual. Patchwork faces, burned, mutilated hands supported in slings, eyes protected from the light with sunglasses and wads of cotton wool. It was nothing to see an 'erk' being pushed in his wheelchair by a group captain. In time the town, with its inhabitants, adopted the hospital. The injured soldiers, sailors and airmen were often guests at the local mansions and smaller dwellings, with McIndoe guest of honour and local hero at many of the house parties of the rich and influential in the locality. Jill Mullins would often be a partner to McIndoe at these functions and they became accepted as a couple. McIndoe would take the opportunity to talk about his work and willingly accepted donations towards the work at the hospital. They were, after all, witnesses to the success of his work in that they saw his patients almost daily.

The Whitehall Restaurant became the local meeting place and watering hole with its convivial landlord Bill Gardner. The downstairs bar provided a haven where a Guinea Pig could be found during most of its opening hours, with the restaurant always able to provide a table when one was required. Jill Mullins and John Hunter went out drinking with their patients regularly, with the maestro himself playing the piano (one of his favourite ways of relaxing), John Hunter telling the jokes and Jill Mullins able to supervise this extension to the post-operative care! On many an occasion she herself would be the centre of attention with her flair for making each of the men feel important in his own right. Later, the reputation established at East Grinstead soon featured in the national press and many VIPs flocked to visit the site including the Duke of Kent, stars of the London theatres and the American actors Walter Pidgeon and Clark Gable. They were all briefed on the kind of sights that they could expect on entering the wards and as a result, all mixed casually in a relaxed atmosphere. The small cottage hospital was gaining celebrity status and attracted the very best in nursing talent as well as those unqualified nursing volunteers who had heard about the work there and wished to be a part of it. Some managed to become successful at their new profession, while others realised that it was not at all glamorous, but very hard work. Slackness was not tolerated. McIndoe used his psychological skills and put the prettiest nurses with the worst injured patients.

McIndoe also had the support of the local press for what he was trying to achieve at East Grinstead in the form of Mrs Clemetson, a local newspaper editor and later editor to a group of newspapers. Mrs Clemetson had her headquarters in Tunbridge Wells, twelve miles from East Grinstead, and she remembers the time when two Guinea Pigs dismounted from a bus, while on a shopping trip in the town, only to be met by the scream from a woman startled by their appearance and the cruel comment: 'They shouldn't be allowed out in that condition,' a comment also made to Richard Hillary while in a Soho pub. 'That attitude would never have been found in East Grinstead,' said Mrs Clemetson.

While on a trip away from the hospital Geoffrey Page also felt the hurtful brunt of insensitive comment. While he was on a bus the conductress said to him: 'Coo, you don't arf look a mess! You ought to see one of them plastic surgeons, mate. It's amazing what they can do for you.'

At Christmas time McIndoe managed to secure a number of items of Christmas fare for the patients in the hutted wards and they duly rewarded him with carefully chosen Christmas gifts. Although wealthy before the war, his share in the business partnership with Gillies was by this time fifty-fifty, taxes were accounting for the majority of his money and he was also finding life difficult devoid of its luxuries, along with the rest of the country. Even his everyday attire was becoming noticeably worn in appearance and the memory of him in rather faded and worn clothes remained with many veterans of Ward 3.

* * *

During the Phoney War period and before the Battle of Britain the air battle over Dunkirk brought in pilots with 'Airman's Burn'. The effects of the treatment on their burns, which had been coated with coagulants and greases such as silver nitrate, gentian violet and sprayed-on acqueous tannic acid, horrified McIndoe and he was convinced that to immerse the injuries in brine would be far more effective.

Convincing his colleagues in the Royal Society for Medicine and the War Wounds Committee of this was going to be far more difficult, although some leading plastic surgeons had noticed how much faster the burns had healed on airmen who had been immersed in the sea. The salt water had not only kept the wounds clean but had seemed to prepare the area for grafts sooner. (Although it was thought at the time that pilots who were burned and who landed in the sea stood a better chance of survival than those who baled out over land, it has since been claimed that this was unlikely to have been due to the salt content of the water, but more probably to the cooling qualities of cold water which perhaps reduced the effects of shock to a survivable level, as well as the pain of the burns.)

McIndoe bombarded the Air Ministry with letters before finally meeting with them:

> Eighty percent of RAF burns involve the hands to a greater or lesser degree. This is due to the peculiar risks which the airman's calling involves, and to his regrettable but understandable failure to wear gloves . . . It is no exaggeration to say that the local treatment of burns in the RAF is dominated by the problem of the burned hand. Therefore any burn occurring on the hands of a man whose technical ability and training make his value to the country of supreme importance must be regarded seriously and treated with the utmost care. Together with the burn of the face in the helmet area, The Airman's Burn, it is a burn which no other can equal as a therapeutic problem or cause of subsequent disability. In the treatment of it, there must be total prohibition of coagulation of the hands and face.

His mentor, Sir Harold 'Giles' Gillies, came to stay with McIndoe at Millfield during this time and he expressed his anger at the current treatment of burns to the older surgeon: 'God damn and blast tannic acid!' McIndoe commented.

'You'll never stop it.' was the reply from Gillies. 'It's laid down as standard medical procedure. Cut the chap's clothes off and then cover him with tannic. They've got the stuff in every home, dressing station and hospital in the land, and they'll use it. Stops the chap from whimpering. Makes him think something's being done. Regulations, Archie. Don't tell me you're trying to change regulations?'

'That's just what I'm going to do,' replied McIndoe. 'I'm writing a paper. I want your backing.'

'What do you want me to do?'

'Spread the word amongst your pals, tell them we're on the warpath. And then call a meeting of the Royal Society of Medicine.'

'If you'll do the big spiel, I'm with you,' Gillies replied.

'If you support me, I'll talk my head off,' McIndoe enthused.

On 11 November he wrote to Adonia in the USA:

> Somehow, between all this, I have to produce a paper on burns for the Royal Society for immediate publication. This follows the show on Wednesday which happened to be the biggest meeting ever held in the RSM on any subject. We won the day hands down and have brought in far-reaching changes in the treatment of burn casualties.

The meeting of the Royal Society of Medicine had heard an impassioned plea from McIndoe to follow his recommended procedures at the end of which it was voted that he produce a document expanding his theories and to have it circulated to all the emergency medical units throughout the country. The RAF chiefs were convinced and ordered an immediate ban on the treatment of third degree burns to the face and hands with tannic acid. It was several months before the other branches of the service got around to it. But why had they ignored such a course of treatment for so long?

Initially, until the meeting with the RSM and the WWC, he had not been able to convince the medical sections at the Air Ministry that the current treatment had to be discontinued, because the time lapse between the application of the tannic acid, silver nitrate and gentian violet was too great. The coating degraded and coagulated into a hard crust which immobilised fingers, toes and eyelids, making the surgeon's job more difficult. The eye specialist's job became nearly impossible, with the grave risk of corneal ulcers and blindness, a very real possibility in Richard's case. The War Wounds Committee however, refused to recognise this as the case, despite his having petitioned them with actual case histories, and would not endorse the use of saline treatment in its place. He wrote a great many letters and in between he used the telephone to pester those in authority to change the system; if the air commodores wouldn't help, then he would try the air vice-marshals. It was at this time that he realised how advantageous it had been for him to have remained out of uniform for he may well have felt the wrath of military discipline in an attempt to have him 'toe the line'.

Regardless, McIndoe had already hastily set up a saline bath unit in Ward 3, which allowed the airmen to be immersed in water maintained at a temperature a little above body temperature. Initially it was an ordinary bath to which the salt was added by hand. Later the bath was modified, the taps were removed to prevent injury to the patient, and a series of pipes fed warm brine from a tank in the roof of the ward, to the bath. A shower attachment was added to enable the injured head and shoulder areas to be sprayed passively. It was not long before the charred and smashed men, victims of the Battle of Britain, came through the doors of the hospital. They referred to it as the 'spa'. An RAF medical orderly nicknamed 'Taffy' featured in Richard's book later passed on his memories of the saline bath:

> I remember the first time we dipped a character in the swill. He had been badly burned somewhere abroad and he was a real mess. The Maestro had already sewn a flap on him and told us to dip him to cool him off. He must have thought the water was boiling hot, or something. Anyway, he jerked the moment he touched the water and you could positively hear the stitches being ripped out. Funny, some of them never could get used to it at first. We had one badly burned child who used to scream every time we carried her to the water, though she just loved it once she was in.

This girl was the 15-year-old whom Richard refers to in *The Last Enemy*. She was in a bed next to the saline bath.

McIndoe had a number of nicknames. To his friends and colleagues he was known as 'Archie', although some called him 'Mac'. To the staff at East Grinstead he was known as 'The Boss' and to his service patients he was known as 'Maestro'.

The hospital was admitting an increasing number of casualties and during September McIndoe wrote to his wife Adonia and said:

> I worked on a child here today with a smashed face and broken leg. She is the only survivor of a family of nine – four younger, four older, all killed last night. Splendid military targets . . . Yesterday I had four shot-down Nazi pilots and they were a lousy lot. Two of them died and the other two, with minor injuries, I sent to a hospital in the East End where they can see what they are doing.

During this period McIndoe was extremely busy, attending a variety of business orientated functions and social events. He still maintained his flat in Chelsea and attended his clinic in Harley Street. Eventually, he closed down his flat and moved to his Sussex home full-time. At East Grinstead, after having operated all day, he would then conduct evening lectures to Red Cross nurses and personnel on the benefits of saline treatment of burns. He told them that their large supplies of tannic acid and gentian violet: '. . . were out, and should be discarded. All I want you to do is keep the wounds clean and sterile and leave the rest to us at the hospital.'

The saline bath and a dusting with sulphur drugs saved many cases which would have been beyond grafting. His success, due to his concerted propaganda campaign and the fact that other units had also adopted this course of treatment, gradually convinced the pedantic individuals on the War Wounds Committee to support and recommend his methods.

In the meantime McIndoe went back to work on the patients at East Grinstead and the hospital would become world famous for the work carried out by him and so many other diligent and caring staff. Although McIndoe spent many hours in the theatre, in time operations were also carried out by five other plastic surgeons at East Grinstead, Jayes, Eckhoff, McLaughlin, Matthews and Moore. But as the Guinea Pig Club became well-known, it was Ward 3 itself and its staff that would ultimately become equally famous for the nature of the work carried out on its patients, with much attention drawn to the patients themselves. It was here in Ward 3, later nicknamed the 'sty', as well as the other two blisters that made up the Emergency Medical Service wards, that the worst burnt individuals were housed. Contrary to popular belief it was not a psychological tool by the chief surgeon who intended that democracy would rule there, and rank would not be recognised. McIndoe had indeed tried for the first year in occupation at East Grinstead to build a ward for officers with separate cubicles for those with jaw and facial fractures. It was noticed that those that were in the communal ward were actually recovering from their injuries and burns at a faster rate than those kept apart.

Companionship seemed to be the answer. Those left on their own would lie brooding about their disfigurement, experiencing the symptoms of stress, not allowing their bodies to recover effectively, including lack of nourishment due to loss of appetite. Once in the hot, noisy, even grim atmosphere of the ward they found those that were suffering from the same problems, and here they found support, companionship and distraction. High-ranking Royal Navy and Royal Air Force officers were lying less than an arm's length from a group of leading aircraftmen and irreverent Australian and Canadian air-gunners; their beds were separated only by a small bedside locker in which to store their few belongings, which in some cases when supplies were short, was only a wooden box. The fact of the matter was that there was just not enough room to segregate the officers and men, not enough staff to look after them, and Ward 3 housed the saline bath facility which was required for the treatment of their injuries. McIndoe had no intention of attempting to instill discipline in Ward 3 as long as the recovery rate was satisfactory, despite the Welfare Committee of the Queen Victoria Hospital receiving a number of complaints; a nurse had asked to be removed from Ward 3 after she had apparently been abused by a patient and there were stories of drunken parties and other goings-on that had reached the committee.

Indeed, crates of beer were kept under some beds, cases of whisky under others. The ward was a cacophony of sound, rowdy patients and loud music. Despite the relaxed 'rowdy-classroom' atmosphere of Ward 3, McIndoe would never allow this behaviour to go beyond certain limits and he was quick to inflict discipline on those who attempted to take things too far. His work in the hospital and, in particular the theatre, was sacrosanct. On that November evening in 1940 when he rose to respond to the complaints made by the Welfare Committee, McIndoe was in no mood for compromise:

I have several things to say, some of which you are not going to like.

The war has been going on for over a year now, yet you as a group obviously wish things to continue as they did in peacetime. You had better realise this.

The Queen Victoria Hospital no longer simply serves the local community. Primarily this hospital is to be used for the physical and mental rebuilding of airmen injured in the course of their duty. I had hoped for some time that you would realise that from now on this hospital will become less and less a civilian organisation as the Services send in their casualties. You have disappointed me. Whether you like it or not, from now on this hospital will cater for the injured airman and his particular problems. Some of you object to pilots and aircrew having alcohol in their wards. Normally I might perhaps agree with you, but in this matter you overlook two points. Firstly, these men are not sick or badly injured. Their bodies may be broken temporarily but their youthful spirits are still with them. Secondly, normal hospital discipline is all very well for a patient who is admitted for a few days or a few weeks, but it has to be relaxed when a man is to be treated for several years. Half my battle is to see that their morale does not suffer through boredom.

The response was positive, and an elderly female member of the committee rose and spoke:

I expect we deserved that rebuke, perhaps we did not think it out too well. But if only Mr McIndoe would take us into his confidence about what he plans to do, it may be in our power to help rather than hinder.

McIndoe took advantage of the offer:

Thank you. Now may I suggest that the next time you go visiting in the wards, forget that these are cases. Think of these boys as human beings – think how you would treat them if they were your own sons – and remember that you're not doing them a favour by visiting them. They're doing a favour by speaking to you.

There is just one more point. You will probably have noticed that I am allowing certain of my patients who are fit to move around to go into East Grinstead. Some of them are not very pretty to look at. A man with a flap hanging down from his face may look like a monster. A man who has lost his nose and is in the process of getting a new one may not exactly resemble Clark Gable – though I seem to recall that he once looked like a pterodactyl until a plastic surgeon altered the shape of his ears!

Invitations to take the patients out for afternoon tea or for a drive were forthcoming, but spurned for quite a while by the injured airmen. Eventually McIndoe realised that away from the comfort of the hospital their disablement could prove embarrassing, particularly when needing assistance when going to the toilet! Fly buttons were a problem for injured hands and eventually Edward Blacksell, the ex-Barnstable school master and physical training (PT) instructor who arrived at the hospital in 1941 and ended up as McIndoe's assistant, discovered an advertisement in an American magazine for the zip-fastener. McIndoe wrote to friends in America and zippers arrived in abundance.

On behalf of his patients at East Grinstead McIndoe also battled against hospital routine and ridiculous Service regulations on their behalf. On one occasion they sent him a batch of garish 'blues' for his convalescing patients to wear when they went into town: 'I'm damned if I'm going to let my boys run around like convicts – no, like invalids, which they are not.' The 'blues' were consigned to the stores.

Later, McIndoe kept half a dozen sets in his office when he introduced the wearing of such unsightly attire as a form of punishment for any patient that was rude to the nurses, rowdy in the hospital, or came in drunk. It proved to be a most efficient deterrent as such a punishment was only ever meted out once with the recipient returning from the town shamefully claiming he had been treated *'like a bloody pi' dog'*. He enforced the letter of the law when the behaviour of certain individuals became intolerable. Stewart Jones, who wore a wig and Ron Pretty who had a false arm were returned to the depot at Uxbridge for continually breaking the rules. One week later with McIndoe's consent, Uxbridge sent them back to East Grinstead as 'hopelessly insubordinate'. Every time Pretty saluted his arm flew through the air and whenever Jones did the same his wig came off!

Ward 3 was a quite fearsome place for new patients, but also for the staff. New additions to the nursing detail found it very difficult to get through the first few shifts. The men could make life extremely difficult. The taunting, the jibes, expletives and raucous behaviour required tolerance and courage as they went about their duties in an environment that they had been totally unprepared for. In addition the windows were kept shut all year round as the high temperature increased the chance of the plastic surgery being successful. It was akin to a Turkish bath at times, and it was Richard's opinion that the ward was not kept clean enough and that the success of some operations suffered as a result, due to the apparent lack of sterility.

In 1947, Archie McIndoe was knighted for his tremendous wartime efforts and his work at East Grinstead. He died in his sleep, from a heart attack, on 13 April 1960, aged 56.

Colin Hodgkinson

'Hoppy' Hodgkinson had been a pilot in the Fleet Air Arm when, on 12 May 1939 at 16.20 hours as a trainee at Gravesend, his Tiger Moth had been in a collision with another Moth flown by an instructor with his trainee 'under the hood'. Neither instructor had seen the other. In the collision, which occurred at 500 feet, the port wing and part of the tail plane of his Moth were sheared away. Hodgkinson's Tiger Moth crashed into a wood next to the A2, the main Rochester to London road. His legs were trapped between the instrument panel and the rudder bar in the impact, and his flying instructor, Spanton, had been killed instantly. The crew of the other Moth managed to carry out a partially controlled descent but had piled up on landing. The instructor received a fractured spine and a fractured skull and, like Colin, was taken to Gravesend Hospital where after an initial period of improvement he died. The pupil, 'Ginger' Taylor, escaped with only minor cuts and abrasions and later visited Colin in hospital. Taylor would return to flying with an operational squadron. He was later shot down over Europe by a flak barrage and posted missing. Colin would also return to operational flying and later met Taylor in Stalag Luft III after he himself had been shot down!

Colin was a red-head and had been 6 feet 1 inch tall before the accident and weighed thirteen and a half stone. He was a belligerent young man who had been powerful, well muscled, very fit and a fine athlete. He qualified as a pilot despite being terrified of flying and suffering quite terrible claustrophobia in the cockpit of his aircraft! The crash and subsequent surgery had reduced his height to 5 feet 10 inches on his tin legs, and his weight to 12 stone. He was invalided out of the Navy with a pension of £3 per week, but having read about Douglas Bader's successful bid to re-join the RAF he was keen to get back into the Fleet Air Arm. He would not be disappointed.

After his accident Colin was rushed to Gravesend Cottage Hospital. He had received serious lacerations to his face where he had impacted with the compass. His seat straps had been kept loose. His right leg had received compound, complex and commutated fractures. The left had received a fractured ankle and a shattered metatarsal. After an initial amputation of the right leg below the knee, gas gangrene set in demanding a life-saving amputation of the leg four inches above the middle thigh. In June he was moved to the Royal Naval Hospital at Greenwich.

On 15 March 1940 Colin had the other leg amputated five inches below the knee. He made his decision based on the fact that it was not healing and he was also rarely without pain. His doctors provided medical advice but the final decision to amputate the limb was left to him. He had also realised that he stood a better chance of returning to operational flying if he had two artificial legs as opposed to one artificial and one crippled leg. He knew that Bader was on operations flying Hurricanes, despite having lost both legs in an accident at Woodley Aerodrome near Reading ten years before the war. Colin was to communicate with Bader during his recovery and from his response, and by example, Bader gave him the impetus to persevere. Colin later went to Roehampton to have artificial legs fitted and to learn how to walk again. He was at Dutton Homestall for a period of convalescence, and met McIndoe. Like so many others he was to benefit from this caring man. Although he had received some plastic surgery on his facial injuries while at Roehampton, McIndoe was to remove a keloid under his left eye which had been inhibiting facial movement. On hearing that Colin was eager to fly again he would be instrumental in helping him get back to operational flying.

Tony Tollemache

Anthony Henry Hamilton Tollemache was born on 3 August 1913 in Suffolk. He was related to the Cambridgeshire family brewery business of Tolly-Cobbold. Tollemache's nickname was 'Tolly'.

The accident that ultimately led to reconstructive surgery at East Grinstead and his meeting with Richard occurred while he was carrying out a searchlight co-operation exercise with an air-gunner, Leading Aircraftman Smith, and a passenger, Lieutenant Sperling of the Welsh Guards, also on board. As he approached the flare path at Manston, having completed the exercise, the Blenheim struck a tree and crashed into a field where it immediately burst into flames. Eyewitness reports state that the Blenheim lost a wing on impact with the tree and was on fire before it hit the ground. Tollemache and LAC Smith found themselves uninjured and were able to scramble clear through the forward hatch of the wreckage which was fast becoming an inferno.

However, on realising that Lieutenant Sperling was still trapped inside, Tollemache returned to the Blenheim and attempted to reach into the cockpit through the forward hatch, on the upper forward section of the fuselage, in an attempt to extricate his passenger from the seat adjacent to his own. With his own body under threat from the fierce heat and exploding ammunition a monumentally courageous effort to save Sperling was defeated. With his own clothing alight he was finally driven back by the intense heat and seering flames. By this time he too had been very badly burned and a local farmer drove the two aircrew back to RAF Manston where Tollemache was initially treated by the station medical officer, Dr Attwood. On realising the severity of his injuries and fearing for the life of the pilot, the MO sent him to Chatham Naval Hospital where, as the dire symptoms of severe burns set in, the next few days saw him fighting for his life.

On 6 August 1940 he was awarded the Medal of the Order of the British Empire for Gallantry (EGM), a rare distinction. This award was exchanged automatically for the George Cross (GC), on its institution on 24 September 1940, with all living holders of the award exchanging their medals at the first convenient investiture.

He was able to return to flying and became ADC to Field Marshal Earl Alexander, governor general of Canada, by 1946. He left the RAF as a squadron leader. He joined Aero Research in 1949 which later became a Ciba-Geigy company for whom he became export manager. At the time of his death he had retired from full-time work with the company, to which he had dedicated himself for so many years, and was retained on a consultancy basis. He hated bureaucracy, was undisciplined in that he did things his way, and always worked very hard. He was a very competent artist, and had an outstanding knowledge of the geography, climate, economics and politics of most of the countries of the world and established a quite considerable network of friends world-wide. He was a connoisseur of good food and particularly fine wines.

He died tragically on 20 February 1977 during a business trip to Paris with his second wife Celia, shortly after taking on his new role as semi-retired export sales consultant to Ciba-Geigy, based at Duxford, Cambridgeshire. Both he and his wife were run down by a taxi while crossing the road. Celia suffered a broken femur, but Tony received terrible head and multiple other injuries including a broken collar bone, hip and leg. He died a few days after the accident at the age of 63. He was buried in Helmingham Churchyard, Suffolk.

Wilfred Handel 'Andy' Miller

Andy Miller was born in North Wales on 27 September 1921 and joined the RAF in August 1941. In January 1942 he was sent to Canada for flying training and returned to 54 OTU, Charterhall.

On the night of 13/14 August 1944, Miller's Mosquito had been damaged by debris from an aircraft he had stalked and then destroyed. It was the first Heinkel He219 to be shot down during World War II. With eleven enemy aircraft destroyed as a night fighter pilot, he saw out the remainder of the war as a prisoner of war.

Andy Miller had flown with Sergeant F.C. Bone as his R/O for his entire operational flying days with 125 and 169 Squadrons. Bone returned to his job in the police force after the war, but suffered from ill health. He died in 1974. Andy Miller retired from the RAF in 1956 in order to be nearer his father who had suffered a heart attack. He then married a girl from Northern Ireland and was offered a job in his father-in-law's large coach building business, producing buses and ambulances. Having settled in Northern Ireland his father-in-law was then also taken ill and the firm had to close. During this period he joined the Ulster RAuxAF, until it disbanded in 1957. Miller then joined Ford in Belfast where he remained for the next 18 years until his retirement in the early 1980s. In May 1985 he was invited to Leeuwarden air base in Holland, as a Dutch aviation archeology team had recently excavated the remains of his Mosquito; whilst there he was taken up in a modern-day two seat Lockheed F-16B fighter.

Apart from his own autographed copy of *The Last Enemy* he hadn't read any other publication concerning the life or death of Richard Hillary until I met him in November 1994. When I informed him that the cause of crash which claimed the lives of Richard Hillary and Wilfrid Fison had remained something of a mystery he explained that as far as he was concerned there was no mystery and has no doubt that the cause of the accident was the same as that which had caused him to abort his own flight minutes before. He strenuously refuted the findings of the crash investigation.

THE *J.B. PROUDFOOT,* WATSON CLASS LIFEBOAT
AND THE CREW OF THE MARGATE LIFEBOAT STATION

In September 1940 Edward Parker, the skipper of the *J.B. Proudfoot*, had been awarded the DSM for gallantry shown when helping with the rescue of soldiers of the BEF from the beaches of Dunkirk as skipper of the No.1 Margate lifeboat, the *Lord Southborough*.

Strewn along the Dunkirk coastline area of a nine mile stretch of sandy beach were queues of thousands of soldiers waiting to be picked up. The waters were very shallow offshore and even at high tide the ships could not come closer than half a mile. The answer was to launch an armada of smaller vessels to relay the soldiers to the larger ships waiting further out. The Ramsgate lifeboat was the first to reach Dunkirk. It had towed eight wherries from Dover and it was just as well as on arrival even the lifeboat could not get in close enough to pick up the men. Each wherry was rowed by a naval or lifeboat man to pick up and relay to the lifeboat eight men at a time. With 160 men on board, the lifeboat set off for the larger ships and transferred the soldiers to there. The Ramsgate lifeboat brought off 800 men that night! Two days later, with the crew totally exhausted and the wherries all sunk by the bad weather and enemy gun-fire, the Ramsgate lifeboat headed back to Dover. They had rescued 2,800 men and not slept for three days.

The Margate lifeboat reached the beaches off Nieuport, 15 miles east of Dunkirk, at midnight on Thursday, 30 May. Edward Parker managed to steer the boat through to the beach where the black lines of waiting soldiers emerged from the gloom of first light. The sound of enemy gun-fire and exploding shells was deafening. Flares momentarily lit up the night sky revealing a grim sight indeed. The scream of falling bombs and the rattle of machine gun fire was almost continuous. The smell of cordite and high explosives was acrid in the damp, dawn air.

The boat responded to the sound of voices calling through the dawn murk and picked up eighty French soldiers. These were then ferried to a waiting barge further offshore that had crossed the Channel with the *Lord Southborough*. The lifeboat then returned to pick up the men of the Border Regiment. Unfortunately the load was so great, that the lifeboat was grounded until the next high tide refloated her. With the Border men now unloaded onto the barge the lifeboat returned to pick up more men. The task for Edward Parker and his crew must have seemed immense. Everywhere they looked there were men in the sea awaiting rescue.

A destroyer was now receiving the rescued men and Edward Parker lost count of the times he ferried between the shore and the destroyer. During this time enemy aircraft continued to swoop down and straffe and bomb anything and everything. The weather became worse until the sight of men drowning as they waded into deeper water, laden with heavy equipment, was more than Edward Parker could stand. He called off the rescue until there was an improvement, in an attempt to avoid more deaths.

Parker headed for Dunkirk and on the way rescued two officers and 15 sailors who were trying to row to a destroyer in a leaky old whaler. The men were all that was left of a 150-strong party that had been working on the beaches for four days.

The weather did not improve and the decision was made to return to Margate. The *Lord Southborough* and her crew had been out for 24 hours and had saved 600 men. The citation on the award of the DSM to Parker and Knight, of the Ramsgate lifeboat read: 'For their gallantry and determination'.

Three other lifeboats arrived at Dover after the Ramsgate and Margate boats had departed, and were given orders to sail for Dunkirk. Led by the skipper of the Hythe lifeboat they refused to sail as, in their experienced opinion, the water was too shallow and they would be grounded offshore. The crews were therefore issued with rail warrants and sent home. Seven more lifeboats arrived at Dover the next morning and, hoping to avoid a similar confrontation, the Navy requisitioned the vessels from the crews and handed them over to Navy officers, despite the RNLI crews expressing great keenness to do the job themselves. The Navy crews were briefly shown their respective tasks on board and, as with the previous three crews, the RNLI men were sent home.

The outcome of this disagreement was a sad one. Three weeks later the RNLI held an enquiry which found that the coxswain of the Hythe lifeboat had persuaded the other two boats not to make the trip across to Dunkirk and he and his mechanic were dismissed. The coxswain expressed the reluctance of some of the crews to take orders from the Navy and stated: 'If the order had come from the Institution to proceed to Dunkirk and do the best you can, there would have been no holding back.'

I'm sure this would have been the case and some sympathy for the treatment of these men would not be inappropriate. They knew that they were the best men for the job, they knew the waters and the hazards, they also knew their own boat. Unfortunately the mission required more of a gung-ho approach under the desperate circumstances.

When the Hythe cox heard of his dismissal he swore that he would carry out rescues in his own fishing boat and two months later he justified his worth by rescuing two British airmen from a ditched bomber. The Hythe lifeboat was the only boat to fail to return from Dunkirk; owing to damage received she was abandoned. No lifeboat returned without bullet holes in their hulls and superstructure. Due to damage received, the *Lord Southborough* was taken out of commission to Routledge for a re-fit. In its absence, the crew were to use the *J.B. Proudfoot* as a temporary rescue boat.

It is interesting to note that Richard's great-great-great-uncle was apparently Lieutenant Colonel Sir William Hillary who, while living in the Isle of Man, founded the RNLI 116 years previously. He himself had been awarded the institution's Gold Medal for gallantry in saving more than 300 lives from shipwrecks off Douglas on the Isle of Man.

Michael Hillary wrote to the RNLI to express his gratitude for his son's rescue:

The Hon Secretary   36 Knightsbridge Court
RNLI   Sloane Street, SW1.
Margate

Dear Sir,
    I am told by my son Pilot Officer R. H. Hillary, who is now an inmate of the Margate Hospital, that he was rescued by the Margate Lifeboat and I want to express the heartfelt thanks of my wife and myself, to the coxswain and his crew for returning him to us.
    It would surely have afforded my ancestor, who founded the service, the liveliest satisfaction to know that his own kith and kin were numbered amongst those who have benefitted by its wonderful work.

                            Yours very truly
                            Michael Hillary

In response the RNLI wrote back to Michael Hillary asking for more information about their family connection to Sir William Hillary and two months after receiving the letter Michael Hillary wrote to them once again:

                                                     36 Knightsbridge Court
                                                     Sloane Street, SW1.

13th December 1940

Dear Sir,
    With further reference to your letter of the 13th September, I have made some enquiries but, owing to people having evacuated their homes and not having access to their papers, I have not been able to find out anything very definite.
    As far as I have been able to discover, my father is a descendant of Richard, a brother of Sir William Hillary, who was one of the three sons of William Hillary of Wensleydale, Yorkshire, so that Sir William Hillary would be my father's great-great-uncle. I hope this will be sufficient for your purpose.

Thank you very much for sending me the literature of the RNLI. I enclose my
cheque for a guinea and shall be glad if you will enrol me as an annual subscriber for
that amount.

Yours faithfully

Michael Hillary
(Signature)

PS. The name of my son who was rescued is Richard also.

The letter was sent to a fellow ex-army officer Lieutenant Colonel C.R. Satterthwaite OBE,
Secretary, RNLI, Lifeboat Depot, Borehamwood, Herts.

And thus Michael Hillary remained a member of the RNLI but had no further contact.

An element of doubt surrounds Richard's family connection to the founder of the RNLI. It has
been suggested that William of Wensleydale's son, Richard, remained a bachelor and had no
known children. This would make the family connection false.

A letter dated 9 April 1965 written by Christopher R. Elliott and addressed to P. Howarth, a
former Public Relations Officer with the RNLI, who was also an author, contained interesting
information:

> You will remember that I am interested in the link between Pilot Officer R.H. Hillary
> who was rescued from the sea by the Margate Lifeboat on 3rd September, 1940, and
> Sir William Hillary, founder of the Lifeboat Service. Pilot Officer Hillary's father, Mr
> Michael Hillary, of 61 Clarewood Court, Seymour Place, London, W.1.
> (Tel:Paddington 0615), told me yesterday, when I saw him for a chat, that as far as he
> knew there was no connection between his family and the founder. Yet there must have
> been some evidence for this belief because representatives from the Margate Lifeboat
> visited Hillary in hospital, very soon after his rescue, and lifeboat representatives
> turned up again at the memorial service in London in 1943. What, then, are we to
> conclude – that someone in 1940 guessed wrongly about the relationship?

A possible explanation for this reaction by Michael Hillary was that, while initially happy to
expound that his family were related to the founder of the RNLI, he had yet to discover
information to confirm the family connection, even though the war was over and access to his
family records was once again possible. Nevertheless, various authors have continued to refer to
this family connection over the years, with only slight variations on the existing version. While it
has not been possible to confirm this point, the common belief today is that Richard Hillary *was*
related to Sir William Hillary, founder of the RNLI and it is one to which I subscribe.

THE MANUSCRIPTS OF RICHARD HILLARY

1.) 1938 – 'Sea Voyage' 45 page short story. Not published.
2.) 1941 – General layout of lectures for the US industrial workers. Loose, typewritten sheets.
3.) 1942 – 'The Pilot and Peace' published in the *RAF Journal* in June 1942.
4.) 1942 – 'The Artist and Fascism' in *The Spectator*. (Based on Richard's 'Where Do We Go
From Here?'
5.) 1942 – 'Fighter Pilot', *John O'London's Weekly*.
6.) 1942 – Reviews of the Sea Rescue film script, *For Those in Peril*.
7.) 1942 – 'The Voyage Back' 11 page short story. Not published. (Discussed with Lovat Dickson,
Eric Linklater and Arthur Koestler at the Savile Club.)
8.) 1942 – *The Last Enemy*, published by Macmillan.

BIBLIOGRAPHY

1. Published sources:

Hector Bolitho, *Combat Report*, Batsford Ltd 1943.
Lewis Brandon DSO, DFC & Bar, *Night Flyer*, William Kimber 1961.
Donald Caldwell, *The JG26 War Diary*, Grub Street 1996.
Michael Charlesworth OBE, *Behind the Headlines – An Autobiography*, Greenbank Press 1994.
Lovat Dickson, *Richard Hillary – A Life*, Macmillan 1950.
Lovat Dickson, *The House of Words*, Macmillan 1963.
Al Deere, *Nine Lives*, Wingham Press 1959.
Lord James Douglas-Hamilton, *The Air Battle for Malta*, Mainstream Publishing 1981
Lord Douglas of Kirtleside, *Years of Command*, Collins 1966.
Lady Winifred Fortescue, *Beauty for Ashes*, Blackwood 1955.
Roger and Anne Gresham Cooke,*Your Uncles*, Private.
Charles Higham and Roy Moseley, *Merle*, New English Library 1983.
Richard Hillary, *The Last Enemy*, Macmillan 1942.
Colin Hodgkinson, *Best Foot Forward*, Odhams 1957.
Arthur Koestler, 'The Birth of a Myth,' first published in *Horizon*, April 1943. Reprinted in his book of essays *The Yogi and the Commissar*, 1945.
Eric Linklater, *Richard Hillary*. An Essay in *The Art of Adventure*, Macmillan 1947.
Leonard Mosley, *Faces From the Fire – The Biography of Sir Archibald McIndoe*, Weidenfeld and Nicholson 1961.
Christine Mill, Norman Collie, *A Life in Two Worlds*, 1987
Hugh McLeave, *McIndoe Plastic Surgeon*, Frederick Muller Ltd 1961.
Frank McEachran, *A Cauldron of Spells*, Greenbank Press 1992. With introduction and memoir by Laurence le Quesne.
Wing Commander George Nelson-Edwards DFC, MA, RAF, *Spit and Sawdust*, Air Forces Publishing Services 1995.
Geoffrey Page, *Shot Down in Flames*, Grub Street 1999.
Dr Alfred Price, *Battle of Britain Day*, Sidgwick and Jackson 1990.
Chris Shores and Clive Williams, *Aces High*, Grub Street 1994.
Bill Simpson, *I Burned My Fingers*, Putnam 1955.
Jack B.Thompson, *The Charterhall Story*, Air Research 1989.
Group Captain Peter Townsend, *Duel of Eagles*, Weidenfeld & Nicholson 1970.
Group Captain Peter Townsend, *Duel in the Dark*, Harrap 1986.
A.P. Walters, *The Margate RNLI Station*, Private, 1997.
Ken Wynn, *The Men of the Battle of Britain*, Gliddon 1989.
Frank Ziegler, *The Story of 609 Squadron*, Crecy 1993.
The Guinea Pig Club Magazine.
The Spectator for the speech made by Richard Hillary at Foyles literary luncheon entitled 'The Artist and Fascism', originally entitled by its author as 'Where Do We Go From Here?'
Richard Hillary, 'The Pilot and Peace,' *RAF Journal*, June 1942. AHB (RAF).
Express Newspapers for the articles by Robert Pitman and Leonard Mosley.
The Sunday Post (Edinburgh/Dundee).

2. Manuscript sources:

The letters of Richard Hillary, Michael and Edwyna Hillary, Denise Maxwell-Woosnam, Rache Lovat Dickson and other friends and colleagues of Richard; along with other papers, photographs and press cuttings held in the Richard Hillary Trust Archive, Trinity College, Oxford.

The private letters of Mary Booker to Richard Hillary, held in the Richard Hillary Trust Archive, Trinity College, Oxford. Permission to read the letters granted by Mr Michael Burn.

The private letters and papers relating to Sergeant Wilfrid Fison, held by the Reverend Geoffrey Fison.

The private letters and flying log-books of Squadron Leader Jim Morton DFC, No.603 (City of Edinburgh) Fighter Squadron, AuxAF.

The flying log books of Squadron Leader Jack Stokoe DFC, No.603 (City of Edinburgh) Fighter Squadron, AuxAF.

The private letters of Flight Lieutenant Ken Macdonald, No.603 (City of Edinburgh) Fighter Squadron, AuxAF.

Documents held by the Oxford University Air Squadron.

No.603 (City of Edinburgh) Fighter Squadron ORB (AIR27 – 2079-2081) & Combat Reports (AIR50 167, I-E), Public Records Office, Kew.

The General Register Office of Scotland.

Photograph Acknowledgements:

Over the years, I have amassed a large collection of photographs of Richard Hillary and No.603 (City of Edinburgh) Squadron, most from private collections. I am grateful to the following sources for their valuable assistance:

Squadron Leader Bruce Blanche – official historian of No.603 Squadron, RAuxAF; the 603 Squadron Archive; Michael Burn; Mrs Fiona Campbell; John Coleman; Joe Crawshaw; Michael Charlesworth and Shrewsbury School; the Reverend Geoffrey Fison, Squadron Leader Chris Goss (The Chris Goss Collection); IWM Photographic Archive (Negatives: E(MOS)1080 and CH6649); Squadron Leader W.H. 'Andy' Miller DFC and Bar, RAF (retired); The Montrose Aerodrome Museum; George Mullay, The National Archives of Canada who provided the following photographs from the Lovat Dickson Collection: PA139031/32, PA139034/5, PA139040-47, PA139053-57; Mrs Pan Nelson-Edwards; Mrs Joan Merton-Jones; Ordnance Survey (Landranger Map 74); The Oxford University Air Squadron; The Richard Hillary Trustees and Trust Archivist Captain A.B. Sainsbury VRD, MA, RNR; Trinity College, Oxford; The RNLI Photographic Achive; and exclusive use of photographs from the family collections of Mrs Jean Blades, the Carbury family, via Desmond W. Carbury, Mrs Jean Cunningham, Mrs Marguerite Morton, Richard and Wendy Roberts, and Squadron Leader BG Stapleton DFC, DFC (Dutch) in conjunction with Ron Hefer Photography, Pinetown, South Africa.

INDEX

NOTES